Administration of Wills, Trusts and Estates, Fourth Edition

Administration of Wills, Trusts and Estates, Fourth Edition

GORDON BROWN & SCOTT MYERS

DELMAR
CENGAGE Learning™

Australia • Brazil • Japan • Korea • Mexico • Singapore • Spain • United Kingdom • United States

DELMAR
CENGAGE Learning™

**Administration of Wills, Trusts and Estates,
Fourth Edition**
Gordon Brown, Scott Myers

Vice President, Career and Professional Editorial:
  Dave Garza

Director of Learning Solutions: Sandy Clark

Acquisitions Editor: Shelley Esposito

Managing Editor: Larry Main

Product Manager: Patricia Osborn

Editorial Assistant: Melissa Zaza

Vice President, Career and Professional
  Marketing: Jennifer McAvey

Marketing Director: Debbie Yarnell

Marketing Coordinator: Jonathan Sheehan

Production Director: Wendy Troeger

Production Manager: Mark Benard

Senior Content Project Manager: Betty Dickson

Senior Art Director: Joy Kocsis

Technology Project Manager: Christopher
  Catalina

Production Technology Analyst: Thomas Stover

For product information and technology assistance, contact us at
Cengage Learning Customer & Sales Support, 1-800-354-9706

For permission to use material from this text or product, submit all requests online at **cengage.com/permissions**
Further permissions questions can be emailed to
permissionrequest@cengage.com

Library of Congress Control Number: 2007941008

ISBN-13: 978-1-4283-2176-2

ISBN-10: 1-4283-2176-4

Delmar Cengage Learning
5 Maxwell Drive
Clifton Park, NY 12065-2919
USA

Cengage Learning is a leading provider of customized learning solutions with office locations around the globe, including Singapore, the United Kingdom, Australia, Mexico, Brazil, and Japan. Locate your local office at:
international.cengage.com/region

Cengage Learning products are represented in Canada by Nelson Education, Ltd.

For your lifelong learning solutions, visit **delmar.cengage.com**

Visit our corporate website at **cengage.com**

NOTICE TO THE READER
Publisher does not warrant or guarantee any of the products described herein or perform any independent analysis in connection with any of the product information contained herein. Publisher does not assume, and expressly disclaims, any obligation to obtain and include information other than that provided to it by the manufacturer. The reader is expressly warned to consider and adopt all safety precautions that might be indicated by the activities herein and to avoid all potential hazards. By following the instructions contained herein, the reader willingly assumes all risks in connection with such instructions. The reader is notified that this text is an educational tool, not a practice book. Since the law in constant change, no rule or statement of law in this book should be relied upon for any service to any client. The reader should always refer to standard legal sources for the current rule or law. If legal advice or other expert assistance is required, the services of the appropriate professional should be sought. The publisher makes no representation or warranties of any kind, including but not limited to, the warranties of fitness for particular purpose or merchantability, nor are any such representations implied with respect to the material set forth herein, and the publisher takes no responsibility with respect to such material. The publisher shall not be liable for any special, consequential, or exemplary damages resulting, in whole or part, from the readers' use of, or reliance upon, this material.

Printed in the United States
2 3 4 5 XX 11 10 09

Dedication

*This text is dedicated, with great love,
to my supportive and generous wife, Lorraine.*

Scott Myers

*For the thirty years that I taught full time at North Shore
Community College, practiced law part time, and wrote text-
books such as this, I have many people to thank. Among them
are talented people in the fields of education, publishing, and
law. The ones who bore the burden of my efforts, however, are
my wife, Jane, for her never-ending support and encourage-
ment, and my children, Steven, Matthew, Deborah, Jennifer,
Timothy, and David. They grew to be outstanding people even
without my being with them during many of their growing-up
activities. It is to these wonderful family members that this
book is dedicated with many thanks and much love.*

Gordon Brown

Contents

Preface

All of law arises from lifetime experiences, including the experience of dying and getting prepared to die. The study of human experiences, which is what one really does when studying law, is one of the things that makes the study of law so interesting. This book attempts to bring to life and make interesting the study of wills, trusts, and estates by interweaving within its pages interesting articles, cases, and observations about many well-known people. The number of celebrity photographs has been doubled in this edition. Authentic probate forms that were filed in the estates of well-known people are included, giving a unique insight into their lives. Frank Sinatra's codicil, for example, is incorporated in the text, as are the spousal property petition of Bo Derek and the probate petitions of George Burns, and John F. Kennedy, Jr. The wills of Theodore Roosevelt, George Burns John F. Kennedy, Jr., Elvis Presley, John Winston Ono Lennon, Richard M. Nixon, Doris Duke, and Jacqueline Onassis are included in Appendix B.

The book continues to be written in a style that is easy to understand, with legal jargon and unnecessary verbiage avoided. Essential legal terms are defined when they are first presented, and many charts, diagrams, and illustrations are included to help students grasp the subject matter and to make it appealing.

Each chapter begins by quoting the "last words" of a recognized individual. This is followed by a scenario entitled "A day at the office ..." that raises genuine law-office issues, which can spark a lively class discussion. Legal ethics are sprinkled throughout the text in diverse ways, and appellate court cases and statutes from many states are used to illustrate points of law. Cases are presented in an analytical style, similar to a legal brief, with the facts summarized, the legal issues identified and answered, and the reason given for the court's decision. Maps and tables are used to identify states that have adopted particular rules of law, and legal forms from a variety of states are used as illustrations.

New subject matter in this edition includes the letter of instruction, the Uniform Nonprobate Transfer on Death Act, dynasty trusts, requirements for inter vivos gifts, long-term care insurance, the family limited partnership, retirement plans including social security, traditional IRAs, Roth IRAs, educational IRAs, SEP, Keogh, and 401(k) plans, and patients without advance directives law. Also included are updated state court forms, federal tax forms, and changes made by the Economic Growth and Tax Relief Reconciliation Act of 2001.

A wealth of pedagogical features continues to be a highlight of this book. "Outcomes" and "Job Competencies" now launch each chapter, and each chapter concludes with a summary and a variety of other reinforcing elements. Questions for review support and sharpen student understanding. Cases to discuss, requiring students to apply the law to factual situations, help to develop analytical skills. Student projects under the heading "Research on the Web," "Sharpening Your Professional Skills," and "Sharpening Your Legal Vocabulary" develop critical thinking abilities.

From Gordon Brown:

I wish to give special thanks to Mary A. McGarry, Acquisitions Editor, Delmar, Cengage Learning, who gave me the opportunity to write a textbook on any subject in the field of law that I desired, and to David J. Sargent, President of Suffolk University, Boston, Massachusetts, who unknowingly affected my life through his outstanding teaching ability, thereby influencing me to choose this subject to write about. I also wish to thank Cynthia Entwistle, Reference Librarian at North Shore Community College, Danvers, Massachusetts, for her research and help in preparing the new celebrity features and obtaining the many photographs for this edition. Thanks also to Lauren Woodward and her beautiful children, Dr. Linda Rose Haley, Jett Williams and her father's estate, The Church of Jesus Christ of Latter-Day Saints, and the Conrad N. Hilton Foundation for providing photographs, and to Modern Maturity, The Salvation Army, Barrett Brothers Publishers, Partnership for Caring, UNOS, and The Living Bank International for providing many forms, maps, and tables for this book.

From Scott Myers:

I wish to thank Shelley Esposito, Acquisitions Editor, and Melissa Riveglia, Senior Product Manager, at Delmar, Cengage Learning and Melissa Berry, Project Manager, at GEX, Inc. for their assistance in ensuring high quality for this edition.

We also wish to thank the following reviewers whose thoughtful observations and suggestions have been very helpful:

Helen L. Bongard, J.D.
Sullivan University

Beverly W. Broman, J.D.
Duff's Business Institute

Patricia Greer, J.D.
Berkeley College

Kent Kauffman
Ivy Tech State College

Clark D. Silliman, J.D.
Edmonds Community College

Laurel A. Vietzen, J.D.
Elgin Community College

Christopher L. Whaley
Roane State Community College

Angie Williams
University of Mississippi

Gordon W. Brown

SUPPORT MATERIAL

This fourth edition is accompanied by a support package that will assist students in learning and aid instructors in teaching:

- An Instructor's Manual and Test Bank prepared by Terri L. Lindfors accompanies this edition and incorporates all changes in the text and to provide comprehensive teaching support. It provides guidance for all featured questions in the core text; including Research on the Web, A Day at the Office, Cases to Discuss, and Sharpening Your Professional Skills, in addition to the standard Review Questions and Key Terms exercises. The Test Bank includes additional True/False and Multiple Choice questions specially tailored for each chapter.

Student CD-ROM

The new accompanying CD-ROM provides additional material to help students master the important concepts in the course. This CD-ROM provides additional cases for futher study including community property cases.

Instructor's e-Resource CD-ROM

The new e-Resource component provides instructors with all the tools they need in one convenient CD-ROM. Instructors will find that this resource provides them with a turnkey solution to help them teach by making available PowerPoint® slides for each chapter, a Computerized Test Bank and an electronic version of the Instructor's Manual.

All of these Instructor materials are also posted on our website, in the Online Resources section.

Online Companion™

The Online Companion provides students with additional support materials in the form of Key Points and Chapter Outlines.Additional information on reading wills and a Probate Checklist file is also provided. The Online Companion™ can be found at www.paralegal.delmar.cengage.com in the Online Companion™ section of the Web Site.

Web Page

Come visit our website at www.paralegal.delmar.cengage.com where you will find valuable information such as hot links and and sample materials to download, as well as other Delmar Cengage Learning products.

> Please note that the Internet resources are of a time-sensitive nature and URL addresses may often change or be deleted.

ABOUT THE AUTHORS

Gordon W. Brown, Professor Emeritus, North Shore Community College, Danvers, Massachusetts, taught law and business subjects, in addition to practicing law, for thirty-eight years. In 1998, Mr. Brown was awarded the Outstanding Educator Award from his alma mater, Salem State College, Salem, Massachusetts. Mr. Brown is also the author of *Legal Terminology* published by Prentice Hall and co-author of *Business Law with UCC Applications* and *Understanding Business and Personal Law* published by Glencoe/McGraw-Hill. Mr. Brown is a member of both the Massachusetts and Federal Bars.

Scott Myers has a J.D. from Rutgers Law School and an M.A. from Rutgers Graduate School. He has been the Director of Paralegal Studies at Marist College in Poughkeepsie, N.Y. for the past 22 years, administering the program while teaching a variety of courses, including Wills, Trusts, and Estates. Under his guidance, the program earned American Bar Association approval in 1988, and has maintained that approval since that date. Scott Myers is also a sole practitioner of law.

Table of
Legal Briefs

Planning an Estate

1

Where There Is a Will

■ CHAPTER OUTLINE

■ CHAPTER OUTCOMES

- Describe the benefits of having a will.
- Recognize the risks in writing one's own will.
- Explain the implications of dying without a will.

■ JOB COMPETENCIES

- Be able to explain to clients the benefits of having a will.
- Be able to caution others about the risks involved with writing one's own will.
- Be able to converse with others about the implications of dying without a will.

◼ A DAY AT THE OFFICE . . .

Marie Cuomo, a paralegal, was the first to arrive at the law office on Monday morning. Although she was not due in the office until 8:30, she usually arrived about 15 minutes early. A woman was waiting near the office doorway.

"Good morning," Marie said to the woman as she unlocked the door.

"Good morning," the woman replied. "Will Attorney Pierce be in this morning?"

"He has to be in court at 9:00," Marie answered. "He usually goes directly to court without stopping here first. Can I help you with anything?"

"Well, my father passed away last week, and I need to talk to Mr. Pierce about his estate."

"Oh, I'm sorry. Why don't you come in?" Marie responded. "Perhaps I can make an appointment for you."

"He was elderly, and he didn't leave a will," the woman continued. "I'm afraid that everything he owned will go to the state."

Marie showed the woman to a chair and took out a yellow legal pad. "What was your father's name?" she asked.

"Vincent Marino," the woman replied, holding up a pillow case. "He was a wonderful father. Look what he wrote on his hospital pillow case before he died. 'I leave all of my property in equal shares to my daughter, Pearl, and my son, Vito.'"

"He signed it, too," Marie observed. "And those look like the signatures of two witnesses."

"Yes," the woman replied, "he had two nurses sign the pillow case. He didn't know that my brother, Vito, died two days before he did. We just didn't have the courage to tell him."

"Oh, I'm so sorry," Marie answered. "Will you be free this afternoon to see Attorney Pierce? I'll make an appointment for you."

Queries:

1. How might Marie have responded to the woman's statement that everything her father owned will go to the state because he died without a will?
2. What would you have told the woman about the words written on the pillow case?
3. In what way, if at all, would these responses raise the issue of practicing law without a license?
4. What further information would you need to have about the woman's brother, Vito?

§ 1.1 WHERE THERE IS A WILL

Wills come in a fascinating variety of shapes, sizes, and sorts. Even a handwritten will written on a greeting card may actually be valid in some states, under certain circumstances. Wills have been written on the backs of envelopes, restaurant place mats, prescription blanks, hospital charts, tractor fenders, and jailhouse walls. A Philadelphia housewife wrote the following will on a page of her handwritten book of kitchen recipes:

Chili Sauce Without Working

4 quarts of ripe tomatoes, 4 small onions, 4 green peppers, 2 teacups of sugar, 2 quarts of cider vinegar, 2 ounces ground allspice, 2 ounces cloves, 2 ounces cinnamon, 12 teaspoons salt. Chop tomatoes, onions, and peppers fine, add the rest mixed together and bottle cold. Measure tomatoes when peeled. In case I die before my husband I leave everything to him.

Even without witnesses, the will was proved and allowed by the probate court in 1913. Pennsylvania statutes allow wills written entirely in the deceased's handwriting to be proved without any witnesses.

Another unusual form for a will was used by William Taylor at a bon voyage party held in his honor. When a guest at the party asked Taylor if he had a will, Taylor replied "no," took a dance invitation from his pocket, and wrote his will on the back of the invitation. When he died several years later, long after returning from the voyage, the 29-word will on the back of the dance invitation was allowed by the probate court.

In a similar situation, George W. Hazeltine had no paper available when he wanted to make his will. One of his nurses lifted her dress and allowed Mr. Hazeltine to write his will on her petticoat. Among other gifts, the will left $10,000 to each of his two nurses as a reward for their devotion. The Los Angeles court disallowed the "petticoat will," however, not because it was written on a petticoat, but because the same two nurses who inherited under it also signed the will as witnesses.

Just as wills may appear in different formats, their lengths vary greatly. The shortest known will, dated January 19, 1967, was written by Karl Tausch of Langen, Hesse, Germany. The will read: "Vse zene," which is Czechoslovakian for "All to wife." A similar will was written by an Englishman at the turn of the century. The will contained three words: "All to mother." The will went to litigation, however, over the meaning of the term *mother*, and the court held that mother meant not his *mother* but his wife.

The longest known will was that of Frederica Evelyn Stilwell Cook. The will was probated in London in 1925 and consisted of four bound volumes containing 95,940 words on 1,066 pages. Cook's estate totaled $100,000.

ONE OF MANY HOWARD HUGHES' WILLS

I Howard R. Hughes being of sound and disposing mind and memory, not acting under duress, fraud or other undue influence of any person whomsoever, and being a resident of Las Vegas, Nevada, declare that this is to be my Last Will and revoke all other Wills previously made by me.

After my death my estate is to be divided as follows:

first: one forth of all my assets to go to Hughes Medical Institute of Miami.

Second: one eight [sic] of assets to be divided among the University of Texas—Rice Institute of Technology of Houston—the University of Nevada and the University of Calif.

Third: one sixteenth to Church of Jesus Christ of Latterday Saints—David O. Makay

Forth: one sixteenth to establish a home for Orphan Children

Fifth: one sixteenth of assets to go to Boy Scouts of America

sixth: one sixteenth to be divided among Jean Peters of Los Angeles and Ella Rice of Houston

seventh: one sixteenth of assets to William R. Loomis of Houston, Texas

eighth: one sixteenth to go to Melvin DuMar of Gabbs, Nevada

ninth: one sixteenth to be divided among my personal aids at the time of my death

tenth: one sixteenth to be used as school scholarship fund for entire country

the spruce goose is to be given to the City of Long Beach, Calif.

the remainder of My estate is to be divided among the key men of the companys I own at the time of my death

I appoint Noah Dietrich as the executor of this will

signed the 19 day of March 1968

Howard R. Hughes

Over 30 wills that were submitted to courts in various states claimed to be that of Howard Hughes, the mysterious and reclusive American billionaire. The famous Melvin Dummar/Mormon Church version printed here inspired the film *Melvin and Howard*, starring Jason Robards as Hughes. The will seems too rough and simplistic to be that of so wealthy and worldly a businessman as Hughes. However, only after a long legal battle was the will finally rejected by the courts. None of the 30 wills was ever admitted to probate. The massive Hughes fortune passed by intestacy to distant relatives whom he hardly knew.

There Is Motivation

In 1927, a Canadian lawyer named Charles Miller left his estate "to the Mother who has given birth in Toronto to the greatest number of children" during the 10 years following his death. A competition, referred to as the "Stork Derby," took place, and $568,000 was eventually divided among four mothers who had each produced nine children within the 10-year period.

There Is Kindness

Remembering what it was like to be without a job and having worn-out shoes, an actor named Conrad Cantzen, who died in 1945, left $226,608.34 "for the people who can't buy shoes, even if they are not paid-up members of Equity. Many times I have been on my uppers, and the thinner the soles of my shoes were, the less courage I had to face the managers in looking for a job." Today, professional actors and actresses who are making the rounds, looking for work in worn-out shoes, can "do the shoe bit." Thanks to Conrad Cantzen, they can obtain money for a pair of shoes from Actors Equity, 226 West 47th Street, New York City, New York.

When he died in 1990, Malcolm Forbes, chairman and editor-in-chief of *Forbes* magazine, left each of his 750 employees an extra week's pay, as well as forgiveness of all personal loans from the company up to $10,000.

In a similar manner, Milton J. Petrie, founder of Petrie Stores, never forgot his modest background. A pawnbroker's son who made millions in the women's apparel business, Petrie continued his lifelong habit of generosity when he died in 1994. Besides establishing a charitable foundation and a family trust, Petrie's 120-page will awarded $90 million in trusts and gifts to 383 individuals. Those named in the will included a policeman paralyzed by an assailant's bullet in 1986, the mother of a murdered transit policeman, a fashion model whose face had been slashed, housekeepers, his barber, an elevator operator at a tennis club, former employees, and even strangers whose misfortune had touched him. Through his will, Petrie maintained his reputation for generosity by providing for those he had supported while alive.

There Is Decision Making

Henry Durrell could not decide which of his three nephews should inherit his stately property located on the shore of Hamilton Harbor, Bermuda. To solve the problem, he stated in his will that the choice should be made by a throw of the dice. On March 15, 1921, dice were thrown by the three nephews, and one of them, Richard Durrell, became the sole owner of the property.

There Is Retribution

The German poet Heinrich Heine wrote a will leaving all his assets to his wife on the condition that she remarry, "[b]ecause then there will be at least one man to regret my death."

In contrast, Patrick Henry, famous for the statement, "Give me liberty or give me death," provided generously for his wife in his will. "But in case my said wife shall marry again . . . I revoke and make void every gift, legacy, authority, or power herein mentioned and order, will and direct, She, my said Wife, shall have no more of my estate than she can recover by law." His widow decided to marry again and take the share that the law provided to wives.

There Is Surprise

Richard J. Cotter, Jr., belonged to the upper crust of Boston society. The son of a prominent Boston lawyer, he graduated from Harvard University and then Harvard Law School, where he befriended former President John F. Kennedy. When Cotter died in April 1999, it was not surprising that the multimillionaire provided generously for his beloved show horses by setting up a $400,000 trust for their care, or that he left $50,000 to the Kentucky man who trained them, and a home to the woman who cared for his prized horses. He similarly bequeathed parts of his estate to a local conservation group, a nonprofit organization that celebrates the children's author Thornton Burgess, and a local visiting nurses association.

What shocked even his executor, who had known him for over 50 years, was that Cotter bequeathed over a million dollars to various neo-Nazis, Holocaust deniers, and white supremacists. William L. Pierce, infamous for writing the *Turner Diaries*, which is said to have inspired the Oklahoma City bombing, received $25,000. Cotter left $100,000 to Ernest Zundel, the leading Holocaust denial propagandist in Canada, and $500,000 to James K. Warner, a founding member of the American Nazi Party whose New Christian Crusade Church advocates extermination of the Jews. Outwardly, Cotter was "kind, generous, a gentleman," in the words of a longtime employee, "but I guess everyone has their own little secrets."

In a different kind of surprise, a New Yorker, who died in 1880, wrote in his will: "I own seventy-one pairs of trousers, and I strictly enjoin my executors to hold a public sale at which these shall be sold to the highest bidder, and the proceeds distributed to the poor of the city. I desire that these garments shall in no way be examined or meddled with, but be disposed of as they are found at the time of my death." The executors did as they were instructed. Following the sale, each pair of trousers was found to contain $1,000 sewn into the lining.

Another secret was kept by the traveling TV personality, Charles Kuralt. When Kuralt died in 1999, his wife, "Petie," learned for the first time that her husband had been having an affair with Patricia Shannon for almost 30 years. Kuralt traveled the country with his mistress, unknown to his wife who stayed in New York. It was only upon Kuralt's death, when his will was entered for probate, that his personal and financial relationship with Shannon became public. (See Chapter 5 for a more complete description of this case.)

There Is Appreciation

Famous for the prizes awarded each year in his honor, Joseph Pulitzer left much of his fortune to employees when he died in 1911. His "faithful valet" received $25,000 (equal to over $325,000 today); his "chief" secretary received $20,000 (over $260,000). He also instructed the executors of his estate to confer with management at the two newspapers he owned and divide $40,000 among "the oldest and most faithful employees . . . giving a special preference on account of loyalty and length of service and to employees receiving salaries of less than $100 a week."

In a similar fashion, when the financier J. P. Morgan died in 1913, his will provided one year's salary to each employee of J. P. Morgan and Company.

More recently, the deli clerks at the Kroger supermarket in suburban Atlanta served the same breakfast every day to the same old man known as "Glenn." The women ignored his grumpy disposition and critical remarks, believing he needed sympathy and compassion. Little did they know that "Glenn" was really James Glenn Dudley, a wealthy, retired podiatrist from Atlanta. When he died of cancer at the age of 85 in 2000, his will reflected his gratitude for their kindness. Each of the four deli clerks was stunned to receive a check for $10,000. The bagger, who carried groceries to Glenn's car every day, received $30,000. Some might say that they earned it.

§ 1.2 THE PRIVILEGE OF HAVING A WILL

This brief overview of the more entertaining aspects of wills does not diminish the significance of making a will. The right to leave property by will is not an inherent right, but a privilege permitted by law. Each state has its own laws, passed by its legislature, setting forth precise rules for the disposition of property by will. Without such laws, one could not make a valid will. Massachusetts Gen. Laws. ch. 191, §1, is an example of a state statute permitting the making of a will:

Every person eighteen years of age or older and of sound mind may by his last will in writing, signed by him or by a person in his presence and by his express direction, and attested and subscribed in his presence by two or more competent witnesses, dispose of his property, real and personal . . . .

Wills are not cast in stone. They are **ambulatory**; that is, they are movable or subject to change. They can be revoked or changed at any time before death. People may change their wills as often as they wish, and it is not uncommon for people to have several wills during their lifetime. People should review their wills about every five years to consider changes in their assets. They may also need to change guardians, executors, and trustees as their circumstances in life change. In addition, it is often necessary, especially in view of today's high divorce rate, when personal or family circumstances warrant, to change one's **beneficiaries—** those who inherit under the will.

■ **ambulatory**

Movable; capable of being changed or revoked; able to walk.

■ **beneficiaries**

1. A person (or organization, etc.) for whose benefit a trust is created. 2. A person to whom an insurance policy is payable. 3. A person who inherits under a will. 4. Anyone who benefits from something or who is treated as the real owner of something for tax or other purposes.

A MODEST WILL FOR A NOBLE MAN

WARREN E. BURGER

Warren E. Burger, who retired as Chief Justice of the Supreme Court of the United States in 1986, died at the age of 87 in 1995. His will surprised many people in the legal community because of its short length and simplicity. Some people felt that his estate could have saved taxes by the use of a more complicated will. Estate planners, however, point out that Burger's estate planning was put into effect a year earlier, when his wife passed away. It is interesting to note that the former Chief Justice typed the will himself on a computer. Apparently, he failed to use the spell-check feature, because the term *executors* is misspelled in the first paragraph.

Last Will and Testament of Warren E. Burger

I hereby make and declare the following to be my last will and testament.

1. My exeuctors will first pay all claims against my estate;

2. The remainder of my estate will be distributed as follows: one-third to my daughter, Margaret Elizabeth Burger Rose and two-thirds to my son, Wade A. Burger;

3. I designate and appoint as executors of this will, Wade A. Burger and J. Michael Luttig.

(continues)

> **A MODEST WILL FOR A NOBLE MAN** (continued)
>
> IN WITNESS WHEREOF, I have hereunto set my hand to this my Last Will and Testament this 9th day of June, 1994.
>
> Warren E. Burger
>
> We hereby certify that in our presence on the date written above WARREN E. BURGER signed the foregoing instrument and declared it to be his Last Will and Testament and that at this request in his presence and in the presence of each other we have signed our names below as witnesses.
>
> Nathaniel E. Brady residing at 120 F St., NW, Washington, DC
>
> Alice M. Khu residing at 3041 Meeting St., Falls Church, VA

§ 1.3 RISKS IN WRITING ONE'S OWN WILL

Writing one's own will can be risky for a layperson, because the law of wills is highly technical and differs widely from state to state. Laypeople who write their own wills are often not aware of the many rules that apply to the writing of a will. In addition, they are not familiar with the true meaning of some of the terms commonly used in wills. Without proper professional assistance, people may die assuming their wills are clear and straightforward when, in fact, the opposite is true. Small errors in will-drafting may result in large depletions of the assets left to beneficiaries.

The DeLong case below illustrates this possible confusion. In deciding the DeLong case, the court of appeals said, "The problems encountered with the will in this case illustrate how treacherous it is to rely on preprinted form wills. At the time the decedent executed the will, she may have saved herself the expense of a lawyer, but in the end, her presumed devisees lost it all to intestacy." Doris DeLong helps to prove the old adage "Pennywise and pound foolish."

Wills must be executed precisely in accordance with the law of the state where they are made, and state laws are not the same. For example, some states require wills to be signed at the end; others do not. Some states require witnesses to sign in each other's presence; others do not. Some states require two witnesses except for wills written in the maker's own handwriting, which require none; other states always require two witnesses; and a few states require three. Because laypeople are not usually familiar with these rules, they can easily make a mistake when executing a will without an attorney. The requirements for executing wills are discussed in Chapter 5. When you study Chapter 5, you will be expected to learn the requirements for executing a will in your state. These particular state formalities are important for paralegals to know because paralegals are key members of the law office team handling the procedure involved in a will's execution.

CASE STUDY   **Matter of Estate of DeLong**

788 P.2d 889 (MT)

FACTS:	Doris I. DeLong wrote her own will using a preprinted form. Following the printed words, "I give, devise and bequeath to," she originally wrote in her own handwriting, "James E. DeLong and Helen DeLong." Thereafter, she lined out the word "and" and substituted the word "or," so that the sentence read, "I give, devise and bequeath to James E. DeLong or Helen DeLong."
LEGAL ISSUE:	Does a will that states "I give, devise and bequeath" to one party "or" another party provide enough information to determine the intent of its maker?
COURT DECISION:	No.
REASON:	By lining out the word "and" and by inserting the word "or," the will does not adequately identify what is to be bequeathed or devised, nor who is to inherit. The will simply does not leave any property to anyone. Because the real and personal property of the decedent are not effectively allocated by her will, that property passes under the laws of intestate succession.

Other rules of law relating to the interpretation of wills are also not usually known by laypeople. For example, if a child is unintentionally omitted from a parent's will, that child may be able to inherit from the parent's estate. Similarly, in some states, if a gift is made in a will to a relative who dies before the person who made the will, the deceased relative's children take their parent's share of the estate. Language can be used in drafting a will to prevent these situations from occurring. Unaware of such technicalities, laypeople who write their own wills may end up leaving their property to unintended heirs. These and other rules of law are discussed more fully in the chapters that follow.

§ 1.4 FINDING THE TESTATOR'S INTENT

The importance of proper legal advice given by a licensed attorney in the preparation of a will cannot be overstated. The language used in a will becomes particularly significant when a court tries to interpret the meaning of a will and determine the intention of the man (**testator**) or woman (**testatrix**) who made the will. The testator's intention must be ascertained from the particular words used in the will itself, from the context in which those words are used, and from the general scope and purposes of the will, read in light of the surrounding and attending circumstances. Elvis Presley's will provides an illustration of the importance and implications of precise wording.

■ **testator**

A person who makes a will.

■ **testatrix**

A female who makes a will.

782 S.W.2d 482 (TN)

FACTS:

Elvis Presley's will (see Appendix B) contained a testamentary trust directing the trustee, among other things, to pay for the support and maintenance of "my daughter, Lisa Marie Presley, and any other lawful issue I might have." Deborah Delaine Presley filed a petition alleging that she is the illegitimate daughter of Elvis A. Presley and is entitled to a share of the estate under this clause. Because it was beyond the scope of the proceeding, the court in this case did not rule on the question of whether Deborah Delaine Presley was the illegitimate daughter of Elvis Presley.

LEGAL ISSUE:

Do the words "lawful issue" in a will include children born outside of wedlock?

COURT DECISION:

No.

REASON:

The court noted that Elvis Presley had been involved in a paternity case and was aware of claims placed against him for children born out of wedlock. At the time the will was executed, Presley had one child from his only marriage. The provision for the child is coupled with the provision "and any other lawful issue I might have." There was no doubt in Mr. Presley's mind that Lisa Marie was his child (**issue**), nor was there any question that she was born in lawful wedlock. With this knowledge of the status of his daughter, he explicitly describes the other subjects of his bounty as "any other lawful issue." The clause provides for issue the testator "might have," indicating his intent to provide for those coming into existence after the execution of the will. The intent of the testator to provide only for legitimate children becomes even more clear when we consider his disposition of the corpus of the trust. Here again, he utilizes the descriptive word *lawful* when referring to his children who should receive his bounty. A will should be construed to give effect to every word and clause contained therein. We are compelled to believe that the word *lawful* was used to denote those born in lawful wedlock.

§ 1.5 WHERE THERE IS NO WILL

When someone dies without a will, his or her property passes according to a specific scheme that has been adopted by the state legislature. The scheme, known as the law of intestate succession, may or may not carry out the wishes of the decedent. **Intestate succession** is the legal name for the process of an heir becoming beneficially entitled to the property of one who dies without a will. In general, **real property** (the ground and anything permanently affixed to it) passes according to the law of intestate succession in the state where the property

■ **issue**

Descendants (children, grandchildren, etc.).

■ **intestate succession**

The distribution of inheritances to heirs according to a state's laws about who should collect. This is done when there is no valid will or when the will does not cover some of a dead person's property.

■ **real property**

Land, buildings, and things permanently attached to land and buildings. Also called realty.

is located. In contrast, **personal property** (everything that can be owned that is not real property) passes according to the law of intestate succession in the state where the decedent was domiciled at the time of death. State laws of intestate succession are not identical. People often die thinking their property will pass one way, when in fact it passes in a different way altogether. The law of intestate succession is discussed thoroughly in Chapter 4, but the major implications of dying without a will are highlighted in this section.

There Can Be No Named Beneficiaries

Without a will, specific individuals or institutions cannot be designated as the appropriate inheritors of an estate. The state, not the deceased, determines who receives the estate and in what proportion they receive it. Some people believe that a will is unnecessary if they own little or no property. What such people overlook is that their financial status may change before they die. For example, a friend or relative may die shortly before them, leaving them sizeable estates. A simple will would have left the unforeseen inheritance according to their wishes rather than according to the scheme developed by the state legislature. Further, the laws of intestate succession provide only for relatives to receive the estate. Friends, step-children, charities, and all others will not participate in any distributions.

There Can Be No Named Guardian

Without a will, a guardian for minor children will not be chosen by the deceased; instead, the court will appoint a guardian. A **guardian** is a person appointed to care for and manage the person, property, or both of a minor or a person who is mentally or physically incapacitated. The one who is cared for is called a **ward**. The law makes a distinction between the guardianship of a minor's person and the guardianship of a minor's property. The two parents or the one surviving parent are the natural **guardians of a child's person**. They are not, however, the natural **guardians of a child's property**.

State laws provide for the division of property among the surviving spouse and the surviving children of a person who dies without a will. If a minor child inherits real or personal property, the surviving spouse loses control of the portion of the property inherited by those young children, because the appointed guardian will oversee the minor's property. In many family situations, it is more desirable to have the surviving spouse inherit the entire estate of a deceased spouse than to split the estate with minor children. And this can be done only if the deceased spouse leaves a will.

■ **personal property**
Having to do with movable property, as opposed to land and buildings.

■ **guardian**
A person who has the legal right and duty to take care of another person or that person's property because that other person (for example, a child) cannot. The arrangement is called *guardianship*.

■ **ward**
A person for whom a guardian has been appointed.

■ **guardians of a child's person**
One who has the care and custody of a child or person who is mentally or physically incapacitated.

■ **guardians of a child's property**
One who has the responsibility of caring for a child's or incapacitated person's property.

AN EXCEPTIONAL FOOTBALL PLAYER

DERRICK THOMAS

The Kansas City Chiefs star linebacker Derrick Thomas died intestate (without a will), at the age of 33 from injuries suffered in a car accident in 2000. He was not married and was survived by seven children by five women, for whom he was paying child support. Thomas's estate was complicated by the fact that he died without a will. He was remembered as an exceptional person and player. Had he left a will, he might have been thought of as being even more special to those he left behind.

There Can Be No Named Personal Representative

personal representative

A general term for the executor or administrator of a dead person's property.

next of kin

1. Persons most closely related to a dead person.
2. All persons entitled to inherit from a person who has not left a will.

public administrator

An official appointed by the court to supervise the estate (property) of a dead person.

Without a will, a personal representative will not be chosen or appointed by the deceased. The **personal representative** is the person who carries out the terms of the will. He or she gathers together the assets, pays the debts and taxes, and distributes the remainder according to the terms of the will. The various types of personal representatives and their duties are discussed in detail in Chapter 11.

The value of choosing a conscientious personal representative is illustrated by the example of John Duncan, a retired hog farmer in North Carolina. Duncan willed his entire estate to orphans and troubled children. He disapproved, however, of using banks as a depository for his money. Instead he carried $50 and $100 bills in his bib overalls and stored cash throughout his property. When he died in 1992, his executor and friend, Robert Lotz, spent more than a year scouring through, under, and around Duncan's property. Lotz's diligence paid off. Under a potato bin, he discovered $2,080; in a medicine tube and a Wheaties box, he found $1,580; inside a pump house cinder block, wrapped in plastic and paper bags, appeared $7,000; and $1,800 showed up in a peanut butter jar stashed in a building column. Because of Lotz's perseverance and honesty, the North Carolina Baptist Children's Home received $13,206 in cash plus the proceeds from the sale of Duncan's home.

When a person dies without a will, the personal representative is appointed by the court following a priority list set by state statute. Generally, surviving spouses are given first priority, followed by **next of kin** (those most nearly related by blood). Next in line, however, are strangers to the decedent, including creditors and **public administrators** (officials appointed by the court to administer estates). Most people would probably not want strangers going through their personal belongings and making decisions about their property, even though they are not around to witness it. Yet that is what can happen when a person dies without a will. Additionally, the professionals appointed by the court will be taking the fees allowed by statute, which are sizeable, depleting the estates assets.

There Can Be No Testamentary Trust

Without a will, a trust that takes effect upon death cannot be established. A **trust** is an arrangement whereby property is held by one person for the benefit of another. Legal title is held by a trustee, who holds the property in trust for the benefit of a beneficiary. Testamentary trusts are vital estate planning tools. Property may be placed in trust in two ways: (1) by creating a living trust, that is, a trust that becomes effective while the person is alive, or (2) by creating a testamentary trust, which is a trust within the body of a will. Without a will, a testamentary trust cannot be created, and a trustee cannot be named. Estate planners consider a will to be a necessity even when a living trust is used as part of the estate plan. Estate planning, taxes, and trusts—important areas of concern to the paralegal—are discussed thoroughly in later chapters.

■ **trust**

An arrangement by which one person holds legal title to money or property for the benefit of another.

BENJAMIN FRANKLIN (1706–1790)

BENJAMIN FRANKLIN

If you would not be forgotten as soon as you are dead and rotten, either write things worth reading, or do things worth the writing.— B.F.

Benjamin Franklin, who was born in Boston and attended grammar schools there, died on April 17, 1790, a citizen of Pennsylvania. His will was dated July 17, 1788, and a codicil to it was dated June 23, 1789. The will and codicil were proved and allowed by the court on April 23, 1790.

In the codicil, Franklin left 1,000 pounds sterling in trust to the town of Boston. He designated the town's "Select Men, united with the Ministers of the oldest Episcopalian, Congregational and Presbyterian churches in that Town" as "managers" of the fund. The codicil directed that for the first 100 years, the money was to be used as a loan fund to help married tradesmen under the age of 25 start their own businesses. In the codicil, Franklin wrote that the managers:

(continues)

BENJAMIN FRANKLIN (1706–1790) (continued)

are to let out the same upon Interest at five per Cent per Annum to such young married Artificers, under the Age of twenty five Years, as have served an Apprenticeship in the said Town; and faithfully fulfilled the Duties required in their Indentures, so as to obtain a good moral Character from at least two respectable Citizens, who are willing to become their Sureties in a Bond with the Applicants for the Repayment of the Monies so lent with Interest according to the Terms herein after prescribed.

Franklin further directed that after 100 years of accumulation, a portion of the fund was to be laid out in public works chosen by the managers. The remainder of the fund was to accumulate for another 100 years, at the end of which time approximately one-fourth of the fund was to be left to the "Disposition of the Inhabitants of the Town of Boston," and approximately three-fourths of the fund was to be left to the "Disposition of the Government of the State."

After 100 years (plus 14 years of litigation), a portion of the fund was withdrawn to help establish the Franklin Institute, a two-year technical college in Boston. The balance of the fund was used to make five percent annual interest loans; in recent years, these loans have gone to medical students. The distribution of the balance of the fund, totaling nearly $5 million, was delayed by a dispute involving the Franklin Institute, the city of Boston, and the state of Massachusetts. In 1993, the Massachusetts Supreme Judicial Court held that the city of Boston and the state, not the Franklin Institute, were entitled to the fund.

The following Massachusetts cases provide an interesting history of Benjamin Franklin's bequest to the city of Boston more than 200 years ago. They also offer some insight into the importance of drafting wills and trusts carefully to avoid expensive litigation:

Higginson v. Turner, 51 N.E. 172 (1898)

Madden v. Boston, 58 N.E. 1024 (1901)

City of Boston v. Doyle, 68 N.E. 851 (1903)

City of Boston v. Curley, 177 N.E. 557 (1931)

Franklin Foundation v. City of Boston, 142 N.E. 367 (1957)

Franklin Foundation v. Attorney General, 163 N.E.2d 662 (1960)

Franklin Foundation v. Collector-Treasurer of Boston, 183 N.E.2d 710 (1962)

Opinion of the Justices to the House of Representatives, 371 N.E.2d 1349 (1978)

Franklin Foundation v. Attorney General, 623 N.E.2d 1109 (1993)

We can presume that the trail of litigation will go on, perhaps as long as the trust.

SUMMARY

Wills have been written on many kinds of strange materials, including the backs of envelopes, restaurant place mats, and recipe books. Wills often cause surprise and may motivate people to take certain courses of action. Wills can also embody acts of kindness, appreciation, gratitude, and retribution.

The right to leave property by will is a privilege permitted by law rather than an inherent right. Each state has its own statutes setting forth precise rules relating to the disposition of property by will. Wills can be revoked or changed at any time before death.

Because the law of wills is highly technical and differs widely from state to state, it is risky for one to write one's own will. Laypeople are usually not aware of the many rules that apply to the writing of a will and may not be familiar with the true meaning of legal terms commonly used in wills.

A will must be executed with the intent to dispose of one's property upon one's death. The language of the will provides the court with the means to determine the intention of the person who made the will.

When people die without a will, their property passes according to the law of intestate succession, which varies from state to state. People who die without a will lose the opportunity to name heirs, guardians, a personal representative, or trustees, and may have needlessly diminished the estate.

■ REVIEW QUESTIONS

1. Generally, how does property pass when someone dies without a will?

2. What are four advantages of having a will?

3. What is meant by the statement, "The right to leave property by will is not an inherent right."

4. How often may people change their wills? How often should people review their wills?

5. In construing the meaning of a will, what does the court seek to determine?

6. Give an example of how state laws differ in their requirements for executing a will.

7. Why can writing one's own will be risky for a layperson?

8. What can happen in some states if a gift is made in a will to a relative who dies before the person who made the will?

■ CASES TO DISCUSS

1. In anticipation of extended travels, Claude Rogers (who was 78 years old and unmarried) and Maxine Robinson invited Maxine's daughter, Judee Dunn; son-in-law, Bill; and a friend, Ina Witherspoon, to dinner. During the evening, Maxine wrote out a two-and-a-half-page will in her own handwriting, at the end of which she signed her name. Beneath her signature she wrote: "Judee Dunn: Claude & I give you full power to do & take care of all our Business & do as you wish

with, with it, with no problems from anyone. You can sell or dispose of all property & monies." This was signed by both Claude and Maxine and witnessed by Bill and Ina. Later, Claude died. Is the instrument the will of Claude? Explain. *Dunn v. Means*, 803 S.W.2d 542 (AR).

2. Father Paul Thomas Quinn executed a will containing the following bequest: "To my housekeeper of many years, Judy Crowe, I give, devise and bequeath an undivided eight per cent share of all the rest and residue of my estate if she be in my employment at the time of my death. If she is not in my employment at the time of my death then this gift to her shall lapse and the same shall be distributed in accordance with the provisions of paragraph Third, part F of this my Last Will and Testament." Later, Father Quinn's health deteriorated. He was hospitalized in September and spent the remainder of his life either in the hospital or a nursing home. During his stay in both places, he told Judy that he wanted her to work for him since he planned to return to his apartment when possible. Judy performed her last duties as housekeeper the following January, when Father Quinn's lease of the apartment was terminated. Father Quinn died in March. Did Judy Crowe inherit under Father Quinn's will? Why or why not? Matter of Estate of Quinn, 450 N.W.2d 432 (SD).

3. Joseph Forti's will stated, "I am married to LUCIA M. FORTI, who is referred to in this Will as 'my wife.' We presently have two children, KENNETH J. FORTI and DENISE A. FORTI who together with any other children of mine born or adopted after the execution of this Will, are referred to in this Will as 'my children.'" Another clause in the will said, "Reference to 'child' and 'children' means lawful descendants in the first degree, whether by blood or adoption." His will left his property to Lucia in trust and upon her death to "each of my children then living." Before making the will, Joseph had committed adultery and become the father of Stephanie, whom he acknowledged as his child. In deciding whether Stephanie should inherit from Joseph's estate, how must the court determine Joseph's intention? *Bell v. Forti*, 584 A.2d 77 (MD).

■ RESEARCH ON THE WEB_____

1. Log on to your state's bar association web site. Look up the ethics rules for your state. In what ways do your state ethics rules apply to the Day at the Office scenario at the beginning of the chapter?

2. Read more about the Howard Hughes "Mormon Will" case at <http://truthandgrace.com/mormonhugheswill.htm>

3. Information about the para-legal field is available online at <http://www.paralegal.edu/profession.html>.

4. Go to <http://celebritycollectables.com/> and look up a celebrity's will that you are curious about.

■ SHARPENING YOUR PROFESSIONAL SKILLS_____

1. Look up your state statute that permits a person to make a will, write down the statutory reference, and photocopy the statute for your notebook.

2. How many witnesses to a will are required under the law of your state? Give the statutory reference where the provision is found.

3. Think of a member of your family whom you believe has no will. Determine who would inherit from that person if he or she died today. Write some disadvantages that would result if that person should die at this time without a will.

4. Who besides Lisa Marie Presley was allotted support and maintenance in Item IV of the will of Elvis Presley (reproduced in Appendix B)?

5. Refer to ARTICLE FOURTEEN of the will of Richard M. Nixon (reproduced in Appendix B) and give a suggestion as to how the case of *Presley v. Hanks*, discussed in this chapter, might have been avoided.

6. How does ARTICLE TWO (A) of the will of Richard M. Nixon (reproduced in Appendix B) ensure that his daughters, Patricia Nixon Cox and Julie Nixon Eisenhower, would be able to have such items of tangible personal property as they wished?

7. Describe the acts of kindness shown in Paragraphs FOUR (A) and FIVE (C)(7) and (8) of the will of Doris Duke (reproduced in Appendix B).

■ SHARPENING YOUR LEGAL VOCABULARY_____

On a separate sheet of paper, fill in the numbered blank lines in the following anecdote with legal terms from this list:

ambulatory

beneficiaries

guardian

intestate succession

living trust

next of kin

personal property

personal representative

public administrator

real property

testamentary trust

testator

testatrix

trust

trustee

Linda Hull asked her lawyer to prepare an instrument called a will, which is a disposition of her property to take effect upon her death. The execution of such an instrument will prevent her property from passing according to the law of (1). Hull was the (2) of the instrument, which was (3), that is, subject to change. Hull named her children as (4) to inherit both her (5) (the ground and anything permanently affixed to it) and her (6) (everything else that can be owned). She named her brother to serve as (7) to care for and manage the person and property of her minor children. Hull's will also contained a(n) (8), that is, an arrangement under which property is divided into two parts, legal title and beneficial title. Because it was also contained in the will, it would be known as a(n) (9). She named her brother as (10), that is, the person to hold legal title. She also named her brother as (11) to carry out the terms of the instrument. If he is able to perform the task, it will be unnecessary for the court to appoint a(n) (12) (public official) to do the job.

■ KEY TERMS

ambulatory	issue	testator
beneficiaries	next of kin	testatrix
guardian	personal property	trust
guardians of a child's person	personal representative	ward
guardians of a child's property	public administrator	
intestate succession	real property	

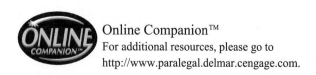

Online Companion™
For additional resources, please go to
http://www.paralegal.delmar.cengage.com.

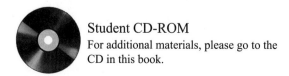

Student CD-ROM
For additional materials, please go to the
CD in this book.

Estate Planning

▪ CHAPTER OUTLINE

▪ CHAPTER OUTCOMES

- Explain the purpose of estate planning.
- Name the members of the estate planning team.
- List the four categories of facts that must be gathered in the estate planning process.
- Identify the principal tools available to the estate planner.
- Describe some postmortem estate planning devices.

▪ JOB COMPETENCIES

- Be able to discuss with others the importance of estate planning.
- Be able to serve as a proficient member of an estate planning team.
- Be able to gather facts that are needed in the development of an estate plan.
- Be able to plan and organize an estate plan under the supervision of an attorney.
- Be able to make recommendations to an attorney regarding possible postmortem estate planning devices.

“Why fear death? Death is only a beautiful adventure.”

LAST WORDS OF CHARLES FROHMAN (1860–1915)

■ A DAY AT THE OFFICE . . .

Tiffany Davis, a paralegal in the law firm of Stearns & MacDonald, was discussing a client's estate with Attorney Stearns.

"Mrs. Bradbury is coming in at 2:00 this afternoon," Attorney Stearns said. "She's still quite despondent about the death of her husband, but we need to begin the probate work."

"It must be hard for her. I'll get the file out right away," Tiffany responded. "Didn't they live in a lot of different states?"

"Yes. If I remember correctly, they owned property in New Mexico, Oregon, and Connecticut, among other places. Now that I think of it," Attorney Stearns continued, "you had better check to see if any of those states are community property states."

"Okay," Tiffany replied, jotting down some notes.

"We could have a domicile problem with this estate," Attorney Stearns thought out loud. "When you go through the file, look for evidence of Mr. Bradbury's domicile."

"There might be an estate planning questionnaire in the file," Tiffany suggested.

"I don't think so," Attorney Stearns countered. "Mr. Bradbury found it hard to talk about death and didn't want to do much more than make out a will when he came in to see us. We did a trust for him, though, and gave Mrs. Bradbury a power of appointment, among other things."

"Oh, that's good. Maybe now that he's gone we can do some postmortem planning for his estate," Tiffany offered.

"You can bet on that," Attorney Stearns responded. "And we'll see what we can do for Mrs. Bradbury before she dies, too."

"That's a good idea. I'll get her file out so that you can review her will while she's here."

"Thanks, Tiffany," Attorney Stearns replied. "If you're free at 2:00, it would be helpful if you could join us."

"Fine. I'll plan on it."

Queries:

1. Are New Mexico, Oregon, and Connecticut community property states?
2. Why did Attorney Stearns say, "We could have a domicile problem with this estate"?
3. Why is an estate planning questionnaire important?
4. When and by whom should an estate planning questionnaire be completed?
5. What could Mrs. Bradbury do with a power of appointment?
6. What are some possibilities with regard to postmortem planning for Mr. Bradbury's estate?

§ 2.1 PURPOSE OF ESTATE PLANNING

Estate planning is the positioning of a person's assets to maintain and protect the family most effectively, both during and after the person's life. The main purpose of all family estate planning is to obtain the maximum benefits of principal and income for the family and to pass on the family property intact (i.e., without any losses). Also important is the disposition of the property according to the client's desires while maintaining family harmony.

The general goal of estate planning is to protect the family unit and provide financial and psychological security. The proper positioning of a person's assets may even make a larger proportion of after-tax income available for the family to save or spend. A thoughtful insurance program can help to create a cash reserve and an estate that would otherwise not exist. Assets that might be depleted or reduced in value can be preserved by appropriate planning. Gifts, trusts, marital deductions, powers of appointment, pension and profit-sharing plans, and other business arrangements are additional devices used by the estate planning team to ensure the family's financial and psychological security and to maximize the assets ultimately shared by the beneficiaries (see Table 2–1). A well-developed estate plan can help do the following:

- clarify the client's intentions regarding the transfer of assets and care of dependents.
- make sure that the client's assets are properly managed and distributed after death.
- reduce transfer taxes so that wealth will be preserved for the benefit of the client's family.
- spare the client's family from complex and expensive legal proceedings following death or incapacity.

Estate planners make use of a wide variety of software programs to assist them with estate planning. You will find many estate planning software programs by searching on the Internet and keying in the words *estate planning software.*

■ **estate planning**
Carrying out a person's wishes for property to be passed on at her death and gaining maximum legal benefit from that property by using the laws of wills, trusts, insurance, property, and taxes.

TABLE 2–1 **Estate Plans Compared**

	No will or trust	Will only	Living trust	Estate tax trust
Can I avoid probate?	No	No	Yes	Yes, if funded during your life
Can I reduce/avoid federal estate taxes?	No	No	No	Yes
Will my estate stay private when I die?	No	No	Yes	Yes, if funded during your life

(continues)

TABLE 2–1   **Estate Plans Compared** (continued)

	No will or trust	Will only	Living trust	Estate tax trust
Can I keep inheritance from my heirs until they reach age thirty or older?	No	No	Yes	Yes
Can I arrange to have funds managed for the benefit of an heir who is handicapped or otherwise unable to handle funds?	No	No	Yes	Yes
Can I make sure my grandchildren will receive my estate after my children die, excluding spouses of my children?	No	No	Yes	Yes
Can I leave assets to children from an earlier marriage, cutting out my present spouse?	No	No	Depends on the state	Depends on the state and how trust is set up
How long should it take after my death until all assets are distributed and the estate is closed, assuming all goes well?	6 mo.– 2 yr.	6 mo.– 2 yr.	2–9 mo.	9 mo.–2 yr.
Can I retain control over my assets while I am alive?	Yes	Yes	Yes	Depends on how trust is set up
Can I change or revoke the plan?	N/A	Yes	Yes	Depends on how trust is set up
Does the plan provide for someone to handle my finances if I become disabled?	No	No	Yes	Yes, if funded during your life
What is the cost for a simple plan?	—	$50– $400	$500– $5,000	$2,000–$6,000

Reproduced with permission from Armond D. Budish, Michael Gilfix, Dennis Clifford, who are all contributors to *Modern Maturity*

§ 2.2 THE PLANNING TEAM

Individuals with different training and abilities, including the paralegal, form the estate planning team. An attorney who specializes in estate planning plays a key role, because many legal issues have to be addressed, legal advice given, and legal documents drafted and signed. The client's accountant can provide information about the client's income taxes, details of assets and liabilities, and realistic appraisals of those assets. A life insurance underwriter can determine the client's need for life insurance, suggest the type and amount required, and prepare an overall, cost-effective life insurance plan for the client.

If a bank is appointed as an executor or trustee, a trust officer of the bank will also be a team member. The trust officer provides advice on how specific investments are to be used in an estate plan. Based on her experience with administrative details, the officer may be able to suggest easier and more economical ways to administer the trust or estate.

An important member of the estate planning team is the well-trained paralegal, who can provide much-needed assistance to the attorney. In the U.S. Supreme Court case of *Missouri v. Jenkins*, 109 S. Ct. 2463, Justice Brennan noted:

> It has frequently been recognized in the lower courts that paralegals are capable of carrying out many tasks, under the supervision of an attorney, that might otherwise be performed by a lawyer and billed at a higher rate. Such work might include, for example, factual investigation, including locating and interviewing witnesses; assistance with depositions, interrogatories, and document production; compilation of statistical and financial data; checking legal citations; and drafting correspondence. Much such work lies in a gray area of tasks that might appropriately be performed either by an attorney or a paralegal.

Paralegals can relieve the attorney of many of the routine details of the estate planning process and thereby reduce the costs and time involved in the process. Paralegals cannot give legal advice to clients because that would be practicing law without a license, which is both illegal and unethical. They can, however, with proper training, assist the attorney in many ways, including the following:

- working with clients to assure that necessary estate planning information is gathered
- assisting with the preparation of estate planning questionnaires
- analyzing client assets and financial information
- drafting legal documents, such as deeds, wills, and trusts
- preparing summaries of provisions of wills and trust agreements
- preparing tax calculations
- monitoring state statutes to ensure that estate plans conform to state law
- reviewing and analyzing insurance policies
- preparing change-of-beneficiary forms
- recording instruments at appropriate registries

§ 2.3 GATHERING INFORMATION

Paralegals are frequently involved in the first, and probably most important, step of the estate planning process: gathering facts. Without these facts the process cannot proceed. Obtaining all the necessary data requires persistence and is the basis for all other procedures. The needed facts can be classified into four categories: (1) domicile, (2) property, (3) beneficiaries, and (4) the individual's objectives.

Domicile

■ **domicile**

A person's permanent home, legal home, or main residence. The words *abode*, *citizenship*, *habitancy*, and *residence* sometimes mean the same as domicile and sometimes not.

The probate court in the place where the testator was **domiciled** at the time of death has primary jurisdiction to administer the decedent's estate. The state where the decedent is domiciled often imposes an estate tax, and this state's law is followed to determine the distribution of personal property. Thus, the estate planner must establish and make clear the client's domicile.

A person can have several residences, but only one domicile at any given time. It is not always easy to determine whether someone has acquired a new domicile. For a new domicile to be established, the person must reside in the new place of residence and, at the same time, have the intent to abandon the former domicile and remain in the new one for an indefinite period of time. As the Winkler and Derricotte cases illustrate, a person's intention regarding domicile is determined by the person's conduct and all the surrounding circumstances. When there is a dispute over domicile, the burden of proving a change of domicile is on the person claiming that it has been changed. So long as a reasonable doubt remains, there is a presumption that the domicile has not been changed.

CASE STUDY ⚖ **Application of Winkler**

567 N.Y.S.2d 53 (App. Div.)

FACTS:	When Frederick E. Winkler died, the question arose as to the location of his domicile. He owned a home in Seaview, Fire Island, Suffolk County, New York, where he lived for seven months of the year. He spent the other months in his two other homes in New York County. His voting records, passport, marriage certificate, and driver's license listed Seaview as his residence, and witnesses' testimony indicated that he intended the home in Seaview to be his domicile.
LEGAL ISSUE:	Is a person's intention to be domiciled in a particular location determined by that person's conduct?

(continues)

CASE STUDY Application of Winkler *(continued)*

COURT DECISION: Yes.

REASON: The intention of one's domicile is determined by the conduct of the person and all the surrounding circumstances that can be proven by acts and declarations. The documentation in this case, as well as witnesses' testimony, were sufficient to show that it was the decedent's intention that his home in Seaview, Fire Island, was to be his domicile.

CASE STUDY In Re Estate of Derricotte

744 A.2d 535 (DC)

FACTS: Elise Derricotte had enjoyed living in the District of Columbia for many years. She sold her house in the district because it was too big and had too many steps for her to climb at her age, and moved to Maryland. She was never happy in her apartment in Maryland and frequently went house hunting in the District. Seven months after her move to Maryland, Ms. Derricotte bought a house in the District and arranged to have her nieces move in with her to assist her. The arrangement fell through, however, before she could move. She sold the house and gave part of the proceeds to a close friend (and licensed broker) to hold as a deposit on another house she expected to buy in the District. She continued to go on weekly outings to find a house in the District, where she continued to do her banking and attend church. Ms. Derricotte died intestate, while a resident of Maryland, at the age of 94—less than four years after leaving the District of Columbia.

LEGAL ISSUE: To establish a new domicile, must a person have the intent to abandon a former domicile?

COURT DECISION: Yes.

REASON: The following facts demonstrated Ms. Derricotte's intent not to abandon her domicile in the District of Columbia: (1) her long and continuing association with the District of Columbia, (2) her dissatisfaction with her apartment in Maryland, (3) her action in purchasing a new residence in the District, and (4) her intention to buy yet another residence there.

Property

All property should be listed in detail, including automobiles, household effects, objects of art, stamp collections, books, and similar possessions. The estate planner must determine the location of all real estate, the form in which title is held, its cost, fair market value, and the amount of all mortgages on the property. All insurance must be listed, with cost, age, present value, face value, cash surrender value, type of policy, and beneficiaries noted. Balance sheets and income statements of all businesses and partnerships must be reviewed. Stocks, bonds, and bank accounts should all be listed individually, and pension plans, profit-sharing plans, and stock option agreements should also be noted. All jointly owned property must be listed, as well as information about gifts made during the client's lifetime.

Beneficiaries

A family tree is a helpful device to visualize a family and all its members. Such a diagram makes concrete the often complex lineal relationships discussed in Chapter 4 (see Exhibit 2–1). Besides this visual aid, however, detailed information about all family members is essential to acknowledge or locate all heirs. Also, as beneficiaries need not be relatives, the location of nonfamilial beneficiaries are needed.

Objectives

The individual objectives of the client are the main focus of estate planning. The client's desires must be clarified and fulfilled in whatever way the client determines. The client may wish to endow the surviving spouse primarily or to favor one child, despite possible family resentment. The legal ramifications of such decisions must be discussed, but ultimately the client's personal preferences are what determine the specific aspects of the estate plan.

Record of Personal and Business Affairs

Estate planners may ask clients to complete a detailed questionnaire or record about their personal and business affairs before the initial interview with the attorney. Completion of the questionnaire in advance reduces the attorney's time and legal fees. Paralegals may have access to the information in the questionnaire or be asked to assist clients in filling out such a questionnaire. It is imperative that paralegals observe proper ethical conduct by not disclosing information that is learned about the client's affairs to anyone other than the attorney.

Many items in the questionnaire may not apply to a particular client; however, using so detailed a questionnaire ensures that all facts will be considered when formulating the best plan for the client. Appendix A illustrates a form that may be followed to record information about a client's personal and business affairs.

§ 2.4 ESTATE PLANNING TOOLS

Estate planning is sometimes called an art rather than a science. It involves a considerable amount of creativity. Every client's unique situation requires a creative approach by the estate planner. The tools available to the estate planner are limitless, but the principal ones used are wills, trusts, gifts, powers of appointment, insurance, retirement plans, and family limited partnerships. Another important tool is the making of a family tree (see Exhibit 2–2).

Wills

A will is considered to be the single most important estate planning instrument. Without a will, state law rather than the wishes of the decedent determines the disposition of the decedent's property. A will has no effect until the testator(rix) dies and may be changed or revoked by the testator(rix) at any time prior to death.

A well-organized will should be outlined before it is drafted. An outline forces the drafter to think through the entire document before focusing on specific details. It provides an overview of what has to be done and helps ensure the final document includes all necessary provisions. An outline also helps weed out potential inconsistencies in the document and furnishes a fail-safe checklist to make sure that everything required has been included.

Any handwritten notes taken by the attorney and the legal assistant during the client interview should be dated and retained in the client's file. These notes are useful in refreshing the attorney's and the legal assistant's recollection in the event of a will contest after the client dies.

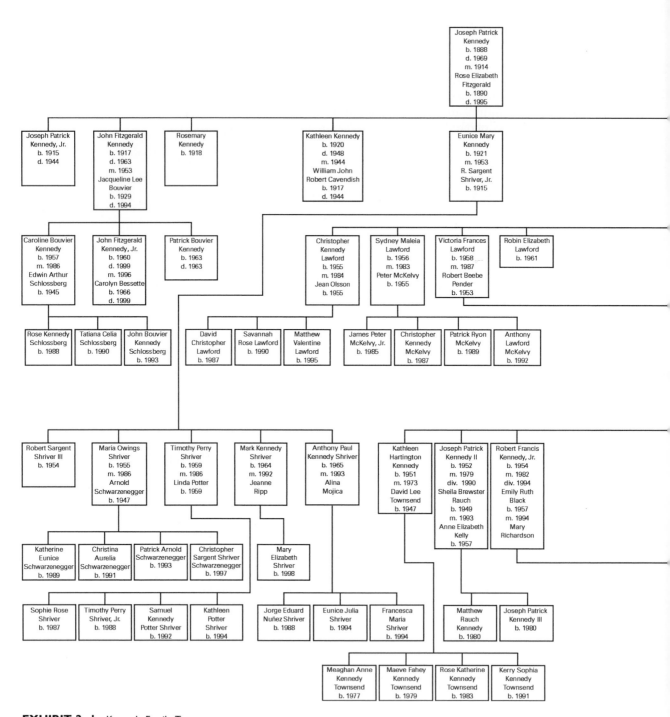

EXHIBIT 2-1   Kennedy Family Tree

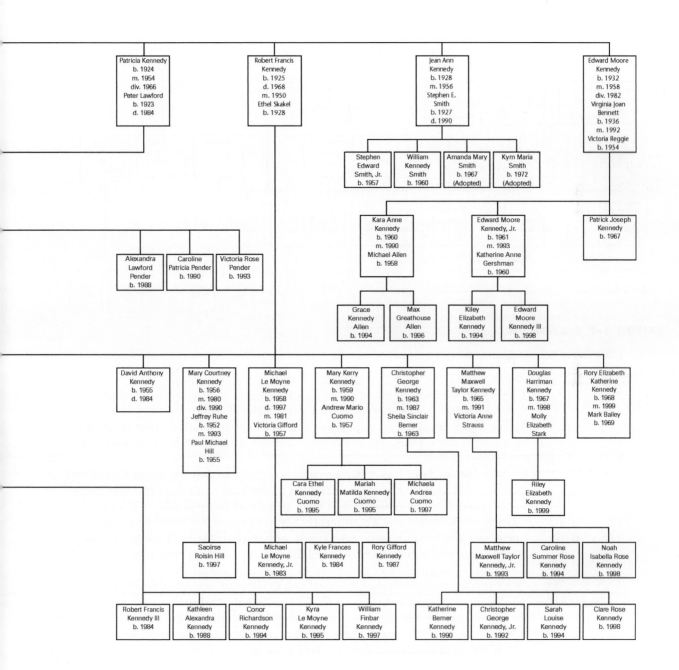

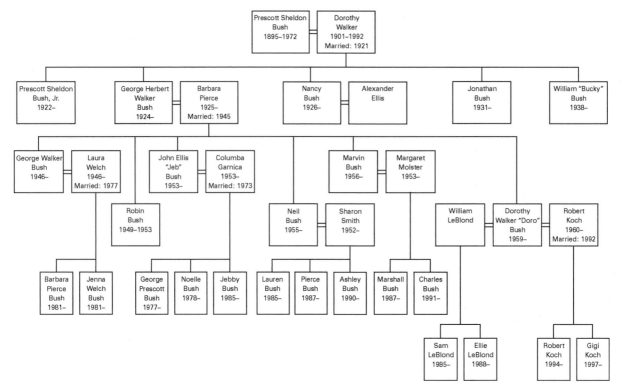

EXHIBIT 2–2 Bush Family Tree

Trusts

Trusts are used by estate planning specialists to reduce problems created by joint ownership, avoid the expense and publicity of probate, and reduce death taxes. Trusts are also used to pass assets on to future generations, provide income for people during their lives, and prevent family assets from being mismanaged or spent unwisely.

As discussed in Chapter 8, trusts may be created so that they come into effect when one is alive, or they may be created in the body of a will so that they come into effect after one passes away. Living trusts may be revocable or irrevocable. Trusts may be funded by life insurance. Spray, or sprinkling, trusts allow the trust principal and income to be distributed in a manner determined by a trustee rather than by the person who created the trust. Spendthrift trusts can be created to protect the interests of beneficiaries who might spend trust funds unwisely. Charitable trusts, credit-shelter trusts, and QTIP trusts are often used to reduce death taxes. So-called dynasty trusts are specially drafted irrevocable trusts with features that enable the trust to continue for many generations. They are designed to shelter assets from transfer taxes and, at the same time, allow generations of family members to receive income from those sheltered assets.

Gifts

The use of gifts during one's lifetime is an important estate planning device that offers tax-saving advantages, as well as providing to the donor the enjoyment of giving while alive. Death taxes can be reduced by giving property away while one is alive, but the gift must be completed. There are three requirements for an *inter vivos* **gift** (a gift between the living) to be completed: (1) the **donor** (the one giving the gift) must intend to make the gift, (2) the gift must be delivered to the **donee** (the one receiving it) and placed beyond the dominion and control of the donor, and (3) the donee must accept the gift. "Dominion and control" means the retention by the donor of power to direct the disposition or manner of enjoyment of the property that was given away. A person claiming an *inter vivos* gift has the burden of showing that a gift was intended by clear and convincing evidence.

A problem arises when a check is given as a gift, and the donor dies before the check is cashed. The Bolton case points out that for the gift to be completed, the check must be honored by the donor's bank before the donor's death.

For tax-saving purposes, gifts made to minors should follow the rules established by the Uniform Transfers to Minors Act. These rules are explained in Chapter 10.

■ *inter vivos* **gift**
An ordinary gift, as opposed to a gift made shortly before dying.

■ **donor**
A person making a gift to another or giving another person power to do something.

■ **donee**
A person to whom a gift is made or to whom a power is given.

CASE STUDY	**Matter of Estate of Bolton**

444 N.W.2d 482 (IA)

FACTS:	Arthur Bolton wrote a check for $20,000 to his daughter, Joyce, intending to make a gift. The check was drawn on the State Bank of Wapello and was mailed to Joyce in Maryland, where she was living. Joyce received the check, endorsed it, and mailed it to her bank in Baltimore with instructions to use it to establish a certificate of deposit in joint tenancy with her father. Bolton died before the check reached the bank on which it was drawn, and that bank refused to honor it.
LEGAL ISSUE:	To be effective, must a gift in the form of a bank check be accepted and honored by the drawee bank prior to the death of the donor?
COURT DECISION:	Yes.
REASON:	Mere delivery of the check to the donee does not place the gift beyond the donor's power of revocation prior to payment or acceptance. Moreover, the death of the drawer effects a revocation of the alleged gift of a check not presented for payment until after such death.

Tax Consequences of Gifts

A donor can give up to $12,000 a year (to be adjusted for inflation) to each of any number of donees without any tax consequences. Under the **split-gift provision** of the Internal Revenue Code, spouses may consent to treat gifts of one spouse as if made one-half by each spouse, and double the amount that may be given away tax free each year. For example, one parent of three children can give as much as $36,000 annually to the children ($12,000 to each) without filing a gift tax return, and both parents, by consenting, could increase the amount to $72,000.

Under the present tax law, a person can make lifetime gifts of up to $2,000,000 in 2007 and 2008, $3,500,000 in 2009, an unlimited exclusion in 2010 and reverting to $1,000,000 in 2011 under the sunset provision of the current tax law, in addition to the $12,000-per-donee-per-year exclusion, without being subject to a gift tax. Furthermore, gifts to the donor's spouse and to charitable institutions are exempt from the tax, as are gifts for tuition and medical care. For reporting purposes, gifts over $12,000 in any one year per donee, other than to a spouse, must be reported to the Internal Revenue Service (IRS) on either Form 709 or Form 709A. Federal estate and gift taxes are explained further in Chapter 13.

A MODEL ESTATE PLAN

JACQUELINE KENNEDY ONASSIS

Strategies used in the will of Jacqueline Kennedy Onassis can be applied to estates worth far less than her many millions. Her 36-page will, reproduced in Appendix B, provides valuable examples of effective estate planning techniques. Here is an analysis of some of the strategies used in writing her will:

Objective	Strategy Used by Onassis	Value of Strategy
Make personal requests	Jacqueline gave her personal papers and letters to her children and requested that her privacy be maintained: "I request, but do not direct, my children to respect my wish for privacy ... and consistent with that wish, to take whatever action is warranted to prevent the display, publication or distribution, in whole or in part, of these papers, letters, and writings."	A will provides the opportunity to make wishes known, while allowing beneficiaries some flexibility.

(continues)

	A MODEL ESTATE PLAN (continued)	
Give material possessions	Items of value or sentimental importance were given to specific individuals (e.g., a copy of John Kennedy's inaugural address signed by the poet Robert Frost given to her lawyer, Alexander Forger).	Specific bequests prevent arguments among heirs and indecision over the decedent's intentions.
Give cash	Taxes on cash gifts to friends, maids, and the butler are directed to be paid from the remainder of the estate.	Unless the will indicates that taxes be paid from the estate, the value of a gift can be drastically reduced.
Give real property	Each of her real properties was clearly devised to a specific heir.	Homes often involve emotional attachment and should be designated for a specific person rather than lumped into the total assets.
Create trusts	After all bequests were made, a charitable trust was established from the remainder of her estate.	For 24 years, the trust will give a specified percentage to charities, then will be divided among her grandchildren.

When heirs do not need income immediately, a charitable trust can be used to reduce estate taxes through donations to charities.

Powers of Appointment

When making a will or a trust, people sometimes do not know who their beneficiaries should be. They cannot predict which family members will be most needy at the time of the testator's death. A power of appointment in a will or trust allows flexibility in determining who will inherit from a decedent's estate. It allows someone besides the decedent to decide, after the decedent's death, who will be the beneficiaries and to what extent.

A **power of appointment** is a right created in a will, trust, or other instrument that allows the holder (the donee) to direct the disposition of property. The testator(rix) or other person who creates the power is known as the donor. The person to whom the power is given—that is, the power holder, the one who has the right to exercise the power—is called the donee. The person for whose benefit the appointment is made is known as the **appointee**. The act of executing the power is called the **appointment**. The property that is subject to the power is known as the **appointive property**.

■ **power of appointment**

The power to decide who gets certain money or property or how it will be used. This power is usually given to a specific person in a deed or will.

■ **appointee**

The person who is to receive the benefit under a power of appointment.

■ **appointment**

The act of putting into effect a power of appointment.

■ **appointive property**

Property that is an estate asset that will be given out by power of appointment.

Powers of appointment may be either general or special. A general power of appointment gives the donee the right to appoint the property to any appointee she desires, including the donee or the donee's estate. In contrast, a special power of appointment limits the appointment of the property to a specified class of persons named by the donor. The following is an example of a special power of appointment in the body of a trust:

> On the death of the donor's wife, the remaining trust property shall be paid over as the donor's wife may in her last will and by express reference to this instrument appoint to any of the donor's issue. Insofar as the donor's wife fails to exercise this power of appointment, the remaining trust property shall be distributed to the donor's then living issue by right of representation.

In view of the language used in this sample power of appointment, the donor's wife must select the appointees from among the donor's issue. The following is an example of a provision that could be used in the wife's will to exercise the power:

> I am the donee of a power of appointment under a declaration of trust dated _____ , 2___ , wherein the settlor is my late husband. I hereby expressly exercise such power by appointing the appointive property thereunder as follows: 50% to my husband's daughter Karen; 25% to my husband's daughter Cynthia; and 25% to my husband's son Charles.

Insurance

Insurance performs many roles in a family estate plan. Most important is its ability to furnish liquidity to an estate. As part of an integrated business plan, insurance may be used to finance the sale of a business interest, thereby guaranteeing sufficient cash to prevent a forced liquidation and the accompanying losses. Insurance may also create an estate that would otherwise be nonexistent. Broadly speaking, life insurance is divided into three general classes: (1) term, (2) whole life, and (3) endowment.

Term life insurance is issued for a particular time period, such as one, five, or 10 years. It offers protection only, with no cash surrender or loan value. The cost of term insurance increases with each new term because the insured is older and at a higher risk of death. Term insurance is the least expensive kind of life insurance, providing maximum protection for the period of coverage at minimum cost. However, it offers no protection after the expiration of the term.

Whole life insurance, also called ordinary life insurance and straight life insurance, provides lifetime protection and builds up a cash surrender value, but payments continue for life. If the policy is cancelled, the policyholder can receive the cash surrender value of the policy, making the insurance a form of savings. **Limited-payment life insurance** requires a greater annual premium, but need

■ **term life insurance**
Life insurance that ends at the end of a certain time period.

■ **whole life insurance**
Life insurance with continuing premium payments (which stop if the policy becomes fully paid), a sum paid at death, and, usually, a cash surrender value.

■ **limited-payment life insurance**
Insurance for which premiums are paid only for the limited period required by the policy, such as 10, 20, or 30 years. After that period, the policy is paid up.

only be paid for the limited period required by the policy, such as 10, 20, or 30 years. After that period, the policy is paid up. Like ordinary life insurance, limited-payment life insurance has a cash surrender value.

Universal (adjustable-premium whole) life insurance, is a flexible type of insurance coverage that allows policy-holders to change the terms of the policy as their needs change. Coverage can be increased or decreased, and cash can be withdrawn without cancelling the policy.

Endowment insurance provides protection for a stated time, generally 20 to 30 years. The face value of the policy is paid to the insured at the end of the stated period, or, if the insured dies before then, the face value is paid to the beneficiary at the time of death. Thus, endowment insurance functions as both a life insurance plan and a way to guarantee funds to the insured if she lives beyond the time during which the insurance is in effect. Basically, an endowment policy is a savings plan guaranteed by life insurance. The cost of endowment insurance is higher than whole life insurance because the policy builds up its cash value more rapidly.

An **annuity** is not really life insurance. Rather, it is a guaranteed retirement income providing period payments over a specified term or for the life of the insured. If the annuity is for a fixed number of years, the beneficiary will receive whatever is left if the insured dies before that time. In contrast, if the annuity is for the life of the insured, any amount remaining after the insured's death is lost. Annuities are purchased either by paying a lump sum or by making periodic payments to the insurer.

Long-term care insurance provides money to pay for nursing home and/or custodial care when an insured becomes chronically debilitated. Many people erroneously believe that either private health insurance or government-based benefits like Medicaid will pay for these needs. Nothing could be further from the truth. Virtually no private health insurance policies pay anything towards custodial care; likewise, Medicaid provides only for acute care benefits. Even benefits for indigent individuals provided through Medicare only pay for nursing home care for a few months, and, of course, Medicare requires that an individual deplete her assets before it can be used. The fear of saving for a lifetime, then seeing all those assets spent on long-term care has spurred an aging American population to consider long-term care insurance as protection.

Some seven million long-term care insurance policies have been sold in the United States in the last 30 years. Policies may vary widely, making comparison shopping difficult, but most good policies can provide peace of mind that care in one's later years will be available and affordable for the insured. Part of that comfort comes from protecting the depletion of assets from expensive long-term care costs, making these policies useful in estate planning. Policies can cover not only nursing home care but should cover care in assisted living facilities, or even home care assistance. The more care options one includes in the policy, however, the more expensive the policy becomes.

■ **universal (adjustable-premium whole) life insurance**
Type of whole life insurance that allows the policyholder flexibility in choosing and changing terms of the policy.

■ **endowment insurance**
An insurance policy that pays a set amount at a set time or, if the person insured dies, pays the money to a beneficiary.

■ **annuity**
1. A fixed sum of money, usually paid to a person at fixed times for a fixed time period or for life. 2. A retirement annuity is a right to receive payments starting at some future date, usually retirement, but sometimes a fixed date. 3. An account with an investment or insurance company that is tax free until retirement.

■ **long-term care insurance**
An insurance policy designed to provide money to pay for nursing home and custodial care when an insured becomes chronically ill.

The trigger for most policies comes either when the insured cannot perform at least two essential daily activities such as bathing, eating, or dressing, or when the insured is cognitively impaired by any dementia such as Alzheimer's disease. When triggered, the policy pays an amount, based on a daily schedule, for the level of care that the policy covers. The policy will pay the daily rate over the term of years that the policy covers. Obviously, the longer the term that the insured's policy covers, the more expensive the policy.

Long-term care insurance is more affordable the younger you are when it is purchased. The American Association of Long-Term Care Insurance, at its Web site (<http://www.aaltci.org>) provides an estimator for costs of this insurance. For example, a healthy 40-year-old would pay an estimated $641 annually for a four-year term comprehensive policy with inflation protection, a 20-day waiting period, and a $100-per-day benefit. The same policy would cost a 50-year-old an estimated $849 per year. If this policy was purchased by a 65-year-old, the estimated cost would be $1,726 per year.

There is no age at which a healthy person cannot qualify for a long-term care policy. However, as an individual ages and her health deteriorates, she may reach a point at which health problems prevent qualification. Also, since the annual costs rise as the starting age rises, the costs can become either out of reach or at least become not cost-effective. For example, at age 75, the previously mentioned policy would cost over $10,000 per year.

Retirement Plans

Retirement plans are an important part of estate planning. Government-sponsored retirement plans include railroad pensions, civil service pensions, military pensions, and Social Security. People who have paid into social security for at least 40 calendar quarters (10 years) are eligible to collect retirement benefits. Retirees may begin collecting reduced Social Security benefits at age 62. They will collect full benefits, however, if they wait until they reach age 65 before starting the process. The latter age increases to 66 and 2 months for people born after 1954, and to 67 for people born after 1960 (see Table 2–2). When collected at 62, Social Security reductions range from about 20 percent for individuals born in 1937 or earlier, to about 30 percent for individuals born in 1960 and later.

In addition to government-sponsored plans, there are a number of different kinds of private retirement plans. **Traditional IRAs** (individual retirement accounts) are individually owned personal pension plans for people (and their nonworking spouses) who are under 70½ years of age and have earned income. The amount that may be contributed to a traditional IRA is $4,000 in 2007, increasing to $5,000 in 2008, for people 49 and younger. An additional $1,000 may be contributed by individuals 50 and older. Contributions are tax deductible if one's income is below a prescribed amount, and interest on the

■ **traditional IRAs**
Bank or investment accounts into which some persons may set aside a certain amount of their earnings each year and have the interest taxed only later when withdrawn.

TABLE 2–2   **Retirement Age to Receive Social Security Benefits**

People Born in	Receive Full Benefits at Age
1938	65 and 2 months
1939	65 and 4 months
1940	65 and 6 months
1941	65 and 8 months
1942	65 and 10 months
1943–54	66
1955	66 and 2 months
1956	66 and 4 months
1957	66 and 6 months
1958	66 and 8 months
1959	66 and 10 months
1960 or later	67

earning is tax deferred until the money is withdrawn. Distributions (withdrawals) made before the age of 59½ are subject to a 10 percent penalty with the exception of an amount for certain home purchases and higher education costs. Distributions from traditional IRAs must begin the year after the contributor reaches the age of 70½.

Roth IRAs are similar to traditional IRAs except that distributions are not required during the owner's lifetime and, when taken after age 59½, are tax free if the account has been in existence for five years. In addition, the amount that passes to the owner's beneficiary at death is not subject to federal income taxes. It is, however, subject to federal estate taxes if the estate is large enough to be taxable. A traditional IRA may be converted to a Roth IRA when the owner's annual adjusted gross income is below $100,000. However, the conversion is taxable on the entire amount of the owner's original deductible contribution as well as on its earnings. Contributions for a Roth IRA are the same as those for a traditional IRA.

In addition to the IRAs mentioned, **education IRAs** (also called Coverdell Education Savings Accounts) can be established for children under the age of 18 by anyone who wishes to put money aside for a child's elementary through postsecondary education. Up to $2,000, through 2010, may be contributed annually for each child. A bank must be the custodian or trustee of the funds in

■ **roth IRAs**
Retirement accounts that are similar to traditional IRAs except that distributions are not required and are tax free when taken after age 59½ if the account has been in existence for 5 years or longer.

■ **education IRAs**
Accounts that can be established for children under the age of 18 for a child's elementary through postsecondary education.

the account. The earnings on an education IRA accumulate tax free, making it a desirable investment for many people. Although contributions are not tax deductible, they are not considered gifts and therefore do not reduce the amount of gifts that can be made tax free by the donor under federal estate and gift tax law. If the particular child does not use the funds for a postsecondary education, the beneficiary can be changed to another child in the family.

All states now have college savings plans, known as 529 plans, for their citizens. Income that is earned on 529 plans is not taxable under federal law, allowing savings to grow at a faster rate. For more information about state college savings plans go to <http://www.collegesavings.org>.

A **401(k) plan** is a company-sponsored retirement plan in which an employee agrees either to take a salary reduction or to forgo a bonus to provide money for retirement. Many employers make matching contributions to the plan based on a percentage of the employee's contribution; however, the law places limits on the amount that can be contributed annually to a 401(k) plan. The money that is invested in the plan and the interest accruing from it are tax free until it is withdrawn at retirement. Withdrawals from a 401(k) pension plan made before the age of 59½ are subject to a 10 percent penalty with the exception of death, disability, termination of employment, or financial hardship.

A **simplified employee pension plan (SEP)** is a pension plan in which an employer withholds money from the employee's salary and deposits it directly into the employee's IRA. Contributions are not currently taxed, and accumulated earnings are tax deferred. There are limits (which are indexed for inflation) to the amount that may be contributed to SEP accounts. Like other private pension plans, withdrawals made before the age of 59½ are subject to a 10 percent penalty (see Table 2–3).

A **Keogh plan** is an optional retirement plan for self-employed people (sole proprietorships and partnerships) and their employees. When a self-employed person elects to adopt a Keogh plan, all employees who have been employed for more than three years and work 1,000 hours or more a year must be included in the plan. Each year, self-employed people may deposit up to 25 percent of their income, or a maximum of $30,000, into the retirement plan account. Whatever percentage contribution employers made to their own account must also be made to their employees' accounts. Contributions to Keogh plans are tax deductible, and the interest they earn is tax deferred until the money is withdrawn. Withdrawals made before the age of 59½ are subject to a 10 percent penalty.

Family Limited Partnership

Estate planners will sometimes recommend placing family-owned businesses into the form of a family limited partnership. A **family limited partnership** is a partnership of family members in which one or more family members (typically

---

■ **401(k) plan**

A company-sponsored retirement plan in which an employee agrees either to take a salary reduction or to forgo a bonus to provide money for retirement.

■ **simplified employee pension plan (SEP)**

An employer's contribution to an employee's IRA that meets certain federal requirements. Self-employed persons often use a SEP.

■ **Keogh plan**

A tax-free retirement account for persons with self-employment income.

■ **family limited partnership**

A partnership of family members in which one or more family members are general partners and one or more family members are limited partners.

TABLE 2–3   **IRA Contribution Limits Increase Gradually**

	Roth and Traditional IRAs		401(k), 403(b), SEP	
Tax Year	Under Age 50	Age 50 and over	Under Age 50	Age 50 and over
2007	$4,000	$5,000	$15,000*	$20,000+
2008	$5,000	$6,000	$15,000*	$20,000+
2009	$5,000	$6,000	$15,000*	$20,000+

* Amounts are adjusted for inflation in $500 increments in these and subsequent years.

+The contribution amount and the catch-up amount (both of which are combined to equal the limit shown) are separately adjusted for inflation in $500 increments in these and subsequent years.

the parents) are general partners and one or more family members (typically the children) are limited partners. **General partners** manage the partnership and have unlimited liability. **Limited partners** have no voice in managing the partnership and have no liability beyond their investment in the partnership. Under this form of ownership, parents can retain control of a business, continue to receive income from it, and make annual gifts of limited-partnership interest to their children at reduced gift-tax rates. The tax rates are reduced because the Internal Revenue Code allows a discount on the value of gifts of limited-partnership shares. The shares are not worth as much because limited partners have restricted rights to the management and sale of the business. Thus, a parent's gift to a child of a $10,000-valued limited-partnership share would be treated as a $7,000 to $7,500 gift rather than as a gift of $10,000.

■ **general partners**
Members of a partnership who run the business and have liability for all partnership debts.

■ **limited partners**
Members of a partnership who partly or fully finance a business, take no part in running it, and have no liability for partnership debts beyond the money they put in or promise to put in.

§ 2.5 POSTMORTEM PLANNING

As unusual as it may seem, estate planning does not end when someone dies; rather, it continues until all possible benefits are identified, explained to heirs, and claimed if possible. Estate planning after a person dies is known as **postmortem planning** and can sometimes be advantageous, especially in saving taxes. An instrument such as a will or a trust cannot be changed or discarded after the death of a decedent; however, decisions can be made and actions taken that can produce tax-saving benefits.

Death taxes can sometimes be reduced when property passes to a family member other than the one who is named in the will to receive it. The gift is renounced or disclaimed and passes by intestacy to other family members in a way that results in a tax savings to the family as a whole.

■ **postmortem planning**
Estate planning done after a person dies.

For example, suppose a son dies intestate, survived by an elderly mother and a sister. Under many state laws, the elderly mother inherits and the estate is subject to estate taxes. Soon thereafter, the mother passes away, leaving everything to her daughter. Like her son's estate, the mother's estate is subject to estate taxes, even though some of it was just taxed. This double taxation could have been avoided if the elderly mother had disclaimed the inheritance from her son and allowed the property to pass to her daughter initially. A **disclaimer** is a formal renunciation of a gift under a will, a trust, or the law of intestate succession. Under federal tax law, a **qualified disclaimer** (illustrated by the Holden case) is defined as an irrevocable and unqualified refusal by a person to accept an interest in property, but only if it is: (1) in writing, (2) received within a specified time, (3) received prior to the acceptance of any benefits, and (4) legally effective to pass the disclosed interest to another person without direction from the person making the disclaimer.

Other devices used in postmortem planning are the release of a power of appointment and the selection of optional provisions in life insurance policies. Also considered are the selection of the tax year for income tax purposes and whether to file a joint return on the decedent's final return. Other strategies include delaying the administration of the decedent's estate and distributing estate assets over a period of time to beneficiaries rather than giving them out all at one time.

■ **disclaimer**

The refusal, rejection, or renunciation of a claim, a power, or property.

■ **qualified disclaimer**

Under federal tax law, an irrevocable and unqualified refusal by a person to accept an interest in property. It is effective only if it is in writing, received within a specified time, received prior to the acceptance of any benefits, and legally effective to pass the disclaimed interest to another person without direction from the person making the disclaimer.

CASE STUDY **Renunciation of Legacy**

20A AMJUR LF WI 266:1093

It is the wish of the undersigned, _____ , that the other members of the family of _____ , deceased, who may be entitled to receive property of the estate under the law may receive it. I therefore decline to accept anything under the will of _____ , deceased, and renounce the same in toto, so far as any interest coming to me is concerned, and leave it to descend under law to the parties entitled, free from any encumbrance on account of the provision naming me in the will.

Dated:

Sometimes taxes can be saved if a spouse exercises elective rights (discussed in Chapter 7). For example, suppose a wife died with a will that left everything to her son. To reduce the estate tax liability on his wife's death, her husband elected to take his intestate share, which qualified for the estate tax marital deduction. The husband's actions resulted in a considerable estate tax savings. The husband then made a gift of his elective share directly to his son's children, reducing the estate taxes ultimately payable upon his son's subsequent death.

CASE STUDY   **In Re Estate of Holden**

539 S.E.2d 703 (SC)

FACTS:	William Holden, Sr., died intestate survived by his wife, two sons, and two grandchildren (one of whom was in gestation when the decedent died). Wishing the entire estate to pass to his mother, each son signed a disclaimer stating, "I hereby disclaim and renounce any interest in the estate and relinquish any claim I may have to it." The sons did not realize that their inheritance, if disclaimed, would pass under intestate law to their children—the lineal descendants of their father—rather than to their mother (see Chapter 4). Learning the legal effect of their disclaimers, the sons filed court documents attempting to revoke their disclaimers.
LEGAL ISSUE:	Can a disclaimer of an inheritance be revoked?
COURT DECISION:	No.
REASON:	A qualified disclaimer is irrevocable under South Carolina statutes, which follow the federal tax law on the subject.

SUMMARY

The primary purpose of all family estate planning is to arrange the affairs of the family unit to obtain the maximum benefits of principal and income for the family and, to the fullest extent possible, to pass on the family property without any loss. The overall goal is to protect the family unit and achieve financial and psychological security to the maximum extent possible.

The first step in planning an estate is to gather the facts, which fall into four categories: (1) domicile, (2) property, (3) beneficiaries, and (4) the individual's objectives. A questionnaire should be completed by the client and returned to the lawyer before any discussion of specific family estate planning proposals. The individual objectives of the client cannot be overlooked in planning an estate.

An attorney who specializes in estate planning, an accountant, and a life insurance underwriter are members of the estate planning team. If a bank is a fiduciary, a trust officer is also included. An important member of the estate planning team is the well-trained legal assistant.

The principal tools used by an estate planner are wills, trusts, gifts, powers of appointment, insurance, retirement plans, and family limited partnerships. A will is considered to be the single most important estate planning instrument. Trusts are used by estate planners to pass assets on to a future generation, provide income for people during their lives, and prevent family assets from being mismanaged or spent unwisely. Trusts also help to reduce problems created by joint ownership, avoid the expense and publicity of probate, and reduce taxes. Gifts are important to reduce death taxes. Powers of appointment allow flexibility in determining who will inherit from a decedent's estate. Insurance can create an estate where otherwise there would be none. It can also furnish liquidity, thus preventing a forced sale of estate property.

Estate planning does not end when a person dies. Postmortem planning can often save estate taxes. Devices such as disclaiming inheritances and exercising a spousal election can sometimes reap tax-saving benefits for beneficiaries.

■ REVIEW QUESTIONS_____

1. Why are paralegals not allowed to give legal advice to clients?

2. What is the primary purpose of all estate planning?

3. Name six members of an estate planning team.

4. What is the first step in estate planning? List the four categories into which the needed facts can be classified.

5. What is required for a new domicile to be established, and why is the determination of domicile important?

6. What are the principal tools used by estate planners?

7. Why are trusts used by estate planners?

8. How can the use of gifts as an estate planning device reduce death taxes?

9. Why might someone use a power of appointment in a will or trust?

10. Describe two postmortem estate planning devices.

■ CASES TO DISCUSS_____

1. Lenora Conger assisted in caring for her uncle, William Westleigh, during his declining years. Westleigh gave Conger $34,000 to keep in her safe deposit box, saying he did not want others to know that he had that amount of money. He also told Conger she could use the money to take care of her parents' medical needs. Conger believed that the money should be retained to cover Westleigh's medical needs and that it would always be available to him if needed. When Westleigh died, approximately $27,000 of the funds remained. Conger claims that the money was a gift to her. Do you agree? Why or why not? *Westleigh v. Conger*, 755 A.2d 518 (ME).

2. John L. Lauricella, Jr., died while living in a house that was owned by his son and located in St. Tammany Parish, Louisiana. Three months before he died, in a codicil to his will, Lauricella declared himself to be a resident of St. Tammany Parish. He also had a checking account there. However, in his last will and testament, executed seven years earlier, Lauricella had declared himself to be a domiciliary of Jefferson Parish. In at least three real estate transactions conducted a month before he died, and in a trust agreement executed 10 days before his death, Lauricella identified himself as a resident or domiciliary of Jefferson Parish. He was a registered voter in Jefferson Parish, and his driver's license, income tax records, and death certificate all identified him as a Jefferson Parish resident. His son stated that his father lived in the St. Tammany Parish

house for insurance purposes. Who has the burden of proving a change of domicile? Was Lauricella domiciled in St. Tammany Parish or in Jefferson Parish? Explain. Succession of Lauricella, 571 So. 2d 885 (LA).

3. Mr. Macklem made a donation to the Church of the Adamic Communion, a religious enterprise founded by Mr. Macklem. Mr. Macklem was the sole member of the church, which was located at his residence. No regular worship services were conducted by or at the church. The church operated to disseminate Mr. Macklem's personal religious views and to proselytize others to his views. Was the gift to the church a completed gift? Why or why not? *Macklem v. United States*, 757 F. Supp. 6 (D. CT).

■ RESEARCH ON THE WEB

1. For an overview of estate planning, see <http://www.law.cornell.edu> and follow the Topics link and then the Estate Planning link.

2. Go to <http://www.lawcrawler.com>. Under the topic Research, click Summaries of Law. Then, scroll down to Trusts & Estates and click Estate Planning. Select a topic of interest and write a report on your findings.

3. To learn more about saving for college, key in <http://www.Google.com>. Then, in the space provided, type "Coverdell Education Savings Accounts."

■ SHARPENING YOUR PROFESSIONAL SKILLS

1. Refer to the will of Theodore Roosevelt (reproduced in Appendix B).

   a. What paragraph contains a power of appointment?

   b. What is the appointive property?

   c. Who is the donee of the power?

   d. Who is the appointee?

2. Draw a diagram of your family (a family tree).

3. Refer to Item XI in the will of Elvis Presley (reproduced in Appendix B). Assume that Elvis's father wishes to exercise the power of appointment, in his own will, by naming John Burns as successor trustee to Elvis's will. Draft a clause that could be used in Elvis's father's will to accomplish this.

4. For what reason do you think paragraph FIRST (D) and (E) and paragraph THIRD (B) and (D) of the will of Jacqueline K. Onassis (reproduced in Appendix B) authorize her children to renounce and disclaim interests in real and personal property?

5. In your own words, explain the meaning of paragraph FOURTH of the will of Jacqueline K. Onassis (reproduced in Appendix B).

■ SHARPENING YOUR LEGAL VOCABULARY_____

On a separate sheet of paper, fill in the numbered blank lines in the following anecdote with legal terms from this list:

401(k) plan

appointees

appointive property

appointments

disclaimer

donee

donor

education IRA

endowment

estate planning

family limited partnership

general partners

general power of appointment

group term life insurance

inter vivos gift

Keogh plan

limited partners

limited payment life insurance

long-term care insurance

ordinary life insurance

postmortem planning

power of appointment

qualified disclaimer

Roth IRA

simplified employee pension (SEP) plan

special power of appointment

split gift provision

straight life insurance

term insurance

traditional IRA

whole life insurance

When Stanley died, his wife, Ruby, realized that Stanley had done some (1), that is, he had arranged his property and estate in the manner best calculated to maintain and protect his family, both during his lifetime and after his death. He was also well insured. He was covered by (2), which furnishes maximum protection for the period covered at minimum cost. In addition, he was covered by (3), also known as (4) or (5), which gives lifetime protection and builds up a cash surrender value but has to be paid for throughout his life. Stanley had decided against buying (6), for which premiums are paid only for the limited period required by the policy and which also has a cash surrender value. He did not have a(n) (7) policy, which would have made a fund available during his lifetime. He did, however, have (8) that provided protection under a master policy, through his employment. The policy was not a(n) (9) policy, under which he would pay only the annual increase in the cash surrender value and the annual premium of the policy. Stanley was eligible to collect retirement benefits from (10) because he had paid into it for more that 40 calendar quarters. He also had two retirement plans: a(n) (11), which is similar to a traditional IRA except that distributions are not required during the owner's lifetime and are tax-free after the age of 59½ and a(n) (12), which is a company-sponsored retirement plan in which an employee agrees either to take a salary reduction or to forgo a bonus to provide money for retirement. When Ruby read Stanley's will, she discovered that Stanley had given her a(n) (13), that is, the right to direct the disposition of Stanley's property. Stanley was called the (14), and Ruby was called the (15). The right was a(n) (16) because it was limited to making (17) to Stanley's children or grandchildren. The people Ruby selects to receive Stanley's property will be called (18). In doing some (19), that is, estate planning after Stanley's death, Ruby decided against making a(n) (20), which is a formal renunciation of her inheritance.

■ KEY TERMS

401(k) plan	estate planning	roth IRAs
annuity	family limited partnership	simplified employee pension plan
appointee	general partners	(SEP)
appointive property	*inter vivos* gift	split-gift provision
appointment	Keogh plan	term life insurance
disclaimer	limited partners	traditional IRAs
domiciled	limited-payment life insurance	universal (adjustable-premium
donee	long-term care insurance	whole) life insurance
donor	postmortem planning	whole life insurance
education IRAs	power of appointment	
endowment insurance	qualified disclaimer	

Online Companion™
For additional resources, please go to
http://www.paralegal.delmar.cengage.com.

Student CD-ROM
For additional materials, please go to the
CD in this book.

3

A Bundle of Rights

■ CHAPTER OUTLINE

§ 3.1 A Bundle of Rights

§ 3.2 Probate Property

§ 3.3 Nonprobate Property

■ CHAPTER OUTCOMES

- Describe the "bundle of rights" concept of property.
- Define probate property and explain its importance in the estate settlement process.
- Distinguish between real property and personal property.
- Describe the different kinds of nonprobate property, and explain its importance in the estate settlement process.

■ JOB COMPETENCIES

- Be able to discuss with clients the difference between probate and nonprobate property.
- Be able to differentiate between probate property and nonprobate property when completing an estate inventory and an estate tax return.

■ A DAY AT THE OFFICE . . .

The phone rang at the desk of Maude Sanders, a paralegal in the office of Cummings & Goyngs. "Good morning," Maude answered.

"Good morning, Maude." The receptionist was on the line. "Ms. Ryan is here. She wants to see an attorney, and there's no one here. Can you talk to her?"

"Sure. I'll come right out." Maude went out to the waiting room, greeted Ms. Ryan, introduced herself as a paralegal, and ushered Ms. Ryan into her office.

"My brother passed away last week, and his wife wants everything that was in my brother's safe-deposit box," Ms. Ryan sputtered angrily.

"Oh, I'm sorry to hear that," Maude replied in a comforting tone. "Were they married long?"

"Three weeks," Ms. Ryan replied. "My brother was a bachelor for 75 years. He died on his honeymoon at a campground on St. John in the Virgin Islands."

"How terrible!"

"His wife's trying to get everything he owned, and it was all joint with me," Ms. Ryan continued. "The house, all the bank books, the stock certificates—they were all in my name and his."

"Do you have a key to the safe-deposit box?" Maude asked.

"No. That's the only thing that was not joint. He didn't want me to know what was in that. He always said it was personal."

"Did he have any life insurance?"

"Yes. But my mother was the beneficiary of the policy, and she died five years ago."

"Did he leave a will?" Maude inquired.

"Yes," Ms. Ryan answered, "I have his will, but I know he didn't know what he was doing when he wrote it. He made it out just before they went on the honeymoon, and he left everything to her. I have a good mind to tear it up."

"You had better not do that," Maude counseled. "I'll make an appointment for you to see Attorney Cummings as soon as possible. Are you free at 4:00 this afternoon?"

Queries:

1. Who will have access to the safe-deposit box?
2. Who will be the beneficiary of the life insurance policy?
3. Are the house, the bank books, and the stock certificates part of the decedent's estate?
4. Why did Maude counsel Ms. Ryan against tearing up the will?

§ 3.1 A BUNDLE OF RIGHTS

Paralegals need a basic understanding of property in its various forms—bank accounts, stock certificates, life insurance, and so on—because property is the basic element underlying wills, estates, and trusts. Without property, there would be nothing to give anyone in a will, nothing to plan about, and nothing to put in a trust.

Property is generally considered anything that people own, such as houses, cars, furniture, bank accounts, stocks, bonds, and money. Indeed, property is sometimes defined as everything that is the subject of ownership. In a legal sense, however, property is not considered to be the item itself. More correctly, it consists of the various rights or interests that people have in the item. Thus, property, in the eyes of the law, is considered to be a "bundle of rights."

The bundle of rights can be considerable and can be spread among various people. For example, many people may have rights to a house and the land that goes with it. The owner (there is often more than one) has the exclusive right to possess the property unless it is leased to someone else, along with the right to bring a trespass action against a trespasser. If someone else has a life estate in the property (discussed later), that person has the exclusive right to possession for his lifetime, and a third person may have a future interest—the right to possession when the life tenant dies. The bank that holds a mortgage on the property has the right to prevent the person in possession from committing waste, that is, damaging the property. The bank also has the right to take the property or sell it if the owner does not pay the mortgage. An attaching creditor who wins a suit against a property owner may have the right to have the property sold by a sheriff in order to obtain the amount of the judgment. Cities and towns have similar rights to sell private property to satisfy liens for overdue taxes.

If the property is leased to a tenant, the tenant has the exclusive right to possession as well as the sole right to bring a trespass action against a trespasser—even against the landlord who owns the property. However, the landlord regains the right to possession once the lease terminates. The holder of an easement over the property has the right to use the property according to the terms of the easement. The holder of a license given by the owner has the right to do whatever the license allows, such as the right to place an advertising billboard on the property. The holder of a **profit à prendre** has the right to go on the property and extract minerals or timber.

■ **profit à prendre**
Describes the right to take the growing crops of another person's land.

Traditionally, things such as wild animals in their natural state, air, running water, and sunlight could not be the subject of ownership and were not considered property, because no one had the exclusive right to possess them. In modern times, however, with increased water shortages and the expanded use of solar energy, state laws give certain property rights even in these areas.

These varied rights that people may have make up the bundle of rights that is usually referred to as real property. Similar rights relating to personal property are also applicable. When people die owning such rights, the rights pass to others according to the law that you are about to study.

§ 3.2 PROBATE PROPERTY

When an estate is settled, the probate court deals only with what is commonly referred to as **probate property** or the **probate estate**. This is real and personal property that was owned by the decedent either solely or with others as a tenant in common (discussed later). Title to real property owned by a decedent **vests** in (accrues to) the decedent's heirs immediately upon death, but is subject to **divestiture** (being taken away) to pay debts of the estate. The probate process is necessary to prove the heir's title. As opposed to real property, title to personal property owned by a decedent passes to the personal representative (executor or administrator) of the decedent's estate; the probate process is necessary to have the executor or administrator appointed and to safeguard the rights of all interested parties.

Real Property

Real property is the ground and anything permanently affixed to it. Land, buildings on the land, trees and perennial plants growing on the land, as well as the airspace above the land, are all considered to be real property. People can own real property either solely or concurrently with others as tenants in common, joint tenants, or, in some states, as tenants by the entirety. To determine the type of ownership that a decedent had in real property, it is necessary to examine the decedent's deed to the property. If the decedent inherited the property, it is necessary to examine the probate court records to determine the decedent's extent of ownership.

Real property that was owned **severally**, that is, apart from others or solely by the decedent, is part of the probate estate and must be included in the list of probate assets. Similarly, the decedent's interest in real property that was owned with others as a tenant in common is also part of the probate estate. **Tenants in common** are two or more persons who own an undivided interest in property in such a way that each owner's interest passes to his heirs upon death rather than to the surviving co-owners. Thus, if a decedent and one other person owned a parcel of real property as tenants in common, the decedent's one-half undivided interest in the property would be included among the assets of the decedent's estate. If, instead, a decedent and five other people owned a parcel of real property as tenants in common, the decedent's one-sixth undivided interest in the property would be included among the assets of the decedent's estate.

■ **probate property**
Property that was owned by the decedent either severally or as a tenant in common with another.

■ **probate estate**
Real and personal property that was owned by the decedent either solely or with others as a tenant in common.

■ **vests**
1. Give an immediate, fixed, and full right.
2. Take immediate effect.

■ **divestiture**
1. Derive, take away, or withdraw.
2. Sell or otherwise dispose of legal title.
For example, you can divest yourself of a car by selling it.

■ **severally**
Separate, individual, independent.

■ **tenants in common**
Persons who each hold a share of land that can be passed on to heirs or otherwise disposed of. This form of ownership is called a tenancy in common.

People become tenants in common when they are deeded or willed property in that manner (see Exhibit 3–1) or when they inherit property under the law of intestate succession.

As the Evans case illustrates below, when co-owners of real property are tenants in common, they have unity of possession. This means that each cotenant is entitled to the possession of the entire premises rather than to a part of it.

Personal Property

■ **personal property**
All property (with the possible exception of intellectual property) that is not land and things attached to or growing on it.

Personal property is everything that can be owned that is not real property. Coins and paper currency, for example, are personal property. **Tangible property** is property that has substance and can be touched. Motor vehicles, household furniture, jewelry, silverware, china, crystal, books, televisions, personal effects, tools, and coin and stamp collections are examples of tangible personal property that are commonly part of decedents' estates. Certificates of title must usually be examined to determine the decedent's title to automobiles, boats, and motor homes.

■ **tangible property**
Property, real or personal, that is capable of being physically touched.

CASE STUDY   *Evans v. Covington*

795 S.W.2d 806 (TX)

FACTS: When J. R. Scott died, his surviving spouse inherited a one-half undivided interest and his children inherited a one-half undivided interest in his real property. James Evans purchased the children's interest, took possession of the property, enclosed it with a chain-link fence, and used it for many years. Scott's surviving spouse conveyed her interest in the property to Roberta Covington. Evans claims that Covington was not a tenant in common with him because she did not use the property during the years that he possessed it.

LEGAL ISSUE: Does a person who purchases several cotenants' interests in property become a tenant in common with the remaining cotenant?

COURT DECISION: Yes.

REASON: When a party claims title under a deed that conveys an interest in an existing cotenancy relationship, he becomes a tenant in common with the other co-owners. The surviving spouse and children became co-owners of the property when Mr. Scott died. Thus, when Evans purchased the undivided interest of the children, he entered into an existing cotenancy, first with Mrs. Scott and later with Roberta Covington. Each cotenant has a right to enter upon the common estate and a corollary right to possess and use the entire estate.

Quitclaim Deed

I, ELIZABETH L. HOLLAND, surviving spouse of EZRA S. HOLLAND, deceased, of Salem, Essex County, Massachusetts, for consideration paid, and in full consideration of $118,300.00

grant to PEARL M. KLINE and WALTER P. MARINO, both of 34 Gallows Hill Rd., Salem, Massachusetts, as tenants in common, with QUITCLAIM COVENANTS

the land with the buildings and improvements thereon, located at 34 Gallows Hill Rd., Salem, Massachusetts, described as follows:

That certain parcel of land on Gallows Hill Rd. in said Salem and shown as Lot One Hundred Seventy-Eight (178) on a plan of land entitled "Plan of Land of Gallows Hill, Salem, Mass.," dated December, 1913, and recorded with Essex South District Registry of Deeds in Plan Book 21, Plan 42; said Lot 178 being more fully described as follows:
Bounded

SOUTHWESTERLY and SOUTHERLY on a curved line by said Gallows Hill Rd., ninety-one (91) feet;

NORTHWESTERLY by Lot 177 as shown on said plan, seventy-seven and 20/100 (77.20) feet;

NORTHEASTERLY by Lot 186 as shown on said plan, twenty-four and 83/100 (24.83) feet; and

EASTERLY by Lot 179 as shown on said plan, seventy-two and 15/100 (72.15) feet.

Being the same premises conveyed to my late husband and me by my deed dated December 9, 1981 and recorded with Essex South District Registry of Deeds in Book 7763, page 129.

Witness my hands and seal this 3rd day of January, 2002.

_____
Elizabeth L. Holland

Commonwealth of Massachusetts

Essex, ss.   January 3, 2002

Then personally appeared the above-named Elizabeth L. Holland and acknowledged the foregoing instrument to be her free act and deed before me.

_____
Notary Public

Pearl M. Kline and Walter P. Marino each own a one-half undivided interest in the property as tenants in common. If either one dies, his or her share passes to his or her heirs rather than to the surviving co-owner.

EXHIBIT 3–1 Quitclaim Deed

THE DEATH OF A PRINCESS

DIANA PRINCESS OF WALES

The will of Diana, Princess of Wales (1961–1997), who died following a tragic car accident, illustrates how little the United States has strayed from its English roots in the drafting of wills. The exordium clause (opening paragraph) reads like a will drawn in the United States:

> I DIANA PRINCESS OF WALES of Kensington Palace London W8 HEREBY REVOKE all former Wills and testamentary dispositions made by me AND DECLARE this to be my last Will which I made this First day of June One thousand nine hundred and ninety three.

In the same way, the testimonium clause reads:

> IN WITNESS whereof I have hereunto set my hand the day and year first above written.

What differs in Princess Diana's will is the common use of the word *chattels*. Present-day lawyers in the United States have replaced that term with such terms as *personal property* and *goods*.

■ **intangible property**
Property that is really a right, rather than a physical object; for example, bank accounts, stocks, copyrights, "goodwill" of a business, etc.

■ **chose in action**
A right to recover a debt or to get damages that can be enforced in court. These words also apply to the thing itself that is being sued on; for example, an accident, a contract, stocks, etc.

Intangible property is property that is not susceptible to the senses and cannot be touched. Such things as stocks, bonds, negotiable instruments (checks, drafts, and promissory notes), patents, copyrights, and trademarks are examples of intangible personal property. They are evidence of the right to property but not the property itself. For example, a stock certificate is evidence of one's ownership in a corporation, and a promissory note is evidence of the right to receive money from a debtor. It is interesting to note that a lease of real property is considered to be an item of intangible personal property.

The legal name for an item of intangible personal property is a **chose in action**. This is a personal right not reduced to possession but recoverable by a suit at law. Other examples of choses in action that are sometimes owned by estates are lawsuits that survive death and that were initially brought by the decedent; rights to collect money due for debts or damages; royalty rights; and the proceeds of life insurance policies and pension benefits when the decedent's estate is named as the beneficiary. Documents such as stock certificates, bond certificates, promissory notes, bank books, insurance policies, and written contracts may be used to prove title to intangible personal property.

§ 3.3 NONPROBATE PROPERTY

Even though all estates need to be entered into probate, not all things that people own are part of their estate. Such nonprobate property includes jointly owned property, transfer-on-death (TOD) accounts, community property, life insurance with named beneficiaries, money in Totten trust accounts (discussed

---

FROM THE DETAILED WILL OF LILLIAN HELLMAN

In her will, Lillian Hellman, one of the most influential playwrights of the twentieth century, reveals her characteristic attention to detail in the precise descriptions of the items designated for her friends. The document reads like an inventory of personal property.

... to MIKE NICHOLS, the Toulouse Lautrec poster in the hall of my New York apartment ...

... to MAX PALEVSKY, the Spanish table presently in the study of my New York apartment ... the framed Russian altar cloth presently over the fireplace in the living room, given to me by Pudovkin, the movie director, as it was executed by a member of his family in 1796 ... and the two chairs against the wall near the sofa in the living room of my New York apartment, made by unknown cabinet makers in Bohemia or possibly France and exchanged by these amateurs one to the other in the early nineteenth century ...

... to ROBERT POIRIER ... the three-step library ladder in the study of my New York apartment; the three (3) Russian china doves, the French secretary and two electrified brass lamps with tulip bulbs in the living room of my New York apartment; and the rare 18th century Biblio bookcase in the bedroom of my New York apartment ...

... to HOWARD BAY, the Forain drawing and the wooden birdcage hanging from the ceiling in the living room of my New York apartment ...

... to WILLIAM ABRAHAMS, the box in the guest bathroom of my New York apartment that has the little foxes on it ...

in Chapter 9), property held in a living trust, pension plan distributions, and individual retirement accounts (IRAs) with named beneficiaries. Although these items pass outside of probate directly to the surviving joint owner or beneficiary, they are part of the decedent's gross estate for estate tax purposes.

As part of their work, paralegals often assist the attorney in gathering the information needed to settle an estate and to complete tax returns. A detailed list of nonprobate property, together with its value, must be obtained by the personal representative of the estate to determine whether the estate is large enough that an estate tax return must be filed. The varied tasks that the paralegal may perform when assisting the personal representative are discussed in Chapter 11.

Jointly Owned Property

Real property that was owned by a decedent and another as joint tenants is not part of the decedent's probate estate. Joint property remains the property of the surviving joint owner or owners when one of the owners dies (see Exhibit 3–2). **Joint tenants** are two or more persons holding one and the same interest, accruing by one and the same conveyance, commencing at one and the same time, and held by one and the same undivided possession. This form of ownership is sometimes referred to as joint tenancy with the right of survivorship. A similar form of ownership, but which can be held only by a husband and wife, is a tenancy by the entirety. **Tenants by the entirety** are a husband and wife who hold title as joint tenants, modified by the common law doctrine that gives the husband the exclusive rights of possession and profits with protection against being taken by creditors and alienation by one spouse alone. This form of ownership is popular because of its protection against attachment by creditors, and some states have modernized the law to give husbands and wives equal rights to possession and profits in property owned as tenants by the entirety (see Exhibit 3–3).

Under the law of some states, such as Massachusetts, ownership of real property by a husband and wife as joint tenants or as tenants by the entirety automatically changes to ownership as tenants in common if the couple is divorced. Thus, after a divorce in Massachusetts, if one marriage partner dies before changing the title to the property, the decedent's interest in the property automatically passes to his heirs rather than to the former spouse. Other states do not follow this rule. In Montana, for example, a divorce does not change a joint tenancy into a tenancy in common.

Another form of ownership that causes property to pass outside of probate is tenancy in partnership. **Tenancy in partnership** is a form of co-ownership of property belonging to members of a partnership. Like a joint tenancy, when one partner dies, the surviving partners, rather than the estate of the decedent, own the partnership property.

■ **joint tenants**

Persons who each hold a share of land that remains the property of the surviving joint owners when a joint owner dies. The joint owners have equal shares that they received at the same time by way of the same conveyance. This form of ownership is called a joint tenancy or a joint tenancy with the right of survivorship.

■ **tenants by the entirety**

Like joint tenants except that they must also be husband and wife and that neither has a share of the land, but both hold the entire land as one individual owner.

■ **tenancy in partnership**

Form of co-ownership of property belonging to members of a partnership.

AFFIDAVIT—DEATH OF JOINT TENANT

STATE OF CALIFORNIA,   )
)   ss.
County of _____)
_____   )

_____, of legal age, being first duly sworn, deposes and says:

That _____, the decedent mentioned in the attached certified copy of Certificate of Death, is the same person as _____ named as one of the parties in that certain _____ dated _____, executed by _____ to _____, as joint tenants, recorded as Instrument No. _____, on _____, in Book/Reel _____, Page/Image _____, of Official Records of _____ County, California, covering the following described property situated in the _____, County of _____, State of California:

That the value of all real and personal property owned by said decedent at date of death, including the full value of the property above described, did not then exceed the sum of $____.

Dated _____ ____
SUBSCRIBED AND SWORN TO before me _____

this ____ day of _____
Signature _____

Title Order No. _____

(This area for official notarial seal)
Escrow or Loan No.

EXHIBIT 3–2   Affidavit—Death of a Joint Tenant

Bank accounts, stocks, bonds, and automobiles are commonly owned by two or more people as joint tenants. Unless it can be shown that a bank account was opened in joint names only for convenience purposes, the account will pass to the surviving depositor when one depositor dies, and will not be part of the decedent's estate. The Parker case illustrates this point.

EXHIBIT 3-3   States that Use Tenants by the Entireties as a Form of Ownership of Real Property by a Husband and Wife

Some states have statutes providing that money in a joint bank account belongs to the joint depositor only when both depositors have signed an agreement to that effect. For example, Texas Probate Code ch. 11, § 439(a), provides:

> Sums remaining on deposit at the death of a party to a joint account belong to the surviving party or parties against the estate of the decedent if, by a written agreement signed by the party who dies, the interest of such deceased party is made to survive to the surviving party or parties. A survivorship agreement will not be inferred from the mere fact that the account is a joint account.

Sometimes a question arises as to whether the contents of a safe-deposit box held in joint names belong to the surviving joint owner when one owner dies. Some courts hold that unless there is an express written agreement saying that the contents of the box belong to the joint owner, the contents of the box belong to the estate of the decedent. The Kulbeth case provides an example of such an agreement.

Frequently, husbands and wives put all of their property in joint names except an automobile, and the estate of the first spouse to die must be probated for the sole purpose of clearing the title to the automobile. Massachusetts has

CASE STUDY   *Parker v. Peavey*

403 S.E.2d 213 (GA)

FACTS:	In addition to establishing certificates of deposit in his own name, Bennie Parker established one in the amount of $86,887 jointly with his wife of one year, Sallie Parker. When he died two years later, his first wife, to whom he had been married 49 years, and his two adult children (who were named in his will) claimed that the joint certificate of deposit was part of his estate.
LEGAL ISSUE:	Does a certificate of deposit that is in the name of two people jointly belong to the estate of the first to die?
COURT DECISION:	No.
REASON:	Sums remaining on deposit at the death of a party of a joint account belong to the surviving party as against the estate of the decedent, unless there is clear and convincing evidence of a different intention at the time the account is created. This right of survivorship vests at the death of a party to a joint account.

addressed the issue by enacting Gen. Laws ch. 90D, ß 15A, which treats a solely owned automobile as joint property of the husband and wife, avoiding the need for probate:

> Upon the death of a married resident owner of a motor vehicle registered as a pleasure vehicle in the Commonwealth, and unless otherwise provided in a will, said motor vehicle, if used for such purposes shall be deemed to have been jointly held property with right of survivorship and the interest of said decedent shall pass to the surviving spouse ... .

Pay-on-Death Accounts

A **pay-on-death (POD) account**, also known as a **Totten trust** (see Chapter 9), is a savings account in the name of the depositor as trustee for another person called a beneficiary. The depositor may withdraw money from the account at any time during the depositor's lifetime. When the depositor dies, however, the money in the account belongs to the beneficiary. If the beneficiary dies before the depositor, the trust terminates and the money belongs to the depositor. Totten trust accounts are not part of the depositor's estate. Instead, they pass directly to the beneficiary, not to the estate of the depositor, unless the trust was revoked by the depositor prior to the depositor's death.

■ **pay-on-death (pod) account**

A trust created by putting money into a bank account in your name as trustee for another person. You can take it out when you want, but if you do not take it out before you die, it becomes the property of that other person.

■ **totten trust**

A savings account in the name of the depositor as trustee for another person called a beneficiary.

CASE STUDY   *Kulbeth v. Purdom*

805 S.W.2d 622 (AR)

FACTS:	Ivan C. Wright leased a safe-deposit box jointly with Pearl Purdom. When Wright died, the box was opened and found to contain $266,150 in cash. The special administrator of Wright's estate claimed the money as an asset of the estate, pointing out that Wright's will bequeathed $100,000 to Purdom. Wright and Purdom had signed the following joint-tenancy agreement when they initially obtained the safe-deposit box:

> In addition to agreeing to the foregoing provisions of safe-deposit box lease which are hereby made a part of this paragraph, the undersigned agree that each, or either of them is joint owner of the present and future contents of said box and said Bank is hereby authorized to permit access to said box by either of the undersigned and that in the event of the death of either of the undersigned the survivor shall have the right to withdraw said contents and upon said withdrawal said Bank shall be automatically relieved of any further obligation or responsibility to the heirs, legatees, devisees or legal representatives of the deceased.

LEGAL ISSUE:	Do the contents of a jointly owned safe-deposit box pass to the co-owner's estate when a co-owner dies when an agreement has been signed by the co-owners that either may withdraw the box's contents?
COURT DECISION:	No.
REASON:	The clause clearly and unequivocally denotes a joint-tenancy agreement with right of survivorship between the lessees, as it contains specific references to the joint ownership of the contents of the box and the right of withdrawal of the contents after the death of either party. The money in the safe-deposit box is not an asset of Wright's estate; it belongs to the co-owner, Purdom.

Uniform Nonprobate Transfer on Death Act

The Uniform Nonprobate Transfer on Death Act is a law that addresses many of the problems that arise when people own bank accounts, securities, and other items in multiple names. The entire act is actually Article VI of the Uniform Probate Code (see Appendix E). Part 2 of the act deals with multiple-person bank accounts; Part 3 covers transfers of securities (stocks and bonds) on death.

Uniform Multiple-Person Accounts

Problems can arise when depositors own bank accounts jointly. This is because there can be a variety of reasons for placing another person's name on an account. The depositor may wish to provide lifetime ownership to all joint owners, or to pass the money to others at death, or simply to allow others to use the account for convenience with no ownership interest. Determining which of these reasons apply to a particular account can lead to litigation when a depositor dies. Part 2 of the Uniform Nonprobate Transfer on Death Act addresses this problem by allowing depositors to establish multiple-person accounts that clearly state the rights of all parties in interest. The states of Alabama, Alaska, Arizona, Colorado, Florida, Montana, Nebraska, New Mexico, and North Dakota have adopted (with some variations) Part 2 of the Act.

Transfers of Securities on Death

Part 3 of the Uniform Nonprobate Transfer on Death Act allows owners of securities to register the title of their securities in transfer-on-death (TOD) form. When this is done, brokers and transfer agents can transfer securities directly to the designated transferees when the owner dies. In contrast with joint ownership, TOD ownership gives no rights to the transferee until the owner dies, leaving the owner in full control of the securities. Every state except Louisiana, Missouri, North Carolina, New York, Tennessee, and Texas has adopted Part 3 of the Act, some with slight modifications.

Community Property

A form of ownership by spouses, called community property, is used in nine states in the United States (see Exhibit 3–4). The primary historical source of our community property laws comes to us from Mexico, which, in turn, inherited the concept from Spain. Originally, the intent was to protect rich women from loosing all their assets if they had a wasteful husband. **Community property** is property (except a gift or inheritance) that is acquired by the personal efforts of either spouse during marriage and which, by law, belongs to both spouses equally. In community property states, a spouse can leave his half of the community property by will to whomever he chooses. Alaska is an opt-in community property state. That is, couples may choose community property ownership by executing a community property agreement or through a community property trust.

■ **community property**

Property owned in common (both persons owning it all) by a husband and wife. "Community property states" are those states that call most property acquired during the marriage the property of both partners no matter whose name it is in.

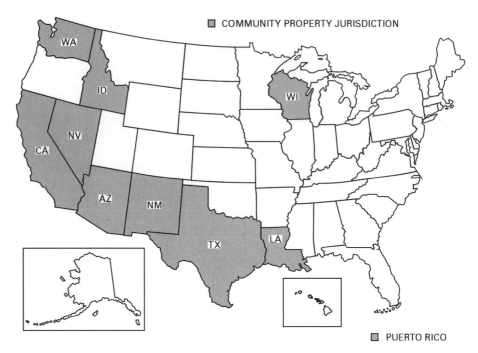

☐ COMMUNITY PROPERTY JURISDICTION

☐ PUERTO RICO

EXHIBIT 3–4 Community Property Jurisdictions

Example

Community Property

20B AMJUR LF WI ß 266:194

I declare that all of the property of my estate which is bequeathed and devised by this will is my one-half interest in the community property of myself and my _____ [husband or wife], _____ [name].

In some community property states, when a spouse dies intestate, all of the community property passes to the surviving spouse (see Exhibit 3–5). In such a situation, the surviving spouse retains his half-interest and inherits the deceased spouse's half-interest, obtaining full title to the entire property. California law mandates an equal splitting of community property. In Texas, a divorce decree may call for an "equitable distribution" of the community property. States may treat community debts differently than community property. California, for example, requires an equal sharing of community property but requires an equitable sharing of community debt.

A number of factors are looked at by the courts in determining an equitable distribution of community property. First, if one spouse has considerably more nonmarital property than the other, the courts may give the spouse with lesser property more marital property in order to leave both spouses with adequate resources. Next, courts may look at the earning powers of the spouses. If one has much greater earning power, then the spouse with the lesser earning power may get more property. Also, if one spouse wasted or dissipated assets during the marriage, then he may receive less community property. In addition, the age and health of the parties may impact community property distributions. Another factor is the tax consequence of the division. Courts would like to minimize the tax burdens of both parties, if possible. Lastly, of course, premarital agreements can predetermine the division of community property assets, such that the courts need not deal with the issue. In truth, courts are able to consider any and all factors to determine an equitable distribution.

The following are not considered to be community property: (1) property owned by either spouse before marriage; (2) property either spouse received as a gift or inherited during marriage; and (3) income, such as rents or interest, earned from the separate property of either spouse. If they wish to do so, spouses can agree to treat separately owned property as community property or vice versa.

Determining what is or is not community property is a constant source of dispute in community property states. Here is an example of just such a dispute.

CASE STUDY **In the Matter of the Marriage of Joyner**

196 S.W.3d 883 (Tx.)

FACTS: On May 29, 2001, Belinda Joyner filed for divorce from her husband, Thomas Joyner. The couple signed a mediated settlement agreement on April 7, 2003, which partitioned most of their property. On July 2, 2003, the couple had a final hearing in court to argue ownership of those few items in dispute. On July 3, 2003, Thomas purchased a winning lottery ticket worth $2,080,000. On June 28, 2004, the court signed their divorce decree.

LEGAL ISSUE: Was the lottery ticket purchased on July 3, 2003, community property?

COURT DECISION: No.

REASONS: Even though the court did not make a final determination on some small property items, the appeals court viewed the decision as to whether the trial court had granted the divorce as having been made. Although the trial court never specifically used the words "rendered the divorce" in open court, the trial judge did state, on July 2, 2003, that the divorce was granted. In addition, he referred to Belinda as Thomas's "former wife." The appeals court felt the trial court had clearly and unambiguously rendered a decision to grant the divorce on July 2, 2003, and that the signed divorce decree simply memorialized that fact. Therefore, the winning lottery ticket was not community property.

DE-221

ATTORNEY OR PARTY WITHOUT ATTORNEY *(Name, state bar number, and address)*	TELEPHONE AND FAX NOS.: (805) 965-1016	*FOR COURT USE ONLY*

ROBERT L. BLETCHER
8 EAST FIGUEROA STREET, #210
SANTA BARBARA, CA 93101
CA STATE BAR #033754
ATTORNEY FOR *(Name)*   BO DEREK

SUPERIOR COURT OF CALIFORNIA, COUNTY OF SANTA BARBARA
STREET ADDRESS: 312 E. Cook St., Bldg C
MAILING ADDRESS: same
CITY AND ZIP CODE: Santa Maria, CA 93454
BRANCH NAME: Cook Division

ESTATE OF *(Name)*:   JOHN DEREK, a.k.a. DEREK DELEVAN HARRIS

DECEDENT

FILED
SANTA BARBARA
SUPERIOR COURT

OCT 13 1998

GARY M. BLAIR
Executive Officer
By: *S. Leyden* Deputy Clerk

SPOUSAL PROPERTY PETITION

CASE NUMBER: 9111036

HEARING DATE: 11-4-98

DEPT: **DEPT ONE**   TIME: 8:30 a.m.

requests

1. Petitioner *(name)*: BO DEREK
   a. [X] determination of property passing to the surviving spouse without administration (Prob. Code, § 13500).
   b. [X] confirmation of property belonging to the surviving spouse (Prob. Code, §§ 100, 101).
   c. [ ] immediate appointment of a probate referee.

2. Petitioner
   a. [X] surviving spouse of the decedent.
   b. [ ] personal representative of *(name)*:   , surviving spouse.
   c. [ ] guardian of the estate or conservator of the estate of *(name)*:   , surviving spouse.

3. Decedent died on *(date)*: 05-22-98
   a. [X] a resident of the California county named above.
   b. [ ] a nonresident of California and left an estate in the county named above.
   c. [X] intestate [ ] testate and a copy of the will and any codicil is affixed as Attachment 3c or 6. *(Attach will.)*

4. a. *(Complete in all cases)* The decedent is survived by
      (1) [X] child as follows: [X] natural or adopted [ ] natural adopted by a third party [ ] no child
      (2) [ ] issue of a predeceased child [X] no issue of a predeceased child.
   b. Decedent [ ] is [X] is not survived by a stepchild or foster child or children who would have been adopted by decedent but for a legal barrier. *(See Prob. Code, § 6454.)*

5. *(Complete only if no issue survived the decedent. Check only the first box that applies.)*
   a. [ ] The decedent is survived by a parent or parents who are listed in item 7.
   b. [ ] The decedent is survived by a brother, sister, or issue of a deceased brother or sister, all of whom are listed in item 7.

6. Administration of all or part of the estate is not necessary for the reason that all or a part of the estate is property passing to the surviving spouse. The facts upon which petitioner bases the allegation that the property described in Attachments 6a and 6b is property that should pass or be confirmed to the surviving spouse are stated in Attachment 6.[1]
   a. [X] Attachment 6a[2] contains the legal description *(if real property add Assessor's Parcel Number)* of the deceased spouse's property that petitioner requests to be determined as having passed to the surviving spouse from the deceased spouse. This includes any interest in a trade or business name of any unincorporated business or an interest in any unincorporated business the deceased spouse was operating or managing at the time of death.
   b. [X] Attachment 6b contains the legal description *(if real property add Assessor's Parcel Number)* of the community or quasi-community property petitioner requests to be determined as having belonged under Probate Code sections 100 and 101 to the surviving spouse upon the deceased spouse's death.

(Continued on reverse, including footnotes)

Form Approved by the
Judicial Council of California
DE 221 (Rev. January 1, 1998)

SPOUSAL PROPERTY PETITION
(Probate)

Probate Code, § 13650

EXHIBIT 3–5a This Spousal Property Petition was filed by Bo Derek in the settlement of the estate of her husband, John Derek

ESTATE OF *(Name)*:   JOHN DEREK, a.k.a. DEREK DELEVAN HARRIS   CASE NUMBER:

DECEDENT

7. The names, relationships, ages, and residence or mailing addresses so far as known to or reasonably ascertainable by petitioner of
   (1) all persons named in decedent's will and codicils, whether living or deceased, and (2) all persons checked in items 4 and 5
   [ ] are listed below   [ ] are listed in Attachment 7.

Name and relationship	Age	Residence or mailing address
BO DEREK, Spouse	Adult	3625 Roblar Avenue Santa Ynez, CA 93460-8722
RUSSEL A. DEREK, Son	Adult	Cottage Care 2415 De La Vina St. Santa Barbara, CA
SEAN CATHERINE DEREK, Daughter	Adult	5321 Tyrone Avenue Sherman Oaks, CA 91401

8. The names and address of all persons named as executors in the decedent's will or appointed as personal representatives
   [ ] are listed below   [ ] are listed in Attachment 8   [X] none.

9. [ ] The petitioner is the trustee of a trust that is a devisee under decedent's will. The names and addresses of all persons
   interested in the trust who are entitled to notice under Probate Code section 13655(b)(2) are listed in Attachment 9.

10. A petition for probate or for administration of the decedent's estate
    a. [ ] is being filed with this petition.
    b. [ ] was filed on *(date)*:
    c. [X] has not been filed and is not being filed with this petition.

11. Number of pages attached: 5

Date: 09-30-98

▶ _____
(SIGNATURE OF ATTORNEY)
ROBERT L. BLETCHER

I declare under penalty of perjury under the laws of the State of California that the foregoing is true and correct.

Date: 09-28-98

BO DEREK
(TYPE OR PRINT NAME)

▶ _____
(SIGNATURE OF PETITIONER)

[1] See Prob. Code, § 13651(b) for the requirement that a copy of the will be attached in certain instances. If required, include in Attachment 3c or 6.
[2] See Prob. Code, § 13658 for required filing of a list of known creditors of a business and other information in certain instances. If required, include in Attachment 6a.

DE-221 (Rev. January 1, 1998)   SPOUSAL PROPERTY PETITION   Page two
                                                    (Probate)

EXHIBIT 3–5b This Spousal Property Petition was filed by Bo Derek in the settlement of the estate of her husband,
John Derek

FACTS TO SUPPORT PROPERTY PASSING TO OR BEING CONFIRMED TO SURVIVING SPOUSE

Decedent, JOHN DEREK, and surviving spouse, BO DEREK, were married on June 10, 1976 in Las Vegas, Nevada and since that date were continuously married to each other until the death of JOHN DEREK on May 22, 1998. At the time of marriage neither party owned any assets of any value and neither inherited assets thereafter from any person. All assets owned by the parties were acquired from their earnings while residing in the State of California and were the community property of the parties.

No agreement defining the rights of the parties in assets, marital or otherwise, was entered into by the parties, either before or after their marriage.

Further, each interest in the properties listed in Attachments 6a and 6b were held in the names of JOHN DEREK and BO DEREK, husband and wife, as community property.

Therefore surviving spouse's interest in each of said properties should be confirmed to her, and decedent's interest in each of said properties should pass to surviving spouse.

PROPERTY PASSING TO SURVIVING SPOUSE

Decedent's community property interest in assets as follows:

1. Undivided one-half interest in real property located in the County of Santa Barbara, State of California and described as follows:

   PARCEL ONE:
   Lot 1 of Tract No. 11572 in the County of Santa Barbara, State of California, as shown on map filed in Book 90, Pages 39 to 41, inclusive, in the Office of the County Recorder of said County.

   PARCEL TWO:
   A non-exclusive easement for road purposes, riding trail, public utilities and drainage purposes as described in the quitclaim and deed of easements to Oak Trail Development Corporation, et al, Recorded March 28, 1973 as Instrument No. 11560 in Book 2453, Page 1429 of Official Records.

   Excepting therefrom those portions lying within the boundaries of Parcel One above.

   [A.P.N. 135-320-71]

2. Undivided one-half interest in real property located in the County of Santa Barbara, State of California and described as follows:

   PARCEL ONE:
   Parcel B of Parcel Map No. 12422, in the County of Santa Barbara, State of California, as per map recorded in Book 18, Pages 97 and 98 of Parcel Maps in the Office of the County Recorder of said County.

   PARCEL TWO:
   A non-exclusive easement for road purposes, riding trail, public utilities and drainage purposes as described in the quitclaim and deed of easements to Oak Trail Development Corporation, et al, Recorded March 28, 1973 as Instrument No. 11560 in Book 2453, Page 1429 of Official Records.

   Excepting therefrom those portions lying within the boundaries of Parcel One above.

   [A.P.N. 135-320-72 and 135-320-76]

Attachment 6a

EXHIBIT 3–5c This Spousal Property Petition was filed by Bo Derek in the settlement of the estate of her husband, John Derek

3. Undivided one-half interest in 200 shares SVENGALI, INC., a California corporation, common stock
4. Undivided one-half interest in 1000 shares ANOTHER, INC., a California corporation, common stock
5. Undivided one-half interest in 1000 shares CRACKAJACK MOVIE COMPANY, a California corporation, common stock
6. Undivided one-half interest in U.S. copyright on screenplay treatment "BOLERO"
7. Undivided one-half interest in U.S. copyright on screenplay treatment "DRAGON LADY"
8. Undivided one-half interest in U.S. copyright on screenplay treatment "DRIVE"
9. Undivided one-half interest in U.S. copyright on screenplay "THE DEEP BLUE SEA"
10. Undivided one-half interest in U.S. copyright on screenplay "THE FLESH IS WEAK"
11. Undivided one-half interest in U.S. copyright on screenplay "THE GIRL WITH THE HUNGRY EYES"
12. Undivided one-half interest in collection of photographs by JOHN DEREK
13. Undivided one-half interest in 1992 Jeep Wrangler automobile
14. Undivided one-half interest in 1970 Chevrolet pickup automobile

Attachment 6b

EXHIBIT 3–5d   This Spousal Property Petition was filed by Bo Derek in the settlement of the estate of her husband, John Derek

Life Insurance and IRAs with Named Beneficiary

A life insurance policy with a named, living beneficiary is not part of the probate estate of the decedent. The proceeds of the policy are paid directly to the beneficiary, bypassing probate altogether. Like jointly owned property, however, life insurance owned by a decedent is part of the decedent's gross estate for estate tax purposes, and must be included on the estate tax return.

In contrast, when decedents name the estate as the beneficiary on life insurance policies, or when the named beneficiary predeceases the insured, the proceeds of the life insurance policy are part of the probate estate and must be listed on the probate inventory.

Individual retirement accounts (IRAs) also contain provisions for selecting beneficiaries. These provisions take precedence over subsequent **testamentary dispositions**—that is, dispositions by will. To illustrate, Massachusetts Gen. Laws. ch. 167D, § 30, provides:

■ **testamentary dispositions**

A bequest or devise. Giving any form of property by will.

> Any designation of any beneficiary in connection with and as provided by an instrument intended to establish a pension, profit-sharing, or other deferred compensation or retirement plan, trust or custodial account ... shall be effective according to its terms, notwithstanding any purported testamentary disposition allowed by statute, by operation of law or otherwise to the contrary.

Living Trusts

A **living trust**, also known as an *inter vivos trust*, is a trust that becomes effective during the lifetime of the person who establishes it. Living trusts can provide for property to be transferred, after a person's death, to those people designated by the trust maker. During the maker's lifetime the maker maintains control over the trust assets. Living trusts can accomplish the same distributions accomplished by a will, without the need for probate.

Distributions done by a living trust can be done much more quickly than distributions done by a will. Additionally, as the living trust does not pass through the probate court, the trust document does not become part of the public record, as opposed to a probated will, which, like most court documents, can be accessed by the public. It should be carefully noted, though, that even though the trust assets pass outside a will, there is no tax advantage to the use of a living trust; all the trust assets are subject to the same estate taxes imposed on assets passed by a will.

Living trusts work as follows: first, the maker (also called a grantor or settler) executes a written trust document establishing a revocable living trust in which he names himself as trustee. He also names himself as trust beneficiary, with his family members, or others, as trust beneficiaries after his death. Assets are then transferred to the trust. Almost anything can be transferred into the trust, including bank accounts, stocks, bonds, and real estate. The maker, as trustee and trust beneficiary, maintains full control over and has the full benefits from the trust assets during his lifetime. Upon his death, the assets transfer to the family members, or others, designated to be the contingent beneficiaries by the trust document.

Although living trusts do save time and do maintain privacy, when comparing them to wills, living trusts are more costly to accomplish. While the cost of a will may start at $250 or $300, the cost for a living trust may start at $2,000. In addition, the establishment of a living trust will incur additional costs to transfer the ownership of the property from the maker personally to the trust itself.

The maker of the living trust still needs a will. The will ensures that property acquired after the trust or property not transferred to the trust initially will transfer as the testator wishes.

To quote Oliver Wendell Holmes, "Put your trust not in money, but put your money in trust." For those who desire living trusts, these are words to live by. Trusts are discussed in more detail in Chapters 8 and 9.

A STINGY PRESIDENT?

LYNDON BAINES JOHNSON

Lyndon Baines Johnson (1908–1973), 36th president of the United States, is shown here in front of the White House in Washington, DC, with First Lady Lynda "Lady Bird" Johnson and their two daughters, Luci and Lynda, with a child.

What is striking about the will of President Lyndon B. Johnson is his apparent lack of concern for his wife. After generously providing for his children and siblings, he designates only minor items—kitchen furniture, musical instruments, books, and jewelry—for his wife. The explanation is that the will was written in the "community state" of Texas: by law a wife is recognized as 50-percent owner of a couple's entire community property. Therefore, Johnson could not will his wife what was legally hers: in this case, half of his more than $10 million estate.

CASE STUDY *Fitzpatrick v. Small*

564 N.E.2d 1035 (MA)

FACTS: Leo Fitzpatrick established six individual retirement accounts (IRAs) naming his brother, Francis, as beneficiary of 100 percent of the benefits at Leo's death. Later, Leo executed a will leaving the same IRA accounts in equal shares to his brother, Francis, and his sister, Claire. Leo died before he changed the beneficiary designation on the IRAs.

LEGAL ISSUE: Does a designation of beneficiary form executed pursuant to an IRA take precedence over a later testamentary disposition directing the distribution of the same IRA proceeds?

COURT DECISION: Yes.

REASON: IRAs are retirement plans governed by statute, which provides that a person who establishes an IRA is free to change the designation of beneficiary under that IRA and that, so long as he does so in the manner specified by the IRA plan, the change will have controlling effects. Although free to change or revoke his designation of beneficiary under his IRAs, the decedent failed to comply with the IRA plans under which he established his IRAs and, instead, apparently sought to change his designation by his will.

Life Estates

A **life estate** is an ownership interest that is limited in duration to either the life of the owner or the life of another person. When the life tenant dies, the property belongs to whoever owns the remainder interest, without the necessity of probate. Life estates have become popular in recent years as a device to save capital gain taxes. This is because, unlike a life tenant, the donee of an outright gift of real property must use the donor's basis (cost plus improvements) when the property is sold, often resulting in a large capital gain. However, if the donor retains a life estate in the property, the donee's basis is the value of the property at the time of the donor's death, usually resulting in a much smaller capital gain. The life tenant's estate, however, will be subject to the federal estate tax if the estate reaches the taxable amount including the life estate property. Estate taxes are discussed in more detail in Chapter 13.

Table 3–1 summarizes the categorization of types of property. Probate property is any property that reverts to the estate of someone who has died; nonprobate property passes outside the estate.

TABLE 3–1 **Items Typically Considered to Be Probate Property and Nonprobate Property**

Probate Property
Real and personal property owned solely by the decedent
Interests in property held as a tenant in common
Nonprobate Property
Property owned in joint tenancy
Community property
Life insurance with named beneficiaries
Pension plan distributions and individual retirement accounts with named beneficiaries
Money held in pay-on-death accounts
Property held in a living trust

SUMMARY

In its legal sense, property is the foundation of wills and consists of a bundle of rights—the various rights or interests that people have in the item.

Probate property is real and personal property that was owned either solely by the decedent or with others as a tenant in common. Tangible personal property is property that has substance and can be touched. Intangible personal property is not susceptible to the senses and cannot be touched.

Nonprobate property includes jointly owned property, community property, life insurance and IRAs with named beneficiaries, money in Totten trust accounts, property held in a living trust, pension plan distributions, and individual retirement accounts with named beneficiaries.

■ REVIEW QUESTIONS

1. Why is it essential for paralegals working in the field of wills, estates, and trusts to have a fundamental understanding of the meaning of property, the various kinds of property, and how it relates to this specialized area of law?

2. In the eyes of the law, what is property considered to be? Why is this so?

3. Name some rights that different persons have to a house and the land that goes with it.

4. When property is leased to a tenant, who has the sole right to bring a trespass action? Against whom may the action be brought?

5. Traditionally, what could not be the subject of ownership and was not considered property? How has this changed?

6. When does title to real property owned by a decedent vest in the decedent's heirs?

7. To whom does title to personal property owned by a decedent pass?

8. What real property owned by a decedent is included among the probate assets?

9. What is the difference between tangible and intangible personal property?

10. What are five kinds of property that are not part of the probate estate?

■ CASES TO DISCUSS

1. In the course of settling an estate, the probate court ordered that costs of administration be paid out of assets, which included a Totten trust account. Is a Totten trust account an asset of the depositor's estate from which costs of administration may be paid? Explain. *Nahar v. Nahar*, 576 So. 2d 862 (FL).

2. Laura Mitchell's will left all of her property to her illegitimate son. When she died, however, Mitchell's attorney did not think the will was valid in form and decided not to present the will to the court. Instead, the attorney began an intestate succession proceeding. Was the attorney correct in making that decision? Explain. *Succession of Mitchell*, 574 So. 2d 500 (LA).

3. Howard and Mary Sander, who were married to each other, purchased land in Montana as joint tenants. They were later divorced but did nothing about the Montana property. Ten years later, when Howard died, his then wife, Jean, claimed the Montana land as an asset of Howard's estate. Mary claimed that it belonged to her after Howard died. How would you decide? Why? *Matter of Estate of Sander*, 806 P.2d 545 (MT).

■ RESEARCH ON THE WEB_____

1. In the opening "Day at the office" scenario, Maude Sanders, a paralegal, talks with a client. What ethical issues should be of concern to Maude? You may find some assistance at <http://www.legalethics.com>.

2. Paralegals are often called upon to conduct legal research on the Internet. Practice your research skills by looking up some information about a topic discussed in this chapter. Try using some of these specialized search engines: <http://www.yahoo.com/Law>, <http://www.catalaw.com>, <http:// www.law.cornell.edu/>,

■ SHARPENING YOUR PROFESSIONAL SKILLS_____

1. Obtain a copy of the deed to your house or that of your parent, relative, or friend. Attach to it a statement as to how the property is owned (either severally, or as tenants in common, joint tenants, or tenants by the entirety). Then state who will own the property if the sole owner or one of the co-owners dies.

2. Under the law of your state, does the dissolution of a marriage change the couple's ownership of real property as joint tenants into ownership as tenants in common? When you find the answer, write down the reference to the statute or the citation to the case in which you found it.

3. Refer to a law dictionary and write the meaning of the term *in specie* as it is used in Item II of the will of Elvis Presley (reproduced in Appendix B).

4. Review paragraph FIRST of the will of Jacqueline K. Onassis (reproduced in Appendix B), and list five items of tangible personal property, two items of intangible personal property, and the legatees of each.

5. Review paragraph THIRD (B) of the will of Jacqueline K. Onassis (reproduced in Appendix B). Under the will, who inherited the real property in Gay Head and Chilmark, Martha's Vineyard, Massachusetts? Explain the meaning of the term tenants in common as used in the will.

6. How does ARTICLE TWO (B) of the will of Richard M. Nixon, (reproduced in Appendix B) dispose of his personal diaries?

7. Read ARTICLE ONE (i) of the will of Richard M. Nixon (reproduced in Appendix B) with respect to the decision of the United States Court of Appeals. Then, in the law library, look up the case of *Nixon v. United States*, 978 F.2d 1269 (D.C. Cir. 1992). State the principal legal issue that was decided by the court, give the court's opinion as to that legal issue, and explain why the case was mentioned in Nixon's will.

8. Refer to the will of Doris Duke (reproduced in Appendix B). Make a chart with the following headings: Paragraph No., Real Property, and Devisee. Then list each item of real property mentioned in the will, name the devisee of that real property, and enumerate the paragraph of the will in which it is devised.

■ SHARPENING YOUR LEGAL VOCABULARY⎯⎯⎯⎯⎯⎯⎯

On a separate sheet of paper, fill in the numbered blank lines in the following anecdote with legal terms from this list:

beneficiary

bundle of rights

chose in action

community property

divesting

intangible personal property

inter vivos trust

joint tenants

joint tenants with the right of survivorship

life estate

living trust

pay-on-death (POD)

personal property

probate estate

probate property

profit à prendre

property

real property

severally

tangible personal property

tenancy in partnership

tenants by the entirety

tenants in common

testamentary

disposition

Totten trust

Uniform Nonprobate

Transfer on Death Act

unity of possession

vested

When Aaron died, the personal representative of his estate, that is, the executrix, made a detailed list of the (1) that was owned (2) (solely, apart from others) by Aaron. In the eyes of the law, it is considered a(n) (3). It was referred to as the (4) or (5). It included (6) (that is, the ground and anything permanently affixed to it) and (7) (that is, other things that can be owned). The former (8) in (accrued to) the heirs immediately upon Aaron's death, subject to (9), that is, being taken away; the latter passed to the executrix of the estate. In addition to an automobile, which was (10) property, Aaron owned some corporate stock, which was (11) and legally considered a(n) (12). He also had a savings bank account in his name as trustee for his niece, Sharon. The account was a(n) (13) account, which is sometimes called a(n) (14). Aaron had co-owned a parcel of land with his sister, Karen, as (15)—sometimes referred to as (16)—which meant that when Aaron died, Karen owned the land outright. Had they owned the land as (17), Aaron's interest would have passed to his heirs, who would have had (18), which means that each cotenant is entitled to the possession of the entire premises. Had Aaron and Karen been husband and wife instead of brother and sister, they could have owned the property as (19) and received protection against having the property taken by creditors. They might also have been able to consider the land as (20), which, in eight states, is property acquired by the personal efforts of either spouse during marriage but which belongs to both spouses equally.

■ KEY TERMS_____

chose in action	pay-on-death (pod) account	tenancy in partnership
community property	personal property	tenants by the entirety
divestiture	probate estate	tenants in common
intangible property	probate property	testamentary dispositions
joint tenants	profit à prendre	totten trust
life estate	severally	vests
living trust	tangible property	

Online Companion™
For additional resources, please go to
http://www.paralegal.delmar.cengage.com.

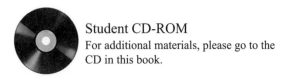

Student CD-ROM
For additional materials, please go to the
CD in this book.

4

Intestate Succession

■ CHAPTER OUTLINE_____

■ CHAPTER OUTCOMES_____

- Contrast the law that governs the passing of real property with the law that governs the passing of personal property when someone dies intestate.

- Describe when property passes according to the law of intestate succession.

- State the share that a surviving spouse inherits under the law of intestate succession in your state.

- Identify the people, other than a surviving spouse, who will inherit and the share each will receive under the law of intestate succession in your state.

- Indicate, under the law of your state, the disposition of property owned by people who die intestate survived by no spouse and no ascertainable kindred.

■ JOB COMPETENCIES_____

- Be able to determine the state law that controls when probating an estate containing property located in two or more states.

"Drink to me!"

**LAST WORDS OF PABLO
PICASSO (1881–1973)**

- Be able to identify the persons who must be given notice when filing a probate petition with the court.

- Be able to determine the persons who will inherit when preparing the final account of an intestate estate.

- Be able to calculate the approximate amount each heir will inherit when preparing the final account of an intestate estate.

■ A DAY AT THE OFFICE . . .

Diane Sherman, a paralegal intern, had been given the task of closing the office and was just about to leave for the day when an obviously upset woman appeared in the waiting room looking for Attorney McKay.

"Mr. McKay has left for the day," Diane told her politely. "May I make an appointment for you to see him?"

"Yes," the woman responded excitedly. "Make it as soon as possible, please. I buried my husband, Will, today and everything we owned was in his name—the checkbook, our bankbooks, the car, even the house."

"Oh, I'm sorry," Diane replied, reaching for a note pad. "What is your name?"

"Gertrude Nullius. You probably read about my husband in the paper. He was murdered by his own son."

"Oh, my heavens. What a tragedy!"

"I still can't believe it! He wasn't my son, thank God. He told me he was going to use the inheritance from his father to hire a good defense lawyer. Can you imagine that? How much do you think he'll inherit?"

"Did your husband have a will?" Diane asked.

"No. He kept putting it off. He was always going to have one made but never got around to it."

"How many children did you have?"

"My husband and I were both married before. I had a daughter by my first husband, and Will had a son—that no-good murderer—by his first wife. We were very happy until this happened. My husband loved my daughter. He treated her just like one of his own. He often said that when he died, he wanted her to share in his estate along with his own children."

"Did your husband have other children?"

"Will and I, we, uh, also had a son of our own who was born a year before we were married. We never told anyone that Will was the real father, you know, because I was still married to my first husband. But Will and I knew the child was ours. In fact, I named him Phil because it rhymes with his father's name, Will. Phil turned out to be a wonderful boy. He can sure use his father's inheritance, too."

"Let me look at Mr. McKay's calendar, Mrs. Nullius. Maybe we can squeeze you in for an appointment early tomorrow morning."

Queries: How should Diane Sherman respond to:

1. Gertrude Nullius's question about how much the son who murdered his father will inherit?
2. Gertrude's statement that her husband wanted her daughter to inherit from him?
3. Gertrude's statement that her son, Phil, can use his father's inheritance?

§ 4.1 INTESTACY

Presidents Abraham Lincoln, Ulysses S. Grant, James A. Garfield, and Andrew Johnson are among the millions of Americans who died without a will. Reasons for postponing the preparation of a will are numerous. Some people may want to avoid the expense of consulting a lawyer. Others may dread any discussion of death or may assume that their assets are not worth enough to require a will. Still others may be well intentioned, but are too busy or too preoccupied with the responsibilities of daily life.

As discussed in Chapter 1, an individual is entitled to make a will at age 18; however, at so young an age, few are motivated to do so. Not until assets increase, or families are formed, or loved ones die, does the need to prepare a will become more apparent to the average person.

When people die without a will, it is said that they die **intestate**. The law of the state where the decedent is domiciled determines how his personal property will pass. In contrast, the law of the state where the property is located determines how real property will pass. Thus, because state laws differ, it is possible for an intestate's real property that is located within the state to pass differently from real property that is located outside the state.

In the past, the rules determining the passing of intestate property were known as the law of descent and distribution. Technically, **descent** refers to the passage of real property, and **distribution** refers to the passage of personal property. Although the words *descent* and *distribution* are still in use today, the more commonly used terminology to describe how intestate property passes is the law of **intestate succession** or **intestacy**. Paralegals who work in the probate field will use these terms frequently.

§ 4.2 THE PASSING OF INTESTATE PROPERTY

It is important for paralegals to know how intestate property passes. This knowledge will be useful when assisting the law firm in settling testate estates as well as intestate estates. This is because in all estates, whether testate or intestate, the **heirs** (those who would have inherited under the law of intestate succession) must be listed on the court petition for probate of a will or administration of an

---

■ intestate

1. Without a will. Dying intestate is dying without having a valid will or one that covers all of the dead person's property. 2. One who dies without a valid will.

■ descent

1. Inheritance from parents or other ancestors. 2. Getting property by inheritance of any type, rather than by purchase or gift.

■ distribution

Division by shares; for example, giving out what is left of a dead person's estate after taxes and debts are paid.

■ intestate succession

The distribution of inheritances to heirs according to a state's laws about who should collect.

■ intestacy

The status of the estate or property of a person who dies without having a valid will.

■ heirs

Persons who inherit property; persons who have a right to inherit property; or those who have a right to inherit property only if another person dies without leaving a valid, complete will.

estate. In addition, the heirs must be notified of the court procedure and given an opportunity to appear if they wish to do so. This is explained further in Chapter 12.

Probate property, as discussed in Chapter 3, passes according to the law of intestate succession when there is property remaining after the decedent's debts, taxes, and administration expenses are paid and the owner dies without a will. In contrast, nonprobate property passes directly to the joint owner or owners and does not pass according to the law of intestate succession.

Even when a person dies with a will, some property may not be included under the terms of the will. That property passes as intestate property according to the state law of intestate succession. This occurs, for example, when a will is drawn without a residuary clause, which distributes all of the testator's property that is not disposed of in other clauses of the will. The Jackson case involves a will that did not include such a clause.

Property may also pass by intestacy when the persons named in the residuary clause of a will die before the testator. The residuary clause is explained more fully in Chapter 6. Similarly, as will be discussed in Chapter 7, children who are omitted unintentionally from their parent's will may be able to take the share they would have received had their parent or grandparent died intestate. The Dorn case involves a granddaughter omitted from her grandmother's will.

Property can also pass by intestacy when someone named to receive a gift in a will refuses to accept it as discussed in Chapter 2.

Simultaneous Death

Sometimes a husband and wife, a parent and child, or other relatives die in a common disaster, and it is impossible to determine who died first. The Uniform Simultaneous Death Act, which has been adopted by almost every state (see Table 10–1 in Chapter 10), allows the property of each person to be distributed as if he had survived, unless a will or trust provides otherwise. For example, if a husband and wife die together in a car accident and each owns separate property, (1) the husband's property will pass to his heirs as though his wife were not living at the time of his death, and (2) the wife's property will pass to her heirs as though her husband were not living at the time of her death.

In the case of property owned jointly by both decedents, the property is distributed equally. Thus, in the preceding example, half of the jointly owned property of the husband and wife will pass to the husband's heirs as though his wife were not living at the time of his death, and the other half will pass to the wife's heirs as though her husband were not living at the time of her death.

CASE STUDY *In Re* Estate of Jackson

793 S.W.2d 259 (TN)

FACTS:

Dorothea Jackson's will established a system for relatives to select desired items of tangible personal property and stated that relatives were to receive nothing more. The will also read: "In the event there is any of said personal property remaining, my Executor is directed to sell the remaining property at public or private sale, as deemed most appropriate by my Executor, and the proceeds therefrom shall be paid to the Eastminster Presbyterian Church, hereinabove referred to." The will contained no residuary clause. A $102,000 certificate of deposit, not specifically bequeathed, was included among the assets of the estate.

LEGAL ISSUE:

How will property not specifically bequeathed pass when a will has no residuary clause?

COURT DECISION:

According to the law of intestate succession.

REASON:

When a will contains no residuary clause, the will makes no disposition of the personal property of the estate other than that which is specifically bequeathed. When there is no residuary clause, property not specifically bequeathed in the will passes as if the deceased had died intestate. A testator can disinherit heirs only by giving his property to others; instructions to exclude the heirs will not be enough to disinherit them unless others are named as the recipients of the property.

CASE STUDY Matter of Estate of Dorn

787 P.2d 1291 (OK)

FACTS:

Laura Mae Dorn's will stated: "I am a widow and my family consists of my son, Richard D. Dorn, presently residing at Oklahoma City, Oklahoma." The will further provided: "I give and bequeath all of my estate, real property, personal or mixed property of whatever character and wheresoever situated of which I die seized or possessed, or which I may own to Richard D. Dorn, my son, to be his forever." The will made no mention of Laura's two deceased children, Kenneth and Jacqueline, nor did it mention her granddaughter, Lynn Mark, the daughter of Jacqueline, who was alive.

LEGAL ISSUE:

May the daughter of a testator's deceased child, who is not named in the will, take the share she would have taken had the testator died intestate?

COURT DECISION:

Yes.

(continues)

CASE STUDY   **Matter of Estate of Dorn** (continued)

REASON: Under the Oklahoma statute: "When any testator omits to provide in his will for any of his children, or for the issue of any deceased child unless it appears that such omission was intentional, such child, or the issue of such child, must have the same share in the estate of the testator, as if he had died intestate, and succeeds thereto as provided in the preceding section." Okla. Stat. tit. 84, § 132 (1981). Thus, as the pretermitted heir of the testator, Lynn Mark was entitled to the same share in the estate of the testatrix as if she had died intestate—that is, one-half of the estate.

When the beneficiary of an insurance policy dies simultaneously with the insured, the proceeds of the policy are payable as if the insured had survived the beneficiary. Thus, if a parent names a child as the beneficiary of a life insurance policy, and the parent and child die together in an accident, the child will be regarded as deceased at the time of the parent's death. The proceeds of the policy will go to the parent's heirs unless an alternate beneficiary is named in the policy. The Uniform Simultaneous Death Act is discussed in more detail in Chapter 10.

In states that have adopted the Uniform Probate Code (see Exhibit 4–1), a specific time period must pass to establish that someone has "survived" an intestate. If someone does not survive the intestate by 120 hours (5 days), she is considered to have died before the intestate. [UPC § 2–104]

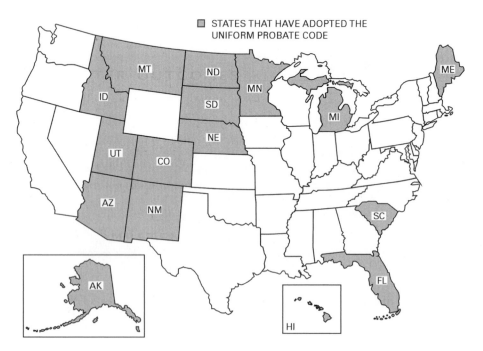

EXHIBIT 4–1   States that Have Adopted the Uniform Probate Code

Homicide by Heir or Devisee

A murderer inheriting from her victim is a repulsive thought. To ensure that people do not benefit from their own wrongdoings, state laws provide that one who is convicted of murdering another cannot inherit from the victim's estate. In the opening "A day at the office" scenario, Gertrude's stepson would not be able to inherit from his father.

Some states, including those that have adopted Uniform Probate Code § 2-803, have passed laws, called **slayer statutes**, to this effect. Other states reach the same conclusion through court decisions. Some courts use a **constructive trust** theory to prevent killers from inheriting from their victims. Under this theory, an heir who murders an intestate takes the inheritance as trustee for the benefit of the persons who would have been heirs if the murderer had died before the victim.

§ 4.3 RIGHTS OF SURVIVING SPOUSE

The first step in determining who will inherit from someone who dies without a will is to find out whether a spouse survived the decedent. When a spouse survives the decedent, the amount that goes to the spouse is determined first, and this amount varies widely from state to state. Some states give only dower or curtesy rights; others merely allow a life estate in real and personal property; still others give property to the surviving spouse and children during widowhood and afterward to the children. Some states give the surviving spouse an absolute interest in the property up to a specified amount; other states deduct an amount from the surviving spouse's share, depending upon the extent of her separately owned assets.

Often, the portion of the estate given to a surviving spouse depends upon who else is alive; that is, if parents, children, grandchildren, or other descendants of the deceased are still living. States adjust the amount given to the surviving spouse according to the existence or absence of parents, children, grandchildren, and descendants of the deceased spouse. Table 4–1 demonstrates the varied approaches to what is considered an appropriate share for the surviving spouse when other relatives are taken into account.

Because a divorce ends a marriage, a divorce also terminates the right of a former spouse to inherit under the laws of intestate succession. (See UPC § 2–802.) A decree of separation (sometimes called a divorce from bed and board) does not terminate a marriage. The right of either spouse to inherit from the other spouse is not affected by a legal separation. Often, however, written separation agreements contain clauses in which the separated spouses renounce their right to elect. That is, they mutually agree to waive their right of election.

■ **slayer statutes**
State laws providing that one who is convicted of murdering another cannot inherit from the victim's estate.

■ **constructive trust**
A situation in which a person holds legal title to property, but the property should, in fairness, actually belong to another person (because the title was gained by fraud, by a clerical error, etc.). In this case, the property may be treated by a court as if the legal owner holds it in trust for the "real" owner.

TABLE 4–1 **Rights of a Surviving Spouse of One Who Dies Intestate**

This general summary of state laws illustrates the wide differences among the states in the laws of intestacy. The summary does not include all variations in every state. Because of the tendency of these laws to change, up-to-date statutes must be checked when looking up a state's intestacy law.

AMOUNT A SURVIVING SPOUSE RECEIVES
If an Intestate Is Survived by:

State	Issue of the Marriage	Issue Not of the Marriage	No Issue But by Parents	No Issue No Parents
Alabama	$50,000 + $\frac{1}{2}$	$\frac{1}{2}$	$100,000 + $\frac{1}{2}$	All
Alaska	All	$100,000 + $\frac{1}{2}$	$200,000 + $\frac{3}{4}$	All
Arizona	All	$\frac{1}{2}$ of separate property	All	All
Arkansas	Dower, Curtesy, and Homestead	Dower, Curtesy, and Homestead	All if married 3 yrs., otherwise $\frac{1}{2}$	All if married 3 yrs., otherwise $\frac{1}{2}$
California	$\frac{1}{2}$ if one child $\frac{1}{3}$ if more than one child	$\frac{1}{2}$ if one child $\frac{1}{3}$ if more than one child	$\frac{1}{2}$	All
Colorado	All	$150,000 + $\frac{1}{2}$ if issue are adults	$200,000 + $\frac{3}{4}$	All
Connecticut	$100,000 + $\frac{1}{2}$	$\frac{1}{2}$	$100,000 + $\frac{3}{4}$	All
Delaware	$50,000 + $\frac{1}{2}$ pp Life estate rp	$\frac{1}{2}$ pp Life estate rp	$50,000 + $\frac{1}{2}$ pp Life estate rp	All
District of Columbia	$\frac{1}{3}$ Life estate rp $\frac{1}{3}$ pp	$\frac{1}{3}$ Life estate rp $\frac{1}{3}$ pp	$\frac{1}{3}$ Life estate rp $\frac{1}{2}$ pp	$\frac{1}{3}$ Life estate rp $\frac{1}{2}$ pp
Florida	$60,000 + $\frac{1}{2}$	$\frac{1}{2}$	All	All
Georgia	Child's share; not less than $\frac{1}{3}$	Child's share; not less than $\frac{1}{3}$	All	All
Hawaii	All	$100,000 + $\frac{1}{2}$	$200,000 + $\frac{3}{4}$	All
Idaho	$\frac{1}{2}$	$\frac{1}{2}$	$\frac{1}{2}$	All
Illinois	$\frac{1}{2}$	$\frac{1}{2}$	All	All
Indiana	$\frac{1}{2}$	$\frac{1}{2}$	$\frac{3}{4}$	All

(continues)

Table 4–1   **Rights of a Surviving Spouse of One Who Dies Intestate** (continued)

AMOUNT A SURVIVING SPOUSE RECEIVES
If an Intestate Is Survived by:

State	Issue of the Marriage	Issue Not of the Marriage	No Issue But by Parents	No Issue No Parents
Iowa	All	$50,000 + $^1\!/_2$	All	All
Kansas	$^1\!/_2$	$^1\!/_2$	All	All
Kentucky	$7,500 + $^1\!/_2$ pp Life estate + $^1\!/_2$ rp	$7,500 + $^1\!/_2$ pp Life estate + $^1\!/_2$ rp	$7,500 + $^1\!/_2$ pp Life estate + $^1\!/_2$ rp	$^1\!/_2$
Louisiana	Life estate	Life estate	Community property	Community property
Maine	$50,000 + $^1\!/_2$	$^1\!/_2$	$50,000 + $^1\!/_2$	All
Maryland	$^1\!/_2$ if minor child $15,000 + $^1\!/_2$ if not	$^1\!/_2$ if minor child $15,000 + $^1\!/_2$ if not	$15,000 + $^1\!/_2$	All
Massachusetts	$^1\!/_2$	$^1\!/_2$	$200,000 + $^1\!/_2$	$200,000 + $^1\!/_2$
Michigan	$150,000 + $^1\!/_2$	$100,000 + $^1\!/_2$	$150,000 + $^3\!/_4$	All
Minnesota	All	$150,000 + $^1\!/_2$	All	All
Mississippi	Child's share	Child's share	All	All
Missouri	$20,000 + $^1\!/_2$	$^1\!/_2$	$20,000 + $^1\!/_2$	All
Montana	All	$100,000 + $^1\!/_2$	$200,000 + $^3\!/_4$	All
Nebraska	$50,000 + $^1\!/_2$	$^1\!/_2$	$50,000 + $^1\!/_2$	All
Nevada	$^1\!/_2$ *	$^1\!/_2$ *	$^1\!/_2$	$^1\!/_2$
New Hampshire	$50,000 + $^1\!/_2$	$^1\!/_2$	$50,000 + $^1\!/_2$	All
New Jersey	$50,000 + $^1\!/_2$	$^1\!/_2$	$50,000 + $^1\!/_2$	All
New Mexico	$^1\!/_4$	$^1\!/_4$	All	All
New York	$50,000 + $^1\!/_2$	$50,000 + $^1\!/_2$	All	All
North Carolina	$^1\!/_2$ if one child rp; $30,000 + $^1\!/_2$ pp; If more than one child: $^1\!/_3$ rp; $30,000 + $^1\!/_3$ pp	$^1\!/_2$ if one child rp; $30,000 + $^1\!/_2$ pp; If more than one child: $^1\!/_3$ rp; $30,000 + $^1\!/_3$ pp	$^1\!/_2$ rp $50,000 + $^1\!/_2$ pp	All

(continues)

TABLE 4–1   **Rights of a Surviving Spouse of One Who Dies Intestate** (continued)

AMOUNT A SURVIVING SPOUSE RECEIVES
If an Intestate Is Survived by:

State	Issue of the Marriage	Issue Not of the Marriage	No Issue But by Parents	No Issue No Parents
North Dakota	$150,000 + $\frac{1}{2}$	$100,000 + $\frac{1}{2}$	$200,000 + $\frac{3}{4}$	All
Ohio	All	$20,000 + $\frac{1}{2}$	All	All
Oklahoma	$\frac{1}{2}$	$\frac{1}{2}$ acquired by joint industry; remainder equal with children	All acquired by joint industry; $\frac{1}{3}$ of remainder	All
Oregon	All	$\frac{1}{2}$	All	All
Pennsylvania	$30,000 + $\frac{1}{2}$	$\frac{1}{2}$	$30,000 + $\frac{1}{2}$	All
Rhode Island	Life estate rp $\frac{1}{2}$ pp	Life estate rp $\frac{1}{2}$ pp	Life estate rp $50,000 + $\frac{1}{2}$ pp	Life estate rp $50,000 + $\frac{1}{2}$ pp
South Carolina	$\frac{1}{2}$	$\frac{1}{2}$	All	All
South Dakota	All	$100,000 + $\frac{1}{2}$	All	All
Tennessee	Greater of $\frac{1}{3}$ or child's share	Greater of $\frac{1}{3}$ or child's share	All	All
Texas	Life estate $\frac{1}{3}$ rp $\frac{1}{3}$ pp	Life estate $\frac{1}{3}$ rp $\frac{1}{3}$ pp	$\frac{1}{2}$ rp All pp	$\frac{1}{2}$ rp All pp
Utah	All	$50,000 + $\frac{1}{2}$	All	All
Vermont	Dower or curtesy Household goods + $\frac{1}{3}$ pp	Dower or curtesy Household goods + $\frac{1}{3}$ pp	$\frac{1}{3}$ rp or $25,000 + $\frac{1}{2}$	$\frac{1}{3}$ rp or $25,000 + $\frac{1}{2}$
Virginia	All	$\frac{1}{3}$	All	All
Washington	$\frac{1}{2}$	$\frac{1}{2}$	$\frac{3}{4}$	All
West Virginia	All unless spouse has child, then $\frac{3}{5}$	$\frac{1}{2}$	All	All
Wisconsin	All	$\frac{1}{2}$	All	All
Wyoming	$\frac{1}{2}$	$\frac{1}{2}$	All	All

* One-third when the deceased is survived by two or more children
   rp = real property   pp = personal property

CASE STUDY   **Estate of Marshall G. Gardiner**

42 P.3d 120 (KS)

FACTS: Marshall G. Gardiner died intestate in Kansas, survived by a wife, to whom he had been married less than a year, and an adult son. His wife, J'Noel, was born a male but had sex reassignment surgery four years before their marriage, making her a "functioning, anatomical female." She had also been given an up-to-date Wisconsin birth certificate, reflecting her new sex and female name. Her husband was apparently aware of the sex change before he married her. In a summary judgment, the lower court found that, for the purposes of marriage under Kansas law, J'Noel was born and remains a male. The court said that the marriage was void under Kansas's statute because it prohibits marriage between persons of the same sex. J'Noel was not entitled to a spousal share under the laws of intestate succession. The case was appealed.

LEGAL ISSUE: When it enacted its marriage law, did the Kansas legislature intend a marriage between a postoperative male-to-female transsexual and a male to be valid?

COURT DECISION: No.

REASON: The Kansas Supreme Court held that the legislature has declared that the public policy of this state is to recognize only the traditional marriage between two parties who are of the opposite sex. The words *sex, male*, and *female* in everyday understanding do not encompass transsexuals. The plain, ordinary meaning of "persons of the opposite sex" contemplates a biological man and a biological woman and not persons who are experiencing gender dysphoria. A male-to-female postoperative transsexual does not fit the common meaning of female. The male organs have been removed, but the ability to "produce ova and bear offspring" does not and never did exist. There is no womb, cervix, or ovaries, nor is there any change in chromosomes.

The Marshall G. Gardiner case illustrates the conflict between present-day society and long-established legal rules. In the Gardiner case, the court quoted the Supreme Court of Vermont, which wrote: "It is not the courts that have engendered the diverse composition of today's families. It is the advancement of reproductive technologies and society's recognition of alternative lifestyles that have produced families in which a biological, and therefore a legal, connection is no longer the sole organizing principle." [In re B.L.V.B, 628 A.2d 1271]

§ 4.4 RIGHTS OF OTHER HEIRS

After determining the amount that goes to the surviving spouse, if there is one, the next step is to determine the rights of other heirs to inherit from the intestate.

Historically, the terms *heirs* and *next of kin* have different meanings. Years ago, under common law, when someone died intestate, the *heirs* were those who inherited the real property, and the *next of kin* inherited the personal property. Modern laws have largely eliminated that distinction, but the two terms are still uniquely different. In most jurisdictions today, heirs are defined as those persons, including the surviving spouse, who are entitled under the statutes of intestate succession to the property of a decedent. [UPC § 1–201(17)] Sometimes the term *heirs* is used in an even broader sense, referring to anyone who inherits property, whether by will or by intestate succession. In contrast, next of kin are those persons who are nearest of kindred to the decedent, that is, those most nearly related by blood. Spouses are not lineally related by blood and are therefore not considered next of kin.

Consanguinity and Affinity

Kindred—people related by blood—are said to be related by **consanguinity**, which means kinship or blood relationship. The relationship may be either lineal or collateral. **Lineal consanguinity** is the relationship between people who are related in a direct line either downward, as between child, grandchild, and great-grandchild, or upward, as between parent, grandparent, and great-grandparent. **Collateral consanguinity**, however, is the relationship between people who have the same ancestors but who do not ascend or descend from each other. Collateral relatives include brothers and sisters, aunts and uncles, nieces and nephews, and cousins. Adopted children are treated identically to blood-related children.

People who are related by marriage are said to be related by **affinity**. They include stepparents, stepchildren, parents-in-law, and daughters- and sons-in-law. Because they are not related by blood to a decedent, they usually do not inherit from the decedent under the laws of intestate succession. A few states have exceptions. Under the Ohio statute (§ 2105.06) for example, intestate property passes to "stepchildren or their lineal descendants *per stirpes*" when there are no next of kin of the decedent.

Half Blood

People who are related by **half blood**, such as a half-brother or half-sister, have the same mother or father in common, but not both parents. The laws of intestate succession differ among the states as to relatives of the half blood. Many states allow half-blood kindred to take equally with whole-blood kindred. For

---

■ **consanguinity**

Having a blood relationship; kinship.

■ **lineal consanguinity**

In a line. Blood relationships such as father and son, grandson and grandmother, etc.

■ **collateral consanguinity**

On the side. Kinship that includes uncles, aunts, and all persons similarly related, but not direct ancestors such as grandparents.

■ **affinity**

Relationship by marriage. For example, a wife is related by affinity to her husband's brother.

■ **half blood**

A relationship between people who have one parent in common but not both parents in common.

example, the Massachusetts statute reads: "the kindred of the half blood shall inherit equally with those of the whole blood in the same degree." [Mass. Gen. Laws Ann. ch. 190, § 4 (West 1990)]. Similarly, Uniform Probate Code § 2–107 reads: "Relatives of the half blood inherit the same share they would inherit if they were of the whole blood."

ART OBJECTS GALORE

When he died without a will in 1973 at age 91, artist Pablo Picasso had produced an astounding number of artworks, making him one of the world's richest men. His estate included 1,885 paintings, 1,228 sculptures, 7,089 drawings, 30,000 prints, 150 sketchbooks, and 3,222 ceramic works, as well as 5 homes, cash, gold, and bonds. Settling the estate involved an intricate network of lawyers, appraisers, catalogers, government-appointed art experts, officials of several government ministries, and even the president of France. After six years of wrangling among Picasso's six heirs, the estate was finally settled—at a cost of over $30 million. The six heirs were: Jacqueline Roque Picasso, the artist's widow (30% or $70 million); Marina and Bernard (20% or $47 million each), the children of Paulo, who was the only one of Picasso's four children born in wedlock; Maya Picasso Widmaier (10% or $23.4 million); and Claude and Paloma (10% or $23.4 million each), the children of Françoise Gilot. To pay the estate tax on this vast wealth of art works, the estate contributed paintings, sculptures, and pottery to France. These works can be seen in the Picasso Museum in Paris.

A FAIR COMPROMISE?

When his 15-year-old daughter died in a car crash in August 1991, James Brindamour did not attend her funeral. However, he did return to Rhode Island three months later to claim one-half of her estate—a $350,000 award to settle a wrongful death suit brought by her mother.

When Brindamour arrived in Rhode Island, he was arrested for failing to pay $66,695 in back child support and interest that had accrued since he had left his wife and daughter a decade earlier. The family court ruled that Brindamour would have to remain in jail until he paid the full amount. Brindamour's solution to his predicament was to request that his share of his daughter's estate be used to pay his debt. After spending 59 days in jail, he was finally released when he agreed to renounce his claim to his daughter's estate. In turn, however, he was relieved of any responsibility for the thousands of dollars he owed in child support.

Some states permit brothers and sisters of the half blood to inherit only if there are no brothers or sisters of the whole blood. Other states give to the half blood only half as much as is given to the whole blood. For example, the Florida Probate Code, Fla. Stat. Ann. § 732.105, reads: "When property descends to the collateral kindred of the intestate and part of the collateral kindred are of the whole blood to the intestate and the other part are of the halfblood, those of the halfblood shall inherit only half as much as those of the whole blood; but if all are of the halfblood they shall have whole parts."

Degrees of Kindred

Under state intestacy laws, the amount remaining after the surviving spouse's share is deducted goes to the next of kin. The method most commonly used in the United States to determine the relatives who are most nearly related by blood is the civil law method. Under this method, each relationship to the decedent is assigned a number called a **degree of kindred** (see Exhibit 4–2). In general, the lowest numbered living kindred inherit the estate to the exclusion of all others. For example, second-degree kindred inherit only when there are no first-degree kindred alive. Similarly, third-degree kindred inherit only when there are no second- or first-degree kindred alive, and so forth.

The degree of kindred of a relative is calculated by counting upward from the decedent to the nearest common ancestor, then downward to the nearest relative. Each generation is called a degree. For example, parents and children of a decedent are related to the decedent in the first degree. Grandparents, grandchildren, brothers, and sisters are related to the decedent in the second degree. Uncles, aunts, nephews, nieces, and great-grandparents are third-degree relatives. First cousins, great-uncles, great-aunts, and great-great-grandparents are fourth-degree relatives. First cousins' children (first cousins once removed) are fifth-degree relatives, and first cousins' grandchildren (first cousins twice removed) are sixth-degree relatives. Second cousins are persons who are related to each other by descending from the same great-grandparents and are also sixth-degree relatives.

A few states follow the common law, or canon law, method of computing degrees of kinship. Under this method, the degree of kinship is determined by counting the nearest common ancestor down to the decedent, and then by taking the longer of the two lines when they are unequal.

Within the degrees of kindred, certain priorities are recognized. For example, the decedent's children receive preference over the decedent's parents, although they are both in the same degree. Similarly, the decedent's brothers and sisters are favored over the decedent's grandparents.

■ **degree of kindred**

The relationship between a deceased person and her relatives to determine who are most nearly related by blood.

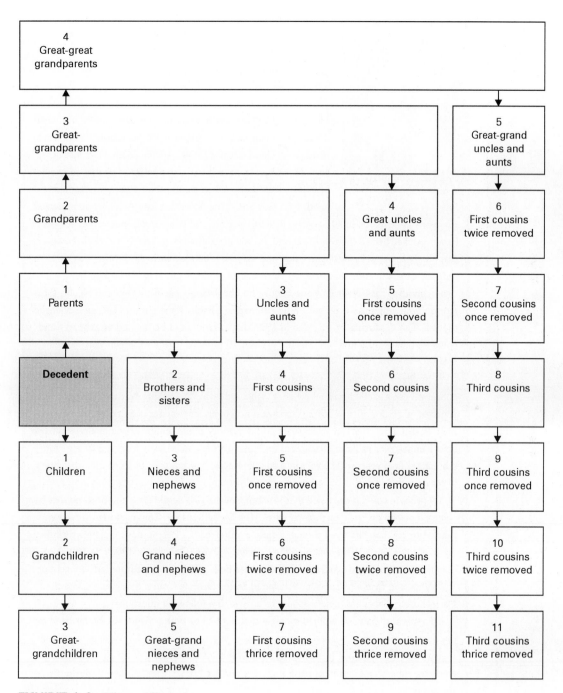

EXHIBIT 4–2 Degrees of Kindred

FROZEN SPERM—DEVELOPING LAW

LAUREN WOODWARD WITH HER DAUGHTERS, MACKENZIE (LEFT) AND MICHAYLA

Photograph by Gordon W. Brown

Edward W. Hart decided to store his sperm for future use when doctors told him that the treatment for his cancer would leave him sterile. Upon learning of his pending death, Hart instructed his wife, Nancy, to have the sperm implanted so that she could bear his child. Nancy did so three months after his death, and Judith Hart was born. The Social Security Administration denied survivor's benefits for Judith, arguing that she was not her father's dependent because her father had died before she was conceived. An administrative law judge ruled in 1995, however, that Hart was the girl's legitimate father and that she is entitled to Social Security benefits. In a separate case, the court has been asked to decide whether Judith is Hart's legal heir.

In another case, William Kane bequeathed his frozen sperm to Deborah Hecht, the woman with whom he lived before he committed suicide. Kane's adult children challenged the will. The California court ruled in 1993 that sperm could be defined as property and could be bequeathed in a will. Hecht received 20 percent (three of fifteen vials) of Kane's sperm.

The first American court of last resort to consider the question of posthumously conceived genetic children's inheritance rights under a state statute was the Massachusetts Supreme Judicial Court in 2002 (*Woodward v. Commissioner of Social Security*, 760 N.E.2d 257). In that case, Warren Woodward had a quantity of his semen stored in a sperm bank before undergoing radiation treatment for leukemia. He passed away from the illness shortly thereafter. Two years after Warren died, his widow, Lauren, gave birth to twin daughters, Michayla and Mackenzie, having been artificially inseminated with her late husband's sperm.

A probate court judge ruled that Warren was the girls' legal father and ordered that his name be placed on their birth certificates. The Social Security Commissioner, however, refused to pay benefits even though a state statute reads, "Posthumous children shall be considered as living at the death of their parent." [Mass. Gen. L. ch. 190, § 8] The commissioner took the position that the statute does not apply to posthumous conception.

When the case was appealed to United States District Court, that court asked the Massachusetts Supreme Judicial Court to answer the following question:

If a married man and woman arrange for sperm to be withdrawn from the husband for the purpose of artificially impregnating the wife, and the woman is impregnated with that sperm after the man, her husband, has died, will children resulting from such pregnancy enjoy the inheritance rights of natural children under Massachusetts's law of intestate succession?

(continues)

FROZEN SPERM—DEVELOPING LAW *(continued)*

The Massachusetts court answered that such inheritance rights exist, but only under certain limited circumstances. The circumstances are that it must be proved that (1) the children are genetically related to the deceased parent, (2) the decedent consented to the posthumous conception, and (3) the decedent consented to the support of any resulting children. In addition, the court said that time limitations may rule out commencing a claim for succession rights, and that notice of any such claim must be given to all interested parties.

Lineal Descendants

As discussed earlier, a lineal relationship exists between a person's children, grandchildren, and great-grandchildren. They all descend from a common ancestor and are referred to as issue or **descendants**. When someone dies intestate, the decedent's children receive what remains after the surviving spouse receives her share. If no surviving spouse exists, the children share the entire estate.

Grandchildren take their parent's share *per stirpes*, that is, by right of representation, when their parents are dead; children stand in place of their deceased parents for purposes of inheritance (see Exhibit 4–3). Under some state laws, when all of the intestate's children have predeceased the intestate, grandchildren inherit **per capita** (by the heads) rather than *per stirpes*. In this method, the number of grandchildren are counted, and each receives an equal share. For example, the Massachusetts statute reads, "if all such descendants are of the same degree of kindred to the intestate, they shall share the estate equally; otherwise, they shall take according to the right of representation." [Mass. Gen. L. ch. 190, § 3].

The law also provides for issue who are not yet alive at the time of the decedent's death. Lineal descendants who are conceived before, but born after, the decedent's death are called **posthumous issue**, or after-born children, and inherit as if they had been born during the lifetime of the decedent. [UPC § 2–108] States are still deciding the question of whether children conceived with frozen sperm after their father's death can inherit from their father.

Adopted Children

For inheritance purposes, modern state statutes generally treat adopted children as kindred or blood relatives of the adopting parents and as strangers to their former blood relatives. Under the Uniform Probate Code, for the purposes of intestate succession, an adopted person is the child of an adopting parent and not of a natural parent. When a child is adopted by the spouse of a natural parent, the relationship between the child and that natural parent remains the

descendants
People who are of the bloodline of an ancestor.

per stirpes
(Latin) "By roots"; by right of representation. Describes a method of dividing a dead person's estate by giving out shares equally "by representation" or by family groups. For example, if John leaves $3,000 to Mary and Sue, and Mary dies, leaving two children (Steve and Jeff), a *per stirpes* division would give $1,500 to Sue and $750 each to Steve and Jeff.

per capita
(Latin) "By heads." By the number of individual persons, each equally.

posthumous issue
A child born after the death of the father.

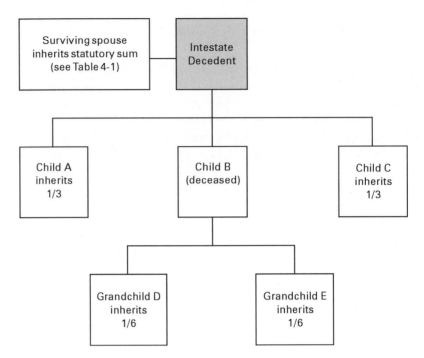

EXHIBIT 4-3   Rights of Children and Grandchildren of Intestate Decedent

same. [UPC § 2–109] Thus, if Alice, the daughter of Janis Akerson, is adopted by Mr. and Mrs. Babson, Alice (adopted child) will inherit from Mr. and Mrs. Babson (adopting parents), not from Janis Akerson (natural mother). If instead Janis Akerson (natural mother) marries John Burns and he adopts Alice, Alice will be able to inherit from both her natural mother, Janis, and her adoptive father, John. The Carlson case illustrates this distinction.

The Massachusetts statute regarding the rights of an adopted child reads: "A person shall by adoption lose his right to inherit from his natural parents or kindred, except when one of the natural parents of a minor child has died and the surviving parent has remarried subsequent to such parent's death, subsequent adoption of such child by the person with whom such remarriage is contracted shall not affect the right of such child to inherit from or through the deceased parent or kindred thereof." [Mass. Gen. L. ch. 210, § 7] In 1994, the Appeals Court of Massachusetts held, in *Shroeder v. Danielson*, 640 N.E.2d 495 (Mass. App. Ct. 1994), that language in a trust leaving property to children of the body had the effect of excluding adopted children and their issue as beneficiaries. The trust contained a sentence providing: "The terms *grandchild* or *grandchildren* wherever used in this agreement shall include only the children of the body of [certain named children]." The person who established the trust had no adopted children or grandchildren when the trust was created.

CASE STUDY *In Re Estate of Carlson*

457 N.W.2d 789 (MN)

FACTS:	Russell Carlson was four years old when he and his two younger brothers were placed in an orphanage after the death of their parents in 1920. Russell went to live with the Klug family but was never adopted. Both of his brothers, however, were adopted by the families with whom they lived. Over the years, the brothers maintained contact with one another through telephone calls, letters, and visits. Russell never married and was childless when he died intestate in 1988. A first cousin once removed claims to be Russell's closest relative for inheritance purposes.
LEGAL ISSUE:	Are adopted-out brothers entitled to inherit from a natural brother's estate?
COURT DECISION:	No.
REASON:	The statutes explicitly provide that adoption eliminates the rights of inheritance from natural relatives. The only exception is when a child is adopted by a spouse of a natural parent.

Nevertheless, the court said that "a trust should be construed to give effect to the intention of the settlor as ascertained from the language of the whole instrument considered in the light of the attendant circumstances." In the Lockwood case, the court held that the Massachusetts adoption statute applies only when a person dies intestate, not when a person leaves a will.

Illegitimate Children

The terminology and rights relating to illegitimate children have changed greatly over time. Under the English common law, children who were born out of wedlock, known as **bastards**, could not be anyone's heir or have any heirs of their own except the heirs of their own body. In those early days, a child born out of wedlock was referred to as a **filius nullius**, which means a child of nobody. Today, such children are referred to as **illegitimate children**, or **nonmarital children**.

In contrast to the English common law, most states in the United States have traditionally had statutes allowing illegitimate children to inherit from their mothers and their maternal ancestors. The rationale was that it is unjust to "visit the sins of the parents upon their unoffending offspring." The right of illegitimate children to inherit from their fathers, however, was not widely acknowledged until 1977. In that year, the United States Supreme Court held that an Illinois law allowing children born out of wedlock to inherit by intestate succession only from their mothers, and not their fathers, violated the equal protection clause of the Fourteenth Amendment to the United States

■ **bastards**

A child born out of lawful wedlock.

■ **filius nullius**

A child of nobody.

■ **illegitimate children**

Describes a child born to an unmarried mother.

■ **nonmarital children**

A child born out of lawful wedlock.

CASE STUDY   *Lockwood v. Adamson*

566 N.E.2d 96 (MA)

FACTS: William P. Wharton executed a will leaving a certain amount of money in trust to his nephew, Dr. Smith, "or his issue by right of representation if he is not living on the date of distribution." Dr. Smith was not living on the date of distribution, but he was survived by four children and one grandchild who was the son of a deceased fifth child. The fifth child divorced his wife and died shortly after his wife remarried. The grandchild was later adopted by the wife's new husband. The exception in the adoption statute [quoted in the text] did not apply because the natural mother remarried *before* the natural father's death.

LEGAL ISSUE: Does the statute, which states that a person shall by adoption lose the right to inherit from natural parents or kindred, apply to testate cases?

COURT DECISION: No.

REASON: Mass. Gen. L. ch. 210, § 7 applies only to the inheritance of property through intestate succession. The word *inherit*, as a legal term of art, though not necessarily in its popular sense, has been defined as referring to intestate succession by an heir and not to transfers of property by will or trust. The Massachusetts Uniform Statutory Will Act provides that "an individual adopted by the spouse of a natural parent is also the child (or issue) of either natural parent" for purposes of construing those terms in wills. Thus, the grandchild is entitled to take his natural father's share of the trust.

Constitution. Since then, most state laws allow nonmarital children to inherit from and through their fathers who have either acknowledged paternity or have been adjudicated to be their fathers in paternity proceedings, as well as from and through their mothers.

Under the Uniform Probate Code, a person born out of wedlock is a child of the mother, and also a child of the father if (1) the natural parents participated in a marriage ceremony before or after the birth of the child, or (2) the paternity is established by an adjudication before the death of the father or is established thereafter by clear and convincing proof. The paternity is ineffective, however, to qualify the father or his kindred to inherit from or through the child unless the father has openly treated the child as his and has not refused to support the child. [UPC § 2–109]

DNA TESTING PROVIDES VINDICATION

No one in the rural town of Adrian, Michigan, believed the 18-year-old live-in housekeeper when she said her employer had raped her one afternoon in 1943. Scorned and ostracized for having an illegitimate daughter, Genevieve Lowery Rindfield moved away, married, and raised five other children.

In 1992, when John Brooks, the employer (and alleged rapist), died at 92 without any children, his relatives assumed the $180,000 estate would be theirs. Instead, Rindfield's daughter, Dianne Burkhard, had the coffin exhumed under a court order. DNA testing of two ribs and muscle tissue proved that Brooks was her father.

Under Michigan law, Burkhard was not entitled to an inheritance from Brooks's estate because Brooks had never acknowledged her as his daughter. Publicity about the case, however, prompted a change in the law in 1993, giving inheritance rights to unacknowledged children. In 1994, a judge awarded $90,000 to Burkhard, $40,000 to be divided among other relatives, and the rest to pay court costs and taxes. For the two women, the victory was far more than monetary; both were vindicated after years of shame.

In 1998, the Pentagon used DNA testing to discover the identity of the "unknown" Vietnam War casualty entombed at Arlington Cemetery. He was Air Force pilot First Lt. Michael Blassie. That same year, the results of DNA tests indicated a probable conclusion (challenged by some critics) that Thomas Jefferson was the father of the child of his slave, Sally Heming.

DNA testing began in the late 1980s. By 2001, according to the Innocence Project, courts nationwide had exonerated, through DNA testing, approximately 90 people who had been wrongfully convicted of serious crimes. Genealogists also use DNA testing to verify family heritage.

A COUNTRY MUSIC LEGEND

HANK AND JETT WILLIAMS

Jett Williams, the illegitimate child of country music legend Hank Williams, Sr., finally inherited a share of her father's estate in 1990, but only after a long, difficult battle to prove her identity. In 1952 Hank signed an agreement with the birth mother, Bonnie Webb Jett, that allowed Lillian Stone, Hank's mother, to assume custody of the baby for two years. Thereafter, Hank would take control. Instead, Hank died days before the child's birth. Until her death in 1955, Mrs. Stone took care of the baby, who was then put up for adoption. Only when Jett turned

(continues)

Lineal Ascendants

We have learned that lineal descendants "descend" from the individual and include a person's children, grandchildren, great-grandchildren, and so on. In the same way, lineal ascendants "ascend" from the individual, include parents, grandparents, and so forth, and have their own distinctive inheritance rights under intestate succession. When no issue of an intestate are alive, both parents, or the surviving parent if one is deceased, inherit what remains after the surviving spouse receives her share (Exhibit 4–4). Parents are entitled to inherit from their child's estate whether or not the parents supported or cared for the deceased child during the child's minority. Even a mother who abandons her infant is entitled to inherit under the laws of intestate succession, as demonstrated by the Hotarek case.

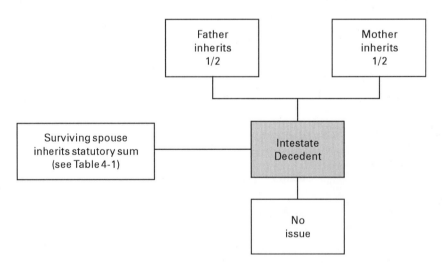

EXHIBIT 4–4 Rights of Parents of Intestate Decedent

CASE STUDY **Matter of Estate of Schneider**

441 N.W.2d 335 (WI)

FACTS: David was born to Mary Ann while she was married to Jack Seng. The birth certificate listed his name as Seng. A few years after David's birth, Mary Ann eloped with Arthur Schneider, taking David with her. David, who now goes by the last name of Schneider, is seeking to inherit Arthur Schneider's estate as a nonmarital child who has been acknowledged as Arthur's son in writings signed by Arthur.

LEGAL ISSUE: Is a husband presumed to be the natural father of his wife's child who is born or conceived during their marriage?

COURT DECISION: Yes.

REASON: This presumption is one of the strongest presumptions known to law. The evidence offered tended to show a strong emotional bond between David and Arthur, but no absence of a biological bond between David and Jack Seng. The evidence was insufficient to rebut the presumption that David is a marital child. David cannot inherit from Arthur's estate as a nonmarital child.

CASE STUDY **Hotarek v. Benson**

557 A.2d 1259 (CN)

FACTS: Paul Hotarek's parents were divorced when he was two years old. His mother abandoned him at the age of three, allegedly having no contact with him after that time. At the age of 15, Paul was killed in a motor vehicle accident. His estate received $300,000 in damages. Seventeen months after Paul was killed, his mother was located in a small town in Utah by a private investigator and told of her son's death. She claimed half of his estate.

LEGAL ISSUE: Is a parent who abandons a three-year-old child entitled to inherit from the child's estate under the laws of intestate succession?

COURT DECISION: Yes.

REASON: By statute, if a person dies intestate leaving no spouse or children, the residue of the intestate's estate shall be distributed equally to the decedent's parent or parents. In the absence of statutory provisions to the contrary, the fact that a parent has abandoned and neglected a deceased minor child does not bar the right of that parent to inherit from the child's estate under the statutes governing descent and distribution.

Some states do, however, have laws that prohibit parents from inheriting from their children if the parents have neglected to support those children. For example, the Pennsylvania statute, 31 Pa. Cons. Stat. § 2106(b), reads:

> Any parent who, for one year or upwards previous to the death of the parent's minor or dependent child, has willfully neglected or failed to perform any duty of support owed to the minor or dependent child or who, for one year, has willfully deserted the minor or dependent child shall have no right or interest ... in the real or personal estate of the minor or dependent child.

Although many state statutes give the decedent's entire estate to the parents or surviving parent when no surviving spouse, child, or descendant of a child exists, some states divide the estate among parents and brothers and sisters.

Siblings

When someone dies intestate survived by no issue and no father or mother, the part of the estate not passing to the surviving spouse usually passes to the decedent's brothers and sisters equally. The children of deceased brothers and sisters (i.e., nieces and nephews) take their parent's share by right of representation (Exhibit 4–5). To illustrate, the Uniform Probate Code provides, "if there is no surviving issue or parent, to the issue of the parents or either of them by representation." [UPC § 2-103(3)]

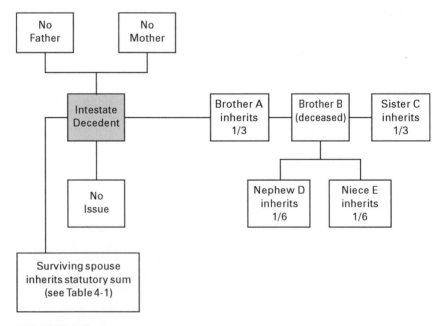

EXHIBIT 4–5   Rights to Siblings of Intestate Decedent

As in the case of grandchildren, some state laws provide that when all of the intestate's brothers and sisters have predeceased the intestate, their issue inherit per capita rather than *per stirpes*. The number of nieces and nephews is counted and each receives an equal share.

Next of Kin

When someone dies intestate survived by no issue, no father or mother, and no brothers or sisters or children of deceased brothers or sisters, the part of the estate not passing to the surviving spouse passes to the decedent's closest kindred. These include grandparents, aunts and uncles, and cousins. (See Exhibit 4–2.)

Grandparents

Existing grandparents usually inherit to the exclusion of aunts, uncles, and cousins because they are more closely related to the intestate. In some states, grandparents inherit equally. In others, if a distribution is to be made to grandparents, the estate is divided into halves and one-half passes to the maternal side and the other half to the paternal side. If there are no grandparents, some states allow great-grandparents to inherit; others do not.

Aunts, Uncles, and Cousins

If no grandparents are living, aunts and uncles are the next in line to inherit, and cousins follow them. Some state statutes provide that intestate property passes to the lineal descendants of the intestate's grandparents by right of representation. Under these statutes, the children of deceased aunts and uncles —that is, cousins—take their parent's share by right of representation.

Other state statutes provide that intestate property passes to the next of kin "in equal degree." Under these statutes, because aunts and uncles are third-degree relatives, they take the entire estate to the exclusion of all others. No one takes by right of representation. Cousins, who are fourth-degree relatives, inherit only when no aunts and uncles are alive when the intestate passes away (see Exhibit 4–6).

Sometimes, in complicated family relationships, the court will require that an affidavit signed by a qualified genealogist be filed as proof of heirship (see Exhibit 4–7).

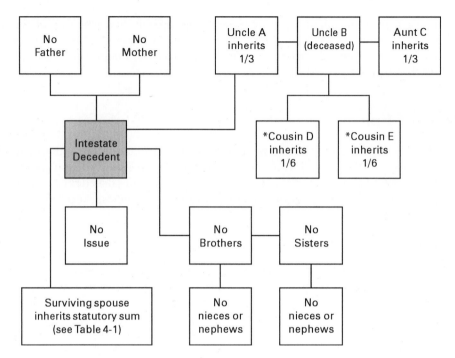

EXHIBIT 4–6   Rights of Extended Family of Intestate Decedent

§ 4.5 ESCHEAT

When people die intestate survived by no spouse and no ascertainable kindred, their property **escheats**, that is, passes or reverts, to the state. Some state laws provide that personal property escheats to the state in which the deceased was domiciled, and real property escheats to the state in which the property is located. Other state laws provide that both real and personal property escheat to the state in which the property is located.

Some state laws provide that an inheritance escheats to the state when the beneficiary under a will cannot be located. For example, a Florida statute provides that when the lawful owner of an inheritance is unknown or cannot be located, the inheritance must be given to the state treasurer to the credit of the state school fund. Under the law, the lawful owner has 10 years to claim the money, after which it escheats to the state for the benefit of the school fund. [Fla. Stat. Ann. § 733.816] In some states, such as Tennessee, an intestate's property escheats if the only surviving relatives are more remote than descendants of grandparents (see Exhibit 4–2). Thus, in Tennessee, second cousins would not inherit; instead, the intestate's property would pass to the state if second cousins were the nearest surviving relatives.

AFFIDAVIT OF DEATH AND HEIRSHIP

STATE OF MICHIGAN)
) ss.
COUNTY OF WAYNE)

NOW COMES Charles Morgan, Jr., of the full age of majority and under no legal disability, who deposes and says:

1. That he is well and personally acquainted with the succession and death of Howard R. Hughes, Jr., deceased.

2. That the decedent died, intestate, on April 5, 1976, with vagabond domicile.

3. Decedent was born a child of Howard R. Hughes, Sr. and Alene Gano, who predeceased the decedent.

4. Howard R. Hughes, Sr. and Alene Gano were married but once, and then to each other. From said marriage, one child was born, to-wit: Howard R. Hughes, Jr.

5. Decedent was twice married, with no issue therefrom. Said marriages ended in divorce, without issue; purported marriage and/or issue concerning the decedent have no evidence, are not supported by fact, record or certified log. There are no adoptions of record or acknowledged children.

6. Decedent's father, Howard R. Hughes, Sr., was a child of Felix Hughes, Sr. and Jean A. Summerlin. They were married but once, and then to each other. From said marriage, four children were born, to-wit:
   A. Howard R. Hughes, Sr., decedent's father;
   B. Felix Hughes, Jr., who predeceased the decedent intestate, without issue;
   C. Gretta Hughes, who predeceased the decedent intestate, without issue;
   D. Rupert Hughes, thrice married; firstly, to Agnes Hedge. From this marriage was born his only child, a cousin of the full blood to the decedent, namely, Elspeth Hughes Lapp.

7. Said Elspeth Hughes Lapp predeceased the decedent and is survived by the following children;
   A. Elspeth DePould, residing Cleveland, Ohio;
   B. Agnes Roberts, residing Cleveland, Ohio;
   C. Barbara Cameron, residing Los Angeles, California.

8. Alene Gano, mother of the decedent, Howard R. Hughes, Jr., is survived by a sister and descendants of a predeceased brother and sister, whose issue are as follows:
   A. Annette Gano, or issue;

EXHIBIT 4–7a   Affidavit of Death and Heirship Filed in the Estate of Howard R. Hughes, Jr.

```
    B. Mrs. J. P. Houston, or issue;
    C. Chilton Gano, or issue.

       9. Said Ganos are maternal cousins and aunt. Said Elspeth DePould,
    Agnes Roberts, and Barbara Cameron are paternal cousins of the full
    blood.

       Affiant is making this affidavit for the sole purpose of establishing
    heirship in the Estate of Howard R. Hughes, Jr.

       Further your affiant sayeth not.

                                            (signed)

                                            _____
                                            CHARLES MORGAN, JR.
                                            Chairman of the Board
                                            Diversified Genealogy Research
                                            1314 City National Bank Building
                                            Detroit, Michigan 48226

    Subscribed and sworn to before
    me this 29th day of April, 1976.
    (signature illegible)
```

EXHIBIT 4–7b   Affidavit of Death and Heirship Filed in the Estate of Howard R. Hughes, Jr.

§ 4.6 INTESTATE SUCCESSION: AN EXAMPLE STATUTE

The New York State Intestacy Statute is typical of these laws. Here is what the New York Law provides.

a. If the decedent is survived by:

1. A spouse and issue, $50,000 and one-half the remaining estate to the spouse, and the balance of the estate to the issue by representation.

2. A spouse and no issue, the entire estate to the spouse.

3. Issue and no spouse, the entire estate to the issue, by representation.

4. One or both parents, and no spouse or issue, the whole to the surviving parent or parents.

5. Issue of the parents, but no spouse, issue or parents, the whole to the issue of the parents, by representation.

6. One or more grandparents, or the issue of grandparents, and no spouse, issue, parent or issue of parents, one-half to the surviving paternal grandparent or grandparents, or if neither of them survive the decedent, to their issue by representation, and the other half to the maternal grandparent or grandparents, or if neither of them survive the decedent, to their issue by representation: provided, that if the decedent was not survived by a grandparent or grandparents on one side or by the issue of such grandparents, the whole to the surviving grandparent or grandparents on the other side, or, if neither of them survive the decedent, to their issue by representation, in the same manner as the one-half. For the purposes of this subparagraph, issue of grandparents shall not include issue more remote than grandchildren of such grandparents.

7. Great-grandchildren of grandparents, and no spouse, issue, parent, issue of parents, grandparent, children of grandparents or grandchildren of grandparents, one-half to the great-grandchildren of the paternal grandparents, per capita, and the other one-half to the great-grandchildren of the maternal grandparents, per capita; provided that if the decedent was not survived by great-grandchildren of the grand-parents on one side, the whole to the great-grandchildren of grand-parents on the other side, in the same manner as the one-half.

b. For the purposes of this section, decedent's relatives of the half-blood shall be treated as relatives of the whole-blood.

c. Distributees of the decedent, conceived before her death, but born alive thereafter, take as if they were born in her lifetime.

d. The right of an adopted child to take a distributive share and the right of succession to the estate of an adoptive child continue as provided in the domestic relations law.

e. A distributive share passing to a surviving spouse under this section is in lieu of any right of dower to which such spouse may be entitled.

A complex formula, easily circumvented by a will.

SUMMARY

When someone dies intestate, the law of the decedent's domicile determines how personal property will pass. In contrast, the law of the place where the property is located determines how real property will pass.

All property that does not pass under a will passes as intestate property, according to the state law of intestate succession.

When people die simultaneously, so that it is impossible to determine who died first, each person's solely owned property is disposed of as if she had survived. In the case of property owned jointly by both decedents, the property is distributed one-half as if one had survived and one-half as if the other had survived. When the beneficiary of an insurance policy dies simultaneously with the insured, the proceeds are payable as if the insured had survived the beneficiary. Any person who fails to survive the intestate by 120 hours is deemed to have predeceased the intestate, under the UPC.

Anyone who is convicted of murdering another cannot inherit from the other's estate. In addition, a divorce terminates the right of a former spouse to inherit from an intestate. People who are related by affinity, such as stepchildren, do not inherit from an intestate. In contrast, half-blood relatives often inherit the same share they would inherit if they were of the whole blood.

The amount that a surviving spouse inherits from a spouse who dies without a will differs from state to state.

The balance remaining after the surviving spouse receives her share passes to the decedent's children equally, with the children of any deceased children taking their parent's share by right of representation. If there are no children or grandchildren, the decedent's parents inherit the estate. If there are no parents, the decedent's brothers and sisters inherit equally, with the children of any deceased brothers and sisters taking their parent's share by right of representation. If there are no brothers, sisters, nieces, nephews, uncles, or aunts, cousins inherit, depending on the state law.

Modern state statutes treat adopted children as strangers to their former relatives and consider adopting parents as though they were legitimate blood relatives to their adopted children. However, adoption of a child by the spouse of a natural parent has no effect on the relationship between the child and that natural parent.

Illegitimate children, under most state laws, inherit from and through their fathers who have either acknowledged paternity or have been adjudicated to be their fathers, as well as from and through their mothers.

When people die intestate survived by no spouse and no ascertainable kindred, their property escheats to the state.

▇ REVIEW QUESTIONS_____

1. What law determines the passing of an intestate's:

    a. out-of-state personal property?

    b. out-of-state real property?

2. When a husband and wife are killed at the same time in an accident, how does the wife's solely owned property pass? How does the husband and wife's jointly owned property pass?

3. What is the rationale for state laws providing that one who is convicted of murdering another cannot inherit from the other's estate?

4. In states that have adopted the Uniform Probate Code, how do relatives of the half blood inherit? How do stepchildren inherit?

5. How does the term *heirs* differ from the term *next of kin*?

6. Under the civil law method, how is the degree of kinship of a relative calculated?

7. Give examples of priorities that are recognized within the degrees of kindred.

8. For inheritance purposes, how do modern state statutes treat adopted children?

9. Since the United States Supreme Court decision in 1977, in what way may nonmarital children inherit from their father and mother who die intestate?

10. When does the property of one who dies intestate pass to the state?

▇ CASES TO DISCUSS_____

1. Mary Holliday was brutally murdered in her home during the evening hours. A grand jury returned an indictment against her son, Craig Holliday, on the charge of murder with the use of a deadly weapon. Holliday was subsequently tried by a jury and acquitted of all charges. Later, a district court determined that Holliday could not inherit from his mother's estate because of the murder. Do you agree? Why or why not? *Holliday v. McMullen*, 756 P.2d 1179 (NV).

2. One year before Delynda was born, her mother, Princess Ann Ricker, and her father, Prince Rupert Ricker, were ceremonially married. The marriage, however, was not valid, because Prince Rupert's divorce from his first wife had not been finalized. Prince Rupert died intestate when Delynda was 18 years old. The Texas court refused to allow her to inherit from her father's estate. A Texas statute prohibited an illegitimate child from inheriting from her father unless her parents had subsequently married, which Delynda's parents had not done. Is the Texas statute valid under the United States Constitution? Explain. *Reed v. Campbell*, 476 U.S. 850.

3. Helen Russell died in the state of Florida, leaving a will that left one-half of her estate to her son, Kenneth Smith, and the other half to her stepchildren, Robert, Ronald, and Patricia Russell. The three stepchildren could not be located. Had Helen died intestate, her only child, Kenneth, would have inherited the entire estate. Kenneth argued that because the stepchildren could not be located, he was entitled to the entire estate. Do you agree? Why or why not? *In re Estate of Russell*, 387 So. 2d 487 (FL).

■ RESEARCH ON THE WEB

1. Log on to the Internet, type in the words <http://www.Google.com>, and press Enter. Then, type in the box the words *intestate succession* and press Enter. Choose one of the many sites that appear (possibly your state), and print out your findings.

2. CataLaw is a catalog of worldwide law on the Internet. It aids legal research by arranging all indexes of law and government into a uniform, universal, and unique index. Find it at <http://www.CataLaw.com>.

3. Read more about the massive problems that arose in settling the estate of Howard Hughes by going to <http://Kingpineapple.com/Hughes/overview.htm.>

■ SHARPENING YOUR PROFESSIONAL SKILLS

1. Refer to the affidavit in Exhibit 4–7 and draw a family tree of the Hughes family. Then, assign a degree of kindred to each person in the family tree, using the information in Exhibit 4–2 on page 89. Finally, determine who should inherit, under the law of intestate succession, from Howard Hughes's estate, being the most nearly related by blood.

2. Look up your state statute that sets forth the right of inheritance of the surviving spouse of a person who dies intestate. Write down the statutory reference, and give the fraction the spouse will inherit (a) if the decedent is survived by issue; (b) if the decedent is survived by no issue but kindred; and (c) if the decedent is survived by no issue and no kindred.

3. A person died intestate. After all debts, taxes, and expenses of administration were paid, the amount remaining to be distributed was $400,000. Under the laws of your state, how will the $400,000 be divided and to whom will it be given if the decedent is survived by: (a) a spouse and two children; (b) a spouse and a father and mother; (c) a spouse but no blood relatives; (d) four children; (e) a brother and two children of a deceased sister; (f) a spouse and a 95-year-old aunt; and (g) no blood relatives and no surviving spouse.

4. (a) List the people who are related to you by lineal consanguinity. (b) List the people who are related to you by collateral consanguinity. (c) List the people who are related to you by affinity. (d) List the people who would inherit from you, and the fractional share each would receive, if you were to die intestate today.

5. In case number 3 of the "Cases to Discuss," how would Helen Russell's estate have passed if she had been domiciled in your state when she died? Provide state statutory references or case citations to back up your answer.

6. Open your book to Exhibit 4–2. Write your name in the square labeled "decedent." Then fill in the other squares, writing in the names of a parent, grandparent, great-grandparent, uncle or aunt, great-uncle or great-aunt, brother or sister, niece or nephew, and so on. Can you name one of your first cousins once removed and one of your second cousins?

7. What is the meaning of the term *per stirpes* as it is used in Item VI of the will of Elvis Presley (reproduced in Appendix B)?

■ SHARPENING YOUR LEGAL VOCABULARY_____

On a separate sheet of paper, fill in the numbered blank lines in the following anecdote with legal terms from this list:

affinity

bastard

collateral consanguinity

consanguinity

descent

distribution

escheat

filius nullius

half blood

heirs

illegitimate child

intestacy

intestate

intestate succession

issue

lineal consanguinity

next of kin

nonmarital child

per capita

per stirpes

posthumous issue

slayer statutes

Conrad Haynes owned both real and personal property when he died (1), that is, without a will. In early times, his real property would have passed according to the law of (2), and his personal property would have passed according to the law of (3). Today, however, the law that determines the passage of Conrad's property is called the law of (4) or (5). His worldly belongings did not (6), that is, pass to the state, because he was survived by people who were related to him by (7), (blood). The relationship between Conrad and his children and grandchildren was one of (8), and the relationship between Conrad and his two sisters was one of (9). Conrad's sister, Norma, was the daughter of his mother but not his father; therefore, she was related to him by the (10). A stepsister, Karen, was related to Conrad by (11), that is, by marriage. The people who inherited from Conrad's estate are called (12). Because they were his nearest kindred, they are also known as his (13). In addition, they were his (14) because they descended from him—a common ancestor. They included two daughters and the son of a deceased daughter who inherited his parent's share (15), that is, by right of representation, rather than (16), which means per head. Another child, who was born out of wedlock, was unable to prove paternity, and therefore did not inherit from Conrad's estate. The law has given such a child various names over the years, including (17), (18), (19), and (20).

■ KEY TERMS

affinity	distribution	intestate succession
bastards	escheats	lineal consanguinity
collateral consanguinity	filius nullius	nonmarital children
consanguinity	half blood	per capita
constructive trust	heirs	*per stirpes*
degree of kindred	illegitimate children	posthumous issue
descendants	intestacy	slayer statutes
descent	intestate	

Online Companion™
For additional resources, please go to
http://www.paralegal.delmar.cengage.com.

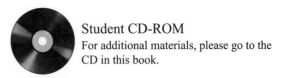

Student CD-ROM
For additional materials, please go to the
CD in this book.

Wills

PART 2

5

The Last Will and Testament

■ CHAPTER OUTLINE

■ CHAPTER OUTCOMES

- Describe the legal requirements for executing a will in your state.
- Explain the methods of changing and revoking wills under the laws of your state.
- Recognize possible grounds for contesting a will.

■ JOB COMPETENCIES

- Be able to assist the attorney in overseeing the process of a client's signing a will.
- Be able to identify signs of a client's possible incapacity to execute a will.
- Be able to prepare an initial draft of a codicil under the supervision of an attorney.
- Be able to recognize situations that could lead to a will contest.

◾ A DAY AT THE OFFICE . . .

Angela Clark, a paralegal in the office of Dillon & Harvey, was given the assignment of interviewing an elderly client in a nursing home for the purpose of drafting the client's will. The client, Mrs. Frothmeyer, acted friendly and smiled pleasantly when she was introduced to Angela by a nursing home attendant. The moment the attendant left, however, Mrs. Frothmeyer whispered to Angela that she needed a will because the people in the nursing home were planning to kill her. Mrs. Frothmeyer said that a bomb had been placed under her bed and was timed to go off at midnight that night; the patient in the next room was scheming to steal all of her furniture. She knew this because she had heard people plotting against her in the middle of the night.

When Angela asked for the names of her children, Mrs. Frothmeyer replied that she had no children. She said that she wanted a new will leaving everything she owned to an aide at the nursing home who had been especially kind to her.

After leaving Mrs. Frothmeyer, Angela inquired at the desk for the name of Mrs. Frothmeyer's guardian and discovered that it was her daughter, Vivian.

Queries:

1. Does Mrs. Frothmeyer have testamentary capacity?
2. What ethical issues arise in this situation?
3. How should they be addressed?

§ 5.1 WILLS AND TESTAMENTS

Paralegals need good judgment and interpersonal skills when interviewing clients for the preparation of the clients' wills. A testator must be of sound mind at the time of execution of the will in order for the will to be valid. As discussed later in this chapter, being able to assess whether a client is of sound mind becomes crucial when the paralegal is asked to witness the will: witnesses may later be asked to vouch for the mental stability of the testator if the will is contested.

Besides dealing with the person behind the will, paralegals must be familiar with specific requirements of the legal document itself: for example, that wills must be in writing in most cases; that specifically two witnesses must be present; that witnesses must sign in each other's presence or in the presence of the person making the will; that real estate is treated differently from personal property. Understanding the rationale behind these details requires a brief look at history.

The law of wills, estates, and trusts of today has its roots in the feudal system that prevailed in England in the eleventh, twelfth, and thirteenth centuries. In those days, it was considered a disgrace to die without a *testament*, which was a will of personal property; wills of real property were not generally allowed. Until the

Reformation, the church, rather than the state, had jurisdiction over the law of testaments of personal property in England. Testaments were received orally by a priest as part of the last confession; the church frequently received gifts of personal property when people died. In fact, much of the law relating to testaments was developed by the church.

In the fourteenth century, a method evolved whereby landowners could bypass the law against making wills of real property. Under this rather ingenious procedure, X (a landowner) would give real property to Y "to the use of X for life and then to the use of X's will." X would then draft a will declaring a use in favor of Z. Since X still had the use of the property and therefore benefited, X was considered the beneficial owner. Y, however, was the legal owner until X died, and then Z became the owner. This arrangement was the forerunner of our present-day trust, discussed in Chapter 8.

LEGAL, BUT ...

JOHN B. KELLY, JR.

Even before his daughter became a movie star and Princess Grace of Monaco, John ("Jack") B. Kelly, Jr., was a prominent figure in Philadelphia, having risen from bricklayer to millionaire contractor. In his unorthodox yet legal will, Kelly replaces legal jargon with personality and wit. He speaks for himself from the beginning:

For years I have been reading Last Wills and Testaments and I have never been able to clearly understand any of them at one reading. Therefore, I will attempt to write my own Will in the hope that it will be understandable and legal. Kids will be called "kids" and not "issue," and it will not be cluttered up with "parties of the first" ... and a lot of other terms that I am not sure are only used to confuse those for whose benefit it is written.

After allocating his property, he speaks to his family:

In this document I can only give you things, but if I had the choice to give you worldly goods or character, I would give you character. The reason I say that, is with character you will get worldly goods because character is loyalty, honesty, ability, sportsmanship and, I hope, a sense of humor. If I don't stop soon, this will be as long as *Gone With the Wind,* so just remember, when I shove off for greener pastures or whatever it is on the other side of the curtain, that I do it unafraid and, if you must know, a little curious.

With characteristic flair, Kelly signed the will in Kelly green ink.

To regain revenues and reduce fraud, England enacted the Statute of Uses in 1536. Under the statute, when X conveyed land to Y "to the use of Z," the use in the hands of Y was destroyed, and full ownership to the property went immediately to Z. Thus, it once again became impossible to dispose of real property by will.

The inability to leave real property by will caused such outrage that England passed the Statute of Wills in 1540, allowing wills of real property to be made "in writing" by most landowners. When feudalism ended in 1660, all land could be disposed of by a written will.

In 1677, more formal requirements were imposed upon wills by the passage of the English Statute of Frauds. That statute declared that a will of real property "shall be in writing, and signed by the party so devising the same, or by some other person in his presence and by his express direction, and shall be attested and subscribed in the presence of the said devisor by three or four credible witnesses."

A will of personal property under the English Statute of Frauds could be oral unless the value exceeded 30 pounds; in that case, the will was not valid unless: (1) it was proved by the oath of three witnesses present when it was made, (2) the testator made the persons present bear witness to the will, (3) the will was made in the last sickness of the testator, and (4) the testimony was given within six months or committed to writing within six days after the will was made.

Technically, the term **will** refers to an instrument that disposes of real property and the term **testament** refers to an instrument that disposes of personal property. Thus, *will and testament* refers to an instrument that disposes of both real and personal property. This distinction is not made, however, in practice in the United States today.

A gift of personal property in a will is called a **bequest** or **legacy** except in states that have adopted the Uniform Probate Code. A person who makes a gift of personal property in a will is known as a **legator**, and a person to whom the gift is given is referred to as a **legatee** or beneficiary. The verb **bequeath** means to give personal property by will.

A gift of real property in a will is called a **devise**. In states that have adopted the Uniform Probate Code, the term *devise* refers to both real and personal property. A person who makes a gift of real property in a will is called a **devisor**, and a person to whom the gift is given is known as a **devisee**. One who is deceased is termed a **decedent**.

§ 5.2 STATE STATUTORY FORMALITIES

Paralegals who work in the field of wills, estates, and trusts must become familiar with their own state statutes governing the formalities of executing a will. This is because each state in the United States has passed its own statutes setting forth the requirements for executing a will. Except for states that have adopted

▪ will
A document in which a person disposes his or her property after death.

▪ testament
A will.

▪ bequest
1. A gift by will, usually of personal property.

▪ legacy
A gift by will, usually of money.

▪ legator
A person who makes a gift of personal property in a will.

▪ legatee
A person who inherits personal property in a will.

▪ bequeath
To give property, usually not real estate, by a will.

▪ devise
1. The gift of land by will.
2. Any gift by will.

▪ devisor
A person who makes a gift of land in a will.

▪ devisee
A person to whom land is given by will.

▪ decedent
A dead person.

the Uniform Probate Code (see Exhibit 4–1), the laws are not uniform. State statutes follow either the requirements of the English Wills Act, the English Statute of Frauds, or a combination of the two. Some differences in the two English statutes are listed here.

1. The English Wills Act required the signature of the testator "at the foot or end thereof." This was not required under the English Statute of Frauds. As you will learn, some states, such as New York, still require a will to be signed by the testator at the end of the will.

2. The English Wills Act required two witnesses, whereas the English Statute of Frauds required three witnesses. Until recently, some states in the United States required two witnesses to a will; others required three. Most states today, however, require only two witnesses to a will.

3. The English Wills Act required that the witnesses be present at the same time, whereas the English Statute of Frauds allowed witnesses to attest separately. Some states today follow the English Wills Act; others follow the English Statute of Frauds relative to the presence of witnesses to the signing of a will.

4. Both statutes required that witnesses attest in the presence of the testator.

Age Requirements

Under the laws of most states, a person must have reached the age of 18 to make a will. People reach the age of 18 on the day before their 18th birthday, because people are considered to have lived the entire day on which they are born. Since the first day of life is counted, infants are 365 days old on the day before their first birthday and are actually one year and one day old on their first birthday.

Some state variations exist on the general age requirement of 18. For example, in Georgia, the age to make a will is 14; in Louisiana, the age is 16; in Texas, married people under the age of 18 may make wills; and in California, emancipated minors may make wills. Members of the armed forces and the merchant marines may make a will at any age in the states of Indiana and Texas.

■ **testamentary capacity**

The mental ability needed to make a valid will.

■ **sound mind**

Whole, healthy mental condition of a person. Sane; mentally competent.

Testamentary Capacity

For a will to be valid, the person making the will must have **testamentary capacity**. This means that he must be of **sound mind** at the time of execution of the will. There is a four-part test to determine soundness of mind. Testators must:

1. know, in a general way, the nature and extent of their bounty (i.e., riches).

2. know, in a general way, who would be the natural objects of their bounty (although they need not leave anything to them).

3. know that they are making a will; and

4. be free from delusions that would influence the disposition of their property.

In the opening "A day at the office ..." scenario, Mrs. Frothmeyer would not pass the test of soundness of mind. Apparently she was having delusions about a bomb being placed under her bed, and she did not know that she had a daughter—a natural object of her bounty.

As suggested earlier, paralegals are often called upon to witness wills, so they may have to determine if an unfamiliar testator is "of sound mind." Conversation is the natural way to explore someone's mental capabilities, especially when dealing with elderly clients. Asking questions about the testator's family, occupation, places of residence, travels, and leisure-time activities can be an effective way to get to know the testator in the short time available. As a matter of practice, carefully annotating the client's file with your discussion and observations of your client's capacity will be useful if questions of competence arise in the future.

The burden of proving the soundness of mind of the testator falls on the **proponent** of the will—that is, the person presenting the will to the court. Establishing the testator's soundness of mind is usually done by offering the will itself, the affidavits of subscribing witnesses, and the judgment admitting the will to probate. In a will contest, witnesses and the testator's physician are usually asked to testify as to the testator's mental capacity. Therefore, the paralegal's role in witnessing wills is a serious responsibility. The paralegal must evaluate the testator's mental capacity exclusively at the time of execution of the will. The *Hedges* case demonstrates that lapses of mental ability in an elderly person do not invalidate the required soundness of mind on the day a will (or codicil) is executed. Capacity is a snapshot event in the law of wills. Only the mental ability at the time of execution is important. The maker's capacity on the day before or the day after is not relevant.

■ **proponent**
The person who offers something, puts something forward, or proposes something.

Necessity of a Writing

With the exception of certain **nuncupative wills** (oral wills) allowed by a few states, wills must be in writing. Many states recognize nuncupative wills of personal property made by soldiers in military service and mariners at sea. Some states also recognize nuncupative wills of very small amounts of personal property and nuncupative wills of personal property made during a last illness when witnesses are present.

■ **nuncupative wills**
An oral will. It is valid in a few states.

■ **holographic will**

A will that is entirely in the handwriting of the signer. Some states require a holographic will to be signed, witnessed, and in compliance with other formalities before it is valid. Other states require less.

A **holographic will** (sometimes spelled **olographic**) is a will that is entirely in the handwriting of the testator and signed by the testator but not witnessed. About half of the states in the United States recognize holographic wills as being valid (see Exhibit 5–1). The rest of the states do not allow them because of the lack of witnesses. Under the UPC, a holographic will is valid if the signature and the material (i.e., important) portions of the document are in the testator's handwriting (see Exhibit 5–2) [UPC § 2-502]. Holographic wills are open to the challenge that they are intended as a rough draft to take to an attorney rather than as the decedent's final draft of the will.

The courts have held that an audiotape recording does not meet the requirements of a holographic will, as illustrated by the *Reed* case. Also, videotaped wills are not valid. Sometimes, you may see an attorney advertise that he does audio or video wills, but the audio or video is a nonbinding, peripheral to the valid formal written will; it is a bit of a gimmick or marketing exercise.

Alternately, if one can present evidence to question competence, one can at least raise a question for the jury.

■ STATES THAT ALLOW HOLOGRAPHIC WILLS

EXHIBIT 5–1   States that Allow Holographic Wills

DE-135

ATTORNEY OR PARTY WITHOUT ATTORNEY *(Name, state bar number, and address):*	TELEPHONE AND FAX NOS.:	*FOR COURT USE ONLY*

ATTORNEY FOR *(Name):*

SUPERIOR COURT OF CALIFORNIA, COUNTY OF
    STREET ADDRESS:
    MAILING ADDRESS:
    CITY AND ZIP CODE:
    BRANCH NAME:

ESTATE OF *(Name):*

DECEDENT

PROOF OF HOLOGRAPHIC INSTRUMENT	CASE NUMBER:

1. I was acquainted with the decedent for the following number of years *(specify):*

2. ☐ I was related to the decedent as *(specify):*

3. I have personal knowledge of the decedent's handwriting which I acquired as follows:
    a. ☐ I saw the decedent write.
    b. ☐ I saw a writing purporting to be in the decedent's handwriting and upon which decedent acted or was charged. It was *(specify):*

    c. ☐ I received letters in the due course of mail purporting to be from the decedent in response to letters I addressed and mailed to the decedent.
    d. ☐ Other *(specify other means of obtaining knowledge):*

4. I have examined the attached copy of the instrument, and its handwritten provisions were written by and the instrument was by the hand of the decedent. *(Affix a copy of the instrument as Attachment 4.)*

I declare under penalty of perjury under the laws of the State of California that the foregoing is true and correct.

Date:

. . . .
(TYPE OR PRINT NAME)   ▶   (SIGNATURE)

. . . .
(ADDRESS)

ATTORNEY'S CERTIFICATION
(Check local court rules for requirements for certifying copies of wills and codicils)

I am an active member of The State Bar of California. I declare under penalty of perjury under the laws of the State of Cali
Attachment 4 is a photographic copy of every page of the holographic instrument presented for probate.

Date:

. . . .
(TYPE OR PRINT NAME)   ▶   (SIGNATURE OF ATTORNEY)

Form Approved by the Judicial Council of California DE-135 [Rev. January 1, 1998] Mandatory Form [1/1/2000]	**PROOF OF HOLOGRAPHIC INSTRUMENT** **(Probate)**	WEST GROUP Official Publisher	Probate Code, § 8222

EXHIBIT 5–2   This Form Is Used in California to Prove a Holographic Will

CASE STUDY   **Matter of Hedges**

473 N.Y.S.2d 529 (NY)

FACTS: On the eve of her 102nd birthday, Nelly Hedges executed a will in which she devised her residence to her long-time friend, Halsey Brower. Seven months later, she signed a codicil to the will revoking the devise to Brower and leaving the residence to her church. After her death, Brower objected to the allowance of the codicil, claiming that Hedges lacked testamentary capacity. Brower offered testimony to indicate that at various times before and after signing the codicil, Hedges had suffered delusions and was irrational and forgetful. No evidence was offered to contradict the testimony of the subscribing witnesses, which established that at the time the codicil was executed, the testatrix was of sound mind and capable of understanding the nature of her action.

LEGAL ISSUE: Is evidence that an elderly testator suffered delusions and was irrational and forgetful before and after signing a codicil, when witnesses testified that she was of sound mind, sufficient to establish lack of testamentary capacity?

COURT DECISION: No.

REASON: It has long been recognized that old age, physical weakness, and senile dementia are not necessarily inconsistent with testamentary capacity as long as the testatrix was acting rationally and intelligently at the time the codicil was prepared and executed. Furthermore, evidence relating to the condition of the testatrix before or after the execution is significant only insofar as it bears upon the strength or weakness of mind at the exact hour of the day of execution. Thus, the evidence adduced at trial was entirely insufficient to establish lack of testamentary capacity at the exact time of the codicil's execution.

CASE STUDY   *Bolan v. Bolan*

611 So.2d 1051 (AL)

FACTS: Charley Bolan died October 8, 1990. He had executed a will on September 6, 1990. There were three witnesses present at the signing; the two people who witnessed the will, and the notary public who notarized the signatures. Several other family members, as well as a neighbor, were also in the house. The witnesses all agreed at trial that the deceased was competent at the signing, but the other people present, all of whom knew

(continues)

CASE STUDY *Bolan v. Bolan* (continued)

Charley well, testified that his mind was not sound, and had been deteriorating for some time. The trial court instructed the jury that the witnesses assertions were definitive as to competence.

LEGAL ISSUE: Should the trial court have judicially determined the competence of the testator?

COURT DECISION: No.

REASON: Although the threshold of competence as to wills is fairly low, when questions of the soundness of the testator arises, conflicting views need be presented to the jury for determination, not judicially determined. "When testamentary capacity is at issue, this Court has held that a very broad factual inquiry is desirable ... "

CASE STUDY **Matter of Estate of Reed**

672 P.2d 829 (WY)

FACTS: Robert G. Reed died without a formally drawn will. However, a sealed envelope was found among his belongings on which was written in his handwriting, "Robert G. Reed To be played in the event of my death only! Robert G. Reed." The envelope contained an audiotape recording of Mr. Reed's directions for the distribution of his assets when he died. The court recognized that the voice-recorded statement did resemble a nuncupative will, but noted that nuncupative wills are not valid in the state of Wyoming.

LEGAL ISSUE: Does an audiotape recording that is placed in a sealed envelope with handwritten instructions that it be played only in the event of death amount to a holographic will?

COURT DECISION: No.

REASON: The envelope notation, standing alone, has no testamentary consequence and cannot be considered a will. Moreover, the statute is not complied with even if the tape and writing are considered together, because no part of the alleged will could be considered to be in the testator's handwriting.

The Will's Execution

Paralegals working in law offices often play key roles in the execution of wills. It is important that they be thoroughly familiar with their state law on signing and witnessing requirements, because wills can be contested if not properly executed. Wills must be signed, attested, and witnessed in accordance with the precise rules of the state in which the will is executed. This is one of the reasons why it is dangerous for lay persons to make their own wills. Most lay persons are not aware of the technical rules that must be followed when executing a will.

Signature Requirements

Written wills must be signed either by the testator or by someone else in the testator's presence who is directed to do so by the testator. A signature may be any mark that the testator intends to be a signature. Thus, a barely discernible signature written by an elderly person's shaking hand, or an X made by someone who cannot write, are accepted as signatures if the intent of the person writing it was to authenticate the instrument.

Signatory intent may be proved by either documentary evidence or the testimony of witnesses with respect to the purpose behind the signing. It may also be proved by the completeness of the document as a testamentary instrument. Thus, if a will is complete, a handwritten name at the beginning may be considered a signature by the court. However, when the document does not appear to be a complete testamentary instrument, a handwritten name located somewhere other than at the end may not be considered valid. To illustrate, Robert Erickson had written notes on three unnumbered three-by-five-inch cards. One card began: "8/22/73 Last Will & Tes I Robert E. Erickson do hereby state that I leave and bequeath to the following persons of my family & others on my demise ... ." The court held that the cards were not a valid holographic will. The court said that the cards did not have sufficient completeness to infer that Erickson intended his name on the first card to be his signature. Nothing indicated the order of the cards or that Erickson had finished his writing [Matter of Estate of Erickson, 806 P.2d 1186 (UT)].

In the states indicated in Exhibit 5–3, the testator's signature must be written at the end of the will. To illustrate, the Pennsylvania statute states, "Every will shall be written and be signed by the testator at the end thereof." The *Hopkins* case points out the danger of making a will without obtaining sound legal advice.

Most states, however, do not require the testator's signature to be at the end of the instrument. For example, in Illinois, "Every will shall be in writing, signed by the testator or by some person in his presence and by his direction and attested in the presence of the testator by two or more credible witnesses" [Ill. Rev. Stat. ch. 110fi para. 4–3 (1985)]. This statute was referred to by the Illinois court in deciding the *Carroll* case.

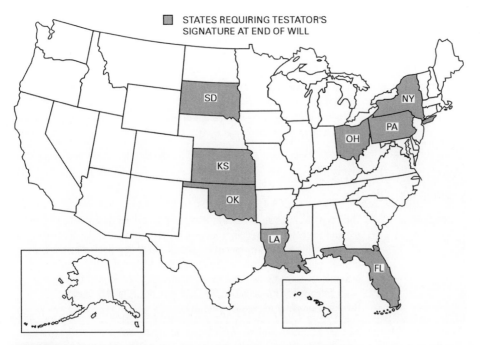

STATES REQUIRING TESTATOR'S
SIGNATURE AT END OF WILL

EXHIBIT 5–3   States that Require Testator's Signature at the End of a Will

FORGERY WHEN STAKES ARE HIGH

When he arrived in the United States as a child in 1906, Stanley Newberg helped his father peddle fruit on the Lower East Side of New York. As an adult, he worked his way through law school before becoming cofounder of two successful aluminum products companies.

When he died at age 81, Newberg left $5.6 million to the United States government as an "expression of deep gratitude for the privilege of residing and living in this kind of government—notwithstanding many of its inequities." At the time of his death, he had no surviving blood relatives. His wife, to whom he had been married for more than 40 years, had died 7 years earlier. She had had three children from a previous marriage, but Newberg never adopted them.

Outraged over the size of his bequest to an "outside" source, the three middle-aged children contested the will. They claimed to have a document signed by Newberg that entitled them to half of his assets upon his death. A handwriting expert concluded, however, that the document had been forged.

The children settled out of court for an unrevealed amount, and Newberg's bequest was sent to the Bureau of Public Debt to help pay general government expenses. The funds covered less than two minutes of government spending, based on the 1994 federal budget of $1.5 trillion.

CASE STUDY *In Re* Estate of Hopkins

570 A.2d 1058 (PA)

FACTS: A four-page document that had been handwritten on lined notepad paper was introduced in court as the will of Edna A. Hopkins. Hopkins had signed her name vertically along the margin of each page, but she failed to sign the document at the end.

LEGAL ISSUE: In Pennsylvania, must a will be signed by the testator at the end of the instrument?

COURT DECISION: Yes.

REASON: The Pennsylvania statute requires that a will be signed by the testator "at the end thereof." This requirement was enacted to prevent the probate of unfinished papers and mere expressions of intent. By signing at the end of a document, the writer has expressed that he has decided on a testamentary scheme and that the writing is not half-formed thoughts never intended to be operative. The will was not allowed, causing Hopkins's property to pass by intestacy.

CASE STUDY *In Re* Estate of Carroll

548 N.E.2d 650 (IL)

FACTS: Genevieve B. Carroll filled out a printed form and signed it on the first line in a sentence declaring the document to be her last will and testament. Near the end of the document, she inserted the date and year in the blank spaces in a line reading: "IN WITNESS WHEREOF I have hereunto set my hand and seal this day of ,19." She did not sign the will a second time. The will was properly witnessed.

LEGAL ISSUE: In Illinois, must a will be signed by the testator at the end of the instrument?

COURT DECISION: No.

REASON: The Probate Act does not require that the testator's signature appear at the end of the will. It is immaterial where in the will the signature of the testator is placed, if it was placed there with the intention of authenticating the instrument. The way the will was filled in suggests that the deceased intended her signature at the beginning of the will to be her authoritative signature.

Will signature requirements, when statutorily provided, must be met exactly in each state. No room for flexibility or interpretation i allowed. This holds true for witness requirements as well.

Witness Requirements

In most states, competent witnesses must witness nonholographic wills in the presence of the testator. With the exception of Pennsylvania (which requires no witnesses except when the testator signs by mark), Louisiana (which requires two witnesses and a notary public), and Vermont (which requires three witnesses), all states in the United States require two witnesses to a will. Some state laws stipulate that the witnesses be in each other's presence when they sign as witnesses to a will. The map in Exhibit 5–4 indicates the states with this requirement. Paralegals who work in one of these states must be aware of the rule, because a violation can cause a will to be invalidated.

The act of witnessing a will consists of two parts, attesting and subscribing. To **attest** means to see the signature or take note mentally that the signature exists as a fact. To **subscribe** means to write beneath or below. Usually courts hold that witnesses to wills must do both. Thus, some cases have held that a will was improperly executed—and therefore void—when the testator refused to allow the witnesses to see his signature, which he had previously written.

■ **attest**

Swear to; act as a witness to; certify formally, usually in writing.

■ **subscribe**

Sign a document (as the person who wrote it, as a witness, etc.).

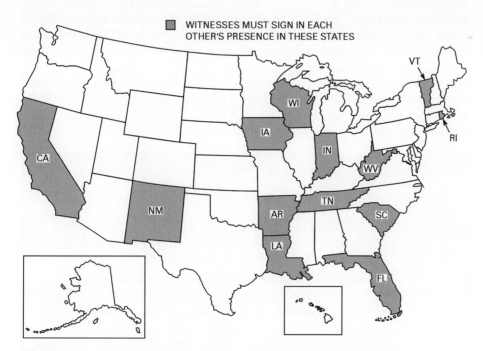

EXHIBIT 5–4 States that Require Witnesses to a Will to Sign in Each Other's Presence

> ## "THE GREAT ONE"
>
> Comedian Jackie Gleason, "the Great One," is probably best known for his role as bus driver Ralph Kramden in the television series *The Honeymooners*. His will is straightforward, but the codicil is unusual. Executed the day before he died, the codicil quadrupled the gift to his secretary from $25,000 to $100,000. The debilitating effects of his cancer made Gleason unable to sign his own name on the codicil. He instructed someone else to sign his name for him, in the presence of two witnesses.

■ **attestation**

The act of witnessing the signing of a document and signing that you have witnessed it.

Some states avoid this problem with **attestation** by the use of suitable language in their statutes. For example, the Virginia law states that a testator's signature:

> ... shall be made or the will acknowledged by him in the presence of at least two competent witnesses, present at the same time; and such witnesses shall subscribe the will in the presence of the testator, but no form of attestation shall be necessary.

The *Robinson* case illustrates that the courts do not interpret the word *subscribe* literally.

In some states, witnesses who are named as beneficiaries under the will lose the inheritance unless there are two other witnesses who inherit nothing under the will. If *Robinson v. Ward* had occurred in Massachusetts, for example, Ward would not have inherited, because she was a witness to the will and two other witnesses were not present. Even spouses of witnesses often lose their inheritances unless there are extra witnesses who do not inherit under the will. Many states, however, protect witnesses who make the mistake of witnessing a will under which they are also beneficiaries. Their laws provide that if the witness would have inherited had the testator died intestate, the witness may inherit the amount in the will, but not more than the intestate share.

CASE STUDY   *Robinson v. Ward*

387 S.E.2d 735 (VA)

FACTS:
When Joane G. Tannehill became ill, she told her very good friend, Katherine D. Ward, to get a legal pad and "Write exactly what I say, and do not interrupt me." As Tannehill dictated, Ward wrote:

To *Katherine D. Ward* I leave everything I own for her lifetime. She is to maintain the farm & provide employment for Penny Guin for as long as Penny cares to stay. I would hope that Katherine can maintain the farm & herself with the income from the farm & interest on my principal. At her

(continues)

CASE STUDY *Robinson v. Ward* (continued)

death, the principal that is left is to be used as an endowment as maintaining this farm, which I wish to go to Covington Boys Home. The farm is to be used by them as a teaching facility. If they do not wish to use it that way then the entire request is to go to VPI to be used in the same manner.

After Ward finished writing the will, Tannehill read it over, signed her name, dated it, and placed it on a bedside table. Shortly thereafter, George A. Knudson, a member of the rescue squad, arrived. Tannehill told Knudson that she had dictated her will to Ward and asked him to read and witness it. He read the will, dated it, wrote "Witness" and signed it in the presence of Tannehill and Ward. Tannehill died that day. The next day, on the advice of an attorney, Ward signed the will below Knudson's signature.

LEGAL ISSUE: Is the signature of a witness on the first line of a will a satisfactory subscription by that witness?

COURT DECISION: Yes.

REASON: Ward did not intend to act as a witness when she wrote her name in the first line of the document. Yet, she was a subscribing witness to the execution of the will within the meaning of the statute. Although the testatrix never formally asked Ward to be a witness to the will, the evidence establishes that Tannehill expected her to act as a witness and treated her as one. (Three judges dissented, saying that Virginia's statutory language requires "signing a will *with the intention of acting as a witness.*")

The 1990 revision of the UPC goes even further, by giving full protection to witnesses when they inherit under the will. The revised law states that the signing of a will by an interested witness does not invalidate the will or any provision of it [UPC § 2-505]. The map in Exhibit 5–5 indicates the states that follow these rules when a witness to a will is also a beneficiary under that will.

Witnesses to a will must be competent. In general, this means competent to be a witness in a court of law. Massachusetts has defined *competency* as being of "sufficient understanding," meaning that the witness understands what a will is and what is taking place when the will is executed. "While age is of importance," a Massachusetts court said,

> it is not the test. To determine whether a person is of "sufficient understanding" to be considered competent the courts of this Commonwealth have long applied a two-prong test: (1) whether the witness has the general ability or capacity to observe, remember, and give expression to that which he or she has seen, heard, or experienced; and (2) whether he or she has understanding sufficient to comprehend the difference between truth and falsehood, the wickedness of the latter

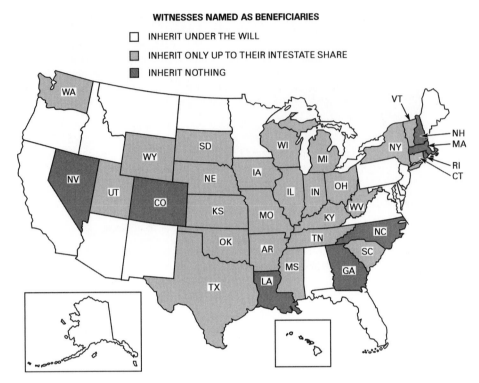

WITNESSES NAMED AS BENEFICIARIES

☐ INHERIT UNDER THE WILL

▦ INHERIT ONLY UP TO THEIR INTESTATE SHARE

■ INHERIT NOTHING

EXHIBIT 5–5   Witnesses Named as Beneficiaries

and the obligation and duty to tell the truth, and, in a general way, belief that failure to perform the obligation will result in punishment [*Commonwealth v. Gamache,* 626 N.E.2d 616].

Although most states have no age requirements for witnesses to wills, Arkansas and Utah require witnesses to be at least 18 years old, Iowa requires them to be at least 16 years old, and Texas requires them to be at least 14 old. As a matter of practice, paralegals and attorneys should only use witnesses of age 18 or older. In addition, engaging witnesses in a conversation, with the intent to establish their orientation as to time and place, is a solid practice. One should annotate the file as to this conversation for future reference if questions arise to the capacity of the witness.

Relaxation of Formalities

The 1990 revision of the UPC contains a section that relaxes the strict, formal requirements concerning the execution of wills if the proponent of the document establishes by clear and convincing evidence that the decedent intended the document to be a will [UPC § 2–503].

Professional Guidelines

To avoid the pitfalls of an improperly executed will, this procedure is recommended:

1. The testator is asked to read the will carefully, being certain that it is accurate, that it expresses the testator's will, and that all aspects of the will are understood.

2. The proper number of witnesses are brought into the room and introduced to the testator; the door is closed, and the group should not be interrupted.

3. The testator declares to the witnesses that the instrument before them is his will and requests them to act as witnesses to its execution. The witnesses do not read the will.

4. The testator signs the will at the end, making sure that all witnesses observe the signature.

5. The testator initials or signs the margin of each page of the will for purposes of authenticity.

6. One witness reads the attestation clause (the clause preceding the witness's signature) aloud. The witnesses then sign their names and write their addresses while the testator and other witnesses observe.

7. If a self-proof clause is used, a notary public, who must also be present, takes the oaths and acknowledgments of the testator and the witnesses.

§ 5.3 CHANGING AND REVOKING WILLS

Just as making a will involves technicalities, changing or revoking a will also requires certain formalities. Paralegals should encourage testators to seek competent legal advice whenever they want to alter their wills in any way.

Changing a Will

Altering the terms of a will is most effectively done through a **codicil**, which is a separate instrument with new provisions that change the original will in some way. In most states, a codicil must refer specifically to the will being changed and must be executed with the same formalities as are required for the execution of a will. The Montana court in the *Kuralt* case, however, did not follow the former rule in its interpretation of a letter serving as a codicil.

A properly executed codicil has the effect of **republishing**, that is, reestablishing, the will. It is said that a codicil breathes new life into a will. Thus, a will with only one witness or a will that has been revoked is reestablished

■ **codicil**
A supplement or addition to a will that adds to it or changes it.

■ **republishing**
Reestablishing the validity of a will that has been revoked.

CASE STUDY In Re the Estate of Charles Kuralt

15 P.3d 931 (MT)

FACTS: Charles Kuralt maintained an intimate personal relationship with Elizabeth Shannon for almost 30 years, without the knowledge of his wife. The couple saw each other regularly and kept in touch by phone and mail. Kuralt was the main source of Shannon's financial support during those years. They built a cabin together on a 20-acre parcel of land in Montana, and Kuralt owned 90 acres of adjoining land. In 1989, Kuralt made a holographic will leaving all of that land to Shannon. Five years later, he executed a formal will leaving everything to his wife and two children. Two months before he died, however, Kuralt deeded the 20-acre parcel with the cabin to Shannon and indicated his intention to deed her the 90-acre site. He became suddenly ill however. After entering a hospital, he wrote Shannon a letter saying among other things, "I'll have the lawyer visit the hospital to be sure you *inherit* the rest of the place in MT if it comes to that."

LEGAL ISSUE: Can a letter expressing one's intent to leave a gift by will be considered a valid holographic codicil to an existing will in Montana?

COURT DECISION: Yes.

REASON: Montana courts are guided by the bedrock principle of honoring the intent of the testator. The letter met the threshold requirements for a valid holographic will. It expressed a present testamentary intent to transfer the property to Shannon. The official comments to the Montana Code states: "when the second will does not make a complete disposition of the testator's estate, the second will is more in the nature of a codicil to the first will." The letter was a codicil as a matter of law because it made a specific bequest of the Montana property and did not purport to bequeath the entirety of the estate.

with a properly executed codicil (see Exhibit 5–6). Unfortunately, the reverse is also possible. One may invalidate, or at least create a question about, a perfectly valid will. If, for example, there is no question of the testator's competence at the time of will execution, but there is a question of competence at the time of the codicil's execution, one may have damaged the original will.

Unfortunately, people often choose to avoid the expense of a lawyer and decide to cross out words or sections of their wills on their own. Such deletions may be accepted without being witnessed if evidence exists that the deletions were done intentionally by the testator. However, proving who made the markings and whether the changes were intended is difficult. Cross-out marks on wills cause confusion, invite contests, and can lead to costly litigation. This is particularly true with holographic wills.

FIRST CODICIL TO WILL OF FRANCIS ALBERT SINATRA
also known as FRANK SINATRA

I, FRANCIS ALBERT SINATRA, also known as FRANK SINATRA, do hereby declare this to be a First Codicil to my Last Will and Testament dated September 3, 1991.

I.

I hereby delete Section C of Clause FIFTH of said Last Will and Testament and in lieu and in place thereof insert the following new Section C:

"C. To ELVINA JOUBERT of Rancho Mirage, California, if she survives me, the sum of One Hundred Fifty Thousand Dollars ($150,000). If ELVINA JOUBERT does not survive me, this gift shall lapse and shall be considered as part of the residue of my estate."

II.

I hereby delete in its entirety Section D of Clause FIFTH of said Last Will and Testament by reason of the death of JILLY RIZZO.

III.

In all other respects I hereby reaffirm and republish my Last Will and Testament dated September 3, 1991.

Signed at RANCHO MIRAGE , California on MAY 1 , 1993.

Frank Sinatra
FRANCIS ALBERT SINATRA
also known as
FRANK SINATRA

ADMITTED TO PROBATE
Date JUN 18 1998
Attest: JOHN A. CLARKE, COUNTY CLERK
by   (signed)   Deputy

ATTESTATION AND DECLARATION

The testator, FRANCIS ALBERT SINATRA, also know as FRANK SINATRA, on the date written above, declared to us, the undersigned, that the foregoing instrument, consisting of two (2) pages, including the page signed by us as witnesses, is his First Codicil to his Last Will dated September 3, 1991 and requested us to act as witnesses to it. Then the testator signed this First Codicil in our presence, all of us being present

EXHIBIT 5–6a   Codicil to Frank Sinatra's Will

at the same time. We now, at his request, in his presence, and in the presence of one another, subscribe our names as witnesses.

Each of us states that the testator and each of us are over eighteen (18) years of age, that the testator appears to be of sound mind, and that we have no knowledge of any facts indicating that the foregoing instrument or any part of it was procured by duress, menace, fraud, or undue influence.

We, each for himself or herself, declare under penalty of perjury under the laws of the State of California that the foregoing is true and correct and that this attestation and this declaration are executed on the 1st day of MAY , 1993, at RANCHO MIRAGE , California.

CONNIE SEDILLOS
(signed)

ROLAND YOUNG
(signed)

EXHIBIT 5–6b   Codicil to Frank Sinatra's Will

Additions to a will following its execution have no legal effect unless the will is re-signed by the testator and reattested by the proper number of witnesses. As discussed earlier, paralegals should encourage testators to seek proper legal expertise when considering changes to their wills. Making a new will or adding a codicil to the existing will is an effective way to avoid future problems.

Either task can be performed easily and speedily through the use of a word processor. Computerized systems allow documents to be easily retrieved and updated. Personal data may have to be changed, as in the case of a marriage, divorce, death, or adoption; a condition or clause in a will (or trust) agreement may no longer be valid. With word-processing software, these changes require a few keyboard strokes and little time. Standardized forms may be retrieved on the computer and then customized for the client. Whole paragraphs may be reworked, deleted, or rearranged with minimal effort and time.

CODICILS BY J. PAUL GETTY

J. PAUL GETTY

The following is a list of codicils to the Will dated September 22, 1958:

1st Codicil: June 18, 1960
2nd Codicil: November 4, 1962
3rd Codicil: December 20, 1962
4th Codicil: January 15, 1963
5th Codicil: March 6, 1963
6th Codicil: September 16, 1965
7th Codicil: March 11, 1966
8th Codicil: January 5, 1967
9th Codicil: November 3, 1967
10th Codicil: February 24, 1969
11th Codicil: March 28, 1969
12th Codicil: June 26, 1970
13th Codicil: March 8, 1971
14th Codicil: July 29, 1971
15th Codicil: March 20, 1973
16th Codicil: June 14, 1973
17th Codicil: October 9, 1973
18th Codicil: July 4, 1974
19th Codicil: January 21, 1975
20th Codicil: August 27, 1975
21st Codicil: March 11, 1976

The number of codicils added to the will of oil magnate J. Paul Getty seems excessive: why a new, updated document was never drafted is anyone's guess. In a time before computerized revisions with word-processing programs, perhaps retyping the entire will required too much time and inconvenience. Or maybe Getty chose the method of adding codicils to show beneficiaries exactly when he no longer approved of them or their actions.

Revoking a Will

State statutes set forth precise methods for **revoking** (canceling) a will. The act of revoking a will must be accompanied by the testator's intent to revoke the will. There are four principal methods of revoking a will:

1. The English Statute of Frauds declared that a will could be revoked by "burning, canceling, tearing, or obliterating." (See sample in Exhibit 5–7.) The English Wills Act prescribed "burning, tearing, or otherwise destroying." Most American statutes use the language of one of these acts.

■ **revoking**
Wipe out the legal effect of something by taking it back, canceling, rescinding, etc.

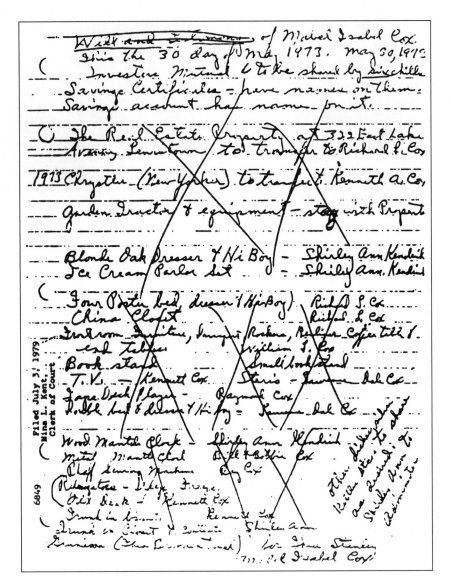

EXHIBIT 5–7 Sample of Canceled Holographic Will

2. In general, the execution of a new will revokes a prior will. To revoke a prior will in some states, however, the new will must either expressly state that it revokes an earlier will or be inconsistent with the old will; otherwise, the new will is treated as a supplement (like a codicil) to the old will. The 1990 revision of the UPC attempts to clarify this rule with the following language:

The testator is presumed to have intended a subsequent will to replace rather than supplement a previous will if the subsequent will makes a complete disposition of the testator's estate [UPC § 2–507(c)]. The testator is presumed to have intended a subsequent will to supplement rather than replace a previous will if the subsequent will does not make a complete disposition of the testator's estate [UPC § 2–507(d)].

Sometimes the act of destroying a will does not revoke it. This occurs when a testator cancels a valid will after making a new one, and the new will turns out to be void. Under a rule known as the doctrine of *dependent relative revocation,* the canceled will is held to be effective in order to avoid intestacy. The reasoning behind the rule is that the testator's intent was to cancel the will only if the new will became effective. If the new will is not effective, the canceled will is revived.

3. The subsequent marriage of a person who has made a will revokes the will in some states unless the will declares that it is made in contemplation of marriage to a particular person. In a small number of jurisdictions, subsequent marriage revokes a will only when a child is born of that marriage. In Georgia, Kansas, Louisiana, and South Dakota, the birth of a child revokes a will unless the child is provided for in the will. In a few states, instead of revoking a will completely, subsequent marriage revokes only gifts made in a will to a former spouse. The map in Exhibit 5–8 indicates the effect of subsequent marriage under the laws of different states.

4. Under the laws of many states, a divorce or dissolution of marriage revokes bequests and devises to a former spouse—but not the will itself —unless the will specifically provides otherwise. In addition, a divorce revokes the appointment of the former spouse as an executor or trustee under the will. See Table 5–1.

State statutes differ with regard to the annulment of a marriage. An annulment revokes the entire will in Maryland and West Virginia. In many states, however, instead of revoking the entire will, an annulment revokes only gifts in the will to a former spouse. The *Knott* case illustrates the Kentucky rule as to the effect of an annulment on a will.

TABLE 5–1   **Effect of Divorce on Bequests to Former Spouse**

A divorce revokes an entire will in:	Connecticut, Georgia
A divorce has no effect on a will in:	Iowa, Louisiana, Mississippi, New Hampshire, Vermont
A divorce revokes all gifts made in a will to a former spouse in:	All other states

EXHIBIT 5–8   Effect of Subsequent Marriage upon Will

CASE STUDY	Knott v. Garriott

784 S.W.2d 803 (KY)

FACTS:	Following his wife's death, Wilbert Martin executed a will. Four years later, Martin married Barbara Mattingly. That marriage was annulled shortly thereafter because of Martin's incapacity to consent to marriage.
LEGAL ISSUE:	Does a marriage, subsequently annulled, revoke a will made prior to the marriage?
COURT DECISION:	No.
REASON:	A decree annulling a marriage is a declaration that no valid marriage ever existed. An annulled marriage is void *ab initio* (from the beginning) and cannot operate to invalidate a will made prior to the marriage.

Sometimes, a testator will leave his entire estate to a particular person without mentioning in the will that he intends to marry that person. Shortly thereafter, the testator marries that person, and the question later arises as to whether the subsequent marriage revoked the will. Courts have held, in recent cases, that the will is not revoked in this situation because there is clear and convincing evidence that the will was made in contemplation of the marriage, even though that fact was not mentioned in the will itself.

§ 5.4 JOINT AND MUTUAL WILLS

A **joint will** is one instrument that serves as the will of two or more people. The instrument is **probated** (proved and allowed by the court) each time a cotestator dies. Generally, it is not good practice to draw joint wills: the parties may separate; one of them, rather than both, may have custody of the will and the other may not know its whereabouts; one of them may destroy the will without the other's knowledge or consent. It is better to draw a separate will for each testator, even if the wills are identical.

Mutual wills (also called **reciprocal wills**) are separate, identical wills for each testator containing reciprocal provisions accompanied by an agreement that neither testator will change his will after the death of the other. The *Johnson* case involved a will that was both joint and mutual and contained a provision requiring mutual agreement for the will to be changed.

CASE STUDY	*In Re* Estate of Johnson
	781 S.W.2d 390 (TX)
FACTS:	Soon after being married, Emma and James Johnson executed a joint will. Both had been previously married and had several children by their prior marriages. The will, among other things, provided for Emma's son and contained the following provision: "… this is our joint and mutual will made by each in consideration of the other so doing and shall be irrevocable excepting by the mutual agreement of both." Four years later, unbeknownst to Emma, James executed a new will, revoking the earlier will and providing for his son instead of Emma's son. Emma learned of the new will when James died seven years later.
LEGAL ISSUE:	May a joint and mutual will stating that it is irrevocable except by mutual consent be revoked by one cotestator without the consent of the other?
COURT DECISION:	No.

(continues)

■ **joint will**

A single instrument that serves as the will of two or more people.

■ **probated**

The process of handling the will and the estate of a dead person.

■ **mutual wills**

Wills that are done together and bilateral (two-sided, two-way, or done one for the other).

■ **reciprocal wills**

Wills that are mutual (done together) and bilateral (two-sided, two-way, or done one for the other). For example, reciprocal wills are wills made by two persons, and enforceable against each other because each person put something in his will that the other asked for.

A written contract to provide for another by will is enforceable in most states; an oral contract is not. However, to prevent unjust enrichment, anyone who furnishes services to another based on the other's oral promise to leave a gift by will can recover the fair value of those services from the other's estate.

§ 5.5 AGREEMENTS TO DEVISE OR BEQUEATH PROPERTY

Agreements to devise or bequeath property to someone in a will must be in writing to be enforceable. This type of agreement occurs most often when a caregiver agrees to care for an elderly person in exchange for receiving something under the elderly person's will. In such cases, the caregiver must be careful not to use undue influence in arranging the transaction, which would invalidate the gift. The Uniform Probate Code (§ 2–514) provides that a contract to make a will or devise, or not to revoke a will or devise, or to die intestate can be established only by:

- provisions of a will stating the material provisions of the contract; or
- an express reference in a will to a contract and extrinsic evidence proving the terms of the contract; or
- a writing signed by the decedent evidencing the contract.

Example

Agreement to Devise or Bequeath Property

20A AMJUR LF WI § 266:29

It is further agreed that if _____ [housekeeper] performs the terms and conditions specified in this agreement until the death of _____ [testator], _____ [testator] will, as part of the compensation for the services performed by _____ [housekeeper], execute a valid will and testament in which the title and all rights to _____ [testator's] house and the land on which it is situated are devised to _____ [housekeeper].

AN ARTISTIC FORTUNE

GEORGIA O'KEEFFE

Artist Georgia O'Keeffe died in 1986 at age 98 with an estate worth over $70 million. Excluded family members contested her will, claiming that Juan Hamilton, her male assistant for over 14 years and more than 50 years her junior, exerted "undue influence" over the aged artist. O'Keeffe had given Hamilton her power of attorney in 1978; as compensation, she left him her ranch and 21 paintings in her will of the following year. Over the years, she became even more liberal: in a second codicil of 1984, Hamilton's share of the estate jumped from 10 to 70 percent, or to an inheritance of over $40 million. What ultimately occurred, however, was a settlement agreement among Hamilton, O'Keeffe's sister, and O'Keeffe's niece. What remained unresolved was whether Hamilton's "influence" was a natural outgrowth of an enduring relationship or deliberate manipulation, and whether O'Keeffe would have favored the final compromise.

§ 5.6 GROUNDS FOR CONTESTING A WILL

To be able to contest a will, a person must have *standing*—that is, have some beneficial interest that will be lost if the will is allowed. This usually means that the person contesting would either inherit under an earlier will or under the law that is applied when someone dies without a will. As mentioned earlier, wills may be contested on the grounds of improper execution and unsound mind. Other grounds for contesting a will are fraud and undue influence.

To successfully contest a will on the ground of fraud, it must be shown that the testator relied on false statements when making the will. To contest a will on the ground of undue influence, it must be shown that the testator's free will was destroyed and, as a result, the testator did something contrary to his true desires. The burden is on the person alleging fraud or undue influence to prove that those conditions existed. When there is fraud or undue influence, the court may disallow only part of the will, instead of the entire will, as in the case of improper execution and unsound mind. The *Home For Incurables of Baltimore* case illustrates how this same rule is applied when part of a will is illegal.

CASE STUDY *Home For Incurables of Baltimore v. University of Maryland*

2002 WL 851083 (MD)

FACTS:

In his will, Dr. Jesse C. Coggins bequeathed almost $30 million to Keswick Multi-Care Center to be held in trust until the death of his wife, Helen. When Helen died 13 years later, the lower court held that the will was illegal because it contained a clause stipulating that the nursing home must use the money only to house white patients. The nursing home told the court that its brochure reads, in part, "Keswick is committed to providing quality care through innovative and futuristic approaches to older adults of all races and creeds," and that it would not honor the will's provision to house only white patients. Nevertheless, the lower court held that the will was unenforceable since it would have required the nursing home to break discrimination laws. The lower court ordered the money to go to the University of Maryland Medical Center, which was named in the will as the alternate beneficiary.

LEGAL ISSUE:

Should the alternate beneficiary named in a will receive the bequest when the gift to the primary beneficiary contains an illegal, racially discriminatory condition?

COURT DECISION: No.

REASON:

Today in Maryland, there are few if any public policies stronger than the policy against discrimination based on race or color. When a condition attached to a bequest is clearly illegal and violates a strong public policy, the illegal portion of the condition should be removed and the bequest enforced without regard to the illegal condition. The provisions of the will should be administered as if the word "white" was not there, giving the bequest to the Keswick Multi-Care Center.

SUMMARY

The law of wills, estates, and trusts has its origins in early England. Wills of real property were not always allowed in England. Until the end of feudalism in 1660, the church, rather than the state, had jurisdiction over the law of testaments, which were often made orally to a priest as part of the last confession.

In general, a person must be 18 years old and of sound mind to make a will. With limited exceptions for personal property, wills must be in writing and signed either by the testator or by someone else in the testator's presence who is directed to do so by the testator. A signature may be any mark that the testator intends to be a signature. Some states require a testator's signature at the end of the instrument; others do not. Nonholographic wills must be witnessed in the presence of the testator by either two or three competent witnesses, depending on state law.

When items are crossed out of a will and there is evidence that the deletion was done intentionally by the testator, the deletion will be accepted even though it was not witnessed. In contrast, when additions are made to a will following its execution, the additions have no legal effect unless the will is re-signed by the testator and reattested by the proper number of witnesses. A codicil must refer specifically to the will being changed and must be executed with the same formalities as are required for the execution of a will. A properly executed codicil has the effect of republishing a will. Wills may be revoked by (1) burning, canceling, tearing, or obliterating; (2) the execution of a new will; (3) subsequent marriage, unless the will declares that it is made in contemplation of marriage to a particular person; and (4) in some states, divorce or annulment with regard to gifts made in a will to a former spouse (but not the will itself), unless the will specifically provides otherwise. A divorce or an annulment also revokes the appointment of the former spouse as an executor or trustee under the will.

A joint will is one instrument that serves as the will of two or more persons. Mutual or reciprocal wills are separate, identical wills for each testator that contain reciprocal provisions accompanied by an agreement that neither testator will change his will after the death of the other.

A person must have standing to contest a will. The most common grounds for contesting a will are (1) improper execution, (2) unsound mind, and (3) fraud or undue influence.

■ REVIEW QUESTIONS

1. What is the technical difference between a will and a testament?

2. Under the law of most states, how old must a person be to make a will? When does a person reach that age?

3. What is the four-part test that determines soundness of mind to make a will?

4. When are nuncupative wills recognized?

5. How may wills be signed by testators?

6. How must nonholographic wills be witnessed?

7. The act of witnessing a will consists of what two parts?

8. Why should testators be discouraged from crossing things out of and adding things to their wills?

9. In what ways may a will be revoked?

10. Name the most common grounds for contesting a will.

■ CASES TO DISCUSS

1. William Cole made a will leaving his entire estate to Catherine Jackson and naming her executrix. The will stated, "I hereby cut off from this will and testament my brothers ... my only heirs-at-law." Nothing in the will mentioned that it was made in contemplation of marriage to Jackson. Six months later, Cole married Jackson. Did the marriage to Jackson revoke Cole's will? Why or why not? *D'Ambra v. Cole*, 572 A.2d 268 (RI).

2. Shortly before her death, Anita P. Clardy, a 79-year-old widow, executed a will leaving her property to various friends and relatives. She left only one dollar to each of her two adopted children "because of their vile attitude towards me since 1953 and the vile names they have called me." The children contested the will on the ground that Mrs. Clardy lacked testamentary capacity. They claimed that Mrs. Clardy had become irrational and experienced false delusional beliefs regarding them and their treatment of her. In finding against the children, the trial court held that the burden of proof rests with the contestants and that the contestants had failed to meet that burden. Was the court's decision correct? Explain. *Clardy v. National Bank*, 555 So. 2d 64 (MS).

3. Margaret C. Mergenthaler's will consisted of four pages. Just before the will was executed, the pages were incorrectly stapled together so that page four, on which the testator signed, came before the residuary clause on page three. The law of that state requires that the testator sign the will "at the end" and provides that matter, other than the attestation clause, following the testator's signature is ineffective. Was the residuary clause in this case ineffective? Why or why not? Will of Mergenthaler, 474 N.Y.S.2d 254 (NY).

4. Susanna H. Proley's will was written in her own handwriting on a four-page printed form. The bottom of page three appeared as follows:

Susanna's signature was written at the middle of the fourth page of the printed form beneath the printed words "Will of," which appeared in a vertical position when the form was folded twice, as indicated on the following photographic reproduction:

Was Susanna's signature written "at the end thereof" as required by Pennsylvania law? Why or why not? *In re* Estate of Proley, 422 A.2d 136 (PA).

■ RESEARCH ON THE WEB

1. Log on to <http://www.lawguru.com> and click on Legal Questions. There, you can search a previously posted question and get the answer, or you can ask your own question.

2. You will discover thought-provoking and practical material of interest to the paralegal at <http://www.legalassistanttoday.com>.

■ SHARPENING YOUR PROFESSIONAL SKILLS

1. Look up your state statute that permits a person to make a will, write down the statutory reference, and look for the answers to the following questions: (a) How old must a person be to make a will? (b) Is a holographic will recognized as valid? (c) How must a will be signed? (d) How must a will be witnessed?

2. Under your state statute, how may a will be revoked? Give the statutory reference where the provision is found.

3. Turn to the will of Stanley P. Goodchild in Chapter 6 (Exhibit 6–1). Draft a codicil, using today's date, naming Stanley's brother, Gilbert G. Goodchild, to serve as alternate guardian of his children. This is necessary because Stanley's sister, Maureen N. Landers, has passed away.

4. Assume that you and your attorney meet with clients, a husband and wife, who would like to make joint wills. The attorney discourages the clients from making joint wills. When the clients leave, you ask the attorney why she discouraged them from doing so. The attorney suggests that you read the case of *Boucher v. Bufford*, 494 S.W.2d 503, and write a brief of the case.

5. Refer to Paragraph FOUR (B) of the will of Doris Duke (reproduced in Appendix B) and attempt to determine, through library research, why the loan was made to Imelda Marcos and whether it has been paid off.

■ SHARPENING YOUR LEGAL VOCABULARY_____

On a separate sheet of paper, fill in the numbered blank lines in the following anecdote with legal terms from this list:

attested

beneficiary

bequeath

bequest

codicil

decedent

dependent relative revocation

devise

devisees

devisor

execute

holographic

intestate

joint will

legacies

legatees

legator

mutual wills

nuncupative

probated

proponent

reciprocal wills

republishing

revoking

sound mind

subscribed

testament

testamentary

testamentary capacity

testate

testator

testatrix

will

will and testament

Jonathan O. Black and his wife, Mable Green-Black, neither of whom sought legal advice, executed one instrument that served as the will of both of them. It was called a(n) (1) and had only one witness who (2), that is, saw the signatures, and (3), that is, signed below Jonathan's and Mable's signatures. Jonathan was the (4). Mable was the (5). If, instead, they had executed separate, identical wills with reciprocal provisions accompanied by an agreement that neither would change their wills after the death of the other, the wills would have been called (6) or (7). Because their will gave gifts of both real and personal property, it was technically known as a(n) (8). Gifts of real property in a will are called (9), and the people who receive them are known as (10). Gifts of personal property in a will are called either (11) or (12), and the people who receive them are known as (13). The will was not a(n) (14) will because it was not written in their handwriting, and it was not a(n) (15) will because it was not oral. Both Jonathan and Mable were in good mental health; therefore, they had (16) and were of (17). One year after executing the will, they decided to change it. They executed a new instrument that referred to the original will and made some changes in it. The new instrument, which was signed and witnessed in the presence of two competent witnesses, was called a(n) (18). Because it was properly executed, the new instrument had the effect of (19) the original will. Prior to their deaths, Jonathan and Mable intentionally tore up the will and codicil, effectively (20) them, and causing Jonathan and Mable to pass away (21).

■ KEY TERMS

attest	holographic will	reciprocal wills
attestation	joint will	republishing
bequeath	legacy	revoking
bequest	legatee	sound mind
codicil	legator	subscribe
decedent	mutual wills	testament
devise	nuncupative wills	testamentary capacity
devisee	probated	will
devisor	proponent	

Online Companion™
For additional resources, please go to
http://www.paralegal.delmar.cengage.com.

Student CD-ROM
For additional materials, please go to the
CD in this book.

Structure of a Model Will

▉ CHAPTER OUTLINE_____

§ 6.1   Guidelines for Drafting a Will
§ 6.2   Introductory Paragraphs
§ 6.3   Main Body
§ 6.4   Fiduciary and Tax Provisions
§ 6.5   Ending Paragraphs
§ 6.6   Letters of Instruction

▉ CHAPTER OUTCOMES_____

- Discuss the guidelines for drafting a will.
- Name and identify the introductory paragraphs of a will.
- Describe the paragraphs that are found in the main body of a will.
- Discuss the fiduciary and tax provisions of a will.
- Name and describe the ending paragraphs of a will.
- Explain letters of instruction.

▉ JOB COMPETENCIES_____

- Be able to prepare an initial draft of a will under the supervision of an attorney.
- Be able to assist the attorney in gathering information and drafting a letter of instruction that accompanies a will.

■ A DAY AT THE OFFICE . . .

Angela Clark introduced herself to Jack Russell, who sat nervously in the waiting room in the office of Dillon & Harvey. Angela apologized for Mr. Dillon's absence, saying that he had been held up in court but should return shortly. She explained that she would begin taking down information that Attorney Dillon would need in drafting a will. Angela ushered Mr. Russell into her office.

After making Mr. Russell feel comfortable by talking with him about how everyone postpones making a will, Angela asked, "May I have your full name?"

"Everybody calls me Jack, but my real name is John. Actually, John is my middle name. My full name is Edward John Russell. I never use Edward, though, except on formal papers, because that was my father's first name. Sometimes I go by E. John Russell, sometimes just John Russell, but my friends call me Jack."

"Do you ever use the name Edward J. Russell?" Angela asked.

"Maybe on a few stock certificates, but that's about all."

"What is your address?"

"Well, I live six months in Fort Myers, Florida, and six months on the Jersey shore. Which address do you want?"

"Why don't you give me both addresses, just to be sure." Angela wrote down the Florida and New Jersey addresses.

"I love warm weather, and I love the beach! In fact, I've never told anybody this, but I want to be cremated and have my ashes dropped in the sea at one of my favorite beaches. And I want that to be in my will. My wife won't like it, though. She's already got a spot picked out for both of us in a cemetery where she grew up in Paramus, New Jersey, but I don't want to be buried there."

"Okay, I'll make a note of that."

"And another thing, while I think of it, I want two copies made of my will—one to keep in Florida and one to keep at the shore. I'll sign both of them. That way there'll be a will nearby wherever I die."

At that moment, Attorney Dillon arrives and joins the conference that Angela is having with Mr. Russell.

Queries:

1. What further questions might Angela Clark ask Jack Russell to determine his domicile?
2. What might Angela Clark tell Jack Russell about his desire to be cremated?
3. How should Angela Clark respond to Mr. Russell's request to sign two copies of his will?

§ 6.1 GUIDELINES FOR DRAFTING A WILL

Before the actual drafting of a will can take place, the attorney must meet with the client and discuss the client's wishes. The attorney asks the client many personal questions and takes down vital information about the client's affairs. Sometimes, the paralegal will be called in to assist in this process. Information that should be obtained from the client and matters that should be considered are found in the checklist in Appendix A. Preparation of the will should be facilitated by having the client prepare a list of assets and debts before coming to the office for the first time. Copies of deeds, mortgages, bank statements, and other financial materials should be brought by the client to the initial interview. Homework is always beneficial.

Paralegals must be especially careful to avoid the unethical practice of law, both when interviewing clients and when drafting documents. At the client interview, the paralegal should be introduced to the client as a "legal assistant" or "paralegal" who is working under the supervision of an attorney. Anything the client says during the interview must be kept confidential. The paralegal may never give legal advice to a client, and all documents prepared by the paralegal must be reviewed and approved by the supervising attorney.

Wills and trusts are usually drafted with the aid of a computer. Software that the firm has developed over the years, as well as software that has been purchased from specialists, is often tailored to fit the particular situation at hand. Each provision in an instrument must be carefully considered to ensure its relevance and accuracy in the present. Paralegals must be computer literate and able to

BOLD BUT BLAND

THEODORE ROOSEVELT

Theodore Roosevelt, America's first "cowboy" president, was a bold and vigorous figure, the former head of the Rough Riders who fought in the Spanish-American War. Roosevelt left a strikingly dull will, however. Earlier presidents had written testaments that revealed personal beliefs, feelings, and sentiments. In contrast, Roosevelt's more "modern" will reveals little of the person, but focuses on the legal terminology necessary to prevent lawsuits. The terms *issue* and *testator* now appear; and beginning with Roosevelt, a president's will is no longer "signed" but "subscribed, sealed, published, acknowledged, and declared by the Testator." His will was drafted in 1912 and penned by a scrivener before the widespread use of typewriters in the law office (see Appendix B).

create documents when called upon to do so. In addition, all wills and other documents must be carefully checked and proofread before being reviewed by the attorney and signed by the client.

The following guidelines can be helpful when drafting a will:

1. A carefully drawn will must be tailored to the individual and personal needs of the testator.

2. Provisions in a will that meet the needs of one testator are often inappropriate and sometimes dangerous for use in another testator's will.

3. Generic forms that meet the laws of one state are not always appropriate under the laws of other states.

4. A carefully drawn will minimizes death taxes to the fullest extent. For this reason, detailed information about the testator's family, assets, liabilities, business, and personal affairs must be obtained and examined by an attorney skilled in estate tax law.

5. As state laws and federal tax laws change, wills drawn under earlier laws must be reevaluated.

6. Because circumstances change in people's lives, testators are well advised to review their wills at least every five years or so to determine whether changes need to be made.

There is no required form for a valid will other than the placement of the signature in some states. Traditionally, however, carefully drawn wills follow a uniform pattern containing certain common elements. The elements of a will include: (1) opening paragraphs, (2) the main body, (3) fiduciary and tax provisions, and (4) ending paragraphs. See Exhibit 6–1.

§ 6.2 INTRODUCTORY PARAGRAPHS

The introductory paragraphs of a will often include the exordium clause, directions for funeral arrangements, and instructions to pay debts.

Exordium Clause

The opening paragraph of a will is called the **exordium clause** or the *publication clause*. Its purposes are: (1) to identify the testator, (2) to state the testator's domicile or residence, (3) to declare the instrument to be the testator's last will, and (4) to revoke all prior wills and codicils made by the testator.

■ **exordium clause**
The introductory clause of a will, stating that it is a valid will, etc. Also known as a *publication clause*.

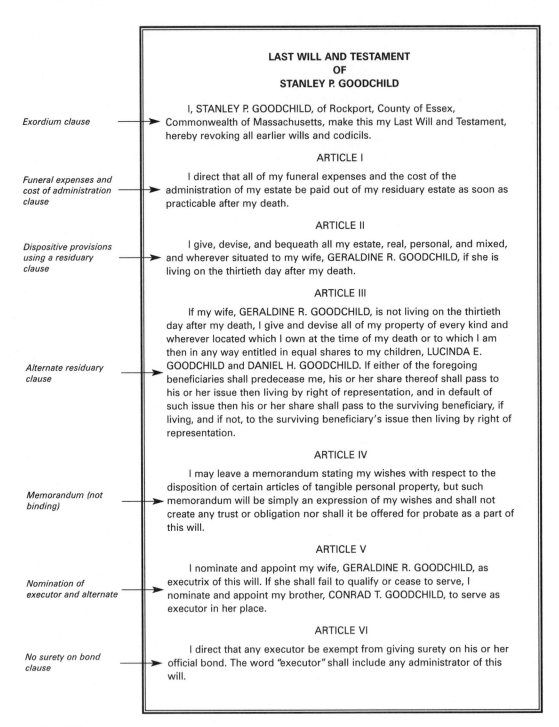

LAST WILL AND TESTAMENT
OF
STANLEY P. GOODCHILD

Exordium clause

I, STANLEY P. GOODCHILD, of Rockport, County of Essex, Commonwealth of Massachusetts, make this my Last Will and Testament, hereby revoking all earlier wills and codicils.

ARTICLE I

Funeral expenses and cost of administration clause

I direct that all of my funeral expenses and the cost of the administration of my estate be paid out of my residuary estate as soon as practicable after my death.

ARTICLE II

Dispositive provisions using a residuary clause

I give, devise, and bequeath all my estate, real, personal, and mixed, and wherever situated to my wife, GERALDINE R. GOODCHILD, if she is living on the thirtieth day after my death.

ARTICLE III

Alternate residuary clause

If my wife, GERALDINE R. GOODCHILD, is not living on the thirtieth day after my death, I give and devise all of my property of every kind and wherever located which I own at the time of my death or to which I am then in any way entitled in equal shares to my children, LUCINDA E. GOODCHILD and DANIEL H. GOODCHILD. If either of the foregoing beneficiaries shall predecease me, his or her share thereof shall pass to his or her issue then living by right of representation, and in default of such issue then his or her share shall pass to the surviving beneficiary, if living, and if not, to the surviving beneficiary's issue then living by right of representation.

ARTICLE IV

Memorandum (not binding)

I may leave a memorandum stating my wishes with respect to the disposition of certain articles of tangible personal property, but such memorandum will be simply an expression of my wishes and shall not create any trust or obligation nor shall it be offered for probate as a part of this will.

ARTICLE V

Nomination of executor and alternate

I nominate and appoint my wife, GERALDINE R. GOODCHILD, as executrix of this will. If she shall fail to qualify or cease to serve, I nominate and appoint my brother, CONRAD T. GOODCHILD, to serve as executor in her place.

ARTICLE VI

No surety on bond clause

I direct that any executor be exempt from giving surety on his or her official bond. The word "executor" shall include any administrator of this will.

EXHIBIT 6–1a   Sample Will with Clauses Defined

ARTICLE VII

Appointment of guardian and alternate no surety on bond clause

I appoint my wife, GERALDINE R. GOODCHILD, as guardian of the person and property of my minor children. If for any reason she shall fail to qualify or cease to serve, I appoint my sister, MAUREEN N. LANDERS, to serve as guardian in her place. No guardian appointed in this will or any codicil need furnish any surety on any official bond.

ARTICLE VIII

Powers of executor

My executor shall have full power of management and authority to sell, either at public or private sale, or to exchange, lease, pledge, or mortgage, in such manner and on such terms as such executor deems advisable, any or all property, real or personal, in my estate and to execute all deeds, assignments, mortgages, leases, or other instruments necessary or proper for these purposes; to compromise claims in favor of or against my estate on such terms as such executor deems advisable; to retain any securities or other property owned by me at the time of my death, although the same may not be considered a proper investment; to make distribution of property in kind, and for such purposes to determine the value of such property; and generally to do any and all such acts and things and execute any and all such written instruments with respect to such property as if the absolute owner thereof.

Testimonium clause with self-proof affidavit

I, the undersigned testator, do hereby declare that I sign and execute this instrument as my last will, that I sign it willingly in the presence of each of said witnesses, and that I execute it as my free and voluntary act for the purposes herein expressed, this 2nd day of January, 2002.

_____
                                        Stanley P. Goodchild

Attestation clause with self-proof affidavit

We, the undersigned witnesses, each do hereby declare in the presence of the aforesaid testator that the testator signed and executed this instrument as his last will in the presence of each of us, that he signed it willingly, that each of us hereby signs this will as witness in the presence of the testator, and that to the best of our knowledge the testator is eighteen (18) years of age or over, of sound mind, and under no constraint or undue influence.

_____   _____
(Witness)   (Address)

_____   _____
(Witness)   (Address)

COMMONWEALTH OF MASSACHUSETTS
COUNTY OF ESSEX

Self-proof affidavits sworn to before notary public

Subscribed, sworn to, and acknowledged before me by the said testator and witnesses this 2nd day of January, 2002.

_____
                                        Notary Public
                                        My commission expires:

EXHIBIT 6–1b Sample Will with Clauses Defined

Example

Exordium Clause

20 AMJUR LF WI § 266:254

I, [name], residing at [address], County, [state], do hereby make, publish, and declare this to be my last will, hereby revoking all former wills and codicils by me at any prior time made.

Identification of Testator

When naming the testator in a will, it is important to include all names that the testator uses in the ownership of all types of property, including real property, personal property, securities, and bank accounts. This is often done by writing the words "also known as ..." after the testator's name. In the interviewing process, the paralegal may need to jog the client's memory so that all variations of names used by the client will be recorded. Failure to list all names used by the testator can cause confusion and lead to the need to obtain court authorization to collect or transfer assets. This process can be expensive and can cause delays in settling the estate. Names used in prior marriages, and the maiden name of a woman who elects to use her husband's family name should be noted.

CASE STUDY   *Hoffman v. Hoffman*

18 N.E.2d (ILL)

FACTS:	Mary Hoffman died on April 26, 1937. She had written a holographic will eight days before her death. The exordium clause of the will contained her handwritten name, but the will was not signed at the end. Illinois statute at the time required that wills be signed. The document was signed by two witnesses, and the deceased had referred to the document as her will.
LEGAL ISSUE:	Was the written name in the exordium clause a signature as required by the Wills Statute in Illinois?
COURT DECISION:	No.
REASON:	The decisive question here is the whether the deceased intended for her name in the exordium clause to be her signature. The testators name in the exordium clause is to identify the testator, not to serve as the required signature, and, barring a preponderance of evidence, the name in the exordium clause is solely descriptive. Here, no such evidence exists.

Domicile of Testator

The testator's domicile establishes the court in which the estate will be settled. The probate court in the place where the testator was domiciled at the time of death has primary jurisdiction to administer the decedent's estate. One's domicile is one's principal place of abode; it is the place to which one intends to return whenever one is absent. A person can have several residences, but only one domicile at any particular time. Once a domicile is established, it continues until a new one is actually acquired. To effect a change of domicile, there must be an actual abandonment of the first domicile, coupled with an intent not to return to it. In addition, physical presence must be established in the other place with the intention of making the last-acquired residence one's permanent home. Such acts as registering to vote and opening a bank account in the new location are evidence of the establishment of a new domicile. In some states, such as Florida, people may file a "Declaration of Domicile" with a government office to establish domicile. The *Elson* case clarifies these distinctions concerning a domicile.

CASE STUDY *In Re* **Estate of Elson**

458 N.E.2d 637 (IL)

FACTS:	Natalie Elson studied recreation and equine sciences at Southern Illinois University. She completed an equestrian internship, taught horseback riding to handicapped children, and trained horses in Illinois. After living her entire life in Illinois, she moved to Pennsylvania to study dressage and to train for the Olympic games. She took her horse and most of her belongings with her, closed out her bank accounts, and opened new accounts in banks near her new residence. Five days later, she died in an automobile accident at the age of 27. In an unmailed letter she had penned the day before her death, Natalie wrote that she had "moved to Pennsylvania."
LEGAL ISSUE:	May a new domicile be established by residing five days in one state after living one's entire life in a different state?
COURT DECISION:	Yes.
REASON:	The question of domicile is largely one of intention. In this case, there is sufficient evidence to establish that Natalie intended to abandon her Illinois domicile permanently and acquire a new domicile in Pennsylvania. Natalie had changed the focus of her life in a permanent manner from Illinois to Pennsylvania in pursuit of her equestrian career.

When a will is made in a place other than the testator's domicile, the exordium clause of the will should state "presently residing in" rather than "of" a certain place. This will help to clarify the fact that the testator is domiciled in another place and may prevent litigation when the will is probated.

The question of domicile is an important tax issue in some cases. This is especially true when people own property in two states, one with higher taxes and one with lower taxes. The state with the higher taxes claims the person is domiciled there and seeks to collect the tax. Here are some suggestions for a person who moves from a northern state to Florida to establish proof of the Florida domicile:

- Sell your house up north, and buy one of equal or greater value in Florida.
- Move your children to schools there.
- Change your car registration and driver's license, and change your address on other forms of identification, including your passport.
- Join a church or synagogue in Florida. Quit your clubs up north, or change to an out-of-state membership.
- Close your northern bank accounts, and open ones in Florida.
- Buy a burial plot in Florida.
- Change the addresses on all credit cards, and other bills, and make all big consumer purchases in your new state.
- Execute all legal documents, including wills and trusts, in Florida.
- File your federal income tax from there.
- Spend your holidays in your new state. Use your new address on all correspondence.
- Find doctors, dentists, lawyers, and accountants in Florida.
- File a "Declaration of Domicile," and apply for homestead exemption in Florida.
- Spend at least six months each year in Florida. Some states use the number of days spent in the state as presumption of domicile.

Revocation of Earlier Wills

One way to revoke a will is to make a new will. In some states, for a revocation to be effective, it is necessary to mention in the new will that it revokes the old one. In other states, a later will revokes an earlier one even though nothing is mentioned in the new will about revocation. By stating in a will that it revokes all prior wills, there can be no questions about the testator's intent when wills with different dates are found after the testator's death, so always state in the new will that previous wills are revoked.

In some states, the subsequent marriage of a person who has made a will revokes the will unless the will declares that it is made in contemplation of marriage to a particular person (see Exhibit 5–7 in Chapter 5). This sentence may be added to the exordium clause to make such a declaration: "I declare that I am contemplating marriage to [name] and that I have made provision in this will for said [name] if my contemplated marriage to [him or her] is consummated."

Funeral Arrangements

It is not always advisable to include funeral and burial arrangements or cremation instructions in a will. This is because such matters must be taken care of immediately, and the will may not be found until later. Courts in some states do not treat the testator's wishes regarding funeral and burial arrangements as binding, deferring instead to the wishes of the surviving spouse or next of kin. Nevertheless, clients often insist that their preferences concerning funeral, burial, or cremation be placed in their wills. Usually a brief statement regarding their wishes is sufficient. These statements have no legal impact, but some client's find them comforting.

Example

Funeral and Burial Directions

20A AMJUR LF WI § 266:371 and § 266:377

I direct that my funeral be held at [address], County, [state], [that it be conducted according to the rites of the (church)], and that my remains be buried in [the family plot or my lot] in the [cemetery] at [address], County, [state].

Cremation

I direct that on my death my remains be cremated, and that the ashes be placed in an urn with my name, my date of birth, which is , and the date of my death inscribed on the urn, and that the urn be placed in the grave of or deposited in the mausoleum in the (cemetery), at (address), County, (state) or (specify other disposition of ashes).

Some people find it desirable to make their funeral arrangements in advance and to pay for the arrangements in advance as well (see Exhibit 6–2 on page 155). Funeral directors often agree to a preestablished price for conducting a funeral, even though the date of death is unknown; the payment for the funeral is held in trust until the time for the funeral arrives. If older clients can be persuaded to make funeral arrangements in advance, the remaining relatives will be spared this added burden while grieving the loss of their loved one.

NOVELTY BY CHARLES DICKENS

CHARLES DICKENS

Charles Dickens, the famous author, wanted little fanfare when he died. In his will, he was specific and forceful: "I emphatically direct that I be buried in an inexpensive, unostentatious, and strictly private manner." He further demanded that "no public announcement be made of the time or place of my burial; that at the utmost not more than three plain mourning coaches be employed." He also ordered that mourners "wear no scarf, cloak, black bow, long hatband, or other such revolting absurdity." All of Dickens's wishes were disregarded: he was eulogized publicly and profusely, with a long cortege, and by a massive audience dressed in the full trappings of mourning.

FROM WHOM WE HAVE GREAT EXPECTATIONS

Example

Funeral Directions

8B AMJUR LF FUN D § 127:9

I request that my personal representative use the services of [funeral home], as I have contacted them regarding my burial arrangements. I have outlined what services I desire with that funeral home. The cost of my burial has been prepaid. If the amount paid to [funeral home] prior to my death is not sufficient, the remainder of the cost of my funeral and burial shall be paid by my estate.

Instructions to Pay Debts

Because the executor is required by law to pay the debts of the decedent, it is not necessary to put a clause in the will instructing the executor to do so. Any instructions to pay debts should be used with caution. Such instructions might require the payment of otherwise uncollectible debts (such as debts that were extinguished by bankruptcy or a statute of limitations), as well as the payment of mortgages on the decedent's real property. Without such a clause, real property will pass to the devisees subject to any existing mortgages on the property. With such a clause, the executor might have to pay off existing mortgages from other assets of the estate so that the real property will pass to the devisees free and clear of all debt.

FUNERAL AGREEMENT

Agreement made _____, between _____ [funeral home], a corporation organized under the laws of the State of _____, and having its principal office at _____ [street address], _____ [city], _____ [county], _____ [state], referred to as funeral director, and _____, of _____ [street address], _____ [city], _____ [county], _____ [state], referred to as beneficiary.

RECITALS

The parties declare:

A. Beneficiary desires to make arrangements in advance for _____ [his or her] funeral and to provide funds for the funeral.

B. Funeral director desires to assure beneficiary that _____ [he or she] will have a funeral in keeping with beneficiary's desires and wishes.

C. The parties desire to establish their mutual rights and obligations.

In consideration of the above recitals, the terms and covenants of this agreement, and other valuable consideration, the receipt of which is acknowledged, the parties agree as follows:

SECTION ONE
DEPOSIT IN SAVINGS ACCOUNT

Concurrently with the execution of this agreement, beneficiary will deposit $_____ in the _____ [name of bank or as the case may be], located at _____ [street address], _____ [city], _____ [state], in a savings account in _____ [his or her] own name, as trustee for the use of beneficiary, which account shall be used in accordance with the terms and conditions provided in this agreement.

SECTION TWO
INTEREST ON ACCOUNT

Beneficiary shall have the right to the interest on the account and shall have the right to withdraw any or all of the account balance at any time.

EXHIBIT 6–2a   Prearranged Funeral Contract [AMJUR LF FUN D § 127:6]

SECTION THREE
MINIMUM BALANCE IN ACCOUNT

If beneficiary reduces the account below the balance stated in Section One of this agreement, funeral director shall have the right to terminate this agreement or to perform its obligations under this agreement, but to furnish service equal in value to such account balance, plus any funeral or burial benefits that may be available upon the death of beneficiary.

SECTION FOUR
EXCESS IN ACCOUNT

If the total amount of the above-referenced account and all of the funeral and burial benefits exceed the balance stated in Section One of this agreement, funeral director agrees to pay any excess to the estate of beneficiary.

SECTION FIVE
APPOINTMENT AS ATTORNEY-IN-FACT

Beneficiary authorizes funeral director to demand and collect any burial and funeral benefits payable on account of the death of beneficiary, and appoints funeral director or its designee as attorney-in-fact, which power shall be coupled with an interest and not revocable by the death of beneficiary, to collect all claims, demands, property, and rights of every kind and description and apply them to the extent necessary to provide the amount of funds stated in Section One of this agreement.

SECTION SIX
SUCCESSOR TO FUNERAL DIRECTOR

In the event funeral director shall consolidate or merge, or its operating assets shall be acquired by any other funeral home, the funeral home shall assume the obligations imposed in this agreement upon funeral director, upon the terms and conditions set forth in this agreement. If the successor business does not agree to assume the obligations, this agreement shall be terminated.

SECTION SEVEN
SERVICES TO BE FURNISHED

If this agreement shall not be terminated as provided above, funeral director agrees to furnish funeral services for the remains of beneficiary in accordance with the instructions that are attached to and made a part of this agreement, which services shall be in the following respective amounts:

Casket and services	$_____
Cemetery charges	$_____
Vault	$_____
Minister	$_____

EXHIBIT 6–2b   Prearranged Funeral Contract [AMJUR LF FUN D § 127:6]

Music	$_____
Flowers	$_____
Transportation	$_____
Notices	$_____
Other	$_____
Total cost of services	$_____
Funeral benefits	$_____
Net deposit	$_____

SECTION EIGHT
BINDING EFFECT

This agreement shall be binding upon and shall inure to the benefit of the heirs, personal representatives, successors, and assigns of the parties to this agreement.

SECTION NINE
GOVERNING LAW

It is agreed that this agreement shall be governed by, construed, and enforced in accordance with the laws of the State of _____.

SECTION TEN
EFFECT ON PARTIAL INVALIDITY

The invalidity of any portion of this agreement shall not be deemed to affect the validity of any other provision. In the event that any provision of this agreement is held to be invalid, the parties agree that the remaining provisions shall be deemed to be in full force and effect as if they had been executed by both parties subsequent to the expungement of the invalid provision.

SECTION ELEVEN
PARAGRAPH HEADINGS

The titles to the paragraphs of this agreement are solely for the convenience of the parties and shall not be used to explain, modify, simplify, or aid in the interpretation of the provisions of this agreement.

SECTION TWELVE
COUNTERPARTS

This agreement may be executed in any number of counterparts, each of which shall be deemed to be an original, but all of which together shall constitute but the same instrument.

In witness, each party to this agreement has caused it to be executed at _____ [place of execution] on the date indicated below.

[Signatures and date(s) of signing]

[Attachment]

EXHIBIT 6–2c   Prearranged Funeral Contract [AMJUR LF FUN D § 127:6]

Example

Instructions to Pay Debts

20A AMJUR LF WI § 266:391

[Use with caution]

I direct that all of my just debts, including the expenses of my last illness, funeral and burial expenses, and expenses of the probate of my will and administration of my estate be paid as soon as possible after this will has been admitted to probate.

---

§ 6.3 MAIN BODY

The main body of a will consists of the dispositive provisions, the residuary clause, and sometimes other miscellaneous clauses. These are shown in summary in Table 6–1 at the end of this section.

Dispositive Provisions

■ **dispositive provisions**

Provisions that clearly settle the disposition of the testator's property.

The **dispositive provisions** of a will are the provisions that dispose of the testator's property. These provisions vary considerably, as they are drafted to meet the needs of the individual client. Gifts under a will may be specific, general, or demonstrative.

Specific Legacies

■ **specific legacy**

Exact. A gift in a will of a precisely identifiable object such as "the family Bible."

In states that have not adopted the Uniform Probate Code (UPC), a **specific legacy** (often called a specific bequest) is a gift in a will of an identifiable item of property (other than real estate), such as a car, a diamond ring, a bank account, or a stock certificate. In states that have adopted the UPC, a legacy or bequest is referred to as a devise.

Example

Specific Legacies

I give and bequeath the following items of personal property if owned by me at the time of my death to the individuals listed below:

(a) To my daughter, [name], if she shall survive me, the portrait of my husband's grandmother.

(b) To my daughter, [name], if she shall survive me, my diamond-ruby-sapphire ring, my Korean satsuma vase, and all pieces of my Friendly Village china.

(c) To my daughter, [name], if she shall survive me, my blue-and-gold vase, and my opal-and-diamond brooch.

(d) To my son, [name], if he shall survive me, my carved marble-top table and my large Chinese platter.

I may leave a memorandum stating my wishes with respect to the disposition of other articles of tangible personal property, but such memorandum will be simply an expression of my wishes and shall not create any trust or obligation, nor shall it be offered for probate as a part of this will.

One advantage of a specific legacy is that it is used for the payment of debts only after the general legacies (money from the general assets of the estate) have been depleted. On the other hand, a specific legacy is subject to **ademption** (extinction; not being owned). If the testator does not own the item at the time of death, the person named to receive it receives nothing. A common type of specific legacy is a gift of all of one's **tangible personal property** (personal property that can be touched).

Example

Bequest of All Tangible Personal Property

I give to my [relationship], [name], all articles of tangible personal property which I own at the time of my death and not otherwise specifically bequeathed by this will, including but not limited to, personal effects, household goods, furniture and furnishings, automobiles, clothing, and jewelry, but not including currency, and securities. If my said [relationship] does not survive me, I give and bequeath the aforesaid property to my [relationship], [name].

Specific Devises

A gift of real property in a will is known as a *devise*. A **specific devise** is a gift in a will of an identifiable parcel of real property. The term includes personal property in states that have adopted the UPC.

When a person dies owning real property solely, or with others as a tenant in common, title to the decedent's share passes to his or her heirs at the moment of death. This contrasts with title to personal property, which passes to the **personal representative** (executor or administrator), who then distributes it to the heirs after paying the estate's debts, taxes, and expenses. Real property can, however, be taken from the heirs and sold by the executor, under a power-of-sale clause in the will or under a license to sell from the court, to pay debts of the estate. Unless a will provides otherwise, real property is usually the last asset to be used for the payment of estate debts.

■ **ademption**
1. Disposing of something left in a will before death, with the effect that the person it was left to does not get it. 2. The gift, before death, of something left in a will to a person who was left it.

■ **tangible personal property**
Personal property that is physically real, capable of being touched.

■ **specific devise**
A gift of a particular, exact piece(s) of real estate (land).

■ **personal representative**
A general term for the executor or administrator of a dead person's property.

Example

Devise of Real Property

To my [relationship], [name], I give my real property consisting of a residence and lot located at [street address], City of , County of , State of , and more particularly described as follows: [insert full description], if [he or she] survives me; but if [he or she] fails to so survive me, I give the above-described property to [relationship], [name], if [he or she] survives me.

General Legacy

■ **general legacy**

A gift of money from the general assets of an estate.

A **general legacy** is a gift of money, or other fungible item, from the general assets of the estate. Gifts given under a residuary clause in a will (discussed later in this section) are also considered to be general. A gift of money in a will, in addition to being a general legacy, is known as a **pecuniary legacy (bequest)**. General bequests, in most states, need not be all or nothing experiences. If insufficient funds exist to satisfy all the general bequests, then the general bequests will be proportionate. That is, if Harry is bequeathed $2,000 and Sharon is bequeathed $1,000 in a will, and there is only $1,500 in the estate, then Harry will receive $1,000 and Sharon $500.

■ **pecuniary legacy (bequest)**

A monetary legacy; a bequest of money.

Example

Pecuniary Bequest

I give to [name], of [address], City of , County of , State of , the sum of Dollars ($), if [he or she] survives me.

Demonstrative Legacy

■ **demonstrative legacy**

A gift of a specific sum of money in a will that is to be paid out of a particular fund where, if the fund has no money, the gift becomes a general legacy on an equal footing with other general legacies.

A **demonstrative legacy** is a gift of a specific sum of money with a direction that it be paid out of a particular fund. It differs from a specific legacy in that the gift is not taken away, that is, adeemed, if there is no money in the fund. Instead, the general assets of the estate are used to fund the gift. Thus, a demonstrative legacy is a special kind of general legacy.

Example

Demonstrative Legacy

I give to [name], of [address], City of , County of , State of , if [he or she] survives me, the sum of Dollars ($), to be paid out of the funds on deposit in my savings account No. , in the [name of bank], at [address], City of , County of , State of .

Residuary Clause

A will should be written so that it allocates all of the testator's property. To do this, a will must contain a residuary clause. The **residuary clause** distributes all of the testator's property that is not disposed of in other clauses of the will. It is a crucial clause because it acts as a safety net, catching any property that falls through the cracks or that is inadvertently omitted from the will. The *Jones* case demonstrates the importance of including a residuary clause.

■ **residuary clause**
Clause in a will that disposes of all items not specifically given away (the "leftovers").

CASE STUDY **Matter of Estate of Jones**

341 N.E.2d 565 (NY)

FACTS: The subject matter of this litigation was a collection of antique, rare, and original books left to the decedent by her father. The lower-court judge held that the rare book collection passed under Article Eleventh of the will. The appellant argues that the collection should pass under Article Fourteenth. The two articles follow:

> ELEVENTH. I give and bequeath all my personal property, consisting of furniture, carpets, curtains, china, linen, miscellaneous prints and pictures, antique chandeliers, Louis XVI mantel, mirror and fireback installed in drawing room in my residence, and miscellaneous bric-a-brac to said Harriet C. Weed to be held and enjoyed by her during the period of her natural life. ... Upon the death of said Harriet C. Weed I give and bequeath to the Minneapolis Institute of Arts ... .

> FOURTEENTH. All the rest, residue and remainder of my estate, both real and personal and wheresoever situate, not herein otherwise disposed of, I give, devise and bequeath to said Harriet C. Weed.

LEGAL ISSUE: Does a bequest of all of one's personal property followed by the words "consisting of" limit the bequest to only the items that follow?

COURT DECISION: Yes.

REASON: Nowhere in the detailed provisions of Article Eleventh is there to be found any reference to books or to the decedent's library. Nor is there any general language susceptible of the interpretation that Article Eleventh was intended as a catch-all paragraph designed to blanket in all tangible personal property not otherwise specifically described. The opening words of the paragraph, "all my personal property," standing alone, would have supported such an interpretation, but these words are then immediately limited by the particularizing phrase, "consisting of," followed by the detailed listing. The diction here was not, for instance, "all my personal property, including, etc.," in which event it could have been argued that the list of specified articles was not intended as an exclusive schedule.

Some situations in which a gift would pass according to the instructions in a residuary clause include:

1. When a gift is void (e.g., in some states when a gift is given to a witness to the will).

2. When a gift is revoked (e.g., when crossed out by the testator).

3. When a gift lapses (e.g., when the legatee or devisee dies before the testator), unless an antilapse statute (discussed in Chapter 7) is available.

4. Without a residuary clause in such situations, the failed gift would pass according to the law of intestacy, as explained in Chapter 4. Property (real and personal) would also pass according to the law of intestacy if a residuary clause is not included in a will. The *Flannery* case illustrates a problem that can arise when a residuary clause is omitted from a will.

CASE STUDY *Flannery v. McNamara, Administrator*

738 N.E.2d 739 (MA)

FACTS:	William H. White died testate, leaving everything to his wife, Katherine. His will stated, in part, "I give, devise, and bequeath all of the property of which I die possessed real, personal, and mixed and wheresoever located to my beloved wife, Katherine M. White."
	The will did not name a contingent beneficiary, and it had no residuary clause. William's wife, Katherine, had passed away two years before William. The couple had no children. In addition to William, Katherine was survived by her two sisters, the Flannerys. The lower court held that William's property passed by intestacy to his first cousins once removed.
	On appeal, the Flannery sisters argued that they should inherit William's estate. They pointed out that they had a close relationship with William, that he was buried in the Flannerys' family plot, and that he told the Flannerys that his residence and its contents "will be [theirs] some day." The sisters contended that the portion of the will that reads, "all to my beloved wife, Katherine M. White," should be either construed or reformed to read, "all to my beloved wife, Katherine M. White, if she survives me, but if not, then to her sisters who survive me."
LEGAL ISSUE:	Is extrinsic evidence admissible to construe an unambiguous will, or can such a will be reformed?
COURT DECISION:	No to both questions.

(continues)

CASE STUDY	*Flannery v. McNamara, Administrator* (continued)
REASON:	Extrinsic evidence is not admissible to explain an unambiguous will. In addition, under Massachusetts law, courts have no power to reform wills. Language cannot be modified to meet unforeseen changes in conditions. The written instrument is the final and unalterable expression of the purpose of the testator. The power of the court is limited to interpretation and construction. It cannot make a new will.

No particular language is necessary for a residuary clause in a will. The clause may begin, "I give, devise, and bequeath the rest, residue, and remainder of my estate to ..." or it may simply say, "I give the residue of my estate to ... ." Similar variations are acceptable as well. As a matter of practice, you should never draft a will without a residuary clause.

Example

Residuary Clause

I direct that all the rest, residue, and remainder of my estate, real, personal, and mixed, of whatever kind and wherever situated, of which I may die seized and possessed, or in which I may have any interest or to which I may be entitled or over which I may have any power of appointment, including any lapsed or deemed legacies (herein called my "residuary estate"), shall be divided into [number] equal shares, to be disposed of as follows: ... .

Miscellaneous Clauses

Wills are drawn to meet the particular needs of individuals, so there is no limit to the variety of clauses that can be included in a will. Also, new clauses are continually written to keep up with changes in state inheritance laws and federal tax laws. A few miscellaneous clauses that are sometimes found in wills are discussed here.

Adopted Children

As was discussed in Chapter 4, modern statutes generally treat adopted children as strangers to their former relatives and consider adopting parents as though they were legitimate blood relatives to their adopted children. However, defining the terms *child* or *children* in a will helps to avoid any possible confusion.

Example

Definition of *Child*

20A AMJUR LF WI § 266:328

The word *child* or *children*, as used in this will, includes any child or children lawfully adopted by me at any time before or after the execution of this will.

Community Property

Community property is property (except a gift or inheritance) acquired by either a husband or a wife during marriage. In community property states (see the map in Exhibit 3–4), such property belongs to both spouses equally. When making a will in a community property state, it is often advisable to clearly state how the testator would like to distribute his or her share of community property.

Example

Community Property

20A AMJUR LF WI § 266:296

I declare that all of the property of my estate which is hereby bequeathed and devised is my one-half interest in the community property of myself and my [wife or husband], [name].

Disinheritance

Some states have laws protecting certain heirs who are omitted from a will. For example, children and certain grandchildren who can prove that they were unintentionally disinherited by a parent may be able to inherit their intestate share from that parent or grandparent. This subject is discussed in detail in Chapter 7. When family members are intentionally disinherited, it is recommended that an explicit declaration be made in the will reinforcing the testator's intention to disinherit those heirs who are not mentioned. A clause to that effect is as follows.

Example

Disinheritance

20A AMJUR LF WI § 266:431

I have, except as otherwise provided in this will, intentionally and with full knowledge, omitted to provide for my heirs who may be living at the time of my death, including any person who may become my heir by reason of marriage or otherwise after the date of the execution of this will.

No-Contest Provision

Sometimes testators believe that one or more disgruntled relatives might attempt to contest the provisions of the will. One way to address this possibility is to provide for such people in the will, and then to stipulate that anyone who contests the will shall lose all interests he or she would otherwise have under the will. A provision eliminating a will contestant from being a beneficiary under the will is called a **no-contest** or *in terrorem clause* (in terror or warning).

Example

No-Contest Clause

20A AMJUR LF WI § 266:411

Every heir, legatee, devisee, or beneficiary under this will [and the trusts herein created, or intended to be created,] who shall contest in any court any provision of this instrument [except as may be permitted by the provisions of (cite statute)] shall not be entitled to any devises, legacies, or benefits under this will or any codicil to this will or any trust created by this will. Any and all devises, legacies, and portions of the income or corpus of my estate, otherwise provided to be paid to such person, shall lapse and shall be paid, distributed, and passed [in accordance with Article hereof or as though such person had died prior to my death leaving no living lawful descendants]. My executor [and trustee] herein named [is or are] specifically authorized to defend at the expense of my estate any contest or attack of any nature upon this will or any codicil to this will, or on any paragraph or provision hereof.

In states that have adopted the UPC, the no-contest provision set forth here would be ineffective. Under the UPC, a provision in a will purporting to penalize any interested person for contesting the will or instituting other proceedings relating to the estate is unenforceable if probable cause exists for instituting proceedings [UPC § 3–905]. You need to check whether your state allows or limits *in terrorem* clauses.

Many people die wanting to leave money for the care of a beloved pet or pets. Money or property cannot be left to animals, but funds can be left to the person who will care for the pet. The assets can be left as an outright gift, a conditional gift, or a trust.

Incorporation by Reference

Occasionally it is desirable to refer in a will to another existing document and to make the other document a part of the will itself. This is known as **incorporation by reference** and may be done only if the other document is in existence at the time the will is executed.

■ **no-contest**

(Latin) "In threat"; "in terror"; "by threat." An *in terrorem* clause in a will "threatens" a beneficiary with revocation of that person's bequest if he or she contests the will. Also known as an *in terrorem* clause.

■ **incorporation by reference**

Making a document a part of something else by mere mention. For example, if document A says that "document B is incorporated by reference," then document B becomes a part of document A even though the words in document B are not rewritten into document A.

Example

Incorporation by Reference

20A AMJUR LF WI § 266:351

I hereby declare that it is my intention to, and I do hereby, incorporate by reference into this will that certain document dated , which is now in existence, located at [address], County, [state], and described as follows: .

TABLE 6–1   **Principal Clauses in a Will**

Clause	Function
Exordium Clause	To identify the testator, state the domicile, declare the instrument to be a will, and revoke prior wills
Funeral Directions	To specify the funeral and burial conditions
Instructions to Pay Debts	To instruct the executor to pay debts (use cautiously)
Dispositive Provisions	To dispose of specific property
Residuary Clause	To distribute all property not otherwise disposed of
Appointment of Fiduciaries	To appoint the executor, guardian, and trustee and their alternates
Powers of Fiduciaries	To provide special powers to the fiduciaries
No Surety on Bond	To avoid a surety on the bond
Tax Clauses	To establish the source for payment of death taxes
Testimonium Clause	To establish the end of the will, introduce the testator's signature, and fix the date of execution of the instrument
Attestation Clause	To introduce the witnesses' signatures and insure compliance with the law of execution of wills
Self-Proof Clause	To prove the will without testimony

§ 6.4 FIDUCIARY AND TAX PROVISIONS

Wills commonly have provisions naming fiduciaries, giving them special powers, and allowing them to serve without furnishing a surety on their official bond. In addition, many wills contain a clause that establishes the source for payment of death taxes.

Appointment of Fiduciaries

Paralegals will have many opportunities to deal with fiduciaries in the course of their work, because the nature of a fiduciary's responsibility often requires working with a law firm. **Fiduciaries** are persons appointed to oversee property that belongs to others and who, therefore, serve in a position of trust. In the case of a will, fiduciaries include executors, guardians, and trustees.

Executor

An important advantage of having a will is that the testator is allowed to select the person who will eventually settle the testator's estate. An **executor** (male) or an **executrix** (female) is a person who is named in a will to serve as the personal representative of the estate. It is common practice also to name an alternate executor to serve in the event the person named as executor is unable to serve in that capacity. The principal task of an executor is to gather the assets, pay the debts (including taxes and expenses of administration), and distribute the remainder according to the terms of the will.

Example

Nomination of Executor and Alternate

I nominate and appoint my [relationship], [name], as executor of this will. If he [or she] shall fail to qualify or cease to serve, I nominate and appoint my [relationship], [name], to serve as executor in [his or her] place.

A testator should consider the items on the following list when appointing an executor in a will [8 AMJUR LF EXEC § 104:6]:

- Individual or corporate executor
- Willingness of appointee to serve
- Competency of appointee
- Familiarity of appointee with estate
- Residency of appointee
- Compensation
- Bond requirement
- Compatibility of appointee with heirs

■ **fiduciaries**
A person who manages money or property for another person and in whom that other person has a right to place great trust.

■ **executor**
A person selected by a person making a will to administer the will and to hand out the property after the person making the will dies.

■ **executrix**
A female executor.

Guardian

Another advantage of having a will is that parents can name one or more guardians for their children in the event they die while their children are minors. There are two kinds of guardians: a guardian of the person and a guardian of the property. A guardian of the person has the care and custody of the child. This is given as a natural right to parents unless they are found to be unfit. In contrast, a guardian of the property has the responsibility of caring for the child's property until the child becomes an adult. Such a guardianship is not a natural right of a parent and may be given by a court to someone other than a parent. Language in a will naming a surviving spouse as guardian of the person and property of minor children, however, is usually followed by the court.

Example

Appointment of Guardian

I appoint my spouse, [name], as guardian of the person and property of my minor children. If for any reason my spouse fails to qualify or ceases to serve as guardian of the person of any minor child of mine, I appoint my friend [or other relationship], [name], as such guardian in my spouse's place. If for any reason my spouse fails to qualify or ceases to serve as guardian of the property of any minor child of mine, I appoint my friend [or other relationship], [name], as such guardian in my spouse's place. No guardian of the person or property appointed in this will need furnish any surety on any official bond.

Trustee

When a will contains a trust, the trust is known as a testamentary trust (see Chapter 8). The will appoints one or more trustees to administer the trust and often provides for the appointment of successor trustees in the event the first-named trustees are unable to serve. The subject matter of trusts is treated in depth in Chapters 8 and 9.

Example

Appointment of Trustee

I nominate and appoint [name] and [name] as trustees of all trusts created hereunder. If any trustee is unwilling, unable, or ceases to serve as trustee, [name] shall serve as successor trustee, and if the successor trustee or any other trustee is unwilling, unable, or ceases to serve as trustee, [name] shall serve as successor trustee. If there is a vacancy in a trusteeship for which no successor has been appointed under the preceding paragraph, the adult beneficiaries entitled to receive a majority of the income may appoint in writing a successor trustee.

Powers of Fiduciaries

The power of a fiduciary to act without court approval is somewhat limited. Unless the will provides otherwise, fiduciaries must seek court approval to do what is necessary for proper administration of the estate. The way to eliminate the need for fiduciaries to seek court approval and thereby to reduce administration costs is to include a powers clause in the will.

Example

Powers of Executor

My executor shall have full power of management and authority to sell, either at public or private sale, or to exchange, lease, pledge, or mortgage, in such manner and on such terms as such executor deems advisable, any or all property, real or personal, in my estate and to execute all deeds, assignments, mortgages, leases, or other instruments necessary or proper for these purposes; to compromise claims in favor of or against my estate on such terms as such executor deems advisable; to retain any securities or other property owned by me at the time of my death, although the same may not be considered a proper investment; to make distribution of property in kind, and for such purposes to determine the value of such property; and generally to do any and all such acts and things and execute any and all such written instruments with respect to such property as if the absolute owner thereof.

No Surety on Bond

Executors are required to post a bond before they can be appointed. By doing so, they become personally liable up to the amount of the bond in the event the estate is mishandled. In some states, unless the will provides otherwise, there must be a surety on the bond. A **surety** is either an insurance company or one or more individuals who stand behind the executor by agreeing to pay the amount of the bond in the event the executor becomes liable on the bond. The cost of a surety can be saved by providing in the will that the executor be exempt from giving surety on his or her bond. When naming a spouse, sibling, or parent as a fiduciary, exempting the fiduciary from the additional cost will help preserve assets.

■ **surety**
A person or company that insures or guarantees that another person's debt will be paid by becoming liable (responsible) for the debt when it is made.

Example

No Surety on Bond

I direct that any executor be exempt from giving surety on his or her official bond. The word *executor* shall include any administrator of this will.

Tax Provision

The purpose of the tax provision in a will is to establish the source for payment of death taxes. The tax clause apportions the burden of federal and state death taxes among the estate assets.

In some states, if a tax clause is not used, taxes imposed on the probate property are paid from the residuary estate and taxes imposed on the nonprobate property are paid from the nonprobate property. Thus, the money to pay the taxes on legacies and devises would come from the residuary clause, the money to pay the taxes on jointly owned property would come from the joint property, and the money to pay the taxes on life insurance would come from the life insurance proceeds. A tax clause is included in a will when payment of estate taxes from a different source is preferable.

When everything in an estate goes to the same person or equally to a group of people, a direction to pay all death taxes from the residuary estate is usually appropriate. However, when items of vastly different value are given to different people, or when there is jointly owned property, life insurance, a pension plan, or a trust, the residuary estate may be an inappropriate source from which to pay death taxes.

Example

Tax Clause

All inheritance, estate, and other taxes in the nature of death taxes, whether state or federal, with respect to any property passing under this Will shall be paid by my Executor out of the residue of my estate, and, in addition, my Executor may in his or her discretion pay from my residue all or any part of such taxes attributable to property not passing under this Will. My Executor shall have full power and authority to pay, compromise, or settle any or all such taxes at any time whether on present or future interests.

■ testimonium clause
The part of a deed or other document that contains who signed and when and where it was signed.

■ signature clause
The clause in a will that falls immediately before the testator's signature.

§ 6.5 ENDING PARAGRAPHS

The ending paragraphs of a will include the testimonium clause, the attestation clause, and the self-proof clause.

Testimonium Clause

The **testimonium clause** (sometimes called the **signature clause**) is the clause that comes immediately before the testator's signature. It is used to establish the end of the will, to introduce the testator's signature, and to fix the date of execution of the instrument. Some attorneys like to have the testator read the testimonium clause out loud to the witnesses before signing it as a declaration that the instrument being signed is the testator's will.

Example

Testimonium Clause

In Witness Whereof, I, the undersigned [name of testator or testatrix], do hereby declare that I willingly sign and execute this instrument as my last will, in the presence of each of the witnesses, who also sign below, and that I execute it as my free and voluntary act for the purposes herein expressed, this day of , 20.

Besides signing on the signature line below the testimonium clause, the testator should either sign or initial all of the other pages of the will. Although not a requirement, signing every page helps to prevent the substitution or loss of pages that come before the testimonium clause.

Only the original of a will should be signed. A will should never be executed in duplicate or triplicate. When more than one signed copy of a will is in existence, the court may require that all copies be produced for probate. If a copy cannot be produced, it may raise a presumption that the testator destroyed the copy with the intention of revoking the will. In the opening "A day at the office ..." scenario, what seemed convenient to the client, Mr. Russell—having a signed copy of his will at both of his residences—could prove dangerously confusing.

Attestation Clause

The **attestation clause** is the clause that follows the testator's signature and precedes the witnesses' signatures. The clause is not required, but is customary and helps to ensure compliance with the law of executing a will. A will is usually executed properly when the directions in the attestation clause are followed precisely.

After the testator has signed the will in the witnesses' presence, it is customary to have one of the witnesses read the attestation clause aloud. When this is done, the witnesses sign below the attestation clause and write their home addresses beside their signatures. Witnesses may have to be contacted after the testator has died in order to prove the will. Neither the testator nor the witnesses should leave the room until all witnesses have finished signing the will in the testator's and each other's presence.

■ **attestation clause**
A clause, usually at the end of a document, that witnesses the signing of the document with a signature of attestation.

A PRESIDENTIAL NEATNIK

GEORGE WASHINGTON

George Washington, a man obsessed with neatness and meticulous detail, prepared his will without any legal assistance. He penned his 15-page will on both sides of watermarked parchment with strict adherence to a justified right margin. The document looks almost computer produced: the lines are precisely spaced and identical in length; dashes or curved strokes fill any empty spaces; words at the end of lines are hyphenated improperly if necessary to maintain the justified margin; each page is signed directly below the center of the last line. No witnesses were necessary, because a handwritten testament without them was legally binding in the 1790s in that state.

Example

Attestation Clause

We, the undersigned witnesses, each do hereby declare in the presence of the aforesaid testatrix that the testatrix signed and executed this instrument as her last will in the presence of each of us, that she signed it willingly, that each of us hereby signs this will as witness in the presence of the testatrix, and that to the best of our knowledge the testatrix is eighteen (18) years of age or over, of sound mind, and under no constraint or undue influence.

Self-Proof Clause

■ **self-proof clause**
A clause in a will containing affidavits of the testator and witnesses that allow a will to be proved without testimony.

In many states, if all of the heirs at law of a decedent do not assent to the allowance of a will, the testimony (or sworn affidavit) of one of the witnesses is required for the will to be allowed. This condition sometimes creates problems: heirs at law cannot always be located; witnesses may have moved or died. To alleviate these complications, some states have enacted a statute that allows a will to be proved without testimony if it is self-proved by affidavits of the testator and the witnesses made before an officer authorized to administer oaths (usually a notary public). The clause, located at the end of the will, is called a **self-proof clause**.

Example

Self-Proof Clause

I, [name], the testator, sign my name to this instrument this day of , 2, and being first duly sworn, do hereby declare to the undersigned authority that I sign and execute this instrument as my last will and that I sign it willingly (or willingly direct another to sign for me), that I execute it as my free and voluntary act for the purposes therein expressed, and that I am eighteen (18) years of age or older, of sound mind, and under no constraint or undue influence.

_____
Testator

We, , , the witnesses, sign our names to this instrument, being first duly sworn, and do hereby declare to the undersigned authority that the testator signs and executes this instrument as his last will and that he signs it willingly (or willingly directs another to sign for him), and that each of us, in the presence and hearing of the testator, hereby signs this will as witness to the testator's signing, and that to the best of our knowledge the testator is eighteen (18) years of age or older, of sound mind, and under no constraint or undue influence.

_____
Witness

_____
Witness

State of_____
County of_____

Subscribed, sworn to, and acknowledged before me by , the testator, subscribed and sworn to before me by , and , witnesses, this day of , 2.

_____
Notary public

§ 6.6 LETTERS OF INSTRUCTION

It is often desirable for a person making a will to write a letter of instruction to the people left behind. A **letter of instruction** furnishes detailed information about the testator's funeral arrangements, assets, location of important documents, and the people to notify when the testator dies. At least three copies of the letter should be made, each placed in a separate envelope marked "Letter of Instruction." One copy should be given to the executor, another placed with the will, and the third placed with the testator's other important papers. A letter of instruction should generally contain the following information [20A AMJUR LF WI § 266:73]:

■ **letter of instruction**

A letter written by a testator to accompany a will, giving detailed information that is not contained in the will.

1. Persons to be notified on testator's death, with their addresses and telephone numbers:

   a. funeral home

   b. relatives

   c. employer

   d. executor

   e. lawyer

   f. partners or business associates

   g. other persons

2. Burial and funeral instructions:

   a. cemetery plot location, deed number, and location of deed

   b. facts needed by funeral director, such as testator's full name, residence, marital status, name of spouse, date of birth, place of birth, father's name and birthplace, mother's maiden name, military service, length of residence in the United States, length of residence in state, social security number, occupation, special wishes and desires

   c. words to be inscribed on gravestone

   d. if cremation is desired, specification as to disposition of ashes

3. Location of all important legal and personal papers:

   a. will

   b. insurance policies

   c. bank books, checkbooks, and certificates of deposits

   d. bonds and stock certificates

   e. Social Security and Medicare cards and papers

   f. title and registration documents of automobiles

   g. titles, deeds, and other relevant papers relating to real property

   h. birth and baptismal certificates

   i. marriage certificate

   j. judgment of dissolution of marriage or divorce decree and separation or settlement agreements

   k. military records

   l. naturalization papers or alien registration card

   m. income tax returns

     n. credit cards

     o. mortgage and other documents relating to outstanding loans

     p. bank statements and cancelled checks

     q. important warranties, such as warranties for major appliances

     r. important receipts, such as receipts for home improvements

     s. other legal papers

4. Location of safe-deposit box, number, in whose name it is registered, location of key, and list of contents

5. Membership in any fraternal or mutual aid association that has as part of its membership death benefits or insurance coverage, address and telephone number of association, person to contact as to procedure for collecting benefit, and location of certificate of membership or certificate of insurance

6. List of life and accident insurance policies, with name and address of company, policy number, amount of coverage, beneficiaries, name, address, and telephone number of insurance agent, and instructions to file claim immediately

7. List of homeowner's, fire, casualty, and other insurance policies, including name and address of company, policy number, amount of coverage, beneficiaries, and name, address, and telephone number of insurance agent

8. List of insurance policies insuring other members of family for which testator has been paying premiums, including name and address of company, policy number, amount of coverage, beneficiaries, and name, address and telephone number of insurance agent

9. Social Security number, with instructions to call local Social Security office to inform them of testator's death, to ask for an appointment and what papers to bring, and instructions to file claim immediately

10. List of bank accounts, with name and address of bank, account number, name or names on the account, type of account, and any special instructions

11. List of all bonds, with their serial numbers, denominations, and names in which they are registered

12. List of all shares of stock, with names of companies, number of shares, in whose names they are issued, and name and address of stockbroker

13. List of pension or profit sharing plans, and the location of any documents relevant thereto

14. List of all credit cards, with the name and address of the issuer and card number

15. List of monetary obligations, including mortgages, with name and address of bank or other lender, account number, name appearing on loan documents, amount of loan, monthly payment, collateral, if any, and whether there was life insurance on loan, and if so, name and address of insurer, with instructions to notify and file claim immediately

16. List of all automobiles, with year, make, model, body type, number of cylinders, color, and identification number

17. List and location of personal effects and other personal property with sentimental value, and names and addresses of persons to whom such property should be given

18. Matters relating to house or condominium, including address, in whose name it is recorded, and legal description. Include a list of home improvements, with the date and cost. Include also a statement as to actual cost of the house, and expenses incurred in purchasing home

19. If renting, name and address of lessor, expiration date of lease, location of lease agreement and receipts of payments

20. If veteran, instructions to notify nearest Veterans Administration office of testator's death and to ask what benefits are available

21. Other special instructions

SUMMARY

The common elements of a will include opening paragraphs, the main body, fiduciary and tax provisions, and ending paragraphs.

A carefully drawn will is tailored to an individual's needs, minimizes death taxes, and follows specific state laws. In addition, it is kept up to date to reflect changes in the law and changes in family circumstances.

When naming the testator in the exordium clause of a will, it is important to use all names that the testator uses in the ownership of all types of property. The probate court in the place where the testator was domiciled at the time of death has primary jurisdiction to administer the decedent's estate. A later will generally revokes an earlier will unless the later will states otherwise. Including funeral and burial arrangements or cremation instructions in a will is not recommended because such matters must be taken care of immediately, and the will may not be found or allowed by the court for several weeks. In addition, the courts in some states do not treat as binding the testator's wishes regarding funeral and burial arrangements. It might be dangerous to put a clause in a will instructing the executor to pay debts because it might require the payment of otherwise uncollectible debts as well as the payment of mortgages on the decedent's real property.

Gifts under a will may be specific, general, or demonstrative. An advantage of a specific legacy is that it is used up only after the general legacies have been depleted for the payment of debts. However, a specific legacy is subject to ademption. When people die owning real property solely, title passes to their heirs at the moment of death; personal property passes to the personal representative of the estate. The residuary clause is very important because it acts as a safety net, covering any property that is otherwise omitted from the will.

Wills often contain clauses that appoint executors, guardians, and trustees, and allow them to serve without furnishing a surety on their bond. Wills often contain clauses that establish the source for payment of death taxes. A powers clause in a will helps to reduce the cost of administration by eliminating the need for the fiduciary to seek court approval when taking certain actions.

The testimonium clause falls immediately before the testator's signature. Only the original of a will should be signed—it should never be executed in duplicate or triplicate. The attestation clause precedes the witnesses' signatures. A will is usually executed properly when the directions in the attestation clause are followed precisely. In some states, a will may be proved without testimony if it contains a self-proof clause.

■ REVIEW QUESTIONS

1. Why is it important, when drafting a will, to use all the names that the testator uses in the ownership of real and personal property?

2. What court has primary jurisdiction to administer a decedent's estate?

3. What words can be written in a will to prevent a subsequent marriage from revoking the will?

4. Why is it not necessarily preferable to include funeral and burial arrangements in a will?

5. What is one advantage and one disadvantage of a specific legacy?

6. When and to whom does title to real property pass when a sole owner dies?

7. How does a demonstrative legacy differ from a specific legacy?

8. When a decedent dies testate and there is no residuary clause in the will, who receives property that is omitted from the will?

9. What is the difference between a guardian of the person and a guardian of the property?

10. Why is a clause giving powers to a fiduciary helpful?

■ CASES TO DISCUSS

1. Article SIXTH of Barnett's codicil provided: "I direct that all the rest, residue and remainder of my estate, including my home and its contents, of whatsoever nature and wheresoever situate, be sold and liquidated and I give and bequeath such remainder, including any legacy which may have lapsed or otherwise not be distributable, to the Federation of Jewish Philanthropies of New York." Did this language create a specific, demonstrative, or residuary gift to the Federation? Explain. *In re Estate of Barnett*, 408 N.Y.S.2d 295 (NY).

2. In her will, Helen Nesmith left all of her tangible personal property to Frederic T. Greenhalge, II, except those items which she designated by a memorandum to be given to others living at the time of her death. Before executing two codicils to her will, she had drafted a "memorandum" which listed 49 specific bequests of tangible personal property to be made upon her death. She had also written in a notebook entitled "List to be given," the following words: "Ginny Clark farm picture hanging over fireplace. Ma's room." Ginny Clark, a neighbor and close friend, had admired the picture, and Nesmith had told two nurses that the picture would go to Clark. Will Clark receive the farm picture under Nesmith's will? Why or why not? *Clark v. Greenhalge*, 582 N.E.2d 949 (MA).

3. Hanna LeSueur had lived for at least 50 years in Lakewood, Cuyahoga County, Ohio. At the age of 96, after being diagnosed as having chronic dementia, she was moved to a Lucas County nursing home, where she died in less than three months. Her will declared her to be a resident of Lakewood, and her funeral services and burial were there also. Her niece, Marjorie, who lived in Fulton County, filed the will for probate in the Fulton County Court of Common Pleas. Does that court have jurisdiction to settle the estate? Explain. *LeSueur v. Robinson*, 557 N.E.2d 796 (OH).

■ RESEARCH ON THE WEB

1. Log on to <http://www.lawguru.com> and click Probate & Wills. Then, scroll down to More LawGuru Probate, Trust, & Wills law Q & A and click your state. Look for questions and answers of interest to you.

2. Go to <http://www.lawguru.com> and click Codes & Statutes. Then click United States followed by the name of your state. See if you can locate your state law on the subject matter of wills.

▨ SHARPENING YOUR PROFESSIONAL SKILLS_____

1. Refer to the "A day at the office …" scenario at the beginning of this chapter and draft the initial part of an exordium clause identifying Jack Russell.

2. Draft an exordium clause for a person who plans to be married and wishes to leave a gift in the will to the future spouse.

3. Obtain a copy of a deed to someone's real property. Using the property description in the deed, draft a clause for a will that devises the specific property to another person.

4. Jack Russell has $15,000 in Account No. 007 64 329 at the Ocean City Savings Bank. (a) Draft a clause for his will leaving a pecuniary bequest of $10,000 to his daughter, Mildred F. Russell. (b) Draft a clause for his will leaving a demonstrative legacy of $10,000 to his son, Michael S. Russell.

5. Jack Russell wishes to leave the residue of his estate in equal shares to his two children, Mildred and Michael. Mildred is adopted. Look up your state statute on adopted children. (a) Cite the statutory reference where it is found. (b) Determine whether it would be necessary to include in the will the clause about adopted children discussed in this chapter.

6. Draft a testimonium clause and an attestation clause for the will of Jack Russell, using the information found in the opening vignette of this chapter.

7. Does the law of your state provide for the self-proving of a will? If so, (a) give the statutory reference where the provision is found, and (b) draft a self-proof clause following your state statute.

8. Who should perform the duties of executor under the will of John F. Kennedy, Jr. (reproduced in Appendix B)? [*Note*: Anthony Stanislaus Radziwill died of cancer a month before JFK Jr.'s death.]

9. How does the will of John Lennon (reproduced in Appendix B) help to establish Lennon's domicile for the purposes of settling his estate?

10. Describe the *in terrorem* clauses in the wills of George Burns and John Lennon (reproduced in Appendix B). George Burns' will would leave the sum of $1.00 only to any devisee, legatee, or beneficiary who contests the will.

11. Who is appointed guardian in the will of John Lennon (reproduced in - Appendix B)? The alternate guardian? Explain the difference between a guardian of the person and a guardian of the property.

12. How does ARTICLE TEN of the will of Richard M. Nixon (reproduced in Appendix B) provide for legacies being distributed to minors?

13. List the legatees and the amount of each pecuniary bequest named in Paragraph FIVE (B) in the will of Doris Duke (reproduced in Appendix B).

■ SHARPENING YOUR LEGAL VOCABULARY_____

On a separate sheet of paper, fill in the numbered blank lines in the following anecdote with legal terms from this list:

attestation clause

community property

demonstrative legacy

dispositive provisions

domicile

executor

executrix

exordium clause

fiduciaries

general legacy

guardian of the person

guardian of the property

incorporation by reference

in terrorem clause

no-contest clause

pecuniary bequest

personal representative

publishing clause

residuary clause

self-proof clause

signature clause

specific bequest

specific devise

specific legacy

surety

tangible personal

property

testamentary trust

testimonium clause

The opening paragraph of Katherine Ganon's will, called the (1) or the (2), stated that she lived at 22 Livingstone Street, Tampa, Florida. Because that address is her principal place of abode, it may be referred to as her (3). The main body of Katherine's will consisted of several paragraphs, known as (4), which disposed of all of her property. She left a valuable painting, which was a(n) (5) to her niece, Myra. The painting is considered to be (6) because it is capable of being touched. She left $10,000 to her nephew, George. This was a(n) (7) because it was a gift of money from the general assets of the estate. It is also known as a(n) (8). Katherine left $10,000 to her niece, Eva, which was to be paid from the funds that Katherine had on deposit in account number 39-778216 at the Century Bank. This was a(n) (9) because it will not adeem if there is no money in the account when she dies. Katherine left her residence located at 22 Livingstone Street, Tampa, Florida, in equal shares to her children, Doris and Daniel. This gift is called a(n) (10). In the (11) of her will, Katherine gave all of her property that was not otherwise disposed of to her children, Doris and Daniel, in equal shares. Katherine named her daughter, Doris, to serve as the personal representative of her estate. Doris will be known as the (12) of the will. Had Daniel been named to serve in that position, he would have been known as the (13). Because Katherine's children were both adults, there was no need to appoint a(n) (14) to have custody of the children or a(n) (15) to care for the children's property. Katherine signed the will on the line that followed the (16). Two of her friends signed as witnesses on the lines that followed the (17). Finally, a notary public signed the will on the line following the (18) after taking the oaths of Katherine and the two witnesses.

■ KEY TERMS

ademption	general legacy	signature clause
attestation clause	incorporation by reference	specific devise
demonstrative legacy	letter of instruction	specific legacy
dispositive provisions	no-contest	surety
executor	pecuniary legacy (bequest)	tangible personal property
executrix	personal representative	testimonium clause
exordium clause	residuary clause	
fiduciaries	self-proof clause	

Online Companion™
For additional resources, please go to
http://www.paralegal.delmar.cengage.com.

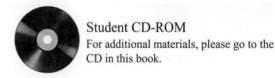

Student CD-ROM
For additional materials, please go to the
CD in this book.

Family Protection, Lapses, and Ademption

■ CHAPTER OUTLINE

■ CHAPTER OUTCOMES

- Explain the laws that have been enacted for the protection of family members.

- Distinguish between lapsed legacies and ademption.

■ JOB COMPETENCIES

- Be able to identify issues, research state law, and draft documents relatin to the protection of widows and children.

- Be alert for legacies that have lapsed and items that have adeemed when preparing probate documents.

◼ A DAY AT THE OFFICE . . .

The office of Dillon & Howard was relatively quiet at 4:00 on the warm Friday afternoon in July. Angela Clark, the legal assistant, was one of the few people remaining in the office when Despina Papadakis walked in, accompanied by her two young children, Nick and Christo. Angela noticed that Mrs. Papadakis looked extremely troubled, greeted her with a sense of concern, and told her that none of the attorneys were in at the moment. Mrs. Papadakis related to Angela that her husband, Vasillios, had recently drowned in a boating accident and that she had no money to support her two children because the bank accounts were in her husband's name.

Angela ushered the distraught woman and her children to a conference room, made them comfortable, and started writing down the facts. Mrs. Papadakis told Angela that, although they owned their own home, they owed many creditors, and she was afraid that she would lose the house to the creditors. Tears ran down her cheeks as she handed Angela a wrinkled legal document and said that her husband had left her out of his will completely. Her grief turned to anger as she mentioned that the will left a large sum of money and a boat to her husband's secretary. The anger turned to rage as she pointed out that the children were also omitted from the will.

Angela tried to calm Mrs. Papadakis down while at the same time listening to her and taking notes. She made an appointment for Mrs. Papadakis to see Attorney Dillon on Monday morning. Mrs. Papadakis laughed as she left the office, saying, "At least she won't get the boat! It sank along with my husband! It was covered by insurance, though."

Queries:

1. Is there any way that Mrs. Papadakis can obtain money from her husband's estate for the immediate support of her family?
2. Is any protection available to Mrs. Papadakis to prevent the loss of her house to creditors?
3. Can Mrs. Papadakis do anything about being left out of her husband's will?
4. Can the children do anything about being left out of their father's will?
5. Will Mr. Papadakis's secretary inherit the insurance from the boat that sank?

§ 7.1 PROTECTION OF FAMILY MEMBERS

The death of a person who provides the fundamental support for a family can be tragic for the survivors who depend on that support. Assets in the decedent's name can be tied up for months while an estate is being settled. Creditors can bring claims against the estate without regard to the needs of survivors. Decedent's occasionally disinherit their spouses or provide for them inadequately in their wills.

Various state laws are in place to give assistance to family members at this difficult time. Although they differ from state to state, they include such things as a family allowance, homestead protection, exemption of property from creditors' claims, dower and curtesy, a spouse's elective share, and pretermitted children laws.

Family Allowance

To provide for the immediate support of the family when a breadwinner dies, state laws generally contain a mechanism for immediate access to money from the decedent's estate. Probate courts have authority to grant an allowance from the estate to the widow or widower and surviving children to provide for their immediate needs after the death of the decedent (see Exhibit 7–1). The allowance is known as the **family allowance** or *widow's allowance.* In some states, the amount of the allowance is discretionary with the court, depending on the size of the estate, the debts of the estate, and the needs of the surviving spouse and children. To illustrate, the Uniform Probate Code (UPC) contains the following provision for a family allowance, in §2–404:

> (a) In addition to the right to homestead allowance and exempt property, if the decedent was domiciled in this state, the surviving spouse and minor children whom the decedent was obligated to support and children who were in fact being supported by him are entitled to a reasonable allowance in money out of the estate for their maintenance during the period of administration, which allowance may not continue for longer than one year if the estate is inadequate to discharge allowed claims. The allowance may be paid as a lump sum or in periodic installments. It is payable to the surviving spouse, if living, for the use of the surviving spouse and minor and dependent children; otherwise to the children, or persons having their care and custody; but in case any minor child or dependent child is not living with the surviving spouse, the allowance may be made partially to the child or his guardian or other person having his care and custody, and partially to the spouse, as their needs may appear. The family allowance is exempt from and has priority over all claims but not over the homestead allowance.

> (b) The family allowance is not chargeable against any benefit or share passing to the surviving spouse or children by the will of the decedent unless otherwise provided, by intestate succession, or by way of elective share. The death of any person entitled to family allowance terminates his right to allowances not yet paid.

The period of time covered by the family allowance coincides with the period during which estate assets are frozen for the protection of creditors, which is usually not more than one year. In Texas, the court may not make an

■ **family allowance**
A state-set percentage of an estate that is given to the immediate family (or the spouse) even if the will gives them less. Also known as a *widow's allowance.*

allowance for the surviving spouse when the survivor has separate property adequate for his or her maintenance. However, as shown by the *Churchill* case, the family allowance must be made in consideration of the whole condition of the estate during the first year after the spouse's death, and for the necessities of the surviving spouse and the circumstances to which he has been accustomed.

Homestead Protection

An important protection for families who own their own residences is the **homestead exemption**. This exemption is available under many state laws, whether or not there is a death in the family, and is designed to place the family residence beyond the reach of creditors. The exemption allows the head of a family to keep the family home up to a certain value regardless of the amount of family debt. It is usually established by state statute but is sometimes found in the state constitution. For example, Article X, Sec. 2 of the North Carolina Constitution reads:

> (2) The homestead, after the death of the owner thereof, shall be exempt from the payment of any debt during the minority of the owner's children, or any of them.

> (3) If the owner of a homestead dies, leaving a surviving spouse but no minor children, the homestead shall be exempt from the debts of the owner, and the rents and profits thereof shall inure to the benefit of the surviving spouse until he or she remarries, unless the surviving spouse is the owner of a separate homestead.

In states that have adopted the UPC, a surviving spouse is entitled to a homestead allowance up to a certain amount of money; if there is no surviving spouse, minor children qualify for the allowance. The homestead allowance is exempt from and has priority over all claims against the estate and is in addition to any share passing to the surviving spouse or minor children by will of the decedent, intestate succession, or by way of an elective share [UPC § 2–401].

In states that have not adopted the UPC, the person who is entitled to the homestead exemption is the **head of household** or the *householder*. In the past, this was the husband. Today, however, many states recognize either a husband or a wife as a head of household. Some states allow only married persons (including widows and widowers) to claim the exemption.

Generally, householders are entitled to the homestead exemption only when they are residing with someone whom they have an obligation to support or who is dependent upon them for support. In a few states, persons who have attained a certain age are entitled to a homestead exemption whether or not they are the head of a household.

■ **homestead exemption**

State laws allowing a head of a family to keep a home and some property safe from creditors other than mortgage holders, or to allow certain persons (such as those over a certain age) to avoid paying real estate or inheritance taxes on their homes.

■ **head of household**

A special category of federal taxpayer. To be taxed at head of household rates, you must meet several requirements; for example, unmarried or legally separated, pay over half the support of your dependents, etc. Also known as *householder*.

AC70

COMMONWEALTH OF MASSACHUSETTS

TO THE HONORABLE THE JUDGES OF THE PROBATE COURT IN AND FOR THE COUNTY OF ESSEX:

RESPECTFULLY represents ....

of .... in the County of ....

that .... late of ....

in said County, whose estate is in course of settlement in said Court, died possessed of personal estate

appraised at $ .... and real estate appraised at $ ....;

that she is his widow and has under her charge a family consisting of

....

....

....

and she further represents that the personal property is insufficient to afford her proper allowance.

    Wherefore, she prays that the Court will allow her—all—part—of the personal estate of said deceased as necessaries for herself and family under her care, in addition to the provisions and other articles by law belonging to her—*and a further sum to be derived from the sale—mortgage—of real property of the deceased.*

    Dated this .... day of .... 19 .

COMMONWEALTH OF MASSACHUSETTS

ESSEX, SS.   PROBATE COURT

    At a Probate Court held at .... in and for said County of Essex, on the .... day of .... in the year of our Lord one thousand nine hundred ....

ON the petition of .... representing

that she is the widow of ....

late of .... in said County, deceased, whose estate is in course of settlement in said Court, and praying to be allowed—all—part—of the personal estate of said deceased as necessaries for herself and family under her care—*and a further sum to be derived from the sale—mortgage—of real property of the deceased.*

    It appearing that she is the widow, and entitled to an allowance as aforesaid; all—part—of the personal estate of said deceased to the amount of ....

.... dollars,—

and a further sum of .... dollars

to be derived from the sale—mortgage—or real property—is hereby allowed to her as necessaries for herself and family under her care, in addition to the provisions and other articles by law belonging to her.

.... *Judge of Probate Court*

EXHIBIT 7–1   Sample Petition for Widow's Allowance (Massachusetts)

CASE STUDY *In Re the Estate of Sullivan*

724 N.W.2d 532(MN)

FACTS:
John Sullivan died in February 2004. He left a will, which was contested, and several children were awarded a family allowance. Nancy Sullivan, one of John's daughters, was denied an allowance. Minnesota statutes require that the recipient of a family allowance be dependent on the deceased in order to be awarded the stipend.

LEGAL ISSUE:
Is an adult daughter entitled to an allowance when she has received periodic funds from the deceased father?

COURT DECISION: No.

REASON:
The daughter, who was 64 years old at the time of her father's death, had received periodic payments for the four years prior to his death. The checks she received were timed randomly and were for different amounts. The daughter testified that some of the money was used to start a business for herself. Social Security documents suggested that the money for the new business was a loan that was to be repaid. She had received no moneys for about six months prior to John's death. The evidence was such that the conclusion of the trial court that she was not a dependent as required by statute was warranted.

MANY WIVES, MANY CHILDREN

BRIGHAM YOUNG

Mormon leader Brigham Young was survived by 17 wives and 48 children when he died in 1877. His carefully drawn will provided: "To avoid any question, the words 'married' or 'marriage' in this will shall be taken to have become consummated between man and woman, either by ceremony before a lawful magistrate or according to the order of the Church of Jesus Christ of Latter-Day Saints, or by their cohabitation in conformity to our custom." The will divided family units into three classes: (1) those with wives with children, (2) those with wives with no children, and (3) those with children of deceased wives. Among other things, each family inherited the house in which it was living. Until all wives died or until the youngest child came of age, the income from the undistributed properties went into a trust to be divided among the various mothers for the support of their children.

CASE STUDY *Churchill v. Churchill*

780 S.W.2d 913 (TX)

FACTS:	Richard Churchill's will made ample provision for his wife, Marian, and other family members. Marian's separate property at the time of her husband's death consisted of jewelry and a residence valued at $51,000. Marian testified that she had annual expenses of $34,161 and that she was accustomed to spending an additional $18,000 to $24,000 per year on golf tournaments with her husband. The trial court awarded Marian a family allowance of $30,000.
LEGAL ISSUE:	Is a surviving spouse entitled to a family allowance when adequate provision was made for her by will and there was no evidence that the spouse's separate property was inadequate for her maintenance?
COURT DECISION:	Yes.
REASON:	The family allowance is to be made in consideration of the whole condition of the estate during the first year after the spouse's death, and of the necessities of the surviving spouse and the circumstances to which he has been accustomed. The evidence was sufficient to show that Marian's separate property was not adequate to her maintenance. In addition, given the testimony showing that Marian's need for maintenance greatly exceeded her income, the court was unable to conclude that the allowance in the amount of $30,000 was excessive.

Although the homestead exemption applies in most states only to real property, a few states allow a homestead exemption on personal property as well. Some states put a limit on the value of the homestead exemption; others have no limitation on the exemption.

The laws of some jurisdictions provide for an automatic homestead exemption; other jurisdictions require the signing and recording in a public place of a written declaration of homestead (see Exhibit 7–2). The written declaration names the homestead owner, describes the homestead property, and states that the homestead is the owner's principal residence.

The owner of a homestead may convey the property to someone else free of the homestead restriction. In some states, this is done simply by signing an ordinary deed; in other states, a statement in the deed specifically releasing the homestead is necessary. Most jurisdictions require that both spouses consent to the conveyance of a homestead. The following clause may be used in some states, to release the right of homestead.

DECLARATION OF HOMESTEAD BY SPOUSE
[9A AMJUR LF HOME § 135:16]

I, _____, hereby declare:

I am the head of a family, I am married, and my spouse's name is
_____. My family consists of my spouse and _____ children.

At the time of making this declaration of homestead, I actually reside with
my family on premises located in _____ County, _____ [state], more
particularly described as follows: _____ [set forth legal description].

I claim and declare the premises, with the dwelling house _____ [and
outbuildings] on it, and its appurtenances, as a homestead for the joint
benefit of myself and my spouse and family.

_____ [No former declaration of homestead had been made by me or
by my spouse, either jointly or separately or A former declaration of
homestead has been made by _____, but it was abandoned before the
execution of this declaration of homestead.]

I estimate the actual cash value of the premises to be _____ Dollars
($_____).

Executed on _____ [Date].

                                                    [Signature]

[Acknowledgment]

EXHIBIT 7–2   Sample Declaration of Homestead by Spouse

Example

Declaration of Abandonment of Homestead

9A AMJUR LF HOME § 135:73

We, _____ [name of husband], and _____ [name of wife], husband and wife, hereby
abandon all claim by us as a homestead to the premises described below, and hereby release and
discharge the premises from any and all claim of homestead by us, and particularly from any claim
under the declaration of homestead recorded _____ [in the office of _____ of
_____ County, _____ (state), in Volume _____ of Declarations of Homestead,
at page _____].

   The premises are situated in _____ [city], _____ County, _____ [state],
and are described as follows: [insert legal description].

   Executed on _____ [Date].

                                        [Signatures]

[Acknowledgment]

When preparing a declaration of homestead, it is necessary to examine the statutes of the state in which the property is located and to include in the declaration all information that the law requires. Homestead exemptions are, in states such as Texas and Florida, essentially unlimited in and are, unfortunately, recognized not only by the surrogate courts in those states, but by the bankruptcy courts as well. This leads to the potential for wealthy corporate criminals to build multimillion dollar homes that are exempt from both estate and bankruptcy proceedings. The late Kenneth Lay, of Enron fame, was building a home in Texas with an estimated value of $5,000,000 that would have satisfied the homestead laws in Texas. The fines and penalties that would have been assessed him in one court could have been discharged in bankruptcy court, with the home exempt from the proceeding. Congress is looking into this potential abuse.

Exempt Property

■ **exempt property**
Certain property of a decedent that passes to the surviving spouse or children without being subject to the claims of general creditors.

Under the laws of some states, certain property of a decedent, called **exempt property**, passes to the surviving spouse or children and is not subject to the claims of general creditors. For example, in states that have enacted the Uniform Probate Code, a surviving spouse is entitled to $3,500 worth of personal property comprising any combination of household furniture, automobiles, furnishings, appliances, and personal effects [UPC § 2–402]. If there is no surviving spouse, children of the decedent are entitled jointly to the same value. These rights are in addition to the homestead allowance, as well as any benefits or share passing to the surviving spouse or children by the will of the decedent, by way of an elective share, or by intestate succession.

THE JOINT IS JUMPIN'

THOMAS "FATS" WALLER

"Money can't buy me love" was a marital theme of jazz great Fats Waller long before the Beatles sang their hit tune. Best known for writing the song "Ain't Misbehaven" for the Broadway hit *Hot Chocolates* featuring Louis Armstrong, Thomas "Fats" Waller died of pneumonia while on board a train near Kansas City, Missouri. In his will, the celebrated jazz pianist and composer of the 1930s, left one dollar to his wife "for reasons best known to her." Instead, a dower right established by law provided her with one-third of the estate.

Read more about this talented person who died at such a young age by logging on to <http://www.Google.com> and key in his name.

Dower and Curtesy

The rights of dower and curtesy originated in early England to provide surviving spouses with a means of support upon the death of a spouse. **Dower,** under English law, was the right of a widow to a one-third life estate in all real property owned by the husband during the marriage. **Curtesy** was the right of a widower to a life estate in all real property owned by the wife during the marriage, but only if issue of the marriage were born alive.

In this day and age, partial interests in real estate can be a hindrance rather than a source of support for a surviving spouse. Many states (including those that have adopted the Uniform Probate Code) have abolished the rights of dower and curtesy altogether [UPC § 2–113]. Other states have changed the early English rules of dower and curtesy to their own liking, making dower and curtesy rights different in each state. The *Del Guercio* case illustrates the New Jersey law, applying the right of dower in 1985.

Dower and curtesy rights arise only upon the death of the other spouse. In addition, these rights do not apply to real property owned by the deceased spouse as a joint tenant with someone else, or to property to which the surviving

■ **dower**

A wife's right to part of her dead husband's property. This right is now regulated by statute and varies from state to state.

■ **curtesy**

A husband's right to part of his dead wife's property. This right is regulated by statute and varies from state to state.

CASE STUDY　　*In Re Del Guercio Estate*

501 A.2d 1072 (NJ)

FACTS: Janet and Fred Del Guercio took title to their residence on September 24, 1970, as tenants by the entireties. On October 24, 1971, Janet conveyed her interest in the property to Fred by bargain-and-sale deed. Some years later, marital difficulties arose between the couple. Janet left the marital residence in 1984 and instituted a divorce action. Fred died before being served with process in that action.

LEGAL ISSUE: Is a widow entitled to a dower interest in real property that was held initially with her husband as a tenant by the entireties but was solely owned by the husband at the time of his death?

COURT DECISION: Yes.

REASON: Under the New Jersey statute, "[t]he widow ... of a person dying intestate or otherwise, shall be endowed for the term of her ... natural life of the full and equal half part of all real property of which the decedent ... was seized of an estate of inheritance at any time during coverture prior to May 28, 1980 to which the widow ... shall not have relinquished her right of dower ... by deed duly executed and acknowledged in the manner provided by law to record deeds.

■ purchase money mortgages

A buyer's financing of part of a purchase by giving a mortgage on the property to the seller as security for the loan.

spouse has released the right of dower or curtesy. In addition, in many states, such rights are subject to **purchase money mortgages** (mortgages given to purchase the property on which the mortgage is placed), whether or not the surviving spouse signed the mortgage. Despite such limitations, dower and curtesy rights have preference over the rights of creditors and can thereby provide protection to surviving spouses in the case of insolvent estates (see Exhibit 7–3).

AC66A

G. L. (Ter. Ed.) c. 189, § 1.

To the Honorable the Judges of the Probate Court in and for the County of Essex:

RESPECTFULLY represents ....

....

of .... in the County of .... that   he is

the widow—*husband*—of ....

....

late of .... in the County of Essex, deceased; that on

the .... day of   19   , the bond of

the execut   —administrat   ....   —of the

        estate—will—of the deceased was approved by this Court, and that   he hereby elects and

claims dower—*curtesy*— ....   in the estate of the deceased, instead of the

interest in real property of the deceased given in section one of chapter one hundred and ninety of the

General Laws.

        And   he also hereby waives any provisions that may have been made in the will of the deceased

for h   and claims such portions of the estate of the deceased as   he would have taken if the

deceased had died intestate.

Dated this .... day of 19   .

EXHIBIT 7–3   Sample Form to Elect the Right of Dower (Massachusetts)

Spouse's Elective Share

To protect surviving spouses from being disinherited, state laws allow surviving spouses to renounce the provisions made for them in the deceased spouse's will. Instead of inheriting under the terms of the will, surviving spouses may elect to take against (i.e., waive) the will and inherit an amount that is set forth in their state's statute. This is often referred to as a **forced share** or an *elective share.*

State laws differ as to the amount a surviving spouse may receive when electing to take against the will. Some states allow the surviving spouse to take a fixed percentage, usually one-third or one-half, of the estate instead of the amount given in the will. Other states allow the surviving spouse to take the amount that he would have received under the state's intestacy laws. Still other states follow a growing trend to allow the surviving spouse to take an amount that is based on the number of years of the marriage. If the marriage lasted only a few years, the percentage given to the surviving spouse would be much less than if the marriage lasted many years.

Particular problems arise when couples enter into second or subsequent marriages with each party having children from earlier marriages. Assets need to be protected for each spouse's children while at the same time providing adequately for the surviving spouse. Improper planning can lead to one's natural children being deprived of their justified inheritance because of a spouse's right to an elective share. Couples in this situation should consider entering into a **prenuptial agreement**. Prenuptual agreements are also called antenuptual agreements in some states. This is a written agreement entered into before marriage in which the parties set forth how their respective properties will be divided upon death or divorce. When spouses sign a prenuptial agreement, they individually agree that the other party's estate plan will be binding, notwithstanding the right of election, the rights of dower or curtesy, or any other statutory rights. Courts enforce these agreements, as long as both parties have fully disclosed their assets prior to the prenuptial; also, courts look to individual representation to demonstrate an arms-length transaction. Another legal device used to assist couples with children from earlier marriages is the use of a qualified terminable interest property (QTIP) trust, explained in Chapter 9.

In some jurisdictions, the forced share is tied to the amount that the survivor would have received if the deceased spouse had died without a will. In the *Spencer* case, a widow opted for the share provided by state statute rather than the amount designated in her husband's will.

In other states, a different formula is used to determine the amount of inheritance when a surviving spouse decides to renounce the provisions of a will and become a **forced heir**. Alabama lists specific amounts in its statute, as shown in the *Barksdale* case.

■ **forced share**

The share a surviving spouse may choose to take in the estate of a deceased spouse. Also known as an *elective share.*

■ **prenuptial agreement**

An antenuptial (before marriage) agreement. A contract between persons about to marry, usually stating the way property will be handled during the marriage, the way it will divide in case of divorce, and the limits on spousal support obligations.

■ **forced heir**

A person who cannot be deprived of a share of an estate unless the testator (person making a will) has a recognized legal cause for disinheriting the person.

CASE STUDY *Spencer v. Williams*

569 A.2d 1194 (DC)

FACTS:
Loy Henderson died at the age of 93. Among other things, his will left $200,000 in trust for the benefit of his wife, Elise, and upon her death to beneficiaries named by Mr. Henderson. If she renounced the will and took the amount provided by statute, Mrs. Henderson would receive $160,000 outright, instead of $200,000 in trust, and be able to name her own beneficiaries upon her death.

LEGAL ISSUE:
May a surviving spouse renounce his deceased spouse's will and take a different share of the estate?

COURT DECISION: Yes.

REASON:
An individual who is predeceased by his spouse, and whose spouse leaves a will, may either take the property left him in the will or, alternatively, take the share provided for by statute—in this jurisdiction, an amount equal to that which the individual would have received had the spouse died intestate, up to a maximum of one-half the net estate.

CASE STUDY *Barksdale v. Barksdale*

551 So. 2d 1006 (AL)

FACTS:
In his will, Elton Barksdale left certain property outright to his wife, Ruby, and the remainder to her for her life. Instead of taking her share under the will, Ruby filed a petition for an elective share of the estate, in addition to claims for homestead and an exempt property allowance.

LEGAL ISSUE:
In Alabama, may a surviving spouse take an elective share in addition to a homestead and exempt property allowance?

COURT DECISION: Yes.

REASON:
The homestead and exempt property allowances are awarded irrespective of a surviving spouse's decision to take an elective share of the spouse's estate. The amounts to be distributed are stated clearly in the Alabama statute: one-third of the estate for the elective share, $3,500 for exempt property, and $6,000 for the homestead allowance.

There is a time limit, ranging from six to nine months, within which a surviving spouse may renounce a deceased spouse's will (see Exhibit 7–4). An election to do so must be made while the surviving spouse is still alive, as illustrated by the *Dahlmann* case.

In states that have adopted the UPC, the subsequent marriage of a testator does not revoke a will [UPC § 2–301]. However, an omitted spouse who married the testator after execution of the will takes the share he or she would have taken had the decedent died intestate, unless (1) it appears from the will that the omission was intentional, or (2) the testator provided for the surviving spouse outside the will in lieu of a testamentary provision. The *Groeper* case involves a clarification of an "omitted spouse."

Divorce ends a marriage, so a person who is divorced from a decedent is not a surviving spouse and does not have the right to an elective share of the decedent's estate. In addition, some states, such as New Jersey, do not allow a surviving spouse to receive an elective share if, at the time of the spouse's death, they were living apart while a divorce was pending and had ceased to cohabit as man and wife. In some states, a spouse who is living in adultery at the time of a spouse's death or who has abandoned a spouse without just cause is prevented from taking any part of the spouse's estate. The *Oliver* case addresses the issue of adulterous cohabitation.

CASE STUDY ⚖ **Estate of *Dahlmann v. Dahlmann***

668 S.W.2d 520 (AR)

FACTS:	William F. Dahlmann died on April 14, 1982. His will acknowledged his wife of 30 years, but left her nothing. Mrs. Dahlmann died two months after her husband without electing to take against his will.
LEGAL ISSUE:	May the estate of a woman who died two months after her husband elect to take against her husband's will?
COURT DECISION:	No.
REASON:	When a spouse dies testate, the surviving spouse must exercise the option to take against the will in his or her lifetime. Otherwise, the right is forfeited, because it is personal and does not survive the surviving spouse.

Prob. 105-H

PROBATE COURT OF _____ COUNTY, OHIO

ESTATE OF_____ , DECEASED

Case No._____ Docket _____ Page _____

CITATION TO SURVIVING SPOUSE TO ELECT TO TAKE UNDER OR AGAINST WILL
Revised Code, Sec. 2107.39

To _____   _____
        Surviving Spouse   **Address**
                                         _____

As decedent's surviving spouse, Ohio law permits you to choose whether to take under decedent's Will, or to take against the Will.

If you elect to take under the Will, you must take under it alone as to property governed by it, unless it plainly appears from the Will that the provisions in it for you are in addition to an intestate share of the estate.

If you elect to take against the Will, you are entitled to one-half of decedent's net estate, unless there are two or more of decedent's children or their lineal descendants surviving, in which case you are entitled to one-third of decedent's net estate.

Whichever choice you make, you will not be barred from your rights to purchase or to remain in the family home for one year, to receive an allowance for support, or to receive an automobile owned by decedent, as and to the extent you may have such rights under the law.

Before making your election, you are entitled to file a complaint in this Court asking that the Will be construed in your favor.

You have one month from the date of service of this citation in which to make your election to take under or against the Will, or to file a complaint for construction of the Will. The Court may extend such time for good cause. If you take no action within the one-month period, it will be conclusively presumed that you elect to take under the Will.

If you elect to take under the Will, you may do so in writing if you wish, but you may also do so merely by taking no action, as explained in the preceding paragraph.

If you elect to take against the Will, you must come to this Court and do so in person. Before accepting your election to take against the Will, the Judge or Referee must explain decedent's Will, your rights under the Will, and your rights in case of your refusal to take under the Will.

It is recommended that you consult your attorney if you are in any doubt as to your rights, as to how to claim them, or as to which course of action would be to your best advantage.

_____   _____
Date   **Probate Judge/Clerk**

FORM 8.0 · CITATION TO SURVIVING SPOUSE TO ELECT TO TAKE UNDER OR AGAINST WILL

EXHIBIT 7–4 Sample Citation to Surviving Spouse (Ohio)

CASE STUDY *Estate of Groeper v. Groeper*

665 S.W.2d 367 (MO)

FACTS: On the day that Walter H. Groeper's first wife, Meta, died, he executed a will leaving his property in equal shares to his five brothers and sisters and Meta's five brothers and sisters, including Melinda, who at the time was the widow of Meta's brother, Hugo. Shortly thereafter, Walter married Melinda. He continued to be married to her until he died, without making a new will.

LEGAL ISSUE: Is a surviving spouse who was a beneficiary under her husband's will as a member of a class (in this case a sister-in-law) considered to be an omitted spouse and thus able to take an intestate share of her husband's estate?

COURT DECISION: Yes.

REASON: When a will that is executed before marriage contains a provision for a named individual who later becomes the testator's spouse, the surviving spouse has the burden of proving that the provision was not made in contemplation of marriage. Because Melinda was the testator's sister-in-law at the time, and the remainder of the class were either brothers, sisters, or in-laws, there is no question that the testator did not contemplate Melinda as a future spouse at the time he executed the will.

CASE STUDY *Oliver v. Estate of Oliver*

554 N.E.2d 8 (IN)

FACTS: Dorothy Oliver, who was suffering from physical ailments associated with diabetes, entered a nursing home. While she was there, her husband, Warren Oliver, began residing in a trailer with another woman. There was evidence that he took the other woman to dinner parties and was living with her at the trailer at the time of his wife's death.

LEGAL ISSUE: May the trial court infer adulterous cohabitation from circumstantial evidence when applying the statute that prevents a surviving spouse who is living in adultery from taking from the estate?

COURT DECISION: Yes.

REASON: Although, admittedly, the circumstantial evidence offered here would have been insufficient to sustain a criminal conviction of adultery, this is a civil case, in which the degree of proof necessary is the lesser preponderance of the evidence standard. Oliver is likewise not aided by a presumption of innocence. The fact of carnal intercourse must in almost every case of adultery be inferred from the circumstances, because direct proof of sex acts between the parties is virtually impossible to produce.

Pretermitted Children

Generally, parents may disinherit children as long as they do so intentionally. If a **pretermitted child** (a child omitted from a parent's will) can prove that the omission was unintentional, the omitted child may be able to inherit an intestate share of the parent's estate. This rule also applies to the issue (lineal descendants) of deceased children who are omitted from a parent's will. In the *Birman* and *Uliscni* cases, the intention of the testator to omit a child is maintained despite a contest.

■ **pretermitted child**

A child (or sometimes any descendant) either unintentionally left out of a will or born after the will is made. Some states have pretermission statutes that allow a child left out by mistake to take a share of the parent's property.

CASE STUDY **Birman v. Sproat**

546 N.E.2d 1354 (OH)

FACTS: Constance Birman, the illegitimate child of Vearl Sproat, contested her father's will. Sproat's will gave $500 each to his son, four stepdaughters, and the Friedens Lutheran Church. The residue was bequeathed to Sproat's wife, Frances. Constance Birman was not mentioned in the will.

LEGAL ISSUE: Can a parent disinherit a child by not mentioning the child in a will?

COURT DECISION: Yes.

REASON: If the testator makes no mention of one of his children in his will and by such will disposes of all his property, such child is as completely disinherited as if the testator had specifically so provided. The specific bequests made by Sproat to his natural son and stepdaughters necessarily imply he meant to exclude Constance Birman from a similar bequest under his will.

CASE STUDY **Matter of Estate of Uliscni**

372 N.W.2d 759 (MN)

FACTS: Michael Uliscni died testate, survived by his only child, Holly Nakari, who was born out of wedlock. Uliscni's will left his entire estate to his nephew. The will contained the following clause: "I do hereby specifically disinherit any and all persons who are or who claim to be my heirs at law except as herein provided." Uliscni's lawyer testified that he had had a conference with Uliscni prior to drafting the will and that Uliscni had told him that he had no children. After Uliscni died, however, the lawyer found in his file a copy of a will he had drawn for Uliscni five years earlier, in which Holly Nakari was specifically named and excluded.

LEGAL ISSUE: Was the evidence sufficient to establish an intentional omission of a child from a will?

(continues)

CASE STUDY **Matter of Estate of Uliscni** *(continued)*

COURT DECISION: Yes.

REASON: In Minnesota, a testator's intent to disinherit need not appear on the face of the will. The evidence is not limited to the will itself. The specific words in a will must be interpreted in light of the circumstances and extrinsic evidence offered in each individual case. Here, the earlier unexecuted will specifically named and disinherited Nakari. There was no evidence of any change in Uliscni's and Nakari's relationship between the making of the two wills that would indicate that Uliscni had decided to provide for Nakari in his will.

In states that have adopted the Uniform Probate Code, the following rules apply to pretermitted children: [UPC § 2–302]

(a) If a testator fails to provide in his will for any of his children born or adopted after the execution of his will, the omitted child receives a share in the estate equal in value to that which he would have received if the testator had died intestate unless:

(1) it appears from the will that the omission was intentional;

(2) when the will was executed the testator had one or more children and devised substantially all his estate to the other parent of the omitted child; or

(3) the testator provided for the child by transfer outside the will and the intent that the transfer be in lieu of a testamentary provision is shown by statements of the testator or from the amount of the transfer or other evidence.

(b) If at the time of execution of the will the testator fails to provide in his will for a living child solely because he believes the child to be dead, the child receives a share in the estate equal in value to that which he would have received if the testator had died intestate.

Clauses in a will such as the following help to make clear the testator's intention as to omitted children.

Example

Persons Not Mentioned

20A AMJUR LF WI § 266:433

I have intentionally omitted all my heirs who are not specifically mentioned herein, and I hereby generally and specifically disinherit each, any, and all persons whomsoever claiming to be or who may be lawfully determined to be my heirs at law, except as otherwise mentioned in this will.

§ 7.2 LAPSED LEGACIES AND DEVISES

It is common for testators to outlive some or all of the individuals to whom they leave gifts in their wills. When legatees or devisees die before the testator, gifts to them in the testator's will are known as **lapsed legacies** or **lapsed devises**. With some exceptions, such gifts become part of the residuary estate and are inherited by the residuary legatees and devisees named in the residuary clause of the will.

Many states have statutes, known as **antilapse statutes**, that minimize the effects of such lapses. The typical antilapse statute provides that if a gift is made to a relative of the testator who dies before the testator and leaves issue surviving the testator, the issue will receive the gift. Some state antilapse statutes apply only to gifts given to children; some apply to gifts given to anyone at all. In states that have adopted the UPC, the antilapse statute applies to gifts given to grandparents and lineal descendants of a grandparent [UPC § 2–605].

Quite often testators do not want the antilapse statute to go into effect. The use of the words, "if he or she shall survive me" accomplishes that result. The clause shown here would prevent the issue of Natalie I. Nichols from inheriting the $50,000 gift if Natalie predeceased the testator:

> I give the sum of Fifty Thousand Dollars ($50,000) to my sister, Natalie I. Nichols, if she shall survive me.

§ 7.3 ADEMPTION

Frequently, property that is specifically bequeathed or devised in a will is not owned by the testator at death. Either the testator disposed of property after executing the will or the property became extinct. A specific legacy or devise is **adeemed** (extinguished or taken away) if the property is not in existence or does not belong to the testator at the time of death. The item is said to adeem by **extinction**. When an item of property adeems, the legatee or devisee of that property simply does not receive it. In addition, he receives nothing in its place, as is pointed out by the *Opperman* case.

Ademption can also come about by a method known as **satisfaction** or *advancement*. This occurs when a gift of property or money is given by the testator, while alive, to a legatee with the intent that the gift or payment be in lieu of the legacy. The *Wolff* case illustrates this method.

■ lapsed legacies

A gift in a will that fails because the legatee predeceased the testator.

■ lapsed devises

A gift of real property in a will that fails because the devisee predeceased the testator.

■ antilapse statutes

State laws that prevent lapsed legacies and lapsed devises.

■ adeemed

Take away.

■ extinction

Put to an end.

■ satisfaction

Property given by a parent to an heir that the parent intends to deduct from the child's eventual share of the parent's estate. Also known as *advancement.*

CASE STUDY *Opperman v. Anderson*

782 S.W.2d 8 (TX)

FACTS: Among other things, Ethel M. Ramchissel's will left one-half of her stock
                in the Pabst Brewing Company to a named individual and all of her
                stock in the Houston Natural Gas Corporation to six named individuals "if
                owned by me at the time of my death." All of the Pabst Brewing stock and
                all but 65 shares of the Houston Natural Gas stock were converted to cash
                before the testatrix died. The remaining 65 shares of stock were redeemed
                for cash after she died.

LEGAL ISSUE: Do the proceeds from shares of stock sold before death pass to the legatee
                of those specific shares of stock?

COURT DECISION: No.

REASON: Mrs. Ramchissel clearly intended that the gifts of stock be specific bequests
                subject to ademption. The will was carefully worded to make the
                bequests of stock operative only in the event that the shares were on hand
                at her death.

CASE STUDY **Matter of Estate of Wolff**

349 N.W.2d 33 (SD)

FACTS: Jacob Wolff, who had three sons, executed a will providing that in the
                event his wife should predecease him, his estate should pass to his sons
                "equally, share and share alike." A year later, he and his wife deeded
                1,000 acres of land to their son, Arthur, and 1,040 acres of land to their
                son, Erwinn, for "$1.00 and other good and valuable consideration." Prior
                to deeding the two tracts of land, Wolff wrote a letter to his third son,
                Jacob, Jr., telling him of the two deeds and saying, "From now on they did
                not have to send any more rent from the land that is deeded to them, and
                about your land, I don't know yet. See how it is turning out. Erwinn can
                buy it or rent for cash, from now on. Or what did you think? I thought if
                Erwinn buys it I can make the Deed to him. If he rents for cash I make the
                Deed to you." Nothing further was done before Jacob died.

LEGAL ISSUE: In South Dakota, may a general legacy adeem by satisfaction?

COURT DECISION: Yes.

REASON: Although there is authority that ademption applies only to specific
                legacies, a South Dakota statute (S.D. Codified Laws ß 29-6–14) allows for
                ademption of general legacies if an intention to adeem is expressed by the
                testator in writing. The testator's letter to his son, Jacob, Jr., satisfied
                the writing requirement of the statute.

SUMMARY

State laws give various kinds of protection to surviving family members when an income provider or spouse dies. With variations from state to state, types of protection include a family allowance, homestead protection, exemption of property from creditors' claims, dower and curtesy, a spouse's elective share, and pretermitted children laws.

Gifts in a will to a devisee or legatee who dies before the testator lapse and fall into the residuary part of the estate, pursuant to the residuary clause of the will, unless they are prevented from doing so by an antilapse statute and pass to the issue of the deceased legatee or devisee.

A specific legacy or devise that is not owned by the testator or was given to the legatee or devisee while the testator was alive is said to have adeemed, and the legatee or devisee receives nothing in its place.

■ REVIEW QUESTIONS

1. What mechanism is provided by state laws to provide for the immediate support of family members when a breadwinner dies?

2. What is the purpose of the homestead exemption, and what does it do?

3. In states that have adopted the Uniform Probate Code, what kind and how much property is considered to be exempt property, and from what is it exempt?

4. What was the difference between dower and curtesy under early English law?

5. Describe generally the provisions of state laws that protect spouses from being disinherited.

6. Under what circumstances may a pretermitted child inherit from a parent's estate?

7. In general, who inherits a gift in a will to a legatee who dies before the testator?

8. What does a typical antilapse statute provide?

9. When a specific legacy or devise in a will is not owned by a testator at death, what does the legatee or devisee receive in its place?

10. How does ademption by satisfaction occur?

■ CASES TO DISCUSS_____

1. George A. Magoon filed a complaint for divorce in the family court on August 12, 1986, and a decree of divorce was entered on March 4, 1987. The court, however, reserved issues related to support and property division for further hearing. Mr. Magoon died on June 6, 1987, before the court was able to conduct a further hearing. Was Mrs. Magoon entitled to receive an elective share of Mr. Magoon's estate? Why or why not? *Magoon v. Magoon*, 780 P.2d 80 (HI).

2. Thomas and Trudy Veit owned real property as tenants by the entireties. The holder of a mortgage on the property brought a foreclosure action for nonpayment of the mortgage. Mrs. Veit argued that, although her husband was still alive, she had a dower interest in her husband's property that prevented the mortgage from being foreclosed. Do you agree with Mrs. Veit? Explain. *Jones v. Veit*, 453 N.E.2d 1299 (OH).

3. After 17 years of marriage, Thomas Carr left his wife, Joyce. A year later, Joyce Carr filed a complaint for divorce on the grounds of desertion. While the case was pending and the parties were living apart, Thomas Carr died, leaving his entire estate to his children from a prior marriage. Was Joyce Carr entitled to an elective share of her husband's estate? Why or why not? *Carr v. Carr*, 576 A.2d 872 (NJ).

■ RESEARCH ON THE WEB_____

1. On the Internet, go to <http://www.findlaw.com>. Under Laws: Cases & Codes, click on States. Next click on Primary Materials, and look up the homestead statute (code) of your state.

2. Learn more about the paralegal profession by going to the National Federation of Paralegal Association's Web site at <http://www.paralegals.org>.

■ SHARPENING YOUR PROFESSIONAL SKILLS_____

1. Look up your state statute, if there is one, relating to each of the following protective devices:

   a. family allowance

   b. exempt property

   c. dower and curtesy

   Write down the statutory reference and make a photocopy of each statute you find.

2. What rights do disinherited surviving spouses have in your state? Give the statutory reference where the provision is found.

3. What rights do disinherited children have in your state? Give the statutory reference where the provision is found.

4. Obtain an actual deed to a family member's or friend's property and draft a declaration of homestead following the form in Exhibit 7–2. Before doing this assignment, look up your state's homestead statute to be sure that the form complies with your state's requirements.

■ SHARPENING YOUR LEGAL VOCABULARY_____

On a separate sheet of paper, fill in the numbered blank lines in the following anecdote with legal terms from this list:

adeemed

antilapse statute

curtesy

dower

elective share

exempt property

extinction

family allowance

forced heir

forced share

head of household

homestead exemption

householder

issue

lapsed devise

lapsed legacy

pretermitted child

purchase money mortgages

satisfaction

widow's allowance

Myrtle Gonzales was left without means of support when her husband, Enrique, passed away in a boating accident. She petitioned the court for a(n) (1), also called a(n) (2), to provide for her immediate financial needs. The family residence was protected because Enrique had qualified for the (3) under state law as the head of household or (4). Myrtle's state had abolished the common law right of (5), which was a right that a widow had, upon the death of her husband, to a one-third life estate in all real property owned by the husband during marriage. Because the will provided for her quite well, Myrtle decided to take under the will instead of a(n) (6) or (7) against the will. She would, therefore, not be known as a(n) (8). One of Enrique's (9) (lineal descendants), a son, Brad, was left out of his father's will, making him a(n) (10). Enrique's daughter, Katherine, died before Enrique, causing the gift to her in his will to be a(n) (11).

Because Katherine had no children, the state's (12) did not prevent the gift to Katherine from passing according to the will's residuary clause. Enrique's will left his boat and automobile to his son, Robert. The boat sank, however, in the accident that caused Enrique's death, and Enrique had already given the automobile to Robert before he died. Thus, the gifts in the will of the boat and automobile (13) (were extinguished), the former by (14) and the latter by (15).

■ KEY TERMS

adeemed	family allowance	lapsed legacies
antilapse statutes	forced heir	prenuptial agreement
curtesy	forced share	pretermitted child
dower	head of household	purchase money mortgages
exempt property	homestead exemption	satisfaction
extinction	lapsed devises	

Online Companion™
For additional resources, please go to
http://www.paralegal.delmar.cengage.com.

Student CD-ROM
For additional materials, please go to the
CD in this book.

Trusts

PART

3

Trusts

■ CHAPTER OUTLINE

■ CHAPTER OUTCOMES

- Define a trust.
- Name the parties to a trust.
- Compare the methods of creating a trust.
- Describe the different kinds of express and implied trusts.

■ JOB COMPETENCIES

- Be able to use correct terminology in the law office when referring to trusts.
- Be able to draft various testamentary and living trusts under the supervision of an attorney.
- Be able to identify implied trusts and make recommendations when they become issues in the law-office setting.

■ A DAY AT THE OFFICE . . .

Lisa Brewer, a legal secretary, entered the office of Tiffany Casey, a paralegal in the law firm of Knight and Francis.

"Hi, Tiffany," Lisa said. "Have you got a minute?"

"Sure. Come on in!"

"I'm working on a living trust for Attorney Fitz, that new attorney who just started Monday ..."

"Oh, yes, the young one who's working with Muriel Knight, right?"

"Yes. He's just out of law school," Lisa replied. "He went to court today with Attorney Knight, so I can't ask him about this trust."

"What's the problem?"

"Well, our client is naming his son as the sole trustee, and, according to the file, the son is a minor. I don't know if Mr. Fitz knows that."

"Who is the beneficiary?" Tiffany asked.

"The same son," Lisa answered. "He's the sole trustee and the sole beneficiary."

"It sounds like there may be a problem there," Tiffany countered. "You had better ask Mr. Fitz about it."

"I think I'll set it up the way Mr. Fitz told me to and print out a draft copy for him to look over tomorrow."

"That's a good idea," Tiffany agreed.

"You look busy today," Lisa observed.

"I am busy. Our client wrote his own will before he died. Listen to this: 'I leave $20,000 to my brother, Carl, and I desire that Carl take care of my sister, Diane, until she reaches the age of 25.' Attorney Knight wants me to research this to see if it creates a trust."

"It sounds interesting," Lisa observed.

"When I'm through with that, I have to go back to a trust that one of our clients had prepared years ago by another firm. The client wants to revoke it, and Attorney Francis put it on my desk with a note to go through the trust with a fine-tooth comb to see if it can be revoked."

"Do you think it can be?" Lisa queried.

"I've read it through once, and there is nothing that says that it's irrevocable," Tiffany responded, "but I haven't found anything that says it can't be revoked, either."

"Good luck, and enjoy your reading!"

Queries:

1. Why did Tiffany say to Lisa, "It sounds like there may be a problem there," when Lisa asked her about the trust?

2. What might Tiffany learn when she researches the problem of the testator leaving money to his brother with the desire that his sister be taken care of until she reaches the age of 25?

3. With the information Tiffany has discovered thus far, can the trust she was reading be revoked?

■ **settlor**

A person who sets up a
trust by providing money
or property for it.

■ **trustee**

A person who holds
money or property for the
benefit of another person
(see trust).

■ **beneficiary (cestui
que trust)**

(French) "He or she who."
For example, a cestui que
trust is a person who has a
right to the property,
money and proceeds being
managed by another. The
modern phrase is
"beneficiary of a trust."

■ **trust res**

Money or property set
aside in a trust or set aside
for special purposes. Also
known as *trust corpus*, *trust
principal*, *trust property*, or
trust fund.

§ 8.1 THE TRUST ARRANGEMENT

Paralegals who work with trusts need to be familiar with terminology that reflects the varied complexities of trust arrangements. Simply stated, a *trust* is an arrangement whereby a person called the **settlor** gives property to a **trustee** (one or more individuals) who holds the property in trust for the benefit of the **beneficiary (cestui que trust)** (one or more individuals) according to the terms of the trust instrument. The property held in trust is known by different names, including the **trust res**, the *trust corpus*, the *trust principal*, the *trust property*, and the *trust fund*. It may include cash, securities, real estate, and other property.

The law requires five elements for the creation of a valid trust. They are:

1. a trustee (also called a settler, or a grantor)

2. trust property

3. a valid trust purpose

4. a trustee

5. a beneficiary

Trusts may be superior to outright gifts or bequests for a variety of reasons, including:

1. The beneficiary may be incapable of receiving or managing the assets, either because of age or infirmity, and having a trustee manage the assets assures the benefit to the beneficiary.

2. Trusts may be multigenerational, guaranteeing to the settler that assets will last for several generations and not be spent by the first generation.

3. Trust property placed in the trust during the settlor's lifetime is not part of the settlor's estate at their death, and therefore, are not subject to will contestations and challenges.

4. If the settler is, by the trust, supporting an individual, the trust may pay taxes at the beneficiary's rate, which may be lower than the settlor's rate, depending on the comparative tax rates of the beneficiary and the settler.

§ 8.2 PARTIES TO A TRUST

The parties to a trust are the *settlor* (also known as the *trustor*, the *grantor*, or the *donor*), the trustee, and the beneficiary (or *cestui que trust*).

The Settlor

To be a settlor of a trust, a person must be competent. This means, generally, that the person must be capable of making a will or entering into a contract. A minor or someone who is insane, for example, would not have the capacity to be the settlor of a trust. In addition to being competent, a settlor must own the property that is to be placed in trust. When property is already held in trust, only the beneficiary has the power to establish another trust in the property.

The Trustee

A valid trust must have a provision for the office of trustee, but it is not necessary that someone be nominated for that position. The court will not allow a trust to fail for lack of a trustee. When no one is nominated or the nominee is deceased, incompetent, or declines the position, and no provision for a replacement is provided, the court has the power to appoint a trustee.

Generally, anyone having the capacity to manage his or her own affairs can be a trustee. This usually excludes someone under a legal disability, such as a minor, a mentally ill person, or a person under guardianship. It is interesting to note, however, that a minor could serve as a trustee and, upon reaching full age, ratify all acts done during minority. A trustee must also be a fit person to perform that task. Whether or not someone is fit to be a trustee lies in the discretion of the court. Banks often serve as trustees because of their investment expertise and probability of continued existence.

The sole trustee of a trust cannot be the sole beneficiary of that trust. However, a trustee can be a beneficiary by combining with other trustees or other beneficiaries. For example, a sole trustee can be a beneficiary if one or more additional beneficiaries are included. Similarly, a trustee can be a sole beneficiary if an additional person serves as a cotrustee. Table 8.1 summarizes these conditions.

TABLE 8–1   **Conditions for Trusteeship**

Rule	*Trustee*	*Beneficiary*
	Who May Be a Trustee	
1. One may be a sole trustee for another.	Oneself	Another person or persons

(continues)

TABLE 8–1   **Conditions for Trusteeship** *(continued)*

Rule	Trustee	Beneficiary
2. One may be a trustee with another for a third person.	Oneself and another person or persons	A third person
3. One may be a sole trustee for oneself and another.	Oneself	Oneself and another person or persons
4. One may be a trustee with another for oneself alone.	Oneself and another person or persons	Oneself
5. One may be a sole trustee for oneself for life if the trust property goes to another at death.	Oneself	Oneself for life; then another person or persons
6. One may be a sole trustee for another for the other's life with the trust property going to oneself at the other's death.	Oneself for another person's life	Oneself at the other person's death

Who May Not Be a Trustee		
1. One may not be a sole trustee for oneself alone.	Oneself	Oneself

Duties of Trustee

■ **fiduciary relationship**

Any relationship between persons in which one person acts for another in a position of trust; for example, lawyer and client or parent and child.

Trustees have a **fiduciary relationship** with their beneficiaries. This is a relationship of trust and confidence requiring the exercise of a high degree of honesty and good faith. Trustees must be loyal to their trust at all times: they cannot profit personally from the trust property; they cannot commingle trust property with their own property; they must treat their beneficiaries fairly; and they cannot delegate the management of the trust to others. Trustees must also keep accurate accounts, showing receipts and disbursements of principal and income. In addition, trustees must exercise reasonable care and prudence in the management of the trust property.

CASE STUDY		Matter of Estate of Ragan

541 N.W.2d 859(IA)

Facts	Dorothy Ragan died in January 1992. She had a will and codicil that named her son-in-law, John Tiffany, the trustee of the testamentary spendthrift trust she established in her will for her daughter, Donna Tiffany. Donna, the trust beneficiary, objected to the appointment of John as trustee. She contends that John is unsuitable to be trustee. Iowa law requires that trustees be qualified to serve. John also has been serving as conservator of a settlement of a lawsuit for his daughter, Pollyann Tiffany. The settlement amount was $19,000.
Legal Issue:	Is John qualified under statute to serve as the trustee of the testamentary trust?
Court Decision:	No.
Reason:	John had a history of questionable money management. Some $10,500 of the lawsuit settlement for his daughter was unaccounted for. He had signed a promissory note to the daughter for this amount, as he had probably used it for his own benefit. The court found that this mismanagement, combined with his total lack of understanding of the requirements of a trustee and his unwillingness to learn them, made him unsuitable to be trustee. The court also found that John's son, Brian Tiffany, who had been named as contingent trustee in Dorothy's will was dominated by John, and, therefore, was also unsuitable to be trustee.

Powers of Trustee

Although trustees have some implied powers and various powers provided by state statutes, the principal powers of a trustee are found in the "powers clause" of the instrument that created the trust. For this reason, trustees should be familiar with the trust instrument that created the trust under which they operate. Similarly, persons dealing with trustees may wish to examine the trust instrument to determine the extent of the trustees' power, especially when purchasing real property from a trustee.

The purposes of a trust can sometimes be thwarted by putting limitations on trustees, so some attorneys and estate planners recommend that settlors select their trustees carefully and then give them very broad powers to perform their duties. The following is an example of a broad powers clause that could be used in a testamentary trust.

Example

Trustee's Powers

17B AMJUR LF TR § 251:827

Trustee shall have the power to do all acts, institute all proceedings, and exercise all rights, powers, and privileges that an absolute owner of the trust property would have, subject always to the discharge of trustee's fiduciary obligations.

Cotrustees must usually join in all fiduciary activity unless a state statute or the trust instrument allows individual trustee action. This is because trustees' powers, like their title, are held jointly by cotrustees. Given the potential for disputes between cotrustees, having a single trustee, whenever possible, is advantageous and reduces the number of disputes and challenges.

The Beneficiary

A beneficiary is an essential party to a trust. Without one, a trust cannot exist. It is not necessary that a particular person be named as beneficiary; it is merely necessary that a beneficiary be capable of being identified and ascertained. At all times during the life of the trust, it must be possible to determine the person or persons for whose benefit the trust was created. The beneficiary need not be in existence when the trust is created. Thus, trusts for the benefit of unborn children are valid.

"TO MY BELOVED DOG, ROVER ..."

"TO MY BELOVED DOG, ROVER ..."

Although guppies, ferrets, pythons, horses, and cockatoos have been named, dogs and cats are the usual beneficiaries in the unusual bequests of pet lovers. Perhaps the largest canine inheritance was that from Eleanor Ritchey, heiress to the Quaker State Refining Corporation, who willed $4.5 million to her 150 dogs in 1968. By the time an agreement was reached with family members who had contested the will, the escrow estate had increased to $14 million. Seventy-seven of the dogs had died, but the remaining dogs were awarded $9 million, or $123,287.69 each for food, grooming, and housing. Two million dollars went to family members; the remainder served as legal fees. The Uniform Probate Code contains an optional provision for validating and limiting the duration of trusts for pets [UPC § 2–907].

Any person who is capable of owning property may be a beneficiary of a trust. Individuals of any age or capacity, corporations, and governmental bodies fall into that category. In some states, unincorporated associations may be beneficiaries; in other states, they may not because such associations are not legal entities. Beneficiaries are not always human beings. Trusts for the benefit of animals and for the upkeep of cemetery lots have been allowed by the courts.

A sole beneficiary of a trust may be a cotrustee with others, but may not be the sole trustee of that trust. When an instrument is drawn naming the sole trustee as the sole beneficiary, the trust fails, and the named trustee becomes the owner of the property outright. The reason for this outcome relates to the crucial distinction between legal title and equitable title, discussed in the next section.

§ 8.3 CREATION OF A TRUST

When a trust is established, the trustee receives the **legal title** to the property —that is, full and absolute ownership, but without a beneficial interest (i.e., without any personal gain or profit). The beneficiary, in contrast, holds what is designated as the **equitable title** (also known as *beneficial title*), which is the right to profit or benefit from the property.

A trust can be created either by a conveyance in trust or by a declaration of trust. In a conveyance in trust, the legal title moves away from the settlor to the trustee. In a declaration of trust, the legal title is retained by the settlor, who becomes the trustee.

Conveyance in Trust

When a trust is created by a **conveyance in trust**, the settlor transfers legal title to someone else—a trustee. The settlor may either retain the equitable title to the property or transfer it to someone else. By definition, whoever has equitable title is the beneficiary of the trust. A conveyance in trust is usually created by a trust agreement (a contract) between the settlor and the trustee. The trust agreement describes the trust property, gives directions for distribution of the principal and income, and spells out the duties and powers of the trustee.

Declaration of Trust

A **declaration of trust** is a trust in which the settlor transfers the equitable title to the trust property to someone else and retains the legal title (see Exhibit 8–1). It is often referred to as a *one-party trust*. The settlor declares that he or she is now holding the property in trust for the benefit of someone else—the beneficiary. The settlor thus becomes the trustee.

legal title
Full and absolute ownership without an equitable or beneficial interest.

equitable title
Ownership of a beneficial interest, with legal title belonging to another. Also known as *beneficial title*.

conveyance in trust
Trust created by a settlor's transfer of legal title to trust property to a trustee for the benefit of either the settlor or someone else.

declaration of trust
A written statement by a person owning property that said property is held for another person. This is one way of setting up a trust.

DECLARATION OF TRUST
[17B AMJUR LF TR § 251:827]

This declaration of trust made on _____, 2___, by _____ of [address], City of _____, County of _____, State of _____, hereinafter referred to as trustor.

Section One
Declaration of Trust

I, _____, as trustor, have assigned myself as trustee and hereby declare that I hold in trust the securities described in Schedule A attached hereto and incorporated herein by this reference, and that I and my successor trustee will hold such securities, and all substitutions therefor and additions thereto, as the trust estate, for the use and benefit of _____, of [address], City of _____, County of _____, State of _____, hereinafter referred to as beneficiary, for the following purposes and on the following terms and conditions:

Section Two
Purpose of Trust

Trustee shall receive and collect the income, profits, interest, and dividends from the trust estate and, after first deducting all taxes, commissions, and other charges against the same, shall pay the income to beneficiary during the period of his [or her] natural life up to _____, 2___.

Section Three
Termination of Trust

On _____, 2___, or on the death of beneficiary, whichever shall first occur, the trust hereby created shall terminate and the principal of the trust estate shall be paid to _____, of [address], City of _____, County of _____, State of _____, absolutely and free from any claim hereunder.

Section Four
Successor Trustee

On my death, resignation, or inability to act as trustee, I name _____, of [address], City of _____, County of _____, State of _____, as successor trustee hereunder, and such successor trustee shall have all the powers and discretions herein given trustee without any further conveyance or transfer of the trust estate.

Any determination of my inability to act as trustee hereunder shall be made (a) by an adjudication of my incompetency by a court of competent

EXHIBIT 8–1a   Sample Declaration of Trust
Courtesy of West Group

jurisdiction, or, in the absence of such adjudication, (b) by the delivery to successor trustee of a written certificate stating that for mental or physical reasons I am incapable of properly managing my business affairs, and executed by any physician currently attending me and by my [spouse and children] who are then living and legally competent. Successor trustee may rely conclusively on any such certificate.

Section Five
Powers and Duties of Trustee

1. *Resignation.* Any trustee may resign by giving _____ days' written notice to me or, if I am not then living or legally competent, by giving such notice to beneficiary. If no successor trustee has been appointed or designated by me hereunder, then beneficiary may appoint any bank or trust company as successor trustee.

2. *Acceptance of Accounts.* With my consent, or with beneficiary's consent if I am not then living or legally competent, any successor trustee may accept without liability the accounts rendered and the assets delivered to it by any predecessor trustee, and any such consent shall discharge the predecessor trustee.

3. *Statement of Receipts and Disbursements.* Trustee shall render a statement of its receipts and disbursements to me, whenever requested by me, and at least [annually] to beneficiary. After my death, beneficiary may approve at any time such statements with the same effect as their approval by a court of competent jurisdiction would have.

4. *Compensation.* The successor trustee herein named shall be entitled to reasonable compensation for services performed by him [or her], and shall be entitled to reimbursement for expenses incurred by him [or her] in the administration of the trust estate.

5. *Court Approval; Bond.* No trustee shall be required to obtain authority from, or the approval of, any court in the exercise of any power conferred upon him [or her] unless such authority or approval is specially required by law and may not be hereby waived.
No trustee, in the absence of an overriding statute or order, shall be required to furnish any bond or other security, or make any reports or accountings to any court.

6. *Specific Powers of Trustee.* Subject to the foregoing, trustee shall have the following specific powers with respect to the trust estate, in addition to the powers herein and by law conferred upon him [or her]: [enumerate specific powers].

EXHIBIT 8–1b Sample Declaration of Trust
Courtesy of West Group

Section Six
Powers Reserved to Trustor

I shall have the right from time to time during my lifetime, by written instrument delivered to the then-acting trustee, to amend or revoke this declaration of trust in whole or in part. However, if a trustee other than myself is serving hereunder, no amendment may change his, her, or its powers, duties, and discretions without such trustee's consent.

If, while I am acting as trustee, any asset of the trust estate is sold and the proceeds are not put in my name as trustee, or if any asset of the trust estate at any time is in my individual name, any such asset shall be conclusively deemed to have been withdrawn from the trust estate.

So long as I am living and legally competent, I shall have the right and power at any time to appoint any additional trustee or trustees, and to remove any trustee with or without the appointment of a successor.

If this declaration is revoked in whole or in part, the trust estate subject to such revocation shall be delivered to me or on my order.

Section Seven
Governing Law

This declaration of trust shall be governed by, and interpreted in accordance with, the laws of the State of _____.

IN WITNESS WHEREOF, I have executed this declaration of trust at [designate place of execution] on the day and year first above written.

[Signature of Trustor]

[Signature of Witness]

EXHIBIT 8–1c Sample Declaration of Trust
Courtesy of West Group

■ **parol**

Oral; not in writing. For example, parol evidence is oral evidence (the evidence a witness gives). It usually refers to evidence about an agreement's meaning that is not clear from the written contract.

Trust Formalities

Although trusts are usually created by some written document, such as a deed, a will, a trust agreement, or some other instrument, a writing is not always necessary to create a trust. **Parol** (oral) trusts dealing with personal property are generally enforceable. Some states require that notice be given to the beneficiary by the grantor when an informal, oral declaration of trust for personal property is made in order to establish the intent necessary to create a trust.

In contrast, trusts dealing with real property must be in writing under many state laws. For example, the Massachusetts statute reads: "No trust concerning land, except such as may arise or result by implication of law, shall be created or declared unless by a written instrument signed by the party creating or declaring the trust or by his attorney" [Mass. Gen. L. ch. 203, § 1].

§ 8.4 EXPRESS TRUSTS

Express trusts, sometimes referred to as **voluntary trusts**, are trusts that are created in explicit terms, either oral or written. No particular words, such as *trust* or *trustee*, are required to create an express trust. However, the intent to create a trust by the settlor is essential and must be evident. The intention that the legal title be vested in one person, to be held in some manner or for some purpose on behalf of another, must be apparent. To be valid, an express trust must include the following elements: (1) a competent settlor, (2) the provision for a trustee, (3) a trust res, and (4) one or more designated beneficiaries. The testamentary trust and the living trust are the most common forms of express trusts.

■ **express trusts**
A trust with terms stated in oral or written words.

■ **voluntary trusts**
With complete free will; intentional. In this sense, a voluntary trust is one set up intentionally, rather than imposed by law.

"GOODBYE, NORMA JEAN ..."

MARILYN MONROE

Before she died in 1962 at age 36 from an overdose of sleeping pills, the legendary actress Marilyn Monroe carefully provided for those closest to her. She established a trust of $100,000 to maintain the institutional care of her mentally ill mother. Neither of her famous ex-husbands (baseball star Joe DiMaggio or playwright Arthur Miller) were named in her will, nor did she have any children to endow. Instead, the major portion of her estate went to her acting mentor, Lee Strasberg; her psychiatrist, Marianne Kris, also inherited a share. Monroe's estate continues to receive more than $1 million a year in licensing fees for use of her image and other rights. The beneficiaries of the original inheritors receive the proceeds: Kris's share goes to a children's psychiatric institute in London, and Strasberg's portion goes to his surviving widow ... whom he married six years *after* Monroe's death.

Go to MarilynMonroe.com on the Net for more information about Marilyn. Her biography, including the titles of her films, images, quotes, poetry, memorabilia, and her will can be found at <http://ellensplace.net/marilyn.html>.

Testamentary Trusts

A **testamentary trust** is a trust in which the trust property is bequeathed or devised in a will to a trustee for the benefit of a beneficiary (see Exhibit 8–2). It is a conveyance in trust created by will and has no effect until the testator(rix) dies. The will must clearly express the testator(rix)'s intent to create a trust by separating the legal title from the equitable title and by conveying the legal title to a trustee for the beneficiary's benefit.

Like the will itself, a testamentary trust is under the control and supervision of the probate court after the death of the testator(rix). The trust becomes a matter of public record, open for anyone to see once the testator dies, and the trustee is required to file annual accounts with the probate court.

For a testamentary trust to become operative, the will must first be proved and allowed, and letters testamentary must be issued by the court. Next, the assets of the estate must be gathered by the executor(rix), and the debts, taxes, and costs of administration paid. Meanwhile, the person named in the will as trustee, or someone else if none is named, files a petition with the court to be appointed trustee. Many states require the filing of a bond when the trustee is appointed. Finally, the executor(rix) makes distribution of the estate assets by turning over to the trustee the property that is to be held in trust according to the directions given in the will. Thus, when there is a testamentary trust, the trustee's job begins when the executor(rix)'s job ends.

Sometimes a testator(rix) will leave money to someone in a will accompanied by a wish or desire that the legatee use the money in a particular way or for a particular purpose. When this happens, the question arises as to whether a trust was created by the *precatory* words: words of entreaty, request, or desire. If a trust was created, the "wish or desire" of the testator(rix) must be carried out; if a trust was not created, the request need not be carried out. A **precatory trust** is a trust that is created by words of entreaty, request, desire, or recommendation rather than by direct command.

A woman, for example, left a will that read:

> I give and bequeath unto my husband the use, income, and improvement of all the estate for and during the term of his natural life, in the full confidence that upon my decease, he will, as he has heretofore done, continue to give and afford my children such protection, comfort, and support as they may stand in need of.

In holding that there was a trust for the children, the court said:

> If the objects of the supposed trust are certain and definite, if the property to which it is to attach is clearly pointed out, if the relations and situation of the testator and the supposed cestuis que trust are such as to indicate a strong interest and motive on the part of the testator in making them partakers of his bounty, and above all, if the recommendatory or precatory clause is so expressed as to warrant the inference

TESTAMENTARY TRUST
FOR A DEVELOPMENTALLY DISABLED CHILD
[17B AMJUR LF TR § 251:363]

PARAGRAPH _____
SPECIAL NEEDS TRUST

I give the sum of _____ Dollars ($ _____) to _____ [trustee], in trust, to be administered and distributed for the benefit of my child _____ [name] in accordance with the following provisions:

1. *Introduction.* It is my primary concern in drafting this testamentary trust that it continue in existence as a supplemental fund to public assistance for my handicapped child, the beneficiary, throughout _____ [his or her] life, as I would provide if I were personally present. Currently there are basic living needs, such as _____ [for example: dental care and outdoor recreation], not provided for by public benefit programs for the developmentally disabled. It is important that my child continue to have access to such programs in order to maintain a level of human dignity and receive humane care. If this trust were to be invaded by creditors, subjected to any liens or encumbrances, or cause public benefits to be terminated, it is likely that the trust corpus would be depleted prior to my child's death, especially since the cost of care for developmentally disabled persons, exclusive of emergency needs, is high. In this event, there would be no coverage for emergencies or supplementation for basic needs. The following trust provisions should be interpreted in light of these concerns and my stated intent.

2. *Special needs.* The trustee shall pay to or apply to the benefit of my child, _____, for _____ [his or her] lifetime, such amounts from the principal or income, up to the whole, as the trustee in its discretion may from time to time deem necessary or advisable for the satisfaction of my child's special needs. Any income not distributed will be added to principal. As used in this instrument, the term "special needs" refers to the requisites for maintaining my child's good health, safety, and welfare when, in the sole discretion of the trustee, such requisites are not deemed provided by any public agency, office, or department of _____ [state], or of any other state, or of the United States. "Special needs" include, but are not limited to, medical and dental expenses, clothing and equipment, programs of training, education, treatment, and essential dietary needs.

3. *Spendthrift.* No interest in the principal or income of this trust shall be anticipated, assigned, or encumbered or shall be subject to any creditor's claim or to legal process, prior to its actual receipt by my child. Furthermore, because this trust is to be conserved and maintained for the special needs of my developmentally disabled child throughout life, no part of the corpus of it, neither principal nor undistributed income, shall be

EXHIBIT 8–2a Sample Testamentary Trust Paragraph in a Will
Courtesy of West Group © 2001

construed as part of my child's "estate" or be subject to the claims of voluntary or involuntary creditors for the provision of care and services, including residential care, by any public entity, office, department or agency of _____ [state], or any other state, or the United States, or any other governmental agency.

4. *Public beneifits.* It is my express intent, that because my child is developmentally disabled and unable to maintain and support _____ [himself or herself] independently, the trustee shall, in the exercise of its best judgment and fiduciary duty, seek support and maintenance from all available public resources including Supplemental Security Income (SSI), _____ [state medical assistance program], Social Security Disability Insurance (SSDI), and the appropriate Regional Center for the developmentally disabled. In making distributions for the special needs defined herein, trustee must take into consideration the applicable resource limitations of the public assistance programs for which my child is eligible. In carrying out the provisions of this article, the trustee must be mindful of the probable future needs of the remainderman of this trust. All public assistance benefits and all earnings for any beneficiary of any trust provided for in this will shall not be commingled with other trust assets but shall be separately held by the trustee. Nothing in this provision shall be construed to require the addition to the trust estate of either public assistance benefits or earnings received by, or on behalf of, any beneficiary.

5. *Supplemental.* No part of the corpus of this trust is to be used to supplement or replace public assistance benefits of any county, state, federal, or other governmental agency having a legal responsibility to serve persons with disabilities that are the same or similar to the impairment or impairments of my child. For purposes of determining the beneficiary's eligibility for any such program, no part of the principal or undistributed income of the trust estate shall be considered available to my child. If the trustee is requested to release trust principal or income to pay for equipment, medication, or services which any such program is authorized to provide were it not for the existence of this trust, or, if the trustee is requested to petition the court or any administrative agency for the release of trust principal or income for that purpose, the trustee is authorized to deny the request and is further authorized in its discretion to take whatever steps, administrative or judicial, as may be necessary to continue eligibility. Such steps may include obtaining instructions from a court of competent jurisdiction and a ruling that the trust corpus is not available to my child for eligibility purposes. Any expenses of the trustee in this regard, including attorney fees, are a proper charge to the trust estate.

6. *Termination.* This trust shall terminate on the death of my child and thereupon the trustee shall distribute and deliver all of the principal and income of the trust estate to the surviving issue of that child, by right

EXHIBIT 8–2b   Sample Testamentary Trust Paragraph in a Will

Courtesy of West Group © 2001

of representation. In the event my child leaves no surviving issue, the remainder of this trust estate shall go to my then-living issue, by right of representation.

7. *Backstop.* Notwithstanding anything to the contrary contained in the other provisions of this trust, in the event that the existence of this trust has the effect of rendering my child ineligible for Supplementary Security Income (SSI), _____ [state medical assistance program], or any other program of public benefits, the trustee is authorized but not required to terminate this trust. The undistributed balance of the trust estate is to be distributed, free of trust, to my then-living issue, other than _____ [beneficiary], by right of representation. It is my wish that the distributee or distributees conserve, manage, and distribute the proceeds of the former trust estate for the benefit of my child, _____ [beneficiary], in accordance with Paragraph 3 of this document. This request is precatory, not mandatory. In determining whether the existence of the trust has the effect of rendering my child ineligible for SSI, _____ [state medical assistance program], or any other program of public benefits, the trustee is granted full and complete discretion to initiate either administrative or judicial proceedings, or both. All costs relating to such proceedings, including attorney fees, are a proper charge to the trust estate.

8. *Expenses.* On the death of my child, _____ [beneficiary], trustee may pay any inheritance, estate, or other death taxes that may be due regarding assets passing in accordance with these provisions or otherwise, all expenses of the last illness and funeral, and expenses related to the administration and distribution of the trust estate if, in the trustee's discretion, other satisfactory provisions have not been made for the payment of those expenses. The trustee shall make no payments for obligations incurred for my child's health, support, and maintenance if the trustee determines, in its discretion, that payment is the obligation of any county, state, federal, or other governmental agency which has a legal responsibility to serve persons with disabilities which are the same or similar to those of the beneficiary herein.

EXHIBIT 8–2c Sample Testamentary Trust Paragraph in a Will
Courtesy of West Group © 2001

that it was designed to be peremptory on the donee, the just and reasonable interpretation is that a trust is created that is obligatory and can be enforced in equity as against the trustee by those in whose behalf the beneficial use of the gift was intended.

Although words such as *wish, request,* and *desire* have been held to be commands creating a precatory trust in some wills, in other cases (like the *McReynolds* one) these same words have been considered only recommendations.

CASE STUDY   **Estate of McReynolds**

800 S.W.2d 798 (MO)

FACTS:	Stanley Hope McReynolds's will left all of his estate in trust for the support of his father and, upon his father's death, to "Rev. Herbert W. Armstrong ... and I request that said legatee shall use the money so received by him in the promotion and furtherance of his Radio Ministry and the spreading of the Gospel as he may see fit, and the Trust shall terminate." Mr. McReynolds's father and the Rev. Armstrong both died before the testator. The will contained no provision for the disposition of the trust property in the event both beneficiaries predeceased the testator. The church contended that the language used in the will created a charitable trust for the church rather than a gift to the Rev. Armstrong for his own personal use.
LEGAL ISSUE:	Does the word "request" standing alone in a will create a precatory trust?
COURT DECISION:	No.
REASON:	A trust is not lightly imposed on mere words of recommendation and confidence when property is given absolutely. A testator's use of the word "request" does not necessarily create a precatory trust, and it never does unless a plain intention appears to create a trust in other parts of the will. Similarly, a charitable trust is created only if the testator manifests an intention that the property be held subject to a legal obligation to devote it to purposes that are charitable. Because both beneficiaries predeceased the testator, the gift in trust lapsed, and the trustee held the trust property in a "resulting trust" for the testator's heirs under the law of intestate succession.

Living Trusts

■ living trust

An ordinary (regular or usual) trust as opposed to one created under a will upon death. Inter vivos (Latin) for "between the living." Also known as an *inter vivos trust.*

A **living trust**, also known as an *inter vivos trust*, is a trust that becomes effective during the settlor's lifetime. It is created by either a conveyance in trust or a declaration of trust (see Exhibit 8–1). A living trust may be funded or unfunded while the settlor is alive. Unlike a testamentary trust, a living trust is not under the control and supervision of the probate court and is not a matter of public record, unless the trust must be recorded to establish title to real property. The lack of court supervision and the element of privacy are considered important advantages of a living trust. Living trusts may be either revocable or irrevocable. See Table 8.2 for a brief overview of living trusts.

TABLE 8–2 **Living Trusts**

Created during lifetime Assets avoid probate	
Revocable	**Irrevocable**
• Can be changed or canceled during lifetime	• Cannot be changed or canceled
• Assets included in taxable estate	• Assets generally not included in taxable estate

Revocable Living Trust

A **revocable living trust** is a living trust in which the settlor retains the right to alter, amend, or revoke the trust during the settlor's lifetime. When the settlor dies, the dispositive provisions of the trust take effect, and the trust then becomes irrevocable. The right to revoke a trust does not survive the settlor's death. Because of its flexibility, a revocable living trust is a commonly used device by estate planners. Such a trust has no tax-saving advantages, however, and is therefore not used for that purpose.

A trust can be altered, amended, or revoked only if the power to do so is expressed in the trust instrument. For that reason, a clause such as the following is essential to make a living trust revocable.

■ **revocable living trust**

Living trust in which the settlor retains the right to alter, amend, or revoke the trust during the settlor's lifetime.

Example

Revocation of Trust

17B AMJUR LF TR § 251:963 and § 251:968

Trustor shall have the right at any time to revoke this trust in whole or in part by [provide method of revocation, such as: an instrument in writing executed by trustor and delivered to trustee].

Amendment of Trust

Trustor, at any time, may alter, amend, or modify any or all of the terms and conditions of this trust instrument by [provide method of amendment, such as: written notice signed by trustor and delivered to trustee].

Settlors can put all of their property into a revocable living trust, receive the income during their lifetime, and give the principal, through the trust instrument, to whomever they designate upon their death. Property that is held in trust does not belong to the settlor's estate; it is owned by the trust, as the trustee has legal title to it. By using trusts, in some states, people can avoid homestead awards and prevent other types of family allowances from being taken from their estate. Homestead awards and family allowances were discussed in Chapter 7.

When the settlor of a revocable living trust wishes to revoke the trust, he or she should notify the trustee in writing to that effect. Although no special words are necessary, a letter such as the one in the following example may be used to notify the trustee of the settlor's intention to revoke the trust. Revocable living trusts can be useful and are popular with older Americans concerned with temporary incapacities or loss of function. With this type of trust they can transfer management of their asset trusts to the contingent trustee, then regain control their affairs as soon as they are able.

Example

Notice to Trustee of Revocation of Trust

17B AMJUR LF TR § 251:1139

To , trustee under a trust instrument, dated , between of [address], [city], County, [state], as trustor, and of [address], [city], County, [state], as trustee:

Pursuant to the right reserved to me as trustor under the described trust instrument, I hereby revoke the trust [in its entirety or if a partial revocation, as to the following-described property:]. I direct that you transfer and deliver all your right, title, and interests to and in the trust property to me.

Dated:

[Signature of trustor]

Irrevocable Living Trust

■ **irrevocable living trust**

Living trust that cannot be revoked or amended by the settlor once it has been established.

An **irrevocable living trust** is a living trust that cannot be revoked or amended by the settlor once it has been established. A trust is irrevocable unless the trust instrument contains a statement that it can be revoked. To make the intent of the settlor clear, however, practitioners usually put the following clause in an irrevocable trust.

Example

Disclaimer of Power to Revoke or Amend

17B AMJUR LF TR § 251:976

This trust shall be irrevocable and shall not be subject to amendment or modification.

The principal advantage of an irrevocable trust is the elimination of the trust property from the settlor's gross estate for federal estate tax purposes. In addition, income from trust property may be shifted from the settlor to the trust itself, which may be in a lower tax bracket than the settlor. The principal disadvantage of an irrevocable trust is that it cannot be changed once it has been established.

Pour-Over Trust

A **pour-over trust** is a provision in a will in which the testator leaves a gift (often the residue of the estate) to the trustee of an existing living trust (see Exhibit 8–3). When the testator(rix) dies, the assets of the estate pour into the existing trust, and are distributed according to the directions contained in the living trust. Although a pour-over trust receives its assets from a will after the death of the settlor, such a trust is considered to be a living trust rather than a testamentary trust because the trust comes into existence while the settlor is alive. In addition, the details of the trust, including the trustee's rights and duties, are contained in the trust instrument rather than in the will.

■ **pour-over trust**
Provision in a will in which the testator(rix) leaves a gift to the trustee of an existing living trust.

**PROVISION IN WILL
FOR "POUR-OVER" TO INTER VIVOS TRUST
[17B AMJUR LF TR § 251:345]**

PARAGRAPH _____
DIVISION OF RESIDUE

All the residue of my estate I give to _____ [name], or _____ [his or her or its] successor in trust, referred to as trustee, as trustee of that trust created under an agreement into which I entered with trustee, the terms of which are set forth in a written instrument dated _____. I direct that the residue of my estate be added to the principal of that trust to be administered, invested, and distributed as a part of the principal of that trust, according to its terms, including any amendments made to it prior to my death, or which may be made to it subsequent to my death.

It is my intent that this provision not create a separate trust or subject the _____ trust, or the property added to it, to the jurisdiction of any probate court.

If the disposition made in this trust is invalid or inoperative, or if the _____ trust has failed or been revoked at the time of my death, then I give the residue of my estate to _____ [name] in trust, to be held, administered, and distributed as follows: _____.

EXHIBIT 8–3   Sample Provision for Pour-Over Trust

Some years ago, a legal problem existed when a living trust was amended after the execution of a will containing a pour-over provision. Some courts held that the pour-over provision was invalid because the living trust had been amended but the will had not. Other courts took an opposite viewpoint. To avoid the conflict, many states have adopted the Uniform Testamentary Additions to Trusts Act [Mass. Gen. L. ch. 203, § 3B]:

> A devise or bequest, the validity of which is determinable by the laws of this state, may be made to the trustee or trustees of a trust established or to be established by the testator or by the testator and some other person or persons or by some other person or persons, including a funded or unfunded life insurance trust, although the trustor has reserved any or all rights of ownership of the insurance contracts, if the trust is identified in the will and the terms of the trust are set forth in a written instrument executed before or concurrently with the execution of the testator's will or set forth in the valid will of a person who has predeceased the testator, regardless of the existence, size or character of the corpus of the trust. The devise or bequest shall not be invalid because the trust is amendable or revocable, or both, or because the trust was amended after the execution of the will or after the death of the testator. Unless the will provides otherwise, the property so devised or bequeathed (a) shall not be deemed to be held under a testamentary trust of the testator, but shall become a part of the trust to which it is given and (b) shall be administered and disposed of in accordance with the provisions of the instrument or will setting forth the terms of the trust including any amendments thereto made before or after the death of the testator. A revocation or termination of the trust before the death of the testator shall cause the devise or bequest to lapse.

§ 8.5 IMPLIED TRUSTS

■ **implied trusts**
A trust that exists by analyzing surrounding circumstances or the action of person(s) involved; a trust known indirectly by the words of another person. Also known as *involuntary trusts*.

Implied trusts, also called *involuntary trusts*, come about by operation of law rather than by the express terms of the settlor. Sometimes, an implied trust comes into existence when an express trust cannot. For example, an express trust for real property requires a writing; an implied trust for real property has no writing requirement. There are two kinds of implied trusts: resulting trusts and constructive trusts.

Resulting Trusts

■ **resulting trust**
A trust created by law (rather than by agreement) for reasons of fairness when one person holds property for another.

A **resulting trust** is a trust that is implied from the intentions of the parties that the person holding legal title is holding it for another's benefit. One of the most common ways that a resulting trust occurs is when one person pays for something and title is placed in another's name.

Resulting trusts also occur when express trusts fail for some reason, or when a fiduciary uses fiduciary funds to buy something and takes title in his or her own name individually. A resulting trust does not occur when the present intent of the person paying for the property is to make a gift of it to the person in whose name the property is placed.

CASE STUDY	*Rainey v. Rainey*
	795 S.W.2d 139 (TN)
FACTS:	William J. Rainey and John R. Rainey, who were brothers, agreed to buy a farm, each agreeing to pay half the purchase price and each owning a one-half interest in the farm. Notwithstanding the agreement, title to the property was taken in the names of J. R. Rainey and Tommy Ray Rainey (John's son). In addition, John paid the entire purchase price for the property. When John died, a dispute arose over the ownership of the farm.
LEGAL ISSUE:	Does a resulting trust arise when property is purchased with the money of one person and title is taken in the name of another person?
COURT DECISION:	Yes.
REASON:	When property is purchased with the money of one person but the title is taken in the name of another, a resulting trust arises. The title holder becomes a trustee for the payor. John supplied the consideration necessary to create a resulting trust in Tommy Ray as his trustee. As a result, John's heirs owned the property when John died.

Constructive Trusts

A constructive trust is a trust that is created by operation of law when someone obtains legal title to property through fraud or other wrongdoing. To avoid unjust enrichment, the court imposes a trust on the person holding legal title, declaring that title is held for the benefit of the one to whom title should belong. In general, the elements that are necessary to establish a constructive trust are: a confidential or fiduciary relationship, a promise by one of the parties, a transfer by the other party in reliance on the promise, and unjust enrichment.

CASE STUDY *Halbersberg v. Berry*

394 S.E.2d 7 (SC)

FACTS:	David Halbersberg entered into an oral partnership with William and Catherine Berry to manufacture and sell neon t-shirts and to share the expenses and profits equally. The parties agreed to lease land on Myrtle Beach, build a building on it to use as a retail outlet, and to rent part of it out. Halbersberg paid the contractor $10,000 toward the construction cost of the building. William Berry paid the contractor the balance and took the lease in his own name. Berry then excluded Halbersberg from the partnership, leased the property out but shared no income with Halbersberg, and made no attempt to return the $10,000.
LEGAL ISSUE:	Does a constructive trust arise when one partner leases property and excludes the other partner from partnership income?
COURT DECISION:	Yes.
REASON:	A constructive trust arises against one who, by fraud, duress, abuse of confidence, commission of a wrong, or any form of unconscionable conduct, either has obtained or holds the right to property that he ought not in equity and good conscience hold and enjoy. Constructive trusts are resorted to in equity to vindicate right and justice or to frustrate fraud. The court held that the partnership agreement had been breached by Berry. The court imposed a constructive trust on the lease income for the benefit of Halbersberg.

SUMMARY

A trust is an arrangement whereby a person called the settlor gives property to a trustee, who holds the property in trust for the benefit of the beneficiary according to the terms of the trust instrument.

To establish a trust, a person must be competent and own the property that is to be placed in trust. The court will not allow a trust to fail for lack of a trustee. Generally, anyone having the capacity to manage his or her own affairs can be a trustee. Trustees have a fiduciary relationship with their beneficiaries and must exercise a high degree of honesty and good faith. The principal powers of a trustee are found in the trust instrument. Without a beneficiary, there can be no trust, and the beneficiary must be capable of being identified and ascertained at all times, even though it need not be in existence. A sole beneficiary may not be a sole trustee; however, a sole beneficiary may be a cotrustee with others.

When a trust is established, legal title is held by one person for the benefit of another person who holds equitable title. In a conveyance in trust, the settlor transfers legal title to a trustee and either retains the equitable title or transfers it to someone else. In a declaration of trust, the settlor transfers the equitable title to someone else and retains the legal title. Except for real property, a writing is not always necessary to create a trust.

No particular words are necessary to create an express trust; however, the intent to create a trust by the settlor is essential. A testamentary trust is under the control and supervision of the probate court, whereas a living trust is not. A trust can be altered, amended, or revoked only if the power to do so is expressed in the trust instrument. An irrevocable living trust has tax-saving advantages; however, it cannot be changed once it has been established. Although a pour-over trust receives its assets from a will after the death of the settlor, it is considered to be a living trust rather than a testamentary trust.

A resulting trust occurs when one person pays for real or personal property and title is placed in another's name. A constructive trust occurs when someone obtains legal title to property through fraud or other wrongdoing.

■ REVIEW QUESTIONS

1. What happens to legal title to the trust property when a trust is created (a) by a conveyance in trust? (b) by a declaration of trust?

2. In what way do the requirements for trusts dealing with personal property differ from those dealing with real property, in many states?

3. To be valid, what elements must an express trust include?

4. Describe the process that must occur for a testamentary trust to become operative and receive trust assets.

5. What three words have been held to create a precatory trust in some wills, but only recommendations in others?

6. In what two ways may a living trust be created?

7. When may a trust be altered, amended, or revoked?

8. What is the principal advantage of an irrevocable trust?

9. How does a resulting trust differ from a constructive trust?

10. When may a trustee also be a beneficiary?

■ CASES TO DISCUSS

1. Maude Keyes paid the full purchase price for a Chevrolet Monte Carlo, but was unable to obtain liability insurance in her name. For that reason, the certificate of title named her son, George W. Keyes, as the owner of the car, and Maude was listed as a lien holder. The car was insured in George's name. When George died, his estate claimed the car. Was his estate entitled to it? Why or why not? *Keyes v. Keyes,* 392 S.E.2d 693 (WV).

2. Before his death, Paul Overmire transferred all of his separate property into a revocable living trust. A bank was named trustee and Paul was to receive the income of the trust during his life. Upon his death, $100,000 of the trust funds were to remain in trust for the benefit of his son by a previous marriage. The balance of the fund was to remain in trust, with the income going to his wife, Sadie, and upon her death, the principal to the Red Cross. Sadie petitioned the court for an award in lieu of homestead of $25,000 and asked that it be charged to the trust, because there were apparently no other funds in the estate. Was Sadie entitled to the $25,000 from the trust? Why or why not? *Estate of Overmire v. Red Cross,* 794 P.2d 518 (WA).

3. Larry Mendal, a 38-year-old college graduate with a degree in economics, lived and worked on his parents' farm. He was befriended by the Hewitts, who were also farmers, and with whom he had transacted farming business. After the death of his parents, Mendal looked to the Hewitts for advice and guidance, and a relationship akin to that of parent and child developed. Mendal alleges that he acceded to the Hewitts' advice to sell his family farm and transfer a large amount of money to the Hewitts to invest in the purchase of another farm as a joint venture with them. Later, Mendal learned that title to the other farm had been conveyed solely to the Hewitts. On what legal grounds might Mendal obtain relief? Explain. *Mendal v. Hewitt,* 555 N.Y.S.2d 899 (NY).

■ RESEARCH ON THE WEB

1. On the Internet, go to Crash Course in Wills and Trusts at <http://www. mtpalermo.com>. Click *Contents,* then scroll down to Comparing Simple Living Trusts and Wills. Write a report on your findings.

2. Log on to the Internet and type in <http://www.Google.com>. Then, in the Google search space, type in the word *trusts.* You will find many items of interest about the subject matter of trusts.

■ SHARPENING YOUR PROFESSIONAL SKILLS_____

1. Does the law of your state require trusts dealing with real property to be in writing? If so, give the statutory reference or case citation where the provision is found.

2. If you have access to a law library, use 17B AMJUR LF TR § 251:341–374 as a guide in drafting the following testamentary provisions:

   a. A trust providing income to someone for life with a reversion to the residuary estate.

   b. A pour-over to an *inter vivos* trust.

   c. A trust for a former spouse pursuant to a property settlement.

   d. A gift of $50,000 in trust for the care, maintenance, and support of a pet cat.

3. Draft a revocable trust agreement in general form. (If you have access to a law library, use 17A AMJUR LF TR § 251:114 as a guide.)

4. Use the facts from the following client information sheet to prepare wills that would meet the requirements of the statutes in your state for Thomas Arthur Scanlon and his wife, JoDee Scanlon:

   a. Names in full: Thomas Arthur Scanlon and JoDee Scanlon

   b. Residence: 2 Brierwood Lane (Home town), (Home state), (zip code)

   c. Children: Jaimie Melissa Scanlon, age 6
                       Abby Jean Scanlon, age 2
                       Taylor Ryan Scanlon, age 2

   d. Disposition of estate: Everything to the surviving spouse. If the spouse is not living, everything in equal shares to the children by right of representation. Testamentary trust for children for support, maintenance, and education; trust estate to be given outright to the children when all children have reached 22 years of age

   e. Executor: Surviving spouse

   f. Alternate: Matthew A. Brown, in each will

   g. Guardian: Surviving spouse

   h. Alternate: Matthew A. Brown, in each will

5. Refer to the will of Elvis Presley (reproduced in Appendix B) and answer the following questions:

   a. What legal term describes the type of trust created in Item IV?

   b. When did the trust come into existence?

   c. Who has control and supervision of the trust?

   d. Name the person or persons who have legal title to the property under the trust.

   e. Name the person or persons who have equitable title to the property under the trust.

6. Refer to the will of Jacqueline K. Onassis (reproduced in Appendix B) and describe the unique way in which Ms. Onassis provided for the children of her sister Lee B. Radziwill.

7. Who are appointed trustees of the trusts created under: (a) Paragraph A of Article SECOND; (b) Paragraph A of Article FIFTH; (c) subparagraph B(3) of Article FIFTH; and (d) Article SIXTH of the will of Jacqueline K. Onassis (reproduced in Appendix B)?

8. What legal term describes the type of trust created in the will of John Lennon (reproduced in Appendix B)?

9. Describe the unusual way in which ARTICLE FOUR (C) of the will of Richard M. Nixon (reproduced in Appendix B) placed the bequests to his grandchildren in trust.

10. How did Doris Duke provide for her dog in Paragraph TWO (G)(3) of her will (reproduced in Appendix B)?

■ SHARPENING YOUR LEGAL VOCABULARY_____

On a separate sheet of paper, fill in the numbered blank lines in the following anecdote with legal terms from this list:

> beneficial title
>
> beneficiary
>
> cestui que trust
>
> constructive trust
>
> conveyance in trust
>
> declaration of trust
>
> donor
>
> equitable title
>
> express trust
>
> fiduciary relationship
>
> grantor
>
> implied trust
>
> *inter vivos* trust
>
> involuntary trust
>
> irrevocable living trust
>
> legal title
>
> living trust
>
> parcel
>
> pour-over trust
>
> precatory trust
>
> resulting trust
>
> revocable living trust
>
> settlor

testamentary trust

trust

trust corpus

trustee

trust fund

trustor

trust principal

trust property

trust res

voluntary trust

   With his winnings from the state lottery, Anton bought a new house and a Lincoln Continental. A fast-talking investment counselor, through fraudulent means, obtained title to the car, but Anton's lawyer got the car back by showing that the counselor held the car in a(n) (1), which is a type of involuntary or (2). Still smarting from that experience, Anton decided to put his house in his sister Babs's name so that people would not know about his wealth. He also decided to set up a(n) (3), which is an arrangement under which title to property is divided into two parts: (4) and (5) (also known as beneficial title). Anton was the (6), also known as the (7), the (8), and the (9). Because Anton was alive when the arrangement came into existence, it was known as a(n) (10) or a(n) (11). Because it was not within the body of a will, it was not a(n) (12), and in view of the fact that it was not created by words of entreaty, request, desire, or recommendation, it was not a(n) (13). Technically, the arrangement was a(n) (14) because Anton transferred beneficial title to his wife, Celeste, and retained legal title to the property, which is also called the (15), the (16), and the (17). Anton was the (18) and Celeste was the (19) or (20). Anton's will contained a provision leaving a gift to the person who had legal title, creating a(n) (21). Because the instrument contained language stating that it could never be revoked, it was called a(n) (22). When Anton died, Babs claimed the house as hers, but the court decided otherwise. The judges said that there was a(n) (23), because Anton had paid the entire purchase price for the property.

■ KEY TERMS

beneficiary (cestui que trust)	irrevocable living trust	revocable living trust
conveyance in trust	legal title	settlor
declaration of trust	living trust	testamentary trust
equitable title	parol	trust res
express trusts	pour-over trust	trustee
fiduciary relationship	precatory trust	voluntary trusts
implied trusts	resulting trust	

Online Companion™
For additional resources, please go to
http://www.paralegal.delmar.cengage.com.

Student CD-ROM
For additional materials, please go to the
CD in this book.

9

Specialized Trusts

■ CHAPTER OUTLINE_____

■ CHAPTER OUTCOMES_____

- Describe a Totten trust.—

- Determine when to use a spendthrift trust and when to use a sprinkling trust.

- Compare assorted marital deduction trusts and the use of each.

- Describe several types of charitable trusts and discuss the use of each.

- Explain the use of a life insurance trust as a way to save taxes.

■ JOB COMPETENCIES_____

- Be able to determine whether the money in a Totten trust bank account is probate or nonprobate property when preparing an estate inventory.

- Be able to draft spendthrift and sprinkling provisions when preparing trusts under the supervision of an attorney.

- Be able to draft marital deduction, charitable, and life insurance trusts under the supervision of an attorney.

▄ A DAY AT THE OFFICE . . .

Tiffany Casey, a paralegal in the office of Knight & Francis, is called into Attorney Knight's office where she is introduced to Mr. and Mrs. DeNunzio, a middle-aged couple.

"We're going to do some estate planning for the DeNunzios, and I'd like you to help them with the estate planning questionnaire," Attorney Knight explains to Tiffany.

"I'll be glad to," Tiffany replies. "The questionnaire is quite complicated."

"Our lives are quite complicated, too," Mrs. DeNunzio interrupts. "We just won the state lottery!"

"Congratulations!" Tiffany exclaims.

"We've only been married for two years, but we were both married before," Mrs. DeNunzio volunteers. "I have six children from my first marriage, and Angelo has eight children from his first marriage."

"That is some family!"

"If I die first, I want Angelo to have enough to live comfortably, but I want my own children to inherit my money. Angelo wants his children to inherit his money, too," Mrs. DeNunzio continues as Angelo looks on quietly.

"We might consider using a special type of trust that will qualify for the marital deduction and save a considerable amount of taxes for your estate," Attorney Knight suggests.

"Good," Mrs. DeNunzio answers. "Right now I have a bank account for each of my children in my name in trust for each child. Will the children get that money if I die?"

"We'll review your bank accounts when we have all the information together, and develop a plan that will be suitable for both of you," Attorney Knight answers.

"Good," Mrs. DeNunzio answers, "Angelo has a daughter who goes through money like water over a dam. If she inherits from Angelo, it won't last very long."

"Tiffany," Attorney Knight suggests, "why don't you take Mr. and Mrs. DeNunzio into your office and go over the estate-planning questionnaire with them? Then you can set up an appointment for us to meet again when we have the information we need."

"Fine," Tiffany replies, ushering Mr. and Mrs. DeNunzio to her office.

Queries:

1. What type of trust might be considered to give the survivor of Mr. and Mrs. DeNunzio a suitable income, while retaining the principal for the children?
2. What is the answer to Mrs. DeNunzio's question about the bank accounts in her name in trust for each child?
3. What might Attorney Knight consider as a way to handle the problem of Angelo's daughter, who spends money "like water over a dam"?

§ 9.1 TOTTEN TRUST

Paralegals who work with trusts must be familiar with a variety of trusts and need to know what type of trust is most suitable in a particular situation. Some of the specialized trusts with which paralegals often work include Totten trusts, spendthrift trusts, sprinkling or spray trusts, marital deduction trusts, charitable trusts, and life insurance trusts. As in the case of Mrs. DeNunzio, people may open bank accounts in their own names "in trust" for someone else, without signing any other trust instrument. The trust that is created when this happens is known as a Totten trust (from a 1904 New York case, *In re Totten*, 71 N.E. 748 (N.Y. 1904)). A Totten trust is a savings bank account in the name of the depositor as trustee for another person. The depositor may withdraw money from the account at any time during the depositor's lifetime. When the depositor dies, the money in the account belongs to the beneficiary, as shown in the *Adams* case. If the beneficiary dies before the depositor, however, the trust terminates; the money belongs to the depositor, not the beneficiary's estate. Totten trusts are not true trusts, because they lack the normal trustee and beneficiary, and the creator has total control over the funds. As trustee in name only, the funds in a Totten trust are subject to claims of creditors of the person who opened the Totten trust.

CASE STUDY	*In Re* Estate of Adams
	587 A.2d 958 (VT)
FACTS:	Bertha Mae Adams deposited her own money in her own name in the Troy Savings Bank "as trustee for Evelyn Lindquist," her daughter. Adams died without making any changes to the bank account.
LEGAL ISSUE:	Does a bank account opened by a depositor in trust for another belong to the depositor's estate when the depositor dies?
COURT DECISION:	No.
REASON:	A deposit of one's own money in one's name as trustee for another is a tentative trust only, revocable at will, until the depositor dies. When the depositor dies before the beneficiary, there is a presumption that an absolute trust was created. This was a valid Totten trust. Evelyn Lindquist was entitled to the balance in the account, not Adams's estate.

§ 9.2 SPECIAL-PURPOSE TRUSTS

There are many types of trusts that are used for special purposes. Among them are spendthrift trusts and sprinkling or spray trusts.

Spendthrift Trusts

A **spendthrift** is a person who spends money profusely and improvidently. A **spendthrift trust** is a trust containing a provision that protects the assets of the trust from creditors and from the beneficiary's reckless spending. With such a provision in a trust, the principal and interest of the trust cannot be reached by creditors until they are received by the beneficiary, and the beneficiary cannot assign the principal and interest before receiving them. Without such a provision, a beneficiary for whom money is being held in trust could take the trust instrument to a bank, borrow on it, and assign the rights to the money to the bank as collateral for the loan.

The restrictions imposed by the spendthrift trust are described in the following provision.

■ **spendthrift**

A person who spends money wildly and whose property the state may allow a trustee to look after.

■ **spendthrift trust**

A trust set up for the protection of a person's property against himself, or creditor. These trusts are also set up privately through wills and trusts to enable one person to give money or property to another without fear that it will be squandered.

Example

Spendthrift Trust Provision

16B AMJUR LF SP T § 237:17

Every beneficiary of this trust is restrained from anticipating, assigning, transferring, selling, or otherwise disposing of his or her interest in the trust estate, and every beneficiary is without power to anticipate, assign, transfer, sell, or otherwise dispose of his or her interest in the trust estate. No such anticipation, assignment, transfer, sale, or other disposition shall be recognized by the trustee, nor shall any attempted anticipation, assignment, transfer, sale, or other disposition by a beneficiary of an interest in the trust estate pass any right, title, or interest to the trust estate. No interest of the beneficiaries under the trust shall be subject to the claims of creditors or other persons, nor to any bankruptcy proceeding, nor to any other liabilities or obligations of any beneficiary.

Sprinkling Trusts

A **sprinkling trust**, which is also known as a *spray trust*, gives the trustee the power to determine how the trust's income or principal or both are to be allocated among a group or class of beneficiaries. This type of trust is also called a *discretionary trust*, because trustees are allowed to use their own discretion in distributing principal and income to the beneficiaries. Trustees have the power to "sprinkle" or "spray" the trust income and principal among the people who are most needy or in a way that will save taxes.

An advantage of this type of trust is that when the trust is established, the settlor does not have to decide specifically who will receive the income and principal. The trustee makes that decision at a later time when the circumstances of potential beneficiaries are better known. Funds can be distributed according to need. The trustee can also take advantage of the tax brackets of the different

■ **sprinkling trust**

A trust that gives income to many persons at different times. Also known as a *spray trust* or *discretionary trust*.

beneficiaries when distributing income, and thereby save income taxes. In addition, estate taxes can often be reduced. Another important advantage of a sprinkling trust is that the spendthrift provision is built in: the trustee can control allotments to a beneficiary who spends money profusely and improvidently.

A disadvantage of a sprinkling trust is that the trustee has ultimate control. Before choosing to use a sprinkling trust, a settlor should trust and respect the prospective trustee greatly: the trustee, not the settlor, will decide exactly who will benefit from the trust within the general group or class of people that the settlor chooses. These types of trusts lend themselves to actions against the trustee for favoritism. The use of a provision like the following in a trust instrument creates a sprinkling trust.

Example

Sprinkling Trust Provision

17B AMJUR LF TR § 251:264

Trustee shall hold, manage, invest, and reinvest the trust estate, and shall apply and distribute the income and principal of the trust as follows:

(a) Distribution of income. Trustee shall pay to or apply for the benefit of my children, herein referred to as income beneficiaries, at least annually, and in such proportions as trustee in its absolute discretion may from time to time determine, all of the net income of the trust estate.

(b) Invasion of principal. At any time and from time to time and notwithstanding any other provision of this agreement, trustee may, in its absolute discretion, in addition to any other payments provided for in this agreement, pay to or apply for the benefit of income beneficiaries such amounts as trustee may, in its absolute discretion, elect from the principal of the trust estate.

(c) Further disposition of trust estate. Income beneficiaries' interests in the trust estate, as provided in subparagraphs (a) and (b) hereof, shall terminate when the youngest beneficiary reaches the age of 30 years. The trust estate shall thereupon be paid and distributed as follows: In equal shares to my issue then living by right of representation.

(d) Shares of income beneficiaries. Payments made to each of income beneficiaries pursuant to this section need not be equal.

§ 9.3 MARITAL DEDUCTION TRUSTS

Under federal estate tax laws, property passing from a decedent to a surviving spouse is not taxable. Instead, it is deductible from the decedent's taxable estate and is known as the **marital deduction**. A trust that is designed to make optimal use of the marital deduction is called a marital deduction trust. A **marital deduction trust** may distribute property to a surviving spouse in various ways, including: (1) an outright gift, (2) a life estate with a general power of appointment, (3) a credit-shelter trust, and (4) a qualified terminable interest property (QTIP) trust.

■ **marital deduction**
The amount of money a wife or husband can inherit from the other without paying estate or gift taxes.

■ **marital deduction trust**
Trust designed to make optimal use of the federal tax marital deduction.

CASE STUDY   *In re* Stoppick's Will

6 Misc.2d 876(NY)

Facts:	Testator Stoppick created a sprinkling trust for the benefit of his minor grandchildren with his residuary estate. The trust was to be paid to the beneficiaries in equal proportion when the oldest grandchild reaches the age of 21 years. The residual estate was apportioned between the testator's wife, who was to receive 80 percent of the residual estate, and the trust, which received the other 20 percent.
Legal Issue:	Are after-born grandchildren entitled to participate in the sprinkling trust established by the testator?
Court Decision:	Yes.
Reason:	The law provides that after-born issue are entitled to the proceeds of a sprinkling trust. However, after-born children are not entitled to accumulations that occurred prior to their birth. Therefore, the grandchildren in existence on the date of death will share the entire trust until the birth of an after-born grandchild, who will share in the trust but not be entitled to profits prior to his or her birth.

Distribution Outright

Sometimes settlors wish to give the entire trust corpus outright to a surviving spouse when they die. This can be done through a simple clause in the trust, such as "Upon the settlor's death, the trustee shall distribute all principal and income, outright and free of trusts, to the settlor's surviving spouse."

The surviving spouse thereby receives full access to and control of the trust property and qualifies for the full estate tax marital deduction. However, choosing this option makes the entire trust property part of the surviving spouse's estate, which may be subject to probate when the surviving spouse dies and become taxable at that time. In addition, the surviving spouse, not the settlor, will have the power to decide who will be the ultimate beneficiaries of the trust property.

Life Estate with Power of Appointment

Another way to qualify for the marital deduction is to leave property in trust to the surviving spouse for life and, upon the spouse's death, to whomever the surviving spouse appoints in a will. This can be done with either a living trust or a testamentary trust.

Example

Testamentary Trust Provision for Spouse

17B AMJUR LF TR § 251:351

With Limited Power of Appointment

PARAGRAPH _____

DIVISION OF RESIDUE

I give the residue of my estate to the trustee, in trust, to be administered, paid or applied as follows:

A. The net income of the trust shall be paid to my [husband or wife] for [his or her] life. If my [husband or wife] does not survive me, the property shall be distributed to my then living children or the issue of any deceased child, *per stirpes*, but if none survive me then to [name].

B. Following the death of my [husband or wife], trustee shall pay and divide the principal and income of the trust estate among my children and the issue of any deceased child, *per stirpes*, in such shares as my [husband or wife] shall by will appoint and subject to such provisions as are set forth in [his or her] will. In default of such appointment, and so far as any appointment extends to persons other than my children living at my death and the issue of any deceased child of mine, the principal and income of the trust shall be paid, in equal shares, to my children. The issue of any deceased child of mine shall take *per stirpes* such share as such child of mine would have taken if then living.

In the preceding trust provision the will leaves the residue of the estate in trust for the surviving spouse to receive the income from the trust for life. Upon death, the trust ends, and the principal of the trust is distributed among the children in whatever fractions are set forth in the surviving spouse's will. To qualify for the marital deduction, the trust, however, must meet specific requirements found in the Internal Revenue Code.

Credit-Shelter Trust

■ **credit-shelter trust**
Trust under which a deceased spouse's estate passes to a trust rather than to the surviving spouse, thereby reducing the possibility of the surviving spouse's estate being taxable. Also called an *A-B trust*, a *bypass trust*, or an *exemption equivalent trust*.

In a **credit-shelter trust**, also known as an *A-B trust*, a *bypass trust*, or an *exemption equivalent trust*, a deceased spouse's estate passes to a trust rather than to the surviving spouse. This strategy reduces the possibility of the surviving spouse's estate being taxable (a drawback noted earlier in the discussion of an outright distribution).

Assume, for example, that a married couple's total assets are several million dollars. The husband dies, leaving everything to his wife. There will be no federal estate tax because of the 100 percent marital deduction. However, when the wife subsequently dies, the amount in her estate that exceeds that year's estate tax exemption will be subject to the estate tax. The tax may be avoided by using a credit-shelter trust.

Under a credit-shelter trust, the will of the first spouse to die leaves the amount that is exempt from the federal estate tax to an irrevocable credit-shelter trust called Trust A. Trust A provides income for the surviving spouse for life; upon that spouse's death, the corpus of Trust A passes to other named beneficiaries, such as children or grandchildren. In addition, the will of the first spouse to die leaves an equal amount to Trust B for the benefit of the surviving spouse, allowing it to qualify for the marital deduction and, therefore, not be taxable. When the second spouse dies, the amount in Trust A is not part of his or her estate and, therefore, is not subject to the estate tax. The only item that is subject to the estate tax is the money in Trust B, but it also is not taxable because it does not exceed the estate tax exemption.

Example

A-B Trust

17B AMJUR LF TR § 251:401

DIVISION OF RESIDUE

In the event that my [husband or wife], [name], survives me, I give to my trustee, [name], to hold and administer as a separate trust, to be designated "Trust A," the marital trust, an amount equal to [fifty] percent of the value of my adjusted gross estate as that term is defined in the Internal Revenue Code, minus the value of any other assets that qualify for the marital deduction allowable in determining the federal estate tax payable with respect to my estate. I specifically empower my trustee to satisfy the transfer to Trust A in cash or in kind, or partly in cash and partly in kind. For purposes of the transfer, any assets distributed in kind shall be valued at their value as finally determined for federal estate tax purposes. My executor shall, consistent with equitable principles requiring impartiality between legatees, act impartially in allocating assets to the satisfaction of the transfer to Trust A for my [husband or wife] so that any noncash distribution or satisfaction shall be made of assets that are fairly representative of appreciation or depreciation in the value of all property thus available for distribution.

Trust B, the residuary trust, shall be equal to the balance of the residue as reduced by Trust A.

QTIP Trust

A third type of trust that qualifies for the marital deduction is a QTIP trust. This type of trust is used when the settlor wants to pass the entire principal of the trust to someone other than the surviving spouse, but wants the spouse to have the income from the trust for life. A **qualified terminable interest property (QTIP)** trust gives all trust income to the surviving spouse for life, payable at least annually. During the surviving spouse's lifetime, no one can appoint the trust property to anyone other than the surviving spouse. This type of trust must also meet specific requirements found in I.R.C. § 2056(b)(7).

■ **qualified terminable interest property (QTIP)**

Trust that gives all trust income to the surviving spouse for life, payable at least annually, and which meets the requirements of I.R.C. § 2056(b)(7).

Suppose, for example, that a woman has three children by her first husband and no children by her second husband to whom she is still married. She wants her children to inherit her property if she dies before her husband, but also wants her husband to live comfortably for the rest of his life. If the estate is large enough to produce sufficient income, a QTIP trust would be appropriate, because the husband would benefit, but would be restricted to the income from the trust for his life. Upon his death, the principal would pass intact to the three children.

An interesting aspect of a QTIP trust is that the decision to actually use the QTIP provision is made after the death of the decedent, even though the trust is created before death. The decedent's executor elects to treat the property as qualified terminable interest property on the estate tax return. Otherwise, the property does not qualify as a QTIP. The executor has the option to either elect or not elect to have the QTIP trust qualify for the marital deduction. The estate planner can look at the circumstances that exist at death, rather than at the time the trust is executed, to make the final decision. Such flexibility makes the QTIP trust an advantageous option in postmortem planning.

§ 9.4 CHARITABLE TRUSTS

■ **charitable trust**

A trust set up for a public purpose such as to support a school, church, or charity. Also called a *public trust.*

A **charitable trust**, sometimes called a *public trust,* is a trust in which the property held by the trustee must be used for public charitable purposes. A charitable trust is created for the benefit of a part of the general public rather than for an individual or designated group of individual persons. In a charitable trust, the actual beneficiaries are indefinite and unascertainable. Such trusts are established for religious, charitable, scientific, or educational purposes, or the like. Because no particular individual can benefit from a charitable trust, no one person can bring suit to enforce the trust. For this reason, charitable trusts are enforced by the attorney general of the state where they are established. Gifts to charities, in general, are exempt from the federal estate tax; however, to be exempt, the recipient of the gift must qualify as a charity under the rules found in I.R.C. §§ 2055 and 2106(a)(2).

■ **cy pres**

(French) "As near as possible." When a dead person's will can no longer legally or practically be carried out, a court may (but is not obligated to) order that the dead person's estate be used in a way that most nearly does what the person would have wanted. The doctrine of *cy pres* is now usually applied only to charitable trusts.

Cy Pres Doctrine

When money or property is left in trust to a charity, and the charity ceases to exist, does the trust also end? Under the doctrine of *cy pres,* which means "as near as possible," if the court finds that the settlor had a general charitable intent, the trust fund will be turned over to another closely related charity. If instead the court finds that the settlor had a specific intent to benefit one charity exclusively, and that charity ends, the trust will also be discontinued, and the trust property will revert to the settlor's heirs. In the *Crawshaw* case, the use of *cy pres* was considered appropriate, and the court allowed a substitution.

In the *Incurables of Baltimore* case, the court followed the doctrine of *cy pres* in making its decision to award Dr. Coggins' bequest to the Keswick Multi-Care Center. The court said in that case:

> The *cy pres* statute directs a Maryland court to salvage a bequest for charity and administer the bequest as nearly as possible in accordance with the testator's intent if, at the time it becomes effective, the bequest "is illegal, or impossible or impracticable of enforcement," as long as "the settlor or testator manifested a general intention to devote the property to charity. ...

> As previously pointed out, the purpose of the *cy pres* statute was to save some charitable bequests that would have failed under prior law. ... Furthermore, where the gift over is also to a charity, it would seem that the testator's general charitable intent is confirmed.

CASE STUDY **Matter of Estate of Crawshaw**

806 P.2d 1014 (KS)

FACTS: After making specific bequests totaling $350 to family members, Chester D. Crawshaw's will left 15 percent of the residue of his estate to the Salvation Army and 85 percent in trust to Marymount College in Salina, Kansas, for school loans to nursing students and other students. If for some reason Marymount College could not accept and administer the trust, the will provided that the bequest go in trust to "the official Board or Association of said college having the legal capacity to accept and administer the herein created trust." One month after Crawshaw died, Marymount College terminated its existence. The Marymount Memorial Educational Trust Fund was established by the college and the Roman Catholic Bishop to administer this and other scholarship funds.

LEGAL ISSUE: Does the doctrine of *cy pres* apply when a testator leaves the bulk of his estate to a named college to provide loans to nursing and other students and the college ceases operation?

COURT DECISION: Yes.

REASON: Under Kansas law, the doctrine of *cy pres* permits a court to implement a testator's intent and save a testamentary charitable gift by substituting beneficiaries only when these conditions are met: First, the gift must be to a charitable organization for a charitable purpose. Second, it must be impossible, impractical, or illegal to carry out the donor's stated charitable purpose. Finally, it must appear that the donor had a general charitable intent. All three requisites are met in this case, and the use of *cy pres* is appropriate.

Rule Against Perpetuities

One feature of a charitable trust is that the rule against perpetuities does not apply: this means that charitable trusts can exist indefinitely, unlike private trusts. Under the common-law **rule against perpetuities**, every interest in property is void unless it must vest, if at all, not later than 21 years plus the period of gestation after some life in being at the time of creation of the interest. For example, if a settlor left money in trust for the settlor's children and then for the lives of the settlor's grandchildren, the rule would be violated, because the grandchildren could include children of an as-yet-unborn child of the settlor, and this might occur more than 21 years after the death of all currently living beneficiaries. Thus, the trust would be void.

The rule against perpetuities has been subject to much criticism and has been changed by statute in many states. Some states have revised the rule to provide that property interests must vest either no later than 21 years after the death of an individual who is alive at the time the interest is created or within

A BENEVOLENT BUSINESSMAN

CONRAD N. HILTON

There is a natural law, a Divine law, that obliges you and me to relieve the suffering, the distressed and the destitute. Charity is a supreme virtue, and the great channel through which the mercy of God is passed onto mankind. It is the virtue that unites men and inspires their noblest efforts.

"Love one another, for that is the whole law"; so our fellow men deserve to be loved and encouraged— never to be abandoned to wander alone in poverty and darkness. The practice of charity will bind us, will bind all men in one great brotherhood.

Conrad N. Hilton was not only an astute businessman who built a worldwide hotel empire; this gentle-looking man was also a compassionate philanthropist, as shown by this excerpt from his will, which was addressed to the directors of the Hilton Foundation. Hilton began the Foundation in 1944 as a trust, then later transferred its assets to a nonprofit corporation. When Hilton died in 1979, the foundation received much of his wealth (over $180 million) to support his philanthropic ideals: "to alleviate human suffering," particularly among disadvantaged children, and to promote the human services activities of the Catholic Sisters worldwide.

90 years of such creation. Under the revised rule, in the preceding example, the trust would not be void if the money would vest in the settlor's grandchildren within 90 years of the trust's creation. In any event, if the settlor left money in trust to a charitable institution, there would be no time limit and the trust could continue for many generations.

Charitable Remainder Trusts (CRATS and CRUTS)

A **charitable remainder trust** is a trust in which the settlor, or a beneficiary, retains the income from the trust for a period of time (usually for life), after which the trust principal is given to a charity. Settlors can use part of such gifts as deductions on their federal income tax returns, thereby increasing their total earning power. In addition, the gift to charity may be deducted from the settlor's federal estate tax. Charitable remainder trusts may be in the form of an annuity trust or a unitrust (see Exhibit 9–1).

Annuity Trusts

A **charitable remainder annuity trust (CRAT)** is a trust in which a fixed amount of income is given to a beneficiary at least annually, and the entire remainder is given to charity. Under Internal Revenue Service (IRS) regulations, the beneficiary must receive annually at least five percent of the amount that was initially given to the trust. The amount can never change, regardless of the needs of the beneficiary or economic inflation. If the income of the trust is insufficient to meet the required annual payment, the difference must be paid from the principal of the trust. If the income of the trust is more than the required payment, the difference remains in the trust. When IRS requirements are met, the settlor receives an income tax deduction for the contributions made to the trust, based on an IRS formula.

■ **charitable remainder trust**

Trust in which the settlor or a beneficiary retains the income from the trust for a period of time (usually for life), after which the trust principal is given to a charity.

■ **charitable remainder annuity trust (CRAT)**

Trust in which a fixed amount of income is given to a beneficiary at least annually, and the entire remainder is given to charity.

Example

Charitable Remainder Annuity Trust Payment Clause

4B AMJUR LF CHAR § 55:9

PAYMENT OF ANNUITY AMOUNT

The Trustee shall pay to [a living individual] (referred to as "the Recipient") in each taxable year of the Trust during the Recipient's life an annuity amount equal to % [at least five] of the net fair market value of the assets of the Trust as of this date. The annuity amount shall be paid in equal quarterly amounts from income and, to the extent income is not sufficient, from principal. Any income of the Trust for a taxable year in excess of the annuity amount shall be added to principal. If the net fair market value of the Trust assets is incorrectly determined, then within a reasonable period after the value is finally determined for federal tax purposes, the Trustee shall pay to the

How You can Receive an Income for Life and Support The Salvation Army:

The Charitable Gift Annuity

A Salvation Army Gift Annuity gives our donors an income for life while making an important investment in the physical, spiritual, and emotional well-being of people who need a helping hand.

○ Frequently a donor names him/herself as the income beneficiary. However, he or she can arrange for someone else - a spouse, another family member or a friend - to benefit from this program.

○ The donor transfers a gift of cash or appreciated securities to The Salvation Army for a Charitable Gift Annuity and receives payments on a monthly, quarterly or semi-annual basis.

○ The donor/income beneficiary receives regular payments for life. When the last income beneficiary is deceased, The Salvation Army uses the remaining principal to help others.

○ There are tax benefits. A portion of the amount a donor transfers is deductible as a charitable gift. Part of each payment a donor and/or beneficiary receives is tax-free.

○ The size of each payment depends on a combination of factors including the amount of cash and/or appreciated securities which funds the annuity and the age of the donor/beneficiary(s) when the annuity is created. Single-life annuity rates range from 6.3% for a 50 year old donor to 12% for a 90 year old donor.

○ Payments are always *guaranteed* and they will always be exactly the same amount for the rest of the beneficiary's life.

ILLUSTRATION

Mrs. Jones, who is 75 years old, transfers $10,000 to a Salvation Army Gift Annuity:

● she receives an 8.2% rate of return or $820.00 per year,

● of that amount, $451.82 is considered tax free income for the course of her life expectancy,

● her charitable contribution deduction is $4,400.90 in the year the gift was made,

● her payments continue, *guaranteed*, for the rest of her life.

EXHIBIT 9–1 Sample Gift Annuity Features

Courtesy of the Salvation Army

Recipient (in the case of an undervaluation) or receive from the Recipient (in the case of an overvaluation) an amount equal to the difference between the annuity amount(s) properly payable and the annuity amount(s) actually paid.

Unitrusts

A **charitable remainder unitrust (CRUT)** is similar to an annuity trust, but does not require the payment of a fixed amount each year to an income beneficiary. Instead, the income beneficiary must receive a fixed percentage—not less than five percent—of the value of the trust property, which is determined annually (see Exhibit 9–2). A unitrust is in effect a type of variable annuity: it offers protection against inflation because the beneficiary's income increases as the value of the trust property increases.

Example

Charitable Remainder Unitrust Payment Clause

4B AMJUR LF CHAR § 55:15

PAYMENT OF UNITRUST AMOUNT

In each taxable year of the trust, the Trustee shall pay to [relation, such as: my wife], [name of life income beneficiary] (the "Recipient"), during [his or her] lifetime, the Unitrust Amount, which shall be equal to % of the net fair market value of the trust assets as of the first day of each taxable year of the trust (the "Valuation Date").

These types of trusts are referred to as "split interest trusts." They provide the benefits of the charitable deduction while providing for other beneficiaries.

§ 9.5 LIFE INSURANCE TRUSTS

If carefully prepared, a life insurance trust may be used to pass money to heirs tax free. First, an irrevocable trust is established; then the trustee purchases a life insurance policy on the settlor's life. The settlor contributes a certain amount of money each year to the trust, which is used by the trustee to pay the premiums on the policy. When the settlor dies, the proceeds of the insurance policy are paid to the trust. If the trust contains Crummey powers (described later), the settlor's spouse may receive the income from the trust for life; upon the spouse's death, the principal passes tax free to the settlor's heirs.

Crummey powers (named from the case of *Crummey v. Commissioner*, 397 F.2d 82 (9th Cir. 1968)), give one or more of the trust beneficiaries the right to withdraw each year the money that is contributed to the trust. The withdrawal

■ **charitable remainder unitrust (CRUT)**

Trust in which a percentage—not less than five percent—of the value of the trust property is determined annually and given to a beneficiary, with the entire remainder going to charity.

■ **crummey powers**

Powers that give trust beneficiaries the right to withdraw each year the money that is contributed to the trust.

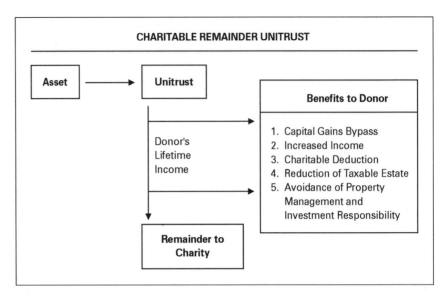

EXHIBIT 9–2   Charitable Remainder Unitrust Structure

amount is usually the amount of the contribution to the trust or the amount of the annual gift tax exclusion ($11,000 per donee, adjusted annually for inflation), whichever is less. Because the contribution may be withdrawn, it is considered a present interest and qualifies for the gift tax annual exclusion. Without these special Crummey powers of withdrawal, the payment of insurance premiums to a trust would normally be considered a taxable gift, not a gift of present interest, and not eligible for the annual gift tax exclusion.

Example

Crummey Withdrawal Provision in Irrevocable Trust

17B AMJUR LF TR § 251:191

The beneficiary shall have the right during each calendar year, upon making written demand upon the trustee therefore, to receive from the trustee outright and free from this trust all or any part of any property transferred or added to such trust by way of *inter vivos* gift during such calendar year. The trustee shall give the beneficiary notice of any such transfer within 10 days of such transfer. However, in no event shall the trustee honor any such demand that exceeds the sum of $_____ per donee in one calendar year. The trustee shall honor any such demand in cash or in kind, in the discretion of the trustee, immediately upon receipt by the trustee of the written demand of the beneficiary. Such payment shall be made from the property transferred to the trust by each donor during that year.

Trust funds must be sufficient to allow for the Crummey withdrawals. Therefore, gifts to an otherwise unfunded trust to pay insurance premiums should be held in trust until the demand period has elapsed. Of course, with this type of trust, the settlor and the beneficiaries would probably want the withdrawal power to lapse each year so that the money could be used to pay the insurance premiums (see Exhibit 9–3).

REVOCABLE TRUST AGREEMENT
[17A AMJUR LF TR § 251:114]

Trust agreement made on _____ [Date], between _____, of _____ [address], _____ [city], _____ County, _____ [state], referred to as trustor, and _____, of _____ [address], _____ [city], _____ County, _____ [state], referred to as trustee.

In consideration of the mutual covenants and promises set forth in this agreement, trustor and trustee agree:

SECTION ONE
TRUST ESTATE

Trustor assigns, transfers, and conveys to trustee the property described in the attached Exhibit _____, which is incorporated by reference, and the receipt of which property is hereby acknowledged by trustee. The property shall be held by trustee in trust on the terms and conditions set forth below.

SECTION TWO
REVOCATION AND AMENDMENT

Trustor reserves the right at any time, by an instrument in writing delivered to trustee _____ [if appropriate, add: and acknowledged in the same manner as a conveyance of real property entitled to be recorded in _____ [state], unless acknowledgment is waived by trustee], to revoke or amend this trust in whole or in part. The duties and liabilities of trustee shall under no circumstances be substantially increased by any amendment of this agreement except with its written consent.

SECTION THREE
ADDITIONS TO TRUST ESTATE

Trustor reserves the right for _____ [himself or herself] or any other person to increase this trust by delivering property to trustee, by having the proceeds of insurance policies made payable to trustee, or by bequest or devise by will. Trustor will notify trustee in writing of any policies made payable to it or will deliver the policies to trustee as custodian. Trustee's

---

EXHIBIT 9–3a General Form of a Revocable Trust Agreement
Courtesy of West Group ©2001

duties and liabilities under this agreement shall under no circumstances be substantially increased by any such additions, except with its written consent.

SECTION FOUR
DISPOSITION OF INCOME AND PRINCIPAL

After paying the necessary expenses incurred in the management and investment of the trust estate, including compensation of trustee for its own services, trustee shall pay the net income of the trust and distribute the principal of the trust in the following manner: _____ [provide for payment of income and distribution of principal of trust].

SECTION FIVE
INVASION OF PRINCIPAL FOR BENEFIT OF TRUSTOR'S SURVIVING SPOUSE AND DESCENDANTS

After trustor's death, trustee may apply so much of the principal of the trust for the use of trustor's _____ [spouse], _____, and trustor's descendants, or any of them, at such time or times as in trustee's discretion it may deem advisable for their proper education, care, or support. The provisions of this section are intended primarily as a means of affording financial assistance to trustor's _____ [spouse] and children in the event of their serious illness, misfortune, or other emergency or unusual condition, and also to assist _____ [his or her] descendants during the period of their education or setting up in business or at the time of their marriage. This enumeration is to serve only as a guide and shall not be construed to restrict the discretionary powers so conferred on trustee. Any amounts so applied to the use of trustor's _____ [spouse] or any descendant shall be charged against, or deducted from, the principal of any share then, or thereafter, set apart for such _____ [spouse] or descendant.

SECTION SIX
DISTRIBUTIONS TO MINORS

Trustee in its discretion may make payment of income or principal applicable to the use of any minor by paying the same to the parent or guardian of the minor, or to any other person having the care and control of the minor, or by expending it in such other manner as trustee in its discretion believes will benefit the minor, provided, that trustee may also pay as an allowance directly to the minor such sums as trustee may deem advisable. Trustee may accumulate for the benefit of any minor so much of any income applicable to the minor's use as trustee in its discretion may deem advisable. Any income so accumulated shall be paid to the minor on his or her attaining majority. Trustee in its discretion may make payment of principal vesting in and payable to a minor, to such minor's parent or guardian, or may defer payment of any part or all of the amount

EXHIBIT 9–3b   General Form of a Revocable Trust Agreement
Courtesy of West Group ©2001

until the minor attains majority, meanwhile applying to the minor's use so much of the principal and income, and at such time or times, as in its discretion it may deem advisable for the minor's proper education, care, or support. Any payment under this section shall operate as a full discharge to trustee with respect to the payment.

SECTION SEVEN
POWERS OF TRUSTEE

_____ [Set forth trustee's powers, as desired.]

SECTION EIGHT
TRANSACTIONS WITH THIRD PERSONS

No person or corporation dealing with trustee shall be required to investigate trustee's authority for entering into any transaction or to administer the application of the proceeds of any transaction.

SECTION NINE
DIVIDENDS

Regular or ordinary cash dividends, although they may be wholly or partly in the nature of a payment in partial liquidation or may wholly or partly represent a distribution of assets of the corporation other than surplus earnings, shall nevertheless be treated wholly as income of the trust. All other liquidating dividends shall be principal. All dividends payable in the stock of the corporation or association declaring or authorizing the same shall be treated as principal. All other extraordinary dividends shall be apportioned between principal and income, as determined by trustee in its absolute discretion.

SECTION TEN
COMPENSATION OF TRUSTEE

_____ [Provide for trustee's compensation or waiver of compensation.]

SECTION ELEVEN
REMOVAL AND RESIGNATION OF TRUSTEE

Trustee may be removed at any time by trustor or after trustor's death by _____ [designate] by written notice to trustee. Trustee may resign by written notice to trustor during trustor's lifetime or after trustor's death to _____. Until the accounts of trustee are settled and trustee is discharged, trustee shall continue to have all the powers and discretions granted to it under this agreement or conferred by law. In the event of the removal or resignation of trustee, trustor or _____ may by written instrument appoint a successor trustee. The successor trustee, on executing a written acceptance of the trusteeship and on the settlement of

EXHIBIT 9–3c   General Form of a Revocable Trust Agreement
Courtesy of West Group ©2001

the accounts and discharge of the prior trustee, shall be vested, without further act on the part of anyone, with all the estate, title, powers, duties, immunities, and discretions granted to the original trustee.

SECTION TWELVE
EMPLOYMENT OF AGENTS: EXPENSES OF TRUST

Trustee may employ agents, including counsel, and pay them reasonable compensation. Trustee shall be entitled to reimbursement therefor and for all other reasonable expenses and charges of the trust out of principal or income, as trustee shall determine.

SECTION THIRTEEN
GOVERNING LAW

This trust shall be governed and construed in all respects according to the laws of _____ [state].

SECTION FOURTEEN
BINDING EFFECT

This agreement shall be binding on trustor, trustor's executor, administrator, successors and assigns, and trustee and trustee's successors and assigns.

In witness whereof, trustor and trustee have executed this agreement at _____ [designate place of execution] the day and year first above written.

[Signatures]

[Acknowledgments]

[Attach exhibit]

EXHIBIT 9–3d   General Form of a Revocable Trust Agreement
Courtesy of West Group ©2001

SUMMARY

A Totten trust is a savings account in the name of the depositor as trustee for another person. The depositor may withdraw money from the account at any time during the depositor's lifetime. When the depositor dies, the money in the account belongs to the beneficiary. If the beneficiary dies before the depositor, the trust terminates, and the money belongs to the depositor.

Spendthrift trusts are used to prevent beneficiaries who spend money profusely or unwisely from having access to trust funds until they are due. Sprinkling trusts give the trustee, rather than the settlor, the power to decide who will receive the trust income and principal.

Property passing to a surviving spouse, called marital deduction property, is not taxable under federal estate tax laws. The deduction may be obtained by an outright gift to the surviving spouse; however, when that spouse dies, his or her estate may be large enough to be taxable. Another way to obtain the deduction is by giving a life estate to the surviving spouse and allowing that spouse to determine who will inherit when he or she dies. This is called a power of appointment. A third way to use the marital deduction is to establish a credit-shelter trust, which passes the deceased spouse's property to a trust for the spouse's benefit (using the estate tax exemption) and any balance to the spouse outright, qualifying for the marital deduction. A QTIP trust gives the income of the trust to the surviving spouse for life, tax free, payable annually, with the balance left intact for whomever the settlor designates.

Charitable trusts are created to benefit a part of the general public rather than individuals and are free of federal estate taxes. Under the doctrine of *cy pres*, if a charity comes to an end and the settlor had a general charitable intent, the trust fund will be turned over to a similar charity. Charitable trusts, unlike private trusts, can exist indefinitely, as exceptions to the rule against perpetuities. A charitable remainder annuity trust provides a fixed amount of income annually to a beneficiary, with the corpus going ultimately to a charity. In contrast, a charitable remainder unitrust offers protection against inflation by providing a percentage (not less than five percent) of the value of the trust property each year to a beneficiary, with the corpus going ultimately to a charity.

A life insurance trust may be used to pass money to heirs tax free if the trust contains Crummey powers, that is, powers given to beneficiaries to withdraw the money that is contributed to the trust.

■ REVIEW QUESTIONS

1. In a Totten trust, who is entitled to the money when the depositor dies before the beneficiary? When the beneficiary dies before the depositor?

2. When would a settlor use a spendthrift trust?

3. Why is a discretionary trust also called a sprinkling or spray trust?

4. What is one advantage and one disadvantage of a sprinkling trust?

5. What is an advantage of leaving the entire corpus of a trust outright to a surviving spouse at one's death? What can be a disadvantage?

6. When a surviving spouse is left property in trust for life with a power of appointment, who receives the trust property when the surviving spouse dies?

7. What type of trust is used when the settlor wants to pass the entire principal of the trust on to someone other than the surviving spouse, but wants the spouse to have the income from the trust for life?

8. What is the rule against perpetuities, and when does it not apply?

9. How does a charitable remainder annuity trust differ from a charitable remainder unitrust?

10. What are Crummey powers, and why are they used?

■ CASES TO DISCUSS_____

1. Joseph Berson deposited $73,544.51 with the Metropolitan Savings Bank in an account entitled "Joseph Berson in Trust for New York City Jewish Defense League." Berson made no further deposits to or withdrawals from the account. When Berson died, the administrator of his estate claimed that the money belonged to the estate. Is the administrator correct? Explain. *In re* Joseph Berson, Deceased, 170 A.D. 2d 504, 566 N.Y.S.2d 74 (NY).

2. Dorothy A. Hewlett left part of the residue of her estate to the New Canaan Inn, Inc. The inn describes itself as a "nonprofit corporation" in its certificate of incorporation. The average age of the inn's residents is 83. The facility provides recreation, health services, housing, and related facilities suited to the special needs and living requirements of the elderly occupants, three meals a day, bed linen, towels, and maid service. Although residents pay monthly, expenses exceed income by $4,000 per resident per year. The additional expenses are paid for by contributions. The residence agreement states, "Once admitted, no resident who has fulfilled all the other elements of this Agreement shall be asked to leave the Inn for inability to pay beyond his or her control." Did Hewlett's gift to the Inn qualify as a gift to charity? Why or why not? *Bannon v. Wise*, 586 A.2d 639 (CN).

3. Robinson's will established a trust for the benefit of his wife for life, with the remainder to their daughter. The executor of the estate did not make an election on the estate tax return to treat the trust property as qualified terminable interest (QTIP) property. Does the amount in the trust qualify for the marital deduction on the estate tax return? Why or why not? *Robinson v. United States*, No. CV489–273, 90–2 U.S.T.C. (S.D. GA).

■ RESEARCH ON THE WEB_____

1. On the Internet, go to <http://www.lawcrawler.com>. Under the topic Research, click Summaries of Law. Then, scroll down to Trusts & Estates, and click Estate Planning. Finally, click Living Trust. Write a report on your findings.

2. Learn more about the legal assistant and paralegal field by going to the National Association of Legal Assistants Web site at <http://www.nala.org/whatis.htm>.

■ SHARPENING YOUR PROFESSIONAL SKILLS_____

1. In your law library, look up and write a brief of the case that decided the current law on Totten trusts, *In re* Totten, 71 N.E. 748 (N.Y. 1904). Then shepardize the case to find a recent reference to it in your state, and brief the latest case you find.

2. Describe a factual situation for which you believe an attorney would recommend the use of:

   a. a spendthrift trust

   b. a sprinkling trust

   c. a credit-shelter trust

   d. a QTIP trust

3. What is the purpose of Item IX in the will of Elvis Presley (reproduced in Appendix B)?

4. Explain the reason for including Paragraph FIFTH (B)(2) in the will of Jacqueline K. Onassis (reproduced in Appendix B).

5. How did ARTICLES ONE and TWO of the will of Richard M. Nixon (reproduced in Appendix B) ensure that the legacies contained in those paragraphs would avoid the federal estate tax?

6. Refer to Paragraphs FIVE (C)(1)–(6) of the will of Doris Duke (reproduced in Appendix B), and explain how the charitable remainder annuity trusts established therein will function.

■ SHARPENING YOUR LEGAL VOCABULARY_____

On a separate sheet of paper, fill in the numbered blank lines in the following anecdote with legal terms from this list:

A-B trust

bypass trust

charitable remainder annuity trust

charitable remainder trust

charitable remainder unitrust

charitable trust

credit-shelter trust

Crummey powers

cy pres doctrine

discretionary trust

exemption equivalent trust

marital deduction

marital deduction trust

public trust

QTIP (qualified terminable interest property) trust

rule against perpetuities

spendthrift

spendthrift trust

split interest trust

spray trust

sprinkling trust

Totten trust

Gino and Dawn considered many types of trusts when they planned their estate. They ruled out a(n) (1) , which is also known as a(n) (2) and a(n) (3) , because it gives the trustee the power to determine how the trust's income and principal will be distributed. They considered a(n) (4) , which is also called a(n) (5), under which the trust property would be used for public charitable purposes. With this type of trust, the length of time the trust is in existence is not a concern because the (6) does not apply. A(n) (7) would allow Gino and Dawn to retain the income from the trust for their lives, after which the principal of the trust would go to charity. If they used a(n) (8) , a fixed amount of income would be given to them annually regardless of inflation, and the remainder would go to charity. In contrast, if they used a(n) (9) , they would receive a percentage of the value of the trust property each year, allowing some protection against inflation. They felt that any charitable trust they established should express a general charitable intent so that the (10) would apply, and the trust would not end. Gino and Dawn were concerned about leaving money to their son, Conrad, because he was a(n) (11) , that is, he spent money profusely and improvidently. They had a bank account in their names "as trustee for Conrad," known as a(n) (12) , but felt that it did not meet their needs. They decided to create a(n) (13) for Conrad because it contained restrictions on the voluntary and involuntary alienation of the trust corpus. In addition, they decided to set up a(n) (14) because it is designed to make optimal use of the (15) , that is, the nontaxable property that passes to the surviving spouse under federal estate tax laws. They decided against a(n) (16) because the surviving spouse would be limited to the income from the trust for life, which they believed would be inadequate. Ultimately, they chose a(n) (17) , which is also known as a(n) (18) , a(n) (19), or a(n) (20) , under which the deceased spouse's estate would pass to a trust rather than to the surviving spouse, thereby reducing the possibility of the surviving spouse's estate being taxable. They also felt they might like to have a life-insurance trust with (21) , giving the beneficiaries the right to withdraw each year the money that is contributed to the trust.

■ KEY TERMS

charitable remainder annuity
    trust (CRAT)

charitable remainder trust

charitable remainder unitrust
    (CRUT)

charitable trust

credit-shelter trust

crummey powers

cy pres

marital deduction

marital deduction trust

qualified terminable interest
    property (QTIP)

rule against perpetuities

spendthrift

spendthrift trust

sprinkling trust

Online Companion™
For additional resources, please go to
http://www.paralegal.delmar.cengage.com.

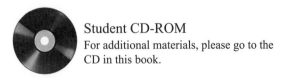

Student CD-ROM
For additional materials, please go to the
CD in this book.

Estate Administration

PART

4

10

Probate Courts and Uniform Laws

"'Tis well."

LAST WORDS OF GEORGE WASHINGTON (1732–1799)

■ CHAPTER OUTLINE

§ 10.1 Probate Jurisdiction

§ 10.2 Probate Records

§ 10.3 Uniform Laws

■ CHAPTER OUTCOMES

- Recognize the courts that have jurisdiction in the field of probate law in your state.

- Identify the office in your state that is responsible for the care and custody of probate records.

- Name and describe uniform laws enacted in your state that deal with probate law.

■ JOB COMPETENCIES

- Be familiar with the courts in your state that have jurisdiction over probate matters.

- Be able to locate, in your law office library and on the Net, the uniform laws affecting probate that have been enacted in your state.

■ A DAY AT THE OFFICE . . .

Claude Vickers, a paralegal, had just returned from his lunch break when he was called into the office of Attorney Zielinski.

"Did you hear about that car accident that happened last night on the interstate, Claude?" Attorney Zielinski inquired.

"Do you mean that head-on collision with a drunk driver that killed two people?" Claude replied.

"Yes. That's the one. The man who was killed had signed an organ donor card, but it wasn't witnessed," Attorney Zielinski continued. "Will you see what our state statute says about that?"

"Right away," Claude responded. "I heard that the couple died instantly."

"That's right. They were both dead when the ambulance arrived at the scene. We have their estates to settle, and I'm on my way over to their house now to talk with the children's grandparents."

"How many children did they have?" Claude asked.

"The man who died, his name was Kenneth Blake, had a three-year-old daughter from a former marriage. The woman's name was Leslie Johnson. She had a seven-year-old son from a former marriage. They were living together but weren't married," Attorney Zielinski explained.

"What a shame. Those poor children."

"Neither parent had a will," Attorney Zielinski continued. "They owned a house together as joint tenants, and they had a joint bank account. I've written some details here in the file. Kenneth owned his own car and a large amount of AT&T stock. Leslie owned her own car and quite a few U.S. savings bonds. Leslie was the beneficiary of Kenneth's life insurance policy. I'd like you to check the simultaneous death statute to see who will inherit their property."

"Okay," Claude replied as Attorney Zielinski put on her coat, preparing to leave the office.

"And while you're at it, see if our statute allows an estate to transfer money to minors," Attorney Zielinski said as she walked out of her office. "Those children are going to inherit quite a bit of property."

"I'll look into that, too," Claude replied, thinking about where he would begin his research.

Queries:

1. Assuming that each child will inherit from his and her parent, what will the daughter inherit? What will the son inherit? Who will receive the proceeds from the life insurance policy?
2. Under your state law, must an organ donor card be witnessed to be valid?
3. Under your state law, may an estate transfer money to minors?

Give statutory references to support your answers.

§ 10.1 PROBATE JURISDICTION

Probate paralegals must be familiar with the probate court systems in the states in which they work. In addition, they must be conversant with the probate law of their states, which may be based on various uniform laws.

In their research, paralegals must often locate state statutes that apply to specific situations and determine what court has jurisdiction. **Jurisdiction** is the power or authority that a court has to hear a case and to make a decision. Without jurisdiction, any decision by a court would be meaningless.

Federal Courts

Federal courts have no jurisdiction to probate a will or to administer an estate. Federal court cases are usually cases involving *in personam* **jurisdiction** (jurisdiction over the person), whereas probate court proceedings are *in rem* **proceedings** (proceedings that are directed against property rather than against persons). The purpose of the proceedings is to determine title to, or the extent of people's interests in, specific property located within a state court's jurisdiction.

Federal courts cannot appoint or control executors, administrators, or guardians. However, once an executor or administrator has been appointed by a state court, a claim against the estate may be brought in a federal court, but only when the parties are citizens of different states and the claim exceeds $75,000.

State Courts

Specific state courts have jurisdiction to probate a will or to administer an estate. This jurisdiction derives from either the state constitution or acts of the state legislature. Many states have established a separate court and empowered it with **probate jurisdiction** (i.e., the authority to probate wills and to administer estates). In most states, this separate court is referred to as the **probate court**. However, some states designate this same court as the *court of chancery*, the *surrogate court*, or the *orphan's court*. States that have not established separate courts give the authority to probate wills and to administer estates to courts of general jurisdiction, such as superior courts, district courts, circuit courts, county courts, and courts of common pleas. Some of these courts of general jurisdiction have separate divisions, one of which is empowered to probate wills and to administer estates.

■ **jurisdiction**

1. The geographical area within which a court (or a public official) has the right and power to operate.
2. The persons about whom and the subject matters about which a court has the right and power to make decisions that are legally binding.

■ *in personam* **jurisdiction**

Jurisdiction over the person.

■ *in rem* **proceedings**

Action directed against a property to enforce rights in a thing as opposed to one brought to enforce rights against another person.

■ **probate jurisdiction**

The authority of the court to process the handling of the will and the estate of a dead person. A probate court handles these matters and sometimes handles the problems of minors and others who are not legally competent to manage their affairs.

§ 10.2 PROBATE RECORDS

In some states, the records of all probate activities are kept in an office called the **Registry of Probate**. In these states, an official, called the Register of Probate, is either elected or appointed to administer the office. The Register of Probate is responsible for the care and custody of all books, documents, and papers filed with the probate court. She must maintain the probate records, compile indexes, and make the records available to the public upon request. In other states, this recordkeeping function is performed by the clerk of court.

The register or clerk keeps a docket of all cases that come before the court and, in general, handles all clerical matters necessary for the court's operation. The Uniform Probate Code contains the following provision relative to court records [UPC § 1–305]:

> The [Clerk of Court] shall keep a record for each decedent, ward, protected person or trust involved in any document that may be filed with the Court under this Code, including petitions and applications, demands for notices or bonds, trust registrations, and of any orders or responses relating thereto by the Registrar or Court, and establish and maintain a system for indexing, filing, or recording that is sufficient to enable users of the records to obtain adequate information. Upon payment of the fees required by law the clerk must issue certified copies of any probated wills, letters issued to personal representatives, or any other record or paper filed or recorded. Certificates relating to probated wills must indicate whether the decedent was domiciled in this state and whether the probate was formal or informal. Certificates relating to letters must show the date of appointment.

In some states, the Registry of Probate is housed in the same building as the **Registry of Deeds**, which is the office that retains deeds, mortgages, and other instruments affecting title to real property. A search of the title to real property often requires the use of both offices. When property is transferred by deed, the Registry of Deeds records the deed. When property is transferred by will or intestacy, no deed is used; the probate records must be examined to determine who has title to the property. Having the two offices in the same building allows title examiners conveniently to examine both types of records.

§ 10.3 UNIFORM LAWS

Uniform laws, sometimes called *model acts*, are laws that have been proposed by the National Conference of Commissioners on Uniform State Laws (a body with representatives from every state) for adoption by state legislatures. These recommendations are not a requirement: states may adopt the uniform laws or pass their own laws. Some uniform laws have been adopted, either in whole or in

---

■ **probate court**

A court that handles matters of wills and estates of a dead person. It sometimes handles the problems of minors and others who are not legally competent to manage their affairs. Some states designate this same court as the *court of chancery*, the *surrogate court*, or the *orphan's court*.

■ **registry of probate**

An office where the records of all probate activities are kept.

■ **registry of deeds**

An office where deeds, mortgages, and other instruments affecting title to real property are kept.

■ **uniform laws**

Laws in various subject areas, proposed by the Commission on Uniform State Laws and the American Law Institute, adopted in whole or in part by many states. Sometimes called *model acts*.

part, by many state legislatures; others have been adopted by only a few state legislatures. The version adopted by a state is often amended by the state legislature, thereby making the "uniform law" no longer uniform. Table 10–1 lists the uniform laws relating to wills, estates, and trusts and the states that have adopted them. Using the index to your state's statutes will help you find your own state's version of any of these uniform laws.

TABLE 10–1   Uniform Laws Relating to Wills, Trusts, and Estates

Name of Uniform Act	*States That Have Adopted Uniform Act*
Anatomical Gift Act (2006)	AR, CO, ID, IN, IA, KS, MN, MT, NV, NM, ND, OR, SD, TN, UT, VA
Custodial Trust Act	AK, AZ, AR, CO, DC, HI, ID, IN, LA, MA, MN, MO, NE, NV, NM, NC, RI, VA, WI
Disclaimer of Property Interests Act (1999)	AZ, AR, DC, FL, HI, IN, IA, MD, NV, NM, ND, OR, VA, WV
Disposition of Community Property Rights at Death Act	AK, AR, CO, CT, FL, HI, KY, MI, MT, NY, NC, OR, VA, WY
Durable Power of Attorney Act	AL, AK, AZ, AR, CA, CO, DE, DC, HI, ID, IA, KS, KY, ME, MD, MA, MI, MN, MS, MT, NE, NV, NH, NJ, NM, NY, NC, ND, OH, OK, OR, PA, RI, SC, SD, TN, TX, VI, UT, VT, VA, WA, WV, WI, WY
Estate Tax Apportionment Act	AR, ID, NM, WA
(1964 Act)	HI, MD, MI, ND, NM, OR, RI, VT
(1958 Act)	AL, MT, NH, WY
Guardianship and Protective Proceeding Act (1997)	AL, CO, HI, MN, MT
Health-Care Decisions Act	AL, AK, DE, HI, ME, MS, NM, WY
Health-Care Information Act	MT, WA
International Wills Act (Uniform Probate Code, Article II, Part 10)	AK, CA, CO, CT, DE, DC, HI, IL, MN, MT, NM, ND, PA, VA

(continues)

TABLE 10–1   **Uniform Laws Relating to Wills, Trusts, and Estates** *(continued)*

Name of Uniform Act	*States That Have Adopted Uniform Act*
Interstate Arbitration of Death Taxes	CA, CO, CT, DE, ME, MA, MI, MN, NE, NV, OR, PA, RI, TN, VT, VA, WA, WV, WI
Interstate Compromise of Death Taxes	AK, CA, CO, DE, DC, IL, KY, ME, MD, MA, MI, MN, MO, NE, NV, NH, NJ, NY, OH, OR, PA, RI, SC, TN, VT, VA, WA, WV
Multiple-Person Accounts Act	AK, AZ, CO, DC, MT, NE, NM, ND, SD
Probate Code	AK, AZ, CO, HI, ID, ME, MI, MN, MT, NE, NJ, NM, ND, PA, SC, SD, UT, WI
Probate of Foreign Wills Act	TX, WI
Simultaneous Death Act (1991)(1993)	AK, AZ, AR, CO, DC, HI, KS, KY, MT, NH, NM, NC, ND, OH, OR, SD, UT, VA, WI
(1940)	AL, CA, DE, FL, GA, ID, IL, IN, IA, ME, MD, MA, MI, MN, MS, MO, NE, NV, NJ, NY, OK, PA, RI, SC, TE, TX, VT, VI, WA, WV, WY
Statutory Form Power of Attorney Act	AR, CA, CO, DC, MT, NM, OH, OK, RI, TX, WI
Statutory Rule Against Perpetuities	AK, AZ, AR, CA, CO, CT, DC, FL, GA, HI, IN, KS, MA, MI, MN, MT, NE, NV, NJ, NM, NC, ND, OR, SC, SD, TN, VA, WV
Testamentary Additions to Trusts Act (1991)	AK, AZ, AR, CT, HI, KY, MN, NE, NM, ND, OH, RI, SD, VA, WV
(1960)	CA, DE, DC, FL, GA, ID, IL, IN, IA, KS, ME, MD, MA, MI, MS, NV, NH, NJ, NY, NC, OK, OR, PA, SC, TN, TX, UT, VT, WA
TOD Security Registration Act	AL, AK, AZ, AR, CA, CO, CT, DE, DC, FL, GA, HI, ID, IL, IN, IA, KS, KY, ME, MD, MA, MI, MN, MS, MO, MT, NE, NV, NH, NJ, NM, NY, NC, ND, OH, OK, OR, PA, RI, SC, SD, TN, UT, VT, VA, WA, WV, WI, WY

(continues)

TABLE 10–1 Uniform Laws Relating to Wills, Trusts, and Estates (continued)

Name of Uniform Act	States That Have Adopted Uniform Act
Transfers to Minors Act	AL, AK, AZ, AR, CA, CO, CT, DE, DC, FL, GA, HI, ID, IL, IN, IA, KS, KY, LA, ME, MD, MA, MI, MN, MS, MO, MT, NE, NV, NH, NJ, NM, NY, NC, ND, OH, OK, OR, PA, RI, SD, TN, TX, UT, VA, WA, WV, WI, WY

Uniform Probate Code

■ **uniform probate code (UPC)**

Uniform law designed to modernize and standardize the laws relating to the affairs of decedents, minors, and certain other persons who need protection.

■ **supervised administration**

Process in which an estate is settled under the continuing surveillance of the court from beginning to end.

■ **unsupervised administration**

Method of administering an estate, under the UPC, without court action unless such action is requested by an interested person.

The **Uniform Probate Code (UPC)** (see Exhibit 4–1) is a law designed to modernize and standardize the laws relating to the affairs of decedents, minors, and certain others who need protection. The law was developed in response to growing dissatisfaction with the high cost, long delays, and unnecessary formalities involved with the old-fashioned probate procedure. Some people resented judicial control and interference by the court in what they considered to be family matters. For some states, the UPC offered welcome changes.

For example, the UPC gives heirs and devisees the option of selecting supervised or unsupervised administration. **Supervised administration** occurs under the continuing authority of the court. In contrast, **unsupervised administration** occurs without court action, unless requested by an interested person. Although there is no court supervision, the Registrar of Probate is given the authority to process any necessary documents and to decide whether they are complete. In unsupervised administration, an interested person can petition the court to resolve a question, such as the validity of the will or the appointment of the personal representative. The court does not become involved unnecessarily; It only settles controversies or doubts.

The purposes of the Uniform Probate Code are [UPC § 1–102]:

1. to simplify and clarify the law concerning the affairs of decedents, missing persons, protected persons, minors, and incapacitated persons.

2. to discover and make effective the intent of a decedent in the distribution of her property.

3. to promote a speedy and efficient system for liquidating the estate of the decedent and making distribution to its successors.

4. to facilitate use and enforcement of certain trusts.

5. to make uniform the law among the various jurisdictions.

Table 10–2 lists the eight articles and contents of the Uniform Probate Code. In 1990, major changes in Article II of the UPC were made in response to the following developments in society:

1. Fewer formalities exist today than in the past.

2. The use of living gifts, jointly owned property, and trusts have increased so much that they constitute a major form of wealth transmission.

3. The advent of a multiple-marriage society, wherein a significant portion of the population marries more than once and has stepchildren and children by previous marriages and wherein a partnership theory of marriage has gained acceptance.

Table 10–2 **Uniform Probate Code Articles and Contents**

Article I	General provisions, definitions, and probate jurisdiction of court
Article II	Intestacy, wills, and donative transfers
Article III	Probate of wills and administration
Article IV	Foreign personal representatives; Ancillary administrations
Article V	Protection of persons under disability and their property
Article VI	Nonprobate transfers on death
Article VII	Trust administration
Article VIII	Effective date and repealer

CASE STUDY		*In re* **Estate of Sky Dancer**

13 P.3d 1231(CO)

FACTS: Sky Dancer died in December 1997. She left a will, which was photocopied by the police. The original will was retained by the police, as one of the beneficiaries was implicated in Sky Dancer's death. As the original will was not available, the court had received the photocopy, which all parties agreed showed probable deficiencies in execution. The will also contained handwritten portions that were not in the testatrix's handwriting.

QUESTION: Should the defective will copy, even with apparent defects that can't be clarified because the original isn't available, be admitted to probate?

COURT DECISION: No.

REASON: The will copy did not satisfy the Colorado statute as its execution was defective, but the legislature had enacted the Uniform Probate Code, which provides that wills that are not in compliance with statutory execution requirements may be treated as a will if clear evidence exists that the document was intended by the deceased to be their will. Here, while the execution defects might be surmountable thanks to the U.P.C. adoption, the handwritten portions, not in the pen of the deceased, was a fatal defect not encompassed by the Uniform Probate Code.

Uniform Simultaneous Death Act

■ **the uniform simultaneous death act**

Uniform law, adopted by most states, that sets forth rules to be followed when the passage of property depends upon the time of one's death, and there is no sufficient evidence that the people died other than at the same time.

When two people die at the same time, as in an automobile accident, plane crash, boating accident, gas poisoning, or house fire, it is often impossible to determine who died first. **The Uniform Simultaneous Death Act** is a uniform law, adopted by most states, that sets forth rules to be followed when the passage of property depends upon the time of death, and no sufficient evidence can establish which person died first.

Before the development of this uniform law, individual states addressed the issue of simultaneous death in different ways. Some states followed the common law rule that required a claimant to prove that one person died before the other, an almost impossible task. Other states developed presumptions that could not be rebutted, many of which were unrealistic. For example, in some states it was conclusively presumed that an adult in good health always survived a minor child. Realistically, however, a parent might very well die attempting to save a child's life.

SIMULTANEOUS DEATHS

JOHN F. KENNEDY, JR. AND CAROLYN BESSETTE

John F. Kennedy, Jr., his wife, Carolyn Bessette-Kennedy, and her sister, Lauren Bessette, died on July 16, 1999, when the airplane John was piloting plummeted into the waters off Martha's Vineyard, Massachusetts. The Uniform Simultaneous Death Act did not apply in the case of JFK Jr. because all of the bequests and devises to his wife in his will were prefaced by the phrase "if she is living on the thirtieth day after my death." (See Exhibit 10–1 and the will of John F. Kennedy, Jr., in Appendix B.)

The following four rules apply under the Uniform Simultaneous Death Act when two or more persons die at the same time:

1. When title to property depends upon priority of death, and there is insufficient evidence that the persons died other than at the same time, the property of each person shall be disposed of as if she had survived. Thus, when a mother's will leaves her entire estate "to my daughter, Kathleen, if living, but if not, to Kathleen's children equally," and the mother and daughter die at the same time in a car accident, the mother's estate will pass directly to the daughter's children.

2. When two or more beneficiaries are designated to take successively or alternatively by survivorship under another person's will or trust, and there is insufficient evidence that they died other than simultaneously, the property shall be divided into as many equal portions as there are successive or alternate beneficiaries and a share distributed to each.

3. When there is no evidence that joint tenants or tenants by the entirety died other than simultaneously, half shall be distributed to each. When there are more than two joint tenants in the same situation, the property is distributed among them all equally.

4. When an insured and a beneficiary of a life insurance policy have died, and there is insufficient evidence that they died other than simultaneously, the proceeds are payable as if the insured had survived the beneficiary.

The law does not apply when there is competent evidence that one person died before the other person, as in the *Sauers* case.

STATE OF NEW YORK
SURROGATE'S COURT: COUNTY OF NEW YORK
————————————————————————X

PROBATE PROCEEDING, WILL OF

    JOHN F. KENNEDY, JR.,

a/k/a JOHN FITZGERALD KENNEDY, JR.,

                         Deceased.
————————————————————————X

PETITION FOR PROBATE AND:

[x] Letters Testamentary
[ ] Letters of Trusteeship
[ ] Letters of Administration c.t.a.

File No. _____5785 - 99_____

To the Surrogate's Court, County of New York
    It is respectfully alleged:

    1.(a)   The name, citizenship, domicile (or, in the case of a bank or trust company, its principal office) and interest in this proceeding of the petitioner are as follows:

Name: _____Timothy P. Shriver_____

Domicile or Principal office: _____JPK Enterprises, 500 Fifth Avenue, Suite 1710_____
                                  (Street and Number)
_____New York_____   _____NY_____   _____10110_____
  (City, Village or Town)   (State)   (Zip Code)

Mailing Address: _____
                       (If different from domicile)

Citizen of: _____United States_____

Name:_____N/A_____

Domicile or Principal office: _____
                          (Street and Number)

    (City, Village or Town)   (State)   (Zip Code)

Mailing Address: _____
                       (If different from domicile)

Citizen of: _____

Interest(s) of Petitioner(s):   [x] Executor(s) named in decedents Will
  (Check one)   [ ] Other (Specify)

    1.(b)   The proposed Executor [ ] is [x] is not an attorney.
            [NOTE: An Executor-Attorney must comply with SCPA 2307-[a]; also see 207.19G Surrogate's Court Rules]
            The death certificate must be filed with this proceeding. If the decedents domicile is different from that shown on the death certificate, attach an affidavit explaining the reason for this inconsistency.

    2.   The name, domicile, date and place of death, and national citizenship of the above named decedent are as follows:

      (a) Name: _____John F. Kennedy, Jr._____

      (b) Date of death: _____July 16, 1999_____

      (c) Place of death: _____Falmouth, Massachusetts_____

      (d) Domicile: Street _____20 North Moore Street, Apt. 9E_____

            City, Town, Village: _____New York_____

            County: _____New York_____   State: _____New York 10013_____

      (e) Citizen of: _____United States_____

    3.   The Last Will, herewith presented, relates to both real and personal property and consists of an instrument or instruments dated as shown below and signed at the end thereof by the decedent and the following attesting witnesses:

December 19, 1997	James S. Benvenuto, Luann Spiotta
(Date of Will)	(Names of All Witnesses to Will)
(Date of Codicil)	(Names of All Witnesses to Will)
(Date of Codicil)	(Names of All Witnesses to Will)

EXHIBIT 10–1   Petition for Probate and Letters Testamentary

CASE STUDY   *Sauers v. Stolz*

218 P.2d 741 (CO)

FACTS:

W. E. Doyle and Mary Edna Doyle, his wife, were killed in a collision between their automobile and a truck. Both were rendered unconscious at the time of the impact and neither ever regained consciousness. Two lay witnesses testified at the trial to determine who should inherit from Mary's intestate estate and whether to apply the Uniform Simultaneous Death Act. Frank W. Hathaway testified that he immediately rushed to the accident scene from a block away. He testified:

Q. And when you arrived at the scene of the accident what did you find?

A. I went to Mrs. Doyle. She was laying on the right-hand side of the car. She was completely out of the car. I tested her to see if she was alive by pressing under the breast and around the arm to see if I could find a heart beat, and I did not find any heart beat.

Q. Where, under her arm, did you press to determine if there was a heart beat?

A. Under the left arm and around by the breast and a little over towards the middle of the chest.

Q. And, from any of your examination, did you determine there was a heart beat of any kind?

A. No, sir.

Q. Did you observe the condition of the body at that time?

A. The body was twisted. It looked like to me it might have been twisted in the hips pretty near clear around.

Q. What do you mean by twisted?

A. She was laying normal in the chest, flat on her back, and at her hips, they were kind of turned around.

Q. About how far?

A. I would say about a three-quarter turn.

Q. Was there any movement on or about the body at all?

A. No.

Q. After examining Mrs. Doyle's body, what did you next do?

(continues)

CASE STUDY *Sauers v. Stolz* (continued)

A. I went around the car to see if there was any other person in the car, and then I found a man on the left side of the car, who was laying with his head over the wheel. I tested him for heartbeat and I found a slight heart beat on him.

Q. Was the man's head on the inside or outside of the car?

A. It was outside.

Q. How did you test the man?

A. Under the left arm I found a slight heart beat.

Q. And was there any movement of his body?

A. I didn't see no movements of his body—only heart beat that I felt.

The other eyewitness, Mr. Williamsen, testified that he was driving behind the truck that collided with the Doyle car and that he was at the scene of the accident within a few minutes after it occurred. He testified:

Q. Will you describe her [Mrs. Doyle's] condition as you saw her at that time?

A. Well, she was laying out of the car with her feet still on the running board and she had just fell out of the car, evidently, to the left side and her body was twisted—looked like it was twisted almost in half. A broken back was what I thought it was; upper half of the body was face up and lower half down.

Q. Did you examine her?

A. I tried to feel a pulse on her arm and there was none; and under the arm and there was none. She had dust both in her nostrils and in her mouth and she hadn't taken a breath from the time of the accident—couldn't possibly have.

Q. Did you make any further examination of the body of Mrs. Doyle at that time?

A. No [the rest of the answer stricken].

Q. Then what did you do?

A. Walked around to the other side of the car.

Q. What did you find?

A. Mr. Doyle was hanging out the left side of the car.

Q. Describe the position of his body.

(continues)

CASE STUDY *Sauers v. Stolz* (continued)

A. His feet was caught between the motor and front seat; his head was twisted back in under the front part of the car; his entire body was hanging out of the car and head twisted back under the running board. It had been dragged.

Q. Did you examine his body?

A. Yes. I pulled his body around straight and he was bleeding quite badly.

Q. How did you examine it?

A. He had pulse on his arm, to start with.

Q. Would you say that was a strong pulse?

A. Yes, it was.

Q. Or a weak pulse?

A. It was strong.

Q. What else did you do at the automobile at that time?

A. Well, he slowly bled to death. He was bleeding quite profusely and certain that is what he died of. He had a very bad split head and that is what he died from.

On cross-examination Williamsen further testified concerning Mr. Doyle:

Q. His head was under the board?

A. Under the running board.

Q. What was the condition of his head? Mr. Doyle's head?

A. It was cracked clear open, sir.

Q. The head was cracked open?

A. Yes, sir. It was bleeding.

Q. Complete skull fracture, would you say?

A. Yes.

Q. And bleeding profusely?

A. Yes. You could see his heart beat. Every time—it would spurt through the top of his head every time the heart beat.

Q. Was his head split wide open? Could you see into his brain?

A. Pretty near see into it—quite bloody.

(continues)

Q. Was he conscious?

A. No, sir.

Williamsen testified on recross-examination that the other eyewitness, Mr. Hathaway, "knelt down by the body and felt for pulse and we discussed at the time that his pulse was fading fast." Dr. Harlan T. Close testified that the spurting of blood from the head, in the manner described by the two eyewitnesses, indicated heartbeats.

LEGAL ISSUE:	Does the Uniform Simultaneous Death Act apply to accident victims when there is uncontradicted testimony that a husband's heart was still beating when no heartbeat could be detected in the wife's body?
COURT DECISION:	No.
REASON:	When two or more persons perish in a common disaster and there is no proof as to which died first, the Uniform Simultaneous Death Act furnishes a guide, in the absence of evidence, by which descent of property may be judicially determined, and creates a presumption that death of the parties was simultaneous. The statute is inapplicable if there is evidence as to which one of the parties survived the other. There being direct evidence that Mr. Doyle survived his wife, there was no occasion for the trial court's resorting to the statutory presumption that Mr. and Mrs. Doyle died simultaneously.

■ **kiddie tax**

Slang for a federal tax on certain unearned income (over a certain amount) of children under 14. The income is taxed at the parent's highest rate to discourage income shifting.

■ **uniform transfers to minors act (UTMA)**

Formerly called Uniform Gifts to Minors Act (UGMA). A uniform law that provides an inexpensive, easy mechanism for transferring property to minors.

Uniform Transfers to Minors Act

Difficulties may arise when gifts are given to minors. Sometimes parents or guardians use the gifts for themselves rather than for the benefit of the minor. At other times, gifts are given to minors and then revoked by the donor before the minor reaches adulthood. In the past, gifts to minors were often used as tax shelters. People would make gifts of money and securities to their children with the aim of shifting unearned income to lower-bracket taxpayers. The IRS stopped this particular practice by establishing a **kiddie tax** that taxes unearned income of children under the age of 14. In 1995, for example, a child's unearned income over $1,300 was taxable at the parent's maximum tax rate if the child had not reached the age of 14.

The **Uniform Transfers to Minors Act (UTMA)**, which has been adopted by most states, prevents some of the problems involved when transfers are made to minors. The UTMA replaces an earlier law known as the Uniform Gifts to Minors Act (UGMA). Besides money and securities, the UTMA allows any kind of property, whether real or personal, tangible or intangible, to be transferred to a custodian for the benefit of a minor. Transfers may be made from trusts, estates, and guardianships as well as from living donors. To be consistent with Internal Revenue Service policy, the UTMA uses the age of 21, rather than 18, to determine when custodianship ends and the former minor receives the property.

Under the uniform law, a transferor (or donor) can register a stock certificate or other security in the name of the transferor (or donor), other adult person, or trust company "as custodian for [name of minor] under the [name of state] Uniform Transfers to Minors Act." Similarly, a transferor (or donor) can open a bank account in the name of the transferor (or donor), other adult person, or trust company "as custodian for [name of minor] under the [name of state] Uniform Transfers to Minors Act." An interest in real property is recorded in the name of the transferor, an adult other than the transferor, or a trust company, followed in substance by the words: "as custodian for [name of minor] under the [name of state] Uniform Transfers to Minors Act."

Each transfer may involve only one minor, and only one person may be the custodian. The minor's Social Security number is used to identify the account, and the income from the securities or bank account is taxable to the minor if she is over the age of 14. A gift to a minor under the Uniform Transfers (or Gifts) to Minors Act is considered to be a completed gift, making it subject to the federal gift tax discussed in Chapter 2.

A custodian must keep custodial property separate and distinct from all other property and must maintain records of all transactions relating to the custodial property. When investing funds, the UTMA requires the custodian to "observe the standard of care that would be observed by a prudent person dealing with the property of another."

A gift made under the act is **irrevocable**: that is, it cannot be taken back. The *McLaughlin* case demonstrates this point of law. Gifts made under the UTMA must be held by the custodian and used only for the minor's support, maintenance, education, and benefit. When the minor becomes 21 years old (18 in some states), the balance of the property held by the custodian must be given to the minor outright.

■ **irrevocable**
Incapable of being called back, stopped, or changed.

CASE STUDY **Matter of Estate of McLaughlin**

483 N.Y.S.2d 943 (NY)

FACTS: Rose McLaughlin established two separate $20,000 bank accounts under the Uniform Gift to Minors Act, one for each of her two daughters. A year later, she closed the accounts and placed the money in two Totten trust accounts in joint names, each naming one of her daughters as a Totten trust beneficiary. When Rose died, the creditors of her estate claimed that the bank accounts should be included as assets of her estate.

(continues)

| CASE STUDY | | **Matter of Estate of McLaughlin** *(continued)* |

LEGAL ISSUE: Can money that is placed by a donor in a custodial account under the Uniform Gifts to Minors Act be returned to the donor?

COURT DECISION: No.

REASON: A gift under the Uniform Gifts to Minors Act is irrevocable and indefeasibly vests title in the donee. The discretionary powers granted to the custodian do not authorize the dissipation of the minors' interest in such property for the purpose of returning the gift to the donor. The custodian in this case wrongfully administered the custodial accounts by restructuring them in the form of joint Totten trusts. The funds in the accounts are neither estate assets nor within the reach of estate creditors. They belong to the children.

Uniform Anatomical Gifts Act

■ **uniform anatomical gifts act (UAGA)**

Uniform law that provides a simplified manner of making a testamentary donation of vital organs for medical research or transplant.

The **Uniform Anatomical Gifts Act (UAGA)** provides an easy way to make a testamentary donation of vital organs for medical research or transplant. All 50 states and the District of Columbia have now adopted either the 1968 or the 1987 version of the act.

Under the 1987 act, no witnesses are required on the document used to make an anatomical gift, such as a donor card or driver's license. In addition, the consent of the next of kin after death is not required. Other provisions of the 1987 act include the following:

1. A donor may revoke the offer of an anatomical gift without advising any specified donee.
2. The designation of a gift of one organ—for example, eyes or a heart— does not restrict the use of other organs as donations after death unless otherwise indicated by the decedent.
3. Hospitals rather than the attending physicians are the donees of anatomical gifts.
4. The sale and purchase of organs and tissue are prohibited.
5. People who act in good faith in accordance with the terms of the act cannot be liable in any civil or criminal action relating to the transplant.

Chapter 14 includes a discussion of anatomical gifts.

SUMMARY

Federal courts have no jurisdiction to probate wills or to administer estates, as their jurisdiction is primarily *in personam* jurisdiction. State courts, exercising *in rem* jurisdiction, have the power to hear probate proceedings to determine title to specific property located within the state. Further, some specific state courts have probate jurisdiction, their authority coming from state constitutions or statutes. Each state has either a separate court or a court of general jurisdiction with jurisdiction over probate matters.

In some states, probate records are kept in the Registry of Probate and are the responsibility of an official known as the Register of Probate. Other states give the responsibility to a clerk of court. Some states house the Registry of Probate in the same building with the Registry of Deeds to facilitate the examination of records in both offices.

Uniform laws are laws that have been proposed by a national committee for adoption by state legislatures. Some uniform laws have been adopted by many states; others have been adopted by only a few states. States sometimes amend uniform laws after adopting them, making them no longer uniform.

The Uniform Probate Code, adopted by 15 states, is designed to reduce the high cost, long delays, and unnecessary formalities involved with probating an estate.

The Uniform Simultaneous Death Act, adopted by most states, establishes rules to be followed when the passage of property depends upon the time of death and no sufficient evidence can establish which person died first.

Either the Uniform Gifts to Minors Act or the Uniform Transfers to Minors Act has been adopted by every state. The law provides an inexpensive, easy mechanism for transferring money and other property to minors. The Gifts to Minors Act provides for making gifts of securities and cash to a custodian for the benefit of a minor. The Transfers to Minors Act, which has been adopted by 38 states, allows the transfer of any kind of property, real or personal, to a custodian for the benefit of a minor. Gifts made to minors under either act are irrevocable.

The Uniform Anatomical Gifts Act, which has been adopted in one form or another by every state, provides for a simplified manner of making a testamentary donation of vital organs for medical research or transplant. The act was amended in 1987 in an attempt to close the gap between the need for organs and tissues and the supply of them.

■ REVIEW QUESTIONS

1. Why do federal courts have no jurisdiction to probate a will or to administer an estate?

2. From what source do state courts obtain their jurisdiction to probate wills and to administer estates?

3. To what courts do states that have not established separate courts with probate jurisdiction give the authority to probate wills and to administer estates?

4. Why is the Registry of Probate housed in the same building as the Registry of Deeds in some states?

5. Must all states adopt uniform laws? Explain.

6. Why did the Uniform Probate Code come into existence?

7. When title to property depends upon priority of death, and there is insufficient evidence that the persons have died other than simultaneously:

   a. How will the property of each person be disposed?

   b. How will the property be disposed when the decedents are two beneficiaries who are designated to take the property successively?

   c. How will the property be disposed when the decedents are joint tenants?

   d. How will the property be disposed when the decedents are an insured and a beneficiary of a life insurance policy?

8. Why does the Uniform Transfers to Minors Act use the age of 21 rather than 18 as the age when custodianship terminates and the property is distributed to the former minor?

9. Under the Uniform Transfers to Minors Act, what language is used to open a bank account for a minor named Irene Buckley whose custodian is Joan M. Peabody?

10. For what two reasons was the Uniform Anatomical Gifts Act revised in 1987?

■ CASES TO DISCUSS

1. Mrs. Roig established three Shearson (investment) accounts valued at $50,000, in which she was the custodian for each of her three children under the Uniform Gifts to Minors Act. Later, in a divorce proceeding, the trial court held that the three accounts were marital property belonging to Mrs. Roig and her husband. Was the trial court correct in its holding? Why or why not? *Roig v. Roig*, 364 S.E.2d 794 (WV).

2. At the time Kathy gave birth to Krystal, Kathy was living as a foster child in Edith's home. Edith petitioned the probate court to be appointed as guardian of Krystal. Under the law of that state, the probate court has equity jurisdiction in all matters relating to wills, trusts, and administration of decedents' estates. Another statute provides that only courts having full equity jurisdiction have power to adjudicate rights as to the custody of infants. Did the probate court have the power to appoint Edith as guardian of Krystal? Why or why not? *In re* Krystal S., 584 A.2d 672 (ME).

■ RESEARCH ON THE WEB

1. Log on to the Internet, type in <http://www.Google.com> and press Enter. Then, in the box type the name of the court that settles estates in your state (either *probate court, surrogate court, orphan's court,* or *court of chancery*). Look for information about your state court and report on your findings.

2. Do an online search for the the Uniform Probate Code. How does the Uniform Code differ from the Probate Code in your state?

3. For information about uniform laws in your state, see the Web site of the National Conference of Commissioners on Uniform State Laws at <http://www.nccusl.org/>.

■ SHARPENING YOUR PROFESSIONAL SKILLS_____

1. What is the name and location of the court in your county that has jurisdiction to probate wills and to administer estates? How near to the Registry of Deeds is the court located?

2. Examine your state statute and determine your state's version of the Uniform Gifts to Minors Act from among the following:

    a. the 1956 version

    b. the 1966 version

    c. its own version

    d. the 1983 version known as the Uniform Transfers to Minors Act

    Give the reference number of that particular statute.

3. Examine Table 10–1, and make a list of the uniform laws that have been adopted by your state.

■ SHARPENING YOUR LEGAL VOCABULARY_____

On a separate sheet of paper, fill in the numbered blank lines in the following anecdote with legal terms from this list:

court of chancery

custodian

in personam jurisdiction

in rem proceedings

irrevocable

jurisdiction

model acts

orphan's court

probate court

probate jurisdiction

Registry of Deeds

Registry of Probate

Supervised administration

surrogate court

Uniform Anatomical Gift Act

Uniform Gifts to Minors Act

uniform laws

Uniform Probate Code (UPC)

Uniform Simultaneous Death Act

Uniform Transfers to Minors Act (UTMA)

unsupervised administration

Enrique made use of one of many (1) (sometimes called (2))—that is, laws proposed by the National Conference of Commissioners on Uniform State Laws for adoption by state legislatures—when he made a gift of money to his five-year-old daughter. The law, called the (3) when it was first formulated in 1956, provides an inexpensive, easy mechanism to transfer gifts of cash and securities to minors. Gifts made to minors under the law are (4), that is they cannot be taken back. Enrique's state has adopted a more recent version of the law, called the (5), which allows any kind of property to be transferred to a(n) (6) for the benefit of a minor. Enrique also made use of another law, known as the (7), when he filled out a simple card providing for the donation of his organs and tissue for medical research or transplant. When Enrique died, his will was probated in a court that had (8), that is, the authority to probate wills and administer estates. Without such (9), any decision by a court would be meaningless. In most states, this court is called the (10). However, some states refer to it as the (11), the (12), or the (13). These court proceedings are (14), which means they are directed against property rather than against persons. Enrique's state had not adopted the (15), which is a law designed to modernize and make uniform the laws relating to the affairs of decedents, minors, and certain other people who need protection. His heirs and devisees did not have the option of selecting (16) (administration under the continuing authority of the court) or (17) (administration without court action). Because Enrique did not die at the same time as one of his heirs or co-owners, the rules under the (18) were not applicable. Enrique's will and other probate papers were filed in an office known as the (19), which was located in the same building as the (20).

■ KEY TERMS

in personam jurisdiction

in rem proceedings

irrevocable

jurisdiction

kiddie tax

probate court

probate jurisdiction

registry of deeds

registry of probate

supervised administration

the uniform simultaneous death act

uniform anatomical gifts act
  (UAGA)

uniform laws

uniform probate code (UPC)

uniform transfers to minors act
  (UTMA)

unsupervised administration

Online Companion™
For additional resources, please go to
http://www.paralegal.delmar.cengage.com.

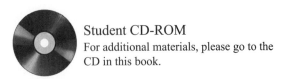

Student CD-ROM
For additional materials, please go to the
CD in this book.

11

The Personal Representative

■ CHAPTER OUTLINE

§ 11.1 Appointment of the Personal Representative

§ 11.2 Personal Representative's Bond

§ 11.3 Duties of Personal Representative

§ 11.4 Titles of Personal Representative

§ 11.5 Removal of Personal Representative

■ CHAPTER OUTCOMES

• Determine, in a given case, who should petition the court for appointment as a personal representative.

• List the duties of a personal representative.

• Distinguish among the titles of personal representatives and determine when each is used.

• Explain the reasons for the removal of a personal representative.

■ JOB COMPETENCIES

• Be able to suggest to the attorney the type of personal representative that would be appropriate in given cases.

• Be able to select the proper forms to use when petitioning the court for appointment of a personal representative.

• Be able to prepare the forms that are used to petition the court for appointment of a personal representative.

"Born in a hotel room —and God damn it— died in a hotel room."

LAST WORDS OF EUGENE O'NEILL (1888–1953)

- Assist the attorney and client in carrying out the duties of a personal representative.

- Be able to make recommendations to the attorney as to the possible removal of a personal representative.

▄ A DAY AT THE OFFICE . . .

It was almost noon when Attorney Serena Hall stopped by the desk of her legal assistant, Ginamarie Orlando. "Ginamarie, I just received a call from Mrs. Greaves about her father's estate. It seems that her brother is the executor of the will, and he's been running their father's business for two years without authority."

"Oh really? What kind of a business is it?"

"It's a truck farm. They grow vegetables and take them into the market to sell. According to Mrs. Greaves, her brother went to a gambling casino in Nevada last year and lost all the money that belongs to the estate."

"Good grief!"

"Apparently, he tried to make up for it by growing a double crop of tomatoes and cucumbers this year, but now he's letting them rot on the vine. He told Mrs. Greaves that he's resigning as executor."

"Nice guy. I hope he was bonded," Ginamarie responded.

"Mrs. Greaves has an appointment with me tomorrow," Attorney Hall continued. "Before she comes, will you look up the state statute to see whether or not an executor can continue running a decedent's business? And, while you're at it, find out what an executor has to do to resign. You might as well draft a petition to have Mrs. Greaves appointed as special administrator. She'll need to be appointed right away to take care of the rotting vegetables."

"I'll begin right after lunch," Ginamarie answered.

"What are you having for lunch today?" queried Attorney Hall.

"A cucumber and tomato sandwich," Ginamarie replied with a smile.

At that moment, the office receptionist entered the room, interrupting the laughter. "Mrs. Greaves is on the phone, Ms. Hall. She said that her brother was rushed to the hospital with a perforated ulcer last night and passed away this morning."

Queries:

1. May an executor legally continue running the decedent's business under the laws of your state?
2. What would be the title of a personal representative who is appointed solely for the purpose of selling the rotting vegetables?
3. Why did Ginamarie say, "I hope he was bonded"?
4. In your state, what would be the title of the person who replaced Mrs. Greaves' brother?

§ 11.1 APPOINTMENT OF THE PERSONAL REPRESENTATIVE

Paralegals may be asked to assist the individual assigned to manage the affairs and settle the estate of someone who dies and owns property. The individual who manages the affairs is known as a personal representative. Because these duties involve good faith, trust, and special confidence, a personal representative is a type of fiduciary and acts in a **fiduciary capacity** (i.e., in a position of trust). The law imposes an unusually high standard of ethical and moral conduct on a fiduciary because he holds property interests for the benefit of others.

When someone dies testate, the person nominated in the will as personal representative, or some other interested person, petitions the court to have the will allowed and to be appointed personal representative (see Exhibit 11–1). When someone dies intestate, one of the heirs, next of kin, or a creditor files a petition with the court requesting the appointment. With variations from state to state, notice of a hearing on the petition is given to all interested parties either by service of process, mail, or publication in a newspaper. A time period of about three to four weeks is established for interested parties to respond to the notice, after which a hearing is held on the petition. The hearing may be dispensed with if no one objects to the petition. If no contest arises, the court allows the will or grants the administration and appoints the personal representative. When a contest does occur, a judge or jury decides the question in dispute.

In many states, the certificate of appointment of a personal representative is called **letters testamentary** in a testate estate and **letters of administration** in an intestate estate (see Exhibit 11–2).

§ 11.2 PERSONAL REPRESENTATIVE'S BOND

In some states, the appointment of a personal representative is not complete until the representative has given bond. A **bond** is a written promise by the personal representative to pay the amount of the bond to the court if the representative does not faithfully perform his or her duties (see Exhibit 11–3). A **surety bond** contains the signature of individuals or insurance companies (sureties) that stand behind a fiduciary by agreeing to pay the amount of the bond to the court in the event the fiduciary fails to meet the obligations of the office. The bond requirement serves to enforce the obligations of the personal representative: suit can be brought on the bond for any losses caused by the personal representative's breach of duty.

■ **fiduciary capacity**
The position of a person who manages money or property for another person. This position implies trust, power, confidence, responsibility, and good faith on the part of both parties.

■ **letters testamentary**
A formal document appointing the executor of the estate of a person who has died testate.

■ **letters of administration**
A formal document appointing the administrator of the estate of a person who has died intestate.

■ **bond**
A document that promises to pay money if a particular future event happens, or a sum of money that is put up and will be lost if that event happens.

■ **surety bond**
A bond that contains an agreement by a third party (*surety*) to pay an obligation if the principal defaults.

☐ District Court ☐ Denver Probate Court

_____ County, Colorado

Court Address:

IN THE MATTER OF THE ESTATE OF:

Deceased:

▲ **COURT USE ONLY** ▲

Attorney or Party Without Attorney (Name and Address):

Case Number:

Phone Number: E-mail:
FAX Number: Atty. Reg.#:   Division   Courtroom

PETITION FOR FORMAL PROBATE OF WILL
AND FORMAL APPOINTMENT OF PERSONAL REPRESENTATIVE

1. Petitioner, (Name) _____

   as _____, is an interested person. (Section 15-10-201, C.R.S.)

2. The decedent died on the date of _____, at the age of _____ years,

   domiciled in the _____ County of _____, State of _____.

3. Venue for this proceeding is proper in this county because the decedent

   ☐ was a domiciliary of this county on the date of death.

   ☐ was not a domiciliary of Colorado, but property of the decedent was located in this county on the date of death.

4. ☐ No personal representative has been appointed in this state or elsewhere.

   ☐ A personal representative of the decedent has been appointed in this state or elsewhere as shown on the attached explanation.
      (Section 15-12-301, C.R.S.)

5. Petitioner

   ☐ has not received a demand for notice and is unaware of any demand for notice of any probate or appointment
      proceeding concerning the decedent that may have been filed in this state or elsewhere.

   ☐ has received, or is aware of, a demand for notice. See attached demand or explanation.

6. The date of decedent's last will is _____. The dates of all codicils are _____
   _____.

   The will and any codicils are referred to as the will. The will

   ☐ was deposited with this Court before the decedent's death. (Section 15-11-515, C.R.S.)

   ☐ has been lodged with this Court since the decedent's death. (Section 15-11-516, C.R.S.)

   ☐ is filed with this petition.

   ☐ has been probated in the State of _____. Authenticated copies of the will and of the statement
      probating it are filed with this petition. (Section 15-12-402, C.R.S.)

   ☐ is lost, destroyed, or otherwise unavailable. See attached explanation. (Section 15-12-402, C.R.S.)

7. Except as may be disclosed on an attached explanation and after the exercise of reasonable diligence, petitioner is unaware of any
   instrument revoking the will, is unaware of any prior wills which have not been expressly revoked by a later instrument, and believes that
   the will is the decedent's last will and was validly executed.

8. ☐ No statutory time limitation applies to the commencement of these proceedings. (Section 15-12-108, C.R.S.)

   ☐ More than 3 years have passed since decedent's death. A statutory time limitation would apply to the commencement
      of these proceedings except for the circumstances described in an attachment to this petition.

9. _____
   Name, address, and telephone number of the nominee for Personal Representative
   _____

   is 21 years of age or older, and has priority for appointment because of:

CPC 9   R7/00   PETITION FOR FORMAL PROBATE OF WILL AND   1
                FORMAL APPOINTMENT OF PERSONAL REPRESENTATIVE

EXHIBIT 11–1a Petition for Formal Probate of Will (Colorado)

❑ nomination by the will.

❑ statutory priority. (Section 15-12-203, C.R.S.)

❑ reasons stated in the attached explanation.

10. The nominee is to serve

    ❑ without bond   ❑ in unsupervised administration

    ❑ with bond (Section 15-12-604, C.R.S.)   ❑ in supervised administration

11. The decedent ❑ was ❑ was not married at time of death.

12. Listed below are the names and addresses of decedent's spouse, children, heirs and devisees, and the names and addresses of guardians or conservators of incapacitated or protected persons. (See instructions below.)

NAME (Include spouse, if any)	ADDRESS (or date of death)	AGE AND DATE OF BIRTH OF MINORS (or nature of disability)	INTEREST AND RELATIONSHIP (See instructions)

PETITIONER REQUESTS that the Court set a time and place of hearing; that notice be given to all interested persons as provided by law; that after notice and hearing, the Court determine the heirs of the decedent and formally admit the decedent's will to probate; that the nominee

    ❑ be formally appointed as personal representative   ❑ be formally confirmed as personal representative

    ❑ without bond   ❑ with bond

    ❑ in unsupervised administration   ❑ in supervised administration (additional fee required)

and that Letters Testamentary be issued to the personal representative or confirmed. Petitioner also requests

    ❑ a setting aside of prior informal findings as to testacy,

    ❑ a setting aside of prior informal appointment of personal representative,

    ❑ _____

Signature of Attorney for Petitioner   Date

(Type or Print name below)

Signature of Petitioner   Date

(Type or Print name, address and tele. # below)

INSTRUCTIONS FOR PARAGRAPH 12:

Include any statements of legal disability or other incapacity required by Rule 10, C.R.P.P.

List the names and dates of death of any deceased devisees. (See applicable antilapse statute, Sections 15-11-601 and 603, C.R.S.)

Where a listed person is an heir, detail the relationship to the decedent which creates heirship. Examples: son, daughter of pre-deceased son. (Sections 15-11-101 to 114, C.R.S.)

Attach additional sheets if necessary.

CPC 9 R7/00 PETITION FOR FORMAL PROBATE OF WILL AND   2
                  FORMAL APPOINTMENT OF PERSONAL REPRESENTATIVE

EXHIBIT 11–1b Petition for Formal Probate of Will (Colorado)

❑ District Court   ❑ Denver Probate Court
_____ County, Colorado
Court Address:

IN THE MATTER OF THE ESTATE OF:

▲   **COURT USE ONLY**   ▲

Case Number:

Deceased

Division: Courtroom:

ORDER ADMITTING WILL TO FORMAL PROBATE AND FORMAL APPOINTMENT OF PERSONAL REPRESENTATIVE

UPON CONSIDERATION of the Petition filed by (Name) _____

_____ for formal probate of will and determination of heirs, and for:

    ❑ formal appointment of personal representative,
    ❑ confirmation of a previous informal appointment of personal representative,
    ❑ setting aside of prior informal findings as to testacy,
    ❑ setting aside of prior informal appointment of personal representative.

THE COURT FINDS, DETERMINES AND ORDERS:

1. Any required notices have been given or waived.

2. Venue is proper.

3. The proceeding was commenced within the time period required by law.

4. The decedent died on the date of _____, domiciled in the City of _____
County of _____, State of _____.

5. The decedent left a will dated _____. The dates of all codicils are
_____

    The will and any codicils are referred to as the will. There are no known prior wills which have not been expressly revoked by a later instrument. The will is the decedent's last will and it is admitted to formal probate.

    ❑ The prior informal finding as to testacy is set aside.

6. The heirs of the decedent are:

NAME	RELATIONSHIP

CPC 10   R7/01   ORDER ADMITTING WILL TO FORMAL PROBATE AND
                  FORMAL APPOINTMENT OF PERSONAL REPRESENTATIVE

Page 1 of 2

EXHIBIT 11–2a   Order Admitting Will to Formal Probate and Formal Appointment of Personal Representative (Colorado)

7. (Name) _____, whose address is _____

_____, telephone (_____)_____,

is entitled to be appointed personal representative.

    ❑ The appointment is made and Letters Testamentary shall be issued.

    ❑ The prior informal appointment and previously issued Letters Testamentary are confirmed.

The personal representative shall serve

    ❑ without bond.

    ❑ with bond in the amount of $_____.

    ❑ in unsupervised administration.

    ❑ in supervised administration as described in an attachment to this order.

    ❑ the prior informal appointment of (Name) _____is set aside.

Dated: _____   BY THE COURT

_____

    ❑ Judge   ❑ Magistrate

CPC 10   R7/01   ORDER ADMITTING WILL TO FORMAL PROBATE AND   Page 2 of 2
                FORMAL APPOINTMENT OF PERSONAL REPRESENTATIVE

EXHIBIT 11–2b   Order Admitting Will to Formal Probate and Formal Appointment of Personal Representative (Colorado)

☐ District Court   ☐ Denver Probate Court

_____ County, Colorado

Court Address:

IN THE MATTER OF THE ESTATE OF:
☐ Deceased ☐ Protected Person

▲   **COURT USE ONLY**   ▲

Attorney or Party Without Attorney (Name and Address):

Case Number:

Phone Number: E-mail:

FAX Number: Atty. Reg.#:

Division   Courtroom

BOND OF   ☐ PERSONAL REPRESENTATIVE   ☐ CONSERVATOR

TO WHOM IT MAY CONCERN: We, _____

(Name)

as principal, and _____of _____

(Name)   (address)

and _____of _____

(Name)   (address)

as surety, are held and firmly bound unto the People of the State of Colorado for the benefit of persons interested in this estate

in the penal sum of _____Dollars,

lawful money of the United States of America, for which payment we, and each of us, do hereby bind ourselves, our heirs,

personal representatives, successors and assigns, jointly and severally.

The condition of this obligation is that if the principal, as ☐ personal representative ☐ conservator of this estate, shall

faithfully discharge the duties of such office as provided by law and orders of Court, then this obligation shall be void

otherwise it shall be and remain in full force and effect.

Executed on _____, at _____, Colorado

(Date)

Approved on _____

(Date)

_____
Signature of Principal

_____
Judge/Registrar

_____
Signature of Principal

_____
Signature of Surety

_____
Signature of Surety

The undersigned, being sworn, states: That the ☐ value of the personal estate of the deceased ☐ aggregate capital value

of the property of the estate of the protected person in the undersigned's control, less the value of such property deposited

with the Clerk of this Court or held subject to Court order, is estimated to be $_____, and that the income

expected from the personal and real property of this estate during the next year is estimated to be $_____

STATE OF _____

_____
Signature of Principal

_____COUNTY OF _____

Subscribed and sworn to before my by _____, as Principal on _____

My commission expires _____.

_____
Notary Public/(Deputy) Clerk of Court

CPC 19   R7/00   BOND OF ☐ Personal representative ☐ Conservator   1

EXHIBIT 11–3a Bond (Colorado)

JUSTIFICATION OF SURETIES

STATE OF _____

_____COUNTY OF _____

I, (Name) _____being sworn, state: That I reside at

_____
and am seized and possessed in my own right, over and above all my just debts, liabilities and liens, of property within the
State of Colorado of a value at least equal to the penal sum of this Bond; that such property is not exempt by law from levy
and sale under execution; that I have made and assigned such property to the People of the State of Colorado, as obligee, for
the use and benefit of all persons interested in this estate; and that such property is described as follows:

_____
Signature of Surety   Date

Subscribed and sworn to before me on _____.

My commission expires _____.   _____
                                                                  Notary Public/(Deputy) Clerk of Court

CPC 19   R7/00   BOND OF ❑ Personal representative   ❑ Conservator   2

EXHIBIT 11–3b Bond (Colorado)

In some states, no bond is required if the will includes a provision like the "No Surety on Bond" provision discussed in Chapter 6, requesting that the personal representative serve without bond. Under some circumstances, a bond is not required if all heirs agree to the appointment without sureties or waive the filing of a bond and the will does not require one. Under the UPC, a bond may be required when an interested person demands that a bond be given (see UPC §§ 3-603 through 3-606).

EXCESSES, INDULGENCES, AND CONSEQUENCES

DORIS DUKE

Doris Duke, daughter of the founder of the American Tobacco Company, lived a life of luxury and generosity from the day she inherited her father's $300 million estate in 1925. When she died in 1993 at age 80, her lavishness continued: she left sums between $500,000 and $3 million to her friends; $10 million each to the Metropolitan Museum of Art and Duke University; even a $100,000 trust fund for her dog. She left the bulk of her fortune, more than $1 billion, to establish a charitable foundation.

Her friend, advisor (and ex-butler), Bernard Lafferty, received a lifetime annuity of $500,000 a year. He was also named executor of the will and trustee of the foundation—positions that would potentially generate millions of dollars in fees. However, in 1995, a Manhattan surrogate ruled Lafferty unfit to continue as executor after he used estate funds irresponsibly to finance his own lavish lifestyle. At estate expense, Lafferty was alleged to have been chauffeured around in Duke's Cadillac and private Boeing 737 jet; with estate credit cards, he allegedly amassed huge bills for antiques, clothing, and jewelry. The ruling of the Manhattan surrogate was appealed. Excerpts of the will of Doris Duke are reproduced in Appendix B.

---

§ 11.3 DUTIES OF PERSONAL REPRESENTATIVE

The duties of a personal representative in general are to collect and preserve the assets of the estate; pay the debts, taxes, and expenses of administration; and distribute the remainder according to the terms of the will or the law of intestate succession if there is no will. Specific rules and regulations for carrying out the duties of a personal representative are set forth in the various state statutes. Under UPC §§ 3–705 through 3–709, the personal representatives must inform the heirs and devisees of the appointment within 30 days, file an inventory of the estate within three months, take possession and control of the decedent's property, and take all steps necessary for the management, protection, and preservation of the property.

The personal representative's duties and responsibilities are numerous and vary greatly depending on the complexity of the estate. In general, they include the following:

1. Locate and read will, if there is one.
   - Ascertain funeral and burial instructions.
   - Verify nomination of executor.
   - Meet key family members.
2. Safeguard the estate assets.
   - Take control of all assets and records.
   - Provide insurance if necessary.
3. Determine the decedent's heirs at law.
4. Petition the court for probate of the will or administration of the estate.
   - Apply for letters.
   - Notify interested parties.
   - Locate witnesses if necessary.
5. Gather and make inventory of all assets.
   - Track down bank accounts, securities, deeds, etc.
   - Notify and file claims with insurance companies.
   - Take possession of safe-deposit box contents.
   - List assets in detail.
   - Obtain appraisal of assets.
   - Manage any real property.
   - Collect accounts due.
   - Oversee any business interests.
6. Administer the estate.
7. Prepare tax returns.
   - Decedent's final state and federal income taxes.
   - Estate state and federal income taxes.
   - Federal and state estate taxes.
8. Settle all claims.
   - Notify creditors.
   - Verify the validity of claims.
9. Distribute the probate estate.
   - Obtain receipts and releases from legatees.

10. Prepare the probate account.

11. Obtain the final discharge.

Unless allowed by state statute or the decedent's will, a personal representative has no authority to continue a decedent's business. Here is the Massachusetts statute (Mass. Gen. Laws ch. 195, § 17) that allows a personal representative to do so:

> The probate court, upon such notice as it considers reasonable, may authorize an executor or administrator to continue the business of the deceased for the benefit of the estate for a period not exceeding one year from the date of his appointment. Such authority may be granted at the time of the appointment of an executor or administrator if the petition for such appointment contains a prayer there for, and may be granted without special notice or with such special notice as the court may order to be given prior to or after the granting of such authority. The court, for cause shown, may extend such authority beyond one year.

Example

Provision in Will Authorizing Continuation of Business

8 AMJUR LF EXEC § 104:73

I empower my personal representative, during the administration of my estate and pending the sale of the property of my estate, to continue all business activities in which I may have been engaged at the time of my death. _____ [He or She] may continue the activities either singly or in a partnership or association with others until the business is sold to the best business advantage as my personal representative shall judge.

Claims against the estate must be presented to the personal representative within a prescribed time period set by state statute. The personal representative must pay all taxes that are due and all legitimate claims against the estate that arose before the death of the decedent. If the assets of the estate are insufficient to pay all claims in full, state statutes provide the order of priority in which they must be paid (see UPC § 3-805).

Once the assets have been collected, the debts and taxes paid, and the time within which creditors may present claims expired, the personal representative may distribute the assets to the rightful heirs. The personal representative files accounts with the court once a year (if the estate cannot be closed) and a final accounting when the estate is closed. The duties of the personal representative end when the final account is allowed by the court.

The paralegal may be asked to assist the personal representative, under the direction of an attorney, with many procedures involved in settling the estate. The paralegal may compile the estate inventory; correspond with institutions (banks, insurance companies, etc.) for asset information; maintain records of creditors' claims, accumulated assets, and the like; file legal documents at the required times; draft legal documents and tax returns; and coordinate dates for filing—thereby ensuring that the complex probate process is manageable and completed correctly.

CASE STUDY   *Pamintuan v. Dosado*

844 A.2d 1010(DE)

FACTS:	Elpidio Rosado died on September 6, 1989. In his will, he specifically directed his executrix to repay a loan to Jose Pamintuan. The rest of the estate, after other debts, went to Elpidio's wife. The primary asset of the estate was a home. Rather than force a sale, Pamintuan allowed the widow to live in the house. The house was now sold, and Pamintuan claimed on the old debt. In Delaware, claims against an estate are barred by a nonclaim statute that precludes payment from an estate unless the claim is submitted in a timely fashion, eight months from date of death.
LEGAL ISSUE:	Did the executrix breach her fiduciary obligation to Pamintuan by not paying the loan as directed by the will?
COURT DECISION:	Yes.
REASON:	Even though the debt was not filed against the estate in a timely fashion, the executrix, who was aware of the debt, established an implied trust by living in the house, as her fiduciary duty required she carry out the financial demands of the estate. As the trust was established in a timely fashion, the claim was not time barred and the executrix/trustee still needed to pay the loan.

---

§ 11.4 TITLES OF PERSONAL REPRESENTATIVE

Under the Uniform Probate Code, a personal representative is known simply as a "personal representative" [§ 1-201(30)]. In states that have not adopted the UPC, personal representatives are given various titles, depending on how they are appointed and the extent of their duties. Some of the different titles are discussed here.

Executor(-trix)

A male who is nominated in a will by a testator to serve as personal representative and carry out the directions in the will is called an executor. A female who is nominated in a will by a testator to serve as personal representative and carry out the directions in the will is called an executrix. State statutes

CASE STUDY		*In Re Estate of Miller*

568 So. 2d 487 (FL)

FACTS:	Pete Miller executed a will naming his nephew, Lloyd Smith, as personal representative of his estate. When Miller died, a relative filed a petition for appointment of a curator, alleging that Smith was improperly disposing of estate assets. (Under Florida law, a curator may be appointed to take charge of an estate before a personal representative is appointed.) Without holding a hearing to determine the validity of the relative's allegations, the trial court appointed the relative as curator rather than appointing Smith as personal representative of the estate.
LEGAL ISSUE:	Unless he or she is disqualified, must the personal representative named in the will be appointed by the court?
COURT DECISION:	Yes.
REASON:	Although courts have a limited amount of discretion to refuse to appoint the personal representative named in the will, the general rule is that trial courts are without discretion to refuse to appoint the personal representative specified by the testator, unless the person is expressly disqualified under the statute or under the court's limited discretion. The Florida statute states that once a petition for administration is filed, "the court shall appoint the person entitled and qualified to be personal representative."

provide that the person named in a will to be the executor or executrix is entitled to be appointed to that position, provided he is legally competent and is generally a suitable person.

The appointment of a coexecutor or coexecutrix is less fraught with difficulties than the appointment of cotrustees. Executors have more time-limited duties, and their tasks are somewhat less judgment calls than those of trustees. As always, though, the potential for judgment gridlock exists when coexecutors or cotrustees are named.

Administrator(-trix)

■ **administrator**

A person appointed by the court to supervise the estate (property) of a dead person. If the supervising person is named in the dead person's will, the proper name is executor.

■ **administratrix**

Female appointed to administer the estate of an intestate decedent.

When someone dies intestate and leaves assets to be administered, the court must appoint a personal representative to perform that task (see Exhibit 11–4). A male appointed to administer the estate of an intestate decedent is called an **administrator**. A female appointed to administer the estate of an intestate decedent is called an **administratrix**. State statutes set forth orders of priority for different people to be appointed administrators. The following is an example.

Administration, To Whom Granted

[Mass. Gen. Laws ch. 193, § 1]

Administration of the estate of a person deceased intestate shall be granted to one or more of the persons hereinafter mentioned and in the order named, if competent and suitable for the discharge of the trust and willing to undertake it, unless the court deems it proper to appoint some other person:

First, the widow or surviving husband of the deceased.

Second, the next of kin or their guardians or conservators as the court shall determine.

Third, if none of the above are competent or if they all renounce the administration or without sufficient cause neglect for thirty days after the death of the intestate to take administration of his estate, one or more of the principal creditors, after public notice upon the petition.

Fourth, if there is no widow, husband, or next of kin within the commonwealth, a public administrator.

Under UPC § 3–203, surviving spouses have first priority to be appointed personal representatives of intestate decedents. Other heirs of the decedent are second in line. Third in line are creditors, but only after 45 days have elapsed after the death of the decedent.

Administrator with the Will Annexed

Except in the case of an executor *de son tort* (discussed later), the only time that a personal representative can be called an "executor" or an "executrix" is when that person is nominated in the will to serve in that capacity. Thus, when a testator dies and someone who is not nominated in the testator's will is appointed by the court to serve as personal representative, that person cannot be called an "executor" but is given another title. He or she is known as an **administrator with the will annexed** (also called an *administrator w.w.a.*) or an *administrator cum testamento annexo* (also called an *administrator c.t.a.*). Such a person is appointed to administer a testate estate in which no executor is nominated, or the named executor declines the nomination or dies or is disqualified before being appointed. As an example, when Harry dies, his named executor is his brother, Bill. Bill, however, is employed in France, and cannot undertake the obligations of executor. The court would need to appoint an administrator with the will annexed to execute the testator's wishes. In at least one state, as shown by the *Dismuke* case, an administrator with the will annexed may be appointed by a majority vote of the beneficiaries under the will.

■ **administrator with the will annexed**

(Latin) "With the will attached." An administrator who is appointed by a court to supervise handing out the property of a dead person whose will does not name executors (persons to hand out property) or whose named executors cannot or will not serve. Also known as *administrator w.w.a.*, *administrator cum testamento annexo*, and *administrator c.t.a.*

Commonwealth of Massachusetts
The Trial Court
_____ Division   **Probate and Family Court Department**   Docket No. _____

Administration With/Without Sureties

Name of Decedent _____

Domicile at Death _____
(Street and No.)   (City or Town)   (County)   (Zip)

Date of Death _____

Name and address of Petitioner(s) _____

_____ Status _____

Heirs at law or next of kin of deceased including surviving spouse:

Name	Residence (minors and incompetents must be so designated)	Relationship

☐ The petitioner(s) hereby certif ____ that a copy of this document, along with a copy of the decedent's death certificate has been sent by certified mail to the **Division of Medical Assistance, P.O. Box 86, Essex Station, Boston, Massachusetts 02112.**

Petitioner(s) pray(s) that he/she/they or some other suitable person_____
of_____ in the County of _____ be appointed
administrat _____ of said estate with/without surety on his/her/their bond(s) and certif_____ under the penalties of perjury that the foregoing statements are true to the best of his/her/their knowledge and belief.

Date_____   Signature(s)_____

_____

The undersigned hereby assent to the foregoing petition.

_____   _____

_____   _____

_____   _____

DECREE

All persons interested having been notified in accordance with the law or having assented and no objections being made thereto, it is decreed that _____
of_____in the
County of_____ be appointed administrat_____ of said estate first giving bond with_____ sureties for the due performance of said trust.

Date_____   _____
                                    JUSTICE OF THE PROBATE AND FAMILY COURT

CJ-P1 (4/99)

EXHIBIT 11–4 Petition for Administration with/without Sureties (Massachusetts)

CASE STUDY *Dismuke v. Dismuke*

394 S.E.2d 371 (GA)

FACTS:	When R. T. Dismuke died, his widow, who was named executrix in the will, renounced the position and selected the decedent's son, Robert, to serve as administrator with the will annexed. A majority of the will's beneficiaries objected, proposing instead that the decedent's daughter, Diane, be appointed administratrix with the will annexed. A statute in that state (applied only to intestate cases) provided that a surviving spouse, upon declining to serve personally as administrator, is entitled to select the person to serve as replacement. A later-enacted statute provided: "in lieu of the foregoing rules, the beneficiaries under a will who are capable of expressing a choice shall be entitled to name an administrator with the will annexed."
LEGAL ISSUE:	Under Georgia law, when an executrix named in a will renounces the position, is the person selected by the majority of beneficiaries, rather than the person selected by the executrix, entitled to be named administrator with the will annexed?
COURT DECISION:	Yes.
REASON:	Although the statute does not provide how the selection of an administrator must be made, clearly it does mandate that its language is to be applied "in lieu of" the remaining rules set forth in the statute—rules that historically have been applied solely in intestacy situations. Because the statute does not declare that *all* of the beneficiaries under the will must agree to the naming of the administrator, we hold that only a majority of the beneficiaries under the will are necessary to name an administrator with the will annexed.

Successor Personal Representative

Sometimes, when an administrator does not fully perform the task of settling an estate, a new administrator must be appointed to do so. The new person so appointed is called an **administrator of goods not administered** or an *administrator de bonis non* (also called an *administrator d.b.n.*).

When an executor or an administrator c.t.a. does not fully perform the task of settling an estate, the new person appointed to complete the task is called an administrator of goods not administered with the will annexed or an administrator *de bonis non cum testamento annexo* (also called an administrator d.b.n.c.t.a.).

■ **administrator of goods not administered**

(Latin) "Of the goods not (already taken care of)." An administrator appointed to hand out the property of a dead person whose executor (person chosen to hand it out) has died. Also called *administrator de bonis non* or *administrator d.b.n.*

The UPC eliminates these long titles and simply calls someone who takes over for another a "successor personal representative." Under UPC § 1–201(41), a **successor personal representative** is a personal representative (other than a special administrator, which is discussed next) who is appointed to succeed a previously appointed personal representative.

Special Administrator

Sometimes the need for someone to take immediate charge of an estate is so urgent that the somewhat slow appointment process must be bypassed. To allow for such a need, the court may at any time appoint a special administrator (see UPC §§ 3-614 through 3-618). A **special administrator** is appointed to handle the affairs of an estate for a limited time for a special purpose (see Exhibit 11–5).

The chief duties of a special administrator are to collect and preserve the assets of the estate until the executor or administrator is appointed. The powers of a special administrator end when a regular executor or administrator is appointed; at that time, the special administrator must turn over the estate assets to the new appointee.

When there is a will contest (a lawsuit over the allowance or disallowance of a will), the court may appoint someone to serve as a personal representative during the suit. Such a person is called an **administrator** *pendente lite* and is a temporary administrator appointed before the adjudication of testacy or intestacy in order to preserve the assets of an estate.

Sometimes it is necessary to appoint an administrator solely for the purpose of a lawsuit other than a will contest. Such an administrator is called an **administrator** *ad litem*. He is appointed by the court to furnish a necessary party to a lawsuit in which a deceased has an interest. The *Traub* case illustrates this situation.

Public Administrator

When an estate must be probated but no eligible person comes forward to serve as administrator, the court will appoint a public administrator to perform the task. A **public administrator** is an official appointed to administer the estate of an intestate decedent when no one appears who is entitled to act as administrator (see Exhibit 11–6). State statutes provide for the appointment by the governor of a limited number of public administrators to serve in each county. The duties and obligations of public administrators are set forth in the statutes of the various states.

Commonwealth of Massachusetts
The Trial Court

_____ Division   **Probate and Family Court Department**   Docket No. _____

Special Administration

Name of Decedent _____

Domicile at Death _____
                  (street and no.)   (city or town)

_____ Date of Death_____
(county)   (zip)

Name and address of Petitioner(s)_____

_____ Status _____

Respectfully represent(s) that said decedent died possessed of goods and estate remaining to be administered, and that there is delay in securing the appointment of_____

_____ of the estate of said decedent by reason

of _____

_____

☐ The petitioner(s) hereby certif ____that a copy of this document, along with a copy of the decedent's death certificate has been sent by <u>certified mail</u> to the **Division of Medical Assistance, P.O. Box 86, Essex Station, Boston, Massachusetts 02112.**

Wherefore your petitioner(s) pray(s) that he/she/they or some other suitable person:_____

of_____
                          (street and no.)

_____may be appointed special
(city or town)   (county)   (zip)

administrator/administratrix of said decedent and may be authorized to take charge of all the real estate of said decedent and to collect rents and make necessary repairs; and may be authorized to continue the business of the decedent for the benefit of his/her estate, and certif_____ under the penalties of perjury that the statements herein contained are true to the best of his/her/their knowledge and belief.

Date_____   Signature_____

The undersigned hereby assent to the foregoing petition.

_____   _____
_____   _____
_____   _____
_____   _____

DECREE

All persons interested having been notified in accordance with the law or having assented and no objections being

made thereto, it is decreed that _____ of _____

_____ in the County of_____ be appointed

administrat _____ of said estate, first giving bond with_____ sureties, for the due performance of said trust.

Date_____   _____
                                         Justice of the Probate and Family Court

CJ-P 8 (12/99)

EXHIBIT 11–5 Petition for Special Administration (Massachusetts)

> ### CASE STUDY 〰 *Traub v. Zlatkiss*
>
> *559 So. 2d 443 (FL)*
>
> | | |
> |---|---|
> | FACTS: | Not long before his death, Sheldon Traub transferred bank accounts and other property to his friend and business partner, Jerrod Zlatkiss. In his will, Traub named Zlatkiss as personal representative of his estate. Traub's estranged wife claimed that the transfers to Zlatkiss were done to deprive her of her elective share of his estate. Florida law permits only a personal representative (in this case, Zlatkiss) to bring an action to rescind (take back) a decedent's prior transfers; therefore, Mrs. Traub could not bring suit to protect her interests. |
> | LEGAL ISSUE: | May an administrator *ad litem* be appointed when the personal representative appears to have an interest that is adverse to the interest of the estate? |
> | COURT DECISION: | Yes. |
> | REASON: | When it is necessary that the estate of a decedent be represented in any probate proceedings and the personal representative is or may be interested adversely to the estate, the court may appoint an administrator *ad litem*, without bond or notice, for that particular proceeding. |

Informal Administrator of Small Estates

State statutes, including UPC § 3–1201, contain provisions for the informal administration of small estates. For an estate to qualify for informal administration, the value of the estate must not exceed an amount set by state statute, a prescribed period of time must have elapsed since the death of the decedent, and a petition for probate of the estate must not have been filed. As examples, New York currently sets the maximum amount of the estate that qualifies as a small estate at $20,000; in New Jersey, the amount is also $20,000, as long as the spouse is the sole heir. Although these amounts may seem small, the amount is adequate when individuals of higher worth have living trusts, as well as for people of modest means. A person who undertakes the informal administration of a small estate is referred to, in some states, as a **voluntary executor** if there is a will, and a **voluntary administrator** if there is no will (see Exhibit 11–7).

A voluntary executor or administrator has limited power. For example, in a negligence action against a surgeon for the wrongful death of a patient, the court held that a voluntary administrator had no power to bring a wrongful death claim or to settle one. The court said that "the status of voluntary administrator may be achieved on fulfillment of essentially administrative formalities and without formal court approval. A voluntary administrator is not required to give bond with sufficient sureties to guarantee the proper performance of his or her trust" (*Marco v. Green*, 615 N.E.2d 928 [Mass. 1993]).

■ **voluntary executor**
Person who undertakes the informal administration of a small testate estate.

■ **voluntary administrator**
Person who undertakes the informal administration of a small intestate estate.

Commonwealth of Massachusetts
The Trial Court

_____ Division   Probate and Family Court Department   Docket No. _____

Public Administration With Sureties

Name of Decedent _____

Domicile at Death _____
(street and no.)   (city or town)

_____ Date of Death _____
(county)   (zip)

Name and address of Public Administrator/Administratrix _____

_____

Decedent left no known widow/widower or heir in this Commonwealth; that said decedent left property in the County
of_____
to be administered,_____
_____

☐ The petitioner is designated by the Department of Public Welfare as the Public Administrat _____ to be appointed pursuant to M.G.L. ch. 194 specifically to pursue a claim against the estate for $_____, the amount alleged due the Department pursuant to M.G.L. ch. 118E. Further, the petitioner states that more than one year has passed from the date of decedent's death, and neither a petition for administration of the decedent's estate nor for admission to probate of the decedent's will has been filed with the Probate and Family Court.

☐ The petitioner hereby certifies that a copy of this document, along with a copy of the decedent's death certificate has been sent by <u>certified mail</u> to the **Department of Public Welfare, P.O. Box 86, Essex Station, Boston, Massachusetts 02112.**

Petitioner prays that he/she be appointed administrator/administratrix of said estate — with — without — sureties on his/her bond and certifies under the penalties of perjury that the foregoing statements are true to the best of his/her knowledge and belief.

Date_____   Signature_____

DECREE

All persons interested having been notified in accordance with the law and no objections being made thereto, it is decreed that said Public Administrat _____ be appointed administrat _____ of said estate, first giving bond with_____ sureties for the due performance of said trust.

Date_____   _____
                                          Justice of the Probate and Family Court

CJ-P 9 (8/92)

EXHIBIT 11–6   Petition for Public Administration with Sureties (Massachusetts)

Commonwealth of Massachusetts
The Trial Court

_____ Division **Probate and Family Court Department** Docket No. _____

Voluntary Administration

Name of Decedent _____

Domicile at Death _____
　　　　　　　　(Street and No.)　　　　　　　　　(City or Town)　　　　(County)　　(Zip)

Date of Death _____

Death Certificate shall be filed with application.

Name and address of Applicant(s) _____

_____ Status _____

Your applicant(s) respectfully state(s) that said estate consisting entirely of personal property the total value of which does not exceed fifteen thousand dollars ($15,000) exclusive of the decedent's automobile as shown by the following schedule of all the assets of said deceased known to the applicant(s):

Name of Property	Estimated Value
_____	$ _____
_____	$ _____
_____	$ _____
_____	$ _____
_____	$ _____
Total	$ _____

That thirty days have expired since the date of death of said deceased and no petition for probate of will or appointment of administration/administratrix has been filed in said Court.

That your applicant(s) ha ___ undertaken to act as voluntary administrator/administratrix of the estate of said deceased and will administer the same according to law and apply the proceeds thereof in conformity with Section 16 of Chapter 195 of the General Laws.

That to the knowledge of the applicant(s) the following are the names and addresses of all persons surviving who, with the deceased, were joint owners of property: also listed are the names and addresses of those who would take under the provisions of Section 3 of Chapter 190 in the case of intestacy.

_____

_____

_____

☐ The applicant(s) hereby certif _____ that a copy of this document, along with a copy of the decedent's death certificate has been sent by <u>certified mail</u> to the **Division of Medical Assistance, P.O. Box 86, Essex Station, Boston, Massachusetts 02112.**

Date _____　　Signature _____

NOTARIZATION

_____ , ss.　　　　Date _____ , _____

Then personally appeared_____
to me known and made oath that the information contained in the foregoing statement is true to the best of his/her/ their knowledge and belief.

Before me, _____
　　　　　　NOTARY PUBLIC/JUSTICE OF THE PEACE

My Commission expires _____

CJ-P7 (10/99)

EXHIBIT 11–7　Petition for Voluntary Administration (Massachusetts)

Executor *de Son Tort*

A person who performs tasks of a personal representative and handles the property of the decedent without authority is called an **executor *de son tort*** (see Table 11–1). He acts like an executor or administrator, but without legal authority. Many states refuse to recognize such an intermeddler as an executor at all. Other states acknowledge such an individual as an executor *de son tort*, but only in order to sue or make him or her liable for the assets that were intermeddled. Some acts of intermeddling that have been considered sufficient to make someone an executor *de son tort* are: collecting money due a decedent, paying a decedent's debts, appropriating growing crops that belong to a decedent, and continuing the business of a decedent. When a lawful executor or administrator has been appointed, no executor *de son tort* can exist, because the assets of the estate can be reached only through the legally appointed or rightful executor or administrator.

■ **executor de son tort**

(French) "Of his own wrong." A person who takes on a duty, such as being executor of a will, without any right to take on the duty, will be held responsible for all actions he takes as executor.

TABLE 11–1 **Titles of Personal Representatives**

administrator	A male appointed by the court to administer an intestate estate
administrator *ad litem*	A person appointed by the court to furnish a necessary party to a lawsuit in which a deceased has an interest
administrator *cum testamento annexo* (c.t.a.); also called *administrator with the will annexed (w.w.a.)*	A person not named in the will who is appointed by the court to administer a testate estate
administrator *de bonis non* (d.b.n.); also called *administrator of goods not administered*	A person appointed by the court to succeed an administrator who did not complete the task of administering an intestate estate
administrator *de bonis non cum testamento annexo* (d.b.n.c.t.a.); also called *administrator of goods not administered with the will annexed*	A person appointed by the court to succeed an administrator *cum testamento annexo* who did not complete the task of administering an intestate estate
administrator *pendente lite*	A person appointed by the court temporarily, before the adjudication of testacy or intestacy, to preserve the assets of an estate
administratrix	A female appointed by the court to administer an intestate estate

(continues)

TABLE 11–1   **Titles of Personal Representatives** (continued)

executor	A male nominated in a will to carry out the terms of the will
executor *de son tort*	A person who performs tasks of a personal representative and intermeddles with the property of a decedent without authority
executrix	A female nominated in a will to carry out the terms of the will
public administrator	An official appointed to administer an estate when no one appears who is entitled to act as executor or administrator
special administrator	A person appointed by the court to handle the affairs of an estate for a limited time for a special purpose
voluntary administrator	A person who undertakes the informal administration of a small intestate estate
voluntary executor	A person who undertakes the informal administration of a small testate estate

§ 11.5 REMOVAL OF PERSONAL REPRESENTATIVE

The death of a personal representative terminates the appointment [UPC § 3–609]. The representative of the deceased personal representative must preserve the estate's assets and turn them over to the successor personal representative.

A personal representative cannot resign without the probate court's consent, and then only when a successor personal representative has been appointed. Under UPC § 3–610d, a personal representative may attempt to resign by filing a written statement to that effect with the court and giving 15 days' notice to persons interested in the estate.

Example

NOTICE OF RESIGNATION

8 AMJUR LF EXEC § 104:4

I, _____ , of _____ [address], City of _____ , County of _____ , State of _____ , appointed by this court on _____ , as personal representative of the estate of _____ , tender my written resignation.

I represent to this court that I stand ready to settle my accounts and deliver all of the property of the estate to the person whom this court shall appoint to receive the property.

Dated: _____ .

[Signature]

If someone comes forward to succeed the personal representative, the resignation takes effect upon the appointment and qualification of the successor representative and delivery of assets to him or her. If no one applies to be successor representative, the attempted resignation is ineffective. The *Nelson* case addresses this distinction.

A personal representative may be removed by the court when it would be in the best interest of the estate to do so [UPC § 3–611]. Grounds for removal include mismanagement of the estate, the disregarding of court orders, failure to perform required duties, breach of a fiduciary duty, and bad character. A personal representative who becomes insane, is incapable of performing the required duties, or is unsuitable to perform the duties may be removed by the court. Any person with an interest in an estate may petition the court for removal of a personal representative for cause at any time. A hearing must be held to determine the cause before the personal representative can be discharged.

CASE STUDY   *In Re* Estate of Nelson

794 P.2d 677 (MT)

FACTS:	Ruth L. Nelson's will appointed Guy L. Robbins, her financial advisor, as personal representative. After Robbins submitted his final accounting to the court, one of the heirs objected to several claims against the estate made by Robbins, charged him with a number of counts of self-dealing, and petitioned for his removal. Robbins subsequently moved out of state, filed bankruptcy, and filed a letter of resignation as personal representative. The court thereafter removed Robbins for cause as personal representative.
LEGAL ISSUE:	May a court remove a personal representative for cause after receiving the representative's letter of resignation?
COURT DECISION:	Yes.
REASON:	A voluntary resignation by a personal representative is effective only upon the appointment and qualification of a successor representative and delivery of the assets to the successor. Robbins's resignation had no effect, because the court did not appoint a successor until it ordered his removal for cause.

As a matter of practice, removing a personal representative is a difficult task. Courts endeavor to carry out the appointment made by the testator. An executor who is difficult for the beneficiaries to deal with is an unpleasant circumstance, but is often a problem without a solution. Indeed, even when personal property disappears from the estate, clear evidence of misconduct is required by the courts. The common, even chronic, complaint of family members who are beneficiaries that items that they knew were in the estate are missing, without concrete proof, falls on deaf judicial ears. Choosing an executor who is effective and trustworthy is an important and substantial task for testators. They need to be encouraged to choose well.

When a will is found after letters of administration have been granted as if there were no will, state laws generally provide that the letters of administration are revoked when the will is proved. Estate assets must be handed over to the executor or the administrator with the will annexed. Under UPC § 3–612, termination of a personal representative's appointment occurs only when a new person takes over; if no one does, the previously appointed personal representative may be appointed personal representative under the subsequently probated will.

CASE STUDY   **District Attorney for Magraw**

628 N.E.2d 24 (MA)

FACTS:	Nancy Magraw executed a will naming her husband, David, as executor. The marriage eventually deteriorated, causing them to separate and negotiate for a divorce settlement. During the negotiations, Nancy was found dead in her home, the victim of a homicide. David, who had assumed his duties as executor of Nancy's estate, was considered a suspect. He impeded the investigation by refusing to waive the confidentiality privilege between his wife and her lawyer and psychotherapist, to whom she had confided her fear of her husband's potential for violence.
LEGAL ISSUE:	May a husband be removed as the executor of his wife's estate because he is a suspect in his wife's death?
COURT DECISION:	Yes.
REASON:	The defendant, as a suspect in his wife's death, had an interest in keeping from authorities any information that might possibly have inculpated him. This interest created reasonable doubt that he honestly, fairly, and dispassionately could execute his responsibilities as executor of his wife's estate.
	[Soon after the *Magraw* case was decided, David Magraw was convicted of first-degree murder and sentenced to life in prison without parole.]

SUMMARY

When someone dies, it is usually necessary for the court to appoint a fiduciary, called a personal representative, to settle the decedent's estate. In testate cases, a person nominated in the will, or some other interested person, petitions the court to have the will allowed and to be appointed as personal representative. In intestate cases, one of the heirs, next of kin, or a creditor files a petition with the court requesting the appointment.

In some states, the appointment of a personal representative is not complete until the representative has given bond. In other states, no bond is required if the will has a provision requesting that the personal representative serve without bond. Under some circumstances, a bond is not required if all heirs at law waive the filing of a bond and the will does not require one. Under the Uniform Probate Code, a bond may be required when an interested person demands that a bond be given.

The duties of a personal representative are to collect and preserve the assets of the estate; pay the debts, taxes, and expenses of administration; and distribute the remainder according to the terms of the will, or the law of intestate succession if there is no will. The paralegal may be asked to assist the personal representative with the many procedures involved in settling the estate. By providing such assistance, the paralegal helps ensure that the complex probate process is manageable and completed correctly.

Once the assets have been collected, the debts and taxes paid, and the time within which creditors may present claims expired, the personal representative may distribute the assets to the rightful heirs. The duties of the personal representative end when the final account is allowed by the court.

Under the Uniform Probate Code, a personal representative is known simply as a "personal representative." In states that have not adopted the UPC, personal representatives are given various titles, depending on how they are appointed and the extent of their duties.

A special administrator is appointed to handle the affairs of an estate for a limited time for a special purpose. The chief duties of a special administrator are to collect and preserve the assets of the estate for the executor or administrator when appointed. The powers of a special administrator end when a regular executor or administrator is appointed.

When it is necessary for an estate to be probated and no one who is eligible comes forward to serve as administrator, the court will appoint a public administrator to perform the task.

State statutes contain provisions for the informal administration of small estates. For an estate to qualify for informal administration, the value of the estate must not exceed an amount set by state statute, a prescribed period of time must have elapsed since the death of the decedent, and a petition for probate of the estate must not have been filed. A person who undertakes the informal administration of a small estate is referred to, in some states, as a voluntary executor if there is a will and as a voluntary administrator if there is no will.

A person who intrudes into the office of personal representative and intermeddles with the property of the decedent without authority is called an executor *de son tort*.

The death of a personal representative terminates the appointment. A personal representative cannot resign without the probate court's consent, and then only when a successor personal representative is appointed. A personal representative may be removed by the court when it would be in the best interest of the estate to do so. Grounds for removal include mismanagement of the estate, the disregarding of court orders, and failure to perform required duties.

■ REVIEW QUESTIONS

1. Why is a personal representative known as a fiduciary?

2. Describe generally the procedure that occurs when a petition for appointment of personal representative is filed with the court.

3. What is the difference between letters testamentary and letters of administration?

4. Why must a personal representative give a bond under the laws of some states?

5. In general, what are the duties of a personal representative?

6. When may a personal representative distribute assets to the rightful heirs? When do the duties of a personal representative end?

7. When is a personal representative known as:

   a. an executrix?

   b. an administrator?

   c. an administrator with the will annexed?

   d. an administratrix *de bonis non*?

   e. an administrator *de bonis non cum testamento annexo*?

8. What are the chief duties of a special administrator, and when do his or her powers end?

9. What is the difference between an administrator *pendente lite* and an administrator *ad litem*? Who is an executor *de son tort*?

10. When may a personal representative resign? When may he be removed?

■ CASES TO DISCUSS_____

1. The probate court admitted the will of Thomas R. McElhenney to probate and issued letters testamentary to Jeff E. Geeslin. Geeslin failed from the outset to assess the income of the estate and its taxes and other obligations, causing the estate to incur interest and penalties of over $150,000. Among other things, Geeslin failed to set aside funds when he became aware that there would be an additional estate-tax liability; he commingled estate funds with the decedent's pension funds; and he failed to make a timely request for an extension of time to pay the federal estate tax. Can Geeslin be removed by the court from his position as executor? Why or why not? *Geeslin v. McElhenney*, 788 S.W.2d 683 (TX).

2. Although William Bearden's will named his wife, Katherine, as executrix, the court appointed someone else as a special administrator when he died, because Katherine was suffering the effects of alcoholism. Later, finding her to be competent, the court appointed Katherine as executrix. Bearden's children of a former marriage appealed the appointment, quoting the state statute: "No person is competent to serve as executor who at the time the will is admitted to probate is adjudged by the court incompetent to execute the duties of the trust by reason of drunkenness." Should Katherine be appointed executrix? Why or why not? *Matter of Estate of Bearden*, 800 P.2d 1086 (OK).

3. Robert O. Hamilton petitioned the court for letters of administration of his father's estate. The petition that he signed contained an oath stating that he "will well, faithfully, and honestly discharge the duties" of the office and "will duly account for all moneys and other property that will come into his hands." Hamilton refused to file a final account, even when ordered to do so, and was held in contempt of court, arrested, and placed in custody. He argued that he did not intentionally violate the court order because he had not maintained the records necessary to prepare an account. Is Hamilton's argument sound? Why or why not? *Matter of Estate of William L. Hamilton, Sr.*, 695 N.Y.S.2d 497 (NY).

■ RESEARCH ON THE WEB_____

1. On the Internet, log on to <http://www.Google.com>. Type the words *personal representative* in the box and look for something of interest to you. Print the information for your notebook.

2. Visit <http://www.westlegalstudies.com> for educational and professional resources for paralegals and legal assistants.

3. Try out the Law Engine: <http://www.thelawengine.com>.

4. Read the appellate court's decision in the Matter of Doris Duke. To find the case, log on to <http://www.findlaw.com>. Click States under Laws: Cases & Codes, then click New York and Primary Materials. At that point, click New York Court of Appeals Opinions from Findlaw since 1992. Finally, click 1996 followed by Matter of Doris Duke, 87 NY2d 465. *Matter of Doris Duke* is also found at 663 N.E.2d 602 and 640 N.Y.S.2d 446.

■ SHARPENING YOUR PROFESSIONAL SKILLS_____

1. In your state, what is the title given to the personal representative appointed by the court:

   a. When an executrix named in the will predeceases the testator?

   b. When an administrator dies before completing his duties?

   c. When an executrix dies before completing her duties?

2. Draft a $500,000 surety bond for an executor, using the form commonly used in your state.

3. Look up your state statute dealing with the powers of executors and administrators. Give the statutory reference where it is found, and determine whether a personal representative can continue running a decedent's business when that power is not provided for in a will.

4. Look up your state statute on special administrators. Give the statutory reference where it is found, and outline the administrators' duties and powers.

5. Who are named as executors of the will of Jacqueline K. Onassis (reproduced in Appendix B) and of the will of John Lennon (reproduced in Appendix B)? How are alternate executors to be selected in each will?

■ SHARPENING YOUR LEGAL VOCABULARY_____

On a separate sheet of paper, fill in the numbered blank lines in the following anecdote with legal terms from this list:

administrator

administrator *ad litem*

administrator *cum testamento annexo*

administrator *de bonis non*

administrator *de bonis non cum testamento annexo*

administrator of goods not administered

administrator of goods not administered with the will annexed

administrator *pendente lite*

administrator with the will annexed

administratrix

bond

executor

executor *de son tort*

executrix

fiduciary

fiduciary capacity

intestate

letters of administration

letters testamentary

personal representative

public administrator

special administrator

successor personal representative

sureties

voluntary administrator

voluntary executor

Alex Pujo, the owner of a truck farm, was killed when his wife, Betsy, accidentally ran over him with a tractor while harvesting the farm's vegetable crop. Betsy was appointed the (1) of his estate. Because Alex died (2), that is, without a will, Betsy was not called a(n) (3). Instead, she was known as a(n) (4). Before she was appointed to that office, however, Carl Pujo took control of Alex's truck farm without authority and started selling the vegetables. In some states, Carl would be known as a(n) (5) because he intermeddled with property of the decedent without authority. Due to the urgent need to care for the vegetables before they spoiled, the court appointed Dan Pujo as a(n) (6) to have the vegetables harvested and sold. Betsy was finally issued (7) (her certificate of appointment) and took office when her (8) (written promise) was approved by the court. It was allowed without (9) because the heirs agreed to accept Betsy's appointment without someone standing behind her. Because Betsy served in a position of trust and confidence, she was called a(n) (10) and served in a(n) (11).

It became necessary, however, for Alex's estate to bring suit against Betsy for Alex's wrongful death. Because Betsy was the personal representative of Alex's estate and was an adverse party, the court appointed a(n) (12) to bring the action against her. Before the estate was settled, Betsy died from sunstroke while picking vegetables on a hot summer day. The court appointed a(n) (13) (also called a(n) (14)) to complete the job of settling Alex's estate. Betsy's relatives contested the allowance of her will, requiring the court to appoint a(n) (15) as a temporary representative prior to the adjudication of testacy or intestacy to preserve the assets of the estate. Dan Pujo, who was nominated in Betsy's will to serve as personal representative of her estate, declined the position, so the court appointed Emily Pujo as a(n) (16) (also known as a(n) (17)) to assume that task. Emily's certificate of appointment was called (18). She began the work but became insane before the estate was settled, requiring the court to appoint a(n) (19) (also called a(n) (20)) to finish the job. Because Betsy's heirs served as personal representatives, it was unnecessary for the court to appoint a(n) (21) to perform that task.

■ KEY TERMS

administrator	administratrix	public administrator
administrator *ad item*	bond	special administrator
administrator of goods not administered	executor *de son tort*	successor personal representative
	fiduciary capacity	surety bond
administrator *pendente lite*	letters of administration	voluntary administrator
administrator with the will annexed	letters testamentary	voluntary executor

Online Companion™
For additional resources, please go to
http://www.paralegal.delmar.cengage.com.

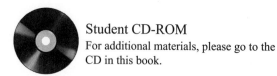

Student CD-ROM
For additional materials, please go to the
CD in this book.

CHAPTER 12

Probating a Will and Administering an Estate

■ CHAPTER OUTLINE

■ CHAPTER OUTCOMES

- Recognize the need for probate in particular cases.

- Outline the steps necessary when formal probate proceedings are undertaken in your state.

- List the steps that are used when informal probate proceedings are undertaken in your state.

- Explain the procedure used in your state when ancillary administration is undertaken.

■ JOB COMPETENCIES

- Be able to explain the reasons for probate proceedings.

- Be able to prepare letters to clients outlining the probate process.

- Be able to gather information that is needed to settle an estate.

- Be able to assist the attorney with the process of settling an estate.

- Be able to prepare documents that are used when various probate proceedings are undertaken.

"Don't turn down the light. I'm afraid to go home in the dark."

LAST WORDS OF O. HENRY (1862–1910)

313

◼ A DAY AT THE OFFICE . . .

Attorney Knutson asked her legal assistant, Lorna Garcia, to come into her office where she was meeting with a client.

"Mr. Notmeyer, this is my assistant, Lorna Garcia," Attorney Knutson said. "She'll be helping me with your father's estate."

"I'm pleased to meet you," Lorna said to Mr. Notmeyer with a smile.

"Mr. Notmeyer's father passed away about two years ago," Attorney Knutson explained, "and he's been handling the estate himself, until now."

"Yes, my brother, Oscar, is threatening to sue me, so I think I need some advice," Mr. Notmeyer volunteered. "I thought I did everything that I was supposed to do. I gave everything to my brothers and sisters equally just like my father wanted—except for my brother, Oscar. My father didn't like him, you know."

"Did your father leave a will?" Lorna asked.

"Yes, but my brother, Oscar, got hold of it first and won't let anyone see it. We think Oscar was left out of the will."

"Did you file any papers with the probate court?" Attorney Knutson asked.

"Oh, no!" Mr. Notmeyer responded. "I just divided by five and gave everyone their share. There are five of us, you know, not counting Oscar."

"Do you know the approximate value of the estate?" Attorney Knutson asked.

"Well, not exactly," Mr. Notmeyer replied. "There were five stock certificates, each worth about $200,000, so I gave each person, except Oscar, one of those. Then I divided the antique furniture five ways."

"Did you have it appraised?" Lorna inquired.

"No. I just gave everyone what they wanted—except for Oscar, of course. I didn't give him anything."

"Did your father own any real estate?" Attorney Knutson asked.

"Yes. He owned a house worth $700,000 and some vacant land on the ocean, somewhere out of state. It's supposed to be quite valuable—worth about $300,000."

"What about debts?" queried Attorney Knutson. "Did your father owe any money to anyone before he died?"

"Well, yes," Mr. Notmeyer answered. "He had quite a few outstanding bills because all his money was tied up in stocks, antiques, and that out-of-state property. I figured that if I didn't let his creditors know he died, by the time they found out, it would be too late for them to collect."

"Mr. Notmeyer, I'm going to leave you with Lorna for a while. She will take down some basic information that we need. Then I'll talk to you about some of the things we'll do to settle your father's estate."

Queries:

1. What is the penalty, under your state law, for failing to turn a decedent's will over to the probate court?

2. What is the most appropriate method that would be used in your state to settle Mr. Notmeyer's estate?
3. Will Mr. Notmeyer's estate be required to file a federal estate tax return? Why or why not?

§ 12.1 THE NEED FOR PROBATE

When someone dies owning property, the property must be protected; the decedent's debts must be paid; those individuals who should own the remainder of the property after the debts are paid must be identified; and the remainder must be distributed accordingly. The term *probate* (to test and to prove) is often used to describe this procedure. **Probating a will** is the process of proving or establishing before the probate court that the document being offered for official recognition as the will of the decedent is in fact genuine. **Administering an estate** means settling and distributing the estate of a deceased person.

The probate process includes the appointment of a personal representative (described in Chapter 11). This appointment gives him or her the legal authority to (1) collect and preserve the assets owned by the decedent, (2) pay the decedent's debts and taxes, and (3) distribute the remainder of the assets according to the terms of the will or the law of intestate succession.

The probate process protects the decedent by seeing that her wishes are carried out. It protects the heirs by assuring that all of the decedent's property is collected and accounted for and by determining the lawful heirs. It also establishes title to property that has been inherited.

■ **probating a will**
Process of proving or establishing before the probate court that the document being offered for official recognition as the will of the decedent is in fact genuine.

■ **administering an estate**
Settling and distributing the estate of a deceased person.

Protection of Decedent

When someone dies, it must first be determined whether there is a will. If a will is found, it must be turned over to the probate court in the county in which the decedent was domiciled, within a time period after death (often 30 days) that is set by state statute. Failure to give the will to the probate court may be a criminal offense. The following is an example of a state statute that allows anyone with an interest in an estate to file a complaint against another suspected of retaining or concealing a deceased person's will [Mass. Gen. Laws ch. 191, § 13]:

A person having custody of a will, other than a register of probate, shall, within thirty days after notice of the death of the testator, deliver such will into the probate court having jurisdiction of the probate thereof, or to the executors named in the will, who shall themselves deliver it into such court within said time; and if a person neglects without reasonable cause so to deliver a will, after being duly cited for that purpose by such court, he may be committed to jail by warrant of the court until he delivers it as above provided, and shall be liable to a person who is aggrieved for the damage sustained by him by reason of such neglect.

Presentation of a will to the court, even if the person in possession of the will considers it to be invalid, is required by law. Normal probate procedure allows a will that is offered for probate to be challenged by evidence that it is not the last will of the decedent or that it was improperly executed, or defective in some way.

Protection of Heirs

■ **heirs at law**

Those persons who would have inherited had the decedent died intestate.

Another important function of the probate procedure is the protection of heirs and next of kin. Heirs, in the term's broadest sense, are all persons who inherit property from a decedent's estate, whether testate or intestate. **Heirs at law** is a narrower term, referring to people who are entitled to inherit from someone under the law of intestate succession. In contrast, next of kin are those most nearly related by blood to the decedent and does not include persons related by marriage, such as a spouse. Heirs at law and next of kin are protected by the probate procedure in that their names must be listed on the petition for probate. They are notified of the probate proceeding and thereby allowed to present objections if the objections are legally sound.

The probate procedure also protects the decedent's property. As discussed later, one of the important duties of the personal representative after being appointed is to file an inventory of the estate with the probate court. The inventory lists all property owned by the decedent and is available for anyone to peruse in order to verify or challenge its contents. This requirement provides some assurance that all of the decedent's property will be listed. In addition, third parties such as banks will release funds from a decedent's bank account only to the personal representative, and then only upon receiving a certified copy of the representative's appointment. The same is true with stock certificates and bonds registered in the decedent's name. The personal representative is the only person who can legally enforce payment to the decedent's estate of money owed by others. Similarly, the personal representative of an estate is the only person who can be sued to collect money owed by the decedent's estate to others.

Establishing Title

The probate process also protects heirs by providing a system for establishing title to inherited property; this assures heirs, legatees, devisees, and future buyers that title is good. If the decedent left a will, legatees and devisees cannot prove their title to the property unless the will is probated. Similarly, in intestate estates, heirs must have the authority of the probate court to establish their title to property they inherit.

§ 12.2 FIRST MEETING WITH CLIENT

Paralegals often work with attorneys and clients from the very beginning of a probate, helping to perform the multitude of tasks that arise when an estate is settled. Their assistance may begin with research, or it may begin with the initial office conference with a probate client. When a client contacts a law office concerning a probate, an initial appointment with the attorney and paralegal who will be working on the file is often scheduled immediately. At times, as when the decedent owned a business, some matters concerning the decedent's estate must be dealt with as soon as possible. In addition, out-of-town relatives who have come to attend the funeral often want to attend the meeting with the attorney. If the deceased is a former client of the law firm, the paralegal is often asked to pull the client's past files for review before the initial meeting with the family. If the firm prepared the decedent's will, at least a copy of the will will be in the file, as well as financial information and useful information concerning family members.

At the first meeting, the following matters are typically addressed:

1. If the decedent died with a valid will, a determination is made with regard to the personal representative named in the will. Is this person willing and able to serve? If not, has an alternate been named?

2. If the decedent died without a valid will, a determination should be made as to which family members are best qualified to serve as administrators of the estate and whether they are willing to do so.

3. A list of all living and deceased heirs of the decedent should be made, including their full legal names, addresses, and relation to the deceased.

4. A plan should be made for keeping the family informed of the progress in handling the estate. Do all family members wish to be notified of all actions taken on behalf of the estate, or do they only wish to be notified of major events during the probate process?

5. The attorney should explain the probate process to the family, including what role each involved individual will fulfill. At this point, a preliminary decision should be made as to the extent of the personal representative's involvement in the probate process. The personal representative may wish to take a very active part in completing and filing all the paperwork necessary to probate the estate, or he or she may defer those duties to the attorney and paralegal.

6. A determination should be made as to any assets that may require immediate attention, such as insurance that may lapse if not paid, or a business that must be run.

7. The paralegal should record the pertinent information gathered from the family members with regard to the decedent's debts and assets and give the family a list of items that must be furnished to the paralegal or attorney when they can be located.

The information to be gathered includes:

1. information concerning bank accounts held by the decedent, including their location and the amount of cash in each account.

2. information concerning real estate in which the decedent held an interest, including deeds, owner's duplicate certificates of title, abstracts, mortgages, and leases.

3. information concerning stocks and bonds held by the decedent.

4. information concerning insurance policies on the life of the decedent or owned by the decedent.

5. copies of the decedent's income tax returns.

6. copies of gift tax returns filed by the decedent.

7. list of the decedent's debts at her date of death.

8. information concerning any pension or profit-sharing plans in which the decedent was a participant.

9. information on any pending estate or trust in which the decedent had an interest.

10. any other information concerning assets, debts, and financial matters of the decedent.

Confidentiality

It is extremely important that paralegals keep confidential all information that is learned at the meeting with the client. The same is true with information that is learned from papers that are in the client's file or by working on the case. The paralegal is an agent of the attorney. Private communications between the attorney, including her agents, and the client are confidential unless the client waives this protection. Every attorney and every attorney's agent have an ethical duty not to disclose confidential information to third parties.

Once documents are filed with the court, however, they are matters of public record and may be accessed by third parties. This information may include details of a family business that could be of benefit to competitors, or financial and personal details of a celebrity, or it may provide details to disgruntled beneficiaries or nonbeneficiaries. These public records are the inevitable result to probate.

§ 12.3 FORMAL PROBATE PROCEEDINGS

Formal probate proceedings are followed when someone dies owning assets above a specific value set by state statute or when it is appropriate to have the court supervise all aspects of the estate's settlement. The Uniform Probate Code (UPC) defines **formal proceedings** as those conducted before a judge with notice to interested persons [UPC § 1–201(15)]. In some states, formal probate proceedings are known as **probate in solemn form**.

Formal probate proceedings involve the following steps:

1. A petition is filed with the court.
2. Notice is given to interested parties.
3. In a testate estate, the will is proved.
4. A bond is given by the personal representative, unless waived.
5. Letters are issued by the court.
6. An inventory is filed.
7. Notice or a time period is given to creditors to make claims.
8. Debts, taxes, and expenses of administration are paid.
9. Distribution is made to the beneficiaries.
10. An account is filed with the court.

Under the UPC, formal probate proceedings can be either supervised or unsupervised. **Supervised administration** is a process whereby an estate is settled under the continued surveillance of the court from beginning to end. **Unsupervised administration** begins formally but becomes less supervised by the court once the personal representative is appointed.

Petition for Probate or Administration

In testate cases, probate proceedings begin when the executor named in the will files a **petition for probate** with the probate court (see Exhibit 12–1). This is a formal, written application asking the court to prove and allow the will and to appoint the petitioner, who is nominated in the will, as executor(-trix). If someone other than the person nominated as personal representative in the will is the petitioner seeking the appointment, a different form, called a **petition for administration with the will annexed**, must be filed with the court. Each state has its own forms for these purposes, and the forms can be obtained from the particular court involved. In states that follow the UPC, the same form is used for both of these mentioned situations. A box on the form is checked to indicate the petitioner's status.

■ **formal proceedings**
Proceedings conducted before a judge with notice to interested persons (UPC § 1–201(15)).

■ **probate in solemn form**
Formal probate proceedings.

■ **supervised administration**
Process in which an estate is settled under the continuing surveillance of the court from beginning to end.

■ **unsupervised administration**
Method of administering an estate, under the Uniform Probate Code, without court action unless such action is requested by an interested person.

■ **petition for probate**
Formal, written application asking the court to prove and allow the will and to appoint the petitioner, who is nominated in the will, as executor (-trix) thereof.

ATTORNEY OR PARTY WITHOUT ATTORNEY (Name and Address): 019453 HERMIONE K. BROWN, ESQ. GANG, TYRE, RAMER & BROWN, INC. 132 South Rodeo Drive Beverly Hills, CA 90212-2403 ATTORNEY FOR (Name): HERMIONE K. BROWN	TELEPHONE NO.: 310-777-4800 TELECOPIER NO.: 310-777-4801

SUPERIOR COURT OF CALIFORNIA, COUNTY OF LOS ANGELES
STREET ADDRESS: 111 North Hill Street
MAILING ADDRESS: 111 North Hill Street
CITY AND ZIP CODE: Los Angeles, CA 90012
BRANCH NAME: Central

FOR COURT USE ONLY

FILED
LOS ANGELES SUPERIOR COURT

AUG 9 - 1996

JOHN A. CLARKE, CLERK
Hector Don Lucas
BY HECTOR DON LUCAS, DEPUTY

ESTATE OF (NAME): GEORGE BURNS,
AKA GEORGE N. BURNS, DECEDENT

CASE NUMBER: **BP042047**

HEARING DATE: *Sept 16*
DEPT: *5* TIME: *9¹⁵*

ATTY PETITION FOR ORDER (For deaths after December 31, 1984)

[X] Probate of Will and for Letters Testamentary
[ ] Probate of Will and for Letters of Administration with Will Annexed
[ ] Letters of Administration
[ ] Letters of Special Administration
[X] Authorization to Administer Under the Independent Administration of Estates Act [ ] with limited authority

GANG, TYRE, RAMER & BROWN, INC.

By *Hermione K. Brown*
(Signature of attorney or party without attorney)

1. Publication will be in (specify name of newspaper): METROPOLITAN NEWS-ENTERPRISE
   a. [X] Publication requested.
   b. [ ] Publication to be arranged.
2. **Petitioner** (name of each): HERMIONE K. BROWN
   requests
   a. [X] decedent's will and codicils, if any, be admitted to probate.
   b. [X] (name): HERMIONE K. BROWN
      be appointed (1) [X] executor   (3) [ ] administrator
      (2) [ ] administrator with will annexed   (4) [ ] special administrator
      and Letters issue upon qualification.
   c. [X] that [X] full [ ] limited authority be granted to administer under the Independent Administration of Estates Act.
   d. [X] bond not be required for the reasons stated in item 3d.
      [ ] $___ bond be fixed. It will be furnished by an admitted surety insurer or as otherwise provided by law. (Specify reasons in Attachment 2d if the amount is different from the maximum required by Probate Code, § 8482.)
      [ ] $___ in deposits in a blocked account be allowed. Receipts will be filed. (Specify institution and location):

3. a. Decedent died on (date): March 9, 1996 at (place): Beverly Hills, California
      [X] a resident of the county named above.
      [ ] a nonresident of California and left an estate in the county named above located at (specify location permitting publication in the newspaper named in item 1):
   b. Street address, city, and county of decedent's residence at time of death:
      720 North Maple Drive, Beverly Hills, County of Los Angeles
   c. Character and estimated value of the property of the estate
      (1) Personal property .... $ over $60,000.00
      (2) Annual gross income from
          (i) [ ] real property .... $ 0.00
          (ii) [ ] personal property .... $ 0.00
                    Total .... $ over $60,000.00
      (3) Real property: $ --0--   (If full authority under the Independent Administration of Estates Act is requested, state the fair market value of the real property less encumbrances.)
   d. [X] Will waives bond. [ ] Special administrator is the named executor and the will waives bond.
      [ ] All beneficiaries are adults and have waived bond, and the will does not require a bond. (Affix waiver as Attachment 3d.)
      [ ] All heirs at law are adults and have waived bond. (Affix waiver as Attachment 3d.)
      [ ] Sole personal representative is a corporate fiduciary.

(Continued on reverse)

Form Approved by the
Judicial Council of California
DE-111 [Rev. July 1, 1989]

PETITION FOR PROBATE

Probate Code, 8002, 10450

CEB

EXHIBIT 12-1a Petition for Probate of Will and Letters Testamentary (California)

ESTATE OF (NAME): GEORGE BURNS,
                   AKA GEORGE N. BURNS,   DECEDENT

CASE NUMBER:

3. e. ☐ Decedent died intestate.
   ☒ Copy of decedent's will dated: 1/26/95   ☐ codicils dated: are affixed as Attachment 3e.
      ☒ The will and all codicils are self-proving (Probate Code, 8220-8221).

   f. **Appointment of personal representative** (check all applicable boxes)
      (1) Appointment of executor or administrator with will annexed
          ☒ Proposed executor is named as executor in the will and consents to act.
          ☐ No executor is named in the will.
          ☐ Proposed personal representative is a nominee of a person entitled to Letters. (Affix nomination as Attachment 3f(1).)
          ☐ Other named executors will not act because of ☐ death ☐ declination ☐ other reasons (specify in Attachment 3f(1)).
      (2) Appointment of administrator
          ☐ Petitioner is a person entitled to Letters. (If necessary, explain priority in Attachment 3f(2).)
          ☐ Petitioner is a nominee of a person entitled to Letters. (Affix nomination as Attachment 3f(2).)
          ☐ Petitioner is related to the decedent as (specify):
      (3) ☐ Appointment of special administrator requested. (Specify grounds and requested powers in Attachment 3f(3).)

   g. Proposed personal representative is a ☒ resident of California ☐ nonresident of California (affix statement of permanent address as Attachment 3g) ☒ resident of the United States ☐ nonresident of the United States.

> Attach a typed copy of a holographic will and a translation of a foreign language will.

4. ☒ Decedent's will does not preclude administration of this estate under the Independent Administration of Estates Act.
5. a. The decedent is survived by
      (1) ☐ spouse ☒ no spouse as follows: ☐ divorced or never married ☒ spouse deceased
      (2) ☒ child as follows: ☒ natural or adopted ☐ natural adopted by a third party ☐ step ☐ foster
          ☐ no child
      (3) ☐ issue of a predeceased child ☒ no issue of a predeceased child
   b. Petitioner ☒ has no actual knowledge of facts ☐ has actual knowledge of facts reasonably giving rise to a parent-child relationship under Probate Code section 6408(b).
   c. ☒ All surviving children and issue of predeceased children have been listed in item 8.
6. (Complete if decedent was survived by (1) a spouse but no issue (only a or b apply); or (2) no spouse or issue. Check the first box that applies):
   a. ☐ The decedent is survived by a parent or parents who are listed in item 8.
   b. ☐ The decedent is survived by issue of deceased parents, all of whom are listed in item 8.
   c. ☐ The decedent is survived by a grandparent or grandparents who are listed in item 8.
   d. ☐ The decedent is survived by issue of grandparents, all of whom are listed in item 8.
   e. ☐ The decedent is survived by issue of a predeceased spouse, all of whom are listed in item 8.
   f. ☐ The decedent is survived by next of kin, all of whom are listed in item 8.
   g. ☐ The decedent is survived by parents of a predeceased spouse or issue of those parents, if both are predeceased, all of whom are listed item 8.
7. (Complete only if no spouse or issue survived the decedent) Decedent ☐ had no predeceased spouse ☐ had a predeceased spouse who (1) ☐ died not more than 15 years before decedent owning an interest in **real property** that passed to decedent, (2) ☐ died not more than five years before decedent owning **personal property** valued at $ 10,000 or more that passed to decedent, (3) ☐ neither (1) nor (2) apply. (If you checked (1) or (2), check only the **first** box that applies):
   a. ☐ The decedent is survived by issue of a predeceased spouse, all of whom are listed in item 8.
   b. ☐ The decedent is survived by a parent or parents of the predeceased spouse who are listed in item 8.
   c. ☐ The decedent is survived by issue of a parent of the predeceased spouse, all of whom are listed in item 8.
   d. ☐ The decedent is survived by next of kin of the decedent, all of whom are listed in item 8.
   e. ☐ The decedent is survived by next of kin of the predeceased spouse, all of whom are listed in item 8.
8. **Listed in Attachment 8** are the names, relationships, ages, and addresses of all persons named in decedent's will and codicils, whether living or deceased, and all persons checked in items 5, 6, and 7, so far as known to or reasonably ascertainable by petitioner, **including** stepchild and foster child heirs and devisees to whom notice is to be given under Probate Code section 1207.
9. ☒ Number of pages attached: 14 (includes Will)

Date: August 7, 1996

Hermione K. Brown
(SIGNATURE OF PETITIONER*)

▶

(SIGNATURE OF PETITIONER*)

I declare under penalty of perjury under the laws of the State of California that the foregoing is true and correct.
Date: August 7, 1996

Hermione K. Brown
(TYPE OR PRINT NAME)

Hermione K. Brown
(SIGNATURE OF PETITIONER*)

* All petitioners must sign the petition. Only one need sign the declaration.

DE-111 [Rev. July 1, 1989]   **PETITION FOR PROBATE**   Page two
                                                                                           CEB

EXHIBIT 12–1b Petition for Probate of Will and Letters Testamentary (California)

■ **petition for administration with the will annexed**

Written application by someone other than the person nominated as personal representative in a will, asking the court to prove and allow the will and to appoint the petitioner as administrator (-trix).

In intestate cases, probate proceedings begin when someone files a form called a **petition for administration** with the probate court. This is a written application by one or more heirs, next of kin, or creditors asking the court to appoint the petitioner or someone else as administrator(-trix) of the estate. Once again, states that follow the UPC, as well as some other states, use the same form for both testate and intestate estates.

Forms for petitions for probate and administration typically provide spaces to write: (1) the name of the decedent, (2) the decedent's domicile, (3) the date of death, (4) the name and address of the petitioner, (5) the names of the decedent's heirs at law (those people who would have inherited had the decedent died intestate), and (6) the petitioner's preference to serve with or without bond or, in some states, without giving a surety on the bond.

■ **petition for administration**

Written application by one or more heirs, next of kin, or creditors asking the court to appoint the petitioner as administrator (-trix) of the estate.

Petition to Open Safe-Deposit Box

Prior to the granting of permanent letters, there are two occasions in which the court may be petitioned for an order to open the decedent's safe-deposit box. The first is if a will cannot be located, and it is suspected that the will may be in the safe-deposit box. The second occasion is when the decedent shared the box with another person and that person needs something from the box. Note that the level of need is quite high. The courts routinely deny requests when what is needed is jewelry or money. If a court grants the request for access, most states require that a bank representative and a state tax representative be present at the opening. If the box is accessed, then only the will, if that is what is requested or the specific necessary items of the co-owner that have been requested may be removed.

Notice to Interested Parties

■ **citation**

A notice to appear in court.

Upon receiving the will and the petition for probate or the petition for administration, the court issues an order, sometimes called a **citation**, requiring the petitioner to notify all heirs at law, devisees, and legatees, either by personal service, newspaper advertising, or both, that the petition has been filed. Personal service may be made either by delivering a copy in hand personally, or, with the consent of the court, by mail. In some states, the citation is prepared by the court; in others, it is prepared by the law office and submitted to the court for issuance. Also, in some states, the citation itself contains the notice that must be given to all interested parties. In other states, a separate form, called a Notice of Probate, is sent to interested parties (see Exhibit 12–2).

00383191-0

ATTORNEY OR PARTY WITHOUT ATTORNEY (Name and Address):

HERMIONE K BROWN ESQ
GANG TYRE RAMER & BROWN
132 S RODEO DR
BEVERLY HILLS CA 90212

TELEPHONE NO.:
(310) 777-4800

FOR COURT USE ONLY

ATTORNEY FOR (Name): Hermione K. Brown

SUPERIOR COURT OF CALIFORNIA, COUNTY OF LOS ANGELES

STREET ADDRESS: 111 N. Hill St.
MAILING ADDRESS: 111 N. Hill St.
CITY AND ZIP CODE: Los Angeles, CA 90012
BRANCH NAME: CENTRAL

ESTATE OF: GEORGE BURNS
         aka GEORGE N. BURNS

DECEDENT

FILED
LOS ANGELES SUPERIOR COURT

AUG 21 1996

JOHN A. CLARKE, CLERK
Hector Don Lucas
BY HECTOR DON LUCAS, DEPUTY

NOTICE OF PETITION TO ADMINISTER ESTATE

OF: GEORGE BURNS
     aka GEORGE N. BURNS

CASE NUMBER:

BP042047

1. To all heirs, beneficiaries, creditors, contingent creditors, and persons who may be otherwise interested in the will or estate, or both, of: GEORGE BURNS
   aka GEORGE N. BURNS

2. A PETITION has been filed by (name of petitioner):   Hermione K. Brown
   in the Superior Court of California, County of (specify): LOS ANGELES

3. THE PETITION requests that (name):   Hermione K. Brown
   be appointed as personal representative to administer the estate of the decedent.

4. [X] THE PETITION requests that the decedent's WILL and codicils, if any, be admitted to probate. The will and any codicils are available for examination in the file kept by the court.

5. [X] THE PETITION requests authority to administer the estate under the Independent Administration of Estates Act. (This authority will allow the personal representative to take many actions without obtaining court approval. Before taking certain very important action, however, the personal representative will be required to give notice to interested persons unless they have waived notice or consented to the proposed action.) The independent administration authority will be granted unless an interested person files an objection to the petition and shows good cause why the court should not grant the authority.

6. [ ] A PETITION for determination of or confirmation of property passing to or belonging to a surviving spouse under California Probate Code section 13650 IS JOINED with the petition to administer the estate.

7. A HEARING on the petition will be held

   on (date): September 16, 1996   at (time): 9:15 AM   in Dept: 5   Room:

   located at (address of court):   111 N. Hill St.
                                    Los Angeles, CA 90012

8. IF YOU OBJECT to the granting of the petition, you should appear at the hearing and state your objections or file written objections with the court before the hearing. Your appearance may be in person or by your attorney.

9. IF YOU ARE A CREDITOR or a contingent creditor of the deceased, you must file your claim with the court and mail a copy to the personal representative appointed by the court within four months from the date of first issuance of letters as provided in section 9100 of the California Probate Code. The time for filing claims will not expire before four months from the hearing date noticed above.

10. YOU MAY EXAMINE the file kept by the court. If you are a person interested in the estate, you may file with the court a formal Request for Special Notice of the filing of an inventory and appraisal of estate assets or of any petition or account as provided in section 1250 of the California Probate Code. A Request for Special Notice form is available from the court clerk.

11. [ ] Petitioner   [X] Attorney for petitioner (name): HERMIONE K BROWN ESQ
    (address): GANG TYRE RAMER & BROWN
               132 S RODEO DR
               BEVERLY HILLS CA 90212

    (SIGNATURE OF) [ ] PETITIONER   [ ] ATTORNEY FOR PETITIONER
                   [X] AGENT FOR ATTORNEY/PETITIONER)

12. This notice was mailed on (date):   AUG 20 1996   at (place):   LOS ANGELES   , California.
    (Continued on reverse)

NOTE: If this notice is published, print the caption, beginning with the words NOTICE OF PETITION, and do not print the information from the form above the caption. The caption and decedent's name must be printed in at least 8-point type and the text in at least 7-point type. Print the case number as part of the caption. Print items preceded by a box only if the box is checked. Do not print the *italicized* instructions in parentheses, the paragraph numbers, the mailing information, or the material on the reverse.

Form Approved by the
Judicial Council of California
DE-121 [Rev. July 1, 1989]   336

NOTICE OF PETITION TO ADMINISTER ESTATE
(Probate)

Probate Code, 8100

EXHIBIT 12–2a   Notice of Petition to Administer Estate (California)

00383191-0

ESTATE OF (NAME): GEORGE BURNS aka GEORGE N. BURNS	CASE NUMBER:
DECEDENT	BP042047

PROOF OF SERVICE BY MAIL

1. I am over the age of 18 and not a party to this cause. I am a resident of or employed in the county where the mailing occurred.

2. My residence or business address is (specify):
   BUSINESS ADDRESS: 210 S. SPRING STREET, LOS ANGELES, CALIFORNIA, 90012

3. I served the foregoing Notice of Petition to Administer Estate on each person named below by enclosing a copy in an envelope addressed as shown below AND
   a. ☐ depositing the sealed envelope with the United States Postal Service with the postage fully prepaid.
   b. ☒ placing the envelope for collection and mailing on the date and at the place shown in item 4 following our ordinary business practices. I am readily familiar with this business' practice for collection and processing correspondence for mailing. On the same day that correspondence is placed for collection and mailing, it is deposited in the ordinary course of business with the United States Postal Service in a sealed envelope with postage fully prepaid.

4. a. Date of deposit: **AUG 20 1996**   b. Place of deposit (city and state): LOS ANGELES, CALIFORNIA

5. ☐ I served with the Notice of Petition to Administer Estate a copy of the petition and other documents referred to in the notice.

I declare under penalty of perjury under the laws of the State of California that the foregoing is true and correct.

Date: **AUG 20 1996**

Jane Iha
(TYPE OR PRINT NAME)

Jane Iha
(SIGNATURE OF DECLARANT)

NAME AND ADDRESS OF EACH PERSON TO WHOM NOTICE WAS MAILED   PAGE # 1 OF 4

01) SANDRA BURNS LUCKMAN
    3383 OCEAN FRONT WALK
    SAN DIEGO CA 92109

02) SANDRA JEAN BURNS
    3383 OCEAN FRONT WALK
    SAN DIEGO CA 92109

03) RONALD BURNS
    941 KAGAWA ST
    PACIFIC PALISADES CA 90272

04) LAURA J GEIS
    980 RANDOLPH RD
    SANTA BARBARA CA 93111

05) LAURA JEAN WILHOITE WRIGHT
    980 RANDOLPH RD
    SANTA BARBARA CA 93111

06) MELISSA G PETERSEN
    7001 OLD REDMOND RD E-318
    REDMOND WA 98052

07) MELISSA WILHOITE SOLEAU
    7001 OLD REDMOND RD E-318
    REDMOND WA 98052

08) GRACE-ANNE WILKINSON
    825 NIANTIC CT NO 4
    SAN DIEGO CA 92109

09) GRACE ANNE LUCKMAN
    825 NIANTIC CT NO 4
    SAN DIEGO CA 92109

10) BROOKE LUCKMAN
    3993 JEWELL ST A-4
    SAN DIEGO CA 92109

DE-121 (Rev. July 1, 1999]

NOTICE OF PETITION TO ADMINISTER ESTATE
(Probate)

Page two

EXHIBIT 12-2b Notice of Petition to Administer Estate (California)

Proof of Will

The procedure for proving a will varies from state to state. Even within a state, several different methods may be used. One method is to have one or more of the attesting witnesses testify before the judge or the clerk of court as to how the will was executed and the testator's competence. A second method is to have one or more of the attesting witnesses sign a written affidavit before the register of probate stating facts about the execution of the will. When witnesses have died or cannot be found, their handwriting may have to be proved. A third method is to obtain written approval of the surviving spouse and the heirs at law. If all interested parties agree to the allowance of a will, neither testimony of witnesses nor affidavits are necessary.

Under the laws of many states, a will containing a self-proof clause (see § 6.5) may be admitted to probate without the testimony or affidavits of witnesses.

The procedure for contesting a will varies from state to state. In some states, the contesting party files with the court an **appearance** (a formal written entry submitting that person to the court's jurisdiction). Following the appearance, the contesting party must file an affidavit of objection to the petition for probate, stating specific facts and grounds upon which the objection is based. In other states, a contesting party files a **caveat**, which is a formal notice or warning to the court to prevent the proving of the will or the granting of administration. Contesting parties must have standing to sue. That is, the individual initiating the lawsuit must stand to personally benefit from having the will wholly or partly invalidated. These individuals may be heirs, if the will is to be invalidated, or beneficiaries named in previous wills.

The grounds for contesting a will are:

1. The will was not properly executed.

2. The testator was not of sound mind at the time of execution of the will.

3. The execution of the will was obtained through fraud or undue influence.

The proponent of the will must show that the document was properly executed by the testator with knowledge of its contents, and that the testator was of sound mind. If undue influence or fraud is alleged, the burden of proof is on the person who claims that fraud or undue influence exists. Only those with an interest in opposing the will, such as a spouse or one of the heirs at law, or a legatee in an earlier-made will, can contest a will.

Allowance of Bond and Issuance of Letters

Some states require all personal representatives to post a bond (see Exhibit 12–3). In addition, they require a surety on the bond unless the will provides otherwise or unless all heirs agree to the appointment without sureties.

■ **appearance**

1. The coming into court as a party (plaintiff or defendant) to a lawsuit. A person who does this "appears." 2. The formal coming into court as a lawyer in a specific lawsuit; often also called "entering" the case.

■ **caveat**

(Latin) "Beware"; warning.

In other states, a bond is not required when the will contains a clause to that effect. In those states, unless the will indicates that a bond is required, the bond can be waived if all beneficiaries named in the will assent to the waiver in writing. Before the probate petition is completed, the will must be reviewed to determine whether the personal representative is allowed to serve without a bond or without giving a surety on the bond.

The amount of the bond varies from state to state. In some states, it must equal the value of the personal property; in other states, it must equal twice the value of the personal property. Real property is not counted in determining the value of the bond unless the property is to be sold by the personal representative and the proceeds from the sale are to become assets of the estate.

Once the personal representative's bond is allowed, the court issues a certificate of appointment known as letters testamentary, for a testate estate, or letters of administration, for an intestate estate (see Exhibit 12–4). This certificate is called *letters of authority* in Michigan. The letters serve as evidence of the right of the fiduciary to take possession of the property in the estate. In some states, the letters remain in full force and effect until completion of the estate or until resignation or removal of the personal representative. In other states, a time limit (such as 15 months) applies to the appointment, after which an extension must be obtained. An authenticated copy of the letters, issued by the court, may be used to establish their validity.

In California, when the petition for probate is allowed, the judge signs an *order for probate* ordering the appointment of the personal representative. The personal representative is given a form explaining the duties and liabilities of the position (Exhibit 12–5), and letters are issued by the court.

In some states, only state residents may be appointed as personal representatives. Other states allow nonresidents to be appointed if they, in turn, appoint a state resident to act as their agent in the event a suit is brought against the estate. In this way, the court obtains personal jurisdiction over the fiduciary.

■ **preliminary letters testamentary**

Certificate, used in some states, giving a preliminary executor the same powers that are given to an ordinary executor, with some limitations, when a delay in probate is anticipated.

In some states, when a delay in probate is anticipated, as in the case of a will contest or a missing heir, the court, upon petition, may issue **preliminary letters testamentary**. Such letters give a preliminary executor the same powers of an ordinary executor but with some limitations. A preliminary executor, for example, cannot make distributions to heirs or dispose of property that is specifically bequeathed or devised in the will. Other restrictions may be placed upon a preliminary executor by the court to protect the rights of all interested persons. By the use of a preliminary executor, an estate can be administered under normal time frames, without waiting for a dispute to be settled or an heir to be located. Preliminary letters are revoked when letters testamentary are issued or when a will is denied probate.

BARRETT BROTHERS, PUBLISHERS, SPRINGFIELD, OHIO

PROBATE COURT OF _____ COUNTY, OHIO

ESTATE OF _____ , DECEASED

Case No. _____ Docket _____ Page _____

FIDUCIARY'S BOND

[For Executors and all Administrators]

Amount of Bond $_____

The undersigned principal, and sureties if any, are obligated to the State of Ohio in the above amount, for payment of which we bind ourselves and our successors, heirs, executors and administrators, jointly and severally.

The principal has accepted in writing the duties of fiduciary in decedent's estate, including those imposed by law and such additional duties as may be required by the Court.

This obligation is void if the principal performs such duties as required.

This obligation remains in force if the principal fails to perform such duties, or performs them tardily, negligently, or improperly, or if the principal misuses or misappropriates estate assets or improperly converts them to his own use or the use of another.

[Check if personal sureties are involved] - ☐ The sureties certify that each of them owns real estate in this county, with a reasonable net value as stated below.

Date	Principal
Surety	Surety
by	by
Attorney in Fact	Attorney in Fact
Typed or Printed Name	Typed or Printed Name
Address	Address

Net value of real estate owned in this county
$ _____

Net value of real estate owned in this county
$ _____

4.2 - FIDUCIARY'S BOND

EXHIBIT 12–3   Fiduciary's Bond (Ohio)

❏ District Court   ❏ Denver Probate Court
_____ County, Colorado

Court Address:

_____

IN THE MATTER OF ❏   THE ESTATE OF:

▲   **COURT USE ONLY**   ▲

Case Number:

❏ **Deceased** ❏ **Protected Person** ❏   **Minor** ❏   **Incapacitated Person**

Division: Courtroom:

LETTERS

(Name) _____was appointed or qualified by this Court or its Registrar

on (date) _____as:

❏ Personal Representative.

  ❏ These are Letters of Administration. (The decedent did not leave a will.)

  ❏ These are Letters Testamentary. (The decedent left a will.)

❏ Special Administrator in ❏ an informal ❏ a formal   proceeding. These are Letters of Special Administration.

❏ Conservator. These are Letters of Conservatorship.

  ❏ The protected person is a minor whose date of birth is _____.

❏ Guardian. These are Letters of Guardianship for:

  ❏ an incapacitated person.   ❏ a minor whose date of birth is _____.

  Appointment or qualification is by ❏ court order. ❏ will. ❏ written instrument.

❏   _____

_____

These Letters evidence full authority, except for the following limitations or restrictions, if any:

_____

_____

Dated: _____   _____
                                        (Deputy) Clerk or Registrar of Court

CERTIFICATION

            Certification Stamp   or   Certified to be a true copy of the original in my
                                                     custody and to be in full force and effect as of:

Dated: _____   _____
                                        (Deputy)Clerk of Court

CPC 17   R7/01   LETTERS

EXHIBIT 12−4 Letters (Colorado)

DE-147

ATTORNEY OR PARTY WITHOUT ATTORNEY (Name, state bar number, and address):

FOR COURT USE ONLY

TELEPHONE NO.:   FAX NO. (Optional):
E-MAIL ADDRESS (Optional):
ATTORNEY FOR (Name):

SUPERIOR COURT OF CALIFORNIA, COUNTY OF
STREET ADDRESS:
MAILING ADDRESS:
CITY AND ZIP CODE:
BRANCH NAME:

ESTATE OF (Name):

DECEDENT

DUTIES AND LIABILITIES OF PERSONAL REPRESENTATIVE
and Acknowledgment of Receipt

CASE NUMBER:

DUTIES AND LIABILITIES OF PERSONAL REPRESENTATIVE

When the court appoints you as personal representative of an estate, you become an officer of the court and assume certain duties and obligations. An attorney is best qualified to advise you about these matters. You should understand the following:

1. MANAGING THE ESTATE'S ASSETS

a. Prudent investments
You must manage the estate assets with the care of a prudent person dealing with someone else's property. This means that you must be cautious and may not make any speculative investments.

b. Keep estate assets separate
You must keep the money and property in this estate separate from anyone else's, including your own. When you open a bank account for the estate, the account name must indicate that it is an estate account and not your personal account. Never deposit estate funds in your personal account or otherwise mix them with your or anyone else's property. Securities in the estate must also be held in a name that shows they are estate property and not your personal property.

c. Interest-bearing accounts and other investments
Except for checking accounts intended for ordinary administration expenses, estate accounts must earn interest. You may deposit estate funds in insured accounts in financial institutions, but you should consult with an attorney before making other kinds of investments.

d. Other restrictions
There are many other restrictions on your authority to deal with estate property. You should not spend any of the estate's money unless you have received permission from the court or have been advised to do so by an attorney. You may reimburse yourself for official court costs paid by you to the county clerk and for the premium on your bond. Without prior order of the court, you may not pay fees to yourself or to your attorney, if you have one. If you do not obtain the court's permission when it is required, you may be removed as personal representative or you may be required to reimburse the estate from your own personal funds, or both. You should consult with an attorney concerning the legal requirements affecting sales, leases, mortgages, and investments of estate property.

2. INVENTORY OF ESTATE PROPERTY

a. Locate the estate's property
You must attempt to locate and take possession of all the decedent's property to be administered in the estate.

b. Determine the value of the property
You must arrange to have a court-appointed referee determine the value of the property unless the appointment is waived by the court. You, rather than the referee, must determine the value of certain "cash items." An attorney can advise you about how to do this.

c. File an inventory and appraisal
Within three months after your appointment as personal representative, you must file with the court an inventory and appraisal of all the assets in the estate.

(Continued on reverse)

Form Adopted for Mandatory Use
Judicial Council of California
DE-147 [Rev. January 1, 2001]
DUTIES AND LIABILITIES OF PERSONAL REPRESENTATIVE
(Probate)
Probate Code, § 8404

EXHIBIT 12–5a   Duties and Liabilities of Personal Representative (California)

CONFIDENTIAL   DE-147S

ESTATE OF *(Name)*:	CASE NUMBER:
DECEDENT	

d. File a change of ownership
At the time you file the inventory and appraisal, you must also file a change of ownership statement with the county recorder or assessor in each county where the decedent owned real property at the time of death, as provided in section 480 of the California Revenue and Taxation Code.

3. NOTICE TO CREDITORS

You must mail a notice of administration to each known creditor of the decedent within four months after your appointment as personal representative. If the decedent received Medi-Cal assistance, you must notify the State Director of Health Services within 90 days after appointment.

4. INSURANCE

You should determine that there is appropriate and adequate insurance covering the assets and risks of the estate. Maintain the insurance in force during the entire period of the administration.

5. RECORD KEEPING

a. Keep accounts
You must keep complete and accurate records of each financial transaction affecting the estate. You will have to prepare an account of all money and property you have received, what you have spent, and the date of each transaction. You must describe in detail what you have left after the payment of expenses.

b. Court review
Your account will be reviewed by the court. Save your receipts because the court may ask to review them. If you do not file your accounts as required, the court will order you to do so. You may be removed as personal representative if you fail to comply.

6. CONSULTING AN ATTORNEY

If you have an attorney, you should cooperate with the attorney at all times. You and your attorney are responsible for completing the estate administration as promptly as possible. **When in doubt, contact your attorney.**

NOTICE: 1. **This statement of duties and liabilities is a summary and is not a complete statement of the law. Your conduct as a personal representative is governed by the law itself and not by this summary.**
2. **If you fail to perform your duties or to meet the deadlines, the court may reduce your compensation, remove you from office, and impose other sanctions.**

ACKNOWLEDGMENT OF RECEIPT

1. I have petitioned the court to be appointed as a personal representative.

2. My address and telephone number are *(specify)*:

3. I acknowledge that I have received a copy of this statement of the duties and liabilities of the office of personal representative.

Date:

▶
_____   _____
(TYPE OR PRINT NAME)   (SIGNATURE OF PETITIONER)

Date:

▶
_____   _____
(TYPE OR PRINT NAME)   (SIGNATURE OF PETITIONER)

CONFIDENTIAL INFORMATION: If required to do so by local court rule, you must provide your date of birth and driver's license number on supplemental Form DE-147S. (Prob. Code, § 8404(b).)

DE-147 [Rev. January 1, 2001]   **DUTIES AND LIABILITIES OF PERSONAL REPRESENTATIVE**   Page two
                                                  (Probate)

EXHIBIT 12–5b Duties and Liabilities of Personal Representative (California)

CONFIDENTIAL

DE-147S

ESTATE OF *(Name)*:

CASE NUMBER:

DECEDENT

CONFIDENTIAL STATEMENT OF BIRTH DATE
AND DRIVER'S LICENSE NUMBER

(Supplement to *Duties and Liabilities of Personal Representative (Form DE-147)*)

*(NOTE: This supplement is to be used if the court by local rule requires the personal representative to provide a birth date and driver's license number. Do **not** attach this supplement to Form DE-147.)*

This separate *Confidential Statement of Birth Date and Driver's License Number* contains confidential information relating to the personal representative in the case referenced above. This supplement shall be kept separate from the *Duties and Liabilities of Personal Representative* filed in this case and shall not be a public record.

INFORMATION ON THE PERSONAL REPRESENTATIVE:

1. Name:

2. Date of birth:

3. Driver's license number: State:

> **TO COURT CLERK:**
> THIS STATEMENT IS **CONFIDENTIAL**. DO NOT FILE
> THIS CONFIDENTIAL STATEMENT IN A PUBLIC COURT FILE.

Form Adopted for Mandatory Use
Judicial Council of California
DE-147S [New January 1, 2001]

**CONFIDENTIAL SUPPLEMENT TO DUTIES AND
LIABILITIES OF PERSONAL REPRESENTATIVE**
(Probate)

Probate Code, § 8404

EXHIBIT 12–5c   Duties and Liabilities of Personal Representative (California)

The Inventory

One of the duties of a personal representative, after receiving letters of appointment, is to file an inventory with the probate court. This task is also one to which the paralegal may be assigned. An **inventory** is a detailed list of property owned by the decedent together with its estimated value as of the decedent's date of death. All property in the estate should be listed on the inventory in detail. The inventory should include serial numbers of automobiles, stock certificates, certificates of deposit, savings bond and savings account numbers, legal descriptions of real property, and the book and page where any deed is recorded at the registry of deeds. States have different time limits within which the inventory must be filed, ranging from one to six months from the date of the personal representative's appointment.

■ **inventory**

A detailed list of articles of property.

Sometimes it is necessary to have a disinterested appraiser assess the value of the estate's real and personal property. Appraisers may be particularly useful in situations in which the heirs disagree on the value, the market value is not easily determinable by a nonexpert, or a dispute about value is anticipated with the tax authorities.

Some assets, such as bank accounts, have a readily ascertainable value and need not be appraised. Requests may be made to financial institutions and brokerage houses for date-of-death values. Sometimes bankbooks must be updated and stock market quotations in newspapers must be reviewed to determine stock values as of the decedent's date of death. If the decedent died on a market day, the proper valuation of stock is the mean between high and low, or bid and asked for that day. If the decedent died on a day the market was closed, the proper valuation is a weighted average of the mean between high and low or bid and asked on the previous market day, and the mean of such quotes on the market day following the decedent's date of death. For variations of these rules see IRS Reg. § 20.2031–2.

After values for all estate assets have been received and the inventory has been prepared, the inventory is filed with the court (see Exhibit 12–6). A copy may be sent to interested persons who request it. In some states, a supplementary or amended inventory is necessary if additional property is discovered or if the value or description of any asset is found to be erroneous. In some states, an inventory is not required if the will or residuary beneficiaries waive the requirement.

The inventory that was filed in 1787 in the Estate of Casparus Cole (shown in Exhibit 12–7) illustrates the extremes that personal representatives sometimes went to in those days to display their honesty. Today, instead of listing each separate item of personal property in the inventory, personal representatives combine the items into general categories. The inventory also points out that slaves were legally considered to be no different from goods and chattels, which passed to others by will or by intestate succession when their owner's died.

BARRETT BROTHERS, SPRINGFIELD, OHIO 1-800-322-7711

PROBATE COURT OF _____ COUNTY, OHIO

ESTATE OF _____ **, DECEASED**

CASE NO. _____

INVENTORY AND APPRAISAL
[R.C. 2115.02]

To the knowledge of the fiduciary the attached schedule of assets in decedent's estate is complete. The fiduciary determined the value of those assets whose values were readily ascertainable and which were not appraised by the appraiser, and that such values are correct.

The estate is recapitulated as follows:

Tangible personal property .... $_____

Intangible personal property .... $_____

Real Estate .... $_____

Total .... $_____

First automobile transferred to surviving spouse
under R.C. 2106.18 .... appraised value $_____
Second automobile transferred to surviving spouse
under R.C. 2106.18 .... appraised value $_____

Total value [not to exceed $40,000.00] .... $_____

[Check if applicable] ☐ The surviving spouse is the sole legatee and devisee under decedent's will, and has not manifested an intention to take against it. It is therefore unnecessary to cite the surviving spouse to make an election.

_____   _____
Attorney   Fiduciary

Attorney Registration No. _____

APPRAISER'S CERTIFICATE

The undersigned appraiser agreed to act as appraiser of decedent's estate, and to appraise the property exhibited truly, honestly, impartially, and to the best of the appraiser's knowledge and ability. The appraiser further says that those assets whose values were not readily ascertainable are indicated on the attached schedule by a check in the "Appraised" column opposite each such item, and that such values are correct.

_____
Appraiser

FORM 6.0 - INVENTORY AND APPRAISAL   4/97

EXHIBIT 12–6a Inventory and Appraisal (Ohio)
Courtesy of Barrett Brothers, Publishers, Springfield, OH

WAIVER OF NOTICE OF TAKING OF INVENTORY
[R.C. 2115.04]

The undersigned surviving spouse hereby waives notice of the time and place of taking the inventory of decedent's estate.

_____
Surviving Spouse

WAIVER OF NOTICE OF HEARING ON INVENTORY
[Use when notice is required by the Court or deemed necessary by the fiduciary]

The undersigned, who are interested in the estate, waive notice of the hearing on the inventory.

_____   _____

_____   _____

_____   _____

_____   _____

_____   _____

_____   _____

_____   _____

ENTRY SETTING HEARING

The Court sets _____ at _____ o'clock _____.M., as the date and time for hearing the inventory of decedent's estate.

_____   _____
Date   Probate Judge

EXHIBIT 12–6b Inventory and Appraisal (Ohio)
Courtesy of Barrett Brothers, Publishers, Springfield, OH

BANK ACCOUNTS TOO SECRET TO FIND

W. C. FIELDS AND CHARLIE MCCARTHY

Almost half of comedian W. C. Fields' estate could never be located. To ensure his privacy and his access to funds wherever he traveled, Fields opened over 200 different bank accounts under assumed names. He did not maintain any records of the deposits or banks, so his executors were probably lucky to locate as many as 45 of the "secret" accounts. The remaining deposits, estimated at $600,000, were never found.

W. C. (William Claude) Fields (1879–1946) was a comedian who played in vaudeville and movies.

Payment of Debts, Taxes, and Expenses

After gathering the assets and preparing an inventory, the next task of the personal representative is to determine the extent of claims against the estate. Here again the paralegal may assist, particularly with preparing correspondence and maintaining records of creditors' claims. Creditors are responsible for bringing claims to the personal representative's attention within a specific time period. Once the deadline has passed, creditors will not be able to collect the money due them. Time periods are established so that personal representatives will know by a specific date the exact amount that is owed to creditors. This knowledge enables the personal representative to make decisions regarding the allocation of estate assets.

Notice to Creditors

Many states have statutes that require personal representatives to publish in a newspaper a notice to creditors, announcing their appointment, giving their addresses, and asking creditors to present their claims within a specific time period (see Exhibit 12–8). In the 1988 *Pope* case, the United States Supreme Court held that actual notice must be given to each creditor if the creditor can be readily identified. Since the Supreme Court decision, all states require that actual notice of the deadline to file a claim against an estate be delivered either by mail or some other means to each known or reasonably ascertainable creditor of the deceased.

Taxes and Expenses

Preparing and filing estate tax returns can be a major part of the work of a personal representative. The paralegal will often be asked to help complete various types of tax returns. State and federal individual income tax returns (Form 1040) often have to be prepared for the decedent's last year of life, up to the date of death. After that, if the estate has income, state and federal estate income tax returns (Form 1041) may have to be prepared from the date of death

---

Estate of Casparus Cole
Inventory

An inventory of the goods & Chattles of the Estate of Casparus Cole, Deceas'd.

Eight milk Cows, Five bulls, one of three years old, one of two, & three of one year old Each two heifers. one of two years, the other of one year old, three yong Calves two steers the other a bull, one old white mare, one Dito Dito horse, one white mare a bay horse & mare of thirteen years old Each. one gray mare three year old, one bay horse colt two years old thirteen dung hill fowls, one old Iron shod wagon, one Dito rack wagon Iron shod, one Dito Dito Cart, one Dito wheel plough, one foot plough without share or colter, one Iron tooth Drag, one wood shod sleigh, one old Iron shod sleigh, one Iron shod sleigh, one sett of old harness, a pair of new wipple trees & Neck yoke painted & Iron shod, one Draft Chain, one Iron wedge, one mans saddle, one womans saddle, & a bridle. three grass syths, two siths, three axes, one stubben how, two broad hows, one hand saw, a(+)one Drawing knife, one gouge, three augers, one weaving Loam. six Reeds & old Harness of Different sorts, one old warpinbars, one pair of sysenbrushes, one temple, one Iron pot Containing 12 Gallons, two Dito 4 1/2 Gallons Each, 2 tramble, one pair of hand Irons old, one tongs, one old Iron Dung shovel, one Iron back, one Dung fork, one Dito hay, one Cubboard, painted Brown, one Bread Cubboard, one Cherry slawbuncks, three tables, two Great Chears, thee old Dito small, three Chests, two Gin Cases with bottles, & one without, one Gallon Guge, one Frying pan, one tea Cittle. Eleven teacups & sausers, one pinte bole, one puter pinte measure, one old puter teapot, one old looking glass, two brasen Candlestick one Iron Candlestick, one snuffer, two silver table spoons, Eight silver Tea spoons, one silver stock buckkels, one pair of silver Clasps, one tin Lanthorn, one Dito Candlemould, one Driping pan, one skemer. one Iron ladle, 2 lb puter spoons. one Dreser in the Citchen,one syder Hogshead & three berrells & one tiers, one meat tub with Iron hoops, one Dito with woddenhoop, two water pails with Iron hoop, Four milktubs & three buttertubs, one Churn with wodden hoops, Four kives &

EXHIBIT 12–7a Inventory (New York, 1787)

ten Forkes, one Large Dutch Bible, one small Dito English, one Psalm Book, Two prayer Books, one Large tinbason, one old straw bed, two pillows & one blanket, one set of old Curtens, two guns, one powder horns & a sword, one pepper mill, one Chery stand, one woolen wheel, one spinning wheel, & three broken spinning wheels, one pair of old wool Cards, one Quill wheel, one tunel, one rasor, a shaven box, three Linnen Draw Collars, one new sleigh line, one skepel measure with Iron hoops. Eighteen sheep & nine Lambs, one straw bench with a knife, one old Corn pin, one riddle, three raw hides, two large Baskets, six smaller sized ones, one kneeding tray, one Largeknot tray, one small knot bole, two knot Dishes, three wood Dishes, one with tray, three wodden sugar Boxes, six fine hair Combs, one pair of stillards, one (+)Gill cup, one Dito sugar Box, one Hundred & a half weight of smoak'd Gammon, (+)lb of pickled pork, twenty lb & three Quarters of smoak'd beef, tho Cart load of (+)y, & a half a Cart load of Good hay in the barn, & in the barrack up to the top (of) the braces, one tin grater, one washing tub, two (berrels?) one head each, Four Flower berrels & Bushel of Patatoes, aflax brackkle,

Inventory of Names & ages of the Blacks belonging to the Estate of the afore mentioned Deceased as follows:

One Negro woman named Dian aged thirty six years, one Dito girl named Nan aged Eleven years, one Dito Named betty Aged seven years, one Negro boy named Harry aged twenty three years, one Dito named tom aged Ninteen years, one Dito named Ben aged Five years, one Dito named Jack aged Nine years, one Dito named (+)uch aged Ninteen months.

Filed May 7, 1787

EXHIBIT 12–7b   Inventory (New York, 1787)

until the year's end. Finally, if the value of the estate exceeds certain limits, state and federal estate tax returns (Form 706) must be prepared. These are discussed in detail in Chapter 3. Federal estate taxes must be paid within nine months after death.

Personal representatives may deduct from the assets of the estate all reasonable expenses incurred during the process of settling the estate. Administrative expenses may include attorney's and appraiser's fees, court costs, amounts paid to newspapers for publishing, and premiums on surety company bonds. In addition, personal representatives are allowed reasonable compensation for their services. The court determines the appropriate amount of compensation, as shown in the *Knight* case.

CASE STUDY — *Tulsa Professional Collection Services, Inc. v. Pope*

108 S. Ct. 1340

FACTS: H. Everett Pope, Jr., died at St. John Medical Center in Tulsa, Oklahoma, after being a patient there for five months. Following the directions of the court, the executrix of his estate published a notice in a newspaper for two consecutive weeks, advising creditors that they must file any claim they had against the estate within two months of the first publication of the notice. Tulsa Professional Collection Services, Inc., which had been assigned the claim from the St. John Medical Center for expenses connected with the decedent's stay at the hospital, did not file a claim within the two-month time period. The Oklahoma Supreme Court held that Collection Services was barred from collecting the money because it had failed to file a timely claim.

LEGAL ISSUE: Must actual notice be given to known and reasonably ascertainable creditors of the time limit within which creditors must file claims against an estate?

COURT DECISION: Yes.

REASON: Under the due process clause of the Fourteenth Amendment, actual notice is a minimum constitutional precondition to a proceeding that could adversely affect the property interests of any party. The executor must make reasonably diligent efforts to uncover the identity of creditors. Known or reasonably ascertainable creditors must be given notice by mail or other means that will ensure actual notice of the time limit for bringing claims. For creditors who are not reasonably ascertainable, publication notice can suffice. The Oklahoma Supreme Court's decision was reversed.

Decedent's Debts

After the expiration of a time period set by state statute, the personal representative pays the claims against the estate. If the estate is **insolvent** (i.e., the assets of the estate are insufficient to pay all the debts), the personal representative pays claims according to a priority list that is established by state statute. Priority lists differ somewhat from state to state. The UPC, in § 3-805, sets forth the following order for the payment of claims:

1. costs and expenses of administration

2. reasonable funeral expenses

3. debts and taxes with preference under federal law

4. reasonable and necessary medical and hospital expenses of the last illness of the decedent, including compensation of persons attending the decedent

5. debts and taxes with preference under state law

6. all other claims

■ **insolvent**

1. The condition of being unable to pay debts as they come due. 2. Having liabilities far greater than assets.

NOTICE OF ADMINISTRATION *
OF THE ESTATE OF

GEORGE BURNS, AKA GEORGE N. BURNS

(NAME)
DECEDENT

FILED

ANGELES SUP...

OCT 4 - 1996

JOHN A. CLARKE, CLERK

B. Barragan

BY L. BARRAGAN, DEPUTY.

NOTICE TO CREDITORS

1. (Name): Hermione K. Brown
    (Address): c/o Gang, Tyre, Ramer & Brown, Inc.
             132 South Rodeo Drive
             Beverly Hills, CA 90212-2403

    (Telephone): 310-777-4800
    is the **personal representative** of the **ESTATE OF** (name): GEORGE BURNS, AKA GEORGE N. BURNS, who is deceased.

2. The personal representative HAS BEGUN ADMINISTRATION of the decedent's estate in the

    a. SUPERIOR COURT OF CALIFORNIA, COUNTY OF (specify): LOS ANGELES

    STREET ADDRESS: 111 North Hill Street
    MAILING ADDRESS: 111 North Hill Street
    CITY AND ZIP CODE: Los Angeles, CA 90012
    BRANCH NAME: Central

    b. Case Number (specify):   BP-042047

3. You must FILE YOUR CLAIM with the court clerk (address in item 2a) AND mail or deliver a copy to the personal representative before the **later** of the following times as provided in section 9100 of the California Probate Code:

    a. **four months after** (date):   September 16, 1996   , the date letters (authority to act for the estate) were
       first issued to the personal representative, OR

    b. **thirty days after** (date):   October 2, 1996   , the date this notice was mailed or personally delivered
       to you.

4. LATE CLAIMS: If you do not file your claim before it is due, you must file a petition with the court for permission to file a late claim as provided in section 9103 of the Probate Code.

WHERE TO GET A CREDITOR'S CLAIM FORM: If a creditor's claim form did not accompany this notice, you may obtain a copy from any superior court clerk or from the person who sent you this notice. (Creditor's Claim, Judicial Council form No. DE-172.) A letter to the court stating your claim is *not* sufficient.

IF YOU MAIL YOUR CLAIM: If you use the mail to file your claim with the court, for your protection you should send your claim by certified mail, with return receipt requested. If you mail a copy of your claim to the personal representative, you should also use certified mail.

NOTE: To assist the creditor and the court, please send a copy of the Creditor's Claim form with this notice.

(Proof of Service on reverse)

* Use this form in estates begun on or after July 1, 1988.

Form Approved by the
Judicial Council of California
DE-157 [Rev. September 30, 1991]

NOTICE OF ADMINISTRATION TO CREDITORS
(Probate)

Probate Code, §§ 9050, 9052

CEB

EXHIBIT 12–8a   Notice to Creditors (California)

[Optional]

PROOF OF SERVICE BY MAIL

1. I am over the age of 18 and not a party to this cause. I am a resident of or employed in the county where the mailing occurred.
2. My residence or business address is (specify):

   132 South Rodeo Drive
   Beverly Hills, CA 90212-2403   including a copy of decedent's death certificate

3. I served the foregoing **Notice of Administration to Creditors** [X] and a blank *Creditor's Claim* form* / on each person named
   below by enclosing a copy in an envelope addressed as shown below AND
   a. ☐ depositing the sealed envelope with the United States Postal Service with the postage fully prepaid.
   b. [X] placing the envelope for collection and mailing on the date and at the place shown in item 4 following our
   ordinary business practices. I am readily familiar with this business' practice for collecting and processing correspondence for mailing. On the same day that correspondence is placed for collection and mailing, it is deposited in the ordinary
   course of business with the United States Postal Service in a sealed envelope with postage fully prepaid.

4. a. Date of deposit: b. Place of deposit (city and state):

   October 2, 1996   Beverly Hills, California

   I declare under penalty of perjury under the laws of the State of California that the foregoing is true and correct.

Date: October 2, 1996

Nancy Cauterucci   ▶ _Nancy Cauterucci_
(TYPE OR PRINT NAME)   (SIGNATURE OF DECLARANT)

NAME AND ADDRESS OF EACH PERSON TO WHOM NOTICE WAS MAILED

Director of Health Services
744 P Street
Mail Station 19-31
Sacramento, CA 95814

CERTIFIED MAIL
RETURN RECEIPT REQUESTED
P 387 834 275

---

*NOTE: To assist the creditor and the court, please send a copy of the Creditor's Claim form with this notice.

DE-157 [Rev. September 30, 1991]   **NOTICE OF ADMINISTRATION TO CREDITORS**   Page two
                                          (Probate)   CEB

EXHIBIT 12–8b Notice to Creditors (California)

CASE STUDY *Estate of Knight v. Knight*

559 N.E.2d 891 (IL)

FACTS:	Teresa Rai Knight requested the sum of $10,334.96 for 145 hours of work and expenses as administratrix of the estate of Arthur B. Knight. The trial judge awarded a fee of $4,000.
LEGAL ISSUE:	Are personal representatives entitled to reasonable compensation for their services?
COURT DECISION:	Yes.
REASON:	Administrators are entitled to reasonable compensation for their services, and the determination of what is reasonable is a matter of discretion for the trial judge. Factors that may be considered include good faith, diligence, time expended, the size of the estate, and the benefits conferred upon the estate. The $4,000 fee in this case was not an abuse of the trial judge's discretion.

No payment is made to creditors of any class until all those of the preceding class or classes have been paid. If assets are inadequate to pay all the debts of any class, the remaining assets are prorated to creditors of that class.

State laws set forth the order in which property is to be consumed for the payment of claims. A legal principle known as **marshaling of assets** ranks estate assets in a certain order for the payment of debts. In some states, unless a will directs otherwise, personal property and then real property is used to pay debts. In addition, property that is specifically bequeathed or devised will not be used to pay debts until after property that is not specifically bequeathed or devised has been exhausted. Then, as between specific legatees and devisees, the remaining debt is usually prorated.

Under UPC § 3–902, no distinction is made between real and personal property in the order that is used to satisfy claims. Property **abates** (is reduced) to pay claims, in the following order: (1) property not disposed of by will; (2) residuary devises; (3) general devises; and then (4) specific devises. In community property states, if the estate consists partly of separate property and partly of community property, community debts are charged against community property and separate debts are charged against separate property and then against the balance of community property.

Sale of Real Property

In most states, title to real property owned by a decedent vests in the decedent's heirs immediately upon death. In contrast, title to personal property vests in the personal representative when he or she is appointed. Therefore, although real property is included in the inventory of the estate, it is not usually

■ marshaling of assets

Collecting assets and claims and arranging the debts into the proper order of priority and then dividing up the assets to pay them off. ... This is done by an executor or administrator of a dead person's estate.

■ abates

1. Destroy or completely end. 2. Greatly lessen or reduce.

included in the final account, because the personal representative has no control over it. When the debts exceed the value of the personal property, however, the personal representative may sell the real property to obtain the money to pay the debts. Such a sale is done under the court's supervision (often by the issuance of a license to sell) unless the will gives the personal representative the power to sell real property without court supervision. The proceeds from the sale of real property are included in the personal representative's final account.

Distribution

After the time has expired for creditors to make claims and the debts and taxes have been paid, the remaining assets of the estate are distributed according to the terms of the will or the law of intestate succession. Some states have special rules allowing the distribution of property *in kind* (as it is), which avoids having to sell the property to distribute cash.

When there are not enough assets to pay the legacies and devises in a will, the rules of abatement, as previously explained, are applied. First, specific legacies and devises are paid in full. Next, general or pecuniary legacies and devises are paid: these abate pro rata if the assets are insufficient to pay them in full.

Final Account

The last task of the personal representative is to prepare and file a *final account* (called a *final return* in some states) with the court. Usually, only one account is filed; however, if an estate is open longer than a year, many states require an account to be filed annually, with a final account at the end.

The account is a listing of everything that the fiduciary has received and disbursed during the period covered in the account. With variations from state to state, a typical account lists receipts in one schedule, disbursements in another schedule, and the balance in a third schedule. If the account is final, no third schedule is necessary (see Exhibit 12–9).

The first schedule begins with the figure that is listed on the inventory as the total value of personal property in the estate. Real estate is not listed unless the personal representative has sold it, in which case the proceeds of the sale are listed. Added to this figure is a list of everything, together with their values, that has come into the estate after the inventory was filed. These include such things as interest, dividends, gains on sales of assets, and later-acquired property. The second schedule lists in detail everything that went out of the estate after the filing of the inventory. This includes the amounts of all bills that the personal

Barrett Brothers, Springfield, Ohio

PROBATE COURT OF _____ COUNTY, OHIO

ESTATE OF _____, DECEASED

CASE NO. _____

FIDUCIARY'S ACCOUNT
[R.C. 2109.30]

[Executors and Administrators]

The fiduciary offers the account given below and on the attached itemized statement of receipts and disbursements, and accompanying vouchers. The fiduciary states that the account is correct, and asks that it be approved and settled.

[Check one of the following]

❑   This is a partial account. A statement of the assets remaining in the fiduciary's hands is attached.

❑   This is a final account. A statement of the assets remaining in the fiduciary's hands for distribution to the beneficiaries is attached.

❑   This is a distributive account and the fiduciary asks to be discharged upon its approval and settlement.

❑   This is a final and distributive account and the fiduciary asks to be discharged upon its approval and settlement.

[Complete if this is a partial account, or if one or more accounts have previously been filed in the estate] The period of this account is from

_____ to _____

[Complete if applicable] Accounts previously filed in the estate, the accounting periods, and the fiduciary and attorney fees paid for each period, are as follows:

Date filed	Accounting Period	Fiduciary Fees Paid	Attorney Fees Paid
		$	$

13.0 - FIDUCIARY'S ACCOUNT   3/1/96

EXHIBIT 12–9a   Fiduciary's Account (Ohio)

This account is recapitulated as follows:

RECEIPTS

Personal property not sold ....$ _____

Proceeds from sale of personal property .... _____

Real estate not sold .... _____

Proceeds from sale of real estate .... _____

Income .... _____

Other receipts .... _____

Total receipts ....$ _____

DISBURSEMENTS

Fiduciary fees this accounting period ....$ _____

Attorney fees this accounting period............................ _____

Other administration costs and expenses.................... _____

Debts and claims against estate................................... _____

Ohio and federal estate taxes .... _____

Personal property distributed in kind .... _____

Real property transferred... _____

Other distributions to beneficiaries .... _____

Other disbursements... _____

Total disbursements ....$ _____

BALANCE REMAINING IN FIDUCIARY'S HANDS ....$ _____

_____   _____
Attorney   Fiduciary

Attorney Registration No. _____   _____
                                                                       Date

ENTRY SETTING HEARING

The Court sets _____at _____o'clock _____M., as the date and time
for hearing the above account.

_____   _____

Date   Probate Judge

EXHIBIT 12–9b Fiduciary's Account (Ohio)

representative paid, losses on sales of assets, and distributions made to devisees and legatees. If the account is final, the total of the first schedule will equal the total of the second schedule with no balance remaining.

In some states, the allowance of the final account by the court formally closes the estate. In other states, the personal representative files a petition for discharge which, when allowed, formally closes the estate. Even after an account is allowed, however, the court may correct manifest error in a judgment or revoke a judgment altogether when the judgment was obtained through fraud.

Estate Administration Battle Plan

As a practical matter, the administration of an estate follows a predictable path for the executor or administrator.

1. Open the safe-deposit box or boxes left by the decedent.
2. Apply for a tax identification number for the estate.
3. Open a checking account for the estate.
4. Compile a list of estate assets.
5. Notify all creditors of the decedent.
6. Collect the releases necessary for distributions.
7. Prepare tax returns.
8. Prepare and file the final accounting for the court.

Providing this basic framework to the personal representative can ease initial fears that they might have as to the scope of their duties. Personal representatives rarely have experience at the job and can be unsure as to their responsibilities.

§ 12.4 INFORMAL PROBATE PROCEEDINGS

Informal proceedings may be followed in most states when someone dies owning assets below a specific value or when there is no reason to have the court supervise all aspects of the estate's settlement. Informal proceedings, sometimes referred to as *unsupervised administration,* are relatively simple, with a minimum amount of paperwork and bureaucratic involvement.

In some states, an informal probate proceeding is known as **independent probate**. Other states refer to it as *probate in common form,* as opposed to probate in solemn form. Still other states provide for the appointment of a voluntary executor or a voluntary administrator to settle small estates by the use of a very simple procedure (see Exhibit 12–10).

■ **informal proceedings**

Proceedings conducted without notice to interested persons by an officer of the court acting as a registrar for probate of a will or appointment of a personal representative (UPC § 1–201(19)).

■ **independent probate**

Informal probate proceedings. Referred to in some states as *probate in common form.*

Commonwealth of Massachusetts
The Trial Court
_____ **Division**   **Probate and Family Court Department**   **Docket No.** _____

Voluntary Executor/Executrix

Name of Decedent _____

Domicile at Death _____
                (Street and No.)   (City or Town)   (County)   (Zip)

Date of Death _____

Will and Death Certificate shall be filed with application.

Name and address of Applicant(s) _____
_____ Status _____

Your Applicant(s) respectfully state(s) that said estate consisting entirely of personal property the total value of which does not exceed fifteen thousand dollars ($15,000) exclusive of the decedent's automobile as shown by the following schedule of all the assets of said deceased known to the applicant(s):

Name of Property	Estimated Value
_____	$ _____
_____	$ _____
_____	$ _____
_____	$ _____
_____	$ _____
Total	$ _____

That thirty days have expired since the date of death of said deceased and no petition for probate of will or appointment of administration/administratrix has been filed in said Court.

That your applicant(s) ha ___ undertaken to act as voluntary executor/executrix of the estate of said deceased and will administer the same according to law and apply the proceeds thereof in conformity with Section 16A of Chapter 195 of the General Laws.

That to the knowledge of the applicant(s) the following are the names and addresses of all persons surviving who, with the deceased, were joint owners of property; also listed are the names and addresses of those who would take under the provisions of Section 3 of Chapter 190 in the case of intestacy, and the names and addresses of those who would take under the provisions of the will.

_____
_____
_____
_____
_____

☐ The applicant(s) hereby certif _____ that a copy of this document, along with a copy of the decedent's death certificate has been sent by <u>certified mail</u> to the **Department of Public Welfare, P.O. Box 86, Essex Station, Boston, Massachusetts 02112.**

Date _____   Signature _____

NOTARIZATION

_____ ss   Date _____

Then personally appeared _____
to me known and made oath that the information contained in the foregoing statement is true to the best of his/her/their knowledge and belief.

Before me, _____
               NOTARY PUBLIC/JUSTICE OF THE PEACE

My Commission expires _____

CJ-P7A (8/92)

EXHIBIT 12–10 Informal Probate Application (Massachusetts)

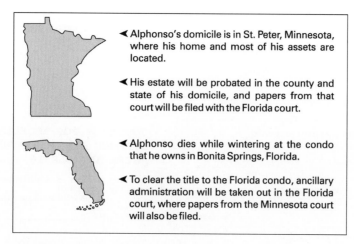

EXHIBIT 12–11   Ancillary Administration

§ 12.5 ANCILLARY ADMINISTRATION

A resident of one state often owns real and personal property in another state. After the decedent's death, the property in the other state must be recovered for the benefit of the decedent's estate, and arrangements must be made for the payment of debts in that state. The term applied to this process is **ancillary administration**, which is the administration of an estate in a state other than where the decedent was domiciled but where the decedent owns property. Exhibit 12–11 illustrates this situation.

Most states have provisions for admitting to record in their probate courts an authenticated copy of a will that has been proved and allowed in another state, together with a certified copy of the personal representative's appointment. Similar provisions are available for intestate estates. This process allows the personal representative to exercise the powers of a local personal representative regarding all local assets. The various states have other methods, as well, for handling ancillary administration (see Exhibit 12–12).

■ **ancillary administration**

A proceeding in a state where a dead person had property, but which is different from the state where that person lived and has her main estate administered.

DO NOT LEAVE ANY ITEMS BLANK

SURROGATE'S COURT OF THE STATE OF NEW YORK
COUNTY OF
---X

ANCILLARY ADMINISTRATION PROCEEDING,

ESTATE OF

a/k/a

a domiciliary of the State of

                                    Deceased.
---X
TO THE SURROGATE'S COURT, COUNTY OF   :

**PETITION FOR ANCILLARY
LETTERS OF ADMINISTRATION
SCPA ARTICLE 16**

[ ] Ancillary Letters of Administration
[ ] Ancillary Letters of
                 Administration d.b.n.

File No. _____

    It is respectfully alleged:
    1. The name, citizenship, domicile (or, in the case of a bank or trust company, its principal office) and interest in this proceeding of the petitioner(s) are as follows:

Name: _____

Domicile or Principal Office: _____
                                          (Street and Number)

_____
   (City, Village or Town)   (State)   (Zip Code)

         Mailing Address:_____
                                (if different from domicile)
Citizen of: _____

Name: _____

Domicile or Principal Office: _____
                                          (Street and Number)

_____
   (City, Village or Town)   (State)   (Zip Code)

         Mailing Address:_____
                                (if different from domicile)
Citizen of: _____

Interest(s) of Petitioner(s): [Check one]
      [ ] Administrator   [ ] Distributee of decedent [State relationship] _____
      [ ] Creditor
      [ ] Other [Specify] _____

    2. The name, domicile, date and place of death, and national citizenship of the above-named decedent are as follow:

      (a) Name: _____

      (b) Date of Death: _____

      (c) Place of death: _____

      (d) Domicile: Street _____

           City, Town, Village _____

           County _____ State _____

      (e) Citizen of: _____

EXHIBIT 12–12a Petition for Ancillary Administration (New York)

AA-1 (4/98) -1-

3. The decedent died **INTESTATE**, leaving no will.

On the _____, letters were issued to _____
by _____ Court, State of _____, being a
competent court of the state of the domicile of decedent having jurisdiction thereof, and the
amount of the security given on the original appointment was $_____.

[If additional space is needed in Paragraphs 4, 5 and 6, attach addendum.]

4.(a) The estimated gross value of decedent's property in the State of New York, consisting
of real property and personal property, is described and valued as follows: [list items and
describe briefly, giving location. If space is insufficient, attach addendum].

Personal Property	$_____
Improved real property in New York State	$_____
Unimproved real property in New York State	$_____
Estimated gross rents for a period of 18 months	$_____
Total	$_____

4.(b) No other assets exist in New York State, nor does any cause of action exist on behalf
of the estate, except as follows: **[Enter "NONE" or specify]**

_____

_____

Exemplified copies of the decree and the letters issued, if any, are submitted as part of this
petition.

5. The names, addresses and interests of all persons entitled to process [(a) New York
State Department of Taxation and Finance, (b) all domiciliary creditors or domiciliaries
claiming to be creditors, and (c) such other persons entitled to letters pursuant to SCPA §1607]
are as follows:

Name	Address	Nature of Interest or Amount of Claim
New York State Department of Taxation and Finance	Albany, New York	_____
_____	_____	_____
_____	_____	_____

EXHIBIT 12–12b Petition for Ancillary Administration (New York)

CASE STUDY ⚖️ *In re* **Estate of Barteau**

736 So.2d 57(FL)

FACTS: Decedent Azalea Barteau left two wills, one in Florida, and one in Mexico. Her Florida beneficiaries claimed the Mexico will was signed under duress, and wish to challenge it in Florida under an ancillary administration proceeding. The trial court dismissed the ancillary proceeding, under a theory of *forum non conveniens*, and both beneficiaries appealed.

LEGAL ISSUE: Can an ancillary administration proceeding be filed for a will executed and located in a foreign country?

COURT DECISION: Yes.

REASON: While no case law existed in Florida allowing the challenging of the validity of a will from a foreign country, cases did exist that provided for this ancillary proceeding regarding wills from different states. The court here felt that these were guiding authority, and that they outweighed the equitable concept of *forum non conveniens*.

SUMMARY

The probate process protects the decedent by seeing that her wishes are carried out. It protects the heirs by assuring that all of the decedent's property is collected and accounted for and by determining the lawful heirs. It also establishes title to property that has been inherited.

Formal probate proceedings involve the following steps: (1) a petition is filed with the court; (2) interested parties are given notice; (3) in a testate estate, the will must be proved; (4) unless waived, a bond is given by the personal representative; (5) letters are issued by the court; (6) an inventory is filed; (7) notice or a time period is given to creditors; (8) debts, taxes, and expenses of administration are paid; (9) distribution is made to the beneficiaries; (10) an account is filed with the court.

Informal probate proceedings may be followed in most states when someone dies owning assets below a specific value or when there is no reason to have the court supervise all aspects of the estate's settlement. Informal proceedings are relatively simple, with a minimum amount of paperwork and bureaucratic involvement.

As part of their ancillary administration provisions, most probate courts admit to record authenticated copies of wills that have been proved and allowed in other states, together with certified copies of the appointment of out-of-state personal representatives.

A checklist of steps for administering a will can be an invaluable guide to the estate's representative or legal assistant, as it helps to ensure that nothing is forgotten and all actions are timely.

◼ REVIEW QUESTIONS

1. What is the consequence of failing to turn over to the probate court a will of a deceased person?

2. How are heirs and next of kin protected by the probate procedure?

3. What steps are followed in formal probate proceedings?

4. How do probate proceedings begin in testate cases? In intestate cases?

5. How do the decedent's heirs learn that a will is being probated?

6. What are three methods that are used to prove a will? Why is a self-proof clause in a will helpful?

7. Describe one of the first duties of a personal representative after receiving letters of appointment.

8. What did the United States Supreme Court hold in 1988 regarding notice to creditors?

9. How do legacies and devises abate when there are not enough assets to pay them?

10. What is one method states use to provide for ancillary administration?

◼ CASES TO DISCUSS

1. Jeremy Mindlin executed a will naming his father, Leo Mindlin, as personal representative. When Jeremy died, the court appointed Jeremy's wife, Karen, rather than Leo, as personal representative. Leo appealed. How would you decide? *Estate of Mindlin v. Mindlin*, 571 So. 2d 90 (FL).

2. Agnes Minkus-Whalen was appointed administratrix of the estate of Stephen J. Minkus. The petition for administration listed three first cousins as the only heirs. Before filing the account, however, the administratrix was notified of the discovery in Lithuania of 11 additional first cousins of the decedent. Without disclosing the discovery, the administratrix filed an account, obtained allowance from the court, and distributed the estate to the three first cousins. Can the allowance of the account be revoked by the court? Explain. *Altshuler v. Minkus-Whalen*, 579 N.E.2d 1369 (MA).

◼ RESEARCH ON THE WEB

1. On the Internet, log on to <http://www.Google.com>. Type the words *probate software* in the box and look for something of interest to you.

2. The Web site at <http://www.paralegalclassifieds.com> contains a database of job listings for paralegals and legal assistants.

3. The following two sites can be extremely helpful when looking for legal information on the Web: <http://www.findlaw.com> and <http://www.lawcrawler.com>.

■ SHARPENING YOUR PROFESSIONAL SKILLS_____

1. Using your state form, prepare a petition for the formal probate of a will. Use a fictitious name, domicile, and date of death of a decedent who is survived by two adult children and one grandchild who is the adopted daughter of a deceased child.

2. From the business section of a newspaper, determine the values to be used in the inventory for each of the following stocks that were owned by a decedent who died on the day before you are doing this assignment:

   a. 55 shares of AT&T

   b. 15 shares of NYNX

   c. 15 shares of Bell South

   d. 24 shares of IBM

   e. 116 shares of Exxon

   Show the calculations you used to determine the values.

3. Using your state form, prepare an inventory for the hypothetical estate used in question 2. Include in the inventory:

   a. a dwelling house

   b. household furniture

   c. personal effects

   d. an automobile

   e. a checking account

   f. a savings account in a different bank

   g. a certificate of deposit in a different bank

   h. 15 Series E U.S. savings bonds

   i. the stocks listed in question 3

   Provide details including values, fictitious account numbers, and fictitious serial numbers for the automobile and the securities.

4. Using your state form, prepare a final account for the hypothetical estate used in questions 2 and 3. Include the following:

   a. interest income from the checking account, savings account, certificate of deposit, and Series E bonds

   b. dividend income from the stocks

   c. gains (or losses) on the sale of the stock certificates

   d. funeral expenses

   e. an outstanding credit card bill

   f. real estate taxes

g. utility bills

h. loss on the sale of the automobile

i. legal fees

j. expenses incurred in settling the estate

k. an executor's fee

l. distribution of the balance to the heirs

■ SHARPENING YOUR LEGAL VOCABULARY_____

On a separate sheet of paper, fill in the numbered blank lines in the following anecdote with legal terms from this list:

abate

administering an estate

ancillary administration

appearance

caveat

citation

formal proceedings

heirs at law

independent probate

informal proceedings

in kind

insolvent

inventory

letters of administration

letters testamentary

marshaling of assets

petition for administration

petition for administration with the will annexed

petition for probate

preliminary letters testamentary

probate

probate in common form

probate in solemn form

probating a will

supervised administration

unsupervised administration

voluntary administrator

voluntary executor

Jack and Jill died accidentally while hiking on a mountain trail. Jack had made a will before he died, but Jill had not. Jack's executrix had the task of (1), that is, establishing before the court that the document offered for official recognition was Jack's genuine will. In contrast, Jill's administrator had the task of (2). The legal process that was used to settle Jack's estate is known as (3) because it was conducted before a judge with notice given to interested persons. In some states, that process is known as (4). Under the Uniform Probate Code, the process may or may not be (5), whereby the estate is settled under the continuing authority of the court from beginning to end. To begin the task of settling Jack's estate, his executrix filed with the court a(n) (6). The court then issued a(n) (7) ordering the executrix to notify all (8), that is, those people who would have inherited from Jack had he died intestate. Because all parties interested assented to the executrix's appointment, and the executrix filed a bond in the appropriate amount, the court issued a certificate of appointment, known as (9). Once appointed, the executrix's first duty was to file a(n) (10), which is a detailed list of property owned by the decedent together with its estimated value as of the date of death. The legal process that was used in settling Jill's estate is known as (11) because it was conducted without notice to interested persons by an officer of the court acting as a registrar. In other states this process may be called (12), (13), or (14). Because of the uncomplicated legal process that was used, the administrator of Jill's estate was not required to file a(n) (15), which is used to begin formal probate proceedings in an intestate estate. Similarly, the court did not issue (16), the usual certificate appointing an administrator. In addition, because neither Jack or Jill owned property out of state, there was no need to take out (17) for either of them.

■ KEY TERMS

abates	independent probate	petition for probate
administering an estate	informal proceedings	preliminary letters testamentary
ancillary administration	insolvent	probate in solemn form
appearance	inventory	probating a will
caveat	marshaling of assets	supervised administration
citation	petition for administration	unsupervised administration
formal proceedings	petition for administration with the	
heirs at law	will annexed	

 Online Companion™
For additional resources, please go to
http://www.paralegal.delmar.cengage.com.

 Student CD-ROM
For additional materials, please go to the
CD in this book.

13

Estate Taxes

CHAPTER OUTLINE

CHAPTER OUTCOMES

- Describe the initial steps that must be taken by a personal representative with regard to the decedent's taxes.

- Identify the income that must be included in the decedent's final income tax return and the fiduciary income tax return.

- Explain the occasion, date due, and form used for filing a federal estate tax return.

- Differentiate between the gross estate and the taxable estate for estate tax purposes.

- Compute a hypothetical estate tax.

JOB COMPETENCIES

- Be able to assist the attorney in identifying a fiduciary's tax obligations.

- Be able to assist the attorney in identifying the forms that must be filed with regard to the decedent's final income tax return.

- Be able to assist the attorney in gathering information needed to prepare the fiduciary income tax return and the estate tax return.

> "I only regret that I have but one life to live for my country."
>
> **LAST WORDS OF NATHAN HALE (1755–1776)**

■ A DAY AT THE OFFICE . . .

It was 9:00 in the morning on December 5. Attorney Knight was discussing the day's activities with Tiffany Casey, the office paralegal.

"My first appointment this morning is at 10:00 with Ms. Shulman. Her father passed away a few days ago, and we're going to be settling his estate."

"I remember when we did Mr. Shulman's will," Tiffany offered. "I was one of the witnesses. He was a jovial man with a nice sense of humor. He used to joke about our Macintosh computer."

"You have a good memory, Tiffany," Attorney Knight replied. "Can you join us at 10:00? I'd like you to help with the estate right from the beginning."

"Sure. I'll be glad to," Tiffany replied. "Let me know when you want me to come in."

Later that morning, Tiffany and Attorney Knight met with Ms. Shulman in Attorney Knight's office.

"I always did my father's income taxes, you know," Ms. Shulman was saying, "but I don't know how to do this year's return."

"We'll help you with that," Attorney Knight responded. "That's part of our work in settling your father's estate. Tiffany, as soon as Ms. Shulman is appointed executrix, we'll need to notify the IRS that a fiduciary relationship exists."

"Right. I'll see that they are notified."

"Also, you'll need to send for an employer identification number from the IRS."

"Yes. I'll do that, too. Ms. Shulman, I'll have some forms for you to sign before you leave today."

"Okay, but one thing is bothering me," Ms. Shulman responded. "My father owned an apple orchard, and the day before he died, he sold $3,000 worth of Macintosh apples to the cannery. When the money comes in, do I declare that as income on his tax return?"

"Don't worry about it," Attorney Knight countered. "We'll do the taxes when the time comes. You've got enough things to worry about for now."

Queries:

1. What income would be included on Mr. Shulman's final income tax return, assuming that Mr. Shulman died on December 1?
2. What form will Tiffany use to notify the IRS of the fiduciary relationship?
3. What form will Tiffany use to obtain an employer identification number (EIN)?
4. What is the money from the sale of the apples called, and on what return will it be reported?

§ 13.1 THE FIDUCIARY'S TAX OBLIGATIONS

The paralegal often plays a key role in assisting the attorney and the personal representative with the many procedures involved in settling an estate. Because a major responsibility of the personal representative is to prepare and file tax returns when they are due, the paralegal often becomes involved with this task as well. Federal and state returns that sometimes must be filed include: (1) a final income tax return for the decedent, (2) an income tax return for the decedent's estate, and (3) an estate tax return. The federal tax returns are discussed in this chapter. (State tax returns differ so much from state to state that discussion of each state's return is beyond the scope of this text.)

Attorneys who specialize in preparing estate taxes frequently use software that is particularly designed for that purpose. Various software products are available for preparing estate tax returns and keeping estate records. One such product is available from Fast-Tax Trust Services at <http://www.zanenet.com>.

Notifying the Internal Revenue Service

The first step in the taxation procedure is to notify the Internal Revenue Service (IRS) that the taxpayer has died and that a fiduciary relationship now exists. Form 56 (Notice Concerning Fiduciary Relationship) is available as a convenience from the IRS for this purpose (see Exhibit 13–1). It is not mandatory that Form 56 be filed. However, by filing the form, any subsequent correspondence from the IRS will be sent to the fiduciary's address rather than to the decedent's last-known address. This will ensure that the fiduciary is informed of all tax liabilities and other tax matters.

Obtaining Identification Number

The next step is to obtain an **employer identification number (EIN)** for the estate. This number is assigned by the IRS to identify an estate and is used in place of a Social Security number. The number is required if any estate tax returns are to be filed or if a bank account is to be opened for estate funds. To obtain the number, it is merely necessary to fill out *Form SS-4* (Application for Employer Identification Number) and file it with the IRS (see Exhibit 13–2). The number will be mailed by the IRS to the person requesting it without delay.

■ **employer identification number (EIN)**

Number assigned by the IRS to identify an estate; used in place of a Social Security number.

| Form **56**
(Rev. April 2002)
Department of the Treasury
Internal Revenue Service | **Notice Concerning Fiduciary Relationship**
(Internal Revenue Code sections 6036 and 6903) | OMB No. 1545-0013 |

Part I   Identification

| Name of person for whom you are acting (as shown on the tax return) | Identifying number | Decedent's social security no. |

Address of person for whom you are acting (number, street, and room or suite no.)

City or town, state, and ZIP code (If a foreign address, see instructions.)

Fiduciary's name

Address of fiduciary (number, street, and room or suite no.)

| City or town, state, and ZIP code | Telephone number (optional)
(   ) |

Part II   Authority

1   Authority for fiduciary relationship. Check applicable box:
- **a(1)** ☐ Will and codicils or court order appointing fiduciary . . . . **(2)** Date of death . . . .
- **b(1)** ☐ Court order appointing fiduciary . . . . **(2)** Date (see instructions) . . . .
- **c** ☐ Valid trust instrument and amendments
- **d** ☐ Other. Describe ▶

Part III   Tax Notices

Send to the fiduciary listed in Part I all notices and other written communications involving the following tax matters:

2   Type of tax (estate, gift, generation-skipping transfer, income, excise, etc.) ▶ . . . .
3   Federal tax form number (706, 1040, 1041, 1120, etc.) ▶ . . . .
4   Year(s) or period(s) (if estate tax, date of death) ▶

Part IV   Revocation or Termination of Notice

Section A—Total Revocation or Termination

5   Check this box if you are revoking or terminating all prior notices concerning fiduciary relationships on file with the Internal Revenue Service for the same tax matters and years or periods covered by this notice concerning fiduciary relationship . ▶ ☐

Reason for termination of fiduciary relationship. Check applicable box:
- **a** ☐ Court order revoking fiduciary authority
- **b** ☐ Certificate of dissolution or termination of a business entity
- **c** ☐ Other. Describe ▶

Section B—Partial Revocation

6a Check this box if you are revoking earlier notices concerning fiduciary relationships on file with the Internal Revenue Service for the same tax matters and years or periods covered by this notice concerning fiduciary relationship . . . . ▶ ☐

b Specify to whom granted, date, and address, including ZIP code.
▶

Section C—Substitute Fiduciary

7   Check this box if a new fiduciary or fiduciaries have been or will be substituted for the revoking or terminating fiduciary(ies) and specify the name(s) and address(es), including ZIP code(s), of the new fiduciary(ies) . . . . ▶ ☐

Part V   Court and Administrative Proceedings

Name of court (if other than a court proceeding, identify the type of proceeding and name of agency)	Date proceeding initiated
Address of court	Docket number of proceeding
City or town, state, and ZIP code	Date	Time	a.m. p.m.	Place of other proceedings

I certify that I have the authority to execute this notice concerning fiduciary relationship on behalf of the taxpayer.

**Please
Sign
Here**

| ▶ Fiduciary's signature | Title, if applicable | Date |
| ▶ Fiduciary's signature | Title, if applicable | Date |

For Paperwork Reduction Act and Privacy Act Notice, see back page.   Cat. No. 16375I   Form **56** (Rev. 4-2002)

EXHIBIT 13–1   Internal Revenue Service Form 56

This form may be used to notify the IRS that a taxpayer has died and that a fiduciary relationship now exists.

Form **SS-4**	**Application for Employer Identification Number**		EIN

Form **SS-4**
(Rev. December 2001)
Department of the Treasury
Internal Revenue Service

Application for Employer Identification Number
(For use by employers, corporations, partnerships, trusts, estates, churches, government agencies, Indian tribal entities, certain individuals, and others.)
▶ See separate instructions for each line.   ▶ Keep a copy for your records.

EIN

OMB No. 1545-0003

Type or print clearly.

1 Legal name of entity (or individual) for whom the EIN is being requested

2 Trade name of business (if different from name on line 1) | **3** Executor, trustee, "care of" name

4a Mailing address (room, apt., suite no. and street, or P.O. box) | **5a** Street address (if different) (Do not enter a P.O. box.)

4b City, state, and ZIP code | **5b** City, state, and ZIP code

6 County and state where principal business is located

7a Name of principal officer, general partner, grantor, owner, or trustor | **7b** SSN, ITIN, or EIN

8a Type of entity (check only one box)
☐ Sole proprietor (SSN) _____
☐ Partnership
☐ Corporation (enter form number to be filed) ▶ _____
☐ Personal service corp.
☐ Church or church-controlled organization
☐ Other nonprofit organization (specify) ▶ _____
☐ Other (specify) ▶

☐ Estate (SSN of decedent) _____
☐ Plan administrator (SSN) _____
☐ Trust (SSN of grantor) _____
☐ National Guard   ☐ State/local government
☐ Farmers' cooperative   ☐ Federal government/military
☐ REMIC   ☐ Indian tribal governments/enterprises
Group Exemption Number (GEN) ▶ _____

8b If a corporation, name the state or foreign country (if applicable) where incorporated | State | Foreign country

9 Reason for applying (check only one box)
☐ Started new business (specify type) ▶ _____
☐ Hired employees (Check the box and see line 12.)
☐ Compliance with IRS withholding regulations
☐ Other (specify) ▶

☐ Banking purpose (specify purpose) ▶ _____
☐ Changed type of organization (specify new type) ▶ _____
☐ Purchased going business
☐ Created a trust (specify type) ▶ _____
☐ Created a pension plan (specify type) ▶ _____

10 Date business started or acquired (month, day, year) | **11** Closing month of accounting year

12 First date wages or annuities were paid or will be paid (month, day, year). **Note:** *If applicant is a withholding agent, enter date income will first be paid to nonresident alien. (month, day, year)* . . . . ▶

13 Highest number of employees expected in the next 12 months. **Note:** *If the applicant does not expect to have any employees during the period, enter "-0-."* . . . . ▶ | Agricultural | Household | Other

14 Check **one** box that best describes the principal activity of your business.   ☐ Health care & social assistance   ☐ Wholesale–agent/broker
☐ Construction   ☐ Rental & leasing   ☐ Transportation & warehousing   ☐ Accommodation & food service   ☐ Wholesale–other   ☐ Retail
☐ Real estate   ☐ Manufacturing   ☐ Finance & insurance   ☐ Other (specify)

15 Indicate principal line of merchandise sold; specific construction work done; products produced; or services provided.

16a Has the applicant ever applied for an employer identification number for this or any other business? . . . . . . ☐ Yes   ☐ No
Note: *If "Yes," please complete lines 16b and 16c.*

16b If you checked "Yes" on line 16a, give applicant's legal name and trade name shown on prior application if different from line 1 or 2 above.
Legal name ▶ _____   Trade name ▶

16c Approximate date when, and city and state where, the application was filed. Enter previous employer identification number if known.
Approximate date when filed (mo., day, year) | City and state where filed | Previous EIN

Third Party Designee	Complete this section **only** if you want to authorize the named individual to receive the entity's EIN and answer questions about the completion of this form.	
	Designee's name	Designee's telephone number (include area code) ( )
	Address and ZIP code	Designee's fax number (include area code) ( )

Under penalties of perjury, I declare that I have examined this application, and to the best of my knowledge and belief, it is true, correct, and complete. | Applicant's telephone number (include area code) ( )

Name and title (type or print clearly) ▶ | Applicant's fax number (include area code) ( )

Signature ▶   Date ▶

For Privacy Act and Paperwork Reduction Act Notice, see separate instructions.   Cat. No. 16055N   Form **SS-4** (Rev. 12-2001)

EXHIBIT 13–2   Internal Revenue Service Form SS-4

This form is used to obtain an employer identification number for an estate. The number is required if any estate tax returns are to be filed or if a bank account is to be opened for estate funds.

EVIDENCE OF GRATEFULNESS

JERRY GARCIA

Using the California Probate Code as a guide, the Marin County Superior Court received more than 30 claims against the estate of Grateful Dead leader, Jerry Garcia, who died in 1995. Claims against his estate were made by ex-lovers, associates, and others to the extent of $38 million—more than its value. Under California community property law, Garcia's wife of 18 months is entitled to half of the assets acquired during marriage. The singer's 18-page will left one-third of the other half of the community property plus one-third of the rest of his estate to his wife, Deborah. The remainder of the estate was divided among his children, his brother, and the daughter of a friend.

Garcia did little to shelter his estate from taxes. He could have used the unlimited marital deduction to leave all of his estate, tax free, to his widow. Similarly, he could have created a qualified terminable interest property (QTIP) trust, which would have excluded the first $600,000 from the estate tax and given his widow the trust's income for her life. Such actions, however, would have delayed inheritances by his children of previous marriages, and it is apparent that he did not want to do this. He seemed grateful for his family.

§ 13.2 THE DECEDENT'S FINAL INCOME TAX RETURN

The personal representative must file the final income tax return of the decedent for the year of death, as well as any returns not filed for preceding years. In the case of a joint return, the surviving spouse may file the return alone if no personal representative has been appointed before the due date.

If an individual died after the close of the tax year, but before the return for that year was filed, the return for the year just closed may not be the final return. The return for that year will be a regular return. The personal representative must file that return for the year before death and the final return for the year in which death occurred.

Income

The decedent's income that is includable on the final return is generally determined in the same way as if the person were still alive, except that the taxable period is usually shorter because it ends on the date of death. Only income that was received up to the date of death is included in the decedent's final income tax return. Income that is received after the date of death (such as bank account interest and stock dividends) is taxable either to the decedent's estate or to a joint owner. For this reason, it is necessary to provide the payor of interest or dividends with the new identification number so that the correct number will be reported to the IRS on the payor's Form 1099. The correct identification number will be either the estate EIN number or the Social Security number of the joint owner.

The amounts reported to the IRS on Forms 1099 (Statement for Recipients of Income) by payors may not be the correct amount that should be reported on the decedent's final tax return. This is because the amount that should be reported is the amount received up to the date of death; amounts received after death are reported either on the estate income tax return or a joint owner's return. If you are preparing a decedent's final return and have received Forms 1099 for the decedent that include amounts paid after the decedent's death, report the total interest and dividends shown on the Forms 1099; then show any interest and dividends belonging to another recipient separately, subtract it, and report the net result.

If an income tax refund is due the decedent, Form 1310 (Statement of Person Claiming Refund Due a Deceased Taxpayer) must be filed together with the decedent's tax return (see Exhibit 13–3).

CASE STUDY *Rollert Trust v. IRS*

752 F.2d 1128(DC)

FACTS: Edward Rollert died on March 2, 1970. He was tentatively awarded a bonus of stock rights three months prior to his death. The rights were enforceable in January, 1971, 1972, and 1973. Rollert's estate was primarily left to the Rollert Trust for the benefit of his children. The decedent's final income tax return did not include these rights, as they were not vested or guaranteed to the deceased.

LEGAL ISSUE: Should these rights been included as income on the final tax return, even though he had no legal right to them?

COURT DECISION: Yes.

REASON: Even though the rights had not vested, nor were they guaranteed, the likelihood of their receipt was substantially certain. Though no legally enforceable right to ownership had vested, the likelihood that they would be paid was substantially certain, and that virtual certainty raised them to the level of income.

Form **1310**
(Rev. March 1995)
Department of the Treasury
Internal Revenue Service

Statement of Person Claiming
Refund Due a Deceased Taxpayer

▶ **See instructions below and on back.**

OMB No. 1545-0073

Attachment
Sequence No. **87**

Tax year decedent was due a refund:
Calendar year _____ , or other tax year beginning _____ , 19 ___ , and ending _____ , 19 ___

	Name of decedent	Date of death	Decedent's social security number

Please type or print

Name of person claiming refund

Home address (number and street). If you have a P.O. box, see instructions. | Apt. no.

City, town or post office, state, and ZIP code. If you have a foreign address, see instructions.

Part I   **Check the box that applies to you.** Check only one box. **Be sure to complete Part III below.**

A ☐ Surviving spouse requesting reissuance of a refund check. See instructions.

B ☐ Court-appointed or certified personal representative. You may have to attach a court certificate showing your appointment.
See instructions.

C ☐ Person, **other** than A or B, claiming refund for the decedent's estate. Also, complete Part II. You may have to attach a copy
of the proof of death. See instructions.

Part II   **Complete this part only if you checked the box on line C above.**

		Yes	No
1	Did the decedent leave a will?		
2a	Has a court appointed a personal representative for the estate of the decedent?		
b	If you answered "**No**" to 2a, will one be appointed?		
	If you answered "**Yes**" to 2a or 2b, the personal representative must file for the refund.		
3	As the person claiming the refund for the decedent's estate, will you pay out the refund according to the laws of the state where the decedent was a legal resident?		
	If you answered "**No**" to 3, a refund cannot be made until you submit a court certificate showing your appointment as personal representative or other evidence that you are entitled under state law to receive the refund.		

Part III   **Signature and verification. All filers must complete this part.**

I request a refund of taxes overpaid by or on behalf of the decedent. Under penalties of perjury, I declare that I have examined this claim, and to
the best of my knowledge and belief, it is true, correct, and complete.

Signature of person claiming refund ▶ _____   Date ▶ _____

EXHIBIT 13–3   Internal Revenue Service Form 1310

This form may have to be filed with the IRS to obtain a tax refund that is due a deceased taxpayer.

Exemptions and Deductions

Generally, the rules for exemptions and deductions allowed to an individual also apply to the decedent's final income tax return. The return should show any deductible items the decedent paid before death.

Medical expenses paid before death by the decedent are deductible on the final income tax return if deductions are itemized. Medical expenses that are not paid before the decedent's death are liabilities of the decedent's estate and are shown on the estate tax return. However, if medical expenses for the decedent are paid out of the estate during the one-year period beginning with the day after death, an election may be made to treat all or part of the expenses as paid by the decedent at the time they were incurred. If the election is made, all or part of the medical expenses can be claimed on the decedent's income tax return rather than on the federal estate tax return (the Form 706 described later).

§ 13.3 FIDUCIARY INCOME TAX RETURN

An estate is a taxable entity that is separate from the decedent. It originates with the death of the individual and exists until the final distribution of its assets to the heirs and other beneficiaries. An estate's income of $600 or more must be reported annually on either a calendar or fiscal year basis. The income is reported on IRS Form 1041 (U.S. Fiduciary Income Tax Return shown in Exhibit 13–4).

Income

Generally, an estate's income is the same as the individual's income, with certain exceptions. Gross income of an estate consists of all income received or accrued during the tax year. It includes interest, dividends, rents, royalties, gain from the sale of property, and income from businesses, partnerships, trusts, and any other sources.

Income in Respect of the Decedent

All gross income that the decedent would have received in a future year had death not occurred is **income in respect of the decedent**. Such income must be included in the gross income of (1) the decedent's estate, if the estate receives it; or (2) the beneficiary, if the right to income is passed directly to the beneficiary and the beneficiary receives it; or (3) any person to whom the estate properly distributes the right to receive it.

For example, suppose that Valerie Miller owned and operated a tomato farm. She used the cash method of accounting and therefore recorded income only when it was received. She sold and delivered $5,000 worth of tomatoes to a canning factory, but did not receive payment before her death. When the estate was settled, payment had not yet been made, and the estate transferred the right to receive the payment to her surviving spouse. When Miller's surviving spouse collects the $5,000, he must include the amount in his income tax return. It should not be reported on the final return of the decedent or on the return of Miller's estate.

Suppose, instead, that Valerie Miller was an author who received royalties (promised future payments against work already performed). Upon Valerie's death, the IRS will estimate the royalties that heirs can expect to receive in the future. This amount must be reported on Line 8 of the estate income tax return (Form 1041), and the full tax must be paid when the return is filed, even though the actual royalty income will not be received by the heirs until years later.

■ **income in respect of the decedent**

All gross income that a decedent would have received, had he not died, that was not properly includable on the decedent's final income tax return.

Department of the Treasury—Internal Revenue Service

Form 1041
U.S. Income Tax Return for Estates and Trusts
2001

For calendar year 2001 or fiscal year beginning _____ , 2001, and ending _____ , 20____

OMB No. 1545-0092

A Type of entity:
- ☐ Decedent's estate
- ☐ Simple trust
- ☐ Complex trust
- ☐ Grantor type trust
- ☐ Bankruptcy estate-Ch. 7
- ☐ Bankruptcy estate-Ch. 11
- ☐ Pooled income fund

B Number of Schedules K-1 attached (see instructions) ▶

Name of estate or trust (If a grantor type trust, see page 10 of the instructions.)

Name and title of fiduciary

Number, street, and room or suite no. (If a P.O. box, see page 10 of the instructions.)

City or town, state, and ZIP code

C Employer identification number

D Date entity created

E Nonexempt charitable and split-interest trusts, check applicable boxes (see page 11 of the instructions):
- ☐ Described in section 4947(a)(1)
- ☐ Not a private foundation
- ☐ Described in section 4947(a)(2)

F Check applicable boxes: ☐ Initial return ☐ Final return ☐ Amended return ☐ Change in fiduciary's name ☐ Change in fiduciary's address

G Pooled mortgage account (see page 12 of the instructions): ☐ Bought ☐ Sold Date:

Income

1	Interest income	1
2	Ordinary dividends	2
3	Business income or (loss) (attach Schedule C or C-EZ (Form 1040))	3
4	Capital gain or (loss) (attach Schedule D (Form 1041))	4
5	Rents, royalties, partnerships, other estates and trusts, etc. (attach Schedule E (Form 1040))	5
6	Farm income or (loss) (attach Schedule F (Form 1040))	6
7	Ordinary gain or (loss) (attach Form 4797)	7
8	Other income. List type and amount _____	8
9	**Total income.** Combine lines 1 through 8	9

Deductions

10	Interest. Check if Form 4952 is attached ▶ ☐	10
11	Taxes	11
12	Fiduciary fees	12
13	Charitable deduction (from Schedule A, line 7)	13
14	Attorney, accountant, and return preparer fees	14
15a	Other deductions **not** subject to the 2% floor (attach schedule)	15a
b	Allowable miscellaneous itemized deductions subject to the 2% floor	15b
16	**Total.** Add lines 10 through 15b	16
17	Adjusted total income or (loss). Subtract line 16 from line 9. Enter here and on Schedule B, line 1 ▶	17
18	Income distribution deduction (from Schedule B, line 15) (attach Schedules K-1 (Form 1041))	18
19	Estate tax deduction (including certain generation-skipping taxes) (attach computation)	19
20	Exemption	20
21	**Total deductions.** Add lines 18 through 20 ▶	21

Tax and Payments

22	Taxable income. Subtract line 21 from line 17. If a loss, see page 17 of the instructions	22
23	**Total tax** (from Schedule G, line 7)	23
24	**Payments: a** 2001 estimated tax payments and amount applied from 2000 return	24a
b	Estimated tax payments allocated to beneficiaries (from Form 1041-T)	24b
c	Subtract line 24b from line 24a	24c
d	Tax paid with extension of time to file: ☐ Form 2758 ☐ Form 8736 ☐ Form 8800	24d
e	Federal income tax withheld. If any is from Form(s) 1099, check ▶ ☐	24e
	Other payments: **f** Form 2439 _____ ; **g** Form 4136 _____ ; Total ▶	24h
25	**Total payments.** Add lines 24c through 24e, and 24h ▶	25
26	Estimated tax penalty (see page 17 of the instructions)	26
27	**Tax due.** If line 25 is smaller than the total of lines 23 and 26, enter amount owed	27
28	**Overpayment.** If line 25 is larger than the total of lines 23 and 26, enter amount overpaid	28
29	Amount of line 28 to be: **a** Credited to 2002 estimated tax ▶ _____ ; **b** Refunded ▶	29

Sign Here

Under penalties of perjury, I declare that I have examined this return, including accompanying schedules and statements, and to the best of my knowledge and belief, it is true, correct, and complete. Declaration of preparer (other than taxpayer) is based on all information of which preparer has any knowledge.

▶ _____ Signature of fiduciary or officer representing fiduciary   Date

▶ _____ EIN of fiduciary if a financial institution

May the IRS discuss this return with the preparer shown below (see page 7)? ☐ Yes ☐ No

Paid Preparer's Use Only

| Preparer's signature | Date | Check if self-employed ☐ | Preparer's SSN or PTIN |
| Firm's name (or yours if self-employed), address, and ZIP code | | EIN | Phone no. ( ) |

For Paperwork Reduction Act Notice, see the separate instructions.

Cat. No. 11370H

Form **1041** (2001)

EXHIBIT 13–4 Internal Revenue Service Form 1041

This form must be filed with the IRS when an estate' annual income amounts to $600 or more.

Exemptions and Deductions

An estate is allowed an exemption of $600 in computing its taxable income. No exemption for dependents is allowed to an estate. Deductions for gifts to charity are allowed only if a specific provision for such gifts is contained in the decedent's will. Generally, an estate can claim a deduction for a loss that it sustains from the sale of property. Losses incurred for casualty and theft during the administration of the estate can be deducted only if they have not been claimed on the federal estate tax return (Form 706).

Expenses of administering an estate can be deducted either from the gross estate in figuring the federal estate tax (Form 706 shown in Exhibit 13–5) or from the estate's gross income in figuring the estate's income tax (Form 1041). However, to prevent a double deduction, these expenses cannot be claimed for both estate tax and income tax purposes.

§ 13.4 ESTATE TAX RETURN

The *federal estate tax* is a tax imposed by the federal government on the amount of a person's estate at the time of death. The estate itself is liable for the tax. However, the estate's beneficiaries (up to the value of the part of the estate they receive) can be held liable if the estate fails to pay it.

The Economic Growth and Tax Relief Reconciliation Act of 2001 made major changes that affect the federal estate tax. Under the act, the federal estate tax phases out in stages until 2010 when there is no estate tax for one year. Then, in 2011, the tax is reinstated automatically unless Congress votes to change it (see Table 13–1).

A federal estate tax return must be filed if the gross estate is more than the exemption amount for that year shown in Table 13–1. If a return must be filed, IRS Form 706 (United States Estate Tax Return) is used. The return is due, and the tax must be paid, within nine months after the date of death, unless an extension of time for filing has been granted. A reasonable extension may be granted if it is impossible or impractical for the return to be completed within nine months after the date of death; however, the extension is usually not for more than six months. Exhibit 13–5 illustrates the first page of the version of Form 706 that was used for decedents who died in 2001. In that year, Congress passed the Victims of Terrorism Relief Act, which reduced the federal estate tax by more than half for victims of the terrorist attacks against the United States on April 19, 1995, and September 11, 2001, and from illness incurred as a result of an anthrax attack after September 11, 2001.

Form **706**		United States Estate (and Generation-Skipping Transfer) Tax Return		
(Rev. November 2001)				OMB No. 1545-0015
Department of the Treasury Internal Revenue Service		Estate of a citizen or resident of the United States (see separate instructions). To be filed for decedents dying after December 31, 2000, and before January 1, 2002. For Paperwork Reduction Act Notice, see page 25 of the separate instructions.		

Part 1.—Decedent and Executor

1a	Decedent's first name and middle initial (and maiden name, if any)	1b Decedent's last name	2 Decedent's Social Security No.
3a	Legal residence (domicile) at time of death (county, state, and ZIP code, or foreign country)	3b Year domicile established 4 Date of birth	5 Date of death
6a	Name of executor (see page 4 of the instructions)	6b Executor's address (number and street including apartment or suite no. or rural route; city, town, or post office; state; and ZIP code)	
6c	Executor's social security number (see page 4 of the instructions)		
7a	Name and location of court where will was probated or estate administered		7b Case number

8 If decedent died testate, check here ▶ ☐ and attach a certified copy of the will.   9 If Form 4768 is attached, check here ▶ ☐

10 If Schedule R-1 is attached, check here ▶ ☐

Part 2.—Tax Computation

1	Total gross estate less exclusion (from Part 5, Recapitulation, page 3, item 12)	1	
2	Total allowable deductions (from Part 5, Recapitulation, page 3, item 23)	2	
3	Taxable estate (subtract line 2 from line 1)	3	
4	Adjusted taxable gifts (total taxable gifts (within the meaning of section 2503) made by the decedent after December 31, 1976, other than gifts that are includible in decedent's gross estate (section 2001(b)))	4	
5	Add lines 3 and 4	5	
6	Tentative tax on the amount on line 5 from Table A on page 12 of the instructions	6	
7a	If line 5 exceeds $10,000,000, enter the lesser of line 5 or $17,184,000. If line 5 is $10,000,000 or less, skip lines 7a and 7b and enter -0- on line 7c . **7a**		
b	Subtract $10,000,000 from line 7a **7b**		
c	Enter 5% (.05) of line 7b	7c	
8	Total tentative tax (add lines 6 and 7c)	8	
9	Total gift tax payable with respect to gifts made by the decedent after December 31, 1976. Include gift taxes by the decedent's spouse for such spouse's share of split gifts (section 2513) only if the decedent was the donor of these gifts and they are includible in the decedent's gross estate (see instructions)	9	
10	Gross estate tax (subtract line 9 from line 8)	10	
11	Maximum unified credit (applicable credit amount) against estate tax . **11**		
12	Adjustment to unified credit (applicable credit amount). (This adjustment may not exceed $6,000. See page 4 of the instructions.) . **12**		
13	Allowable unified credit (applicable credit amount) (subtract line 12 from line 11)	13	
14	Subtract line 13 from line 10 (but do not enter less than zero)	14	
15	Credit for state death taxes. Do not enter more than line 14. Figure the credit by using the amount on line 3 less $60,000. See Table B in the instructions and **attach credit evidence** (see instructions)	15	
16	Subtract line 15 from line 14	16	
17	Credit for Federal gift taxes on pre-1977 gifts (section 2012) (attach computation) **17**		
18	Credit for foreign death taxes (from Schedule(s) P). (Attach Form(s) 706-CE.) **18**		
19	Credit for tax on prior transfers (from Schedule Q) . **19**		
20	Total (add lines 17, 18, and 19)	20	
21	Net estate tax (subtract line 20 from line 16)	21	
22	Generation-skipping transfer taxes (from Schedule R, Part 2, line 10)	22	
23	Total transfer taxes (add lines 21 and 22)	23	
24	Prior payments. Explain in an attached statement . **24**		
25	United States Treasury bonds redeemed in payment of estate tax . **25**		
26	Total (add lines 24 and 25)	26	
27	Balance due (or overpayment) (subtract line 26 from line 23)	27	

Under penalties of perjury, I declare that I have examined this return, including accompanying schedules and statements, and to the best of my knowledge and belief, it is true, correct, and complete. Declaration of preparer other than the executor is based on all information of which preparer has any knowledge.

Signature(s) of executor(s)   Date

Signature of preparer other than executor   Address (and ZIP code)   Date

Cat. No. 20548R

EXHIBIT 13–5 Internal Revenue Service Form 706

This particular version of Form 706 was used only for the estate of people who died in 2001. Lines 6–9 of the form contain special instructions that apply to the estates of individuals who died as a result of wounds or injuries incurred from the terrorist attacks against the United States on April 19, 1995 and September 11, 2001, and from illness incurred as a result of an attack involving anthrax after September 11, 2001.

TABLE 13–1 **Federal Estate and Gift Tax Phase-Out Schedule**

Year	Top Estate Tax Rate	Exemption Amount
2007	45%	$2,000,000
2008	45%	$2,000,000
2009	45%	$3,500,000
2010	Repealed	N/A
2011	55%	$1,000,000

The federal estate and gift tax phases out gradually until 2010 when there is no estate tax for one year. Then, in 2011, the tax is reinstated automatically unless Congress votes to change it.

The Gross Estate

One of the first steps required in preparing an estate tax return is to determine the decedent's gross estate. The **gross estate** is all of the property owned by a decedent that is subject to the federal estate tax. It includes individually owned property, jointly owned property, property held in trust, life insurance, pensions and annuities, and certain gifts made over the decedent's lifetime. As a general rule, all property that the decedent had the right to use and enjoy or over which the decedent had control will be part of the decedent's gross estate. Form 706 has a separate schedule to list each type of property that is included in the gross estate.

Valuation

Generally, the value of the decedent's property interest for estate tax purposes is its fair market value at the date of death. The **fair market value** is the price that a willing buyer would pay a willing seller when neither is under pressure to buy or sell and both have knowledge of the relevant facts. The personal representative may elect to use the **alternate valuation method**, which allows property to be valued as of six months after the date of death. The purpose of the alternate valuation method is to permit a reduction of the tax liability if the total value of the estate's property has decreased since the date of death. The election applies to all of the property in the estate and cannot be used for only part of the property.

■ **gross estate**

The total value of a dead person's property from which deductions are subtracted (and to which certain gifts made during life are added) to determine the amount on which federal estate and gift taxes will be paid.

■ **fair market value**

The price to which a willing seller and a willing buyer would agree for an item in the ordinary course of trade.

Real Estate

Real estate owned solely by the decedent is reported on Schedule A. Look for all schedules at <http://www.irs.gov>. The decedent's community property interest in real estate and any real estate the decedent contracted to buy should be reported. Each parcel of real estate must be described on the return in sufficient detail so that the IRS can inspect the property to determine its value. An appraisal by a competent appraiser is often necessary to determine the fair market value of the property.

If any interest in real property is subject to a mortgage for which the estate is liable, the full value of the property must still be listed. The mortgage indebtedness will be listed on Schedule K (described later) and subtracted from the gross estate.

Stocks and Bonds

All of the decedent's individually owned stocks and bonds are reported on Schedule B. Stocks must be listed in detail, including the number of shares, whether common or preferred, the issue, the par value, the price per share, the exact name of the corporation, the principal exchange upon which the stock is sold, and the CUSIP number if available. The **CUSIP**(Committee on Uniform Security Identification Procedures) **number** is a nine-digit number that is assigned to all stocks and bonds traded on major exchanges and many unlisted securities. Usually, the number is printed on the face of the stock certificate. Bonds must indicate the quantity and denomination, name of obligor, date of maturity, interest rate, interest due date, principal exchange, and CUSIP number.

The fair market value of the stocks and bonds must be listed. The fair market value is the mean between the highest and lowest selling prices quoted on the valuation date. For example, suppose a person dies owning 100 shares of Home Depot stock, and the executor of the estate decides to use the date-of-death valuation. Suppose further that the highest selling price of Home Depot stock for the date of death was 40.80 and the lowest selling price for that day was 40.06. The fair market value would be 40.43 (40.80 + 40.06 = 80.86 ÷ 2 = 40.43). Selling prices for most stocks can be obtained from the stock quotations listed in the newspaper.

Mortgages, Notes, and Cash

All of the decedent's individually owned interests in mortgages, notes, bank accounts, and cash are reported on Schedule C. This includes cash on hand and in safe-deposit boxes, cash in banks, mortgages and notes owed to the decedent, and contracts made by the decedent to sell (but not to buy) real estate.

Bank accounts must be listed in detail, including the name and address of the bank, the account number, the amount, and the nature of the account, such as checking, savings, or time deposit.

Insurance on Decedent's Life

Insurance on the decedent's life is reported on Schedule D. Insurance must be listed if the proceeds are receivable by or for the benefit of the decedent's estate or the decedent possessed any incident of ownership in the policy. **Incidents of ownership** include the power to change the beneficiary, to surrender or cancel the policy, to assign the policy, to revoke an assignment, to pledge the policy for a loan, or to obtain a loan against the policy's cash surrender value. The *Perry* case illustrates this definition.

For every policy of life insurance listed on the schedule, a statement on Form 712 (Life Insurance Statement) must be obtained from the insurance company that issued the policy. The forms must be attached to Schedule D of the return.

Jointly Owned Property

All property, of whatever kind or character, in which the decedent held an interest, either as a joint tenant with the right of survivorship or as a tenant by the entirety, must be entered on Schedule E. Although all joint property must be reported, only one-half of property held jointly with the surviving spouse is includable in the decedent's gross estate—the other half is excludable as

■ **incidents of ownership**

Indications of ownership of life insurance, such as the power to change the beneficiary, surrender or cancel the policy, assign the policy, revoke an assignment, pledge the policy for a loan, or obtain a loan against the policy's cash surrender value.

CASE STUDY ⚖ ***Estate of Perry v. Commissioner***

927 F.2d 209 (5th Cir.)

FACTS: Less than a year before he died of gunshot wounds sustained in a hunting accident, Frank Perry filled out applications for two life insurance policies with face amounts totaling $600,000. Perry paid the premiums that were due on the policies before his death. Perry's sons were designated as the owners and beneficiaries of both policies. Following Perry's death, the proceeds of both policies were paid in lump sums to Perry's sons. The proceeds were not included in the gross estate on the decedent's federal estate tax return.

LEGAL ISSUE: Must the proceeds of life insurance policies in which the decedent had no incidents of ownership, but for which the decedent paid the premiums, be included in the decedent's gross estate for federal estate tax purposes?

COURT DECISION: No.

REASON: The proceeds were not includable in the decedent's gross estate because the decedent possessed no incidents of ownership in the insurance policies. The policies and all incidents of ownership were owned from their inception by the decedent's sons.

belonging to the surviving spouse. The entire value of property the decedent held jointly with anyone except the surviving spouse is presumed to be includable in the gross estate. However, this presumption can be rebutted by an affidavit showing that the other joint owner furnished some of the purchase price, or that the property was acquired by the decedent and the other joint owner by gift, bequest, devise, or inheritance from a third person.

Other Miscellaneous Property

All items that must be included in the gross estate that are not reported on any other schedule are reported on Schedule F. Items to be reported include household effects, clothing, automobiles, boats, aircraft, jewelry, antiques, objects of art, collections, accrued salary, vacation pay and bonuses due the decedent, individual proprietorships and business ventures, professional practices, farm machinery, livestock and growing crops, partnership interests, patents and copyrights, insurance on the life of another, remainders and reversionary interests, interests in other estates and trusts, unsecured debts due the decedent, claims due the decedent, royalties, judgments, and uncashed checks payable to the decedent.

Transfers During Decedent's Life

Transfers made during the decedent's life are reported on Schedule G. These include transfers in which the decedent reserved a life estate to the property itself or to its income. These also include transfers over which the decedent reserved the right to designate who shall possess or enjoy the property or its income.

The types of transfers reportable on this schedule include transfers of an interest in a life insurance policy made within three years before death, gift taxes paid within three years before death, assets contained in a revocable trust, assets contained in a Totten trust, assets held by the decedent under the Uniform Gifts to Minors Act if the decedent was also the donor, and transfers made by the decedent in which the decedent had the power to determine who will receive the property transferred.

Powers of Appointment

■ **power of appointment**

The power to decide who gets certain money or property or how it will be used. This power is usually given to a specific person in a deed or will.

The value of property over which the decedent possessed, exercised, or released certain powers of appointment must be reported on Schedule H. A **power of appointment** is a right created in a will, trust, or other instrument that allows the holder to direct the disposition of property. The term *general power of appointment*, with some limitations, means a power that can be exercised in favor of the decedent, the decedent's estate, the decedent's creditors, or the creditors of the decedent's estate.

Annuities

The value of any annuity receivable by a beneficiary because of the decedent's death, under which the decedent had certain rights, must be reported on Schedule I. An annuity is a right to receive fixed, periodic payments either for life or for a term of years. For tax purposes, the term includes one or more payments extending over any period of time. Typical annuities are those under employer-sponsored plans. Also included are payments to a beneficiary under an individual retirement account (IRA).

The Taxable Estate

After the gross estate is computed, certain items are deducted to reach the amount of the estate that is taxable. The **taxable estate** is the gross estate minus administration and funeral expenses, claims against the estate, outstanding obligations, casualty and theft losses, the marital deduction, and the charitable deduction.

■ **taxable estate**
The property of a dead person (or a gift) that will be taxed after subtracting for allowable expenses, deductions, and exclusions.

Administration and Funeral Expenses

The estate is entitled to deduct administration and funeral expenses on Schedule J. Administration expenses include personal representative's commissions, attorney's fees, court filing fees, appraisal fees, accountant's fees, and expenses for collecting, protecting, maintaining, and selling assets. Funeral expenses include funeral director's charges; monument, mausoleum, and burial charges; perpetual care payments; cost of transporting the body to the place of burial; and payments to clergy officiating at the funeral.

Claims Against the Estate

All enforceable personal obligations of the decedent at the time of death may be deducted as claims against the estate on Schedule K. These claims include such things as medical expenses, outstanding tax bills, unpaid mortgages, utility bills, credit card bills, and other obligations that were due at the time of death.

Casualty and Theft Losses

Losses from thefts, fires, storms, shipwrecks, or other casualties that occurred during the settlement of the estate are deductible on Schedule L. They are deductible only to the extent that the losses are not compensated for by insurance or by someone who caused the loss.

Marital Deduction

The marital deduction is a deduction from the gross estate of the value of property that passes to a surviving spouse. All property passing to a surviving spouse qualifies for the marital deduction and is reported on Schedule M. Included in this category are such things as outright bequests and devises to the surviving spouse, life insurance proceeds in which the spouse was the beneficiary, and property owned jointly with the surviving spouse. Marital deduction trusts, including credit-shelter trusts and QTIP trusts (discussed in chapter 9), are commonly used devices to reduce estate taxes.

Charitable Deduction

A deduction is allowed on Schedule O for the value of property in the gross estate that the decedent transfers to a public or charitable organization. To qualify, charitable organizations must be organized and operated exclusively for religious, charitable, scientific, literary, or educational purposes. In addition to legacies given to charitable organizations, charitable remainder annuity trusts and unitrusts (discussed in chapter 9) are popular estate planning devices to reduce estate taxes. However, "split-interest" bequests (i.e., bequests of the same property to both charitable and noncharitable beneficiaries, without distinguishing the amount to each) cannot be deducted as a gift to charity.

Estate Tax Computation

The estate tax computation begins by subtracting the various deductions from the gross estate to yield the taxable estate previously discussed. Then the value of all taxable gifts that were made while the decedent was alive after 1976 are added to the taxable estate.

A BROADWAY LEGACY

Books and Lyrics by
ALAN JAY LERNER
"What's Up"—1943
"The Day Before Spring"—1945
"Brigadoon"—1947
"Love Life"—1948
"Paint Your Wagon"—1951
"My Fair Lady"—1956
"Gigi"—1958
"Camelot"—1960

(continues)

A BROADWAY LEGACY (continued)

"On a Clear Day You Can See Forever"—1965

"Coco"—1969

"1600 Pennsylvania Avenue"—1976

"Carmelina"—1979

Alan Jay Lerner, prolific lyricist and playwright, collaborated with the composer Frederick Loewe to make musical theater history. Both men quickly amassed fortunes from the proceeds of the shows as well as film and recording rights. Despite his prosperity, however, Lerner experienced financial difficulties as a result of seven divorce settlements and his extravagant lifestyle. When Lerner died in June 1986, the IRS was still trying to recover $1.4 million in back taxes and penalties.

Taxable Gifts

A federal gift tax is imposed, with exceptions, on gifts totaling more than $1,000,000 during one's lifetime. Usually, the donor (the person making the gift) must pay the tax; however, if that person does not pay it, the donees (the persons receiving the gift) may have to pay the gift tax. In 1976, the federal government unified—that is, combined—the estate tax with the gift tax, making them one tax. In 2001, the government gradually phased out the estate tax over a nine-year period but retained the tax on total gifts exceeding $1,000,000 during one's lifetime.

Each year, anyone can make gifts of up to $12,000 ($24,000 for a husband and wife) per donee to any number of persons without being subject to the gift tax or having to file a gift-tax return. In future years, this $11,000 annual gift-tax exemption will be adjusted for inflation in increments of $1,000. Gifts exceeding these amounts, except to one's spouse, must be reported in any year they occur to the IRS on Form 709 for informational purposes only (see Exhibit 13–6). Unless the donor's lifetime gifts exceed $1,000,000 (in addition to the $12,000-per-donee-per-year exclusion mentioned above), the gift tax is not paid when Form 709 is filed. Instead, the amount is included in the decedent's gross estate on Form 706, and any tax due is payable nine months after the decedent's death. The *Dillingham* case addresses the issue of lifetime gifts.

Credits Against the Tax

A tentative tax, called the **gross estate tax**, is computed by applying a unified rate schedule that is supplied with the instructions for Form 706. Then, various credits are deducted from the gross estate tax, including (1) an applicable credit amount (see Table 13–2); (2) state death taxes, up to a certain

■ **gross estate tax**
Tentative estate tax computed by applying the unified rate schedule to the sum of the taxable estate and all taxable gifts.

limit, paid by the estate; (3) gift taxes paid before 1976 on gifts that are included in the gross estate; (4) taxes paid on certain prior transfers; and (5) foreign death taxes paid by the estate.

The **net estate tax** is the amount determined by deducting the credits mentioned here from the gross estate tax. Generation-skipping transfer taxes (if any) are added to the net estate tax to determine the amount of tax that must be paid to the government.

■ **net estate tax**

Amount of estate tax that must be paid to the government; determined by deducting certain allowable credits, including a unified credit of $192,000, from the gross estate tax.

CASE STUDY *Dillingham v. Commissioner*

903 F.2d 760 (10th Cir. 1990)

FACTS: On December 24, 1980, Elizabeth Dillingham delivered six checks to various people, each in the amount of $3,000. (In that year, the annual exclusion for gift-tax purposes was $3,000 per donee. Since then, the annual exclusion per donee has increased to $11,000.) The checks were presented to the bank for payment on January 28, 1981, and paid. That same day, January 28, 1981, Dillingham delivered six additional $3,000 checks to the same donees. These checks were paid by the bank on the day they were drawn. Dillingham died on June 7, 1981.

LEGAL ISSUE: For gift-tax purposes, do checks drawn in one year and paid the next year constitute a gift made during the year in which they are drawn?

COURT DECISION: No.

REASON: Checks drawn in one year and paid the next year constitute a gift made during the year in which they are paid by the bank. Under U.S. Treasury regulations, a gift is complete when the donor has so parted with dominion and control over the property as to leave in the donor no power to change its disposition. "A gift is incomplete when a donor reserves the power to revest the beneficial title to the property in himself." Under Oklahoma law (where this case occurred), absent consideration from the payee to the drawer of a check, a stop-payment order by the drawer operates to extinguish liability of the drawer to the payee. Thus, under Oklahoma law, the decedent retained the power to stop payment and thereby defeat the claims of the donees from the time the checks were delivered in 1980 until they were cashed in 1981. Accordingly, the decedent retained dominion and control over the checks during 1980.

Form **709** | **United States Gift (and Generation-Skipping Transfer) Tax Return** | OMB No. 1545-0020

(Section 6019 of the Internal Revenue Code) (For gifts made during calendar year 2001)

2001

Department of the Treasury
Internal Revenue Service

▶ **See separate instructions.**

Part 1—General Information

1 Donor's first name and middle initial	2 Donor's last name	3 **Donor's social security number**
4 Address (number, street, and apartment number)		5 Legal residence (domicile) (county and state)
6 City, state, and ZIP code		7 Citizenship

		Yes	No
8	If the donor died during the year, check here ▶ ☐ and enter date of death ...., ...		
9	If you received an extension of time to file this Form 709, check here ▶ ☐ and attach the Form 4868, 2688, 2350, or extension letter		
10	Enter the total number of separate donees listed on Schedule A—count each person only once. ▶		
11a	Have you (the donor) previously filed a Form 709 (or 709-A) for any other year? If the answer is "No," do not complete line 11b		
11b	If the answer to line 11a is "Yes," has your address changed since you last filed Form 709 (or 709-A)?		
12	Gifts by husband or wife to third parties.—Do you consent to have the gifts (including generation-skipping transfers) made by you and by your spouse to third parties during the calendar year considered as made one-half by each of you? (See instructions.) (If the answer is "Yes," the following information must be furnished and your spouse must sign the consent shown below. **If the answer is "No," skip lines 13–18 and go to Schedule A.**)		
13	Name of consenting spouse — 14 SSN		
15	Were you married to one another during the entire calendar year? (see instructions)		
16	If the answer to 15 is "No," check whether ☐ married ☐ divorced or ☐ widowed, and give date (see instructions) ▶		
17	Will a gift tax return for this calendar year be filed by your spouse?		

18 **Consent of Spouse**—I consent to have the gifts (and generation-skipping transfers) made by me and by my spouse to third parties during the calendar year considered as made one-half by each of us. We are both aware of the joint and several liability for tax created by the execution of this consent.

Consenting spouse's signature ▶ **Date** ▶

Part 2—Tax Computation

		Line	Amount	
1	Enter the amount from Schedule A, Part 3, line 15	1		
2	Enter the amount from Schedule B, line 3	2		
3	Total taxable gifts (add lines 1 and 2)	3		
4	Tax computed on amount on line 3 (see Table for Computing Tax in separate instructions)	4		
5	Tax computed on amount on line 2 (see Table for Computing Tax in separate instructions)	5		
6	Balance (subtract line 5 from line 4)	6		
7	Maximum unified credit (nonresident aliens, see instructions)	7	220,550	00
8	Enter the unified credit against tax allowable for all prior periods (from Sch. B, line 1, col. C)	8		
9	Balance (subtract line 8 from line 7)	9		
10	Enter 20% (.20) of the amount allowed as a specific exemption for gifts made after September 8, 1976, and before January 1, 1977 (see instructions)	10		
11	Balance (subtract line 10 from line 9)	11		
12	Unified credit (enter the smaller of line 6 or line 11)	12		
13	Credit for foreign gift taxes (see instructions)	13		
14	Total credits (add lines 12 and 13)	14		
15	Balance (subtract line 14 from line 6) (do not enter less than zero)	15		
16	Generation-skipping transfer taxes (from Schedule C, Part 3, col. H, Total)	16		
17	Total tax (add lines 15 and 16)	17		
18	Gift and generation-skipping transfer taxes prepaid with extension of time to file	18		
19	If line 18 is less than line 17, enter **balance due** (see instructions)	19		
20	If line 18 is greater than line 17, enter **amount to be refunded**	20		

Attach check or money order here.

Sign Here

Under penalties of perjury, I declare that I have examined this return, including any accompanying schedules and statements, and to the best of my knowledge and belief, it is true, correct, and complete. Declaration of preparer (other than donor) is based on all information of which preparer has any knowledge.

▶ Signature of donor — Date

Paid Preparer's Use Only

Preparer's signature ▶ — Date — Check if self-employed ▶ ☐

Firm's name (or yours if self-employed), address, and ZIP code ▶ — Phone no. ▶ ( )

For Disclosure, Privacy Act, and Paperwork Reduction Act Notice, see page 12 of the separate instructions for this form. Cat. No. 16783M Form **709** (2001)

EXHIBIT 13–6 Internal Revenue Service Form 709

This form must be filed with the IRS in any year that the total of all gifts for that year exceed the annual gift tax exculsion.

TABLE 13–2   **Applicable Credit Amounts**

Year	Credit
2007	$ 780,800
2008	$ 780,800
2009	$ 1,455,800
2010	N/A
2011	$ 345,800

Generation-Skipping Transfer Tax

■ **generation-skipping transfer tax**

A tax imposed when property exceeding an amount set by Congress is transferred to a person who is two or more generations below the donor or decedent.

A **generation-skipping transfer tax** is a tax imposed when property exceeding $1,060,000 (increased to $1.5 million in 2004) is transferred to a person who is two or more generations below the donor or decedent, thereby skipping the generation directly below the transferor. For example, a trust established for the benefit of a grandchild, with the trust property passing to the grandchild's estate on the grandchild's death, would be a direct skip and would be subject to this tax. The person receiving the property in a generation-skipping transfer is called a **skip person**. Paragraph FIFTH of the will of Jacqueline K. Onassis (reproduced in Appendix B) contains a generation-skipping provision. The residue of her estate is to be placed in a charitable trust for 24 years, after which it will skip her children and be divided among her grandchildren. The generation-skipping transfer tax is reported on Schedule R of Form 706.

■ **skip person**

Person receiving the property in a generation-skipping transfer.

SUMMARY

State and federal tax returns must sometimes be filed by the personal representative of an estate; among these is an estate tax return. The IRS may be notified of a fiduciary relationship by filing Form 56. An estate identification number (which replaces the Social Security number) may be obtained by filing Form SS-4.

The final income tax return must be filed by the personal representative. Only income that was received up to the date of death is included on the final return. Medical expenses paid before death by the decedent are deductible on the final income tax return if deductions are itemized. Form 1310 must be filed with the decedent's final return if a refund is due the decedent.

An estate's income of $600 or more must be reported to the IRS on Form 1041. Gross income consists of all items of income received or accrued during the tax year. An estate is allowed an exemption deduction of $600. In addition, an estate can deduct losses from the sale of property, losses incurred for casualty and theft, and expenses of administration.

A federal estate tax return must be filed within nine months after the date of death if the gross estate is more than the amount prescribed for that year. The gross estate includes individually owned property, jointly owned property, property held in trust, life insurance, pensions and annuities, and certain gifts made over the decedent's lifetime. The taxable estate is the gross estate minus administration and funeral expenses, claims against the estate, outstanding obligations, casualty and theft losses, the marital deduction, and the charitable deduction. The gross estate tax is computed by applying the unified rate schedule, which is supplied with the instructions for Form 706, to the sum of the taxable estate and all taxable gifts. The net estate tax is computed by deducting the following from the gross estate tax: an applicable credit amount, state death taxes up to a certain limit, gift taxes paid before 1976, taxes paid on certain prior transfers, and foreign death taxes.

■ REVIEW QUESTIONS

1. What three tax returns must often be filed by the personal representative of an estate?

2. For what purpose is an employer identification number used for an estate, and how is one obtained?

3. What income is included in the decedent's final income tax return?

4. How is "income in respect of the decedent" reported to the IRS?

5. How much income must an estate earn before it must be reported to the IRS? On what form is the income reported?

6. On what tax returns may expenses of administering an estate be deducted?

7. On what occasion must a federal estate tax return be filed? What form is used? On what date must the return be filed and the tax paid?

8. What property does the gross estate include?

9. What is the difference between the gross estate and the taxable estate?

10. How is the gross estate tax computed? How is the net estate tax computed?

■ CASES TO DISCUSS_____

1. Forrest J. Johnson's will established one trust with three purposes: to support his three sisters; to maintain the Johnson family gravesite; and to create a charitable trust to pay for religious education in certain Catholic parishes. After Johnson's death, money from the trust was set aside for the support of his sisters and $235,398.30 was used to fund a charitable trust, as he had requested. Can the amount in the charitable trust be used as a deduction on Johnson's estate tax return? Explain. *Estate of Johnson v. United States,* 941 F.2d 1318 (5th Cir.).

2. Before she died, Jennie Owen transferred 251 shares of stock as gifts to 29 different people. The recipients did not know that they were receiving gifts of stock and believed they were merely participating in stock transfers. Each recipient's share was less than $10,000. Upon receiving the stock certificates, the recipients endorsed them over to members of the decedent's family, whose shares exceeded $10,000. Can the gifts of stock be excluded from the decedent's gift tax return? Why or why not? *Heyen v. United States,* 945 F.2d 359 (10th Cir.).

■ RESEARCH ON THE WEB_____

1. IRS forms and publications can be downloaded free at <http://www.irs.gov>.

2. To locate estate tax software, log on to <http://www.Google.com>. Type the words *estate tax software* in the box.

3. For additional estate tax software, go to <http://www.zanenet.com>.

■ SHARPENING YOUR PROFESSIONAL SKILLS_____

Refer to "A day at the office ..." scenario at the beginning of this and make the following calculations:

1. Assume that Mr. Shulman owned 100 shares of Exxon Mobile stock and 250 shares of General Electric stock when he died on December 1. The highest selling price for Exxon Mobile on that day was 41.24; the lowest selling price was 40.40. The highest selling price for GE on that day was 39.35; the lowest selling price was 38.95. Calculate the fair market value of all of the stock as of December 1.

2. In December 2003, Mrs. Nichols gave gifts of $20,000 to her son, Bruce; $20,000 to her son and daughter-in-law, David and Cheryl; $15,000 to a favorite nephew; and $10,000 to each of her seven grandchildren. What amount must Mrs. Nichols report to the IRS on her 2003 gift-tax return? Please show your calculations.

■ SHARPENING YOUR LEGAL VOCABULARY

On a separate sheet of paper, fill in the numbered blank lines in the following anecdote with legal terms from this list:

alternate valuation method

annuity

CUSIP number

donee

donor

employer identification number

fair market value

Form 56

Form 706

Form 709

Form 712

Form 1041

Form 1099

Form 1310

Form SS-4

general power of appointment

generation-skipping transfer tax

gross estate

gross estate tax

incident of ownership

income in respect of the decedent

marital deduction

net estate tax

power of appointment

skip person

taxable estate

When Dawn DiCarlo received her appointment as executrix of the estate of Anthony Amenta, she notified the IRS of the fiduciary relationship by filing (1). She also obtained a number, that is, a(n) (2) by filing (3) with the IRS. The following February, after all copies of (4) (Statements for Recipients of Income) had been received, DiCarlo completed Amenta's final income tax return. Because Amenta was entitled to a refund, DiCarlo filed (5) along with the decedent's tax return. Amenta was entitled to some royalty income from a publishing company, but the money had not yet arrived before he died and could not be included on Amenta's final return. When the royalty check did arrive, it was called (6) and was included in the gross income of the decedent's estate. Because Amenta's estate earned income of more than $600, the estate was required to file (7), the United States Fiduciary Income Tax Return. In addition, because the decedent's (8), that is, all the property the decedent owned that was subject to the federal estate tax, was more than the exemption amount for that year, (9) (the United States Estate Tax Return) had to be filed. The executrix valued the property at the (10), which is the price at which the property would change hands between a willing buyer and a willing seller if neither one were under any compulsion to buy or sell, and if both had reasonable knowledge of all relevant facts. The executor chose not to use the (11), which allows property to be valued as of a date other than the date of death. The executrix listed on Schedule D all life insurance in which the decedent possessed any (12), which included the power to change the beneficiary. For every policy listed on Schedule D, the executrix had to obtain a(n) (13) (life insurance statement) from the insurance company. To determine the (14), certain expenses and claims were deducted from the gross estate. Also deducted was the (15), which was the value of property that passed to the surviving spouse. Because the decedent made no annual gifts exceeding $11,000 in his lifetime, it was never necessary for him to file (16), the United States Gift Tax return. A tentative tax, called the (17), was computed by applying the unified rate schedule to the sum of the taxable estate and all taxable gifts. Finally, certain credits, including an applicable credit amount, were deducted to obtain the (18), the amount that was due the government. Because Amenta gave no property directly to his grandchildren that exceeded $1,060,000 (increased to $1.5 million in 2004), the (19) was not imposed.

■ KEY TERMS

alternate valuation method	generation-skipping transfer tax	net estate tax
CUSIP number	gross estate	power of appointment
employer identification number (EIN)	gross estate tax	skip person
	incidents of ownership	taxable estate
fair market value	income in respect of the decedent	

Online Companion™
For additional resources, please go to
http://www.paralegal.delmar.cengage.com.

Student CD-ROM
For additional materials, please go to the
CD in this book.

CHAPTER 14

Final Choices

■ CHAPTER OUTLINE

§ 14.1 The Right to Die
§ 14.2 Advance Directives
§ 14.3 Anatomical Gifts
§ 14.4 The Decedent's Body

■ CHAPTER OUTCOMES

- Summarize the law as it applies to the right to refuse medical treatment.
- Describe the types of advance directives that are commonly used in your state.
- Explain the methods of making anatomical gifts.
- Determine who usually has the right to possession of the decedent's body and the duty of burial.

■ JOB COMPETENCIES

- Be able to explain to clients the meaning and importance of advance directives.
- Be able to prepare an advance directive, under the supervision of an attorney.
- Be able to discuss with others the need for people to make anatomical gifts and the process of doing so.

"Win one for the Gipper!"

LAST WORDS OF GEORGE GIPP (1895–1920)

381

◼ A DAY AT THE OFFICE . . .

"Good morning, Marie," Attorney Pierce said to Marie Perez, the office paralegal. "I've got a little research project for you to start off the day."

"Fine, I could use something besides coffee to wake me up," Marie replied with a smile.

Attorney Pierce handed Marie a document. "This is an ordinary power of attorney that was on our computer. Will you look up our state statute to see what language we need to add to it to make it a durable power of attorney?"

"Sure," Marie said eagerly. "I think our state has adopted the Uniform Durable Power of Attorney Act, and the language is right in the statute."

"Good. After you've found it, draw up a durable power of attorney for Mr. LaBella. He's mentally sound now, but he's getting along in years and needs to be protected. Here's his file."

"Okay. Who does he want to name as his agent in the durable power of attorney?" Marie asked.

"His daughter," replied Attorney Pierce. "You'll find her name and address in my notes in the file—if you can read them. Oh, and while you're at it, you had better draw up a living will for Mr. LaBella. He mentioned to me that if he ever went into the hospital, he wouldn't want to be kept alive by artificial means."

"That's a good idea."

"We may have trouble with his daughter, though. She told Mr. LaBella that he has a constitutional right to die and doesn't need a living will."

"I hope he believes you instead of his daughter," Marie responded.

"She also told him he shouldn't sign an anatomical gift card because his body would be disfigured at his funeral, and it wouldn't be very pleasant."

"She is certainly uninformed about the details of dying!"

Queries:

1. Why might Mr. LaBella need a living will?
2. Was Mr. LaBella's daughter correct when she said that his body would be disfigured if he made an anatomical gift?

§ 14.1 THE RIGHT TO DIE

Paralegals may have to help educate the law firm's clients about the details of death when discussing the various legal options concerning organ donations and the decision to extend or terminate life.

The question of whether a person should have the right to choose a swift, natural death instead of involuntary prolongation has been debated for some time. The dilemma arose when medical technology developed faster than the ethical guidelines for dealing with the effects of that technology. Doctors, health care professionals, judges, lawyers, politicians, clergy, ethicists, and others have grappled with the conflicting issues for many years. In a case decided as long ago as 1976, the New Jersey Supreme Court wrote (*In re* Quinlan, 70 N.J. 10, 355 A.2d 647):

> Medicine, with its combination of advanced technology and professional ethics, is both able and inclined to prolong biological life. Law, with its felt obligation to protect the life and freedom of the individual, seeks to assure each person's right to live out his human life until its natural and inevitable conclusion. Theology, with its acknowledgment of man's dissatisfaction with biological life as the ultimate source of joy ... , defends the sacredness of human life and defends it from all direct attack.

A body of law has begun to develop that deals with the right of a dying person to refuse extraordinary treatment to prolong life. The cases and statutes emerging from this relatively new body of law are often referred to as *right-to-die* laws.

The United States Supreme Court discussed the question for the first time in 1990 in *Cruzan v. Director, Missouri Department of Health*. Although the case decided a very narrow question of law, it was significant in that the Court answered some important questions about the right to die. The Court recognized the common law right of a competent individual to refuse medical treatment. In addition, the Court stated that the right to refuse medical treatment is found in, and protected by, the "liberty interest" created by the Fourteenth Amendment. The Court also said that the individual's interest must be balanced against the state's interest in protecting and preserving the lives of its citizens. It further stated that incompetent individuals have the same rights as competent ones, but their rights must be exercised by some sort of surrogate decision maker.

CASE STUDY 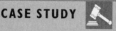 *Cruzan v. Director, Missouri Department of Health*

110 S. Ct. 2841, 111 L. Ed. 2d 224

FACTS: At the age of 25, Nancy Cruzan sustained severe injuries in an automobile accident, which left her in a persistent vegetative state. She remained unconscious for nearly five years, nourished by a feeding and hydration tube. Nancy's parents asked the Missouri court for permission to remove their daughter's feeding tube so that she could die as they believed she would want. The lower court approved the request, but on appeal, the Supreme Court of Missouri reversed the lower court's decision. The appeals court said that no person can assume the choice of terminating medical treatment for an incompetent person in the absence of either the formalities required under the living will statute or "clear and convincing, inherently reliable evidence" of the patient's wishes.

(continues)

CASE STUDY   *Cruzan v. Director, Missouri Department of Health* (continued)

LEGAL ISSUE:	Is it constitutional for a state to require that an incompetent's wishes as to the withdrawal of life-sustaining treatment be proven by clear and convincing evidence?
COURT DECISION:	Yes.
REASON:	A state can assert an unqualified interest in the preservation of human life. It can legitimately seek to safeguard the personal element of the choice between life and death of an incompetent individual through the imposition of heightened evidentiary requirements. A state can also guard against potential abuses in situations in which family members either are unavailable to serve as surrogate decision makers or would not act to protect a patient.

§ 14.2 ADVANCE DIRECTIVES

■ **advance directives**

A document such as a durable power of attorney, health-care proxy, or living will that specifies your health-care decisions and who will make decisions for you if you cannot make your own. Advance directives often specify a DNR (do-not-resuscitate) order.

In 1997, the U.S. Supreme Court reaffirmed the constitutional right of competent patients to refuse unwanted medical treatment in the cases of *Washington v. Glucksberg* and *Vacco v. Quill.* The court, in those cases, emphasized the use of advance directives as a means of safeguarding that right if patients were to become incompetent. **Advance directives** are written instruments in which individuals give instructions for future medical care in the event they become unable to speak for themselves. A living will, a health-care proxy, and a durable power of attorney are the principal types of advance directives. They enable people to make important decisions about their future medical care at a time when they are competent rather than waiting until they are unable to do so. Since the fine points of advance-directive legislation vary from state to state, it is well to check your own state law before using a generic form. It is now common practice for attorneys to draft advance directives for clients at the same time they draft their wills.

People can register their advance directives with the U.S. Living Will Registry. This is a free nationwide service that stores advance directives electronically and makes them available 24 hours a day to health care providers across the country. Information about the U.S. Living Will Registry is available at <http://www.uslivingwillregistry.com>.

■ **living will**

An advance directive by which you authorize your possible future removal from an artificial life support system.

The Living Will

A **living will** is a written expression of one's wishes to be allowed to die a natural death and not be kept alive by heroic measures or artificial means. The purpose of a living will is to guide family members and doctors in deciding how aggressively to use medical treatments to delay death. Every state in the United States except Massachusetts, Michigan, and New York has enacted a living will statute. Even so, New York has court decisions recognizing a writing as one way to establish clear and convincing evidence of a patient's wishes. Exhibit 14–1 shows pregnancy restrictions in living will statutes. A living will is referred to by different names. In some states it is called a **directive to physicians**, in others a **medical directive**, and in still others a **health-care declaration**, as shown in Exhibit 14–2.

Living will laws vary from state to state. Generally, they provide a procedure for people to leave instructions that will permit them to die a natural death. If properly executed, the instructions are binding on health care providers. Some states require that living wills be witnessed; others do not. Some states require them to be acknowledged before a notary public; others do not. Some states require the use of a particular form; others have no particular form. Exhibit 14–3 shows a sample living will.

Health Care Proxy Laws

A **health care proxy** authorizes an **agent** or **surrogate** (one appointed to act in place of another) to make medical treatment decisions for the principal in the event of the principal's incapacity. Agents are to receive full medical information from their principal's doctor before making decisions. Doctors may rely on an agent decision without fear of liability when the agent is acting under a health care proxy (see Exhibit 14–4). A health care proxy can be completed by any competent adult and must usually be signed in the presence of two witnesses.

The great majority of states in the United States have statutes that authorize the appointment of health care agents. Exhibits 14–5 and 14–6 describe the reciprocity provisions and the pregnancy restrictions that are contained in statutes authorizing health care agents.

Durable Power of Attorney

Prior to the 1960s, when someone became incapacitated, the only option was to have a guardian or conservator appointed by a court to handle the person's affairs. A guardian is a person appointed to care for and manage the person, property, or both of a minor or incompetent. A **conservator** is appointed to care for the property of persons who, by reason of their advanced age, mental weakness, or physical incapacity, are unable to do so themselves, but who are not mentally ill. Obtaining such an appointment from the court can be time consuming and expensive, requiring affidavits by attending physicians and court appearances by attorneys. To make it easier and less expensive for someone to act on behalf of an incompetent, all states in the United States have enacted legislation authorizing the durable power of attorney.

■ **directive to physicians**
Another name for a living will.

■ **medical directive**
See advance directive.

■ **health-care declaration**
Another name for a living will.

■ **health care proxy**
Written statement authorizing an agent or surrogate to make medical treatment decisions for a principal in the event of the principal's incapacity.

■ **agent**
A person authorized (requested or permitted) by another person to act for him or her; a person entrusted with another's business.

■ **surrogate**
A person who stands in for, takes the place of, or represents another.

■ **conservator**
A guardian or preserver of another person's property appointed by a court because the other person cannot legally manage it.

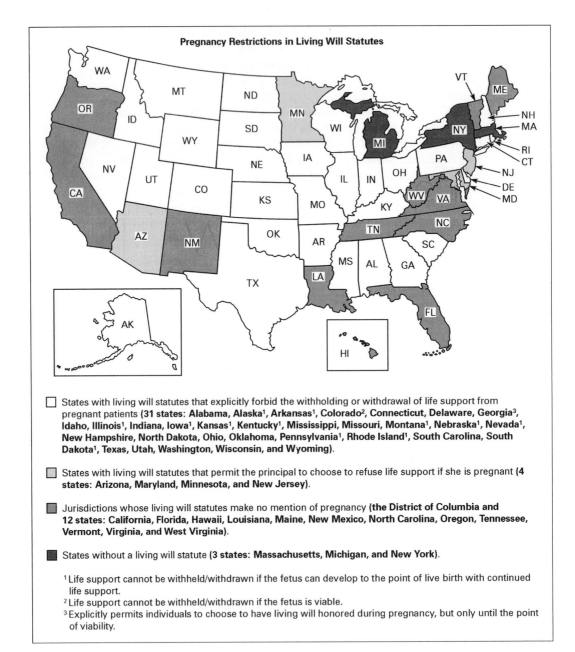

Pregnancy Restrictions in Living Will Statutes

☐ States with living will statutes that explicitly forbid the withholding or withdrawal of life support from pregnant patients (**31 states: Alabama, Alaska[1], Arkansas[1], Colorado[2], Connecticut, Delaware, Georgia[3], Idaho, Illinois[1], Indiana, Iowa[1], Kansas[1], Kentucky[1], Mississippi, Missouri, Montana[1], Nebraska[1], Nevada[1], New Hampshire, North Dakota, Ohio, Oklahoma, Pennsylvania[1], Rhode Island[1], South Carolina, South Dakota[1], Texas, Utah, Washington, Wisconsin, and Wyoming**).

▨ States with living will statutes that permit the principal to choose to refuse life support if she is pregnant (**4 states: Arizona, Maryland, Minnesota, and New Jersey**).

▦ Jurisdictions whose living will statutes make no mention of pregnancy (**the District of Columbia and 12 states: California, Florida, Hawaii, Louisiana, Maine, New Mexico, North Carolina, Oregon, Tennessee, Vermont, Virginia, and West Virginia**).

■ States without a living will statute (**3 states: Massachusetts, Michigan, and New York**).

[1] Life support cannot be withheld/withdrawn if the fetus can develop to the point of live birth with continued life support.
[2] Life support cannot be withheld/withdrawn if the fetus is viable.
[3] Explicitly permits individuals to choose to have living will honored during pregnancy, but only until the point of viability.

EXHIBIT 14–1 Pregnancy Restrictions in Living Will Statutes, March 2001

Reprinted by permission of Partnership for Caring, Inc., 1620 Eye Street, NW, Suite 202, Washington, DC 20006, 800-989-9455, **www.partnershipforcaring.org.** © 2001

INSTRUCTIONS

PRINT YOUR NAME

CHECK THE OPTIONS WHICH REFLECT YOUR WISHES

ADD PERSONAL INSTRUCTIONS (IF ANY)

© 2000
PARTNERSHIP FOR CARING, INC.

PENNSYLVANIA DECLARATION

I, _____, being of sound mind, willfully and voluntarily make this declaration to be followed if I become incompetent. This declaration reflects my firm and settled commitment to refuse life-sustaining treatment under the circumstances indicated below.

I direct my attending physician to withhold or withdraw life-sustaining treatment that serves only to prolong the process of my dying, if I should be in a terminal condition or in a state of permanent unconsciousness.

I direct that treatment be limited to measures to keep me comfortable and to relieve pain, including any pain that might occur by withholding or withdrawing life-sustaining treatment.

In addition, if I am in the condition described above, I feel especially strongly about the following forms of treatment:
   I ( ) do ( ) do not want cardiac resuscitation.
   I ( ) do ( ) do not want mechanical respiration.
   I ( ) do ( ) do not want tube feeding or any other artificial or
                     invasive form of nutrition (food) or hydration (water).
   I ( ) do ( ) do not want blood or blood products.
   I ( ) do ( ) do not want any form of surgery or invasive diagnostic
                     tests.
   I ( ) do ( ) do not want kidney dialysis.
   I ( ) do ( ) do not want antibiotics.

I realize that if I do not specifically indicate my preference regarding any of the forms of treatment listed above, I may receive that form of treatment.

Other instructions:

EXHIBIT 14–2a   Pennsylvania Declaration

Reprinted by permission of Partnership for Caring, Inc., 1620 Eye Street, NW, Suite 202, Washington, DC 20006,
800-989-9455, **www.partnershipforcaring.org**. © 2000

PENNSYLVANIA DECLARATION — PAGE 2 OF 2

APPOINTING A SURROGATE

Surrogate decisionmaking:

I ( ) do ( ) do not want to designate another person as my surrogate to make medical treatment decisions for me if I should be incompetent and in a terminal condition or in a state of permanent unconsciousness.

PRINT THE NAME, ADDRESS AND PHONE NUMBER OF YOUR SURROGATE

Name: _____

Address: _____

Phone: _____

Name and address of substitute surrogate (if surrogate designated above is unable to serve):

PRINT THE NAME, ADDRESS AND PHONE NUMBER OF YOUR ALTERNATE SURROGATE

Name: _____

Address: _____

Phone: _____

PRINT THE DATE

I made this declaration on the _____ day of _____.
                              (day)   *(month, year)*

SIGN THE DOCUMENT AND PRINT YOUR ADDRESS

Declarant's signature: _____

Declarant's address: _____

WITNESSING PROCEDURE

The declarant, or the person on behalf of and at the direction of the declarant, knowingly and voluntarily signed this writing by signature or mark in my presence.

YOUR TWO WITNESSES MUST SIGN AND PRINT THEIR ADDRESSES

Witness's signature: _____

Witness's address: _____

Witness's signature: _____

Witness's address: _____

© 2000
PARTNERSHIP FOR CARING, INC.

Courtesy of **Partnership for Caring, Inc.**   6/96
1035 30th Street, NW Washington, DC 20007 800-989-9455

EXHIBIT 14–2b   Pennsylvania Declaration

Reprinted by permission of Partnership for Caring, Inc., 1620 Eye Street, NW, Suite 202, Washington, DC 20006, 800-989-9455, **www.partnershipforcaring.org.** © 2000

INSTRUCTIONS

NEW YORK LIVING WILL

This Living Will has been prepared to conform to the law in the State of New York, as set forth in the case <u>In re Westchester County Medical Center</u>, 72 N.Y.2d 517 (1988). In that case the Court established the need for "clear and convincing" evidence of a patient's wishes and stated that the "ideal situation is one in which the patient's wishes were expressed in some form of writing, perhaps a 'living will.'"

PRINT YOUR NAME

I, _____, being of sound mind, make this statement as a directive to be followed if I become permanently unable to participate in decisions regarding my medical care. These instructions reflect my firm and settled commitment to decline medical treatment under the circumstances indicated below:

I direct my attending physician to withhold or withdraw treatment that merely prolongs my dying, if I should be in an **incurable or irreversible mental or physical condition with no reasonable expectation of recovery,** including but not limited to: (a) **a terminal condition**; (b) a **permanently unconscious condition**; or (c) **a minimally conscious condition in which I am permanently unable to make decisions or express my wishes.**

I direct that my treatment be limited to measures to keep me comfortable and to relieve pain, including any pain that might occur by withholding or withdrawing treatment.

While I understand that I am not legally required to be specific about future treatments **if I am in the condition(s) described above I feel especially strongly about the following forms of treatment:**

CROSS OUT ANY STATEMENTS THAT DO NOT REFLECT YOUR WISHES

    I do not want cardiac resuscitation.
    I do not want mechanical respiration.
    I do not want artificial nutrition and hydration.
    I do not want antibiotics.

    However, I **do want** maximum pain relief, even if it may hasten my death.

EXHIBIT 14–3a   New York Living Will

Reprinted by permission of Partnership for Caring, Inc., 1620 Eye Street, NW, Suite 202, Washington, DC 20006, 800-989-9455, **www.partnershipforcaring.org.** © 2000

	NEW YORK LIVING WILL — PAGE 2 OF 2
ADD PERSONAL INSTRUCTIONS (IF ANY)	Other directions:
	These directions express my legal right to refuse treatment, under the law of New York. I intend my instructions to be carried out, unless I have rescinded them in a new writing or by clearly indicating that I have changed my mind.
SIGN AND DATE THE DOCUMENT AND PRINT YOUR ADDRESS	Signed _____ Date _____ Address _____
WITNESSING PROCEDURE	I declare that the person who signed this document appeared to execute the living will willingly and free from duress. He or she signed (or asked another to sign for him or her) this document in my presence.
YOUR WITNESSES MUST SIGN AND PRINT THEIR ADDRESSES	Witness 1 _____ Address _____ Witness 2 _____ Address _____
© 2000 **PARTNERSHIP FOR CARING, INC.**	*Courtesy of* **Partnership for Caring, Inc.** 12/00 1035 30th Street, NW Washington, DC 20007 800-989-9455

EXHIBIT 14–3b   New York Living Will

Reprinted by permission of Partnership for Caring, Inc., 1620 Eye Street, NW, Suite 202, Washington, DC 20006, 800-989-9455, **www.partnershipforcaring.org.** © 2000

FLORIDA DESIGNATION OF HEALTH CARE SURROGATE

— — — — — — — — — — — — — — — — — — —

INSTRUCTIONS
———

PRINT YOUR NAME

Name:_____
    (Last)   *(First)*   *(Middle Initial)*

In the event that I have been determined to be incapacitated to provide informed consent for medical treatment and surgical and diagnostic procedures, I wish to designate as my surrogate for health care decisions:

PRINT THE NAME, HOME ADDRESS AND TELEPHONE NUMBER OF YOUR SURROGATE

Name:_____

Address: _____

_____ Zip Code: _____

Phone: _____

If my surrogate is unwilling or unable to perform his or her duties, I wish to designate as my alternate surrogate:

PRINT THE NAME, HOME ADDRESS AND TELEPHONE NUMBER OF YOUR ALTERNATE SURROGATE

Name: _____

Address: _____

_____ Zip Code: _____

Phone: _____

I fully understand that this designation will permit my designee to make health care decisions and to provide, withhold, or withdraw consent on my behalf; to apply for public benefits to defray the cost of health care; and to authorize my admission to or transfer from a health care facility.

ADD PERSONAL INSTRUCTIONS (IF ANY)

Additional instructions (optional):

© 2000
PARTNERSHIP FOR CARING, INC.

EXHIBIT 14–4a Florida Designation of Health Care Surrogate

FLORIDA DESIGNATION OF HEALTH CARE SURROGATE — PAGE 2 OF 2

I further affirm that this designation is not being made as a condition of treatment or admission to a health care facility. I will notify and send a copy of this document to the following persons other than my surrogate, so they may know who my surrogate is:

PRINT THE NAMES AND ADDRESSES OF THOSE WHO YOU WANT TO KEEP COPIES OF THIS DOCUMENT

Name: _____

Address: _____

Name: _____

Address: _____

SIGN AND DATE THE DOCUMENT

Signed: _____

Date: _____

WITNESSING PROCEDURE

TWO WITNESSES MUST SIGN AND PRINT THEIR ADDRESSES

Witness 1:

  Signed: _____

  Address: _____

Witness 2:

  Signed: _____

  Address: _____

© 2000
PARTNERSHIP FOR CARING, INC.

Courtesy of **Partnership for Caring, Inc.**   10/99
1035 30th Street, NW Washington, DC 20007 800-989-9455

EXHIBIT 14–4b   Florida Designation of Health Care Surrogate

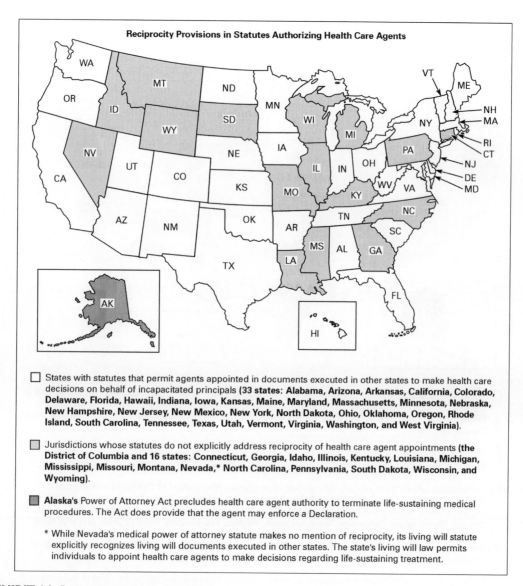

Reciprocity Provisions in Statutes Authorizing Health Care Agents

☐ States with statutes that permit agents appointed in documents executed in other states to make health care decisions on behalf of incapacitated principals **(33 states: Alabama, Arizona, Arkansas, California, Colorado, Delaware, Florida, Hawaii, Indiana, Iowa, Kansas, Maine, Maryland, Massachusetts, Minnesota, Nebraska, New Hampshire, New Jersey, New Mexico, New York, North Dakota, Ohio, Oklahoma, Oregon, Rhode Island, South Carolina, Tennessee, Texas, Utah, Vermont, Virginia, Washington, and West Virginia).**

☐ Jurisdictions whose statutes do not explicitly address reciprocity of health care agent appointments **(the District of Columbia and 16 states: Connecticut, Georgia, Idaho, Illinois, Kentucky, Louisiana, Michigan, Mississippi, Missouri, Montana, Nevada,* North Carolina, Pennsylvania, South Dakota, Wisconsin, and Wyoming).**

☐ **Alaska's** Power of Attorney Act precludes health care agent authority to terminate life-sustaining medical procedures. The Act does provide that the agent may enforce a Declaration.

* While Nevada's medical power of attorney statute makes no mention of reciprocity, its living will statute explicitly recognizes living will documents executed in other states. The state's living will law permits individuals to appoint health care agents to make decisions regarding life-sustaining treatment.

EXHIBIT 14–5   Reciprocity Statutes, March 2001

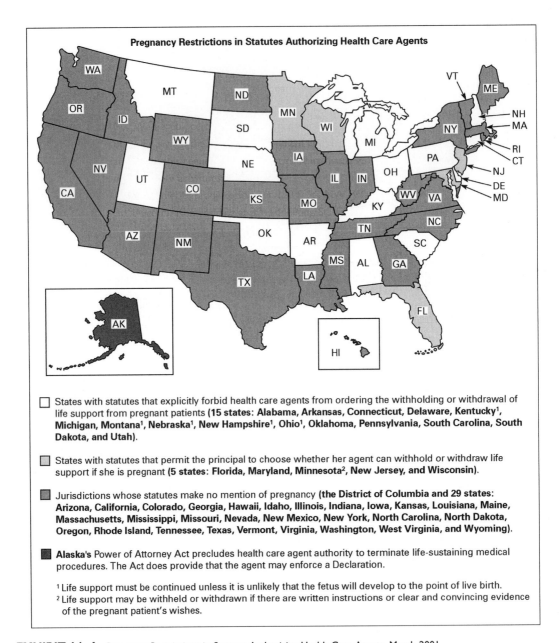

Pregnancy Restrictions in Statutes Authorizing Health Care Agents

☐ States with statutes that explicitly forbid health care agents from ordering the withholding or withdrawal of life support from pregnant patients **(15 states: Alabama, Arkansas, Connecticut, Delaware, Kentucky[1], Michigan, Montana[1], Nebraska[1], New Hampshire[1], Ohio[1], Oklahoma, Pennsylvania, South Carolina, South Dakota, and Utah).**

☐ States with statutes that permit the principal to choose whether her agent can withhold or withdraw life support if she is pregnant **(5 states: Florida, Maryland, Minnesota[2], New Jersey, and Wisconsin).**

■ Jurisdictions whose statutes make no mention of pregnancy **(the District of Columbia and 29 states: Arizona, California, Colorado, Georgia, Hawaii, Idaho, Illinois, Indiana, Iowa, Kansas, Louisiana, Maine, Massachusetts, Mississippi, Missouri, Nevada, New Mexico, New York, North Carolina, North Dakota, Oregon, Rhode Island, Tennessee, Texas, Vermont, Virginia, Washington, West Virginia, and Wyoming).**

■ **Alaska's** Power of Attorney Act precludes health care agent authority to terminate life-sustaining medical procedures. The Act does provide that the agent may enforce a Declaration.

[1] Life support must be continued unless it is unlikely that the fetus will develop to the point of live birth.
[2] Life support may be withheld or withdrawn if there are written instructions or clear and convincing evidence of the pregnant patient's wishes.

EXHIBIT 14–6 Pregnancy Restrictions in Statutes Authorizing Health Care Agents, March 2001

CASE STUDY *Owens v. National Health Corp.*

2006 WL 1865009(TN)

FACTS:	Mary King executed a health care proxy, naming Gwen Daniel to make medical decisions on her behalf. In addition, Dorothy Owens had been named conservator of King's assets. Daniel signed an admission application and contract with a local nursing home owned by National Health Corporation. The contract waived the patient's right to a jury trial in favor of arbitration should a dispute arise. Owens filed suit against National Health, alleging negligence in their care of King.
LEGAL ISSUE:	Can a health care proxy sign a contract for care that waives the right to a jury trial?
COURT DECISION:	Yes.
REASON:	When health care decisions are made, they almost inevitably require financial decisions and obligations regarding the care. As well, the contracts often contain agreements as to where disputes will be resolved. Given the intertwining of the care, the necessary contract for the care, and the choice of forum in the contract, the patient can be bound by the health care representative for all three.

An ordinary **power of attorney** is a written instrument authorizing another person to perform certain specified acts on one's behalf. One who authorizes another to act on one's behalf is called a **principal**. One who is authorized to act on another's behalf is called either an *agent* or an **attorney-in-fact**. A **durable power of attorney** is a power of attorney with language indicating that the power is to survive incapacity or become effective when the principal becomes incapacitated. See UPC § 5–501. The durable power of attorney must be executed by the principal at a time when he or she is in good mental health and is still capable of handling her own affairs.

In some states, a power of attorney is made durable by such language as: "This power of attorney shall not be affected by subsequent disability or incapacity of the principal." With this provision, the power becomes effective when the document is executed and continues to be effective even though the principal becomes incapacitated (see Exhibit 14–7). In other states, the following words are used to make a power of attorney durable: "This power of attorney shall become effective upon the disability or incapacity of the principal." This is known as a *springing power* because the document does not become effective unless and until the principal becomes incapacitated.

■ **power of attorney**

A document authorizing a person to act as attorney *in fact* for the person signing the document.

■ **principal**

A person or anyone else who has another person (an agent) do things for him or her.

■ **attorney-in-fact**

Any person who acts formally for another person.

■ **durable power of attorney**

A power of attorney that lasts as long as a person remains incapable of making decisions, usually about health care. It is a form of advance directive.

DURABLE POWER OF ATTORNEY
OF JANE P. DOE

I, JANE P. DOE, of Mytown, Smith County, Massachusetts, appoint my son, DAVID J. DOE, my attorney to conduct all my affairs, with full power and authority to act in my name and on my behalf as fully as I could do if personally present. Without limiting the generality of his powers, I specifically authorize him to do the following:

1. To manage and have the general control and supervision of all my property and interests in property, real or personal, tangible or intangible, including power to buy, sell, lease, and mortgage.

2. To maintain bank accounts for me in my name, or in the name of my said attorney, and to make deposits or withdrawals of money belonging to me in such accounts, and to disburse any money from such accounts on the signature of my said attorney.

3. To pay all my bills and to expend funds for any purposes which my said attorney deems for my benefit.

4. To collect, demand and receive any income, interest, dividends, rents, profits, or other property due or payable to me.

5. To borrow money on my behalf, to execute contracts on my behalf, and to execute on my behalf any other deed or instrument in my name or in the name of my said attorney, which in the discretion of my said attorney, appears to be necessary or advisable in the management of my affairs.

6. To have access to all safe deposit boxes in my name and the right to remove their contents.

7. To prepare or have prepared and to sign tax returns of any sort on my behalf.

8. To prosecute or defend or submit to arbitration any claim by or against me or my property and to receive and give full or partial releases of any kind.

9. To consent to surgery or any other medical procedures or assistance to me.

10. To transfer funds or property of mine to any trust established by me, whether before or after the date of this instrument.

11. To substitute another to act under this power of attorney and to revoke the substitution at any time.

12. To do any of the foregoing in the Commonwealth or elsewhere in the U.S.A.

No person dealing with my said attorney shall be required to see to the application of any funds or property paid or transferred to him. Any person may rely on this power of attorney or a copy of it certified by a notary public until notified in writing of its revocation.

I intend that this power of attorney shall not be affected by my subsequent disability or incapacity.

EXHIBIT 14–7a Sample Durable Power of Attorney

```
IN WITNESS WHEREOF, I hereunto set my hand and seal this
_____ day of _____, 2____.

                                    _____
                                    Jane P. Doe


            COMMONWEALTH OF MASSACHUSETTS

_____ County, ss.    _____, 2____

    Then personally appeared the above-named JANE P. DOE and
acknowledged the foregoing instrument to be her free act and deed,
before me,

                                    _____
                                    Notary Public
```

EXHIBIT 14–7b Sample Durable Power of Attorney

Under the UPC, all acts done by an attorney-in-fact under a durable power of attorney during any period of disability or incapacity of the principal have the same effect as if the principal were competent and not disabled [UPC § 5–502]. If a guardian or conservator is appointed to handle the affairs of the principal, the attorney-in-fact is accountable to the guardian or conservator, and the latter may revoke or amend the power of attorney [UPC § 5–503(a)].

In some states, a *durable power of attorney for health care,* sometimes called a *medical power of attorney,* is used instead of a living will. In these states, the statutes set forth the exact form to be used, along with rules for the form's execution. The statutes also grant immunity to health care providers. In addition to other powers, they authorize:

1. access to medical records and other personal information.
2. the employment and discharge of health care personnel.
3. the giving and withholding of consent to medical treatment.
4. the granting of releases to medical personnel.

Patient Self-Determination Act

To encourage the use of advance directives, Congress passed the Patient Self-Determination Act in 1991. Under that act, health care facilities that participate in Medicare and Medicaid are required to advise patients of their right to sign advance directives for health care decisions.

Health care facilities must do the following:

- Provide written information to patients about their right to make decisions concerning treatment by completing advance directives.

- Ensure compliance with the requirements of state law.

- Maintain written policies and procedures with respect to advance directives.

- Document in the individual's medical record whether or not the individual has executed an advance directive.

- Educate their staff and the communities they serve about state law governing advance directives.

- Not condition the provision of care or otherwise discriminate against an individual based on whether or not the individual has executed an advance directive.

Patients Without Advance Directives

■ **surrogate decision-making laws**

Laws, passed by most states, that permit a close relative or friend to make health-care decisions for patients who have no advance directives.

A majority of states have passed statutes called **surrogate decision-making laws** (see Exhibit 14–8) that permit a close relative or friend to make health-care decisions for patients who have no advance directives. The laws make unnecessary the need to seek court permission by allowing family members to make decisions about life-sustaining treatment. Exhibit 14–9 shows state law addressing this issue.

Some states' laws are similar to the *Uniform Health-Care Decisions Act* (adopted with variations by California, Delaware, Hawaii, Maine, Mississippi, and New Mexico). Under this Act, when there is no advance directive, the following family members in descending order of priority may act as a surrogate: (1) the spouse, unless legally separated, (2) an adult child, (3) a parent, or (4) an adult brother or sister. If none of these people are available, an adult who has exhibited special care and concern for the patient and who is familiar with the patient's personal values may act as the surrogate.

§ 14.3 ANATOMICAL GIFTS

Each year, organ and tissue donations save the lives of thousands of grateful recipients and give sight and mobility to many more. Surgeons can recover the heart, lungs, pancreas, liver, and kidneys from brain-dead donors and transplant them successfully 80 to 95 percent of the time. Doctors can also transplant tissues, including skin grafts to burn victims, heart valves to patients with congenital heart

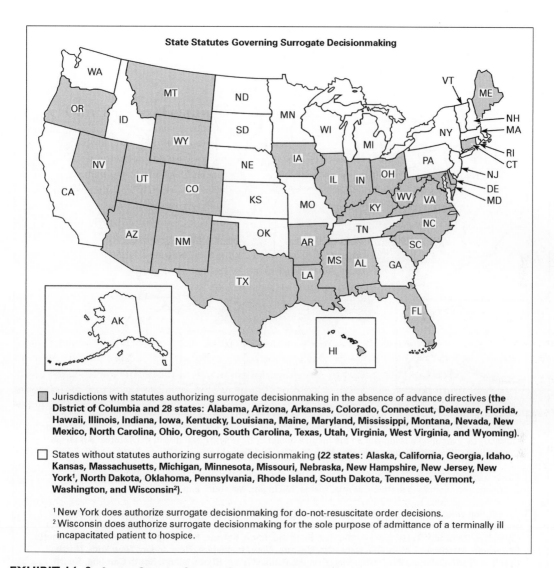

State Statutes Governing Surrogate Decisionmaking

☐ Jurisdictions with statutes authorizing surrogate decisionmaking in the absence of advance directives (**the District of Columbia and 28 states: Alabama, Arizona, Arkansas, Colorado, Connecticut, Delaware, Florida, Hawaii, Illinois, Indiana, Iowa, Kentucky, Louisiana, Maine, Maryland, Mississippi, Montana, Nevada, New Mexico, North Carolina, Ohio, Oregon, South Carolina, Texas, Utah, Virginia, West Virginia, and Wyoming**).

☐ States without statutes authorizing surrogate decisionmaking (**22 states: Alaska, California, Georgia, Idaho, Kansas, Massachusetts, Michigan, Minnesota, Missouri, Nebraska, New Hampshire, New Jersey, New York[1], North Dakota, Oklahoma, Pennsylvania, Rhode Island, South Dakota, Tennessee, Vermont, Washington, and Wisconsin[2]**).

[1] New York does authorize surrogate decisionmaking for do-not-resuscitate order decisions.
[2] Wisconsin does authorize surrogate decisionmaking for the sole purpose of admittance of a terminally ill incapacitated patient to hospice.

EXHIBIT 14–8   Statutes Governing Surrogate Decisionmaking, March 2001

Reprinted by permission of Partnership for Caring, Inc., 1620 Eye Street, NW, Suite 202, Washington, DC 20006, 800-989-9455, **www.partnershipforcaring.org.** © 2001

disease, corneas to the sightless, and ligaments to persons crippled by sports injuries. Because of organ donors, many people are able to walk again, to see, to survive severe burns, and to live a better quality of life.

The United Network for Organ Sharing (UNOS) created the system through which people receive transplants in the United States. UNOS is the administrator of the National Organ Procurement and Transplantation network and the U.S.

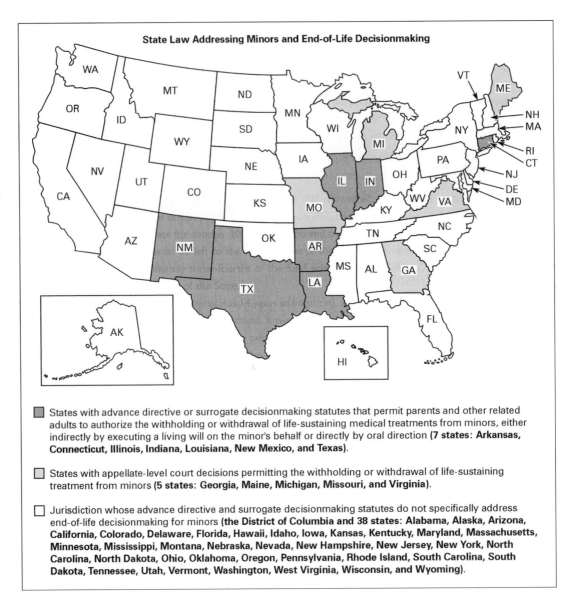

State Law Addressing Minors and End-of-Life Decisionmaking

■ States with advance directive or surrogate decisionmaking statutes that permit parents and other related adults to authorize the withholding or withdrawal of life-sustaining medical treatments from minors, either indirectly by executing a living will on the minor's behalf or directly by oral direction (**7 states: Arkansas, Connecticut, Illinois, Indiana, Louisiana, New Mexico, and Texas**).

▢ States with appellate-level court decisions permitting the withholding or withdrawal of life-sustaining treatment from minors (**5 states: Georgia, Maine, Michigan, Missouri, and Virginia**).

□ Jurisdiction whose advance directive and surrogate decisionmaking statutes do not specifically address end-of-life decisionmaking for minors (**the District of Columbia and 38 states: Alabama, Alaska, Arizona, California, Colorado, Delaware, Florida, Hawaii, Idaho, Iowa, Kansas, Kentucky, Maryland, Massachusetts, Minnesota, Mississippi, Montana, Nebraska, Nevada, New Hampshire, New Jersey, New York, North Carolina, North Dakota, Ohio, Oklahoma, Oregon, Pennsylvania, Rhode Island, South Carolina, South Dakota, Tennessee, Utah, Vermont, Washington, West Virginia, Wisconsin, and Wyoming**).

EXHIBIT 14–9 State Laws Addressing Minors and End-of-Life Decisionmaking, March 2001

Scientific Registry on Organ Transplantation. Under contract with the U.S. Department of Health and Human Services, UNOS develops transplant allocation policy.

Every state in the United States has enacted the Uniform Anatomical Gifts Act (UAGA). An **anatomical gift** is a donation of all or part of a human body, which donation takes effect upon or after death. Under the UAGA, any individual who is at least 18 years of age may give all or any part of her body upon death to a donee. The donee may be a hospital, physician, surgeon, medical or dental school, college or university, organ bank or storage facility, or any specified individual for therapy or transplantation. Some specific information on transplants is provided in Table 14–1.

■ **anatomical gift**
A donation of all or part of a human body.

TABLE 14–1   **Facts About Transplantation in the United States**

Number of Transplants Performed in March 28, 2008.*	
Type of Transplant	**Number**
Kidney alone transplants	16,624
Liver transplants	6,492
Pancreas alone transplants	469
Kidney-pancreas transplants	862
Intestine transplants	198
Heart transplants	2,210
Heart-lung transplants	30
Lung transplants	1,469
Total	28,354

*Based on OPTN data as of March 28, 2008. Double Kidney, double lung, and heart-lung transplants are counted as one transplant. Note: Data subject to change due to future data submission or correction

Source: United Network for Organ Sharing (UNOS), 1100 Boulders Parkway, Suite 500, P.O. B 13770, Richmon, VA23225-8770, **http://www.UNOS.org**

Donation by Will

Under the UAGA, a gift of all or part of a decedent's body may be made by will. The gift becomes effective upon the death of the testator, without waiting for probate. If the will is not probated or if it is declared invalid for testamentary purposes, the gift is nevertheless valid to the extent that it has been acted upon in good faith [UAGA § 4(a)].

Example

Gift of Body Organs

7A AMJUR LF DEAD B § 84:39

I direct that on my death, the _____ [executor or executrix] of my estate immediately contact _____ [hospital], at _____ [address] City of _____ , County of _____ , State of _____ , and offer any of the organs of my body to whomever, without limitation of any kind, such hospital deems might benefit from such organs.

Because of my utmost confidence in the staff of _____ [hospital], it is my desire that the appropriate staff member have sole and exclusive authority to decide if such organ or organs might benefit another human, and should such staff member decide that such organ or organs can and should be used, I direct that the staff member be permitted to remove same from my body and utilize them as the staff member sees fit.

I further direct that my estate indemnify and hold harmless such staff member and _____ [hospital] from and against any and all liability resulting from such act.

Donation by Signed Document

A gift of all or part of a decedent's body may also be made by a document other than a will. The document, often called an **organ-tissue donor's card**, must be signed by the donor in the presence of two witnesses, who must also sign the document in the donor's presence. If the donor cannot sign, the document may be signed by someone else at the donor's request, in her presence, and in the presence of two witnesses.

In addition to keeping a card on their persons, organ-tissue donors may register with the Living Bank, P.O. Box 6725, Houston, TX 77265, or call toll free 1-800-528-2971 (24 hours a day). To register, a donor fills out a simple form (see Exhibit 14–10) and mails it to the Living Bank. The information is kept in a networked computer system, and a donor card is sent to all registered members. There is no charge for the service.

The Living Bank is a national multiorgan donor registry. It is not a medical or storage facility. If the Living Bank is notified of a registrant's imminent death, the case is referred to the regional organ procurement agency to comply with the donor's wishes. Medical professionals will make decisions as to what is medically acceptable for transplant. Once organs and tissues are removed, the family has the responsibility of arranging for burial or cremation. Organ and tissue donation does not delay or increase costs of the funeral arrangements, and the decedent's body is not disfigured.

The Registry of Motor Vehicles in many states has programs that allow people to make anatomical gifts as a part of the process of issuing and renewing licenses. A person's driver's license, under this method, identifies the individual as a donor of an anatomical gift.

■ **organ-tissue donor's card**

Document, signed by a donor in the presence of two witnesses, donating all or part of the donor's body; the donation takes effect upon or after death.

The Living Bank International
P.O. Box 6725, Houston, TX 77265 – 1-800-528-2971
www.livingbank.org
E-mail: info@livingbank.org

Uniform Anatomical Gift Act
DONOR REGISTRATION FORM

Instructions: <u>When this form is completed and mailed to the address below, a donor card will be sent to you to be carried with you at all times.</u> The form and the card are legal documents in all 50 states under the Uniform Anatomical Gift Act and similar laws. You must sign the form and have it witnessed by two persons of legal age. Your next of kin is preferred as a witness, to make sure he/she knows of your decision. If you are under 18, a parent or guardian must sign. Federal law prohibits any payment or charge to you for signing this form, and any payment or charge to you or any other entity for your donated organs.
PLEASE TYPE OR PRINT. COMPLETE LINES 1 THROUGH 15.

1. Social Security #_____   2. Date of Birth_____

3. Donor's Full Name: _____   Phone: (   ) _____

4. Mailing Address: _____   E-mail: _____

5. City: _____ 6. State: _____ 7. Zip: _____-_____

8. Name of Donor's Next of Kin: _____ 9. Relationship: _____

10. Full Address: _____   Phone: (   ) _____

11. In the hope that I may help others, I hereby make this anatomical gift, if medically acceptable, to take effect upon my death. The words and marks below indicate my desires.

I give   ☐ Any needed organs and tissues.   ☐ Only the organs and tissues listed below:

_____

12. Donor's Signature: _____   13. Date Signed: _____

14. Witnessed: _____   15. Witnessed: _____

Critical Facts About Organ and Tissue Donation
Currently, the National Waiting List exceeds 78,000 patients.
Every 14 minutes another name is added to the list.
In 2000, 5,597 people died because an organ was not available in time.
Even though 2.1 million died in the U.S. last year, there were only 22,854 organ transplants.

Thank you for your decision to become an Organ/Tissue Donor.
Please share this decision with your family.

Return this page to:
The Living Bank International
P.O. Box 6725
Houston, TX 77265-6725

Upon receipt your data will be entered in a national database of Organ/Tissue Donors.

To find out how to implement this program in your community, call 800-528-2971.

EXHIBIT 14–10 Uniform Anatomical Gift Act Donor
Courtesy of The Living Bank, Houston, TX

MORE THAN A BASEBALL STAR

MICKEY MANTLE

Mickey Mantle was a Hall of Famer whose speed, switch hitting, and overall ability on the baseball diamond made him a living legend in the 1950s and 1960s. He was also a man whose years of heavy drinking led to a liver transplant in 1995 at the age of 63.

The speed with which he received a donor liver (18 hours after doctors announced he "may die waiting") ignited a debate over whether celebrities awaiting transplants receive preferential treatment. Complaints prompted a review by the United Network for Organ Sharing, the organization committed to ensuring an impartial system of organ allocation nationwide. No policy violations were found at Baylor University Medical Center or at the Southwest Organ Bank in Dallas.

Organ Bank officials maintained that patients in Mantle's severe condition wait about 3.3 days, whereas less serious cases may wait 130 days. Many factors influence the choice of a specific recipient, including degree of illness, blood type, organ size, even geographical distance between donor and recipient. Celebrity status was not one.

Mantle died, two months after the transplant, from the cancer that had spread from his old liver to other organs. Although his celebrity status prompted some charges of favoritism, that same reputation helped to sharply increase public awareness of the need for organ donations. The head of the transplant program at Baylor described Mantle's impact as his "ultimate home run." After his transplant operation, requests for organ donor cards at the Southwest Organ Bank jumped from 12 per week to 700 a week.

Over 10,000 donor cards were distributed at the ballpark in Arlington at an event related to the all-star game on July 11. In his last public appearance that same day, Mantle announced that he hoped to live long enough to promote the need for organ donation by establishing the Mickey Mantle Foundation—a legendary farewell.

Besides a written document, the decedent may use a telegraphic, recorded telephonic, or other recorded message to authorize an anatomical donation. The gift may be made to a specified donee or without specifying a donee. In the latter case, the gift may be accepted by the attending physician as donee upon or following the donor's death.

If a gift is made to a specified donee who is not available at the time and place of the donor's death, the attending physician may accept the gift as donee, unless instructed otherwise by the donor. However, in this situation, the physician who becomes a donee may not participate in the medical procedures for removing or transplanting a part.

Example

Refusal to Make Anatomical Gift

7A AMJUR LF DEAD B § 84:38

According to the provisions of the Uniform Anatomical Gift Act, I hereby refuse to make any anatomical gifts. Any such gift authorized by my representative after death is expressly against my wishes.

Date of Birth _____

Date Signed _____

      [Signature of Declarant]

      [Address of Declarant]

Donors may amend or revoke their gifts either orally or in writing. If an amendment or revocation is made orally, the oral statement must be made either in the presence of two persons and communicated to the donee, or by a statement to a physician during a terminal illness that is known to the donee. If it is done in writing, the writing must be signed by the donor and delivered to a specified donee or retrieved after death. An anatomical gift that is not revoked by the donor before death is irrevocable and does not require the consent or concurrence of any person, including next of kin, after the donor's death.

Donation by Others

Unless the decedent has indicated otherwise, the following persons, listed in order of priority, may also make a gift of all or any part of a decedent's body: a surviving spouse, adult son or daughter, parent, brother or sister, or guardian. A gift may not be made in this manner, however, if an objection is made by someone of the same or higher priority on the list.

§ 14.4 THE DECEDENT'S BODY

When someone dies, a decision must be made as to what to do with the decedent's body. Occasionally family members will disagree about arrangements, such as the type of funeral service, the place of burial, or cremation of the remains. Sometimes these questions must be decided by a court.

Under early English common law, no one had any rights in a dead body, and a decedent's wishes made in a will or otherwise prior to death did not have to be carried out. Even today, some courts hold that a dead body is not an "effect" within the meaning of the "persons, houses, papers, and effects" clause of the Fourth Amendment to the U.S. Constitution, because it is neither real nor personal property. In recognizing family members' rights to possession of a deceased's body for purposes of preparation, mourning, and burial, courts hold that it is merely a possessory right, not a property right. No one can own a dead body.

State laws differ as to whether directions in a will for the disposal of a body must be carried out. Some courts take the position that every person has the right to determine the disposition of her body after death. Others declare that the wishes of the decedent will be carried out as far as possible, but that such wishes are not absolute and will be governed by rules of propriety and reasonableness. Oral statements as to funeral and burial arrangements made by a person before death will sometimes take precedence over contradictory directions found in an earlier-made will.

A clause that is sometimes used in wills to give directions for one's funeral and burial appears in an earlier-made will. The following example may be used in a will when funeral directions have been given to a funeral director.

Example

Clause in Will Providing for Funeral and Burial

20A AMJUR LF WI § 266:372

I direct that my funeral and burial is to be conducted in accordance with my written instructions therefor which are on file at [name of funeral director or mortician] at [address], _____ County, [state]. The said written instructions are hereby incorporated into and made a part of this will.

Usually, the decedent's surviving spouse has the right to possession of the decedent's body, along with the duty of burial or other disposal. If there is no surviving spouse, this right and duty is given to the decedent's next of kin, that is, those persons who are most nearly related by blood. The executor or administrator of the decedent's estate has no right or duty relating to the decedent's body unless the will provides otherwise or unless there is no surviving spouse and no next of kin.

Ordinarily, the person who has the right of burial is entitled to select the place of burial, giving due consideration to any expressed wishes of the decedent. A court will not order or permit a body to be **disinterred** (unearthed) unless there is a strong showing that it is necessary and that the interests of justice require it. However, there is no universal rule, and each case depends on its own

■ **disinterred**

Unearth.

facts and circumstances. As the *Estes* case illustrates, a decedent's spouse who has consented to the burial of the decedent's body in a certain place cannot afterward remove the remains against the will of the decedent's next of kin.

GRAVE DIGGING

ZACHARY TAYLOR

In 1991, the crypt of Zachary Taylor, 12th President of the United States, was opened to determine if his death in 1850 resulted from arsenic poisoning. Questions about the cause of his death were raised by an author who was preparing a Taylor biography and who suspected that political enemies had poisoned and, therefore, murdered Taylor. Tests of the remains revealed, however, that Taylor had *not* been poisoned. If he had been, history would have changed dramatically: Abraham Lincoln, the nation's 16th president, would no longer have been the first president to have been assassinated.

In 1995, relatives of the assassin John Wilkes Booth and descendants of the outlaw Jesse James sought to have the bodies exhumed for positive identification.

Legend had Booth escaping from Union soldiers in 1865 to live another 38 years in Mississippi, Texas, and the Oklahoma Territory. In 1903, Booth supposedly killed himself; his body was mummified and toured with sideshows for years. The Baltimore Circuit Court, however, was not convinced by such conjecture, and did not allow the remains to be exhumed.

Legend had Jesse James faking his death in 1882 after a member of his gang shot him in the head for a $10,000 reward. Would-be descendants claimed that James used aliases to remain alive and father more children. Two such "descendants" were on the research team that was allowed to disinter a skull, an upper rib cage, arm and leg bones, and 14 teeth, including a gold one which James is known to have had.

Preliminary DNA tests showed that the remains exhumed from the grave of Jesse James are probably those of the notorious bandit.

In 1996, a coroner's jury in Tennessee decided that the remains of explorer Meriwether Lewis should be exhumed to determine whether he committed suicide or was murdered 187 years ago. The exhumation would require the approval of the National Park Service because Lewis is buried under a monument on the Nanchez Trace National Parkway. The National Park Service refused to allow the exhumation in 1999 saying, "In our opinion, national parks throughout the country entrusted with the stewardship of burial sites could be profoundly affected if this project were allowed to go forward."

CASE STUDY	*Estes v. Woodlawn Memorial Park, Inc.*

780 S.W.2d 759 (TN)

FACTS: When his wife died, A. M. Estes signed a paper authorizing his wife's niece to make the funeral arrangements. He had lost his daughter six months earlier. Estes attended his wife's funeral and burial and made no objections to having her buried in a family plot near their daughter. Two years later, Estes wanted his wife and daughter buried in another place, but his wife's niece objected.

LEGAL ISSUE: Can the paramount right of a surviving husband and parent to select the final burial place for his deceased wife and daughter be overridden by the wishes of the wife's relatives?

COURT DECISION: Yes.

REASON: Disinterment of a body is not favored in the law. Except in cases of necessity and for laudable purposes, it is the policy of the law that the sanctity of the grave should be maintained and that a body, once suitably buried, should remain undisturbed.

In a Pennsylvania case, the court refused to follow the directions in a decedent's will that he be buried next to his ex-wife, saying that it would be a great injustice to the surviving spouse. The decedent, it seems, had led a double life: he had been secretly married to two women and had separate families in separate locations. The court held that the decedent, by his own deceitfulness and activities, had forfeited any right to have consideration given to his desires as to a final resting place.

SUMMARY

In the *Cruzan* case, the U.S. Supreme Court recognized the right to refuse medical treatment. The Court held that the rights of incompetent individuals must be exercised by some sort of surrogate decision maker and that a state can require clear and convincing evidence of an incompetent's wishes.

At least 80 percent of the states have enacted living will laws that set forth procedures for people to leave instructions allowing them to die a natural death. Some states have passed laws allowing people to execute a written health-care proxy, which appoints an agent to make health care decisions in the event of incapacity. Still other states have authorized the use of a durable power of attorney for health care, which empowers another person to make health care decisions when one is incapacitated. The federal Patient Self-Determination Act requires health facilities to advise patients of state law, as well as of their own policies, regarding advance directives. Facilities must also note in patients' medical records whether patients have executed an advance directive.

Because of organ donors, many people are able to walk again, to see, to survive severe burns, and to live a better quality of life. Every state in the United States has enacted the Uniform Anatomical Gifts Act, under which any individual who is at least 18 years of age may give all or any part of her body upon death to a donee.

Some states take the position that every person has the right to determine the disposition of her body after death. Others hold that the wishes of the decedent will be carried out so far as possible, but that such wishes are not absolute and will be governed by rules of propriety and reasonableness.

Usually the decedent's surviving spouse has the right to possession of the decedent's body, along with the duty of burial. If there is no surviving spouse, this right and duty are given to the decedent's next of kin. The person who has the right of burial is entitled, in most situations, to select the place of burial, giving due consideration to any expressed wishes of the decedent.

■ REVIEW QUESTIONS

1. What did the United States Supreme Court say about the right to refuse medical treatment in *Cruzan v. Director?*

2. For what reason have all states enacted legislation authorizing the durable power of attorney?

3. a. What sentence creates a durable power of attorney in some states? When does the power become effective?

   b. What sentence is used in other states? When does the power become effective?

4. Who may be a donor under the Uniform Anatomical Gifts Act? Who may be a donee?

5. When a gift of all or part of a person's body is made by will, when does the gift become effective? What happens to the gift if the will is declared to be invalid for testamentary purposes?

6. How many people are required to witness the signature of the donor on an organ-tissue donor statement or card?

7. How may organ-tissue donors revoke their gifts orally? How may they revoke their gifts in writing?

8. Under what circumstances and by whom may someone other than the decedent make a gift of all or any part of a decedent's body?

9. In what way do the states differ as to whether directions in a will for the disposal of a body must be carried out?

10. Who usually has the right to possession of the decedent's body, along with the duty of burial?

■ CASES TO DISCUSS_____

1. Sidney Greenspan, age 76, suffered a stroke that left him permanently and irreversibly unconscious. He was placed in a nursing home where he lay in a fetal position and received nasogastric tube feeding for some five years. Earlier, Greenspan had told his wife many times that he would "rather be shot than reside in a nursing home." He had discussed the *Quinlan* case with his daughter and said that he would not want to live under such conditions. On the very day of his stroke, he discussed the disability of a mutual friend with a former coworker and said that he would never wish to be either on life support or in a nursing home. May a state require that an incompetent's wishes as to the withdrawal of life-sustaining treatment be proven by clear and convincing evidence? Explain. *In re* Greenspan, 558 N.E.2d 1194 (IL).

2. Steven Brotherton was found "pulseless" in an automobile and taken to a hospital where he was pronounced dead. When asked if she would consider an anatomical gift, the decedent's wife refused because of her husband's strong feelings against such a gift. An autopsy was performed and, without asking the family or looking at hospital records, the coroner's office permitted the decedent's corneas to be removed and utilized as anatomical gifts. In a suit that followed, the question arose as to whether family members have property rights in a deceased's body. What is your opinion? Explain. *Brotherton v. Cleveland,* 733 F. Supp. 56 (S.D. OH).

3. John Hough, an alcoholic, died from injuries suffered during a fall down the basement stairs. Because of questions about the cause of his death, an inquest was held. The jury found that his death was accidental. Later, over the objections of Hough's widow, his daughter sought to have Hough's body disinterred for further medical tests. When and for what reason will a court permit a body to be disinterred? *Hough v. Weber,* 560 N.E.2d 5 (IL).

■ RESEARCH ON THE WEB_____

1. Log on to <http://www.partnershipforcaring.org>, click Advance Directives, then click State-Specific Documents. Finally, click the name of your state and print your state's advance directive that appears on the screen.

2. For information about organ sharing in America go to <http://www.unos.org>.

3. Go to <http://www.legalhire.com>. to look for employment opportunities.

4. Read the latest legal news and locate legal forms and documents at <http://www.lpig.org>.

■ SHARPENING YOUR PROFESSIONAL SKILLS_____

1. Look up the Uniform Durable Power of Attorney Act in your state, make a note of its statutory reference, and write down the sentence that is used to create a durable power of attorney. Does this create an immediate power or a springing power?

2. Under your state statute, who has the right to make decisions as to the disposition of a dead body? Give the statutory reference where the provision is found.

3. Describe the anatomical gift that was made in the will of Doris Duke (reproduced in Appendix B).

■ SHARPENING YOUR LEGAL VOCABULARY_____

On a separate sheet of paper, fill in the numbered blank lines in the following anecdote with legal terms from this list:

advance directive

anatomical gift

attorney in fact

conservator

disinterred

durable power of attorney

guardian

health-care proxy

living will

organ-tissue donor's card

power of attorney

principal

right-to-die laws

springing power

surrogate

After witnessing a horrible accident in which her sister was severely burned, Tiffany Andrews decided to make a(n) (1), that is, a donation of all or part of her body to take effect upon or after her death. To accomplish this, she signed a(n) (2) in the presence of two witnesses, who also signed in her presence. Seeing her sister so ill in the hospital made her think about the possibility of being kept alive in a vegetative state for years. Tiffany decided she did not want to be in that position. She had heard about (3), that is, cases and statutes dealing with the right of a dying person to refuse extraordinary treatment to prolong life. Also, her Aunt Agnes, who lived out of state, had a(n) (4) (a type of (5)), which is a written expression of one's wishes to be allowed to die a natural death and not be kept alive by heroic measures or artificial means. However, Tiffany's attorney said that her state had a law allowing her to sign a(n) (6), which is a written statement authorizing an agent or (7) to make health care decisions for her in the event she is unable to do so herself. Because Tiffany was a young adult in good mental and physical health, she was not in need of a(n) (8), that is, a person who is appointed to care for and manage the person, property, or both of a minor or incompetent. For the same reason, she did not need a(n) (9), that is, one appointed to care for the property of persons who by reason of their advanced age, mental weakness, or physical incapacity are unable to do so themselves, but who are not mentally ill. In addition, Tiffany did not need a(n) (10), that is, a written instrument authorizing another person to perform certain specified acts on her behalf. Tiffany felt, however, that her sister should have a(n) (11), that is, a power of attorney with language indicating that the power is to survive incapacity or become effective when the principal becomes incapacitated. In Tiffany's state, the following words are used to make a power of attorney durable: "This power of attorney shall become effective upon the disability or incapacity of the principal." This is known as a(n) (12) because the document does not become effective unless and until the (13) (person giving the power) becomes incapacitated. At that time, the (14) (person receiving the power) is empowered to act.

■ KEY TERMS

advance directives

agent

anatomical gift

attorney-in-fact

conservator

directive to physicians

disinterred

durable power of attorney

health care proxy

health-care declaration

living will

medical directive

organ-tissue donor's card

power of attorney

principal

surrogate

surrogate decision-making laws

Online Companion™
For additional resources, please go to
http://www.paralegal.delmar.cengage.com.

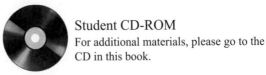

Student CD-ROM
For additional materials, please go to the
CD in this book.

Appendices

Note: Article II of the 1969 version of the UPC appears on
pages 479 through 491. The 1990 version of Article II is found
on pages 452 through 479.

A

Record of Testator's Personal Information and Business Affairs

[20A AMJUR LF WI § 266:3]
© 2001 WEST GROUP

Record of Personal Information and Business Affairs of ———————— [Name]

A. Introduction

This document was prepared on ———————— [date], at ———————— [address], ———————— [city], ———————— [state], and constitutes a record of the personal information and private and business affairs of ———————— [name] ("testator").

B. General Information; Vital Statistics

  1. Name:

    a. Full name of testator: ————————.

    b. Names, other than the one set out above, by which testator has been or is now known: ————————.

  2. Address; Residence:

    a. Present address: ———————— .

    b. Residences other than above address: ————————.

    c. Average length of time spent annually at each address: ————————.

    d. If testator has more than one residence, specify which one testator considers to be testator's permanent residence: ————————.

3. Telephone Numbers:
   a. Residence: ――――――――――.
   b. Business: ――――――――――.

4. Social Security Numbers:
   a. Testator's number: ――――――――――.
   b. Spouse's number: ――――――――――.

5. Birth Date:
   a. Date of birth: ――――――――――.
   b. Place of birth: ――――――――――.
   c. Does testator have birth certificate: ――――――――――.
   d. If yes, where is birth certificate located: ――――――――――.

6. Citizenship:
   a. Citizenship of testator: ――――――――――.
   b. If citizenship of United States, is citizenship by birth or naturalization: ――――――――――.
   c. If citizenship is by naturalization, specify dates and place of naturalization: ――――――――――.
   d. Naturalization certificate located at: ――――――――――.

C. Family Information; Marital Status

1. Marital Status at Present Time:
   a. Married: ――――――――――.
   b. Divorced or marriage dissolved or annulled: ――――――――――.
   c. Separated: ――――――――――.
   d. Widowed: ――――――――――.
   e. Never married: ――――――――――.

2. If Married:
   a. Date of marriage: ――――――――――.
   b. Location of marriage certificate: ―――――――――― [place, street, city and state].
   c. Name of spouse: ――――――――――.
   d. Age of spouse: ――――――――――.
   e. Address of spouse: ――――――――――.
   f. Spouse previously married: ――――――――――.
   g. If spouse was previously married, such marriage was terminated by: ――――――――――[death or divorce or dissolution of marriage or annulment].
      (1) If marriage was terminated by divorce, dissolution of marriage or annulment, specify details, including court, date, place, property settlement agreement, etc.: ――――――――――.
      (2) If marriage terminated by death, specify date and place of death and status of decedent's estate, etc.: ――――――――――.

h. Testator previously married: —————————.

i. If testator previously married, such marriage terminated by [death or divorce or dissolution of marriage or annulment]: —————————.

    (1) If marriage terminated by divorce, dissolution of marriage or annulment, specify details, including court, date, place, property settlement agreement, etc.: —————————.

    (2) If marriage terminated by death, specify date and place of death and status of decedent's estate, etc.: —————————.

j. Will executed by spouse: —————————.

k. If will executed by spouse, will executed before or after marriage to testator: —————————.

l. Location of spouse's will: —————————.

m. Testator party to any antenuptial agreement: —————————.

    (1) Location of instrument: —————————[place, street, city, and state].

    (2) General content of agreement: —————————.

n. Testator party to any postnuptial property agreement: —————————.

    (1) Location of instrument: —————————[place, street, city, and state].

    (2) General content of agreement: —————————.

3. If Divorced or Marriage Dissolved or Annulled:

a. Name of state and court in which decree of divorce, dissolution, or annulment was entered: —————————.

b. Date of decree: —————————.

c. Location of testator's copy of decree: —————————.

d. General contents of decree concerning support and property rights: —————————.

e. General contents of property settlement agreement, alimony or support agreement, alimony trusts, etc.: —————————.

4. If Separated:

a. Name of state and court in which separation decree was entered: —————————.

b. Date of decree: —————————.

c. Location of testator's copy of decree: —————————.

d. General contents of decree concerning support and property rights: —————————.

e. General contents of separation agreement concerning support and property rights: —————————.

5. If Widowed:

a. Date and place of spouse's death: —————————.

b. Spouse died testate or intestate: —————————.

c. Spouse's estate has been or is being administered: —————————.

d. Court and state in which spouse's estate was or is being administered: —————————.

e. If estate is being administered, general status of administration: —————————.

f. Testator's interest (as heir, legatee, devisee, creditor, or otherwise) in spouse's estate: —————————.

6. Next of Kin: [Note: Include adopted children and children of deceased children.]

Name	Address	Date of Birth If Known	Adult or Minor	Relationship
a. _____	_____	_____	_____	_____
b. _____	_____	_____	_____	_____
c. _____	_____	_____	_____	_____

D. Employment and Employment Benefits

   1. If Employed:

     a. Name of Employer: _____ .

     b. Address: _____ .

     c. Telephone Number: _____ .

     d. Date employed: _____ .

     e. Employee benefits: [Note: Specify beneficiary whenever appropriate.]

       (1) Health and accident insurance: _____ .

       (2) Life insurance: _____ .

       (3) Vacation: _____ .

       (4) Pension: _____ .

       (5) Stock options: _____ .

       (6) Profit sharing: _____ .

       (7) _____ [Other benefits].

   2. If Self-Employed:

     a. Nature of business: _____ .

     b. Address of business: _____ .

     c. Telephone number: _____ .

   3. If Retired:

     a. Date of retirement: _____ .

     b. Source of pension benefits other than social security benefits: _____ [such as private or employer's plan].

E. Military Service

   1. United States military service: _____ .

     a. Army: _____ .

     b. Air Force: _____ .

     c. Navy: _____ .

     d. Marine Corps: _____ .

     e. Coast Guard: _____ .

2. Military service in foreign countries: —————————.

    a. Country: —————————.

    b. Branch of service —————————.

3. If discharged, location of discharge papers: —————————.

F. Bank, Savings and Loan, and Credit Union Accounts

   1. Personal Accounts:

Firm	Address	Account Number	Type of Account	Account in Name of	Balance	Location of Pass Book
a. ————	————	————	————	————	————	————
b. ————	————	————	————	————	————	————
c. ————	————	————	————	————	————	————

   2. Joint Accounts:

Firm	Address	Account Number	Type of Account	Account in Name of	Balance	Location of Pass Book
a. ————	————	————	————	————	————	————
b. ————	————	————	————	————	————	————
c. ————	————	————	————	————	————	————

   3. Business Accounts:

Firm	Address	Account Number	Type of Account	Account in Name of	Balance	Location of Pass Book
a. ————	————	————	————	————	————	————
b. ————	————	————	————	————	————	————
c. ————	————	————	————	————	————	————

   4. Fiduciary Accounts:

Firm	Address	Account Number	Type of Account	Account in Name of	Balance	Location of Pass Book
a. ————	————	————	————	————	————	————
b. ————	————	————	————	————	————	————
c. ————	————	————	————	————	————	————

G. Safe Deposit Boxes

    1. Box numbers: ————————— .

    2. Name of bank or trust company where located: ————————— .

    3. Address of bank or trust company: ————————— .

    4. Name of person or persons who have right to enter box: ————————— .

H. Real Property

	Form of Ownership	Description	Holder of Encumbrance	Location of Deed and Title Ins. Policy
1.	————————	————————	————————	————————
2.	————————	————————	————————	————————
3.	————————	————————	————————	————————

I. Personal Property

    1. Furniture and Furnishings; Household Goods and Appliances:

	Article and Description	Location
a.	————————	————————
b.	————————	————————
c.	————————	————————

    2. Motor Vehicles; Boats; Aircraft:

        a. ———————— [make]   ———————— [model].
           ———————— [year]   Located:———————— .

        b. ———————— [make]   ———————— [model].
           ———————— [year]   Located: ———————— .

        c. ———————— [make]   ———————— [model].
           ———————— [year]   Located: ———————— .

    3. Jewelry:

	Type	Value	Located
a.	————————	————————	————————
b.	————————	————————	————————
c.	————————	————————	————————

4. Stamp and Coin Collections, Paintings and Other Art Objects:

Description	Value	Location
a. _____	_____	_____
b. _____	_____	_____
c. _____	_____	_____

5. Other Property:

a. _____ [Specify other items.]

b. _____ [Specify other items.]

J. Insurance

1. Life Insurance:

Policy No.	Amount	Company	Location of Policy
a. _____	_____	_____	_____
b. _____	_____	_____	_____
c. _____	_____	_____	_____

2. Other Insurance (Fire, Health, Marine, etc.):

Kind	Amount	Company	Policy Number	Location of Policy
a. _____	_____	_____	_____	_____
b. _____	_____	_____	_____	_____
c. _____	_____	_____	_____	_____

K. Securities; Stocks and Bonds

Type	Company	Number or Amount	Located	Acquired by Purchase; Gift; Inheritance	Date Acquired and Price Paid
1. _____	_____	_____	_____	_____	_____
2. _____	_____	_____	_____	_____	_____
3. _____	_____	_____	_____	_____	_____

L. Patents, Copyrights, Franchises, Licenses, Mineral Rights, etc.

Type	Testator's Interest	Date of Acquisition	Value
1. _____	_____	_____	_____
2. _____	_____	_____	_____
3. _____	_____	_____	_____

M. Joint Venture, Partnerships, Sole Proprietorships, etc.

Type of Organization	Name of Business	Nature of Business	Net Worth	Testator's Interest	Testator's Position
1. _____	_____	_____	_____	_____	_____
2. _____	_____	_____	_____	_____	_____
3. _____	_____	_____	_____	_____	_____

N. Obligations Owed Testator

Nature of Debt	Evidenced by (as Note)	Balance Due	Debtor	Address
1. _____	_____	_____	_____	_____
2. _____	_____	_____	_____	_____
3. _____	_____	_____	_____	_____

O. Inter Vivos Trusts Established by Testator

Beneficiaries	Revocable or Nonrevocable	Date	Trustee
1. _____	_____	_____	_____
2. _____	_____	_____	_____
3. _____	_____	_____	_____

P. Gifts, Transfers, and Advancements Made by Testator

Donee	Type of Gift	Value	Date
1. _____	_____	_____	_____
2. _____	_____	_____	_____

3. Gift tax returns filed: _____.

4. If filed: Prepared by _____ [name and address].

Q. Testator's Interest in Trusts and Estates

1. Testator Beneficiary of Trust: _____.

   a. Location of instrument: _____ [place, street, city, and state].

   b. General content: _____.

2. Testator's expectancy of inheritance from persons other than deceased spouse: ——————.

    a. Place of administration: —————— [court and state].

    b. General analyses of status and rights: ——————.

R. Fiduciary Capacity; Power of Appointment

    1. Testator's Fiduciary Capacities: ——————.

        a. Manner created: ——————.

        b. General description of status: ——————.

    2. Power of Appointments: ——————.

        a. Instrument creating power: —————— [place, street, city, and state].

        b. Location of instrument: ——————.

        c. General content: ——————.

S. Obligations Owed by Testator

Nature of Obligation	Creditor	Address	Amount
1. ——————	——————	——————	——————
2. ——————	——————	——————	——————
3. ——————	——————	——————	——————

T. Tax Returns

    1. Location of return (state and federal estate, gift, income, information, fiduciary, etc.): —————— [place, street, city, and state].

    2. Location of supporting documents: —————— [place, street, city, and state].

    3. Returns prepared by: —————— [name and address].

U. Wills and Codicils

1. Will executed by testator: ——————————.

2. Date will executed: ——————————.

3. Place will executed: ——————————.

4. Location of will: —————————— [place, street, city, and state].

5. Attorney who prepared will: —————————— [name], —————————— [address].

6. Executor: —————————— [name], —————————— [address].

7. Trustee (if any): —————————— [name].

8. Guardian (if any) for minor children: —————————— [guardian's name], —————————— [address].

9. Codicils executed by testator: ——————————.

10. Date codicils executed: ——————————.

11. Places where codicil or codicils executed: ——————————.

12. Location of codicil or codicils: —————————— [place, street, city, and state].

13. Changed conditions (such as marriage, divorce, death, children adopted or born, devised assets conveyed, mortgaged, etc.) which could affect provisions of will or codicil: ——————————.

Sample Last Wills and Testaments

Last Will and Testament of
Theodore Roosevelt

I, Theodore Roosevelt, of Oyster Bay, County of Nassau, and State of New York, hereby make and do publish and declare this to be my Last Will and Testament, revoking all former wills by me made.

FIRST: As I have given to my daughter Alice all the silver given as wedding presents on my marriage with her mother, I give my other silver, plate, and plated-ware to my other children to be divided as equally between them according to value as may be possible.

SECOND: I direct my Executors who shall qualify or take upon them the execution of my will to divide the trust fund of Sixty thousand dollars given by the third clause of my Father's will to his Executors in Trust for my benefit into as many shares of equal value as I shall have children who or issue of whom are living at my decease, and I devise and bequeath one of such shares to each one of my surviving children, and one to the issue, collectively and according to their stocks, of each of my children who may die before me leaving such issue respectively.

THIRD: All the rest, residue and remainder of my estate, both real and personal, wheresoever and whatsoever, including any legacies which may lapse and all other property which I have power to appoint and dispose of by will, I devise and bequeath to my Executors who shall qualify, the survivor of them and their successors in trust:

I. To collect and receive the rents, profits, interest and income, and apply them to the use of my wife, Edith Kermit Roosevelt, during her life:

II. I authorize and empower my wife by last Will and Testament published and executed after my decease, to dispose of the principal of this trust to and among any one or more of my issue, in such shares and portions, and either absolutely or upon any trust or limitation, respectively, as she shall declare.

III. In default of any such testamentary disposition by my wife after my decease, I devise and bequeath all said rest, residue and remainder of my estate, both real and personal, wheresoever and whatsoever, including any legacies which may lapse and all other property which I have power to appoint or dispose of by will, to my children who survive my wife and to the issue surviving her of any deceased child of mine, according to their stocks.

FOURTH: I direct my Executors to hold each share of my estate which any infant legatee or devisee may be or become entitled to absolutely under this will until such infant attains the age of twenty-one years, and that, in the mean time, they collect and receive the income of each share so held respectively and apply them to the use of the infant legatee.

FIFTH: I direct that my Executors shall not be required to file any inventory of my estate or give security for the same or any part thereof. I authorize and empower my Executors and Trustees, the survivor of them and their successors, to sell and partition my real and personal estate all at one time or different parcels from time to time, and to consent to the sale or partition of any real estate in which I may be interested. Such sales may be either public or private, and they are authorized to execute all proper instruments for carrying such sales and partition into effect. I also authorize them to personally appraise my real and personal property and divide and allot the same to the various trusts and among the several legatees and devisees in accordance with such appraisement which shall be final and conclusive beyond any dispute or appeal. I also authorize them to retain and hold, at the risk of the share to which the same may be allotted, as an investment for any trust hereby created or for any infant legatee any investment, real or personal, which I may leave; and I authorize them to invest and reinvest the whole or any part of the proceeds of real and personal property sold, and all money or personal property held or received by them as Trustees or for any infant legatee in and upon real estate, or bonds secured by mortgage on railroads, or on real estate, or the bonds, stocks, or obligations of corporations, or in such other stocks, evidences of debt, or property, real or personal, whether of or situated in the United States or any other country, as in their own personal judgment may seem best; and, from time to time to sell any real or personal property held or purchased by them, and to change the investments as and whenever they please; and they shall not be responsible for any losses arising therefrom.

SIXTH: I further authorize my Executors and Trustees out of the income of each share held in trust and of each share held during the minority of a legatee or devisee respectively, to pay all taxes, assessments and expenses for repairs or insurance thereon; also, from time to time, in their discretion, to make leases of the real estate forming any part thereof upon such terms and conditions, not however exceeding twenty-one years, as to them may seem desirable; also to build upon, alter or improve any such real estate, expending for the purpose any of the other principal if such share, as in their own personal judgment may seem wise.

SEVENTH: I name and appoint my wife Edith Kermit Roosevelt and my son Theodore Roosevelt Jr. and George Emlen Roosevelt, Executrix and Executors of and Trustees under this my will. In case any of them, or any one who may be from time to time appointed Executor and Trustee pursuant to this clause of my will, shall fail to qualify or cease to act from any cause, I direct that the trusts and powers herein contained shall vest in and may be fully executed by the one or ones who shall be qualified or acting, and I authorize my duly qualified and acting Executors or Trustees, and the survivor of them, by an instrument in writing duly acknowledged to appoint a new Executor and Trustee to fill each vacancy as it may occur, and the person so appointed shall thereupon become vested with all the estate and powers of an Executor and Trustee hereunder, the same as if named by me herein as such.

IN WITNESS WHEREOF, I have hereunto subscribed my name and set my seal this 13th day of December, in the year of our Lord one thousand nine hundred and twelve.

Theodore Roosevelt

Subscribed, sealed, published, acknowledged, and declared by the Testator, Theodore Roosevelt, as, for, and to be his Last Will and Testament in our sight and presence, whereupon, at his request and in his sight and presence, and in the sight and presence of each other, we and each of us do sign our names as attesting witnesses the day and year last above written.

/s/Frank Harper

/s/George Douglas Wardrop.

STATE OF NEW YORK	)	
County of Nassau	) ss.:
SURROGATE'S COURT	)	

Recorded in the office of the Surrogate of Nassau County, in Liber 20 of Wills of Real Estate, page 620 the foregoing last Will and Testament of Theodore Roosevelt deceased, as a will of real and personal estate, and the decree admitting the same to probate in the Surrogate's Court in the said County of Nassau, which record is signed and hereby certified by me pursuant to the provisions of the statutes of the State of New York.

IN TESTIMONY WHEREOF, I have hereunto set my hand and affixed the official seal of the said Surrogate's Court at the Surrogate's office aforesaid, this 11th day of March 1919.

[seal]
[signed]
Clerk of the Surrogate's Court.

Last Will and Testament of George Burns

I, GEORGE BURNS, a resident of the County of Los Angeles, State of California, being of sound and disposing mind and memory, and not acting under fraud, duress, menace or undue influence of any person whomsoever, declare this to be my Last Will and Testament.

FIRST: I hereby revoke all wills, codicils to wills, or other testamentary dispositions at any time heretofore made by me.

SECOND: I declare that I am a widower. I was formerly married to GRACE ALLEN BURNS ("my wife"), who died many years ago. I have two children, legally adopted by my wife and myself, to-wit: my daughter, SANDRA JEAN BURNS ("Sandra"), and my son, RONALD JON BURNS ("Ronald"). Sandra has four children now living, to-wit: LAURA JEAN WILHOITE WRIGHT, MELISSA WILHOITE SOLEAU, GRACE ANNE LUCKMAN and BROOKE LEE LUCKMAN. Ronald has three children now living, to-wit: BRENT JON BURNS, BRAD ALLEN BURNS and BRYAN GEORGE BURNS. Except as hereinabove specified, I have not been married and I have had no children.

THIRD: It is my intention by this will to dispose of all property over which I have power of disposition by will. I expressly declare that I do not intend by any general language in this will to exercise any power of appointment which I may have (if any) in the absence of a provision in this will, or any codicil to it, specifically referring to and expressing my intent to exercise such power.

FOURTH: I hereby designate HERMIONE K. BROWN as executor of my will hereunder. If for any reason whatsoever Hermione K. Brown is unable or unwilling to qualify as executor, or having qualified, should for any reason whatsoever be unable or unwilling to continue in such capacity, then HAROLD ZIVETZ is designated as alternate executor in her place. If Harold Zivetz also is unable or unwilling to act or continue as executor, the then acting executor may designate one or more individuals and/or a bank or trust company duly qualified to carry on a trust business in California to act as a successor executor, such designation to be by notice in writing to such designated fiduciary and filed with the Court having jurisdiction over my estate. Any successor executor may similarly designate his successor. The latest designation of an executor pursuant to this article prior to the actual qualification of such executor, shall be deemed to revoke all prior designations.

I specifically direct that no bond be required of any individual named herein or designated, as hereinabove provided, as an executor.

Subject only to such confirmation or other Court order as may be provided by law, I hereby authorize my executor in his discretion: (i) to sell, lease or mortgage the whole or any part of my estate, whether real or personal, at either public or private sale, with or without notice; (ii) to invest and reinvest any surplus funds or sale proceeds at any time held by my executor in such investments, as my executor deems advisable; (iii) to continue to hold, manage or operate any property, business or enterprise that may be held or owned by me at the time of my death; and (iv) to continue as a general or limited partner in any partnership in which I was a partner at the date of my death; the profits or losses from all of the foregoing to inure to or be chargeable to my estate and not to my executor. Moreover, I authorize my executor to act as a so-called "independent executor" to the fullest extent permitted by law, and if my executor so acts, I expressly exonerate him from any liability by reason of his actions as such, as fully as though such actions had been taken with the approval or authorization of the Probate Court.

I further give to my executor full power to make all decisions and elections (including tax decisions and elections) which are available to my estate, including, but not by way of limitation, the power to treat expenses of administration, taxes, and other items as deductions from my federal estate tax return or from the income tax returns of the executor, whichever the executor, in his discretion, shall deem most advantageous, and the power to allocate the generation-skipping tax exemption. The decision of my executor made in good faith shall be conclusive and not subject to attack by any beneficiary or other person. Notwithstanding any claimed or actual conflict of interest, my executor shall not be liable to any beneficiary or other person by reason of the effects of any such decision; and my executor may, but shall not be required to, prorate or adjust any charges or savings therefrom as among any of the beneficiaries.

My executor may engage such attorneys, custodians, accountants, investment advisors, agents, personal managers and other personnel as my executor deems advisable to assist in the performance of his duties hereunder, the costs thereof to be a charge against my estate and not to diminish the fees to which my executor may otherwise be entitled; and my executor may rely upon the advice of such experts.

The word "executor", though used herein with the masculine singular pronoun, shall be deemed to refer to the individual or individuals (irrespective of gender) and/or corporate fiduciary from time to time qualified and functioning in such capacity.

All income of my estate during administration (other than income from property specifically devised) less only such taxes and other expenses of administration as my executor shall elect to treat as charges against said income rather than against principal of my estate shall constitute net income and shall be allocated to the residue of my estate. No interest shall be payable on any gift or legacy under this will or any codicil to it, whether outright or in trust. Notwithstanding the foregoing, if any gift is satisfied in whole or in part with property other than cash, such property shall be value at the value thereof at the date or dates of distribution; and all pecuniary gifts and payments which are not paid or funded within 15 months of decedent's death shall bear interest thereafter at the rate as provided in § 12001 of the California Probate Code.

FIFTH: I authorize my executor to pay, or reimburse any person who shall have paid on my behalf, my just debts, last illness and funeral expenses. I direct that all federal estate taxes and all other estate, inheritance, succession and transfer taxes (all collectively "death taxes") including without limitation any generation skipping transfer taxes ("GST taxes") payable upon, resulting from, or by reason of my death attributable to property passing under this will shall be paid without apportionment out of the residue of my probate estate. Any non-probate property which is included in my estate for death tax purposes shall bear its proportionate share of all death taxes, and my executor shall recover from the recipients of such property their respective shares of all such taxes, to the extent and in the manner provided by law. In this connection I declare that I have earlier this day completely restated my living trust, pursuant to a Declaration of Trust identified as the "George Burns Living Trust (1995 Restatement)". I direct that all death taxes imposed by reason of my death attributable to property which is included in the George Burns Living Trust (1995 Restatement), including without limitation any GST taxes, shall be paid out of said trust and (except as said trust may otherwise provide) shall be charged against the trust balance thereof in the manner provided in said George Burns Living Trust (1995 Restatement).

SIXTH: Upon my death, all of the rest, residue and remainder of my estate of every kind and character whatsoever and wheresoever situate ("residue") is given, devised and bequeathed to the Trustee designated in the George Burns Living Trust (1995 Restatement) to be held, administered and disposed of as therein provided (including any changes therein or amendments thereto made before my death regardless of whether made before or after the execution of this will) as contemplated and permitted under California Probate Code § 6300.

If for any reason the disposition set forth in the preceding paragraph shall not be operative or shall be invalid or the George Burns Living Trust (1995 Restatement) shall have failed or been revoked prior to my death, in such event I give, devise and bequeath the residue of my estate hereunder to the Trustee designated in the George Burns Living Trust (1995 Restatement), as a testamentary trustee and I hereby incorporate the George Burns Living Trust (1995 Restatement) into this will as this place as if it were set forth herein in full and adopt its terms as part of this will, to govern the disposition of my estate hereunder, it being my intent and my direction that in such event my estate shall be distributed as testamentary dispositions under the provisions set forth in said George Burns Living Trust (1995 Restatement). To the extent permitted by law, it is my intention that each reference to the George Burns Living Trust (1995 Restatement) in this will shall also include any future amendments to said trust (except, of course, for an amendment revoking said trust in its entirety). However, if amendments to the George Burns Living Trust (1995 Restatement) made after the execution of this will may not be given effect under applicable law existing at the date of my death with respect to incorporation by reference into a testamentary instrument, then I direct that each reference to the George Burns Living Trust (1995 Restatement) as contained in this will shall be to said trust as it exists at the date of execution of this will.

SEVENTH: If my executor is a member of a law firm, accounting firm or business management firm which renders professional services to my estate, my executor shall be entitled to regular compensation for his services hereunder; and the law firm, accounting or business management firm with which such executor is associated shall, in addition, be entitled to reasonable fees for the professional services rendered.

EIGHTH: This document shall be construed and interpreted according to the laws of the State of California where this will is executed and its validity and the validity of any of its provisions shall be determined by and in accordance with the laws of said state.

NINTH: I have, except as otherwise in this will specified, intentionally and with full knowledge omitted to provide for my heirs living at the time of my decease.

TENTH: If any devisee, legatee or beneficiary under this will, or any person claiming under or through any devisee, legatee or beneficiary, or any person who would be entitled to share in my estate through inheritance or intestate succession (all therein referred to as "party") shall, in any manner whatsoever, directly or indirectly, contest this will or the George Burns Living Trust (1995 Restatement) or attack, oppose or in any manner seek to impair or invalidate any provision hereof or thereof, or shall in any manner whatsoever conspire or cooperate with any party or parties attempting to do any of the acts or things aforesaid, or shall acquiesce in or fail to oppose such proceedings, then in each of the above-mentioned cases, I hereby bequeath to such party or parties the sum of $1.00 only, and all other bequests, devises and interest in this will given to such party or parties shall be deemed to have lapsed and shall be distributed among the beneficiaries entitled to the trust balance under the George Burns Living Trust (1995 Restatement) as shall not in any manner have participated in, and as shall have opposed such acts or proceedings. If, as a result of any attack or contest of this will, an intestacy would otherwise result as to all or any portion of my estate, then and in such event, with respect to any such portion of my estate, I hereby give, devise and bequeath such portion of my estate to the beneficiaries entitled to the trust balance under the George Burns Living Trust (1995 Restatement), excluding any parties attacking, contesting, opposing and/ or cooperating or acquiescing in any such attack, contest or opposition or their issue. For the purpose of this article, an action for declaratory relief or a petition for instructions or to determine heirship or to set aside property or any similar action or proceeding shall be deemed to constitute an attack upon this will where the purpose of the institution of such action or proceeding would be to oppose, impair or invalidate any provision hereof or to diminish the size of my probate estate or of the George Burns Living Trust (1995 Restatement) or otherwise defeat my testamentary intent as expressed in this will and the George Burns Living Trust (1995 Restatement). The provisions of this article shall also apply with respect to any codicils hereto or amendments to the George Burns Living Trust (1995 Restatement) hereafter made by me.

ELEVENTH: If any provision or provisions of this will be invalid or be held illegal or unenforceable, then notwithstanding any invalidity, illegality or unenforceability of such provision or provisions, the remainder of this will shall subsist and shall be in full force and effect as though such invalid, illegal or unenforceable provisions had been omitted from this will.

IN WITNESS WHEREOF, I have hereunto set my hand this <u>26th</u> day of <u>January</u>, 1995.

George Burns
George Burns

The foregoing instrument, consisting of ten (10) pages, including the page signed by the testator and the page signed by us as witnesses thereto, was at the date hereof, by GEORGE BURNS, signed as and declared to be his Last Will and Testament. Such signature and declaration were made in the presence of all of us who, at his request and in his presence, and in the presence of one another, have subscribed our names as witnesses thereto. We each have observed the signing of this will by GEORGE BURNS and by each other subscribing witness and have personally observed that each signature is the true signature of the person whose name was signed. Each of us is now more than eighteen (18) years of age and a competent witness and resides at the address set forth after his name. Each of us is acquainted with George Burns. At this time, he is over the age of eighteen (18) years, and to the best of our knowledge he is of sound mind and is not acting under fraud, duress, menace or undue influence.

Each of the undersigned does hereby declare under penalty of perjury under the laws of the State of California that the foregoing is true and correct.

Executed on <u>January 26</u>, 1995.

[The signatures and addresses of the three witnesses are illegible.]

Last Will and Testament of
John F. Kennedy, Jr.

Filed September 24, 1999

I, JOHN F. KENNEDY, JR., of New York, New York, make this my last will, hereby revoking all earlier wills and codicils. I do not by this will exercise any power of appointment.

FIRST: I give all my tangible property (as distinguished from money, securities and the like), wherever located, other than my scrimshaw set previously owned by my father, to my wife, Carolyn Bessette-Kennedy, if she is living on the thirtieth day after my death, or if none, by right of representation to my then living issue, or if none, by right of representation to the then living issue of my sister, Caroline Kennedy Schlossberg, or if none, to my said sister, Caroline, if she is then living. If I am survived by issue, I leave this scrimshaw set to said wife, Carolyn, if she is then living, or if not, by right of representation, to my then living issue. If I am not survived by issue, I give said scrimshaw set to my nephew John B.K. Schlossberg, if he is then living, or if not, by right of representation to the then living issue of my said sister, Caroline, or if none, to my said sister Caroline, if she is then living. I hope that whoever receives my tangible personal property will dispose of certain items of it in accordance with my wishes, however made unknown, but I impose no trust, condition or enforceable obligation of any kind in this regard.

SECOND: I give and devise all my interest in my cooperative apartment located at 20-26 Moore Street, Apartment 9E, in said New York, including all my shares therein and any proprietary leases with respect thereto, to my said wife, Carolyn, if she is living on the thirtieth day after my death.

THIRD: If no issue of mine survive me, I give and devise all my interests in real estate, wherever located, that I own as tenants in common with my said sister, Caroline, or as tenants in common with any of her issue, by right of representation to Caroline's issue who are living on the thirtieth day after my death, or if none, to my said sister Caroline, if she is then living.

References in this Article THIRD to "real estate" include shares in cooperative apartments and proprietary leases with respect thereto.

FOURTH: I give and devise the residue of all the property, of whatever kind and wherever located, that I own at my death to the ten trustees of the John F. Kennedy Jr. 1983 Trust established October 13, 1983 by me, as Donor, of which John T. Fallon, of Weston, Massachusetts, and I are currently the trustees (the "1983 Trust"), to be added to the principal of the 1983 Trust and administered in accordance with the provisions thereof, as amended by a First Amendment dated April 9, 1987 and by a Second Amendment and Complete Restatement dated earlier this day, and as from time to hereafter further amended whether before or after my death. I have provided in the 1983 Trust for my children and more remote issue and for the method of paying all federal and state taxes in the nature of estate, inheritance, succession and like taxes occasioned by my death.

FIFTH: I appoint my wife, Carolyn Bessette-Kennedy, as guardian of each child of our marriage during minority. No guardian appointed in this will or a codicil need furnish any surety on any official bond.

SIXTH: I name my cousin Anthony Stanislaus Radziwill as my executor; and if for any reason, he fails to qualify or ceases to serve in that capacity, I name my cousin Timothy P. Shriver as my executor in his place. References in this will or a codicil to my executor" mean the one or more executors (or administrators with this will annexed) for the time being in office. No executor or a codicil need furnish any surety on any official bond. In any proceeding for the allowance of an account of my executor, I request the Court to dispense with the appointment of a guardian ad litem to represent any person or interest. I direct that in any proceeding relating to my estate, service of process upon any person under a disability shall not made when another person not under a disability is a party to the proceeding and has the same interest as the person under the disability.

SEVENTH: In addition to other powers, my executor shall have power from time to time at discretion and without license of court: To retain, and to invest and reinvest in, any kind or amount of property; to vote and exercise other rights of security holders; to make such elections for federal and state estate, gift, income and generation-skipping transfer tax purposes as my executor may deem advisable; to compromise or admit to arbitration any matters in dispute; to borrow money, and to sell, mortgage, pledge, exchange, lease and contract with respect to any real or personal property, all without notice to any beneficiary and in such manner, for such consideration and on such terms as to credit or otherwise as my executor may deem advisable, whether or not the effect thereof extends beyond the period settling my estate; and in distributing my estate, to allot property, whether real or personal, at then current values, in lieu of cash.

WITNESS my hand this 19 day of Dec., 1997.

John F. Kennedy, Jr.

Signed, scaled, published and declared by the above-named John F. Kennedy, Jr. and for his last will, in the presence of us two who, at his request and in his presence and in the presence of each other, hereto subscribe our names as witnesses, all on the date last above written.

[Signatures of two witnesses appear here]

STATE OF NEW YORK   )
                                              ), ss.
COUNTY OF NEW YORK   )

Each of the undersigned, individually and severally being duly sworn, deposes and says:

The within will was subscribed in our presence and sight at the end thereof by John F. Kennedy, Jr., the within named testator, on the 19th day of December, 1997, at 500 Fifth Avenue, New York.

Said testator at the time of making such subscription declared the instrument so subscribed to be his last will.

Each of the undersigned thereupon signed his or her name as a witness at the end of said will at the request of said testator and in his presence and sight and in the presence and sight of each other.

Said testator was, at the time of so executing said will, over the age of 18 years and, in the respective opinions of the undersigned, of sound mind, memory and understanding and not under any restraint or in any respect incompetent to make a will.

The testator, in the respective opinions of the undersigned, could read, write and converse in the English language and was suffering from no defect of sight, hearing or speech, or from any other physical or mental impairment which would affect his capacity to make a valid will. The will was executed as a single, original instrument and was not executed in counterparts.

Each of the undersigned was acquainted with said testator at such time and makes this affidavit at his request.

The within will was shown to the undersigned at the time this affidavit was made, and was examined by each of them as to the signature of said testator and of the undersigned.

The foregoing instrument was executed by the testator and witnessed by each of the undersigned affiants under the supervision of Robert W. Corcoran, attorney-at-law.

[Signature]

[Signature]

Severally sworn to before me this 19th day of December, 1997.

Virginia DeSario
Notary Public
My Commission Expires:

VIRGINIA DESARIO
Notary Public State of New York
No. 43-4886020
Qualified in Richmond County
Certificate Filed in New York County
Commission Expires Sept. 3, 1999

Last Will and Testament of
Elvis A. Presley, Deceased

Filed August 22, 1977

I, Elvis A. Presley, a resident and citizen of Shelby County, Tennessee, being of sound mind and disposing memory, do hereby make, publish and declare this instrument to be my last will and testament, hereby revoking any and all wills and codicils by me at any time heretofore made.

Item I
Debts, Expenses and Taxes

I direct my Executor, hereinafter named, to pay all of my matured debts and my funeral expenses, as well as the costs and expenses of the administration of my estate, as soon after my death as practicable. I further direct that all estate, inheritance, transfer and succession taxes which are payable by reason under this will, be paid out of my residuary estate; and I hereby waive on behalf of my estate any right to recover from any person any part of such taxes so paid. My Executor, in his sole discretion, may pay from my domiciliary estate all or any portion of the costs of ancillary administration and similar proceedings in other jurisdictions.

Item II
Instruction Concerning Personal Property:
Enjoyment in Specie

I anticipate that included as a part of my property and estate at the time of my death will be tangible personal property of various kinds, characters and values, including trophies and other items accumulated by me during my professional career. I hereby specifically instruct all concerned that my Executor, herein appointed, shall have complete freedom and discretion as to disposal of any and all such property so long as he shall act in good faith and in the best interest of my estate and my beneficiaries, and his discretion so exercised shall not be subject to question by anyone whomsoever.

I hereby expressly authorize my Executor and my Trustee, respectively and successively, to permit any beneficiary of any and all trusts created hereunder to enjoy in specie the use or benefit of any household goods, chattels, or other tangible personal property (exclusive of choses in action, cash, stocks, bonds or other securities) which either my Executor or my Trustees may receive in kind, and my Executor and my Trustees shall not be liable for any consumption, damage, injury to or loss of any tangible property so used, nor shall the beneficiaries of any trusts hereunder or their executors or administrators be liable for any consumption, damage, injury to or loss of any tangible personal property so used.

Item III
Real Estate

If I am the owner of any real estate at the time of my death, I instruct and empower my Executor and my Trustee (as the case may be) to hold such real estate for investment, or to sell same, or any portion thereof, as my Executor or my Trustee (as the case may be) shall in his sole judgment determine to be for the best interest of my estate and the beneficiaries thereof.

Item IV
Residuary Trust

After payment of all debts, expenses and taxes as directed under Item I hereof, I give, devise, and bequeath all the rest, residue, and remainder of my estate, including all lapsed legacies and devices, and any property over which I have a power of appointment, to my Trustee, hereinafter named, in trust for the following purposes:

(a) The Trustee is directed to take, hold, manage, invest and reinvent the corpus of the trust and to collect the income therefrom in accordance with the rights, powers, duties, authority and discretion hereinafter set forth. The Trustee is directed to pay all the expenses, taxes and costs incurred in the management of the trust estate out of the income thereof.

(b) After payment of all expenses, taxes and costs incurred in the management of the trust estate, the Trustee is authorized to accumulate the net income or to pay or apply so much of the net income and such portion of the principal at any time and from time to time for health, education, support, comfortable maintenance and welfare of: (1) My daughter, Lisa Marie Presley, and any other lawful issue I might have, (2) my grandmother, Minnie Mae Presley, (3) my father, Vernon E. Presley, and (4) such other relatives of mine living at the time of my death who in the absolute discretion of my Trustees are in need of emergency assistance for any of the above mentioned purposes and the Trustee is able to make such distribution without affecting the ability of the trust to meet the present needs of the first three numbered categories of beneficiaries herein mentioned or to meet the reasonably expected future needs of the first three classes of beneficiaries herein mentioned. Any decision of the Trustee as to whether or not distribution, to any of the persons described hereunder shall be final and conclusive and not subject to question by any legatee or beneficiary hereunder.

(c) Upon the death of my Father, Vernon E. Presley, the Trustee is instructed to make no further distributions to the fourth category of beneficiaries and such beneficiaries shall cease to have any interest whatsoever in this trust.

(d) Upon the death of both my said father and my said grandmother, the Trustee is directed to divide the Residuary Trust into separate and equal trusts, creating one such equal trust for each of my lawful children then surviving and one such equal trust for the living issue collectively, if any, of any deceased child of mine. The share, if any, for the issue of any such deceased child, shall immediately vest in such issue in equal shares but shall be subject to the provisions of Item V herein. Separate books and records shall be kept for each trust, but it shall not be necessary that a physical division of the assets be made as to each trust.

The Trustee may from time to time distribute the whole or any part of the net income or principal from each of the aforesaid trusts as the Trustee, in its uncontrolled discretion, considers necessary or desirable to provide for the comfortable support, education, maintenance, benefit and general welfare of each of my children. Such distributions may be made directly to such beneficiary or to the guardian of the person of such beneficiary and without responsibility on my Trustee to see to the application of any such distributions and in making such distributions, the Trustee shall take into account all other sources of

funds known by the Trustee to be available for each respective beneficiary for such purpose.

(e) As each of my respective children attains the age of twenty-five (25) years and provided that both my father and my grandmother are deceased, the trust created hereunder for such child care [shall] terminate, and all the remainder of the assets then contained in said trust shall be distributed to such child so attaining the age of twenty-five (25) years outright and free of further trust.

(f) If any of my children for whose benefit a trust has been created hereunder should die before attaining the age of twenty five (25) years, then the trust created for such a child shall terminate on his death, and all remaining assets then contained in said trust shall be distributed outright and free of further trust and in equal shares to the surviving issue of such deceased child but subject to the provisions of Item V herein; but if there be no such surviving issue, then to the brothers and sisters of such deceased child in equal shares, the issue of any other deceased child being entitled collectively to their deceased parent's share. Nevertheless, if any distribution otherwise becomes payable outright and free of trust under the provisions of this paragraph (f) of the Item IV of my will to a beneficiary for whom the Trustee is then administering a trust for the benefit of such beneficiary under provisions of this last will and testament, such distribution shall not be paid outright to such beneficiary but shall be added to and become a part of the trust so being administered for such beneficiary by the Trustee.

Item V
Distribution to Minor Children

If any share of corpus of any trust established under this will become distributable outright and free of trust to any beneficiary before said beneficiary has attained the age of eighteen (18) years, then said share shall immediately vest in said beneficiary, but the Trustee shall retain possession of such share during the period in which such beneficiary is under the age of eighteen (18) years, and, in the meantime, shall use and expend so much of the income and principal for the care, support, and education of such beneficiary, and any income not so expended with respect to each share so retained all the power and discretion had with respect to such trust generally.

Item VI
Alternate Distributees

In the event that all of my descendants should be deceased at any time prior to the time for the termination of the trusts provided for herein, then in such event all of my estate and all the assets of every trust to be created hereunder (as the case may be) shall then be distributed outright in equal shares to my heirs at law per stirpes.

Item VII
Unenforceable Provisions

If any provisions of this will are unenforceable, the remaining provisions shall, nevertheless, be carried into effect.

Item VIII
Life Insurance

If my estate is the beneficiary of any life insurance on my life at the time of my death, I direct that the proceeds therefrom will be used by my Executor in payment of the debts, expenses and taxes listed in Item I of this will, to the extent deemed advisable by the Executor. All such proceeds not so used are to be used by my Executor for the purpose of satisfying the devises and bequests contained in Item IV herein.

Item IX
Spendthrift Provision

I direct that the interest of any beneficiary in principal or income of any trust created hereunder shall not be subject to claims of creditors or others, nor to legal process, and may not be voluntarily or involuntarily alienated or encumbered except as herein provided. Any bequests contained herein for any female shall be for her sole and separate use, free from the debts, contracts and control of any husband she may ever have.

Item X
Proceeds from Personal Services

All sums paid after my death (either to my estate or to any of the trusts created hereunder) and resulting from personal services rendered by me during my lifetime, including, but not limited to, royalties of all nature, concerts, motion picture contracts, and personal appearances shall be considered to be income, notwithstanding the provisions of estate and trust law to the contrary.

Item XI
Executor and Trustee

I appoint as executor of this, my last will and testament, and as Trustee of every trust required to be created hereunder, my said father.

I hereby direct that my said father shall be entitled by his last will and testament, duly probated, to appoint a successor Executor of my estate, as well as a successor Trustee or successor Trustees of all the trusts to be created under my last will and testament.

If, for any reason, my said father be unable to serve or to continue to serve as Executor and/or as Trustee, or if he be deceased and shall not have appointed a successor Executor or Trustee, by virtue of his last will and testament as stated above, then I appoint National Bank of Commerce, Memphis, Tennessee, or its successor or the institution with which it may merge, as successor Executor and/or as successor Trustee of all trusts required to be established hereunder.

None of the appointees named hereunder, including any appointment made by virtue of the last will and testament of my said father, shall be required to furnish any bond or security for performance of the respective fiduciary duties required hereunder, notwithstanding any rule of law to the contrary.

Item XII
Powers, Duties, Privileges and Immunities of the Trustee

Except as otherwise stated expressly to the contrary herein, I give and grant to the said Trustee (and to the duly appointed successor Trustee when acting as such) the power to do everything he deems advisable with respect to the administration of each trust required to be established under this, my last will and Testament, even though such powers would not be authorized or appropriate for the Trustee under statutory or other rules of law. By way of illustration and not in limitation of the generality of the foregoing grant of power and authority of the Trustee, I give and grant to him plenary power as follows:

(a) To exercise all those powers authorized to fiduciaries under the provisions of the Tennessee Code Annotated, Sections 35-616 to 35-618, inclusive, including any amendments thereto in effect at the time of my death, and the same are expressly referred to and incorporated herein by reference.

(b) Plenary power is granted to the Trustee, not only to relieve him from seeking judicial instruction, but to the extent that the Trustee deems it to be prudent, to encourage determinations freely to be made in favor of persons who are the current income beneficiaries. In such instances the rights of all subsequent beneficiaries are subordinate, and the Trustee shall not be answerable to any subsequent beneficiary for anything done or omitted in favor of a current income beneficiary may compel any such favorable or preferential treatment. Without in anywise minimizing or impairing the scope of this declaration of intent, it includes investment policy, exercise of discretionary power to pay or apply principal and income, and determination [of] principal and income questions;

(c) It shall be lawful for the Trustee to apply any sum that is payable to or for the benefit of a minor (or any other person who in the Judgment of the Trustee, is incapable of making proper disposition thereof) by payments in discharge of the costs and expenses of educating, maintaining and supporting said beneficiary, or to make payment to anyone with whom said beneficiary resides or who has the care or custody of the beneficiary, temporarily or permanently, all without intervention of any guardian or like fiduciary. The receipt of anyone to whom payment is so authorized to be made shall be a complete discharge of the Trustees without obligation on his part to see to the further application hereto, and without regard to other resource that the beneficiary may have, or the duty of any other person to support the beneficiary;

(d) In dealing with the Trustee, no grantee, pledge, vendee, mortgage, lessee or other transference of the trust properties, or any part thereof, shall be bound to inquire with respect to the purpose or necessity of any such disposition or to see to the application of any consideration therefore paid to the Trustee.

Item XIII
Concerning the Trustee and the Executor

(a) If at any time the Trustee shall have reasonable doubt as to his power, authority or duty in the administration of any trust herein created, it shall be lawful for the Trustee to obtain the advice and counsel of reputable legal counsel without resorting to the courts for instructions; and the Trustee shall be fully absolved from all liability and damage or detriment to the various trust estates of any beneficiary thereunder by reason of anything done, suffered or omitted pursuant to advice of said counsel given and obtained in good faith, provided that nothing contained herein shall be construed to prohibit or prevent the Trustee in all proper cases from applying to a court of competent jurisdiction for instructions in the administration of the trust assets in lieu of obtaining advice of counsel.

(b) In managing, investing, and controlling the various trust estates, the Trustee shall exercise the judgment and care under the circumstances then prevailing, which men of prudence, discretion and judgment exercise in the management of their own affairs, not in regard to speculation, but in regard to the permanent disposition of their funds, considering the probable income as well as the probable safety of their capital, and, in addition, the purchasing power of income distribution to beneficiaries.

(c) My Trustee (as well as my Executor) shall be entitled to reasonable and adequate compensation for the fiduciary services rendered by him.

(d) My Executor and his successor Executor and his successor Executor shall have the same rights, privileges, powers and immunities herein granted to my Trustee wherever appropriate.

(e) In referring to any fiduciary hereunder, for purposes of construction, masculine pronouns may include a corporate fiduciary and neutral pronouns may include an individual fiduciary.

Item XIV
Law Against Perpetuities

(a) Having in mind the rule against perpetuities, I direct that (notwithstanding anything contained to the contrary in this last will and testament) each trust created under this will (except such trusts as have heretofore vested in compliance with such rule or law) shall end, unless sooner terminated under other provisions of this will, twenty-one (21) years after the death of the last survivor of such of the beneficiaries hereunder as are living at the time of my death; and thereupon that the property held in trust shall be distributed free of all trust to the persons then entitled to receive the income and/or principal therefrom, in the proportion in which they are then entitled to receive such income.

(b) Notwithstanding anything else contained in this will to the contrary, I direct that if any distribution under this will become payable to a person for whom the Trustee is then administering a trust created hereunder for the benefit of such person, such distribution shall be made to such trust and not to the beneficiary outright, and the funds so passing to such trust shall become a part thereof as corpus and be administered and distributed to the same extent and purpose as if such funds had been a part of such a trust at its inception.

Item XV
Payment of Estate and Inheritance Taxes

Notwithstanding the provisions of Item X herein, I authorize my Executor to use such sums received by my estate after my death and resulting from my personal services as identified in Item X as he deem necessary and advisable in order to pay the taxes referred to in Item I of my said will.

In WITNESS WHEREOF, I, the said ELVIS A. PRESLEY, do hereunto set my hand and seal in the presence of two (2) competent witnesses, and in their presence do publish and declare this instrument to be my Last Will and Testament, this 3 day of March, 1977.

[Signed by Elvis A. Presley]
ELVIS A. PRESLEY

The foregoing instrument, consisting of this and eleven (11) preceding typewritten pages, was signed, sealed, published and declared by ELVIS A. PRESLEY, the Testator, to be his Last Will and Testament, in our presence, and we, at his request and in his presence and in the presence of each other, have hereunto subscribed our names as witnesses, this 3 day of March, 1977, at Memphis, Tennessee.

[Signed by Ginger Alden]
Ginger Alden residing at 4152 Royal Crest Place

[Signed by Charles F. Hodge]
Charles F. Hodge residing at 3764 Elvis Presley Blvd.

[Signed by Ann Dewey Smith]
Ann Dewey Smith residing at 2237 Court Avenue.

State of Tennessee
County of Shelby

Ginger Alden, Charles F. Hodge, and Ann Dewey Smith, after being first duly sworn, make oath or affirm that the foregoing Last Will and Testament, in the sight and presence of us, the undersigned, who at his request and in his sight and presence, and in the sight and presence of each other, have subscribed our names as attesting witnesses on the 3 day of March, 1977, and we further make oath or affirm that the Testator was of sound mind and disposing memory and not acting under fraud, menace or undue influence of any person, and was more than eighteen (18) years of age; and that each of the attesting witnesses is more than eighteen (18) years of age.

[Signed by Ginger Alden]
Ginger Alden

[Signed by Charles F. Hodge]
Charles F. Hodge

[Signed by Ann Dewey Smith]
Ann Dewey Smith

Sworn To And Subscribed before me this 3 day of March, 1977.

Drayton Beecker Smith II Notary Public

My commission expires: August 8, 1979

Admitted to probate and Ordered Recorded August 22, 1977

Joseph W. Evans, Judge

Recorded August 22, 1977

B.J. Dunavant, Clerk

By: Jan Scott, D.C.

Last Will and Testament
of John Winston Ono Lennon

I, JOHN WINSTON ONO LENNON, a resident of the County of New York, State of New York, which I declare to be my domicile do hereby make, publish and declare this to be my Last Will and Testament, hereby revoking all other Wills, Codicils and Testamentary dispositions by me at any time heretofore made.

FIRST: The expenses of my funeral and the administration of my estate, and all inheritance, estate or succession taxes, including interest and penalties, payable by reason of my death shall be paid out of and charged generally against the principal of my residuary estate without apportionment or proration. My Executor shall not seek contribution or reimbursement for any such payments.

SECOND: Should my wife survive me, I give, devise and bequeath to her absolutely, an amount equal to that portion of my residuary estate, the numerator and denominator of which shall be determined as follows:

1. The numerator shall be an amount equal to one-half (1/2) of my adjusted gross estate less the value of all other property included in my gross estate for Federal Estate Tax purposes and which pass or shall have passed to my wife either under any other provision of this Will or in any manner outside of this Will in such manner as to qualify for and be allowed as a marital deduction. The words "pass", "have passed", "marital deduction" and "adjusted gross estate" shall have the same meaning as said words have under those provisions of the United States Internal Revenue Code applicable to my estate.

2. The denominator shall be an amount representing the value of my residuary estate.

THIRD: I give, devise and bequeath all the rest, residue and remainder of my estate, wheresoever situate, to the Trustees under a Trust Agreement dated November 12, 1979, which I signed with my wife YOKO ONO, and ELI GARBER as Trustees, to be added to the trust property and held and distributed in accordance with the terms of that agreement and any amendments made pursuant to its terms before my death.

FOURTH: In the event that my wife and I die under such circumstances that there is not sufficient evidence to determine which of us has predeceased the other, I hereby declare it to be my will that it shall be deemed that I shall have predeceased her and that this, my Will, and any and all of its provisions shall be construed based upon that assumption.

FIFTH: I hereby nominate, constitute and appoint my beloved wife, YOKO ONO, to act as the Executor of this my Last Will and Testament. In the event that my beloved wife YOKO ONO shall predecease me or chooses not to act for any reason, I nominate and appoint ELI GARBER, DAVID WARMFLASH and CHARLES PETTIT, in the order named, to act in her place and stead.

SIXTH: I nominate, constitute and appoint my wife YOKO ONO, as the Guardian of the person and property of any children of the marriage who may survive me. In the event that she predeceases me, or for any reason she chooses not to act in that capacity, I nominate, constitute and appoint SAM GREEN to act in her place and stead.

SEVENTH: No person named herein to serve in any fiduciary capacity shall be required to file or post any bond for the faithful performance of his or her duties, in that capacity in this or in any other jurisdiction, any law to the contrary notwithstanding.

EIGHTH: If any legatee or beneficiary under this will or the trust agreement between myself as Grantor and YOKO ONO LENNON and ELI GARBER as Trustees, dated November 12, 1979 shall interpose objections to the probate of this Will, or institute or prosecute or be in any way interested or instrumental in the institution or prosecution of any action or proceeding for the purpose of setting aside or invalidating this Will, then and in each such case, I direct that such legatee or beneficiary shall receive nothing whatsoever under this Will or the aforementioned Trust.

IN WITNESS WHEREOF, I have subscribed and sealed and do publish and declare these presents as and for my Last Will and Testament, this 12th day of November, 1979.

/s/ John Winston Ono Lennon

THE FOREGOING INSTRUMENT consisting of four (4) typewritten pages, including this page, was on the 12th day of November, 1979, signed, sealed, published and declared by JOHN WINSTON ONO LENNON, the Testator therein named, as and for his Last Will and Testament, in the present of us, who at his request, and in his presence, and in the presence of each other, have hereunto set our names as witnesses.

[The names of the three witnesses are illegible.]

Last Will and Testament
of Richard M. Nixon

I, RICHARD M. NIXON, residing in the Borough of Park Ridge, County of Bergen and State of New Jersey, being of sound and disposing mind and memory, do hereby make, publish and declare this to be my Last Will and Testament, revoking all prior Wills and codicils.

ARTICLE ONE

I give and bequeath to THE RICHARD NIXON LIBRARY AND BIRTHPLACE (hereinafter sometimes referred to as the "Library") for its uses, an amount equal to the "adjusted proceeds amount" (as hereinafter defined); provided, however, that if there are any outstanding and unpaid amounts on pledges I have made to the Library, including, specifically, any amounts unpaid on the One Million Two Hundred Thousand Dollar pledge made in 1993, then the adjusted proceeds amount under this bequest shall be paid first directly to the Library to the extent necessary to satisfy such charitable pledge or pledges, and provided further, that if at the time of my death or distribution the Library is not an organization described in Sections 170(c) and 2055(a) of the Internal Revenue Code of 1986, as amended (the "Code"), which would entitle the estate to a charitable deduction for Federal Estate Tax purposes, I give and bequeath such property to THE NIXON BIRTHPLACE FOUNDATION, provided further, if THE NIXON BIRTHPLACE FOUNDATION is not then an organization described in Sections 170(c) and

2055(a) of the Code, I give and bequeath such property to such organization or organizations described in said Sections of the Code in such shares as my executors shall designate by written and acknowledged instrument filed within six months from the date of my death with the clerk of the court in which this Will shall have been admitted to probate.

In the event such property is distributed to an organization other than the RICHARD NIXON LIBRARY & BIRTHPLACE, I request such organization to bear in mind my wish that such property ultimately repose in such Library, if and when it qualifies as a charitable organization under Sections 170(c) and 2055(a) of the Code.

The term "adjusted proceeds amount" shall be defined as the excess of

(i) the amount due or paid to me and/or my estate under the judgment entered following the decision of the United States Court of Appeals for the District of Columbia Circuit in the case of Richard Nixon v. United States of America, decided on November 17, 1992, and/or any concurrent or subsequent proceedings relating or pertaining thereto, and any related or subsequent case, provided that any such amounts paid during my life shall only be included as adjusted proceeds to the extent such amounts as of the date of my death are held or invested in a segregated and traceable account or accounts over

(ii) the sum of (a) the amount of all attorneys' fees and other costs or expenses, whether previously paid or unpaid, associated with or incurred in connection with such proceedings or any case similar to or relating thereto and all other attorneys' fees from 1974 on, which my estate or I have paid or which are outstanding, excluding, however, any attorneys' fees paid to the firm of which William E. Griffin has been a member, and (b) One Million Four Hundred Fifty Thousand Dollars, the amount equal to my contribution to the Library made in 1992. The amounts under (a) and (b) of this subparagraph (ii) shall be part of my residuary estate.

It is my intention, by this bequest, to make a charitable gift of any "windfall" received under the lawsuits referred to above, and to first make my family whole by recovering all of the legal expenses I have incurred or my estate is to incur because of these and other lawsuits.

ARTICLE TWO

A. Subject to the restrictions contained in this paragraph and any other restrictions contained in this Will, I give and bequeath all items of tangible personal property that I shall own at my death which relate to events of my official or personal life or the official or personal life of my deceased wife, PATRICIA R. NIXON, which have had historical or commemorative significance, except for my "personal diaries", which are defined and disposed of in Paragraph B of this Article, to THE RICHARD NIXON LIBRARY & BIRTHPLACE; provided, however, that if at the time of my death or distribution such Library is not an organization described in Sections 170(c) and 2055(a) of the Code, which would entitle the estate to a charitable deduction for Federal Estate Tax purposes, I give and bequeath such property to THE NIXON BIRTHPLACE FOUNDATION, provided further that if THE NIXON BIRTHPLACE FOUNDATION is not then an organization described in Sections 170(c) and 2055(a) of the Code, I give and bequeath such property to such organization or organizations described in said Sections of the Code in such shares

as my executors shall designate by written and acknowledged instrument filed within six months from the date of my death with the clerk of the court in which this Will shall have been admitted to probate.

In the event such property is distributed to an organization other than the RICHARD NIXON LIBRARY & BIRTHPLACE, I request such organization to bear in mind my wish that such property ultimately repose in such Library, if and when it qualifies as a charitable organization under Sections 170(c) and 2055(a) of the Code. Such tangible personal property shall include, without limitation, awards, plaques, works of art of all kinds, medals, membership or achievement certificates, commemorative stamps and coins, religious items, commemorative and personal photographs and all correspondence, documents, notes, memoranda, letters and all other writings that I own at my death, of whatever kind and nature, personal or public, whether inscribed by me or not inscribed by me and whether written by me or to me. I direct that the determination as to which items of my tangible personal property are included in this bequest, and which items are items of tangible personal property disposed of under Paragraph C of this Article, shall be based on the decision of my executors; however, it is my wish that my executors consult with my surviving daughters in making this determination. The determination of my executors shall be conclusive and binding upon all parties interested in my estate.

Notwithstanding the above provisions, my daughters, PATRICIA NIXON COX and JULIE NIXON EISENHOWER, or the survivor, or if neither daughter is surviving, my executors, shall have the right, within six months of my date of death, to go through all of such tangible personal property, to take any such property appraised at no value, or any other items of such tangible personal property, provided that under no circumstances shall the amount of such property taken by my daughters exceed in value three (3%) percent of the total value of all such property included in this Paragraph A.

B. I give and bequeath my "personal diaries" (as hereinafter defined) in equal shares to my daughters, JULIE NIXON EISENHOWER and PATRICIA NIXON COX, or all to the survivor. If either or both of my daughters shall, disclaim some or all or parts of my "personal diaries", such disclaimed items shall be distributed to THE RICHARD NIXON LIBRARY AND BIRTHPLACE (the "Library") for its uses; provided, however, that if at the time of my death or distribution the Library is not an organization described in Sections 170(c) and 2055(a) of the Internal Revenue Code of 1986, as amended (the "Code"), which would entitle the estate to a charitable deduction for Federal Estate Tax purposes, I give and bequeath such property to THE NIXON BIRTHPLACE FOUNDATION, provided further that if THE NIXON BIRTHPLACE FOUNDATION is not then an organization described in Sections 170(c) and 2055(a) of the Code, I give and bequeath such property to such organization or organizations described in said Sections of the Code in such shares as my executors shall designate by written and acknowledged instrument filed within six months from the date of my death with the clerk of the court in which this Will shall have been admitted to probate.

In the event such property is distributed to an organization other than the RICHARD NIXON LIBRARY & BIRTHPLACE, I request such organization to bear in mind my wish that such property ultimately repose in such Library, if and when it qualifies as a charitable organization under Sections 170(c) and 2055(a) of the Code.

If neither of my daughters survives me, I direct my executors to collect and destroy my "personal diaries." Notwithstanding any other provisions of this Will, if neither of my daughters survives me, the property constituting my "personal diaries" shall be subject to the following restrictions: At no time shall my executors be allowed to make public, publish, sell, or make available to any individual other than my executor (or except as required for Federal tax purposes) the contents or any part or all of my "personal diaries" and, provided further,

that my executors shall, within one year from the date of my death or, if reasonably necessary, upon the later receipt of a closing estate tax letter from the Internal Revenue Service, destroy all of my "personal diaries".

My "personal diaries" shall be defined as any notes, tapes, transcribed notes, folders, binders, or books that are owned by me or to which I may be entitled under a judgment of law including, but not limited to, folders, binders, or books labeled as Richard Nixon's Diaries, Diary Notes, or labeled just by dates, that may contain my daily, weekly or monthly activities, thoughts or plans. The determination of my executors as to what property is included in this bequest shall be conclusive and binding upon all parties interested in my estate; however, it is my wish that my executors consult with my surviving daughters and/or my office staff in making this determination.

C. If at the time of my death any lawsuit or lawsuits are pending regarding the ownership of any of my tangible personal property including, but not limited to, all of the tangible personal property listed in Paragraph A above, I specifically direct my executors to continue such lawsuits for as long as they, in their discretion, deem it appropriate to do so, knowing my wishes in this matter.

D. I give and bequeath the balance of the tangible personal property I shall own at my death, not otherwise effectively disposed of in this Will, to my issue, per stirpes. If both of my daughters, PATRICIA NIXON COX and JULIE NIXON EISENHOWER, shall survive me, such tangible personal property shall be divided between my daughters in such manner as they shall agree, or in the absence of agreement, or if any child is a minor, as my executors determine, which determination shall be conclusive upon all persons interested in my estate.

E. I authorize and empower my executors to pay, and to charge as administration expenses of my estate, the expenses of storing, packing, insuring and mailing or delivering any article of tangible personal property hereinabove disposed of.

ARTICLE THREE

A. If my granddaughter, MELANIE EISENHOW-ER, survives me, I give and bequeath to her the sum of Seventy Thousand ($70,000.00) Dollars.

B. If my grandson, ALEXANDER RICHARD EISENHOWER, survives me, I give and bequeath to him the sum of Thirty Thousand ($30,000.00) Dollars.

C. If my grandson, CHRISTOPHER COX, survives me, I give and bequeath to him the sum of Ten Thousand ($10,000.00) Dollars.

The specific bequests to my grandchildren named above are made to equalize the gifts made to all of my grandchildren during my life. The disparity in amounts, or lack of a bequest, is not intended and should not be interpreted as a sign of favoritism for one grandchild over another.

ARTICLE FOUR

All of the rest, residue and remainder of my estate, real and personal, wherever situated, including any lapsed or ineffective legacies or devises (but excluding any property over which I may have a power of appointment, it being my intention not to exercise any such power), herein sometimes referred to as my "residuary estate", I dispose of as follows:

A. I give and bequeath the sum of Fifty Thousand ($50,000.00) Dollars to each grandchild of mine who survives me.

B. I give, devise and bequeath the balance of my residuary estate to my issue, per stirpes.

C. Notwithstanding any other provisions of this will, if any bequest or share of my estate under this Article FOUR would be payable to a grandchild of mine for whose benefit a separate trust created under the Will of my deceased wife, PATRICIA R. NIXON, is then in existence, I direct that such bequest or share of my estate shall be distributed to the trustee(s) of such trust to be added to, administered and disposed of as part of the principal of such trust in accordance with the terms of such trust; and, provided further, that if the addition of any portion or all of this residuary bequest or share of my estate to a trust for a grandchild under the Will of PATRICIA R. NIXON shall cause such trust to have an inclusion ratio greater than zero for purposes of the Generation Skipping Transfer Tax provisions of Article 13 of the Code (the "GST tax"), then any portion, up to the whole, of such bequest or share of my estate, that is not exempt from the GST tax shall not be added to the trust, but shall be given to such trustee(s) to be held in a separate trust under the same terms and conditions, my intention being to create two separate trusts, one of which has, for GST tax purposes, an inclusion ratio of zero, and one of which has an inclusion ratio greater than zero.

ARTICLE FIVE

If upon my death no issue of mine shall then be living, I give, devise and bequeath my residuary estate, or the then remaining principal and, except as hereinabove otherwise provided, any undistributed or accrued income of such trust as the case may be, to THE RICHARD NIXON LIBRARY & BIRTHPLACE, and if such organization is not then in existence, to the persons who would have been my heirs under the laws of intestate distribution of New Jersey then in effect had I died on the date of the event requiring a distribution.

ARTICLE SIX

I direct that all estate, inheritance and other death taxes (including any interest and penalties thereon) imposed by any jurisdiction whatsoever by reason of my death upon or with respect to any property includable in my estate for the purposes of any such taxes, or upon or with respect to any person receiving any such property, whether such property shall pass under or outside, or shall have passed outside, the provisions of this Will, except for additional estate taxes imposed by Section 4980(A)(d) of the Code and generation-skipping transfer taxes imposed under Section 13 of the Code ("GST taxes") which may be payable by reason of my death, shall be paid, without apportionment, from the principal of my residuary estate. Any GST tax payable by reason of my death shall be charged and the liability for the payment of such GST taxes shall be determined according to the law of the jurisdiction imposing such GST tax.

ARTICLE SEVEN

If any beneficiary under this Will and I shall die simultaneously or in such circumstances as to render it difficult or impossible to determine who predeceased the other, it shall conclusively be presumed for the purposes of this Will that I survived.

ARTICLE EIGHT

I hereby nominate, constitute and appoint my friends, WILLIAM E. GRIFFIN, and JOHN R. TAYLOR, to be the co-executors of this Will.

The appointment of my attorney, WILLIAM E. GRIFFIN, as a co-executor is made with my knowledge and approval of his receipt of commissions as provided by law, and his law firms receipt of compensation for legal services rendered to my estate.

The individuals named in the foregoing paragraph are granted the continuing discretionary power, exercisable while in office, and exercisable only unanimously if more than one of them is then in office, to designate one or more successors or co-fiduciaries or a succession of successors or co-fiduciaries in such office to act one at a time or together with co-fiduciaries, to fill any vacancy occurring in such office after any successor designated herein shall have failed to qualify or ceased to act, by written instrument, duly acknowledged, and to revoke any such designation prior to the happening of the event upon which it is to become effective, by a written instrument, duly acknowledged, and a new designation may be made as above provided. If there shall be more than one such designation of successor fiduciary or co-fiduciary in effect and unrevoked, they shall be effective in the reverse of the order in which they were made.

Any fiduciary may resign at any time by delivering or mailing a notice in writing of such resignation to his or her co-fiduciaries, or, if none, to his or her designated successor, if such designee has indicated his or her willingness to act, and thirty days thereafter such res-

ignation shall take effect. If any fiduciary becomes disabled, that determination of disability shall also constitute that individual's immediate resignation as a fiduciary without any further act. For the purposes of this paragraph, a person shall be considered disabled if either (i) a committee, guardian, conservator or similar fiduciary shall have been appointed for such person or (ii) a court shall have determined, or two physicians shall have certified, that the person is incompetent or otherwise unable to act prudently and effectively in financial affairs.

Each successor fiduciary and co-fiduciary shall have all rights and discretions which are granted to the executors named herein, except those which may be specifically denied in this will.

At any time that there are two or more fiduciaries then in office, all decisions regarding my estate shall be made by both or the majority of my fiduciaries in such office. However, my fiduciaries may from time to time authorize one of their number, or each of them acting singly, to execute instruments of any kind on their behalf (including, but not by way of limitation, any check, order, demand, assignment, transfer, contract, authorization, proxy, consent, notice or waiver). Insofar as third parties dealing with my fiduciaries are concerned instruments executed and acts performed by one fiduciary pursuant to such authorization shall be fully binding as if executed or performed by all of them. An authorization shall be valid until those acting in reliance on it receive actual notice of its revocation.

No fiduciary shall be required to give any bond or other security for the faithful performance of such fiduciary's duties in any jurisdiction whatsoever; or if any such bond shall be required, no such fiduciary shall be required to furnish any surety thereon. No executor shall be required to file a bond to secure the return of any payment or payments on account of commissions of such executor.

My individual executors may receive the commissions allowable under New Jersey Law from time to time during the period of the administration of my estate and any trusts hereunder.

Any corporate executor serving hereunder shall receive compensation in accordance with its Schedule of Fees in effect from time to time during the period over which its services are performed.

ARTICLE NINE

I give to my fiduciaries, with respect to any and all property, whether real or personal, which I may own at the time of my death, or which shall at any time constitute part of my estate, including funds held hereunder for persons under the age of 21 years, and whether constituting principal or income therefrom, in addition to the authority and power conferred upon them by law, express authority and power to be exercised by them as such fiduciaries, in their discretion, for any purpose, without application to, authorization from, or confirmation by any court:

a) To retain and to purchase or otherwise acquire stocks, whether common or preferred, bonds, obligations, shares or interests in investment companies or investment trusts, securities issued by or any common trust fund maintained by any corporate fiduciary, partnership interests, or any other property, real or personal, of whatsoever nature, wheresoever situated, without duty to diversify, whether or not productive of income and whether or not the same may be authorized by law for the investment of estate funds, it being my intention to give my fiduciaries the same power of investment which I myself possess with respect to my own funds.

b) To deposit funds in the savings or commercial department of any corporate fiduciary or of any other bank without limit as to duration or amount.

c) To sell, without prior authorization or confirmation of the court, at public or private sale, exchange, mortgage, lease without statutory or other limitation as to duration, partition, grant options in excess of six months on, alter, improve, demolish buildings, or otherwise deal with any property, real or personal, upon any terms and whether for cash or upon credit, and to execute and deliver deeds, leases, mortgages or other instruments relating hereto.

d) To exercise in person or by proxy all voting, conversion, subscription, or other rights incident to the ownership of any property, including the right to participate in any corporate reorganization, merger or other transaction and to retain any property received thereunder and the right to delegate discretionary power.

e) To borrow from any person, including any corporate fiduciary, and to lend money to any person, including any person beneficially interested hereunder, with or without security.

f) To compromise or arbitrate claims, to prepay or accept prepayment of any debt, to enforce or abstain from enforcing, extend, modify or release any right or claim, or to hold any claim after maturity without extension, with or without consideration.

g) To hold separate shares or trusts in solido, and to hold property in bearer form or in the name of a nominee or nominees.

h) To execute and deliver deeds or other instruments, with or without covenants, warranties and representations and with or without consideration, including releases which shall discharge the recipient from responsibility for property receipted for thereby.

i) To abstain from rendering or filing any inventory or periodic account in any court.

j) Without the consent of any beneficiary, to make division or distribution in cash or in kind or partly in each. Any such distribution in kind shall be made at the fair market value on the date or dates of distribution and may be made without regard to the tax basis of such property and without any duty to distribute such assets pro rata among beneficiaries or to equalize the tax basis recovered by such beneficiaries, any provision of this will or rule of law to the contrary notwithstanding.

k) To employ legal and investment counsel, custodians, accountants and agents for the transaction of any business of my estate or any trust hereunder or for services or advice, to pay reasonable compensation therefor out of my estate or such trust, as may be applicable, and to rely and act or decline to rely or act upon any information or opinion furnished by them.

l) To retain or acquire the stock of any corporation in which any individual fiduciary hereunder or any officer or director of any corporate fiduciary hereunder may have an interest, whether as officer, director, employee or otherwise.

m) To make or join in elections and joint returns under any tax law; to agree in the apportionment of any joint tax liability; to exercise or forbear to exercise any income, gift or estate tax options; to determine the allocation of exemptions or exercise other elections available to my executors for generation-skipping transfer tax purposes; and to make or refrain from making adjustments between principal and income or between shares of my estate by reason of any deduction taken for income tax instead of estate tax purposes or any election as to the date of valuation of my estate for estate tax purposes, all in such manner as my executor may deem advisable, and any such determination made by my executor shall be conclusive and binding upon all persons affected thereby.

n) To pay out of my general estate in respect of any real or tangible personal property situated outside the state of the principal administration of my estate at the time of my death any administration expense payable under the laws of the state or country where such property is situated.

o) To pay themselves, individually, at such time or times and without prior approval of any court or person interested in my estate or, any trust hereunder or payment of interest or the securing of any bond or rendering of any annual statement, account or computation thereof, such sum or sums on account of commissions to which they may eventually be entitled hereunder as they, in their discretion, may determine to be just and reasonable, to charge the same wholly against principal or wholly against income, or partially against principal and partially against income, as they may, in their discretion, determine advisable, and in the case of any trustee, to retain commissions which they may determine shall be payable out of income from income derived from any year preceding or succeeding the year with respect to which such commissions shall have been earned.

p) Generally, to exercise in good faith and with reasonable care all investment and administrative powers and discretions of an absolute owner which may lawfully be conferred upon a fiduciary.

ARTICLE TEN

A. Whenever income or principal is to be distributed or applied for the benefit of a person under the age of 21 years (referred to as a "minor" in this Article) or a person who in the sole judgment of my fiduciaries is incapable of managing his or her own affairs, my fiduciaries may make payment of such property in any or all of the following ways:

1. By paying such property to the parent, guardian or other person having the care and control of such minor for such minor's benefit or to any authorized person as custodian for such minor under any applicable Gifts to Minors Act, with authority to authorize any such custodian to hold such property until the minor attains the age of 21 years where permitted under applicable law.

2. By paying such property to the guardian, committee, conservator or other person having the care and control of such incapable person.

3. By paying directly to such minor or incapable person such sums as my fiduciaries may deem advisable as an allowance.

4. By expending such property in such other manner as my fiduciaries in their discretion shall determine will benefit such minor or incapable person.

B. If principal becomes vested in and payable to a minor, my fiduciaries may make payment thereof in any of the ways set forth in the preceding paragraph of this Article, or may, defer payment of any part or all thereof meanwhile paying or applying to or for the use of such minor so much or all of such principal and of the income therefrom, as my fiduciaries in their discretion may deem advisable. Any income not so expended by my fiduciaries shall be added to principal. My fiduciaries shall pay any remaining principal to such minor upon such minor's attaining the age of 21 years or to such minor's estate upon death prior to such payment in full.

C. Any payment or distribution authorized in this Article shall be a full discharge to my fiduciaries with respect thereto.

ARTICLE ELEVEN

All interests hereunder, whether in principal or income, while undistributed and in the possession of my executors, and even though vested or distributable, shall not be subject to attachment, execution or sequestration for any debt, contract, obligation or liability of any beneficiary, and, furthermore, shall not be subject to pledge, assignment conveyance or anticipation by any beneficiary.

ARTICLE TWELVE

The account (intermediate or final) of any executor may be settled by agreement with the adult beneficiaries interested in the account and a parent or guardian of those beneficiaries who are minors, who shall have the full power on the basis of such settlement to release such fiduciary from all liability for such fiduciary's acts or omissions as executor for the period covered thereby. Such settlement and release shall be binding upon all interested parties hereunder including those who may be under legal disability or not yet in being and shall have the force and effect of a final decree, judgment or order of a court of competent jurisdiction rendered in an action or proceeding for an accounting in which jurisdiction was duly obtained over all necessary and proper parties. The foregoing provisions, however, shall not preclude any fiduciary from having such fiduciary's accounts judicially settled if such fiduciary shall so desire. In any probate, accounting or other persons interested in my estate are required by law to be served with process, if a party to the proceeding has the same interest as or a similar interest to a person under a legal disability (including, without limitation, an infant or an incompetent) it shall not be necessary to serve process upon the person under a disability or otherwise make such person a party to the proceeding, it being my intention to avoid the appointment of a guardian ad litem wherever possible.

ARTICLE THIRTEEN

The validity, construction, effect and administration of the testamentary dispositions and the other provisions contained in this will shall, in any and all events, be administered in accordance with, and construed and regulated by, the laws of the State of New Jersey from time to time existing.

ARTICLE FOURTEEN

A. Wherever "child", "children" or "issue" appears in this Will, it shall be deemed to include only lawful natural issue and persons deriving their relationship to or through their parent or ancestor by legal adoption prior to such adopted person's attainment of the age of 18 years.

B. A disposition in this Will to the descendants of a person per stirpes shall be deemed to require a division into a sufficient number of equal shares to make one share for each child of such person living at the time such disposition becomes effective and one share for each then deceased child of such person having one or more descendants then living, regardless of whether any child of such person is then living, with the same principle to be applied in any required further division of a share at a more remote generation.

ARTICLE FIFTEEN

A. All references herein to this Will shall be construed as referring to this Will and any codicil or codicils hereto that I may hereafter execute.

B. Wherever necessary or appropriate, the use herein of any gender shall be deemed to include the other genders and the use herein of either the singular or the plural shall be deemed to include the other.

C. Except as otherwise specifically, provided in this will:

　1. Each reference to my "fiduciaries" shall be deemed to mean and refer to my executor and, where applicable, to a custodian hereunder;

2. Each reference to my "executors" shall be deemed to mean and refer to the fiduciary or fiduciaries, natural or corporate, who shall be acting hereunder in such capacity from time to time; and

3. Any and all power, authority and discretion conferred upon my executor or my fiduciaries may be exercised by the fiduciary or fiduciaries who shall qualify and be acting hereunder from time to time in the capacity in which such power, authority and discretion are exercised.

IN WITNESS WHEREOF, I have hereunto set my hand and seal this (24th) day of February, 1994.

/s/ Richard M Nixon

ATTESTATION CLAUSE

WE the undersigned, do hereby certify that on the 24th of February, 1994, RICHARD M. NIXON, the Testator above named did, in the presence of the undersigned and of each of us, subscribe, publish and declare the foregoing instrument to be his last Will and Testament and then and there requested us and each of us to sign our names thereto as witnesses to the execution thereof, which we hereby do in the presence of the said Testator and of each other on this 24th day of February, 1994.

(signed by three witnesses)

each being duly sworn, depose and say:

That they witnessed the execution of the Will of RICHARD M. NIXON, dated February 24, 1994, consisting of eighteen pages. That the Will was executed at Woodcliff Lake, New Jersey, under the supervision of Karen J. Walsh an attorney at law with offices at 51 Pondfield Road, Bronxville, New York. That this affidavit is made at the request of the Testator.

That the Testator, in our presence, subscribed his name to the Will at the end thereof, and at the time of making such subscription, published and declared the same to be his Last Will and Testament; thereupon we, at his request and in his presence and in the presence of each other, signed our names thereto as subscribing witnesses.

That the said Testator, at the time of such execution, was more than 18 years of age and, in our opinion, of sound mind, memory and understanding, not under any restraint or in any respect incompetent to make a Will.

That the Testator indicated to us that he had read the Will, knew the contents thereof, and that the provisions therein contained expressed the manner in which his Estate is to be administered and distributed.

That the Testator could read, write and converse in the English language and was suffering from no defect of sight, hearing or speech, or from any physical or mental impairment which would affect his capacity to make a valid Will.

That the Testator signed only of the said Will on said occasion.

Sworn to before me this 25th day of February, 1994.

PAUL G. AMICUCCI
Notary Public, State of New York
No. 5001747
Qualified in Westchester County

Last Will and Testament of
Doris Duke [excerpted]

I, DORIS DUKE, a resident of and domiciled in the State of New Jersey, do hereby make, publish and declare this to be my Last Will and Testament, hereby revoking all wills and codicils at any time heretofore made by me.

ONE: A. I direct that there be no funeral service or memorial service of any kind for me and that I be buried at sea.

B. I give my eyes to THE EYE BANK FOR SIGHT RESTORATION INC., New York, New York, and I hereby ratify all that anyone theretofore may have done toward carrying out this gift.

TWO: A. 1. I give, devise and bequeath all of my right, title and interest in and to a certain portion of my real property located in Somerville, New Jersey, known as the "parks area" to my Trustees hereinafter named to be held as a new and separate wholly charitable trust which shall be created upon my death and which shall be known as the DORIS DUKE FOUNDATION FOR THE PRESERVATION OF ENDANGERED WILDLIFE, and such separate wholly charitable trust shall be administered and distributed subject to the provisions of Article NINE for the purposes hereinafter set forth in this Paragraph 1. All references in this Will to the DORIS DUKE FOUNDATION FOR THE PRESERVATION OF ENDANGERED WILDLIFE shall refer to such wholly charitable trust. I direct the DORIS DUKE FOUNDATION FOR THE PRESERVATION OF ENDANGERED WILDLIFE to use the parks area to provide an enclosure to protect endangered species of all kinds, both flora and fauna, from becoming extinct. The funds necessary to operate the DORIS DUKE FOUNDATION FOR THE PRESERVATION OF ENDANGERED WILDLIFE shall be provided by the DORIS DUKE CHARITABLE FOUNDATION as set forth in Article EIGHT hereof.

2. I give, devise and bequeath all of my right, title and interest in and to a certain portion of my real property located in Somerville, New Jersey, known as the "farmland and growing areas" to my Trustees hereinafter named to be held as a new and separate wholly charitable trust which shall be created upon my death and which shall be known as the DORIS DUKE FOUNDATION FOR THE PRESERVATION OF NEW JERSEY FARMLAND AND FARM ANIMALS, and such separate wholly charitable trust shall be administered and distributed subject to the provisions of Article NINE for the purposes hereinafter set forth in this Paragraph 2. All references in this Will to the DORIS DUKE FOUNDATION FOR THE PRESERVATION OF NEW JERSEY FARMLAND AND FARM ANIMALS shall refer to such wholly charitable trust. The DORIS DUKE FOUNDATION FOR THE PRESERVATION OF NEW JERSEY FARMLAND AND FARM ANIMALS shall be authorized to lease this property at an annual rental of One Dollar ($1.00) to a college or university specializing in farming education. In all events, I direct that this property be used solely for agricultural and horticultural purposes, including research (provided that no animals are used to conduct such research), and that this property be used for the exclusive purpose of maintaining and protecting the wildlife located on the property. I direct that the DELAWARE VALLEY COLLEGE OF SCIENCE AND AGRICULTURE, Doylestown, Pennsylvania, be given the first right to so lease such property, provided that such COLLEGE pay all of the expenses of operating such property during the term of any such lease. The funds necessary for the DORIS DUKE FOUNDATION FOR THE PRESERVATION OF NEW JERSEY FARMLAND AND FARM ANIMALS to make required capital improvements and to purchase farm equipment shall be provided by the DORIS DUKE CHARITABLE FOUNDATION as set forth in Article EIGHT hereof.

3. I give, devise and bequeath all of my right, title and interest in and to the balance of my real property, located in Somerville, New Jersey, and all structures

and improvements located thereon, to my Trustees hereinafter named to be held as a new and separate wholly charitable trust which shall be created upon my death and which shall be known as the DORIS DUKE CHARITABLE FOUNDATION, and such separate wholly charitable trust shall be administered and distributed subject to the provisions of Article NINE for the purposes hereinafter set forth in Subdivisions A through J of Article EIGHT and Subdivision K of this Article. All references in this Will to the DORIS DUKE CHARITABLE FOUNDATION shall refer to such wholly charitable trust. In no event shall the wholly charitable trust which shall be known as the DORIS DUKE CHARITABLE FOUNDATION be confused with "The Doris Duke Foundation," which was incorporated in Delaware in 1934 and which was originally known as "Independent Aid, Inc." It is my intention that the Doris Duke Foundation receive no benefit from my estate under this Will or the exercise of any power of appointment under this Will.

4. I give and bequeath all of my clothing, jewelry and other personal effects located at my residence in Somerville, New Jersey at my death to the DORIS DUKE CHARITABLE FOUNDATION.

5. The Thai and Burmese objects of art located at my Somerville, New Jersey residence and the Thai houses that have been dismantled and that are presently stored on my Somerville, New Jersey property are owned by the FOUNDATION FOR SOUTHEAST ASIAN ART AND CULTURE. It is my hope and expectation that after my death, such property will either (i) be sold by the FOUNDATION FOR SOUTHEAST ASIAN ART AND CULTURE, with the proceeds thereof to be used for the general charitable purposes that I have supported or (ii) be returned to their respective countries of origin under appropriate conditions.

6. I give and bequeath all of my furniture, furnishings, books, linen, silver, china, glassware and other household effects, automobiles and all other similar tangible personal property of whatsoever description (hereinafter "Other Tangible Personal Property") located at my residence in Somerville, New Jersey at my death to

the DORIS DUKE CHARITABLE FOUNDATION, to be used at its principal headquarters.

B. I give, devise and bequeath my real property located in Montague City, New Jersey to the Morristown, New Jersey chapter of the NATURE CONSERVANCY INC., upon the conditions that such property be kept in its natural state and that such property be leased for One Dollar ($1.00) per year to the Trail Blazers Camp so long as such Camp shall be in existence and shall use such property for its campsite. If the NATURE CONSERVANCY INC. shall not agree to accept such property on these conditions or if the Trustees of the DORIS DUKE CHARITABLE FOUNDATION determine in their absolute discretion that either or both of such conditions shall have been violated at any time, I direct that such property shall be distributed to the DORIS DUKE CHARITABLE FOUNDATION, to be held by it upon the conditions set forth in the preceding sentence, or if that is not feasible for any reason, then for the general charitable purposes for which the DORIS DUKE CHARITABLE FOUNDATION is being administered.

C. I give, devise and bequeath my real property, known as the Quarry, in Whitehorse Station, New Jersey (approximately 3.83 acres) to the DORIS DUKE CHARITABLE FOUNDATION.

D. 1. I give, devise and bequeath all of my right, title and interest in and to my real property, and the structures and improvements thereon, known as Rough Point, in Newport, Rhode Island, to the NEWPORT RESTORATION FOUNDATION, which shall be charged with the responsibility and obligation of maintaining Rough Point in accordance with the usual standards for preserving historical properties located in Newport, Rhode Island. I direct that the first two (2) floors of the residence (together with the tangible personal property described in Paragraph 3 of this Subdivision D) be set aside for public viewing similar to the manner in which the other "summer cottages" are operated by the Preservation Society and that the top floor of the residence be used for the NEWPORT RESTORATION FOUNDATION's offices. (Accordingly, it is my expectation that the house at Two Marlborough Street owned by the NEWPORT RESTORATION FOUNDATION be used as a rental property since it will no longer be used as office space.) Funds to maintain Rough Point shall be provided by the DORIS DUKE CHARITABLE FOUNDATION as set forth in Article EIGHT hereof.

2. I give and bequeath all of my clothing, jewelry, and other personal effects located at my residence known as Rough Point, in Newport, Rhode Island at my death to the DORIS DUKE CHARITABLE FOUNDATION.

3. I give and bequeath all of my Other Tangible Personal Property (as hereinbefore defined) located at my residence known as Rough Point, in Newport, Rhode Island at my death to the NEWPORT RESTORATION FOUNDATION, to be set aside for public viewing as explained in Paragraph I of this Subdivision D.

E. I give, devise and bequeath such portion of my real property in Middletown, Rhode Island which is contiguous to the Prescott Farm Museum (approximately four (4) acres) to the NEWPORT RESTORATION FOUNDATION, to be used as a part of such Museum. I direct that the balance of my Middletown, Rhode Island property be sold and the net sales proceeds thereof be disposed of as a part of my residuary estate in accordance with the provisions of Article EIGHT hereof.

F. 1. I give, devise and bequeath all of my right, title and interest in and to my real property, and the structures and improvements located thereon, known as Shangri La, in Kaalawai, Honolulu, Hawaii to a new and separate wholly charitable trust which my Trustees hereinafter named shall create upon my death and which shall be known as the DORIS DUKE FOUNDATION FOR ISLAMIC ART, and such separate wholly charitable trust shall be held, administered and distributed subject to the provisions of Article NINE for the purposes hereinafter set forth in this Paragraph 1. All references in this Will to the DORIS DUKE FOUNDATION FOR ISLAMIC

ART shall refer to such wholly charitable trust. The DORIS DUKE FOUNDATION FOR ISLAMIC ART shall promote the study and understanding of Middle Eastern art and culture. I direct that the DORIS DUKE FOUNDATION FOR ISLAMIC ART make this property available to scholars, students and others interested in the furtherance and preservation of Islamic art and make the premises open to the public subject to the payment of a reasonable fee to be fixed by the Trustees of the DORIS DUKE FOUNDATION FOR ISLAMIC ART. In addition, I direct that the Honolulu Academy of Arts be permitted to use the premises for display of its collection of Middle Eastern art without any charge to the Academy. In the event that the funds derived from admission fees charged to the public are inadequate to staff and maintain properly the land, grounds, buildings, furniture, furnishings and art held by the DORIS DUKE FOUNDATION FOR ISLAMIC ART, supplemental funds for such purposes shall be provided by the DORIS DUKE CHARITABLE FOUNDATION as set forth in Article EIGHT hereof.

2. I give and bequeath all of my clothing, jewelry and other personal effects located at my residence known as Shangri La, in Kaalawai, Honolulu, Hawaii at my death to the DORIS DUKE CHARITABLE FOUNDATION.

3. I give and bequeath all of my other Tangible Personal Property located at my residence known as Shangri La, in Kaalawai, Honolulu, Hawaii at my death to the DORIS DUKE FOUNDATION FOR ISLAMIC ART.

G. 1. I give, devise and bequeath all of my right, title and interest in and to my real property, and the structures and improvements thereon, known as Falcon's Lair, in Beverly Hills, California to the DORIS DUKE CHARITABLE FOUNDATION.

2. I give and bequeath all of my clothing, jewelry, other personal effects and Other Tangible Personal Property located at my residence known as Falcon's Lair, in Beverly Hills, California at my death to the DORIS DUKE CHARITABLE FOUNDATION.

3. If I shall be survived by a dog owned by me and residing at my death at my residence known as Falcon's Lair, in Beverly Hills, California, I give such dog to the caretaker of such property at my death or, if such caretaker is at any time unwilling or unable to care for such dog, to one of the foundations created under this Will or of which I was a member, director, trustee or officer at my death which is caring for other dogs of mine. If I shall be survived by a dog owned by me and located at my death at Falcon's Lair, I give and bequeath the sum of One Hundred Thousand Dollars ($100,000) to my Trustees, to be held by them in a separate trust for the benefit of such dog, with the income and principal thereof to be disposed of as follows:

a. My Trustees, at any time and from time to time, shall apply such part or all or none of the net income and principal of the trust for the benefit of such dog, at such times and in such amounts as my Trustees, in their absolute discretion, shall deem necessary for the care, feeding, comfort, maintenance and medical treatment of such dog, even though any such application or applications may result in the termination of the trust. At the end of each year of the trust, my Trustees shall accumulate and add to principal any net income not so applied, any such capitalized income thereafter to be disposed of as a part of such principal.

b. Upon the earlier to occur of (i) the death of such dog and (ii) twenty-one (21) years after my death, the trust shall terminate. Upon such termination, the principal of the trust remaining at that time, and any accrued and undistributed income, shall be added to my residuary estate and disposed of in accordance with the provisions of Article EIGHT hereof.

H. 1. I give and bequeath all of my right, title and interest in and to my cooperative apartment, known as Penthouse B, located at 475 Park Avenue, New York, New York, including the proprietary lease and shares of stock relating thereto, to the DORIS DUKE CHARITABLE FOUNDATION.

2. I give and bequeath all of my clothing, jewelry, other personal effects and Other Tangible Personal Property located at my New York City cooperative apartment at my death to the DORIS DUKE CHARITABLE FOUNDATION.

I. To the extent, if any, that my Other Tangible Personal Property, as hereinbefore defined, or any of my clothing, jewelry, personal effects or real property shall not otherwise be effectively disposed of in the preceding provisions of this Article, I give and bequeath such property to the DORIS DUKE CHARITABLE FOUNDATION.

J. I give and bequeath my two (2) camels, two (2) horses and donkey to the DORIS DUKE FOUNDATION FOR THE PRESERVATION OF ENDANGERED WILDLIFE.

K. If, upon semi-annual investigation into the expenditures and needs of the NEWPORT GARDENS FOUNDATION, INC., the Trustees of the DORIS DUKE CHARITABLE FOUNDATION determine that the NEWPORT GARDENS FOUNDATION, INC. is operating at a deficit, and if they determine that the deficit is not created by substantial waste or mismanagement, they shall pay over to the NEWPORT GARDENS FOUNDATION, INC. from the DORIS DUKE CHARITABLE FOUNDATION sufficient monies to offset any justified operating deficit and in addition shall supply the NEWPORT GARDENS FOUNDATION, INC. with operating funds sufficient for a period not in excess of sixty (60) days from the date of payment if the NEWPORT GARDENS FOUNDATION, INC. is then a tax-exempt organization, as hereinafter defined. In the event that the NEWPORT GARDENS FOUNDATION, INC. reports that funds are required for capital improvements or major repairs, the Trustees of the DORIS DUKE CHARITABLE FOUNDATION shall retain the services of a qualified engineer and, to the extent that the engineer confirms the need for such funds, the Trustees of the DORIS DUKE CHARITABLE FOUNDATION shall pay over such funds to the NEWPORT GARDENS FOUNDATION, INC., which shall promptly render a full and complete accounting of the funds disbursed for such purposes.

L. Any expenses which may be incurred by my Executors in selling, storing, packing, shipping and insuring any of my tangible personal property, including any expenses which may be incurred in delivering such property to the designated beneficiary or beneficiaries thereof, shall be charged against the principal of my residuary estate and treated as an expense of administering my estate.

M. I direct that (i) my Executors, in their absolute discretion, shall be authorized to determine what property, if any, shall be disposed of under each provision of this Will, and (ii) all such determinations by my Executors shall be binding and conclusive upon all interested persons.

THREE: I direct that my Executors sell the airplane owned by Newport Farms, Inc., a New Jersey corporation of which I own one hundred percent (100%) of the stock, and then liquidate such corporation and add the net sales proceeds thereof to my residuary estate to be disposed of in accordance with the provisions of Article EIGHT hereof.

FOUR: A. The following loans were owed to me as of August, 1991:

1. DR. ROBERT NIXON: Fifty-Eight Thousand Dollars ($58,000).

2. ELEANOR LAWSON: Sixteen Thousand Five Hundred Dollars ($16,500).

3. FRANCO ROSSELLINI: One Hundred Fifty-Eight Thousand Dollars ($158,000).

4. VERA CYCKMAN: Ten Thousand Dollars ($10,000).

5. EDWARD LEIATO: Thirty Thousand Dollars ($30,000).

6. RAPHAEL RECTO: One Hundred Thousand Dollars ($100,000).

I direct that, to the extent that these loans shall be outstanding at the time of my death, such loans shall be forgiven.

B. I direct that my Executors make reasonable arrangements with IMELDA MARCOS (or the legal representatives of her estate, if she shall not survive me) for the repayment of the Five Million Dollars ($5,000,000), plus accrued interest, that I loaned to her pursuant to a demand note dated March 6, 1990, such repayment to be made when Mrs. Marcos and the Philippines government settle their financial dispute or at such other time as my Executors shall deem appropriate in their absolute discretion.

C. I have made a loan in the current principal amount of Six Hundred Thousand Dollars ($600,000), plus accruing interest, to HEALTH MAINTENANCE PROGRAMS, INC., which loan is convertible to common stock in such corporation. I direct my Executors to convert such loan (as the same shall be outstanding at my death) into common stock and to add such stock to my residuary estate to be disposed of in accordance with the provisions of Article EIGHT hereof.

D. I direct my Executors not to seek a refund for the relinquishment of my memberships at the Newport Country Club and the Spouting Rock Beach Association.

FIVE: A. I give and bequeath the following sums to the following organizations:

1. Ten Million Dollars ($10,000,000) to DUKE UNIVERSITY, Durham, North Carolina.

2. Five Hundred Thousand Dollars ($500,000) to the SELF-REALIZATION FELLOWSHIP, Los Angeles, California.

3. Ten Million Dollars ($ 10,000,000) to the METROPOLITAN MUSEUM OF ART, New York, New York.

4. One Million Dollars ($1,000,000) to the NEW YORK ZOOLOGICAL PARK operated by the New York Zoological Society, Bronx, New York.

B. I give and bequeath the following sums to such of the following persons as shall survive me:

1. Three Million Dollars ($3,000,000) to ELEANOR JOHNSON LAWSON.

2. One Million Dollars ($1,000,000) to DOROTHY MCCAWLEY.

3. One Million Dollars ($1,000,000) to ROSEANNA TODD.

4. Five Hundred Thousand Dollars ($500,000) to ANNA LUNDY LEWIS.

5. One Million Dollars ($1,000,000) to REVEREND LAWRENCE ROBERTS, in his individual capacity, whether or not he is, at the date of my death, affiliated with the First Baptist Church of Nutley, New Jersey.

6. Five Hundred Thousand Dollars ($500,000) to CONSTANCE PITTS SPEED.

7. Two Hundred Thousand Dollars ($200,000) to JOHN GOMEZ.

8. One Million Dollars ($1,000,000) to ANNA KENNESAY.

C. 1. The bequests to my employees under this Subdivision C are in gratitude for their past services rendered to me and my foundations. It is my hope and expectation that my Executors and Trustees and the foundations in which I am a member, director, trustee or officer at my death or which are to be created under this Will shall employ as many of these persons as reasonably possible in order to maintain my various properties and to operate these foundations after my death. The determination of my Executors as to the persons to receive a bequest under this Subdivision C and the amount of each such bequest shall be binding and conclusive on all interested persons.

2. If BERNARD LAFFERTY shall survive me and shall at my death be in my employ or in the employ of The Doris Duke Foundation, the Foundation for Southeast Asian Art and Culture, the Duke Gardens Foundation, Inc., the Newport Restoration Foundation (such foundations being hereinafter collectively referred to as the "Applicable Foundations") or of any other foundation of which I am a member, director, trustee or officer at my death, I give and bequeath to my Trustees the sum of Ten Million Dollars ($10,000,000). Such sum shall be held by my Trustees in a separate charitable remainder annuity trust, with the income and principal thereof to be disposed of in accordance with the provisions of Paragraph 6 of this Subdivision C.

3. If NUKU MAKASIALE shall survive me and shall at my death be in my employ or in the employ of any of the Applicable Foundations or of any other foundation of which I am a member, director, trustee or officer at my death, I give and bequeath to my Trustees a sum which my Executors, in their absolute discretion, determine shall be necessary, assuming that such sum will generate interest at a rate of five percent (5%) per annum, to produce income on an annual basis which shall equal the sum of (i) the annual salary that NUKU MAKASIALE received from me or such foundation, as the case may be, for the twelve (12) month period immediately preceding my death plus (ii) Fifty-Eight Thousand Dollars ($58,000). Such sum shall be held by my Trustees in a separate charitable remainder annuity trust, with the income and principal of such trust to be disposed of in accordance with the provisions of Paragraph 6 of this Subdivision C.

4. If JINADASA DESILVA shall survive me and shall at my death be in my employ or in the employ of any of the Applicable Foundations or of any other foundation of which I am a member, director, trustee or officer at my death, I give and bequeath to my Trustees a sum which my Executors, in their absolute discretion, determine shall be necessary, assuming that such sum will generate interest at a rate of five percent (5%) per annum, to produce income on an annual basis which shall equal the sum of (i) the annual salary that JINADASA DESILVA received from me or such foundation, as the case may be, for the twelve (12) month period immediately preceding my death plus (ii) Eighteen Thousand Dollars ($18,000). Such sum shall be held by my Trustees in a separate charitable remainder annuity trust, with the income and principal of such trust to be disposed of in accordance with the provisions of Paragraph 6 of this Subdivision C.

5. With respect to each of NILZA MOORE, SHIZUE HAMAMOTO, GEORGE REED and BENJAMIN REED who shall survive me and shall at my death be in my employ or in the employ of any of the Applicable Foundations or of any other foundation of which I am a member, director, trustee or officer at my death, I give and bequeath to my Trustees a sum which my Executors, in their absolute discretion, determine shall be necessary, assuming that such sum will generate interest at a rate of five percent (5%) per

annum, to produce income on an annual basis which shall equal such person's annual salary from me or such foundation, as the case may be, for the twelve (12) month period immediately preceding my death. With respect to each such person, such sum shall be held by my Trustees in a separate charitable remainder annuity trust, with the income and principal of each such trust to be disposed of in accordance with the provisions of Paragraph 6 of this Subdivision C.

6. Pursuant to the foregoing provisions of this Subdivision C, certain property is to be held by my Trustees in a separate charitable remainder annuity trust for the benefit of a certain person. I direct that the income and principal of each such trust shall be disposed of as follows:

a. Commencing as of the date of my death and continuing during the lifetime of the person for whose benefit the trust has been established (the "Beneficiary"), my Trustees shall, in each taxable year of the trust, pay to the Beneficiary an annuity amount equal to five percent (5%) of the initial net fair market value of the property which constitutes the principal of the trust (the "Annuity Amount"), provided, however, that the payout percentage (as adjusted to reflect the time and frequency of the annuity payments) shall not exceed the percentage that would result in a five percent (5%) probability that the principal of the trust shall be exhausted before the death of the Beneficiary, determined as of the date of my death (or the alternate valuation date, if applicable).

b. Upon the death of the Beneficiary, the principal and income of the trust remaining at that time, other than any such principal and income which may be required to be distributed to the Beneficiary or the Beneficiary's estate in satisfaction of the final Annuity Amount payment, shall be distributed outright to the DORIS DUKE CHARITABLE FOUNDATION. If the DORIS DUKE CHARITABLE FOUNDATION is not a tax-exempt organization, as hereinafter defined, at the time when any principal or income of the trust is to be distributed to it, then my Trustees shall distribute such principal and income to such one or more tax-exempt organizations as my Trustees shall determine in their absolute discretion.

c. The trusts held pursuant to this Paragraph 6 of Subdivision C shall be administered in accordance with the provisions of Subdivision D of this Article.

7. I give and bequeath to each other person who shall survive me and who my Executors shall determine in their absolute discretion shall be on my payroll or the payroll of any of the Applicable Foundations or of any other foundation of which I am a member, director, trustee or officer at my death on a salaried (but not an hourly) basis, other than a person who is a beneficiary under another provision of this Will, a sum equal to one (1) month's salary for each full year of such employment prior to my death (rounded to the nearest Five Hundred Dollars ($500)), but in no case less than One Thousand Five Hundred Dollars ($1,500).

8. I give and bequeath to each other person who shall survive me and who my Executors shall determine in their absolute discretion shall be on my payroll or the payroll of any of the Applicable Foundations or of any other foundation of which I am a member, director, trustee or officer at my death on an hourly basis, other than a person who is a beneficiary under another provision of this Will, a sum equal to one (1) month's salary for each full year of such employment prior to my death (rounded to the nearest Five Hundred Dollars ($500)), but in no case less than One Thousand Five Hundred Dollars ($1,500). For purposes of this Paragraph 8, one month's salary shall be deemed to equal one-twelfth (1/12) of the income such person received from me or such foundation, as the case may be, in the year prior to my death based on such person's Form W-2 for such year.

9. Notwithstanding anything herein which might suggest a contrary result, I hereby specifically state that I do not intend by the provisions of Paragraph 7 or 8 of this Subdivision C to make any gift or bequest to any person or entity that I, any of the Applicable Foundations or any other foundation retain as an independent contractor to perform services, including lawyers, accountants, physicians, nurses and others who are not my employees, the employees of an Applicable Foundation or the employees of any other foundation of which I am a member, director, trustee or officer at my death.

10. I request that each of NILZA MOORE, GEORGE REED and BENJAMIN REED who are at my death in the employ of any of the Applicable Foundations or of any other foundation of which I am a member, director, trustee or officer at my death have a residence provided for them by one of such foundations after my death. If possible, I expect that the DORIS DUKE CHARITABLE FOUNDATION shall provide such a residence for each of NILZA MOORE and GEORGE REED and that the NEWPORT RESTORATION FOUNDATION shall provide such a residence for BENJAMIN REED.

Last Will and Testament of Jacqueline K. Onassis

I, JACQUELINE K. ONASSIS, of the City, County and State of New York, do make, publish and declare this to be my Last Will and Testament, hereby revoking all wills and codicils at any time heretofore made by me.

FIRST: A. I give and bequeath to my friend RACHEL (BUNNY) L. MELLON, if she survives me, in appreciation of her designing the Rose Garden in the White House my Indian miniature "Lovers watching rain clouds," Kangra, about 1780, if owned by me at the time of my death, and my large Indian miniature with giltwood frame "Gardens of the Palace of the Rajh," a panoramic view of a pink walled garden blooming with orange flowers, with the Rajh being entertained in a pavilion by musicians and dancers, if owned by me at the time of my death.

B. I give and bequeath to my friend MAURICE TEMPELSMAN, if he survives me, my Greek alabaster head of a woman if owned by me at the time of my death.

C. I give and bequeath to my friend ALEXANDER D. FORGER, if he survives me, my copy of John F. Kennedy's Inaugural Address signed by Robert Frost if owned by me at the time of my death.

D. Except as hereinabove otherwise effectively bequeathed, I give and bequeath all my tangible personal property, including, without limitation, my collection of letters, papers and documents, my personal effects, my furniture, furnishings, rugs, pictures, books, silver, plate, linen, china, glassware, objects of art, wearing apparel, jewelry, automobiles and their accessories, and all other household goods owned by me at the time of my death to my children who survive me, to be divided between them by my Executors, in the exercise of sole and absolute discretion, in as nearly equal portions as may be practicable, having due regard for the personal preferences of my children.

I authorize and empower my children, within a period of nine (9) months from the date of my death, to renounce and disclaim all interest in any part or all of the tangible personal property bequeathed to them pursuant to this Paragraph D of Article FIRST. Any such disclaimer shall be by instrument in writing, duly executed and filed in the court in which this Will has been admitted to original probate.

E. Any interests in my tangible personal property which are disclaimed by my children shall be disposed of as follows:

1. I give and bequeath such items of said tangible personal property and interests therein which relate to the life and work of my late husband, John F. Kennedy, to JOHN FITZGERALD KENNEDY LIBRARY INCORPORATED, Boston, Massachusetts, or if said library shall not be a qualified charitable beneficiary, as defined in Paragraph A of Article SECOND hereof, at the time of my death, to such one or more qualified charitable beneficiaries with similar purposes as my Executors, in the exercise of sole and absolute discretion, shall select.

2. I direct that the balance of said tangible personal property shall be sold and the net proceeds of sale shall be added to my residuary estate, thereafter to be held, administered and disposed of as a part thereof.

F. I give and bequeath all copyright interests owned by me at the time of my death in my personal papers, letters or other writings by me, including any royalty or other rights with respect thereto, to my children who survive me, in equal shares. I request, but do not direct, my children to respect my wish for privacy with respect to such papers, letters and writings and, consistent with that wish, to take whatever action is warranted to prevent the display, publication or distribution, in whole or in part, of these papers, letters and writings.

SECOND: A. I have made no provision in this my Will for my sister, Lee B. Radziwill, for whom I have great affection because I have already done so during my lifetime. I do wish, however, to remember her children and, thus, I direct my Executors to set aside the amount of Five Hundred Thousand Dollars ($500,000) for each child surviving me of my sister, Lee B. Radziwill, and I give and bequeath the sum so set aside to the Trustees hereinafter named, IN TRUST, NEVERTHELESS, to hold the same, and to manage, invest and reinvest the same, to collect the income thereof and to dispose of the net income and principal for the following uses and purposes and subject to the following terms and conditions:

1. Payment of Annuity Amount. The Trustees shall hold and manage the trust property for a term (the "trust term") which shall commence with the date of my death and shall end on the tenth (10th) anniversary thereof. At the end of each taxable year of the trust during the trust term (other than any short taxable year thereof for which specific provisions are hereinafter made), the Trustees shall pay over to such organization or organizations, to be selected by the Trustees, in the exercise of sole and absolute discretion, and only to such organization or organizations as are described in and satisfy the requirements of both of sections 170(c) and 2055(a) of the Internal Revenue Code of 1986, as amended (hereinafter sometimes referred to as the "Code"), at the time any such payment or payments to such organization or organizations are made (such organization or organizations shall herein be referred to collectively as the "qualified charitable beneficiaries") in such amounts or proportions, equal or unequal, as the Trustees, in the exercise of sole and absolute discretion, shall determine, such amount or amounts as shall, in the aggregate, equal ten percent (10%) of the initial net fair market value of the trust assets as finally determined for federal estate tax purposes. Such aggregate amount shall hereinafter be referred to as the "annuity amount."

The annuity amount shall be paid first from the ordinary taxable income of the trust (including short term capital gains) which is not unrelated business income and, to the extent not so satisfied, the annuity amount shall be paid from the long term capital gains, the unrelated business income, the tax exempt income and finally out of the principal of the trust, in that order. In any taxable year of the trust in which the net income exceeds the annuity amount, the excess, at the end of such taxable year, shall be added to trust principal and thereafter shall be held, administered and disposed of as a part thereof. Should the initial net fair market value of the assets comprising the trust, and hence the annuity amount, be incorrectly determined, then within a reasonable period after the value of such assets is finally determined for federal tax purposes, the Trustees shall pay over to the qualified charitable beneficiaries, in the case of an undervaluation, or, in the case of an overvaluation, shall receive from such beneficiaries to which amounts from the trust were paid, in proportion to the payments made to each, an aggregate amount equal to the difference between the annuity amount properly payable and the annuity amount actually paid during such taxable year.

2. Distribution at End of Trust Term. Upon the expiration of the trust term, the trust created under this Paragraph A shall terminate, and the Trustees shall thereupon transfer, convey and pay over the trust assets, as they are then constituted (other than any amount due to the qualified charitable beneficiaries), to the then living descendants of my sister, Lee B. Radziwill, per stirpes.

3. Proration of Annuity Amount. To determine the proper aggregate amount payable from the trust to the qualified charitable beneficiaries in any short taxable year of the trust's existence, the Trustees shall

prorate the annuity amount, on a daily basis, in accordance with the applicable provisions of Treas. Dept. Reg. § 1.664-2.

4. Deferral Provision. The obligation to pay the annuity amount to the qualified charitable beneficiaries shall commence with the date of my death, but payment of the annuity amount may be deferred from the date of my death until the end of the taxable year of the trust in which occurs the complete funding of the trust. Within a reasonable time after the end of the taxable year in which complete funding of the trust occurs, the Trustees shall pay to the qualified charitable beneficiaries, in the case of an underpayment, or shall receive from the qualified charitable beneficiaries, in the case of an overpayment, in proportion to the payments made to each, the difference between: (1) any annuity amounts actually paid, plus interest, compounded annually, computed for any period at the rate of interest that the Treasury Regulations under section 664 of the Code prescribe for the trust for such computation for such period, and (2) the annuity amounts properly payable, plus interest, compounded annually, computed for any period at the rate of interest that the Treasury Regulations under section 664 of the Code prescribe for the trust for such computation for such period.

5. Additional Contributions. No additional contribution shall be made to the trust after the initial contribution which shall consist of all property passing to the trust by reason of my death.

6. Prohibited Transactions. Notwithstanding any other provision in this my Will, during the trust term, the Trustees are expressly prohibited (a) from engaging in any act of self-dealing as defined in section 4941(d) of the Code, (b) from retaining any excess business holdings as defined in section 4943(c) of the Code which would subject the trust to tax under section 4943 of the Code, (c) from making any investments which would subject the trust to tax under section 4944 of the Code, and (d) from making any taxable expenditures as defined in section 4945(d) of the Code. The Trustees shall make distributions at such time and in such manner as not to subject the trust to tax under section 4942 of said Code.

7. Taxable Year; Code References. As used in this Paragraph A, the term "taxable year" of the trust shall mean the calendar year and the term "initial net fair market value" of the trust assets shall mean the initial net fair market value of those assets as the term is used in section 664(d)(1) of the Code. All references to sections of the Code and the regulations and rulings issued thereunder in this Paragraph A shall be deemed to include future amendments to such sections, regulations and rulings as well as corresponding provisions of future Internal Revenue laws, regulations, and rulings.

8. Intention. It is my intention to insure that the interest committed to the qualified charitable beneficiaries by this Paragraph A shall be deductible for income and estate tax purposes under the provisions of the Code. Further, I intend that payments of gross income made by the Trustees to qualified charitable beneficiaries qualify as income tax charitable deductions. Accordingly, I direct that all provisions of this Paragraph A and this my Will shall be construed to effectuate this intention, that all provisions of this Paragraph A and this my Will shall be construed, and the trust be administered, solely in a manner consistent with sections 170(c), 642(c), and 2055 of the Code, and with regulations and rulings which may be promulgated from time to time with respect to trusts creating charitable interests, that none of the powers granted to the Trustees by this my Will shall be exercised in a manner as to disqualify the trust for such deductions, and specifically, but without limiting the foregoing, that nothing in this my Will shall be construed to restrict the Trustees from investing the trust assets in a manner which could result in the annual realization of a reasonable amount of income or gain from the sale or disposition of trust assets. I hereby grant to my Executors and the Trustees all the administrative powers necessary to act in compliance with the requirements of the Code, as in effect at the time of my death and from time to time thereafter, so as to qualify the interest committed to the qualified charitable beneficiaries hereunder for the estate and income tax charitable deductions. Should any provisions of this my Will be inconsistent or in conflict with

the sections of the Code and the regulations and rulings governing charitable lead trusts as in effect from time to time, then such sections, regulations and rulings shall be deemed to override and supersede such inconsistent or conflicting provisions. If such sections, regulations and rulings at any time require that instruments creating charitable lead trusts contain provisions which are not expressly set forth in this my Will, then such provisions shall be incorporated herein by reference and shall be deemed to be a part of this my Will to the same extent as though they had been expressly set forth herein.

9. Trustees' Limited Power of Amendment. The Trustees shall have the power, acting alone, to amend the provisions governing this trust contained in this my Will in any manner required for the sole purpose of ensuring that the trust qualifies and continues to qualify as a charitable lead annuity trust.

B. I give and bequeath the amount of Two Hundred and Fifty Thousand Dollars ($250,000) to each child of mine who survives me.

C. I give and bequeath to NANCY L. TUCKER-MAN, if she survives me, the amount of Two Hundred and Fifty Thousand Dollars ($250,000).

D. I give and bequeath to MARTA SQUBIN, if she survives me, the amount of One Hundred and Twenty-Five Thousand Dollars ($125,000).

E. I give and bequeath to my niece ALEXANDRA RUTHERFURD, if she survives me, the amount of One Hundred Thousand Dollars ($100,000).

F. I give and bequeath to PROVIDENCIA PARE-DES, if she survives me, the amount of Fifty Thousand Dollars ($50,000).

G. I give and bequeath to LEE NASSO, if she survives me, the amount of Twenty-Five Thousand Dollars ($25,000).

H. I give and bequeath to MARIE AMARAL, if she survives me, the amount of Twenty-Five Thousand Dollars ($25,000).

I. I give and bequeath to EFIGENIO PIN-HEIRO, if he survives me, the amount of Twenty-Five Thousand Dollars ($25,000).

THIRD: A. I give and devise any and all interest owned by me at the time of my death in the real property located in the City of Newport, State of Rhode Island, which I inherited from my mother, Janet Lee Auchincloss, and which is known as "Hammersmith Farm," including all buildings thereon and all rights and easements appurtenant thereto and all policies of insurance relating thereto, to HUGH D. AUCHIN-CLOSS, JR., if he survives me, or, if he does not survive me, to his children who survive me, in equal shares as tenants-in-common.

B. I give and devise all real property owned by me at the time of my death and located in the Towns of Gay Head and Chilmark, Martha's Vineyard, Massachusetts, including all buildings thereon and all rights and easements appurtenant thereto and all policies of insurance relating thereto, to my children who survive me, in equal shares as tenants-in-common, or, if only one of my children survive me, to such survivor, or, if none of my children survive me, I authorize, but do not direct, my Executors to sell such real property and I direct that the net proceeds of sale together with any such real property not so sold be added to my residuary estate to be held, administered and disposed of as a part thereof.

I authorize and empower my children, within a period of nine (9) months from the date of my death, to renounce and disclaim all interest in any part or all of said real property devised to them pursuant to this Paragraph B of Article THIRD. Any such disclaimer shall be by instrument in writing, duly executed and filed in the court in which this Will has been admitted to original probate.

I direct that any such interest in my real property in Martha's Vineyard, Massachusetts which is disclaimed by my children shall be sold, and the net proceeds of sale shall be added to my residuary estate, thereafter to be held, administered and disposed of as a part thereof.

C. Except as hereinbefore otherwise effectively devised, I give and devise all real property owned by me at the time of my death, including all buildings thereon and all rights and easements appurtenant thereto and all policies of insurance relating thereto, to my children who survive me, in equal shares as tenants-in-common, or, if only one of my children survive me, to such survivor, or, if none of my children survive me, I authorize, but do not direct, my Executors to sell any such real property and I direct that the net proceeds of sale together with any such property not so sold be added to my residuary estate and thereafter held, administered and disposed of as a part thereof.

I authorize and empower my children, within a period of nine (9) months from the date of my death, to renounce and disclaim all interest in any part of all of said real property devised to them pursuant to this Paragraph C of Article THIRD. Any such disclaimer shall be by instrument in writing, duly executed and filed in the court in which this Will has been admitted to original probate.

I direct that any such interest in my real property which is disclaimed by my children shall be sold, and the net proceeds of sale shall be added to my residuary estate, thereafter to be held, administered and disposed of as a part thereof.

D. I give, devise and bequeath all stock owned by me at the time of my death in any corporation which is the owner of any building in which I have a cooperative apartment, together with any lease to such apartment and all right, title and interest owned by me at the time of my death in and to any agreements relating to said building and the real property on which it is located, to my children who survive me, in equal shares as tenants in common, or, if only one of my children survive me, to such survivor, or, if none of my children survive me, I authorize, but do not direct, my Executors to sell any such stock and I direct that the net proceeds of sale together with any such stock not so sold be added to my residuary estate and thereafter held, administered and disposed of as a part thereof.

I authorize and empower my children, within a period of nine (9) months from the date of my death, to renounce and disclaim all interest in any part or all of said stock devised to them pursuant to this Paragraph D of Article THIRD. Any such disclaimer shall be by instrument in writing, duly executed and filed in the court in which this Will has been admitted to original probate.

I direct that any such interest in said stock which is disclaimed by my children shall be sold, and the net proceeds of sale shall be added to my residuary estate, thereafter to be held, administered and disposed of as a part thereof.

FOURTH: Under the Will of my late husband, John Fitzgerald Kennedy, a marital deduction trust was created for my benefit over which I was accorded a general power of appointment. I hereby exercise such power of appointment and direct that, upon my death, all property subject to such power be transferred, conveyed and paid over to my descendants who survive me, per stirpes.

FIFTH: All the rest, residue and remainder of my property and estate, both real and personal, of whatsoever kind and wheresoever situated, of which I shall die seized or possessed or of which I shall be entitled to dispose at the time of my death (my "residuary estate"), after the payment therefrom of the taxes directed in Article NINTH hereof to be paid from my residuary estate (my "net residuary estate"), I give, devise and bequeath to the Trustees hereinafter named, IN TRUST, NEVERTHELESS, to hold as THE C & J FOUNDATION (sometimes hereinafter referred to as the "Foundation") and to manage, invest and reinvest the same, to collect the income thereof and to dispose of the net income and principal thereof for the following uses and purposes subject to the following terms and conditions:

A. 1. Payment of Annuity Amount. The Trustees shall hold and manage the Foundation property for a primary term which shall commence with the date of my death and shall end on the 24th anniversary thereof. [In no event, however, shall the Foundation's primary term extend beyond a period of twenty-one (21) years after the death of the last to die of those descendants of my former father-in-law Joseph P. Kennedy who were in being at the time of my death.] At the end of each taxable year of the Foundation during the primary term (other than any short taxable year thereof for which specific provisions are hereinafter made), the independent Trustees (i.e., the Trustees of the Foundation other than any Trustee who has disclaimed any property of my Estate which becomes a part of the Foundation) shall pay over to such organization or organizations, to be selected by the independent Trustees, in the exercise of sole and absolute discretion, and only to such organization or organizations as are described in and satisfy the requirements of both of sections 170(c) and 2055(a) of the Code, at the time any such payment or payments to such organization or organizations are made (such organization or organizations shall herein be referred to collectively as the "qualified charitable beneficiaries") in such amounts or proportions, equal or unequal, as the independent Trustees, in the exercise of sole and absolute discretion, shall determine, such amount or amounts as shall, in the aggregate, equal eight percent (8%) of the initial net fair market value of the assets of the Foundation as finally determined for federal estate tax purposes. Such aggregate amount shall hereinafter be referred to as the "annuity amount."

The annuity amount shall be paid first from the ordinary taxable income of the foundation (including short term capital gains) which is not unrelated business income and, to the extent not so satisfied, the annuity amount shall be paid from the long term capital gains, the unrelated business income, the tax exempt income and finally out of the principal of the trust, in that order. In any taxable year of the Foundation in which the net income exceeds the annuity amount, the excess, at the end of such taxable year, shall be added to the principal of the Foundation and thereafter shall be held, administered and disposed of as a part thereof. Should the initial net fair market value of the assets comprising the Foundation, and hence the annuity amount, be incorrectly determined, then within a reasonable period after the value of such assets is finally determined for federal tax purposes, the Trustees shall pay over to the qualified charitable beneficiaries, in the case of an undervaluation, or, in the case of an overvaluation, shall receive from such beneficiaries to which amounts from the Foundation were paid, in proportion to the payments made to each, an aggregate amount equal to the difference between the annuity amount properly payable and the annuity amount actually paid during such taxable year.

I have accorded the independent Trustees sole and absolute discretion in selecting the qualified charitable beneficiaries to receive all or any portion of the annuity amount referred to in this Paragraph A of Article FIFTH, stipulating only that at the time any payment from the Foundation is made to a qualified charitable beneficiary so selected it be an organization described in sections 170(c) and 2055(a) of the Code. It is my wish, however, that in selecting the particular qualified charitable beneficiaries which shall be the recipients of benefits from the Foundation the independent Trustees give preferential consideration to such eligible organization or organizations the purposes and endeavors of which the independent Trustees feel are committed to making a significant difference in the cultural or social betterment of mankind or the relief of human suffering. To assist the independent Trustees I authorize, but do not direct, that they retain my close friend and confidante Nancy L. Tuckerman to assist them in the administration of the Foundation. Should the independent Trustees deem it advisable to retain Nancy L. Tuckerman, they shall pay to her from the assets of the Foundation reasonable compensation for the services she shall render. But such compensation shall not be charged against the annuity amount in any full taxable year of the Foundation nor against the appropriate fraction of said amount, determined as herein provided, payable to the qualified charitable beneficiaries in any short taxable year of the Foundation but shall rather be paid from the assets of the Foundation at large.

2. Proration of the Annuity Amount. To determine the proper aggregate amount payable from the Foundation to the qualified charitable beneficiaries in any short taxable year of the Foundation's existence, the independent Trustees shall prorate the annuity amount, on a daily basis, in accordance with the applicable provisions of Treas. Dept. Reg. § 1.664-2.

3. Deferral Provision. The obligation to pay the annuity amount to the qualified charitable beneficiaries shall commence with the date of my death, but payment of the annuity amount may be deferred from the date of my death until the end of the taxable year of the Foundation in which occurs the complete funding of the Foundation. Within a reasonable time after the end of the taxable year in which complete funding of the Foundation occurs, the independent Trustees shall pay to the qualified charitable beneficiaries, in the case of an underpayment, or shall receive from the

qualified charitable beneficiaries, in the case of an overpayment, in proportion to the payments made to each, the difference between (1) any annuity amounts actually paid, plus interest, compounded annually, computed for any period at the rate of interest that the Treasury Regulations under section 664 of the Code prescribe for the Foundation for such computation during such period, and (2) the annuity amounts properly payable, plus interest, compounded annually, computed for any period at the rate of interest that the Treasury Regulations under section 664 of the Code prescribe for the Foundation for such computation during such period.

4. Additional Contributions. No additional contributions shall be made to the Foundation after the initial contribution which shall consist of all property passing to the Foundation by reason of my death.

5. Prohibited Transactions. Notwithstanding any other provision in this my Will, during the primary term, the Trustees are expressly prohibited (a) from engaging in any act of self-dealing as defined in section 4941(d) of the Code, (b) from retaining any excess business holdings as defined in section 4943(c) of the Code which would subject the Foundation to tax under section 4943 of the Code, (c) from making any investments which would subject the Foundation to tax under section 4944 of the Code, and (d) from making any taxable expenditures as defined in section 4945(d) of the Code. The Trustees shall make distributions at such time and in such manner as not to subject the Foundation to tax under section 4942 of the Code.

6. Taxable Year; Code References. As used in this Paragraph A, the term "taxable year" of the Foundation shall mean the calendar year and the term "initial net fair market value" of the assets of the Foundation shall mean the initial net fair market value of those assets as the term is used in section 664(d)(1) of the Code. All references to sections of the Code and the regulations and rulings issued thereunder in this Paragraph A shall be deemed to include future amendments to such sections, regulations and rulings as well as corresponding provisions of future Internal Revenue laws, regulations and rulings.

7. Intention. It is my intention to insure that the interest committed to the qualified charitable beneficiaries by this Paragraph A shall be deductible for income and estate tax purposes under the provisions of the Code. Further, I intend that payments of gross income made by the independent Trustees to qualified charitable beneficiaries qualify as income tax charitable deductions. Accordingly, I direct that all provisions of this Paragraph A and this my Will shall be construed to effectuate this intention, that all provisions of this Paragraph A and this my Will shall be construed, and the Foundation be administered, solely in a manner consistent with sections 170(c), 642(c), and 2055 of the Code, and with regulations and rulings which may be promulgated from time to time with respect to trusts creating charitable interests, that none of the powers granted to the Trustees by this my Will shall be exercised in a manner as to disqualify the Foundation for such deductions, and specifically, but without limiting the foregoing, that nothing in this my Will shall be construed to restrict the Trustees from investing the assets of the Foundation in a manner which could result in the annual realization of a reasonable amount of income or gain from the sale or disposition of the assets of the Foundation. I hereby grant to my Executors and the Trustees all the administrative powers necessary to act in compliance with the requirements of the Code, as in effect at the time of my death and from time to time thereafter, so as to qualify the interest committed to the qualified charitable beneficiaries hereunder for the estate and income tax charitable deductions. Should any provisions of this my Will be inconsistent or in conflict with the sections of the Code and the regulations and rulings governing charitable lead trusts as in effect from time to time, then such sections, regulations and rulings shall be deemed to override and supersede such inconsistent or conflicting provisions. If such sections, regulations and rulings at any time require that instruments creating charitable lead trusts contain provisions which are not expressly set forth in this my Will, then such provisions shall be incorporated herein by reference and shall be deemed to be a part of this my Will to the same extent as though they had been expressly set forth herein.

8. Trustees' Limited Power of Amendment. The Trustees shall have the power, acting alone, to amend the provisions governing this Foundation contained in this my Will in any manner required for the sole purpose of ensuring that the Foundation qualifies and continues to qualify as a charitable lead annuity trust.

B. Upon the expiration of the Foundation's primary term the assets of the Foundation (other than any amount due to the qualified charitable beneficiaries) shall be disposed of in the following manner:

1. If no descendant of any child of mine is then living, the assets of the Foundation shall be transferred, conveyed and paid over as follows: (a) one-half (?) thereof (or the entire amount thereof if neither my sister, Lee B. Radziwill, nor any descendant of hers is then living) to the then living descendants of my cousin Michel Bouvier, per stirpes; and (b) the other one-half (?) thereof (or the entire amount thereof if no descendant of my cousin Michel Bouvier is then living) to the then living descendants of my sister, Lee B. Radziwill, per stirpes, or, if no such descendant of hers is then living, to my said sister, if she shall then be living.

2. If one or more descendants of any child of mine is then living but no such descendant was in being at the time of my death, the assets of the Foundation shall be transferred, conveyed and paid over as follows: (a) one-half (?) thereof (or the entire amount if no descendant of my son, John F. Kennedy, Jr., is then living) to then then living descendants of my daughter, Caroline B. Kennedy, per stirpes; and (b) one-half (?) thereof (or the entire amount if no descendant of my daughter, Caroline B. Kennedy, is then living) to the then living descendants of my son, John F. Kennedy, Jr., per stirpes.

3. If any descendant of any child of mine is then living and if at least one of those then living descendants was in being at the time of my death, the assets of the Foundation shall be divided into a sufficient number of equal shares so that there shall be set aside one (1) such share for the collective descendants who are then living of my daughter, Caroline B. Kennedy, if any such descendant is then living, and one (1) such share for the collective descendants who are then living of my son, John F. Kennedy, Jr., if any such

descendant is then living, such shares to be disposed of as follows: Each such share shall be transferred, conveyed and paid over to the Trustees hereinafter named to be held in separate trust for a secondary trust term for the benefit of the descendants living from time to time of the child of mine for whose benefit the share has been set aside (such descendants shall hereinafter be referred to as the "beneficiaries"). The secondary term for any particular trust created hereunder shall terminate upon the death of the last to die of the beneficiaries, except that the secondary terms of all trusts created pursuant to this paragraph 3 shall in all events terminate simultaneously no later than twenty-one (21) years after the death of the last to die of the descendants of my former father-in-law Joseph P. Kennedy who were in being at the time of my death. The Trustees shall manage, invest and reinvest the principal of each trust created hereunder, shall collect the income thereof and shall pay over or apply the net income, to such extent and at such time or times as the independent Trustees (i.e., the Trustees of each particular trust created hereunder other than any Trustee who is also a beneficiary of that trust or of any other trust hereunder and other than any Trustee who has disclaimed any property of my Estate which becomes a part of this trust), in the exercise of sole and absolute discretion, deem advisable, to or for the use of such one or more of the beneficiaries, as the independent Trustees, in the exercise of sole and absolute discretion, determine. Any net income not so paid over or applied shall be accumulated and added to the principal of the trust at least annually and thereafter shall be held, administered and disposed of as a part thereof. I authorize and empower the independent Trustees of each trust created hereunder at any time and from time to time to pay over to any one or more of the beneficiaries, or to apply for his, her or their benefit, out of the principal of such trust, such amount or amounts, including the whole thereof, as the independent Trustees, in the exercise of sole and absolute discretion, deem advisable. Each trust established under this subparagraph 3 shall terminate upon the death of the last to die of the beneficiaries thereof, and, notwithstanding the foregoing, each trust established under this subparagraph 3 shall terminate no later than twenty-one (21) years after the death of the last to die of the descendants of my former father-in-law Joseph P. Kennedy who were in being at the time of my death.

The principal of any trust created hereunder which has terminated by reason of the death of the last to die of the beneficiaries thereof, as such principal is the constituted, shall be transferred, conveyed and paid over to the Trustees of the other trust or trusts created hereunder, if any such trust is still in existence, to be held, administered and disposed of as a part thereof. If no other trust created hereunder is then in existence upon the occurrence of such termination, the principal of the last trust created hereunder to terminate, as then constituted, shall be transferred, conveyed and paid over as follows:

(a) If any descendant of any child of mine is then living, (i) one-half (?) thereof (or the entire amount if no descendant of my son, John F. Kennedy, Jr., is then living) to the then living descendants of my daughter, Caroline B. Kennedy, per stirpes; and (ii) one-half (?) thereof (or the entire amount if no descendant of my daughter, Caroline B. Kennedy, is then living) to the then living descendants of my son, John F. Kennedy, Jr., per stirpes.

(b) If no descendant of any child of mine is then living, (i) one-half (?) thereof (or the entire amount thereof if neither my sister, Lee B. Radziwill, nor any descendant of hers is then living) to the then living descendants of my cousin Michel Bouvier, per stirpes; and (ii) the other one-half (?) thereof (or the entire amount thereof if no descendant of my cousin Michel Bouvier is then living) to the then living descendants of my sister, Lee B. Radziwill, per stirpes, or, if no such descendant of hers is then living, to my said sister, if she shall then be living.

Should any trust created hereunder terminate by reason of expiration of a period of twenty-one (21) years after the death of the last to die of the descendants of my former father-in-law Joseph P. Kennedy in being at the time of my death, the principal of each such terminating trust, as then constituted, shall be transferred, conveyed and paid over to the then living beneficiaries of that trust in equal shares.

SIXTH: A. Unless it shall not be permissible under the applicable rules of law to create a trust of the property described in this Paragraph A, if any individual under the age of twenty-one (21) years becomes entitled to any property from my estate upon my death or any property from any trust created hereunder upon the termination thereof, such property shall be held by, and I give, devise and bequeath the same to, the Trustees hereinafter named, IN TRUST, NEVERTHELESS, for the following uses and purposes: To manage, invest and reinvest the same, to collect the income and to apply the net income and principal to such extent (including the whole thereof) for such individual's general use and at such time or times as the independent Trustees (i.e., the Trustees of each particular trust created hereunder other than any Trustee who is also a beneficiary of that trust or of any other trust hereunder and other than any Trustee who has disclaimed any property of my Estate which becomes a part of this trust), in the exercise of sole and absolute discretion, shall determine, until such individual reaches the age of twenty-one (21) years, and thereupon to transfer, convey and pay over the principal of the trust, as it is then constituted, to such individual. Any net income not so applied shall be accumulated and added to the principal of the trust at least annually and thereafter shall be held, administered and disposed of as a part thereof. Upon the death of such individual before reaching the age of twenty-one (21) years, the Trustees shall transfer, convey and pay over the principal of the trust, as it is then constituted, to such individual's executors or administrators.

If my Executors or the independent Trustees, as the case may be, in the exercise of sole and absolute discretion, determine at any time not to transfer in trust or not to continue to hold in trust any part or all of such property, as the case may be, they shall have full power and authority to transfer and pay over such property, or any part thereof, without bond, to such individual, if an adult under the law of the state of his or her domicile at the time of such payment, or to his or her parent, the guardian of his or her person or property, or to a custodian for such individual under any Uniform Gifts to Minors Act pursuant to which a custodian is acting or may be appointed.

The receipt of such individual, if an adult, or the parent, the guardian or custodian to whom any principal or income is transferred and paid over pursuant to any of the above provisions shall be a full discharge to my Executors or the Trustees, as the case may be, from all liability with respect thereto.

B. If it shall not be permissible under the applicable rules of law to create a trust of the property hereinabove described in Paragraph A, and if such individual is a minor as hereinafter defined, in that event such property shall vest absolutely in such minor, subject to the following: I hereby authorize and empower the Trustees hereinafter named to retain such minor's property without bond, as donees of a power in trust for the following uses and purposes: To manage, invest and reinvest the same, to collect the income and to apply the net income and principal to such extent (including the whole thereof) for such minor's general use and at such time or times as the independent Trustees, in the exercise of sole and absolute discretion, shall determine, until such minor reaches the age of majority, and thereupon to transfer, convey and pay over the property, as it is then constituted, to such minor. Any net income not so applied shall be accumulated and added to principal at least annually and thereafter shall be held, administered and disposed of as a part thereof. Upon the death of such minor before reaching his or her majority, the Trustees shall transfer, convey and pay over the property, as it is then constituted, to such minor's executors or administrators.

If my Executors or the independent Trustees, as the case may be, in the exercise of sole and absolute discretion, determine at any time not to transfer to the Trustees as such donees of a power in trust or not to continue to hold any part or all of such property as hereinabove provided, as the case may be, they shall have full power and authority to transfer and pay over such property or any part thereof, without bond, to such minor's parent or to the guardian of such minor's person or property, or to a custodian for such minor under any Uniform Gift to Minors Act pursuant to which a custodian is acting or may be appointed.

The receipt of the parent, guardian or custodian to whom any property is transferred and paid over pursuant to any of the above provisions shall be a full discharge to my Executors or the Trustees, as the case may be, from all liability with respect thereto.

As compensation for their services under this Paragraph B the Trustees shall be entitled to commissions at the rates and in the manner allowed to trustees of testamentary trusts under the laws of the State of New York in effect from time to time.

In administering any property pursuant to this Paragraph B, the Trustees shall have all of the powers conferred upon them under this Will.

The term "minor" as used in this Paragraph B shall be deemed to refer to an individual under the age at which such individual may execute a binding contract to dispose of real or personal property under the laws of the State of his or her domicile.

SEVENTH: Any application of the net income or principal of any trust herein created may be by the payment of bills rendered for the support, maintenance, education or general welfare of the beneficiary for whose use the application is to be made or by the payment of net income or principal to such person or persons, including, in the case of a minor, his or her parent, the guardian of his or her person or property or the person with whom such minor resides, as the Trustees, in the exercise of sole and absolute discretion, deem appropriate. Any such payment or application may be made without bond, without intervention of any guardian or committee, without order of court, without regard to the duty of any person to support the beneficiary and without regard to any other funds which may be available for the purpose. The receipt of the person or persons to whom any net income or principal is paid pursuant to this Article shall be a full discharge to the Trustees from all liability with respect thereto.

EIGHTH: In the event that any beneficiary or beneficiaries hereunder upon whose survivorship any gift, legacy or devise is conditioned and the person or persons, including myself, upon whose prior death such gift, legacy or devise takes effect shall die simultaneously or under such circumstances as to render it impossible or difficult to determine who survived the other, I hereby declare it to be my will that such beneficiary or beneficiaries shall be deemed not to have survived but to have predeceased such person or persons, and that this my Will and any and all of its provisions shall be construed on such assumption and basis.

NINTH: A. All estate, inheritance, legacy, succession or transfer or other death taxes (including any interest and penalties thereon) imposed by any domestic or foreign taxing authority with respect to all property owned by me at the time of my death and passing under this my Will (other than any generation-skipping transfer tax imposed by Chapter 13 of the Code, or any successor section or statute of like import, and any comparable tax imposed by any other taxing authority) shall be paid without apportionment out of my residuary estate and without apportionment within my residuary estate and with no right of reimbursement from any recipient of any such property. By directing payment of the aforesaid taxes from my residuary estate only in so far as those taxes are generated by property passing under this my Will, it is my express intention that the property over which I possess a general power of appointment and to which I refer in Article FOURTH of this my Will shall bear its own share of such taxes.

B. Should my Estate, after payment of all of my debts and funeral expenses, the expenses of estate administration and the taxes referred to in this Article NINTH, be insufficient to satisfy in full all of the pre-residuary bequests and devises which I make under Articles FIRST through THIRD hereof, I direct that the bequests and devises in (1) Paragraphs A, B and C of Article FIRST, (2) Article SECOND and (3) Paragraph A of Article THIRD shall abate last after the abatement of the bequests and devises in Paragraphs D and E of Article FIRST and Paragraphs B, C and D of Article THIRD.

TENTH: A. My Executors may make such elections under the tax laws (including, but without limitation, any election under Chapter 13 of the Code) as my Executors, in the exercise of sole and absolute discretion, deem advisable, regardless of the effect thereof on any of the interests under this Will, and I direct that there shall be no adjustment of such interests by reason of any action taken by my Executors pursuant hereto.

B. My Executors may, in the exercise of sole and absolute discretion, disclaim or renounce any interest which I or my estate may have under any other will, under any trust agreement or otherwise.

C. The determination of my Executors with respect to all elections, disclaimers and renunciations referred to in this Article shall be final and conclusive upon all persons.

D. I authorize my Executors, in the exercise of sole and absolute discretion, to divide (whether before or after any trust is funded and whether before or after any allocation of GST exemption under section 2631 of the Code is made) any trust or any property used or to be used to fund or augment any trust created under this Will into two or more fractional shares. The shares shall be held and administered by the Trustees as separate trusts, but may be managed and invested in solido. Some of the purposes for granting this authority are to provide an inclusion ratio (within the meaning of section 2642(a) of the Code) of zero for the separate trust receiving the fractional share to which the allocation of GST exemption is made.

Whenever two trusts created under this Will are directed to be combined into a single trust (for example, because property of one trust is to be added to the other trust), whether or not the trusts have different inclusion ratios with respect to any common transferor or have different transferors for generation-skipping transfer tax purposes, the Trustees are authorized, in the exercise of sole and absolute discretion, instead of combining said trusts, to administer them as two separate trusts with identical terms in accordance with the provisions that would have governed the combined trusts. However, the Trustees may manage and invest such separate trusts in solido.

The Trustees are authorized, in the exercise of sole and absolute discretion, to combine any one or more trusts with identical terms for an identical beneficiary or beneficiaries created under this Will as a single trust. The Trustees are also authorized, in the exercise of sole and absolute discretion, later to divide such trust as provided above in this Paragraph. Without in any way limiting the sole and absolute discretion of the Trustees granted by this Paragraph, I envision that the Trustees will not elect to combine two or more trusts with different inclusion ratios for generation-skipping transfer tax purposes.

ELEVENTH: In addition to, and not by way of limitation of, the powers conferred by law upon fiduciaries, subject, however, to the directions and prohibitions in Article FIFTH hereof, I hereby expressly grant to my Executors with respect to my estate and the Trustees with respect to each of the trust estates herein created, including any accumulated income thereof, the powers hereinafter enumerated, all of such powers so conferred or granted to be exercised by them as they may deem advisable in the exercise of sole and absolute discretion:

(1) To purchase or otherwise acquire, and to retain, whether originally a part of my estate or subsequently acquired, any and all stocks, bonds, notes or other securities, or any variety of real or personal property, including securities of any corporate fiduciary, or any successor or affiliated corporation, interest in common trust funds and securities of or other interests in investment companies and investment trusts, whether or not such investments be of the character permissible for investments by fiduciaries; and to make or retain any such investment without regard to degree of diversification.

(2) To sell (including to any descendant of mine), lease, pledge, mortgage, transfer, exchange, convert or otherwise dispose of, or grant options with respect to, any and all property at any time forming a part of my estate or any trust estate, in any manner, at any time or times, for any purpose, for any price and upon any terms, credits and conditions; and to enter into leases which extend beyond the period fixed by statute for leases made by fiduciaries and beyond the duration of any trust.

(3) To borrow money from any lender, including any corporate fiduciary, for any purpose connected with the protection, preservation or improvement of my estate or any trust estate, and as security to mortgage or pledge upon any terms and conditions any real or personal property of which I may die seized or possessed or forming a part of any trust estate.

(4) To vote in person or by general or limited proxy with respect to any shares of stock or other security; directly or through a committee or other agent, to oppose or consent to the reorganization, consolidation, merger, dissolution or liquidation of any corporation, or to the sale, lease, pledge or mortgage of any property by or to any such corporation; and to make any payments and take any steps proper to obtain the benefits of any such transaction.

(5) To the extent permitted by law, to register any security in the name of a nominee with or without the addition of words indicating that such security is held in a fiduciary capacity; and to hold any security in bearer form.

(6) To complete, extend, modify or renew any loans, notes, bonds, mortgages, contracts or any other obligations which I may owe or to which I may be a party or which may be liens or charges against any of my property, or against my estate, although I may not be liable thereon; to pay, compromise, compound, adjust, submit to arbitration, sell or release any claims or demands of my estate or any trust against others or of others against my estate or any trust upon any terms and conditions, including the acceptance of deeds to real property in satisfaction of bonds and mortgages; and to make any payments in connection therewith.

(7) To make distributions in kind (including in satisfaction of pecuniary bequests) and to cause any distribution to be composed of cash, property or undivided fractional shares in property different in kind from any other distribution without regard to the income tax basis of the property distributed to any beneficiary or any trust.

(8) Whenever no corporate fiduciary is acting hereunder, to place all or any part of the securities which at any time are held by my estate or any trust estate in the care and custody of any bank or trust company with no obligation while such securities are so deposited to inspect or verify the same and with no responsibility for any loss or misapplication by the bank or trust company; to have all stocks and registered securities placed in the name of such bank or trust company or in the name of its nominee; to appoint such bank or trust company agent and attorney to collect, receive, receipt for and disburse any income, and generally to perform the duties and services incident to a so-called "custodian" account; and to allocate the charges and expenses of such bank or trust

company to income or to principal or partially to income and partially to principal.

(9) To appoint, employ and remove, at any time and from time to time, any accountants, attorneys, investment counselors, expert advisers, agents, clerks and employees; and to fix and pay their compensation from income or principal or partially from income and partially from principal. Nothing herein contained, however, shall be construed to permit any person or entity to receive compensation in excess of what is reasonable, as defined for purposes of sections 4941(d)(2)(E) and 4945 (d)(5) of the Code and under the laws of the State of New York, if such compensation is a charge, directly or indirectly, against any charitable lead trust created hereunder.

(10) Whenever permitted by law, to employ a broker-dealer as custodian for all or any part of the securities at any time held by my estate or any trust estate and to register such securities in the name of such broker-dealer.

(11) With respect to securities in any closely-held corporations, or any interests of my estate or any trust estate in any unincorporated business enterprises, to retain any such securities or interests and to allow any assets of my estate or any trust estate invested in any such corporations or businesses to remain so invested for such time as may appear desirable without liability for any such retention of any such stock, to advance money to any such corporations or businesses in order to aid them in their operations or with the view to maintaining or increasing the value of the interest therein of my estate or any trust estate; to provide for the management, operation and conduct of such businesses, either singly or in conjunction with others interested therein; to engage and delegate duties and powers to any employees, managers or other persons, without liability for any delegation except for negligence in selection; to borrow money for such corporations or businesses, and to secure such loans by a pledge or mortgage not only of interests held in such corporations or businesses but also of any other assets held in my estate or any trust estate; to vote any stock so as to effect the election as an officer or director, or both, of any such corporations of any fiduciary hereunder and also to provide for reasonable compensation to

such officer or director (which compensation shall be in addition to and not in lieu of any compensation to which such fiduciary may be entitled for acting hereunder); to enter into agreements for voting trusts and to deposit securities with the voting trustees, to delegate duties to such trustees with all powers of an absolute owner of such stock, to authorize such trustees to incur and pay expenses and receive compensation, and to accept and retain any property received under such agreements; to take business risks in the management, operation, conduct and disposition of any such corporations and business enterprises, notwithstanding that my estate or any trust estate shall have an interest therein; to sell the securities or assets of any such corporations or businesses, or to liquidate, dissolve or otherwise dispose of the same; and to organize, either singly or in conjunction with others, a corporation or corporations to carry on any business enterprise, transferring assets or cash thereto for stock.

(12) To manage, insure against loss, subdivide, partition, develop, improve, mortgage, lease or otherwise deal with any real property or interests therein which may form at any time a part of my estate or any trust estate; to satisfy and discharge or extend the term of any mortgage thereon; to demolish, rebuild, improve, repair and make alterations from time to time in any structures upon any such real property; to plat into lots and prepare any such real property for building purposes; to construct and equip buildings and other structures upon any such real property and to make any and all other improvements of any kind or character whatsoever in connection with the development and improvement thereof; to execute the necessary instruments and covenants to effectuate the foregoing powers, including the granting of options in connection therewith.

(13) To divide any trust created under this Will into one or more separate trusts for the benefit of one or more of the beneficiaries of the trust (to the exclusion of the other beneficiaries) so divided, as the Trustees, in the exercise of sole and absolute discretion, determine and to allocate to such divided trust some or all of the assets of the trust estate for any reason including, but not limited to, enabling any such trust or trusts to qualify as an eligible shareholder of a

subchapter S corporation as described in sections 1361(c)(2)(A)(i) or 1361(d)(3) of the Code, as the case may be, or for any other purpose.

(14) To delegate any duties or powers, discretionary or otherwise, to a co-fiduciary for such periods and upon such terms and conditions as may be designated in a written instrument acknowledged in such form as would entitle a deed of real property to be recorded and delivered to such co-fiduciary; and the fiduciary so delegating any duties or powers hereunder shall have no further responsibility with respect to the exercise of such duties or powers so long as such delegation shall remain in effect; and any such delegation shall be revocable by a similar instrument so delivered at any time, provided, however, that no duties or powers described in Paragraph J of Article TWELFTH hereof may be delegated to a Trustee who is a beneficiary of any trust created hereunder.

(15) To manage any trust created hereunder in solido with any other trust created hereunder which has similar terms, conditions and beneficiaries.

(16) To execute and deliver any and all instruments to carry out any of the foregoing powers, no party to any such instrument being required to inquire into its validity or to see to the application of any money or other property paid or delivered to the terms of any such instrument.

TWELFTH: A. I appoint ALEXANDER D. FORGER and MAURICE TEMPELSMAN Executors of this my Last Will and Testament. If either of them should fail to qualify or cease to act as Executor hereunder, I authorize, but do not direct, the other, in the exercise of sole and absolute discretion, to appoint as a co-Executor such individual or such bank or trust company as he, in the exercise of sole and absolute discretion, shall select. Any such appointment shall be made by an instrument in writing filed with the clerk of the appropriate court.

If at any time and for any reason there is only one Executor acting hereunder, I authorize, but do not direct, such Executor to appoint such individual or such bank or trust company as such Executor, in the exercise of sole and absolute discretion, shall select as successor Executor to act in his or her place if he or she should cease to act. Any such appointment shall

be made by an instrument in writing filed with the clerk of the appropriate court and may be revoked by such Executor during his or her lifetime and succeeded by a later appointment, the last such appointment to control.

B. Should it be necessary for a representative of my estate to qualify in any jurisdiction wherein any Executor named herein cannot or may not desire to qualify as such, any other Executor acting hereunder shall, without giving any security, act as Executor in such jurisdiction and shall have therein all the rights, powers, privileges, discretions and duties conferred or imposed upon my Executor by the provisions of this my Will, or, if no Executor can or wishes to qualify as Executor in such other jurisdiction, or, if at any time and for any reason there shall be no Executor in office in such other jurisdiction, I appoint as Executor therein such person or corporation as may be designated by the Executors acting hereunder. Such substituted Executor shall, without giving any security, have in such other jurisdiction all the rights, powers, privileges, discretions and duties conferred or imposed upon my Executors by the provisions of this my Will.

C. I appoint ALEXANDER D. FORGER and MAURICE TEMPELSMAN Trustees of the trust created under Paragraph A of Article SECOND of this my Will. If either of them should fail to qualify or cease to act as a Trustee hereunder, I authorize, but do not direct, the other, in the exercise of sole and absolute discretion, to appoint as a co-Trustee such individual or such bank or trust company as he, in the exercise of sole and absolute discretion, shall select. Any such appointment shall be made by an instrument in writing filed with the clerk of the appropriate court.

If at any time and for any reason there is only one Trustee acting for said trust, I authorize, but do not direct, such Trustee to appoint such individual or such bank or trust company as such Trustee, in the exercise of sole and absolute discretion, shall select as successor Trustee to act in his or her place if he or she should cease to act. Any such appointment shall be made by an instrument in writing filed with the clerk of the appropriate court and may be revoked by such Trustee during his or her lifetime and succeeded by a later appointment, the last such appointment to control.

D. I appoint my daughter, CAROLINE B. KENNEDY, my son, JOHN F. KENNEDY, JR., ALEXANDER D. FORGER and MAURICE TEMPELSMAN Trustees of the trust created under Paragraph A of Article FIFTH of this my Will and therein designated THE C & J FOUNDATION provided, however, that, if my daughter and/or my son disclaims any property of my Estate which becomes part of the trust created under Paragraph A of Article FIFTH, my daughter and/or my son who has so disclaimed shall only serve as an Administrative Trustee. An Administrative Trustee is only authorized to take such actions as are necessary to preserve and maintain the trust property within the meaning of Treas. Reg. § 25.2518-2(d)(2) and, accordingly, is prohibited from participating in the exercise, or decision not to exercise, any discretion over payments, distributions, applications or accumulations of income or principal by the Trustees, including the selection of the charitable beneficiaries of the annuity interest.

Should any one or more of the Trustees herein designated fail to qualify or cease to act as a Trustee of said Foundation without having designated his or her successor in the manner authorized by Paragraph H of this Article, I direct the Trustees or Trustee continuing in office to exercise that right so that there shall be a minimum of two (2) Trustees in office for the Foundation at all times.

E. I appoint CAROLINE B. KENNEDY and JOHN F. KENNEDY, JR., or the survivor of them, Trustees of each trust created under subparagraph B(3) of Article FIFTH of this my Will provided, however, that, if my daughter and/or my son disclaims any property of my Estate which becomes part of the trust created under Paragraph B(3) of Article FIFTH, my daughter and/or my son who has so disclaimed shall only serve as an Administrative Trustee. An Administrative Trustee is only authorized to take such actions as are necessary to preserve and maintain the trust property within the meaning of Treas. Reg. § 25.2518-2(d)(2) and, accordingly, is prohibited from participating in the exercise, or decision not to exercise, any discretion over payments, distributions, applications or accumulations of income or principal by the Trustees. In addition, I appoint as co-Trustee or

co-Trustees of each such trust such person or persons and/or bank or trust company as my son and daughter, or the survivor of them, shall agree upon and designate as co-Trustee or co-Trustees by an instrument in writing to be filed with the clerk of the appropriate court. It shall not be necessary to appoint successors to any individual acting as a Trustee of any trust created under subparagraph B(3) of Article FIFTH hereof if and during such time as a bank or trust company shall be acting hereunder.

F. I appoint my daughter, CAROLINE B. KENNEDY, and my son, JOHN F. KENNEDY, JR., Trustees of any trust created under Article SIXTH of this my Will, and I authorize any one parent of any individual for whom any such trust is created to qualify as a co-Trustee of such trust if he or she cares to do so provided, however, that, if my daughter and/or my son disclaims any property of my Estate which becomes part of the trust created under Article SIXTH, my daughter and/or my son who has so disclaimed shall only serve as an Administrative Trustee. An Administrative Trustee is only authorized to take such actions as are necessary to preserve and maintain the trust property within the meaning of Treas. Reg. § 25.2518-2(d)(2) and, accordingly, is prohibited from participating in the exercise, or decision not to exercise, any discretion over payments, distributions, applications or accumulations of income or principal by the Trustees.

G. Any Executor or Trustee may resign from office without leave of court at any time and for any reason by filing a written instrument of resignation with the clerk of the appropriate court.

H. I authorize and empower any individual acting as a Trustee of any one or more of the trusts created hereunder to appoint at any time and from time to time any individual or bank or trust company (unless a bank or trust company is then acting as Trustee of such trust) to act as successor Trustee of any one or more of such trusts in the event that the person so making the appointment shall cease to act as a Trustee of such trust or trusts due to his or her death or resignation. If more than one Trustee is acting hereunder, and at any time or from time to time there shall be a vacancy in the office of co-Trustee of any one or more of the trusts created hereunder due to the death or resignation of a co-Trustee and no successor Trustee willing and able to serve shall have been appointed herein or by such co-Trustee as hereinabove provided, then I authorize and empower the remaining individual Trustee, if any, of such trust or trusts to appoint any individual or corporation to act as co-Trustee of such trust or trusts.

I. In the event that the only acting Trustee or Trustees of any trust created hereunder are prohibited from taking certain actions which are necessary or appropriate, I appoint as co-Trustee such individual or bank or trust company as shall be selected, in the exercise of sole and absolute discretion, by the then acting Trustee or Trustees. Any such appointment shall be made by an instrument in writing filed with the clerk of the appropriate court.

J. Notwithstanding any other provision of this my Will, no Trustee who is a beneficiary of any trust created hereunder or who is under a duty to support a beneficiary shall ever participate in (i) the exercise, or decision not to exercise, any discretion over payments, distributions, applications, accumulations, or uses of income or principal by the Trustees, (ii) the exercise of discretion to allocate receipts or expenses between principal and income, or (iii) the exercise of any general power of appointment described in sections 2041 or 2514 of the Code.

K. Except as provided by law, I direct that my Executors shall not be required to file any inventory or render any account of my Estate and that no Executor, Trustee, or donee of a power in trust shall be required to give any bond. If, notwithstanding the foregoing direction, any bond is required by any law, statute or rule of court, no sureties shall be required thereon.

L. I authorize and empower the Trustees or Trustee of each trust created hereunder to transfer the trust assets to, and to hold and administer them in, any jurisdiction in the United States and to account for the same in any court having jurisdiction over said assets.

M. I direct that any and all powers and discretion conferred by law and by this my Will upon my Trustees including, but not by way of limitation, the right to appoint successor and co-Trustees, may be exercised by the Trustees from time to time qualified and acting hereunder.

N. Whenever the terms "Executors" or "Executor" and "Trustees" or "Trustee" are used in this my Will, they shall be deemed to refer to the Executors or Executor or the Trustees or Trustee acting hereunder from time to time.

THIRTEENTH: A. A disposition in this Will to the descendants of a person per stirpes shall be deemed to require a division into a sufficient number of equal shares to make one share for each child of such person living at the time such disposition becomes effective and one share for each then deceased child of such person having one or more descendants then living, regardless of whether any child of such person is then living, with the same principle to be applied in any required further division of a share at a more remote generation.

B. As used in this Will, the terms "child," "children," "descendant" and "descendants" are intended to include adopted persons and the descendants of adopted persons, whether of the blood or by adoption.

FOURTEENTH: In accordance with the provisions of section 315(5) of New York's Surrogate's Court Procedure Act, in any proceeding involving my estate or any trust estate created hereunder it shall not be necessary to serve process upon or to make a party to any such proceeding any person under a disability where another party to the proceeding has the same interest as the person under a disability.

FIFTEENTH: No trust created under this my Will shall be subject to the provisions of section 11-2.1(k) of New York's Estates, Powers and Trusts Law (the "EPTL"), nor shall the Trustees of any such trust be obliged to make any allocation to income in respect of any property held as a part of any trust created hereunder which at any time is underproductive within the meaning of section 11-2.1(k)(1) of the EPTL.

IN WITNESS WHEREOF, I, JACQUELINE K. ONASSIS, have to this my Last Will and Testament subscribed my name and set my seal this <u>22</u> day of <u>March</u>, in the year One Thousand Nine Hundred and Ninety-Four.

Jacqueline K Onassis
Jacqueline K. Onassis

Subscribed and sealed by the Testatrix in the presence of us and of each of us, and at the same time published, declared and acknowledged by her to us to be her Last Will and Testament, and thereupon we, at the request of the said Testatrix, in her presence and in the presence of each other, have hereunto subscribed our names as witnesses this 22nd day of March 1994.

Georgiana J. Slade _____

    residing at

    417 Park Avenue _____

    New York, N.Y. _____

Samuel S. Polk _____

    residing at

    Guard Hill Road _____

    Bedford, New York _____

_____

    residing at

NOTE: ATTESTING WITNESSES SHOULD READ CAREFULLY BEFORE SIGNING THIS AFFIDAVIT—NOTARY SHOULD NOT BE A PARTY OR WITNESS

STATE OF NEW YORK   )
                      : ss.:
COUNTY OF NEW YORK   )

Each of the undersigned, individually and severally being duly sworn, deposes and says:

The within Will was subscribed in our presence and sight at the end thereof by JACQUELINE K. ONASSIS, the within-named Testatrix, on the 22nd day of March , 1994, at 1040 Fifth Avenue in the State of New York.

Said Testatrix at the time of making such subscription declared the instrument so subscribed to be her Last Will and Testament.

Each of the undersigned thereupon signed his or her name as a witness at the end of said Will at the request of said Testatrix and in her presence and sight and in the presence and sight of each other.

Said Testatrix was, at the time of so executing said Will, over the age of 18 years and, in the respective opinions of the undersigned, of sound mind, memory and understanding and not under any restraint or in any respect incompetent to make a will.

The Testatrix, in the respective opinions of the undersigned, could read, write and converse in the English language and was suffering from no defect of sight, hearing or speech or from any other physical or mental impairment which would affect her capacity to make a valid will. The Will was executed as a single, original instrument and was not executed in counterparts.

Each of the undersigned was acquainted with said Testatrix at said time and makes this affidavit at her request.

The within Will was shown to the undersigned at the time this affidavit was made, and was examined by each of them as to the signature of said Testatrix and of the undersigned.

The foregoing instrument was executed by the Testatrix and witnessed by each of the undersigned affiants under the supervision of Georgiana J. Slade , an attorney-at-law.

Georgiana J. Slade _____
Samuel S. Polk _____

Severally sworn to before me this 22nd day of March, 1994.

Carole A. Mahoney _____

Notary Public

CAROLE A. MAHONEY
Notary Public, State of New York
No. 31-4880120
Qualified in New York County
Commission Expires: December 15, 1994

Uniform Simultaneous Death Act

An Act providing for the disposition of property where there is no sufficient evidence that persons have died otherwise than simultaneously, and to make uniform the law with reference thereto.

§ 1. NO SUFFICIENT EVIDENCE OF SURVIVORSHIP

Where the title to property or the devolution thereof depends upon priority of death and there is no sufficient evidence that the persons concerned have died otherwise than simultaneously, the property of each person shall be disposed of as if he had survived, except as otherwise provided in this act.

§ 2. SURVIVAL OF BENEFICIARIES

If property is so disposed of that the right of a beneficiary to succeed to any interest therein is conditional upon his surviving another person, and both persons die, and there is no sufficient evidence that the two have died otherwise than simultaneously, the beneficiary shall be deemed not to have survived. If there is no sufficient evidence that two or more beneficiaries have died otherwise than simultaneously and property has been disposed of in such a way that at the time of their death each of such beneficiaries would have been entitled to the property if he had survived the others, the property shall be divided into as many equal portions as there were such beneficiaries and these portions shall be distributed respectively to those who would have taken in the event that each of such beneficiaries had survived.

§ 3. JOINT TENANTS OR TENANTS BY THE ENTIRETY

Where there is no sufficient evidence that two joint tenants or tenants by the entirety have died otherwise than simultaneously the property so held shall be distributed one-half as if one had survived and one-half as if the other had survived. If there are more than two joint tenants and all of them have so died the property thus distributed shall be in the proportion that one bears to the whole number of joint tenants.

The term "joint tenants" includes owners of property held under circumstances which entitled one or more to the whole of the property on the death of the other or others.

§ 4. COMMUNITY PROPERTY

Where a husband and wife have died, leaving community property, and there is no sufficient evidence that they have died otherwise than simultaneously, one-half of all the community property shall pass as if the husband had survived [and as if said one-half were his separate property,] and the other one-half thereof shall pass as if the wife had survived [and as if said other one-half were her separate property.]

§ 5. INSURANCE POLICIES

Where the insured and the beneficiary in a policy of life or accident insurance have died and there is no sufficient evidence that they have died otherwise than simultaneously the proceeds of the policy shall be distributed as if the insured had survived the beneficiary, [except if the policy is community property of the insured and his spouse, and there is no alternative beneficiary except the estate or personal representatives of the insured, the proceeds shall be distributed as community property under Section 4.]

§ 6. ACT DOES NOT APPLY IF DECEDENT PROVIDES OTHERWISE

This act shall not apply in the case of wills, living trusts, deeds, or contracts of insurance, or any other situation where provision is made for distribution of property different from the provisions of this act, or where provision is made for a presumption as to survivorship which results in a distribution of property different from that here provided.

§ 7. UNIFORMITY OF INTERPRETATION

This act shall be so construed and interpreted as to effectuate its general purpose to make uniform the law in those states which enact it.

§ 8. SHORT TITLE

This act may be cited as the Uniform Simultaneous Death Act.

§ 9. REPEAL

All laws or parts of laws inconsistent with the provisions of this act are hereby repealed.

§ 10. SEVERABILITY

If any of the provisions of this act or the application thereof to any persons or circumstances is held invalid such invalidity shall not affect other provisions or applications of the act which can be given effect without the invalid provisions or application, and to this end the provisions of this act are declared to be severable.

§ 11. TIME OF TAKING EFFECT

This act shall take effect _____.

UNIFORM TRANSFERS TO MINORS ACT

§ 1. Definitions.

In this [Act]:

(1) "Adult" means an individual who has attained the age of 21 years.

(2) "Benefit plan" means an employer's plan for the benefit of an employee or partner.

(3) "Broker" means a person lawfully engaged in the business of effecting transactions in securities or commodities for the person's own account or for the account of others.

(4) "Conservator" means a person appointed or qualified by a court to act as general, limited, or temporary guardian of a minor's property or a person legally authorized to perform substantially the same functions.

(5) "Court" means [————————— court].

(6) "Custodial property" means (i) any interest in property transferred to a custodian under this [Act] and (ii) the income from and proceeds of that interest in property.

(7) "Custodian" means a person so designated under Section 9 or a successor or substitute custodian designated under Section 18.

(8) "Financial institution" means a bank, trust company, savings institution, or credit union, chartered and supervised under state or federal law.

(9) "Legal representative" means an individual's personal representative or conservator.

(10) "Member of the minor's family" means the minor's parent, stepparent, spouse, grandparent, brother, sister, uncle, or aunt, whether of the whole or half blood or by adoption.

(11) "Minor" means an individual who has not attained the age of 21 years.

(12) "Person" means an individual, corporation, organization, or other legal entity.

(13) "Personal representative" means an executor, administrator, successor personal representative, or special administrator of a decedent's estate or a person legally authorized to perform substantially the same functions.

(14) "State" includes any state of the United States, the District of Columbia, the Commonwealth of Puerto Rico, and any territory or possession subject to the legislative authority of the United States.

(15) "Transfer" means a transaction that creates custodial property under Section 9.

(16) "Transferor" means a person who makes a transfer under this [Act].

(17) "Trust company" means a financial institution, corporation, or other legal entity, authorized to exercise general trust powers.

§ 2. Scope and Jurisdiction.

(a) This [Act] applies to a transfer that refers to this [Act] in the designation under Section 9(a) by which the transfer is made if at the time of the transfer, the transferor, the minor, or the custodian is a resident of this State or the custodial property is located in this State. The custodianship so created remains subject to this [Act] despite a subsequent change in residence of a transferor, the minor, or the custodian, or the removal of custodial property from this State.

(b) A person designated as custodian under this [Act] is subject to personal jurisdiction in this State with respect to any matter relating to the custodianship.

(c) A transfer that purports to be made and which is valid under the Uniform Transfers to Minors Act, the Uniform Gifts to Minors Act, or a substantially similar act, of another state is governed by the law of the designated state and may be executed and is enforceable in this State if at the time of the transfer, the transferor, the minor, or the custodian is a resident of the designated state or the custodial property is located in the designated state.

§ 3. Nomination of Custodian.

(a) A person having the right to designate the recipient of property transferable upon the occurrence of a future event may revocably nominate a custodian to receive the property for a minor beneficiary upon the occurrence of the event by naming the custodian followed in substance by the words: "as custodian for ———————— (name of minor) under the [name of Enacting State] Uniform Transfers to Minors Act." The nomination may name one or more persons as substitute custodians to whom the property must be transferred, in the order named, if the first nominated custodian dies before the transfer or is unable, declines, or is ineligible to serve. The nomination may be made in a will, a trust, a deed, an instrument exercising a power of appointment, or in a writing designating a beneficiary of contractual rights which is registered with or delivered to the payor, issuer, or other obligor of the contractual rights.

(b) A custodian nominated under this section must be a person to whom a transfer of property of that kind may be made under Section 9(a).

(c) The nomination of a custodian under this section does not create custodial property until the nominating instrument becomes irrevocable or a transfer to the nominated custodian is completed under Section 9. Unless the nomination of a custodian has been revoked, upon the occurrence of the future event the custodianship becomes effective and the custodian shall enforce a transfer of the custodial property pursuant to Section 9.

§ 4. Transfer by Gift or Exercise of Power of Appointment.

A person may make a transfer by irrevocable gift to, or the irrevocable exercise of a power of appointment in favor of, a custodian for the benefit of a minor pursuant to Section 9.

§ 5. Transfer Authorized by Will or Trust.

(a) A personal representative or trustee may make an irrevocable transfer pursuant to Section 9 to a custodian for the benefit of a minor as authorized in the governing will or trust.

(b) If the testator or settlor has nominated a custodian under Section 3 to receive the custodial property, the transfer must be made to that person.

(c) If the testator or settlor has not nominated a custodian under Section 3, or all persons so nominated as custodian die before the transfer or are unable, decline, or are ineligible to serve, the personal representative or the trustee, as the case may be, shall designate the custodian from among those eligible to serve as custodian for property of that kind under Section 9(a).

§ 6. Other Transfer by Fiduciary.

(a) Subject to subsection (c) a personal representative or trustee may make an irrevocable transfer to another adult or another trust company as custodian for the benefit of a minor pursuant to Section 9, in the absence of a will or under a will or trust that does not contain an authorization to do so.

(b) Subject to subsection (c), a conservator may make an irrevocable transfer to another adult or trust company as custodian for the benefit of the minor pursuant to Section 9.

(c) A transfer under subsection (a) or (b) may be made only if (i) the personal representative, trustee, or conservator considers the transfer to be in the best interest of the minor, (ii) the transfer is not prohibited by or inconsistent with provisions of the applicable will, trust agreement, or other governing instrument, and (iii) the transfer is authorized by the court if it exceeds [$10,000] in value.

§ 7. Transfer by Obligor.

(a) Subject to subsections (b) and (c), a person not subject to Section 5 or 6 who holds property of or owes a liquidated debt to a minor not having a conservator may make an irrevocable transfer to a custodian for the benefit of the minor pursuant to Section 9.

(b) If a person having the right to do so under Section 3 has nominated a custodian under that section to receive the custodial property, the transfer must be made to that person.

(c) If no custodian has been nominated under Section 3, or all persons so nominated as custodian die before the transfer or are unable, decline, or are ineligible to serve, a transfer under this section may be made to an adult member of the minor's family or to a trust company unless the property exceeds [$10,000] in value.

§ 8. Receipt for Custodial Property.

A written acknowledgment of delivery by a custodian constitutes a sufficient receipt and discharge for custodial property transferred to the custodian pursuant to this [Act].

§ 9. Manner of Creating Custodial Property and Effecting Transfer; Designation of Initial Custodian; Control.

(a) Custodial property is created and a transfer is made whenever:

(1) an uncertificated security or a certificated security in registered form is either:

(i) registered in the name of the transferor, an adult other than the transferor, or a trust company, followed in substance by the words: "as custodian for _____ (name of minor) under the [Name of Enacting State] Uniform Transfers to Minors Act"; or

(ii) delivered if in certificated form, or any document necessary for the transfer of an uncertificated security is delivered, together with any necessary endorsement to an adult other than the transferor or to a trust company as custodian, accompanied by an instrument in substantially the form set forth in subsection (b);

(2) money is paid or delivered to a broker or financial institution for credit to an account in the name of the transferor, an adult other than the transferor, or a trust company, followed in substance by the words: "as custodian for _____ (name of minor) under the [Name of Enacting State] Uniform Transfers to Minors Act";

(3) the ownership of a life or endowment insurance policy or annuity contract is either:

(i) registered with the issuer in the name of the transferor, an adult other than the transferor, or a trust company, followed in substance by the words: "as custodian for _____ (name of minor) under the [Name of Enacting State] Uniform Transfers to Minors Act"; or

(ii) assigned in a writing delivered to an adult other than the transferor or to a trust company whose name in the assignment is followed in substance by the words: "as custodian for _____ (name of minor) under the [Name of Enacting State] Uniform Transfers to Minors Act";

(4) an irrevocable exercise of a power of appointment or an irrevocable present right to future payment under a contract is the subject of a written notification delivered to the payor, issuer, or other obligor that the right is transferred to the transferor, an adult other than the transferor, or a trust company, whose name in the notification is followed in substance by the words: "as custodian for _____ (name of minor) under the [Name of Enacting State] Uniform Transfers to Minors Act";

(5) an interest in real property is recorded in the name of the transferor, an adult other than the transferor, or a trust company, followed in substance by the words: "as custodian for _____ (name of minor) under the [Name of Enacting State] Uniform Transfers to Minors Act";

(6) a certificate of title issued by a department or agency of a state or of the United States which evidences title to tangible personal property is either:

(i) issued in the name of the transferor, an adult other than the transferor, or a trust company, followed in substance by the words: "as custodian for _____ (name of minor) under the [Name of Enacting State] Uniform Transfers to Minors Act"; or

(ii) delivered to an adult other than the transferor or to a trust company, endorsed to that person followed in substance by the words: "as custodian for _____ (name of minor) under the [Name of Enacting State] Uniform Transfers to Minors Act"; or

(7) an interest in any property not described in paragraphs (1) through (6) is transferred to an adult other than the transferor or to a trust company by a written instrument in substantially the form set forth in subsection (b).

(b) An instrument in the following form satisfies the requirements of paragraphs (1)(ii) and (7) of subsection (a):

"TRANSFER UNDER THE [NAME OF ENACTING STATE] UNIFORM TRANSFERS TO MINORS ACT

I, _____ (name of transferor or name and representative capacity if a fiduciary) hereby transfer to _____ (name of custodian), as custodian for _____ (name of minor) under the [Name of Enacting State] Uniform Transfers to Minors Act, the following: (insert a description of the custodial property sufficient to identify it).

Dated: _____

_____
(Signature)

_____ (name of custodian) acknowledges receipt of the property described above as custodian for the minor named above under the [Name of Enacting State] Uniform Transfers to Minors Act.

Dated: _____

_____
(Signature)

(c) A transferor shall place the custodian in control of the custodial property as soon as practicable.

§ 10. Single Custodianship.

A transfer may be made only for one minor, and only one person may be the custodian. All custodial property held under this [Act] by the same custodian for the benefit of the same minor constitutes a single custodianship.

§ 11. Validity and Effect of Transfer.

(a) The validity of a transfer made in a manner prescribed in this [Act] is not affected by:

(1) failure of the transferor to comply with Section 9(c) concerning possession and control;

(2) designation of an ineligible custodian, except designation of the transferor in the case of property for which the transferor is ineligible to serve as custodian under Section 9(a); or

(3) death or incapacity of a person nominated under Section 3 or designated under Section 9 as custodian or the disclaimer of the office by that person.

(b) A transfer made pursuant to Section 9 is irrevocable, and the custodial property is indefeasibly vested in the minor, but the custodian has all the rights, powers, duties, and authority provided in this [Act], and neither the minor nor the minor's legal representative has any right, power, duty, or authority with respect to the custodial property except as provided in this [Act].

(c) By making a transfer, the transferor incorporates in the disposition all the provisions of this [Act] and grants to the custodian, and to any third person dealing with a person designated as custodian, the respective powers, rights, and immunities provided in this [Act].

§ 12. Care of Custodial Property.

(a) A custodian shall:

(1) take control of custodial property;

(2) register or record title to custodial property if appropriate; and

(3) collect, hold, manage, invest, and reinvest custodial property.

(b) In dealing with custodial property, a custodian shall observe the standard of care that would be observed by a prudent person dealing with property of another and is not limited by any other statute restricting investments by fiduciaries. If a custodian has a special skill or expertise or is named custodian on the basis of representations of a special skill or expertise, the custodian shall use that skill or expertise. However, a custodian, in the custodian's discretion and without liability to the minor or the minor's estate, may retain any custodial property received from a transferor.

(c) A custodian may invest in or pay premiums on life insurance or endowment policies on (i) the life of the minor only if the minor or the minor's estate is the sole beneficiary, or (ii) the life of another person in whom the minor has an insurable interest only to the extent that the minor, the minor's estate, or the custodian in the capacity of custodian, is the irrevocable beneficiary.

(d) A custodian at all times shall keep custodial property separate and distinct from all other property in a manner sufficient to identify it clearly as custodial property of the minor. Custodial property consisting of an undivided interest is so identified if the minor's interest is held as a tenant in common and is fixed. Custodial property subject to recordation is so identified if it is recorded, and custodial property subject to registration is so identified if it is either registered, or held in an account designated, in the name of the custodian, followed in substance by the words: "as a custodian for _____ (name of minor) under the [Name of Enacting State] Uniform Transfers to Minors Act."

(e) A custodian shall keep records of all transactions with respect to custodial property, including information necessary for the preparation of the minor's tax returns, and shall make them available for inspection at reasonable intervals by a parent or legal representative of the minor or by the minor if the minor has attained the age of 14 years.

§ 13. Powers of Custodian.

(a) A custodian, acting in a custodial capacity, has all the rights, powers, and authority over custodial property that unmarried adult owners have over their own property, but a custodian may exercise those rights, powers, and authority in that capacity only.

(b) This section does not relieve a custodian from liability for breach of Section 12.

§ 14. Use of Custodial Property.

(a) A custodian may deliver or pay to the minor or expend for the minor's benefit so much of the custodial property as the custodian considers advisable for the use and benefit of the minor, without court order and without regard to (i) the duty or ability of the custodian personally or of any other person to support the minor, or (ii) any other income or property of the minor which may be applicable or available for that purpose.

(b) On petition of an interested person or the minor if the minor has attained the age of 14 years, the court may order the custodian to deliver or pay to the minor or expend for the minor's benefit so much of the custodial property as the court considers advisable for the use and benefit of the minor.

(c) A delivery, payment, or expenditure under this section is in addition to, not in substitution for, and does not affect any obligation of a person to support the minor.

§ 15. Custodian's Expenses, Compensation, and Bond.

(a) A custodian is entitled to reimbursement from custodial property for reasonable expenses incurred in the performance of the custodian's duties.

(b) Except for one who is a transferor under Section 4, a custodian has a noncumulative election during each calendar year to charge reasonable compensation for services performed during that year.

(c) Except as provided in Section 18(f), a custodian need not give a bond.

§ 16. Exemption of Third Person from Liability.

A third person in good faith and without court order may act on the instructions of or otherwise deal with any person purporting to make a transfer or purporting to act in the capacity of a custodian and, in the absence of knowledge, is not responsible for determining:

(1) the validity of the purported custodian's designation;

(2) the property of, or the authority under this [Act] for, any act of the purported custodian;

(3) the validity or propriety under this [Act] of any instrument or instructions executed or given either by the person purporting to make a transfer or by the purported custodian; or

(4) the propriety of the application of any property of the minor delivered to the purported custodian.

§ 17. Liability to Third Persons.

(a) A claim based on (i) a contract entered into by a custodian acting in a custodial capacity, (ii) an obligation arising from the ownership or control of custodial property, or (iii) a tort committed during the custodianship, may be asserted against the custodial property by proceeding against the custodian in the custodial capacity, whether or not the custodian or the minor is personally liable therefor.

(b) A custodian is not personally liable:

(1) on a contract properly entered into in the custodial capacity unless the custodian fails to reveal that capacity and to identify the custodianship in the contract; or

(2) for an obligation arising from control of custodial property or for a tort committed during the custodianship unless the custodian is personally at fault.

(c) A minor is not personally liable for an obligation arising from ownership of custodial property or for a tort committed during the custodianship unless the minor is personally at fault.

§ 18. Renunciation, Resignation, Death, or Removal of Custodian; Designation of Successor Custodian.

(a) A person nominated under Section 3 or designated under Section 9 as custodian may decline to serve by delivering a valid disclaimer [under the Uniform Disclaimer of Property Interests Act of the Enacting State] to the person who made the nomination or to the transferor or the transferor's legal representative. If the event giving rise to a transfer has not occurred and no substitute custodian able, willing, and eligible to serve was nominated under Section 3, the person who made the nomination may nominate a substitute custodian under said Section 3; otherwise the transferor or the transferor's legal representative shall designate a substitute custodian at the time of the transfer, in either case from among the persons eligible to serve as custodian for that kind of property under Section 9(a). The custodian so designated has the rights of a successor custodian.

(b) A custodian at any time may designate a trust company or an adult other than a transferor under Section 4 as successor custodian by executing and dating an instrument of designation before a subscribing witness other than the successor. If the instrument of designation does not contain or is not accompanied by the resignation of the custodian, the designation of the successor does not take effect until the custodian resigns, dies, becomes incapacitated, or is removed.

(c) A custodian may resign at any time by delivering written notice to the minor if the minor has attained the age of 14 years and to the successor custodian and by delivering the custodial property to the successor custodian.

(d) If a custodian is ineligible, dies, or becomes incapacitated without having effectively designated a successor and the minor has attained the age of 14 years, the minor may designate as successor custodian, in the manner prescribed in subsection (b), an adult member of the minor's family, a conservator of the minor, or a trust company. If the minor has not attained the age of 14 years or fails to act within 60 days after the ineligibility, death, or incapacity, the conservator of the minor becomes successor custodian. If the minor has no conservator or the conservator declines to act, the transferor, the legal representative of the transferor or of the custodian, an adult member of the minor's family, or any other interested person may petition the court to designate a successor custodian.

(e) A custodian who declines to serve under subsection (a) or resigns under subsection (c), or the legal representative of a deceased or incapacitated custodian, as soon as practicable, shall put the custodian property and records in the possession and control of the successor custodian. The successor custodian by action may enforce the obligation to deliver custodial property and records and becomes responsible for each item as received.

(f) A transferor, the legal representative of a transferor, an adult member of the minor's family, a guardian of the person of the minor, the conservator of the minor, or the minor if the minor has attained the age of 14 years may petition the court to remove the custodian for cause and to designate a successor custodian other than a transferor under Section 4 or to require the custodian to give appropriate bond.

§ 19. Accounting by and Determination of Liability of Custodian.

(a) A minor who has attained the age of 14 years, the minor's guardian of the person or legal representative, an adult member of the minor's family, a transferor, or a transferor's legal representative may petition the court (i) for an accounting by the custodian or the custodian's legal representative; or (ii) for a determination of responsibility, as between the custodial property and the custodian personally, for claims against the custodial property unless the responsibility has been adjudicated in an action under Section 17 to which the minor or the minor's legal representative was a party.

(b) A successor custodian may petition the court for an accounting by the predecessor custodian.

(c) The court, in a proceeding under this [Act] or in any other proceeding, may require or permit the custodian or the custodian's legal representative to account.

(d) If a custodian is removed under Section 18(f), the court shall require an accounting and order delivery of the custodial property and records to the successor custodian and the execution of all instruments required for transfer of the custodial property.

§ 20. Termination of Custodianship.

The custodian shall transfer in an appropriate manner the custodial property to the minor or to the minor's estate upon the earlier of:

(1) the minor's attainment of 21 years of age with respect to custodial property transferred under Section 4 or 5;

(2) the minor's attainment of [majority under the laws of this State other than this [Act]] [age 18 or other statutory age of majority of Enacting State] with

respect to custodial property transferred under Section 6 or 7; or

(3) the minor's death.

§ 21. Applicability.

This [Act] applies to a transfer within the scope of Section 2 made after its effective date if:

(1) the transfer purports to have been made under [the Uniform Gifts to Minors Act of the Enacting State]; or

(2) the instrument by which the transfer purports to have been made uses in substance the designation "as custodian under the Uniform Gifts to Minors Act" or "as custodian under the Uniform Transfers to Minors Act" of any other state, and the application of this [Act] is necessary to validate the transfer.

§ 22. Effect on Existing Custodianships.

(a) Any transfer of custodial property as now defined in this [Act] made before [the effective date of this Act] is validated notwithstanding that there was no specific authority in [the Uniform Gifts to Minors Act of the Enacting State] for the coverage of custodial property of that kind or for a transfer from that source at the time the transfer was made.

(b) This [Act] applies to all transfers made before the effective date of this [Act] in a manner and form prescribed in [the Uniform Gifts to Minors Act of the Enacting State], except insofar as the application impairs constitutionally vested rights or extends the duration of custodianships in existence on the effective date of this [Act].

(c) Sections 1 and 20 with respect to the age of a minor for whom custodial property is held under this [Act] do not apply to custodial property held in a custodianship that terminated because of the minor's attainment of the age of [18] after [date prior Act was amended to specify [18] as age of majority] and before [the effective date of this Act].

§ 23. Uniformity of Application and Construction.

This [Act] shall be applied and construed to effectuate its general purpose to make uniform the law with respect to the subject of this [Act] among states enacting it.

§ 24. Short Title.

This [Act] may be cited as the "[Name of Enacting State] Uniform Transfers to Minors Act."

§ 25. Severability.

If any provisions of this [Act] or its application to any person or circumstance is held invalid, the invalidity does not affect other provisions or applications of this [Act] which can be given effect without the invalid provision or application, and to this end provisions of this [Act] are severable.

§ 26. Effective Date.

This [Act] takes effect _____.

§ 27. Repeals.

[Insert appropriate reference to the existing Gifts to Minors Act of the Enacting State or other jurisdiction] is hereby repealed. To the extent that this [Act], by virtue of Section 22(b), does not apply to transfers made in a manner prescribed in [the Gifts to Minors Act of the Enacting State] or to the powers, duties, and immunities conferred by transfers in that manner upon custodians and persons dealing with custodians, the repeal of [the Gifts to Minors Act of the Enacting State] does not affect those transfers or those powers, duties, and immunities.

Uniform Probate Code (Abridged)

Official Text Approved by the National Conference of Commissioners on Uniform State Laws

ARTICLE II
INTESTACY, WILLS, AND DONATIVE TRANSFERS (1990)

This version of Article II is followed in Alaska, Arizona, Colorado, Hawaii, Minnesota, Montana, New Mexico, North Dakota and South Dakota.

(See page 479 for the earlier version of this article.)

Part 1
Intestate Succession

§ 2-101. [Intestate Estate.]

(a) Any part of a decedent's estate not effectively disposed of by will passes by intestate succession to the decedent's heirs as prescribed in this Code, except as modified by the decedent's will.

(b) A decedent by will may expressly exclude or limit the right of an individual or class to succeed to property of the decedent passing by intestate succession. If that individual or a member of that class survives the decedent, the share of the decedent's intestate estate to which that individual or class would have succeeded passes as if that individual or each member of that class had disclaimed his [or her] intestate share.

§ 2-102. [Share of Spouse.]

The intestate share of a decedent's surviving spouse is:

(1) the entire intestate estate if:

(i) no descendant or parent of the decedent survives the decedent; or

(ii) all of the decedent's surviving descendants are also descendants of the surviving spouse and there is no other descendant of the surviving spouse who survives the decedent;

(2) the first [$200,000], plus three-fourths of any balance of the intestate estate, if no descendant of the decedent survives the decedent, but a parent of the decedent survives the decedent;

(3) the first [$150,000], plus one-half of any balance of the intestate estate, if all of the decedent's surviving descendants are also descendants of the surviving spouse and the surviving spouse has one or more surviving descendants who are not descendants of the decedent;

(4) the first [$100,000], plus one-half of any balance of the intestate estate, if one or more of the decedent's surviving descendants are not descendants of the surviving spouse.

[ALTERNATIVE PROVISION FOR COMMUNITY PROPERTY STATES]

§ 2-102A. [Share of Spouse.]

(a) The intestate share of the surviving spouse in separate property is:

(1) the entire intestate estate if:

(i) no surviving issue or parent of the decedent, the entire intestate estate;

(ii) if there is no surviving issue but the decedent is survived by a parent or parents, the first [$50,000], plus one-half of the balance of the intestate estate;

(2) the first [$200,000], plus three-fourths of any balance of the intestate estate, if no descendant of the decedent survives the decedent, but a parent of the decedent survives the decedent;

(3) the first [$150,000], plus one-half of any balance of the intestate estate, if all of the decedent's surviving descendants are also descendants of the surviving spouse and the surviving spouse has one or more surviving descendants who are not descendants of the decedent;

(4) the first [$100,000], plus one-half of any balance of the intestate estate, if one or more of the decedent's surviving descendants are not descendants of the surviving spouse.

(b) The one-half of community property belonging to the decedent passes to the [surviving spouse] as the intestate share.

§ 2-103. [Share of Heirs Other Than Surviving Spouse.]

Any part of the intestate estate not passing to the decedent's surviving spouse under Section 2-102, or the entire intestate estate if there is no surviving spouse, passes in the following order to the individuals designated below who survive the decedent:

(1) to the decedent's descendants by representation;

(2) if there is no surviving descendant, to the decedent's parents equally if both survive, or to the surviving parent;

(3) if there is no surviving descendant or parent, to the descendants of the decedent's parents or either of them by representation;

(4) if there is no surviving issue, parent or descendant of a parent, but the decedent is survived by one or more grandparents or descendants of grandparents, half of the estate passes to the decedent's paternal grandparents equally if both survive, or to the surviving paternal grandparent, or to the descendants of the decedent's paternal grandparents or either of them if both are deceased, the descendants taking by representation; and the other half passes to the decedent's maternal relatives in the same manner; but if there is no surviving grandparent or descendant of a grandparent on either the paternal or the maternal side, the entire estate passes to the decedent's relatives on the other side in the same manner as the half.

§ 2-104. [Requirement That Heir Survive Decedent For 120 Hours.]

An individual who fails to survive the decedent by 120 hours is deemed to have predeceased the decedent for purposes of homestead allowance, exempt property and intestate succession, and the decedent's heirs are determined accordingly. If it is not established by clear and convincing evidence that an individual who would otherwise be an heir survived the decedent by 120 hours, it is deemed that the individual failed to survive for the required period. This section is not to be applied if its application would result in a taking of intestate estate by the state under Section 2-105.

§ 2-105. [No Taker.]

If there is no taker under the provisions of this Article, the intestate estate passes to the [state].

§ 2-106. [Representation.]

(a) [Definitions.] In this section:

(1) "Deceased descendant," "deceased parent," or "deceased grandparent" means a descendant, parent or grandparent who either predeceased the decedent or is deemed to have predeceased the decedent under Section 2-104.

(2) "Surviving descendant" means a descendant who neither predeceased the decedent nor is deemed to have predeceased the decedent under Section 2-104.

(b) [Decedent's Descendants.] If, under Section 2-103(1), a decedent's intestate estate or a part thereof passed "by representation" to the decedent's descendants, the estate or part thereof is divided into as many equal shares as there are (i) surviving descendants in the generation nearest to the decedent which contains one or more surviving descendants and (ii) deceased descendants in the same generation who left surviving descendants, if any. Each surviving descendant in the nearest generation is allocated one share. The remaining shares, if any, are combined and then divided in the same manner among the surviving descendants of the deceased descendants as if the surviving descendants who were allocated a share and their surviving descendants had predeceased the decedent.

(c) [Descendants of Parents or Grandparents.] If, under Section 2-103(3) or (4), a decedent's intestate estate or a part thereof passed "by representation" to the descendants of the decedent's deceased parents or either of them or to the descendants of the decedent's deceased paternal or maternal grandparents or either of them, the estate or part thereof is divided into as many equal shares as there are (i) surviving descendants in the generation nearest the deceased parents or either of them, or the deceased grandparents or either of them, that contains one or more surviving descendants and (ii) deceased descendants in the same generation who left surviving descendants, if any. Each surviving descendant in the nearest generation is allocated one share. The remaining shares, if any are combined and then divided in the same manner among the surviving descendants of the deceased descendants as if the surviving descendants who were allocated a share and their surviving descendants had predeceased the decedent.

§ 2-107. [Kindred of Half Blood.]

Relatives of the half blood inherit the same share they would inherit if they were of the whole blood.

§ 2-108. [Afterborn Heirs.]

An individual in gestation at a particular time is treated as living at that time if the individual lives 120 hours or more after birth.

§ 2-109. [Advancements.]

(a) If an individual person dies intestate as to all or a portion of his [or her] estate, property the decedent gave during the decedent's lifetime to an individual who, at the decedent's death, is an heir is treated as an advancement against the heir's intestate share only if (i) the decedent declared in a contemporaneous writing or the heir acknowledged in writing that the gift is an advancement or (ii) the decedent's contemporaneous writing or the heir's written acknowledgment otherwise indicates that the gift is to be taken into account in computing the division and distribution of the decedent's intestate estate.

(b) For purposes of subsection (a), property advanced is valued as of the time the heir came into possession or enjoyment of the property or as of the time of the decedent's death, whichever first occurs.

(c) If the recipient of the property fails to survive the decedent, the property is not taken into account in computing the division and distribution of the decedent's intestate estate, unless the decedent's contemporaneous writing provides otherwise.

§ 2-110. [Debts to Decedent.]

A debt owed to a decedent is not charged against the intestate share of any individual except the debtor. If the debtor fails to survive the decedent, the debt is not taken into account in computing the intestate share of the debtor's descendant.

§ 2-111. [Alienage.]

No individual is disqualified to take as an heir because the individual or an individual through whom he [or she] claims is or has been an alien.

[§ 2-112. [Dower and Curtesy Abolished.]

The estates of dower and curtesy are abolished.]

§ 2-113. [Persons Related to Decedent Through Two Lines.]

An individual who is related to the decedent through two lines of relationship is entitled to only a single share based on the relationship that would entitle the individual to the larger share.

§ 2-114. [Parent and Child Relationship.]

(a) Except as provided in subsections (b) and (c), for purposes of intestate succession by, through, or from a person, an individual is the child of his [or her] natural parents, regardless of their marital status. The parent and child relationship may be established under [the Uniform Parentage Act] [applicable state law] [insert appropriate statutory reference].

(b) An adopted individual is the child of his [or her] adopting parent or parents and not of his [or her] natural parents, but adoption of a child by the spouse of either natural parent has no effect on (i) the relationship between the child and that natural parent or (ii) the right of the child or a descendant of the child to inherit from or through the other natural parent.

(c) Inheritance from or through a child by either natural parent or his [of her] kindred is precluded unless that natural parent has openly treated the child as his [or hers], and has not refused to support the child.

Part 2
Elective Share of Surviving Spouse

§ 2-201. [Elective Share.]

(a) Elective-Share Amount. The surviving spouse of a decedent who dies domiciled in this State has a right of election, under the limitations and condition stated in this Part, to take an elective-share amount equal to the value of the elective-share percentage of the augmented estate, determined by the length of time the spouse and the decedent were married to each other, in accordance with the following schedule:

If the decedent and the spouse were married to each other:	The elective-share percentage is:
Less than 1 year	Supplemental Amount Only.
1 year but less than 2 years	3% of the augmented estate.
2 years but less than 3 years	6% of the augmented estate.
3 years but less than 4 years	9% of the augmented estate.
4 years but less than 5 years	12% of the augmented estate.
5 years but less than 6 years	15% of the augmented estate.
6 years but less than 7 years	18% of the augmented estate.
7 years but less than 8 years	21% of the augmented estate.
8 years but less than 9 years	24% of the augmented estate.
9 years but less than 10 years	27% of the augmented estate.
10 years but less than 11 years	30% of the augmented estate.
11 years but less than 12 years	34% of the augmented estate.
12 years but less than 13 years	38% of the augmented estate.
13 years but less than 14 years	42% of the augmented estate.
14 years but less than 15 years	46% of the augmented estate.
15 years or more	50% of the augmented estate.

(b) Supplemental Elective-Share Amount. If the sum of the amounts described in Sections 2-202(b)(3) and (4), 2-207(a)(1) and (3), and that part of the elective-share amount payable from the decedent's probate and reclaimable estates under Sections 2-207(b) and (c) is less than [$50,000], the surviving spouse is entitled to a supplemental elective-share amount equal to [$50,000], minus the sum of the amounts described in those sections. The supplemental elective-share amount is payable from the decedent's probate estate and from recipients of the decedent's reclaimable estate in the order of priority set forth in Sections 2-207(b) and (c).

(c) Non-Domiciliary. The right, if any, of the surviving spouse of a decedent who dies domiciled outside this State to take an elective share in property in this State is governed by the law of the decedent's domicile at death.

§ 2-202. [Augmented Estate.]

(a) Definitions.

(1) In this section:

(i) "Bona fide purchaser" means a purchaser for value in good faith and without notice of an adverse claim. The notation of a state documentary fee on a recorded instrument pursuant to [insert appropriate reference] is prima facie evidence that the transfer described therein was made to a bona fide purchaser.

(ii) "Nonadverse party" means a person who does not have a substantial beneficial interest in the trust or other property arrangement that would be adversely affected by the exercise or nonexercise of the power that he [or she] possesses respecting the trust or other property arrangement. A person having a general power of appointment over property is deemed to have a beneficial interest in the property.

(iii) "Presently exercisable general power of appointment" means a power of appointment under which, at the time in question, the decedent by an exercise of the power could have created an interest, present or future, in himself [or herself] or his [or her] creditors.

(iv) "Probate estate" means property, whether real or personal, movable or immovable, wherever situated, that would pass by intestate succession if the decedent died without a valid will.

(v) "Right to income" includes a right to payments under an annuity or similar contractual arrangement.

(vi) "Value of property owned by the surviving spouse at the decedent's death" and "value of property to which the surviving spouse succeeds by reason of the decedent's death" include the commuted value of any present or future interest then held by the surviving spouse and the commuted value of amounts payable to the surviving spouse after the decedent's death under any trust, life insurance settlement option, annuity contract, public or private pension, disability compensation, death benefit or retirement plan, or any similar arrangement, exclusive of the federal Social Security system.

(2) In subsections (b)(2)(iii) and (iv), "transfer" includes an exercise or release of a power of appointment, but does not include a lapse of a power of appointment.

(b) Property Included in Augmented Estate. The augmented estate consists of the sum of:

(1) the value of the decedent's probate estate, reduced by funeral and administration expenses, homestead allowance, family allowances and exemptions, and enforceable claims;

(2) the value of the decedent's reclaimable estate. The decedent's reclaimable estate is composed of all property, whether real or personal, movable or immovable, wherever

situated, not included in the decedent's probate estate, of any of the following types:

(i) property to the extent the passing of the principal thereof to or for the benefit of any person, other than the decedent's surviving spouse, was subject to a presently exercisable general power of appointment held by the decedent alone, if the decedent held that power immediately before his [or her] death or if and to the extent the decedent, while married to his [or her] surviving spouse and during the two-year period next preceding the decedent's death, released that power or exercised that power in favor of any person other than the decedent or the decedent's estate, spouse, or surviving spouse;

(ii) property, to the extent of the decedent's unilaterally severable interest therein, held by the decedent and any other person, except the decedent's surviving spouse, with right of survivorship, if the decedent held that interest immediately before his [or her] death or if and to the extent the decedent, while married to his [or her] surviving spouse and during the two-year period preceding the decedent's death, transferred that interest to any person other than the decedent's surviving spouse;

(iii) proceeds of insurance, including accidental death benefits, on the life of the decedent payable to any person other than the decedent's surviving spouse, if the decedent owned the insurance policy, had the power to change the beneficiary of the insurance policy, or the insurance policy was subject to a presently exercisable general power of appointment held by the decedent alone immediately before his [or her] death if and to the extent the decedent, while married to his [or her] surviving spouse and during the two-year period next preceding the decedent's death, transferred that policy to any person other than the decedent's surviving spouse; and

(iv) property transferred by the decedent to any person other than a bona fide purchaser at any time during the decedent's marriage to the surviving spouse, to or for the benefit of any person, other than the decedent's surviving spouse, if the transfer is of any of the following types:

(A) any transfer to the extent that the decedent retained at the time of his [or her] death the possession or enjoyment of, or right to income from, the property;

(B) any transfer to the extent that, at the time of or during the two-year period next preceding the decedent's death, the income or principal was subject to a power, exercisable by the decedent alone or in conjunction with any other person or exercisable by a nonadverse party, for the benefit of the decedent or the decedent's estate;

(C) any transfer of property, to the extent the decedent's contribution to it, as a percentage of the whole, was made within two years before the decedent's death, by which the property is held, at the time of or during the two-year period next preceding the decedent's death, by the decedent and another, other than the decedent's surviving spouse, with right of survivorship; or

(D) any transfer made to a donee within two years before the decedent's death to the extent that the aggregate transfers to any one donee in either of the years exceed $10,000.00;

(3) the value of property to which the surviving spouse succeeds by reason of the decedent's death, other than by homestead allowance, exempt property, family allowance, testate succession, or intestate succession, including the proceeds of insurance, including accidental death benefits, on the life of the decedent and benefits payable under a retirement plan in which the decedent was a participant, exclusive of the federal Social Security system; and

(4) the value of property owned by the surviving spouse at the decedent's death, reduced by enforceable claims against that property or that spouse, plus the value of amounts that would have been includible in the surviving spouse's reclaimable estate had the spouse predeceased the decedent. But amounts that would have been includible in the surviving spouse's reclaimable estate under subsection (b)(2)(iii) are not valued as if he [or she] were deceased.

(c) [Exclusions.] Any transfer or exercise or release of a power of appointment is excluded from the decedent's reclaimable estate (i) to the extent the decedent received adequate and full consideration in money or money's worth for the transfer, exercise, or release or (ii) if irrevocably made with the written consent or joinder of the surviving spouse.

(d) [Valuation.] Property is valued as of the decedent's death, but property irrevocably transferred during the two-year period next preceding the decedent's death which is included in the decedent's reclaimable estate under subsection (b)(2)(i), (ii), and (iv) is valued as of the time of the transfer. If the terms of more than one of the subparagraphs or sub-subparagraphs of subsection (b)(2) apply, the property is included in the augmented estate under the subparagraph or sub-subparagraph that yields the highest value. For the purposes of this subsection, an "irrevocable transfer of property" includes an irrevocable exercise or release of a power of appointment.

(e) [Protection of Payors and Other Third Parties.]

(1) Although under this section a payment, item of property, or other benefit is included in the decedent's reclaimable estate, a payor or other third party is not liable for having made a payment or transferred an item of property or other benefit to a beneficiary designated in a governing instrument, or for having taken any other action in good faith reliance on the validity of a governing instrument, upon request and satisfactory proof of the decedent's death, before the payor or other third party received written notice from the surviving spouse or spouse's representative of an intention to file a petition for the elective share or that a petition for the elective share has been filed. A payor or other third party is liable for payments made or other actions taken after the payor or other third party received written notice of an intention to file a petition for the elective share or that a petition for the elective share has been filed.

(2) The written notice of intention to file a petition for the elective share or that a petition for the elective share has been filed must be mailed to the payor's or other third party's main office or home by registered or certified mail, return receipt requested, or served upon the payor or other third party in the same manner as a summons in a civil action. Upon receipt of written notice of intention to file a petition for the elective share or that a petition for the elective share has been filed, a payor or other third party may pay any amount owed or transfer or deposit any item of property held by it to or with the court having jurisdiction of the probate proceedings relating to the decedent's estate, or if no proceedings have been commenced, to or with the court having jurisdiction of probate proceedings relating to decedents' estates located in the county of the decedent's residence. The court shall hold the funds or item of property and, upon its determination under Section 2-205 (d), shall order disbursement in accordance with the determination. If no petition is filed in the court within the specified time under Section 2-205(a) or, if filed, the demand for an elective share is withdrawn under Section 2-205(c), the court shall file disbursement to the designated beneficiary. Payments, transfers, or deposits

made to or with the court discharge the payor or other third party from all claims for the value of amounts paid to or items of property transferred to or deposited with the Court.

(3) Upon petition to the probate court by the beneficiary designated in a governing instrument, the court may order that all or part of the property be paid to the beneficiary in an amount and subject to conditions consistent with this section.

(f) [Protection of Bona Fide Purchasers; Personal Liability of Recipient.]

(1) A person who purchases property from a recipient for value and without notice, or who receives a payment or other item of property in partial or full satisfaction of a legally enforceable obligation, is neither obligated under this Part to return the payment, item of property, or benefit nor is liable under this Part for the amount of the payment or the value of the item of property or benefit. But a person who, not for value, receives a payment, item of property, or any other benefit included in the decedent's reclaimable estate is obligated to return the payment, item of property, or benefit, or is personally liable for the amount of the payment or the value of the item of property or benefit, as provided in Section 2-207.

(2) If any section or part of any section of this Part is preempted by federal law with respect to a payment, an item of property or any other benefit included in the decedent's reclaimable estate, a person who, not for value, receives the payment, item of property, or any other benefit is obligated to return that payment, item of property, or benefit, or is personally liable for the amount of that payment or the value of that item of property or benefit, as provided in Section 2-207, to the person who would have been entitled to it were that section or part of that section not preempted.

§ 2-203. [Right of Election Personal to Surviving Spouse.]

(a) [Surviving Spouse Must Be Living at Time of Election.] The right of election may be exercised only by a surviving spouse who is living when the petition for the elective share is filed in the court under Section 2-205(a). If the election is not exercised by the surviving spouse personally, it may be exercised on the surviving spouse's behalf by his [or her] conservator, guardian, or agent under the authority of a power of attorney.

(b) [Incapacitated Surviving Spouse.] If the election is exercised on behalf of a surviving spouse who is an incapacitated person, that portion of the elective-share and supplemental elective-share amounts due from the decedent's probate estate and recipients of the decedent's reclaimable estate under Sections 2-207(b) and (c) must be placed in a custodial trust for the benefit of the surviving spouse under the provisions of the [Enacting state] Uniform Custodial Trust Act, except as modified below. For the purposes of this subsection, an election on behalf of a surviving spouse by an agent under a durable power of attorney is presumed to be on behalf of a surviving spouse who is an incapacitated person. For purposes of the custodial trust established by this subsection, (i) the electing guardian, conservator, or agent is the custodial trustee, (ii) the surviving spouse is the beneficiary, (iii) the custodial trust is deemed to have been created by the decedent spouse by written transfer that takes effect at the decedent spouse's death and that directs the custodial trustee to administer the custodial trust as for an incapacitated beneficiary.

(c) [Custodial Trust.] For the purposes of subsection (b), the [Enacting state] Uniform Custodial Trust Act must be applied as if Section 6(b) thereof were repealed and Sections 2(e), 9(b), and 17(a) were amended to read as follows:

(1) Neither an incapacitated beneficiary nor anyone acting on behalf of an incapacitated beneficiary has a power to terminate the custodial trust; but if the beneficiary regains capacity, the beneficiary then acquires the power to terminate the custodial trust by delivering to the custodial trustee a writing signed by the beneficiary declaring the termination. If not previously terminated, the custodial trust terminates on the death of the beneficiary.

(2) If the beneficiary is incapacitated, the custodial trustee shall expend so much or all of the custodial trust property as the custodial trustee considers advisable for the use and benefit of the beneficiary and individuals who were supported by the beneficiary when the beneficiary became incapacitated, or who are legally entitled to support the beneficiary. Expenditures may be made in the manner, when, and to the extent that the custodial trustee determines suitable and proper, without court order but with regard to other support, income, and property of the beneficiary [exclusive of] [and] benefits of medical or other forms of assistance from any state or federal government or governmental agency for which the beneficiary must qualify on the basis of need.

(3) Upon the beneficiary's death, the remaining custodial trust property, in the following order: (i) under the residuary clause, if any, of the will of the beneficiary's predeceased spouse against whom the elective share was taken, as if that predeceased spouse died immediately after the beneficiary; or (ii) to that predeceased spouse's heirs under Section 2-711 of [this State's] Uniform Probate Code.

[STATES THAT HAVE NOT ADOPTED THE UNIFORM CUSTODIAL TRUST ACT SHOULD ADOPT THE FOLLOWING ALTERNATIVE SUBSECTION (B) AND NOT ADOPT SUBSECTION (B) OR (C) ABOVE]

[(b) [Incapacitated Surviving Spouse.] If the election is exercised on behalf of a surviving spouse who is an incapacitated person, the court must set aside that portion of the elective-share and supplemental elective-share amounts due from the decedent's probate estate and recipients of the decedent's reclaimable estate under Section 2-207(b) and (c) and must appoint a trustee to administer that property for the support of the surviving spouse. For the purposes of this subsection, an election on behalf of a surviving spouse by an agent under a durable power of attorney is presumed to be on behalf of a surviving spouse who is an incapacitated person. The trustee must administer the trust in accordance with the following terms and such additional terms as the court determines appropriate:

(1) Expenditures of income and principal may be made in the manner, when, and to the extent that the trustee determines suitable and proper for the surviving spouse's support, without court order but with regard to other support, income, and property of the surviving spouse [exclusive of] [and] benefits of medical or other forms of assistance from any state or federal government or governmental agency for which the surviving spouse must qualify on the basis of need.

(2) During the surviving spouse's incapacity, neither the surviving spouse nor anyone acting on behalf of the surviving spouse has a power to terminate the trust; but if the surviving spouse regains capacity, the surviving spouse then acquires the power to terminate the trust and acquire full ownership of the trust property free of trust, by delivering to the trustee a writing signed by the surviving spouse declaring the termination.

(3) Upon the surviving spouse's death, the trustee shall transfer the unexpended trust property in the following order: (i) under the residuary clause, if any, of the will of the predeceased spouse against whom the elective share was taken, as if that predeceased spouse died immediately after the surviving spouse; or (ii) to that predeceased spouse's heirs under Section 2-711.]

§ 2-204. [Waiver of Right to Elect and of Other Rights.]

(a) The right of election of a surviving spouse and the rights of the surviving spouse to homestead allowance, exempt property, and family allowance, or any of them, may be waived, wholly or partially, before or after marriage, by a written contract, agreement, or waiver signed by the surviving spouse.

(b) A surviving spouse's waiver is not enforceable if the surviving spouse proves that:

(1) he [or she] did not execute the waiver voluntarily; or

(2) the waiver was unconscionable when it was executed and, before execution of the waiver, he [or she]:

(i) was not provided a fair and reasonable disclosure of the property or financial obligations of the decedent;

(ii) did not voluntarily and expressly waive, in writing, any right to disclosure of the property or financial obligations of the decedent beyond the disclosure provided; and

(iii) did not have, or reasonably could not have had, an adequate knowledge of the property or financial obligations of the decedent.

(c) An issue of unconscionability of a waiver is for decision by the court as a matter of law.

(d) Unless it provides to the contrary, a waiver of "all rights" or equivalent language, in the property or estate of a present or prospective spouse or a complete property settlement entered into after or in anticipation of separation or divorce is a waiver of all rights to elective share, homestead allowance, exempt property, and family allowance by each spouse in the property of the other and a renunciation by each of all benefits that would otherwise pass to him [or her] from the other by intestate succession or by virtue of the provisions of any will executed before the waiver or property settlement.

§ 2-205. [Proceeding for Elective Share; Time Limit.]

(a) Except as provided in subsection (b), the election must be made by filing in the court and mailing or delivering to the personal representative, if any, a petition for the elective share within nine months after the decedent's death, or within six months after the probate of the decedent's will, whichever limitation later expires. The surviving spouse must give notice of the time and place set for hearing to persons interested in the estate and to the distributees and recipients of portions of the augmented estate whose interests will be adversely affected by the taking of the elective share. Except as provided in subsection (b), the decedent's reclaimable estate, described in Section 2-202(b)(2), is not included within the augmented estate for the purpose of computing the elective share, if the petition is filed later than nine months after the decedent's death.

(b) Within nine months after the decedent's death, the surviving spouse may petition the court for an extension of time for making an election. If, within nine months after the decedent's death, the spouse gives notice of the petition to all persons interested in the decedent's reclaimable estate, the court for cause shown by the surviving spouse may extend the time for election. If the court grants the spouse's petition for an extension, the decedent's reclaimable estate, described in Section 2-202(b)(2), is not excluded from the augmented estate for the purpose of computing the elective-share and supplemental elective-share amounts, if the spouse makes an election by filing in the court and mailing or delivering to the personal representative, if any, a petition for the elective share within the time allowed by the extension.

(c) The surviving spouse may withdraw his [or her] demand for an elective share at any time before entry of a final determination by the court.

(d) After notice and hearing, the Court shall determine the elective-share amounts, and supplemental elective-share amounts, and shall order its payment from the assets of the augmented estate or by contribution as appears appropriate under Section 2-207. If it appears that a fund or property included in the augmented estate has not come into the possession of the personal representative, or has been distributed by the personal representative, the court nevertheless shall fix the liability of any person who has any interest in the fund or property or who has possession thereof, whether as trustee or otherwise. The proceeding may be maintained against fewer than all persons against whom relief could be sought, but no person is subject to contribution in any greater amount than he [or she] would have been under Section 2-207 had relief been secured against all persons subject to contribution.

(e) An order or judgment of the court may be enforced as necessary in suit for contribution or payment in other courts of this State or other jurisdictions.

§ 2-206. [Effect of Election on Statutory Benefits.]

If the right of election is exercised by or on behalf of the surviving spouse, the surviving spouse's homestead allowance, exempt property, and family allowance, if any, are not charged against but are in addition to the elective-share and supplemental elective-share amounts.

§ 2-207. [Charging Spouse with Owned Assets and Gifts Received; Liability of Others for Balance of Elective Share.]

(a) [Elective-Share Amount Only.] In a proceeding for an elective share, the following are applied first to satisfy the elective-share amount and to reduce or eliminate any contributions due from the decedent's probate estate and recipients of the decedent's reclaimable estate:

(1) amounts included in the augmented estate which pass or have passed to the surviving spouse by testate or intestate succession;

(2) amounts included in the augmented estate under Section 2-202(b)(3);

(3) amounts included in the augmented estate which would have passed to the spouse but were disclaimed; and

(4) amounts included in the augmented estate under Section 2-202(b)(4) up to the applicable percentage thereof. For the purposes of this subsection, the "applicable percentage" is twice the elective-share percentage set forth in the schedule in Section 2-201(a) appropriate to the length of time the spouse and the decedent were married to each other.

(b) [Unsatisfied Balance of Elective Share-amount; Supplemental Elective-Share Amount.] If, after the application of subsection (a), the elective share is not fully satisfied or the surviving spouse is entitled to a supplemental elective-share amount, amounts included in the decedent's probate estate and that portion of the decedent's reclaimable estate other than amounts irrevocably transferred within two years before the decedent's death are applied first to satisfy the unsatisfied balance of the elective-share amount or the supplemental elective-share amount. The decedent's probate estate and that portion of the decedent's reclaimable estate are so applied that liability for the unsatisfied balance of the elective-share amount or for the supplemental elective-share amount is equitably apportioned among the recipients of the decedent's probate estate and that portion of the decedent's reclaimable estate in proportion to the value of their interests therein.

(c) [Unsatisfied Balance of Elective-Share and Supplemental Elective-Share Amounts.] If, after the application of subsections (a) and (b), the elective-share or supplemental elective-share amount is not fully satisfied, the remaining portion of the decedent's reclaimable estate is so applied that liability for the unsatisfied balance of the elective-share or supplemental elective-share amount is equitably apportioned among the recipients of that portion of the decedent's reclaimable estate in proportion to the value of their interests therein.

(d) [Liability of Recipients of Reclaimable Estate and Their Donees.] Only original recipients of the reclaimable estate described in Section 2-202(b)(2), and the donees of the recipients of the reclaimable estate to the extent the donees have the property or its proceeds, are liable to make a proportional contribution toward satisfaction of the surviving spouse's elective-share or supplemental elective-share amount. A person liable to make contribution may choose to give up the proportional part of the reclaimable estate or to pay the value of the amount for which he [or she] is liable.

Part 3
Spouse and Children Unprovided for in Wills

§ 2-301. [Entitlement of Spouse; Premarital Will.]

(a) If a testator's surviving spouse married the testator after the testator executed his [or her] will, the surviving spouse is entitled to receive, as an intestate share, no less than the value of the share of the estate he [or she] would have received if the testator had died intestate as to that portion of the testator's estate, if any, that neither is devised to a child of the testator who was born before the testator married the surviving spouse and who is not a child of the surviving spouse nor is devised or passes under Sections 2-603 or 2-604 to a descendant of such a child, unless:

(1) it appears from the will or other evidence that the will was made in contemplation of the testator's marriage to the surviving spouse;

(2) the will expresses the intention that it is to be effective notwithstanding any subsequent marriage; or

(3) the testator provided for the spouse by transfer outside the will and the intent that the transfer be in lieu of a testamentary provision is shown by the testator's statements or is reasonably inferred from the amount of the transfer or other evidence.

(b) In satisfying the share provided by this section, devises made by the will to the testator's surviving spouse, if any, are applied first, and other devises, other than a devise to a child of the testator who was born before the testator married the surviving spouse and who is not a child of the surviving spouse or a devise or substitute gift under Sections 2-603 or 2-604 to a descendant of such a child, abate as provided in Section 3-902.

§ 2-302. [Omitted Children.]

(a) Except as provided in subsection (b), if a testator fails to provide in his [or her] will for any of his [or her] children born or adopted after the execution of the will, the omitted after-born or after-adopted child receives a share in the estate as follows:

(1) If the testator had no child living when [or she] executes the will, an omitted after-born or after-adopted child receives a share in the estate equal in value to that which the child would have received had the testator died intestate, unless the will devised all or substantially all the estate to the other parent of the omitted child and that other parent survives the testator and is entitled to take under the will.

(2) If the testator had one or more children living when he [or she] executed the will, and the will devised property or an interest in property to one or more of the the-living children, an omitted after-born or after-adopted child is entitled to share in the testator's estate as follows:

(i) The portion of the testator's estate in which the omitted after-born or after-adopted child is entitled to share is limited to devises made to the testator's then-living children under the will.

(ii) The omitted after-born or after-adopted child is entitled to receive the share of the testator's estate, as limited in subparagraph (i), that the child would have received had the testator included all omitted after-born or after-adopted children with the children to whom devises were made under the will and had given an equal share of the estate to each child.

(iii) To the extent feasible, the interest granted and omitted after-born or after-adopted child under this section must be of the same character, whether equitable or legal, present or future, as that devised to the testator's then-living children under the will.

(iv) In satisfying a share provided by this paragraph, devises to the testator's children who were living when the will was executed abate ratably. In abating the devises of the then-living children, the court shall preserve to the maximum extent possible the character of the testamentary plan adopted by the testator.

(b) Neither subsection (a)(1) nor subsection (a)(2) applies if:

(1) it appears from the will that the omission was intentional; or

(2) the testator provided for the omitted after-born or after-adopted child by transfer outside the will and the intent that the transfer be in lieu of a testamentary provision is shown by testator's statements or is reasonably inferred from the amount of the transfer or other evidence.

(c) If at the time of execution of the will the testator fails to provide in his [or her] will for a living child solely because he believes the child to be dead, the child receives a share in the estate equal in value to that which the child would have received had the testator died intestate.

(d) In satisfying a share provided by subsection (a)(1) or (c), devises made by the will abate as provided in Section 3-902.

Part 4
Exempt Property and Allowances
§ 2-401. [Applicable Law.]

This Part applies to the estate of a decedent who dies domiciled in this State. Rights to homestead allowance, exempt property, and family allowance for a decedent who dies not domiciled in this State are governed by the law of the decedent's domicile at death.

§ 2-402. [Homestead Allowance.]

A decedent's surviving spouse is entitled to a homestead allowance of [$15,000]. If there is no surviving spouse, each minor child and each dependent child of the decedent is entitled to a homestead allowance amounting to [$15,000] divided by the number of minor and dependent children of the decedent. The homestead allowance is exempt from and has priority over all claims against the estate. Homestead allowance is in addition to any share passing to the surviving spouse or minor or dependent child by the will of the decedent, unless otherwise provided, by intestate succession, or by way of elective share.

[§ 2-402A. [Constitutional Homestead.]

The value of any constitutional right of homestead in the family home received by a surviving spouse or child must be charged against that spouse or child's homestead allowance to the extent that the family home is part of the decedent's estate or would have been but for the homestead provision of the constitution.]

§ 2-403. [Exempt Property.]

In addition to the homestead allowance, the decedent's surviving spouse is entitled from the estate to a value, not exceeding $10,000 in excess of any security interests therein, in household furniture, automobiles, furnishings, appliances and personal effects. If there is no surviving spouse, the decedent's children are entitled jointly to the same value. If encumbered chattels are selected and the value in excess of security interests, plus that of other exempt property in the estate, is less than $10,000, or if there is not $10,000 worth of exempt property in the estate, the spouse or children are entitled to other assets of the estate, if any, to the extent necessary to make up the $10,000 value. Rights to exempt property and assets needed to make up a deficiency of exempt property have priority over all claims against the estate, but the right to any assets to make up a deficiency of exempt property abates as necessary to permit earlier payment of homestead allowance and family allowance. These rights are in addition to any benefit or share passing to the surviving spouse or children by the decedent's will, unless otherwise provided, by intestate succession, or by way of elective share.

§ 2-404. [Family Allowance.]

(a) In addition to the right to homestead allowance and exempt property, the decedent's surviving spouse and minor children whom the decedent was obligated to support and children who were in fact being supported by the decedent are entitled to a reasonable allowance in money out of the estate for their maintenance during the period of administration, which allowance may not continue for longer than one year if the estate is inadequate to discharge allowed claims. The allowance may be paid as a lump sum or in periodic installments. It is payable to the surviving spouse, if living, for the use of the surviving spouse and minor and dependent children; otherwise to the children, or persons having their care and custody. If a minor child or dependent child is not living with the surviving spouse, the allowance may be made partially to the child or his [or her] guardian or other person having the child's care and custody, and partially to the spouse, as their needs may appear. The family allowance is exempt from and has priority over all claims except the homestead allowance.

(b) The family allowance is not chargeable against any benefit or share passing to the surviving spouse or children by the will of the decedent, unless otherwise provided, by intestate succession, or by way of elective share. The death of any person entitled to family allowance terminates his right to allowances not yet paid.

§ 2-405. [Source, Determination, and Documentation.]

(a) If the estate is otherwise sufficient, property specifically devised may not be used to satisfy rights to homestead allowance or exempt property. Subject to this restriction, the surviving spouse, the guardians of minor children, or children who are adults may select property of the estate as homestead allowance and exempt property. The personal representative may make those selections if the surviving spouse, the children, or the guardians of the minor children are unable or fail to do so within a reasonable time or if there is no guardian of the minor child. The personal representative may execute an instrument or deed of distribution to establish the ownership of property taken as homestead allowance or exempt property. The personal representative may determine the family allowance in a lump sum not exceeding $18,000 or periodic installments not exceeding $1,500 per month for one year, and may disburse funds of the estate in payment of the family allowance and any part of the homestead allowance payable in cash. The personal representative or any interested person aggrieved by any selection, determination, payment, proposed payment, or failure to act under this section may petition the court for appropriate relief, which relief may include a family allowance other than that which the personal representative determined or could have determined.

(b) If the right to an elective share is exercised on behalf of a surviving spouse who is an incapacitated person, the personal representative may add any unexpended portions payable under the homestead allowance, exempt property, and family allowance to the trust established under Section 2-203(b).

Part 5
Wills, Will Contracts, and Custody and Deposit of Wills

§ 2-501. [Who May Make Will.]

An individual 18 or more years of age who is of sound mind may make a will.

§ 2-502. [Execution; Witnessed Wills; Holographic Wills.]

(a) Except as provided in subsection (b) and in Sections 2-503, 2-506, and 2-513, a will must be:

(1) in writing;

(2) signed by the testator or in the testator's name by some other individual in the testator's conscious presence and by the testator's direction; and

(3) signed by at least two individuals, each of whom signed within a reasonable time after he [or she] witnessed either the signing of the will as described in paragraph (2) or the testator's acknowledgment of that signature or acknowledgment of the will.

(b) A will that does not comply with subsection (a) is valid as a holographic will, whether or not witnessed, if the signature and material portions of the document are in the testator's handwriting.

(c) Intent that the document constitute the testator's will can be established by extrinsic evidence, including, for holographic wills, portions of the document that are not in the testator's handwriting.

§ 2-503. [Writings Intended as Wills, etc.]

Although a document or writing added upon a document was not executed in compliance with Section 2-502, the document or writing is treated as if it had been executed in compliance with that section if the proponent of the document or writing establishes by clear and convincing evidence that the decedent intended the document or writing to constitute (i) the decedent's will, (ii) a partial or complete revocation of the will, (iii) an addition to or an alteration of the will, or (iv) a partial or complete revival of his [or her] formerly revoked will or of a formerly revoked portion of the will.

§ 2-504. [Self-proved Will.]

(a) A will may be simultaneously executed, attested, and made self-proved, by acknowledgment thereof by the testator and affidavits of the witnesses, each made before an officer authorized to administer oaths under the laws of the state in which execution occurs and evidenced by the officer's certificate, under official seal, in substantially the following form:

I, _____, the testator, sign my name to this instrument this _____ day of _____, 19_____, and being first duly sworn, do hereby declare to the undersigned authority that I sign if willingly (or willingly direct another to sign for me), that I execute it as my free and voluntary act for the purposes therein expressed, and that I am eighteen years of age or older, of sound mind, and under no constraint or undue influence.

_____
Testator

We, _____, _____, the witnesses, sign our names to this instrument, being first duly sworn, and do hereby declare to the undersigned authority that the testator signs and executes this instrument as his [her] last will and that [he] [she] signs it willingly (or willingly directs another to sign for [him] [her]), and that each of us, in the presence and hearing of the testator, hereby

signs this will as witness to the testator's signing, and that to the best of our knowledge the testator is eighteen years of age or older, of sound mind, and under no constraint or undue influence.

_____
Witness

_____
Witness

The State of _____
County of _____

Subscribed, sworn to and acknowledged before me by _____, the testator and subscribed and sworn to before me by _____, and _____, witness, this _____ day of _____.

(Seal)

(Signed) _____
(Official capacity of officer)

(b) An attested will may be made self-proved at any time after its execution by the acknowledgment thereof by the testator and the affidavits of the witnesses, each made before an officer authorized to administer oaths under the laws of the state in which the acknowledgment occurs and evidenced by the officer's certificate, under the official seal, attached or annexed to the will in substantially the following form:

The State of _____
County of _____

We, _____, _____, and _____, the testator and the witnesses, respectively, whose names are signed to the attached or foregoing instrument, being first duly sworn, do hereby declare to the undersigned authority that the testator signed and executed the instrument as his last will and that [he] [she] had signed willingly (or willingly directed another to sign for [him] [her]), and that [he] [she] executed it as [his] [her] free and voluntary act for the purposes therein expressed, and that each of the witnesses, in the presence and hearing of the testator, signed the will as witness and that to the best of [his] [her] knowledge the testator was at that time eighteen years of age or older, of sound mind and under no constraint or undue influence.

_____
Testator

_____
Witness

_____
Witness

Subscribed, sworn to and acknowledged before me by _____, the testator, and subscribed and sworn to before me by _____, and witnesses, this _____ day of _____.

(Seal)
(Seal)

(Signed) _____
(Official capacity of officer)

(c) A signature affixed to a self-proving affidavit attached to a will is considered a signature affixed to the will, if necessary to prove the will's due execution.

§ 2-505. [Who May Witness.]

(a) An individual generally competent to be a witness may act as a witness to a will.

(b) The signing of a will by an interested witness does not invalidate the will or any provision of it.

§ 2-506. [Choice of Law as to Execution.]

A written will is valid if executed in compliance with Section 2-502 or 2-503 or if its execution complies with the law at the time of execution of the place where the will is executed, or of the law of the place where at the time of execution or at the time of death the testator is domiciled, has a place of abode, or is a national.

§ 2-507. [Revocation by Writing or by Act.]

(a) A will or any part thereof is revoked:

(1) by executing a subsequent will that revokes the previous will or part expressly or by inconsistency; or

(2) by performing a revocatory act on the will, if the testator performed the act with the intent and for the purpose of revoking the will or part or if another individual performed the act in the testator's conscious presence and by the testator's direction. For purposes of this paragraph, "revocatory act on the will" includes burning, tearing,

canceling, obliterating, or destroying the will or any part of it. A burning, tearing, or canceling is a "revocatory act on the will," whether or not the burn, tear, or cancellation touched any of the words on the will.

(b) If a subsequent will does not expressly revoke a previous will, the execution of the subsequent will wholly revokes the previous will by inconsistency if the testator intended the subsequent will to replace rather than supplement the previous will.

(c) The testator is presumed to have intended a subsequent will to replace rather than supplement a previous will if the subsequent will makes a complete disposition of the testator's estate. If this presumption arises and is not rebutted by clear and convincing evidence, the previous will is revoked; only the subsequent will is operative on the testator's death.

(d) The testator is presumed to have intended a subsequent will to supplement rather than replace a previous will if the subsequent will does not make a complete disposition of the testator's estate. If this presumption arises and is not rebutted by clear and convincing evidence, the subsequent will revokes the previous will only to the extent the subsequent will is inconsistent with the previous will; each will is fully operative on the testator's death to the extent they are not inconsistent.

§ 2-508. [Revocation by Change of Circumstances.]

Except as provided in Sections 2-803 and 2-804, a change of circumstances does not revoke a will or any part of it.

§ 2-509. [Revival of Revoked Will.]

(a) If a subsequent will that wholly revoked a previous will is thereafter revoked by a revocatory act under Section 2-507(a)(2), the previous will remains revoked unless it is revived. The previous will is revived if it is evident from the circumstances of the revocation of the subsequent will or from the testator's contemporary or subsequent declarations that the testator intended the previous will to take effect as executed.

(b) If a subsequent will that partly revoked a previous will is thereafter revoked by a revocatory act under Section 2-507(a)(2), a revoked part of the previous will is revived unless it is evident from circumstances of the revocation of the subsequent will or from the testator's contemporary or subsequent declarations that the testator did not intend the revoked part to to take effect as executed.

(c) If a subsequent will that revoked a previous will in whole or in part is thereafter revoked by another, later, will, the previous will remains revoked in whole or in part, unless it or its revoked part is revived. The previous will or its revoked part is revived to the extent it appears from the terms of the later will that the testator intended the previous will to take effect.

§ 2-510. [Incorporation by Reference.]

A writing in existence when a will is executed may be incorporated by reference if the language of the will manifests this intent and describes the writing sufficiently to permit its identification.

§ 2-511. [Testamentary Additions to Trusts.]

(a) A will may validly devise property to the trustee of a trust established or to be established (i) during the testator's lifetime by the testator, or by the testator and some other person, or by some other person, including a funded or unfunded life insurance trust, although the settlor has reserved any or all rights of ownership of the insurance contracts, or (ii) at the testator's death by the testator's devise to the trustee, if the trust is identified in the testator's will and its terms are set forth in a written instrument, other than a will, executed before, concurrently with, or after the execution of the testator's will or in another individual's will if that other individual has predeceased the testator, regardless of the existence, size, or character of the corpus of the trust. The devise is not invalid because the trust is amendable or revocable, or because the trust was amended after the execution of the will or the death of the testator.

(b) Unless the testator's will provides otherwise, property devised to a trust described in subsection (a) is not held under a testamentary trust of the testator, but it becomes a part of the trust to which it is devised, and must be administered and disposed of in accordance with the provisions of the governing instrument setting forth the terms of the trust, including any amendments thereto made before or after the testator's death.

(c) Unless the testator's will provides otherwise, a revocation or termination of the trust before the testator's death causes the devise to lapse.

§ 2-512. [Events of Independent Significance.]

A will may dispose of property by reference to acts and events that have significance apart from their effect upon the dispositions made by the will, whether they occur before or after the execution of the will or before or after the testator's death. The execution or revocation of another individual's will is such an event.

§ 2-513. [Separate Writing Identifying Devise of Certain Types of Tangible Personal Property.]

Whether or not the provisions relating to holographic wills apply, a will may refer to a written statement or list to dispose of items of tangible personal property not otherwise specifically disposed of by the will, other than money. To be admissible under this section as evidence of the intended disposition, the writing must be signed by the testator and must describe the items and the devisees with reasonable certainty. The writing may be referred to as one to be in existence at the time of the testator's death; it may be prepared before or after the execution of the will; it may be altered by the testator after its preparation; and it may be a writing which has no significance apart from its effect on the dispositions made by the will.

§ 2-514. [Contracts Concerning Succession.]

A contract to make a will or devise, or not to revoke a will or devise, or to die intestate, if executed after the effective date of this Article, may be established only by (i) provisions of a will stating material provisions of the contract, (ii) an express reference in a will to a contract and extrinsic evidence proving the terms of the contract, or (iii) a writing signed by the decedent evidencing the contract. The execution of a joint will or mutual wills does not create a presumption of a contract not to revoke the will or wills.

§ 2-515. [Deposit of Will with Court in Testator's Lifetime.]

A will may be deposited by the testator or the testator's agent with any court for safekeeping under rules of the court. The will must be sealed and kept confidential. During the testator's lifetime, a deposited will must be delivered only to the testator or to a person authorized in writing signed by the testator to receive the will. A conservator may be allowed to examine a deposited will of a protected testator under procedures designed to maintain the confidential character of the document to the extent possible, and to ensure that it will be resealed and kept on deposit after the examination. Upon being informed of the testator's death, the court shall notify any person designated to receive the will and deliver it to that person on request; or the court may deliver the will to the appropriate court.

§ 2-516. [Duty of Custodian of Will; Liability.]

After death of a testator and on request of an interested person, a person having custody of a will of the testator shall deliver it with reasonable promptness to a person able to secure its probate and if none is known, to an appropriate court. A person who wilfully fails to deliver a will is liable to any person aggrieved for any damages that may be sustained by the failure. A person who wilfully refuses or fails to deliver a will after being ordered by the court in a proceeding brought for the purpose of compelling delivery is subject to penalty for contempt of court.

§ 2-517. [Penalty Clause for Contest.]

A provision in a will purporting to penalize an interested person for contesting the will or institution other proceedings relating to the estate is unenforceable if probable cause exists for instituting proceedings.

Part 6
Rules of Construction Applicable Only to Wills
§ 2-601. [Scope.]

In the absence of a finding of a contrary intention, the rules of construction in this Part control the construction of a will.

§ 2-602. [Will May Pass All Property and After-Acquired Property.]

A will may provide for the passage of all property the testator owns at death and all property acquired by the estate after the testator's death.

§ 2-603. [Antilapse; Deceased Devisee;Class Gifts.]

(a) [Definitions.] In this section:

(1) "Alternative devise" means a devise that is expressly created by the will and, under the terms of the will, can take effect instead of another devise on the happening of one or more events, including survival of the testator or failure to survive the testator, whether an event is expressed in condition-precedent, condition-subsequent, or any other form. A residuary clause constitutes an alternative devise with respect to a nonresiduary devise only if the will specifically proves that, upon lapse or failure, the nonresiduary devise, or nonresiduary devises in general, pass under the residuary clause.

(2) "Class member" includes an individual who fails to survive the testator but who would have taken under a devise in the form of a class gift had he [or she] survived the testator.

(3) "Devise" includes an alternative devise, a devise in the form of a class gift, and an exercise of a power of appointment.

(4) "Devisee" includes (i) a class member if the devise is in the form of a class gift, (ii) the beneficiary of a trust but not the trustee, (iii) an individual or class member who was deceased at the time the testator executed his [or her] will as well as an individual or class member who was then living but who failed to survive the testator, and (iv) an appointee under a power of appointment exercised by the testator's will.

(5) "Stepchild" means a child of the surviving, deceased, or former spouse of the testator or of the donor of a power of appointment, and not of the testator or donor.

(6) "Surviving devisee" or "surviving descendant" means a devisee or a descendant who neither predeceased the testator nor is deemed to have predeceased the testator under Section 2-702.

(7) "Testator" includes the donee of a power of appointment if the power is exercised in the testator's will.

(b) [Substitute Gift.] If a devisee fails to survive the testator and is a grandparent, a descendant of a grandparent, or a stepchild of either the testator or the donor of a power of appointment exercised by the testator's will, the following apply:

(1) Except as provided in paragraph (4), if the devise is not in the form of a class gift and the deceased devisee leaves surviving descendants, a substitute gift is created in the devisee's surviving descendants. They take by representation the property to which the devisee would have been entitled had the devisee survived the testator.

(2) Except as provided in paragraph (4), if the devise is in the form of a class gift, other than a devise to "issue," "descendants," "heirs of the body," "heirs," "next of kin," "relatives," or "family," or a class described by language of similar import, a substitute gift is created in the deceased devisee or devisee's surviving descendants. The property to which the devisees would have been entitled had all of them survived the testator passes to the surviving devisees and the surviving descendants of the deceased devisees. Each surviving devisee takes the share to which he [or she] would have been entitled had the deceased devisees survived the testator. Each deceased devisee's surviving descendants who are substituted for the deceased devisee take by representation the share to which the deceased devisee would have been entitled had the deceased devisee survived the testator. For the purposes of this paragraph, "deceased devisee" means a class member who failed to survive the testator and left one or more surviving descendants.

(3) For the purposes of Section 2-601, words of survivorship, such as in a devise to an individual "if he survives

me," or in a devise to "my surviving children," are not, in the absence of additional evidence, a sufficient indication of an intent contrary to the application of this section.

(4) If the will creates an alternative devise with respect to a devise for which a substitute gift is created by paragraph (1) or (2), the substitute gift is superseded by the alternative devise only if an expressly designated devisee of the alternative devise is entitled to take under the will.

(5) Unless the language creating a power of appointment expressly excludes the substitution of the descendants of an appointee for the appointee, a surviving descendant of a deceased appointee of a power of appointment can be substituted for the appointee under this section, whether or not the descendant is an object of the power.

(c) [More Than One Substitute Gift; Which One Takes.] If, under subsection (b), substitute gifts are created and not superseded with respect to more than one devise and the devises are alternative devises, one to the other, the determination of which of the substitute gifts takes effect is resolved as follows:

(1) Except as provided in paragraph (2), the devised property passes under the primary substitute gift.

(2) If there is a younger-generation devise, the devised property passes under the younger-generation substitute gift and not under the primary substitute gift.

(3) In this subsection:

(i) "Primary devise" means the devise that would have taken effect had all the deceased devisees of the alternative devises who left surviving descendants survived the testator.

(ii) "Primary substitute gift" means the substitute gift created with respect to the primary devise.

(iii) "Younger-generation devise" means a devise that (A) is to a descendant of a devisee of the primary devise, (B) is an alternative devise with respect to the primary devise, (C) is a devise for which a substitute gift is created, and (D) would have taken effect had all the deceased devisees who left surviving descendants survived the testator except the deceased devisee or devisees of the primary devise.

(iv) "Younger-generation substitute gift" means the substitute gift created with respect to the younger-generation devise.

§ 2-604. [Failure of Testamentary Provision.]

(a) Except as provided in Section 2-603, a devise, other than a residuary devise, that fails for any reason becomes a part of the residue.

(b) Except as provided in Section 2-603, if the residue is devised to two or more persons, the share of a residuary devisee that fails for any reason, his share passes to the other residuary devisee, or to other residuary devisees in proportion to the interest of each in the remaining part of the residue.

§ 2-605. [Increase in Securities; Accessions.]

(a) If a testator executes a will that devises securities and the testator then owned securities that meet the description in the will, the devise includes additional securities owned by the testator at death to the extent the additional securities were acquired by the testator after the will was executed as a result of the testator's ownership of the described securities and are securities of any of the following types:

(1) securities of the same organization acquired by reason of action initiated by the organization or any successor, related, or acquiring organization, excluding any acquired by exercise of purchase options;

(2) securities of another organization acquired as a result of a merger, consolidation, reorganization, or other distribution by the organization or any successor, related, or acquiring organization; or

(3) securities of the same organization acquired as a result of a plan of reinvestment.

(b) Distributions in cash before death with respect to a described security are not part of the devise.

§ 2-606. [Nonademption of Specific Devises; Unpaid Proceeds of Sale, Condemnation, or Insurance; Sale by Conservator or Agent.]

(a) A specific devisee has a right to the remaining specifically devised property in the testator's estate at death and:

(1) any balance of the purchase price, together with any security agreement, owing from a purchaser to the testator at death by reason of sale of the property;

(2) any amount of a condemnation award for the taking of the property unpaid at death;

(3) any proceeds unpaid at death on fire or casualty insurance on or other recovering for injury to the property;

(4) property owned by the testator at death and acquired as a result of foreclosure, or obtained in lieu of foreclosure, of the security interest for a specifically devised obligation;

(5) real or tangible personal property owned by the testator at death which the testator acquired as a replacement for specifically devised real or tangible personal property; and

(6) unless the facts and circumstances indicate that ademption of the devise was intended by the testator or ademption of the devise is consistent with the testator's manifested plan of distribution, the value of the specifically devised property to the extent the specifically devised property is not in the testator's estate at death and its value or its replacement is not covered by paragraphs (1) through (5).

(b) If specifically devised property is sold or mortgaged by a conservator or an agent acting within the authority of a durable power of attorney for an incapacitated principal, or if a condemnation award, insurance proceeds, or recovery for injury to the property are paid to a conservator or to an agent acting within the authority of a durable power of attorney for an incapacitated principal, the specific devisee has the right to a general pecuniary devise equal to the net sale price, the amount of the unpaid loan, the condemnation award, the insurance proceeds, or the recovery.

(c) The right of a specific devisee under subsection (b) is reduced by any right the devisee has under subsection (a).

(d) For the purposes of the references in subsection (b) to a conservator, subsection (b) does not apply if after the sale, mortgage, condemnation, casualty, or recovery, it was adjudicated that the testator's incapacity ceased and the testator survived the adjudication by one year.

(e) For the purposes of the reference in subsection (b) to an agent acting within the authority of a durable power of attorney for an incapacitated principal, (i) "incapacitated principal" means a principal who is an incapacitated person, (ii) no adjudication of incapacity before death is necessary, and (iii) the acts of an agent within the authority of a durable power of attorney are presumed to be for an incapacitated principal.

§ 2-607. [Nonexoneration.]

A specific devise passes subject to any mortgage interest existing at the date of death, without right of exoneration, regardless of a general directive in the will to pay debts.

§ 2-608. [Exercise of Power of Appointment.]

In the absence of a requirement that a power of appointment be exercised by a reference, or by an express of specific reference, to the power, a general residuary clause in a will, or a will making general disposition of all of the testator's property, expresses an intention to exercise a power of appointment held by the testator only if (i) the power is a general power and the creating instrument does not contain a gift if the power is not exercised or (ii) the testator's will manifests an intention to include the property subject to the power.

§ 2-609. [Ademption by Satisfaction.]

(a) Property which a testator gave in his [or her] lifetime to a person is treated as a satisfaction of a devise in whole or in part, only if (i) the will provides for deduction of the lifetime gift, (ii) the testator declared in a contemporaneous writing that the gift is in satisfaction of the devise or that its value is to be deducted from the devise, or (iii) the devisee acknowledges in writing that the gift is in satisfaction of the devise or that its value is to be deducted from the value of the devise.

(b) For purposes of partial satisfaction, property given during lifetime is valued as of the time the devisee came into possession or enjoyment of the property or at the testator's death, whichever occurs first.

(c) If the devisee fails to survive the testator, the gift is treated as a full or partial satisfaction of the devise, as appropriate, in applying Sections 2-603 and 2-604, unless the testator's contemporaneous writing provides otherwise.

Part 7
Rules of Construction Applicable to Donative Dispositions in Wills and Other Governing Instruments

§ 2-701. [Scope.]

In the absence of a finding of a contrary intention, the rules of construction in this Part control the construction of a governing instrument. The rules of construction in this Part apply to a governing instrument of any type, except as the application of a particular section is limited by its terms to a specific type or types of donative disposition or governing instrument.

§ 2-702. [Requirement of Survival by 120 Hours.]

(a) [Requirement of Survival by 120 Hours Under Probate Code.] For the purposes of this Code, except for purposes of Part 3 of Article VI [Uniform TOD Security Registration Act] and except as provided in subsection (d), an individual who is not established by clear and convincing evidence to have survived an event, including the death of another individual, by 120 hours is deemed to have predeceased the event.

(b) [Requirement of Survival by 120 Hours under Donative Provision of Governing Instrument.] Except as provided in subsection (d) and except for a security registered in beneficiary form (TOD) under Part 3 of Article VI [Uniform TOD Security Registration Act], for purposes of a donative provision of a governing instrument, an individual who is not established by clear and convincing evidence to have survived an event, including the death of another individual, by 120 hours is deemed to have predeceased the event.

(c) [Co-owners with Right of Survivorship; Requirement of Survival by 120 Hours.] Except as provided in subsection (d), if (i) it is not established by clear and convincing evidence that one of two co-owners with right of survivorship survived the other co-owner by 120 hours, one-half of the property passes as if one had survived by 120 hours and one-half as if the other had survived by 120 hours and (ii) there are more than two co-owners and it is not established by clear and convincing evidence that at least one of them survived the others by 120 hours, the property passes in the proportion that one bears to the whole number of co-owners. For the purposes of this subsection, "co-owners with right of survivorship" includes joint tenants, tenants by the entireties, and other co-owners of property or accounts held under circumstances that entitles one or more to the whole of the property or account on the death of the other or others.

(d) [Exceptions.] This section does not apply if:

(1) the governing instrument contains anguage dealing explicitly with simultaneous deaths or deaths in a common disaster and that language is operable under the facts of the case;

(2) the governing instrument expressly indicates that an individual is not required to survive an event, including the death of another individual, by any specified period or expressly requires the individual to survive the event by a specified period;

(3) the imposition of a 120-hour requirement of survival would cause a nonvested property interest or a power of appointment to fail to qualify for validity under Section 2-901(a)(1), (b)(1), or (c)(1) or to become invalid under Section 2-901(a)(2), (b)(2), or (c)(2); or

(4) the application of this section to multiple governing instruments would result in an unintended failure or duplication of a disposition.

(e) [Protection of Payors and Other Third Parties.]

(1) A payor or other third party is not liable for having made a payment or transferred an item of property or any other benefit to a beneficiary designated in a governing instrument who, under this section, is not entitled to the payment or item of property, or for having taken any other action in good faith reliance on the beneficiary's apparent entitlement under the terms of the governing instrument, before the payor or other third party received written notice of a claimed lack of entitlement under this section. A payor or other third party is liable for a payment made or other action taken after the payor or other third party received written notice of a claimed lack of entitlement under this section.

(2) Written notice of a claimed lack of entitlement under paragraph (1) must be mailed to the payor's or other third party's main office or home by registered or certified mail, return receipt requested, or served upon the payor or other third party in the same manner as a summons in a civil action. Upon receipt of written notice of a claimed lack of entitlement under this section, a payor or other third party may pay any amount owed or transfer or deposit any item of property held by it to or with the court having jurisdiction of the probate-proceedings relating to the decedent's estate, or if no proceedings have been commenced, to or with the court having jurisdiction of probate proceedings relating to decedents' estates located in the county of the decedent's residence. The court shall hold the funds or item of property and, upon its determination under this section, shall order disbursement in accordance with the determination. Payments, transfers, or deposits made to or with the court discharge the payor or other third party from all claims for the value of amounts paid to or items of property transferred to or deposited with the court.

(f) [Protection of Bona Fide Purchaser; Personal Liability of Recipient.]

(1) A person who purchases property for value and without notice, or who receives a payment or other item of property in partial or full satisfaction of a legally enforceable obligation, is neither obligated under this section to return the payment, item of property, or benefit nor is liable under this section for the amount of the

payment or the value of the item of property or benefit. But a person who, not for value, receives a payment, item of property or any other benefit to which the person is not entitled under this section is obligated to return the payment, item of property, or benefit, or is personally liable for the amount of the payment or the value of the item of property or benefit, to the person who is entitled to it under this section.

(2) If this section or any part of this section is preempted by federal law with respect to a payment, an item of property, or any other benefit covered by this section, a person who, not for value, receives the payment, item of property, or any other benefit to which the person is not entitled under this section is obligated to return the payment, item of property, or benefit or is personally liable for the amount of the payment or the value of the item of property or benefit, to the person who would have been entitled to it were this section or part of this section not preempted.

§ 2-703. [Choice of Law as to Meaning and Effect of Donative Dispositions.]

The meaning and legal effect of a donative disposition is determined by the local law of the state selected by the transferor in the governing instrument, unless the application of that law is contrary to the provisions relating to the elective share described in Part 2, the provisions relating to exempt property and allowances described in Part 4, or any other public policy of this State otherwise applicable to the disposition.

§ 2-704. [Power of Appointment; Meaning of Specific Reference Requirement.]

If a governing instrument creating a power of appointment expressly requires that the power be exercised by a reference, an express reference, or a specific reference, to the power or its source, it is presumed that the donor's intention, in requiring that the donee exercise the power by making reference to the particular power or to the creating instrument, was to prevent an inadvertent exercise of the power.

§ 2-705. [Class Gifts Construed to Accord With Intestate Succession.]

(a) Adopted individuals and individuals born out of wedlock, and their respective descendants if appropriate to the class, are included in class gifts and other terms of relationship in accordance with the rules for intestate succession. Terms of relationship that do not differentiate relationships by blood from those by affinity, such as "uncles," "aunts,"

"nieces," or "nephews," are construed to exclude relatives by affinity. Terms of relationship that do not differentiate relationships by the half blood from those by the whole blood, such as "brothers," "sisters," "nieces," or "nephews," are construed to include both types of relationships.

(b) In addition to the requirements of subsection (a), in construing a donative disposition by a transferor who is not the natural parent, an individual born to the natural parent is not considered the child of that parent unless the individual lived while a minor as a regular member of the household of that natural parent or of that parent's parent, brother, sister, spouse, or surviving spouse.

(c) In addition to the requirements of subsection (a), in construing a donative disposition by a transferor who is not the adopting parent, an adopted individual is not considered the child of the adopting parent unless the adopted individual lived while a minor, either before or after the adoption, as a regular member of the household of the adopting parent.

§ 2-706. [Life Insurance; Retirement Plan; Account With POD Designation; Transfer-on-Death Registration; Deceased Beneficiary.]

(a) [Definitions.] In this section:

(1) "Alternative beneficiary designation" means a beneficiary designation that is expressly created by the governing instrument and, under the terms of the governing instrument, can take effect instead of another beneficiary designation on the happening of one or more events, including survival of the decedent or failure to survive the decedent, whether an event is expressed in condition-precedent, condition-subsequent, or any other form.

(2) "Beneficiary" means the beneficiary of a beneficiary designation and includes (i) a class member if the beneficiary designation is in the form of a class gift and (ii) an individual or class member who was deceased at the time the beneficiary designation was executed as well as an individual or class member who was then living but who failed to survive the decedent.

(3) "Beneficiary designation" includes an alternative beneficiary designation and a beneficiary designation in the form of a class gift.

(4) "Class member" includes an individual who fails to survive the decedent but who would have taken under a beneficiary designation in the form of a class gift had he [or she] survived the decedent.

(5) "Stepchild" means a child of the decedent's surviving, deceased, or former spouse, and not of the decedent.

(6) "Surviving beneficiary" or "surviving descendant" means a beneficiary or a descendant who neither predeceased the decedent nor is deemed to have predeceased the decedent under Section 2-702.

(b) [Substitute Gift.] If a beneficiary fails to survive the decedent and is a grandparent, a descendent of a grandparent, or a stepchild of the decedent, the following apply:

(1) Except as provided in paragraph (4), if the beneficiary designation is not in the form of a class gift and the deceased beneficiary leaves surviving descendants, a substitute gift is created in the beneficiary's surviving descendants. They take by representation the property to which the beneficiary would have been entitled had the beneficiary survived the decedent.

(2) Except as provided in paragraph (4), if the beneficiary designation is in the form of a class gift, other than a beneficiary designation to "issue," "descendants," "heirs of the body," "heirs," "next of kin," "relatives," or "family," or a class described by language of similar import, a substitute gift is created in the deceased beneficiary or beneficiaries' surviving descendants. The property to which the beneficiaries would have been entitled had all of them survived the decedent passes to the surviving beneficiaries and the surviving descendants of the deceased beneficiaries. Each deceased beneficiary's surviving descendants takes the share to which he [or she] would have been entitled had the deceased beneficiaries survived the decedent. Each deceased beneficiary's surviving descendants who are substituted for the deceased beneficiary take by representation the share to which the deceased beneficiary would have been entitled had the deceased beneficiary survived the decedent. For the purposes of this paragraph, "deceased beneficiary" means a class member who failed to survive the decedent and left one or more surviving descendants.

(3) For the purposes of Section 2-701, words of survivorship, such as in a beneficiary designation to an individual "if he survives me," or in a beneficiary designation to "my surviving children," are not, in the absence of additional evidence, a sufficient indication of an intent contrary to the application of this section.

(4) If a governing instrument creates an alternative beneficiary designation with respect to a beneficiary designation for which a substitute gift is created by paragraph (1) or (2), the substitute gift is superseded by the alternative beneficiary designation only if an expressly designated beneficiary of the alternative beneficiary designation is entitled to take.

(c) [More Than One Substitute Gift; Which One Takes.] If, under subsection (b), substitute gifts are created and not superseded with respect to more than one beneficiary designation and the beneficiary designations are alternative beneficiary designations, one to the other, the determination of which of the substitute gifts takes effect is resolved as follows:

(1) Except as provided in paragraph (2), the devised property passes under the primary substitute gift.

(2) If there is a younger-generation beneficiary designation, the devised property passes under the younger-generation substitute gift and not under the primary substitute gift.

(3) In this subsection:

(i) "Primary beneficiary designation" means the beneficiary designation that would have taken effect had all the deceased beneficiaries of the alternative beneficiary designations who left surviving descendants survived the decedent.

(ii) "Primary substitute gift" means the substitute gift created with respect to the primary beneficiary designation.

(iii) "Younger-generation beneficiary designation" means a beneficiary designation that (A) is to a descendant of a beneficiary of the primary beneficiary designation, (B) is an alternative beneficiary designation with respect to the primary beneficiary designation, (C) is a beneficiary designation for which a substitute gift is created, and (D) would have taken effect had all the deceased beneficiaries who left surviving descendants survived the testator except the deceased beneficiary or beneficiaries of the primary beneficiary designation.

(iv) "Younger-generation substitute gift" means the substitute gift created with respect to the younger-generation beneficiary designation.

(d) [Protection of Payors.]

(1) A payor is protected from liability in making payments under the terms of the beneficiary designation until the payor has received written notice of a claim to a substitute gift under this section. Payment made before the receipt of written notice of a claim to a substitute gift under this section discharges the payor, but not the recipient, from all claims for the amounts paid. A payor is liable for a payment made after the payor has received written notice of the claim. A recipient is liable for a payment received, whether or not written notice of the claim is given.

(2) The written notice of the claim must be mailed to the payor's main office or home by registered or certified mail, return receipt requested, or served upon the payor in the same manner as a summons in a civil action. Upon receipt of written notice of the claim, a payor may pay any amount owed by it to the court having jurisdiction of the probate proceedings relating to the decedent's estate, or if no proceedings have been commenced, to the court having jurisdiction of probate proceedings relating to decedents' estates located in the county of the decedent's residence. The court shall hold the funds and, upon its determination under this section, shall order disbursement in accordance with the determination. Payment made to the court discharges the payor from all claims for the amounts paid.

(e) [Protection of Bona Fide Purchasers; Personal Liability of Recipient.]

(1) A person who purchases property for value and without notice, or who receives a payment or other item of property in partial or full satisfaction of a legally enforceable obligation, is neither obligated under this section to return the payment, item of property, or benefit nor is liable under this section for the amount of the payment or the value of the item of property or benefit. But a person who, not for value, receives a payment, item of property, or any other benefit to which the person is not entitled under this section is obligated to return the payment, item of property, or benefit, or is personally liable for the amount of the payment or the value of the item of property or benefit, to the person who is entitled to it under this section.

(2) If this section or any part of this section is preempted by federal law with respect to a payment, an item of property or any other benefit covered by this section, a person who, not for value, receives the payment, item of property, or any other benefit to which the person is not entitled under this section is obligated to return the payment, item of property, or benefit, or is personally liable for the amount of that payment or the value of that item of property or benefit, to the person who would have been entitled to it were this section or part of this section not preempted.

§ 2-707. [Survivorship with Respect to Future Interests Under Terms of Trust; Substitute Takers.]

(a) Definitions. In this section:

(1) "Alternative future interest" means an expressly created future interest that can take effect in possession or enjoyment instead of another future interest on the happening of one or more events, including survival of an event or failure to survive an event, whether an event is expressed in condition-precedent, condition-subsequent, or any other form. A residuary clause in a will does not create an alternative future interest with respect to a future interest created in a nonresiduary devise in the will, whether or not the will specifically provides that lapsed or failed devises are to pass under the residuary clause.

(2) "Beneficiary" means the beneficiary of a future interest and includes a class member if the future interest is in the form of a class gift.

(3) "Class member" includes an individual who fails to survive the distribution date but who would have taken under a future interest in the form of a class gift had he [or she] survived the distribution date.

(4) "Distribution date," with respect to a future interest means the time when the future interest is to take effect in possession or enjoyment. The distribution date need not occur at the beginning or end of a calendar day, but can occur at a time during the course of a day.

(5) "Future interest" includes an alternative future interest and a future interest in the form of a class gift.

(6) "Future interest under the terms of a trust" means a future interest that was created by a trust or to an existing trust or by an exercise of a power of appointment to an existing trust, directing the continuance of an existing trust, designating a beneficiary of an existing trust, or creating a trust.

(7) "Surviving beneficiary" or "surviving descendant" means a beneficiary or a descendant who neither predeceased the distribution date nor is deemed to have predeceased the distribution date under Section 2-702.

(b) [Survivorship Required: Substitute Gift.] A future interest under the terms of a trust is contingent on the beneficiary's surviving the distribution date. If a beneficiary a future interest under the terms of a trust fails to survive the distribution date, the following apply:

(1) Except as provided in paragraph (4), if the future interest is not in the form of a class gift and the deceased beneficiary leaves surviving descendants, a substitute gift is created in the beneficiary's surviving descendants. They take by representation the property to which the beneficiary would have been entitled had the beneficiary survived the decedent.

(2) Except as provided in paragraph (4), if the future interest is in the form of a class gift, other than a future interest to "issue," "descendants," "heirs of the body," "heirs," "next of kin," "relatives," or "family," or a class described bylanguage of similar import, a substitute gift is created in the deceased beneficiary or beneficiaries' surviving descendants. The property to which the beneficiaries would have been entitled had all of them survived the distribution date passes to the surviving beneficiaries and the surviving descendants of the deceased beneficiaries. Each surviving beneficiary takes the share to which he [or she] would have been entitled had the deceased beneficiaries survived the distribution date. Each deceased beneficiary's surviving descendants who are substituted for the deceased beneficiary take by representation the share to which the deceased beneficiary would have been entitled had the deceased beneficiary survived the distribution date. For the purposes of this paragraph, "deceased beneficiary" means a class member who failed to survive the distribution date and left one or more surviving descendants.

(3) For the purposes of Section 2-701, words of survivorship, attached to a future interest are not, in the absence of additional evidence, a sufficient indication of an intent contrary to the application of this section. Words of survivorship include words of survivorship that relate to the distribution date or to an earlier or an unspecified time, whether those words of survivorship are expressed in condition-precedent, condition- subsequent, or any other form.

(4) If a governing instrument creates an alternative future interest with respect to a future interest for which a substitute gift is created by paragraph (1) or (2), the substitute gift is superseded by the alternative future interest only if an expressly designated beneficiary of the alternative future interest is entitled to take in possession or enjoyment.

(c) [More Than One Substitute Gift; Which One Takes.] If, under subsection (b), substitute gifts are created and not superseded with respect to more than one future interest and the future interests are alternative future interests, one to the other, the determination of which of the substitute gifts takes effect is resolved as follows:

(1) Except as provided in paragraph (2), the property passes under the primary substitute gift.

(2) If there is a younger-generation future interest, the property passes under the younger-generation substitute gift and not under the primary substitute gift.

(3) In this subsection:

(i) "Primary future interest" means the future interest that would have taken effect had all the deceased beneficiaries of the alternative future interests who left surviving descendants survived the distribution date.

(ii) "Primary substitute gift" means the substitute gift created with respect to the primary future interest.

(iii) "Younger-generation future interest" means a future interest that (A) is to a descendant of a beneficiary of the primary future interest, (B) is an alternative future interest with respect to the primary future interest, (C) is a future interest for which a substitute gift is created, and (D) would have taken effect had all the deceased beneficiaries who left surviving descendants survived the distribution date except the deceased beneficiary or beneficiaries of the primary future interest.

(iv) "Younger-generation substitute gift" means the substitute gift created with respect to the younger-generation future interest.

(d) [If No Other Takers, Property Passes Under Residuary Clause or to Transferor's Heirs.] If after the application of subsections (b) and (c), there is no surviving taker, the property passes in the following order:

(1) if the trust was created in a nonresiduary devise in the transferor's will or in a codicil to the transferor's will, the property passes under the residuary clause in the transferor's will; for purposes of this section, the residuary clause is treated as creating a future interest under the terms of a trust.

(2) if no taker is produced by the application of paragraph (1), the property passes to the transferor's heirs under Section 2-711.

§ 2-708. [Class Gifts to "Descendants," "Issue," or "Heirs of the Body"; Form of Distribution if None Specified.]

If a class gift in favor of "descendants," "issue," or "heirs of the body" does not specify the manner in which the property is to be distributed among the class members, the property is distributed among the class members who are living when the interest is to take effect in possession or enjoyment, in such shares as they would receive, under the applicable law of intestate succession, if the designated ancestor had then died intestate owning the subject matter of the class gift.

§ 2-709. [Representation; Per Capita at Each Generation; Per Stirpes.]

(a) [Definitions.] In this section:

(1) "Deceased child" or "deceased descendant" means a child or a descendant who either predeceased the distribution date or is deemed to have predeceased the distribution date under Section 2-702.

(2) "Distribution date," with respect to an interest means the time when the interest is to take effect in possession or enjoyment. The distribution date need not occur at the beginning or end of a calendar day, but can occur at a time during the course of a day.

(3) "Surviving ancestor," "surviving child," or "surviving descendant" means an ancestor, a child, or a descendant who neither predeceased the distribution date nor is deemed to have predeceased the distribution date under Section 2-702.

(b) [Representation; Per Capita at Each Generation.] If an applicable statute or a governing instrument calls for property to be distributed "by representation" or "per capita at each generation," the property is divided into as many equal shares as there are (i) surviving descendants in the generation nearest to the designated ancestor which contains one or more surviving descendants (ii) and deceased descendants in the same generation who left surviving descendants, if any. Each surviving descendant in the nearest generation is allocated one share. The remaining shares, if any, are combined and then divided in the same manner among the surviving descendants of the deceased descendants as if the surviving descendants who were allocated a share and their surviving descendants had predeceased the distribution date.

(c) [Per Stirpes.] If a governing instrument calls for property to be distributed "per stirpes," the property is divided into as many equal shares as there are (i) surviving children of the designated ancestor and (ii) deceased children who left surviving descendants. Each surviving child is allocated one share. The share of each deceased child with surviving descendants is divided in the same manner, with subdivision repeating at each succeeding generation until the property is fully allocated among surviving descendants.

(d) [Deceased Descendant With No Surviving Descendant Disregarded.] For the purposes of subsection (b) and (c), an individual who is deceased and left no surviving descendant is disregarded, and an individual who leaves a surviving ancestor who is a descendant of the designated ancestor is not entitled to a share.

§ 2-710. [Worthier-Title Doctrine Abolished.]

The doctrine of worthier title is abolished as a rule of law and a rule of construction. Language in a governing instrument describing the beneficiaries of a donative disposition as the transferor's "heirs," "heirs at law," "next of kin," "distributees," "relatives," or "family," or language of similar import, does not create or presumptively create a reversionary interest in the transferor.

§ 2-711. [Future Interests in "Heirs" and Like.]

If an applicable statue or a governing instrument calls for a future distribution to or creates a future interest in a designated individual's "heirs," "heirs at law," "next of kin," "relatives," or "family," or language of similar import, the property passes to those persons, including the state under Section 2-105, and in such shares as would succeed to the designated individual's intestate estate under the intestate succession law of the designated individual's domicile if the designated individual died when the donative disposition is to take effect in possession or enjoyment. If the designated individual's surviving spouse is living but is remarried at the time the interest is to take effect in possession or enjoyment, the surviving spouse is not an heir of the designated individual.

Part 8
General Provisions Concerning Probate and Nonprobate Transfers

§ 2-801. [Disclaimer of Property Interests.]

(a) [Right to Disclaim Interest in Property.] A person or the representative to whom an interest in or with respect to property or an interest therein devolves by whatever means may disclaim it in whole or in part by delivering or filing a written disclaimer under this section. The right to disclaim exists notwithstanding (i) any limitation on the interest of the disclaimant in the nature of a spendthrift provision or similar restriction or (ii) any restriction or limitation on the right to disclaim contained in the governing instrument. For purposes of this subsection, the "representative of a person" includes a personal representative of a decedent, a conservator of a disabled person, a guardian of a minor or incapacitated person and an agent acting on behalf of the person within the authority of a power of attorney.

(b) [Time of Disclaimer.] The following rules govern the time when a disclaimer must be filed or delivered:

(1) If the property or interest has devolved to the disclaimant under a testamentary instrument or by the laws of intestacy, the disclaimer must be filed, if of a present

interest not later than [nine] months after the death of the deceased owner or deceased donee of a power of appointment and, if of a future interest, not later than [nine] months after the event determining that the taker of the property or interest is finally ascertained and his [or her] interest is indefeasibly vested. The disclaimer must be filed in the [probate] court of the county in which proceedings for the administration of the estate of the deceased owner or deceased donee of the power have been commenced. A copy of the disclaimer must be delivered in person or mailed by registered or certified mail, return receipt requested, to any personal representative or other fiduciary of the decedent or donee of the power.

(2) If a property or interest has devolved to the disclaimant under a nontestamentary instrument or contract, the disclaimer must be delivered or filed, if of a present interest, not later than [nine] months after the effective date of the nontestamentary instrument or contract and, if of a future interest, not later than [nine] months after the event determining that the taker of the property or interest is finally ascertained and his [or her] interest is indefeasibly vested. If the person entitled to disclaim does not know of the existence of the interest, the disclaimer must be delivered or filed not later than [nine] months after the person learns of the existence of the interest. The effective date of a revocable instrument or contract is the date on which the maker no longer has power to revoke it or to transfer to himself [or herself] or another the entire legal and equitable ownership of the interest. The disclaimer of a copy thereof must be delivered in person or mailed by registered or certified mail, return receipt requested, to the person who has legal title to or possession of the interest disclaimed.

(3) A surviving joint tenant [or tenant by the entireties] may disclaim as a separate interest any property or interest therein devolving to him [or her] by right of entire interest in any property or interest therein that is the subject of a joint tenancy [or tenancy by the entireties] devolving to him [or her], if the joint tenancy [or tenancy by the entireties] was created by act of a deceased joint tenant [or tenancy by the entireties], the survivor did not join in creating the join tenancy [or tenancy by the entireties], and has not accepted a benefit under it.

(4) If real property or an interest therein is disclaimed, a copy of the disclaimer may be recorded in the office of the [Recorder of Deeds] of the county in which the property or interest disclaimed is located.

(c) [Form of Disclaimer.] The disclaimer must (i) describe the property or interest disclaimed, (ii) declare the disclaimer and extent thereof, and (iii) be signed by the disclaimant.

(d) [Effect of Disclaimer.] The effects of a disclaimer are:

(1) If property or an interest therein devolves to a disclaimant under a testamentary instrument, under a power of appointment exercised by a testamentary instrument, or under the laws of intestacy, and the decedent has not provided for another disposition of that interest, should it be disclaimed, or of disclaimed or failed interests in general, the disclaimed interest devolves as if the disclaimant had predeceased the decedent, but if by law or under the testamentary instrument the descendants of the disclaimant would take the disclaimant's share by representation were the disclaimant to predecease the decedent, then the disclaimed interest passes by representation to the descendants of the disclaimant who survive the decedent. A future interest that takes effect in possession or enjoyment after the termination of the estate or interest disclaimed takes effect as if the disclaimant had predeceased the decedent. A disclaimer relates back for all purposes to the date of death of the decedent.

(2) If property or an interest therein devolves to a disclaimant under a nontestamentary instrument, and the instrument or contract does not provide for another disposition of that interest, should it be disclaimed, or of disclaimed or failed interests in general, the disclaimed interest devolves as if the disclaimant had predeceased the effective date of the instrument or contract, but if by law or under the nontestamentary instrument or contract the descendants of the disclaimant would take the disclaimant's share by representation were the disclaimant to predecease the effective date of the instrument, then the disclaimed interest passes by representation to the descendants of the disclaimant who survive the effective date of the instrument. A disclaimer relates back for all purposes to that date. A future interest that takes effect in possession or enjoyment at or after the termination of the disclaimed interest takes effect as if the disclaimant had died before the effective date of the instrument or contract that transferred the disclaimed interest.

(3) The disclaimer or the written waiver of the right to disclaim is binding upon the disclaimant or person waiving and all persons claiming through or under either of them.

(e) [Waiver and Bar.] The right to disclaim property or an interest therein is barred by (i) an assignment, conveyance, encumbrance, pledge, or transfer of the property or interest, or a contract therefor, (ii) a written waiver of the right to disclaim, (iii) an acceptance of the property or interest or benefit under it, or (iv) a sale of the property or interest under judicial sale made before the disclaimer is made.

(f) [Remedy Not Exclusive.] This section does not abridge the right of a person to waive, release, disclaim, or renounce property or an interest therein under any other statute.

(g) [Application.] An interest in property existing on the effective date of this section as to which, if a present interest, the time for filing a disclaimer under this section has not expired or, if a future interest, the interest has not become indefeasibly vested or the taker finally ascertained, may be disclaimed within [nine] months after the effective date of this section.

§ 2-802. [Effect of Divorce, Annulment, and Decree of Separation.]

(a) An individual who is divorced from the decedent or whose marriage to the decedent has been annulled is not a surviving spouse unless, by virtue of a subsequent marriage, he [or she] is married to the decedent at the time of death. A decree of separation that does not terminate the status of husband and wife is not a divorce for purposes of this section.

(b) For purposes of Parts 1, 2, 3 & 4 of this Article, and of Section 3-203, a surviving spouse does not include:

(1) an individual who obtains or consents to a final decree or judgment of divorce from the decedent or an annulment of their marriage, which decree or judgment is not recognized as valid in this State, unless subsequently they participate in a marriage ceremony purporting to marry each to the other or live together as man and wife;

(2) an individual who, following an invalid decree or judgment of divorce or annulment obtained by the decedent, participates in a marriage ceremony with a third individual; or

(3) an individual who was a party to a valid proceeding concluded by an order purporting to terminate all marital property rights.

§ 2-803. [Effect of Homicide on Intestate Succession, Wills, Trusts, Joint Assets, Life Insurance, and Beneficiary Designations.]

(a) [Definitions.] In this section:

(1) "Disposition or appointment of property" includes a transfer of an item of property or any other benefit to a beneficiary designated in a governing instrument.

(2) "Governing instrument" means a governing instrument executed by the decedent.

(3) "Revocable," with respect to a disposition, appointment, provision, or nomination, means one under which the decedent, at the time of or immediately before death, was alone empowered, by law or under the governing instrument, to cancel the designation in favor of the killer, whether or not the decedent was then empowered to designate himself [or herself] in place of his [or her] killer and or the decedent then had capacity to exercise the power.

(b) [Forfeiture of Statutory Benefits.] An individual who feloniously and intentionally kills the decedent forfeits all benefits under this Article with respect to the decedent's estate, including an intestate share, an elective share, an omitted spouse's or child's share, a homestead allowance, exempt property, and a family allowance. If the decedent died intestate, the decedent's intestate estate passes as if the killer disclaimed his [or her] intestate share.

(c) [Revocation of Benefits Under Governing Instrument.] The felonious and intentional killing of the decedent:

(1) revokes any revocable (i) disposition or appointment of property made by the decedent to the killer in a governing instrument, (ii) provision in a governing instrument conferring a general or nongeneral power of appointment on the killer, and (iii) nomination of the killer in a governing instrument, nominating or appointing the killer to serve in any fiduciary or representative capacity, including a personal representative, executor, trustee, or agent; and

(2) severs the interests of the decedent and killer in property held by them at the time of the killing as joint tenants with the right of survivorship [or as community property with the right of survivorship], transforming the interests of the decedent and killer into tenancies in common.

(d) [Effect of Severance.] A severance under subsection (c)(2) does not affect any third-party interest in property acquired for value and in good faith reliance on an apparent title by survivorship in the killer unless a writing declaring the severance has been noted, registered, filed, or recorded in records appropriate to the kind and location of the property which are relied upon, in the ordinary course of transactions involving such property, as evidence of ownership.

(e) [Effect of Revocation.] Provisions of a governing instrument that are not revoked by this section are given effect as if the killer disclaimed all revoked provisions or, in the case of a revoked nomination in a fiduciary or representative capacity, as if the killer predeceased the decedent.

(f) [Wrongful Acquisition of Property.] A wrongful acquisition of property or interest by a killer not covered by this section must be treated in accordance with the principle that a killer cannot profit from his [or her] wrong.

(g) [Felonious and Intentional Killing; How Determined.] After all right to appeal has been exhausted, a judgment of conviction establishing criminal accountability for the felonious and intentional killing of the decedent conclusively establishes the convicted individual as the decedent's killer for purposes of this section. In the absence of a conviction, the court, upon the petition of an interested person must determine whether, under the preponderance of evidence standard, the individual would be found criminally accountable for the felonious and intentional killing of the decedent. If the court determines that, under that standard, the individual would be found criminally accountable for the felonious and intentional killing of the decedent, the determination conclusively establishes that individual as the decedent's killer for purposes of this section.

(h) [Protection of Payors and Other Third Parties.]

(1) A payor or other third party is not liable for having made a payment or transferred an item of property or any other benefit to a beneficiary designated in a governing instrument affected by an intentional and felonious killing, or for having taken any other action in good faith reliance on the validity of the governing instrument, upon request and satisfactory proof of the decedent's death, before the payor or other third party received written notice of a claimed forfeiture or revocation under this section. A payor or other third party is liable for a payment made or other action taken after the payor or other third party received written notice of a claimed forfeiture or revocation under this section.

(2) Written notice of a claimed forfeiture or revocation under paragraph (1) must be mailed to the payor's or other third party's main office or home by registered or certified mail, return receipt requested, or served upon the payor or other third party in the same manner as a summons in a civil action. Upon receipt of written notice of a claimed forfeiture or revocation under this section, a payor or other third party may pay any amount owed or transfer or deposit any item of property held by it to or with the court having jurisdiction of the probate proceedings relating to the decedent's estate, or if no proceedings have been commenced, to or with the court having jurisdiction of probate proceedings relating to decedents' estates located in the county of the decedent's residence. The court shall hold the funds or item of property and, upon its determination under this section, shall order disbursement in accordance with the determination. Payments, transfers, or deposits made to or with the court discharge the payor or other third party from all claims for the value of amounts paid to or items of property transferred to or deposited with the court.

(i) [Protection of Bona Fide Purchasers; Personal Liability of Recipient.]

(1) A person who purchases property for value and without notice, or who receives a payment or other item of property in partial or full satisfaction of a legally enforceable obligation, is neither obligated under this section to return the payment, item of property, or benefit nor is liable under this section for the amount of the payment or the value of the item of property or benefit. But a person who, not for value, receives a payment, item of property, or any other benefit to which the person is not entitled under this section is obligated to return the payment, item of property, or benefit, or is personally liable for the amount of the payment or the value of the item of property or benefit, to the person who is entitled to it under this section.

(2) If this section or any part of this section is preempted by federal law with respect to a payment, an item of property or any other benefit covered by this section, a person who, not for value, receives the payment, item of property, or any other benefit is obligated to return that payment, item of property, or benefit, or is personally liable for the amount of that payment or the value of that item of property or benefit, to the person who would have been entitled to it were that section or part of that section not preempted.

§ 2-804. [Revocation of Probate and Nonprobate Transfers by Divorce; No Revocation by Other Changes of Circumstances.]

(a) [Definitions.] In this section:

(1) "Disposition or appointment of property" includes a transfer of an item of property or any other benefit to a beneficiary designated in a governing instrument.

(2) "Divorce or annulment" means any divorce or annulment, or any dissolution or declaration of invalidity of a marriage, that would exclude the spouse as a surviving spouse within the meaning of Section 2-802. A decree of separation that does not terminate the status of husband and wife is not a divorce for purposes of this section.

(3) "Divorced individual" includes an individual whose marriage has been annulled.

(4) "Governing instrument" means a governing instrument executed by the decedent.

(5) "Relative of the divorced individual's former spouse" means an individual who is related to the divorced individual's former spouse by blood, adoption, or affinity and who, after the divorce or annulment, is not related to the divorced individual by blood, adoption, or affinity.

(6) "Revocable," with respect to a disposition, appointment, provision, or nomination, means one under which the divorced individual, at the time of the divorce or annulment, was alone empowered, by law or under the governing instrument, to cancel the designation of his [or her] former spouse or former spouse's relative, whether or not the divorced individual was then empowered to designate himself [or herself] in place of his [or her] former spouse or in place of his [or her] former spouse's relative and whether or not the divorced individual then had capacity to exercise the power.

(b) [Revocation Upon Divorce.] Except as provided by the express terms of a governing instrument, a court order, or a contract relating to the division of the marital estate made between the divorced individuals before or after the marriage, divorce, or annulment, the divorce or annulment of a marriage:

(1) revokes any revocable (i) disposition or appointment of property made by a divorced individual to his [or her] former spouse in a governing instrument and any disposition or appointment created by law or in a governing instrument to a relative of the divorced individual's former spouse, (ii) provision in a governing instrument conferring a general or nongeneral power of appointment on the divorced individual's former spouse or on a relative of the divorced individual's former spouse, and (iii) nomination in a governing instrument, nominating a divorced individual's former spouse or a relative of the divorced individual's former spouse to serve in any fiduciary or representative capacity, including a personal representative, executor, trustee, conservator, agent, or guardian; and

(2) severs the interests of the former spouses in property held by them at the time of the divorce as joint tenants with the right of survivorship [or as community property with the right of survivorship], transforming the interests of the former spouses into tenancies in common.

(c) [Effect of Severance.] A severance under subsection (b)(2) does not affect any third-party interest in property acquired for value and in good faith reliance on an apparent title by survivorship in the former spouses unless a writing declaring the severance has been noted, registered, filed, or recorded in records appropriate to the kind and location of the property which are relied upon, in the ordinary course of transactions involving such property, as evidence of ownership.

(d) [Effect of Revocation.] Provisions of a governing instrument that are not revoked by this section are given effect as if the former spouse and relatives of the former spouse disclaimed the revoked provisions or, in the case of a revoked nomination in a fiduciary or representative capacity, as if the former spouse and relatives of the former spouse died immediately before the divorce or annulment.

(e) [Revival if Divorce Nullified.] Provisions revoked solely by this section are revived by the divorced individual's remarriage to the former spouse or by a nullification of the divorce or annulment.

(f) [No Revocation for Other Change of Circumstances.] No change of circumstances other than as described in this section and in Section 2-803 effects a revocation.

(g) [Protection of Payors and Other Third Parties.]

(1) A payor or other third party is not liable for having made a payment or transferred an item of property or any other benefit to a beneficiary designated in a governing instrument affected by a divorce, annulment, or remarriage, or for having taken any other action in good faith reliance on the validity of the governing instrument, before the payor or other third party received written notice of the divorce, annulment, or remarriage. A payor or other third party is liable for a payment made or other action taken after the payor or other third party received written notice of a claimed forfeiture or revocation under this section.

(2) Written notice of the divorce, annulment, or remarriage under subsection (g)(2) must be mailed to the payor's or other third party's main office or home by registered or certified mail, return receipt requested, or served upon the payor or other third party in the same manner as a summons in a civil action. Upon receipt of written notice the divorce, annulment, or remarriage, a payor or other third party may pay any amount owed or transfer or deposit any item of property held by it to or with the court having jurisdiction of the probate proceedings relating to the decedent's estate, or if no proceedings have been commenced, to or with the court having jurisdiction of probate proceedings relating to decedents' estates located in the county of the decedent's residence. The court shall hold the funds or item of property and, upon its determination under this section, shall order disbursement in accordance with the determination. Payments, transfers, or deposits made to or with the court discharge the payor or other third party from all claims for the value of amounts paid to or items of property transferred to or deposited with the court.

(h) [Protection of Bona Fide Purchasers; Personal Liability of Recipient.]

(1) A person who purchases property from a former spouse, relative of a former spouse, or any other person for value and without notice, or who receives from a former spouse, relative of a former spouse, or any other person a payment or other item of property in partial or full satisfaction of a legally enforceable obligation, is neither obligated under this section to return the payment, item of property, or benefit nor is liable under this section for the amount of the payment or the value of the item of property or benefit. But a former spouse, relative of a former spouse, or any other person who, not for value, receives a payment, item of property, or any other benefit to which that person is not entitled under this section is obligated to return the payment, item of property, or benefit, or is personally liable for the amount of the payment or the value of the item of property or benefit, to the person who is entitled to it under this section.

(2) If this section or any part of this section is preempted by federal law with respect to a payment, an item of property or any other benefit covered by this section, a former spouse, relative of a former spouse, or any other person who, not for value, received a payment, item of property, or any other benefit to which that person is not entitled under this section is obligated to return that payment, item of property, or benefit, or is personally liable

for the amount of that payment or the value of that item of property or benefit, to the person who would have been entitled to it were this section or part of this section not preempted.

Part 9
Statutory Rule Against Perpetuities; Honorary Trusts

SUBPART 1. STATUTORY RULE AGAINST PERPETUITIES

§ 2-901. [Statutory Rule Against Perpetuities.]

(a) [Validity of Nonvested Property Interest.] A nonvested property interest is invalid unless:

(1) when the interest is created, it is certain to vest or terminate no later than 21 years after the death of an individual then alive; or

(2) the interest either vests or terminates within 90 years after its creation.

(b) [Validity of General Power of Appointment Subject to a Condition Precedent.] A general power of appointment not presently exercisable because of a condition precedent is invalid unless:

(1) when the power is created, the condition precedent is certain to be satisfied or become impossible to satisfy no later than 21 years after the death of an individual then alive; or

(2) the condition precedent either is satisfied or becomes impossible to satisfy within 90 years after its creation.

(c) [Validity of Nongeneral or Testamentary Power of Appointment.] A nongeneral power of appointment or a general testamentary power of appointment is invalid unless:

(1) when the power is created, it is certain to be irrevocably exercised or otherwise to terminate no later than 21 years after the death of an individual then alive; or

(2) the power is irrevocably exercised or otherwise terminates within 90 years after its creation.

(d) [Possibility of Post-death Child Disregarded.] In determining whether a nonvested property interest or a power of appointment is valid under subsection (a)(1), (b)(1), or (c)(1), the possibility that a child will be born to an individual after the individual's death is disregarded.

(e) [Effect of Certain "Later-of" Type Language.] If, in measuring a period from the creation of a trust or other property arrangement, language in a governing instrument (i) seeks to disallow the vesting or termination of any interest or trust beyond, (ii) seeks to postpone the vesting or termination of any interest or trust until, or (iii) seeks to operate in effect in any similar fashion upon, the later of (A) the expiration of a period of time not exceeding 21 years after the death of the survivor of specified lives in being at the creation of the trust or other property arrangement or (B) the expiration of a period of time that exceeds or might exceed 21 years after the death of the survivor of lives in being at the creation of the trust or other property arrangement, that language is inoperative to the extent it produces a period of time that exceeds 21 years after the death of the survivor of the specified lives.

§ 2-902. [When Nonvested Property Interest or Power of Appointment Created.]

(a) Except as provided in subsections (b) and (c) and in Section 2-905(a), the time of creation of a nonvested property interest or a power of appointment is determined under general principles of property law.

(b) For purposes of Subpart 1 of this Part, if there is a person who alone can exercise a power created by a governing instrument to become the unqualified beneficial owner of (i) a nonvested property interest or (ii) a property interest subject to a power of appointment described in Section 2-901(b) or (c), the nonvested property interest or power of appointment is created when the power to become the unqualified beneficial owner terminates. [For purposes of Subpart 1 of this Part, a joint power with respect to community property or to marital property under the Uniform Marital Property Act held by individuals married to each other is a power exercisable by one person alone.]

(c) For purposes of Subpart 1 of this Part, a nonvested property interest or a power of appointment arising from a transfer of property to a previously funded trust or other existing property arrangement is created when the nonvested property interest or power of appointment in the original contribution was created.

§ 2-903. [Reformation.]

Upon the petition of an interested person, a court shall reform a disposition in the manner that most closely approximates the transferor's manifested plan of distribution and is within the 90 years allowed by Section 2-901(a)(2), 2-901(b)(2), or 2-901(c)(2) if:

(1) a nonvested property interest or a power of appointment becomes invalid under Section 2-901 (statutory rule against perpetuities);

(2) a class gift is not but might become invalid under Section 2-901 (statutory rule against perpetuities) and the time has arrived when the share of any class member is to take effect in possession or enjoyment; or

(3) a nonvested property interest that is not validated by Section 2-901(a)(1) can vest but not within 90 year after its creation.

§ 2-904. [Exclusions from Statutory Rule Against Perpetuities.]

Section 2-901 (statutory rule against perpetuities) does not apply to:

(1) a nonvested property interest or a power of appointment arising out of a nondonative transfer except a nonvested property interest or a power of appointment arising out of (i) a premarital or postmarital agreement, (ii) a separation or divorce settlement, (iii) a spouse's election, (iv) a similar arrangement arising out of a prospective, existing, or previous marital relationship between the parties, (v) a contract to make or not to revoke a will or trust, (vi) a contract to exercise or not to exercise a power of appointment, (vii) a transfer in satisfaction of a duty of support, or (viii) a reciprocal transfer;

(2) a fiduciary's power relating to the administration or management of assets, including the power of a fiduciary to sell, lease, or mortgage property, and the power of a fiduciary to determine principal and income;

(3) a power to appoint a fiduciary;

(4) a discretionary power of a trustee to distribute principal before termination of a trust to a beneficiary having an indefeasibly vested interest in the income and principal;

(5) a nonvested property interest held by a charity, government, or governmental agency or subdivision, if the nonvested property interest is preceded by an interest held by another charity, government or governmental agency or subdivision;

(6) a nonvested property interest in or a power of appointment with respect to a trust or other property arrangement forming part of a pension, profit-sharing, stock bonus, health, disability, death benefit, income deferral, or other current or deferred benefit plan for one or more employees, independent contractors, or their beneficiaries or spouses, to which contributions are made for the purpose of distributing to or for the benefit of the participants or their beneficiaries or spouses the property, income, or principal in the trust or other property arrangement, except a nonvested property interest or a power of appointment that is created by an election of a participant or a beneficiary or spouse; or

(7) a property interest, power of appointment, or arrangement that was not subject to the common-law rule against perpetuities or is excluded by another statute of this State.

§ 2-905. [Prospective Application.]

(a) Except as extended by subsection (b), Subpart 1 of this Part applies to a nonvested property interest or a power of appointment that is created on or after the effective date of Subpart 1 of this Part. For purposes of this section, a nonvested property interest or a power of appointment is created when the power is irrevocably exercised or when a revocable exercise becomes irrevocable.

(b) If a nonvested property interest or a power of appointment was created before the effective date of Subpart 1 of this Part and is determined in a judicial proceeding, commenced on or after the effective date of Subpart 1 of this Part, to violate this State's rule against perpetuities as that rule existed before the effective date of Subpart 1 of this Part, a court upon the petition of an interest person may reform the disposition in the manner that most closely approximates the transferor's manifested plan of distribution and is within the limits of the rule against perpetuities applicable when the nonvested property interest or power of appointment was created.

§ 2-906. [Supersession] [Repeal.]

Subpart 1 of this Part [supersedes the rule of the common law known as the rule against perpetuities] [repeals (list statutes to be repealed)].

SUBPART 2. HONORARY TRUSTS

[Optional provision for validating and limiting the duration of so-called honorary trusts and trusts for pets.]

§ 2-907. [Honorary Trusts; Trusts for Pets.]

(a) [Honorary Trust.] A trust for a noncharitable corporation or unincorporated society or for a lawful noncharitable purpose may be performed by the trustee for [21] years but no longer, whether or not there is a beneficiary who can seek the trust's enforcement or termination and whether or not the terms of the trust contemplate a longer duration.

(b) [Trust for Pets.] Subject to this subsection, a trust for the care of a designated domestic or pet animal and the animal's offspring is valid. Except as expressly provided otherwise in the trust instrument:

(1) No portion of the principal or income may be converted to the use of the trustee or to any other use than for the benefit of a covered animal.

(2) The trust terminates at the earlier of [21] years after the trust was created or when no living animal is covered by the trust.

(3) Upon termination, the trustee shall transfer the unexpended trust property in the following order:

(i) as directed in the trust instrument;

(ii) if the trust was created in a nonresiduary clause in the transferor's will or in a codicil to the transferor's will; and

(iii) if no taker is produced by the application of subparagraph (i) or (ii), to the transferor's heirs under Section 2-711.

(4) For the purposes of Section 2-707, the residuary clause is treated as creating a future interest under the terms of the trust.

(5) The intended use of the principal or income can be enforced by an individual designated for that purpose in the trust instrument or, if none, by an individual appointed by a court upon application to it by an individual.

(6) Except as ordered by the court or required by the trust instrument, no filing, report, registration, periodic accounting, separate maintenance of funds, appointment, or fee is required by reason of the existence of the fiduciary relationship of the trustee.

(7) A governing instrument must be liberally construed to bring the transfer within this section, to presume against the merely precatory or honorary nature of the disposition, and to carry out the general intent of the transferor. Extrinsic evidence is admissible in determining the transferor's intent.

(8) A court may reduce the amount of the property transferred, if it determines that that amount substantially exceeds the amount required for the intended use. The amount of the reduction, if any passes as unexpended trust property under subsection (b)(3).

(9) If no trustee is designated or no designated trustee is willing or able to serve, a court shall name a trustee. A court may order the transfer of the property to another trustee, if required to assure that the intended use is carried out and if no successor trustee is designated in the trust instrument or if no designated successor trustee agrees to serve or is able to serve. A court may also make such other orders and determinations as shall be advisable to carry out the intent of the transferor and the purpose of this section.

The following version of UPC Article II is the earlier one, which precedes the 1990 amendment. It is reproduced here for reference in states that have not adopted the newer version.

Here begins Article II of the 1969 UPC.

ARTICLE II
INTESTATE SUCCESSION AND WILLS (1969)

This 1969 version of Article II is followed in Florida, Idaho, Maine, Michigan, Nebraska, South Carolina, and Utah.

Part 1
Intestate Succession

§ 2-101. [Intestate Estate.]

Any part of the estate of a decedent not effectively disposed of by his will passes to his heirs as prescribed in the following sections of this Code.

§ 2-102. [Share of the Spouse.]

The intestate share of the surviving spouse is:

(1) if there is no surviving issue or parent of the decedent, the entire intestate estate;

(2) if there is no surviving issue but the decedent is survived by a parent or parents, the first [$50,000], plus one-half of the balance of the intestate estate;

(3) if there are no surviving issue all of whom are issue of the surviving spouse also, the first [$50,000], plus one-half of the balance of the intestate estate;

(4) if there are surviving issue one or more of whom are not issue of the surviving spouse, one-half of the intestate estate.

ALTERNATIVE PROVISION FOR COMMUNITY PROPERTY STATES

[§ 2-102A. [Share of the Spouse.]

The intestate share of the surviving spouse is as follows:

(1) as to separate property

(i) if there is no surviving issue or parent of the decedent, the entire intestate estate;

(ii) if there is no surviving issue but the decedent is survived by a parent or parents, the first [$50,000], plus one-half of the balance of the intestate estate;

(iii) if there are surviving issue all of whom are issue of the surviving spouse also, the first [$50,000], plus one-half of the balance of the intestate estate;

(iv) if there are surviving issue one or more of whom are not issue of the surviving spouse, one-half of the intestate estate.

(2) as to community property

(i) The one-half of community property which belongs to the decedent passes to the [surviving spouse].]

§ 2-103. [Share of Heirs Other Than Surviving Spouse.]

The part of the intestate estate not passing to the surviving spouse under Section 2-102, or the entire intestate estate if there is no surviving spouse, passes as follows:

(1) to the issue of the decedent; if they are all of the same degree of kinship to the decedent they take equally, but if of unequal degree, then those of more remote degree take by representation;

(2) if there is no surviving issue, to his parent or parents equally;

(3) if there is no surviving issue or parent, to the issue of the parents or either of them by representation;

(4) if there is no surviving issue, parent or issue of a parent, but the decedent is survived by one or more grandparents or issue of grandparents, half of the estate passes to the paternal grandparents if both survive, or to the surviving paternal grandparent, or to the issue of the paternal grandparents if both are deceased, the issue taking equally if they are all of the same degree of kinship to the decedent, but if of unequal degree those of more remote degree take by representation; and the other half passes to the maternal relatives in the same manner; but if there be no surviving grandparent or issue of grandparent on either the paternal or the maternal side, the entire estate passes to the relatives on the other side in the same manner as the half.

§ 2-104. [Requirement That Heir Survive Decedent For 120 Hours.]

Any person who fails to survive the decedent by 120 hours is deemed to have predeceased the decedent for purposes of homestead allowance, exempt property and intestate succession, and the decedent's heirs are determined accordingly. If the time of death of the decedent or of the person who would otherwise be an heir, or the times of death of both, cannot be determined, and it cannot be established that the person who would otherwise be an heir has survived the decedent by 120 hours, it is deemed that the person failed to survive for the required period. This section is not to be applied where its application would result in a taking of intestate estate by the state under Section 2-105.

§ 2-105. [No Taker.]

If there is no taker under the provisions of this Article, the intestate estate passes to the [state].

§ 2-106. [Representation.]

If representation is called for by this Code, the estate is divided into as many shares as there are surviving heirs in the nearest degree of kinship and deceased persons in the same degree who left issue who survive the decedent, each surviving heir in the nearest degree receiving one share and the share of each deceased person in the same degree being divided among his issue in the same manner.

§ 2-107. [Kindred of Half Blood.]

Relatives of the half blood inherit the same share they would inherit if they were of the whole blood.

§ 2-108. [Afterborn Heirs.]

Relatives of the decedent conceived before his death but born thereafter inherit as if they had been born in the lifetime of the decedent.

§ 2-109. [Meaning of Child and Related Terms.]

If, for purposes of intestate succession, a relationship of parent and child must be established to determine succession by, through, or from a person,

(1) an adopted person is the child of an adopting parent and not of the natural parents except that adoption of a child by the spouse of a natural parent has no effect on the relationship between the child and either natural parent.

(2) In cases not covered by Paragraph (1), a person is the child of its parents regardless of the marital status of its partners and the parent and child relationship may be established under the [Uniform Parentage Act].

Alternative subsection (2) for states that have not adopted the Uniform Parentage Act.

[(2) In cases not covered by Paragraph (1), a person born out of wedlock is a child of the mother. That person is also a child of the father, if:

(i) the natural parents participated in a marriage ceremony before or after the birth of the child, even though the attempted marriage is void; or

(ii) the paternity is established by an adjudication before the death of the father or is established thereafter by clear and convincing proof, but the paternity established under this subparagraph is ineffective to qualify the father or his kindred to inherit from or through the child unless the father has openly treated the child as his, and has not refused to support the child.]

§ 2-110. [Advancements.]

If a person dies intestate as to all his estate, property which he gave in his lifetime to an heir is treated as an advancement against the latter's share of the estate only if declared in a contemporaneous writing by the decedent or acknowledged in writing by the heir to be an advancement. For this purpose the property advanced is valued as of the time the heir came into possession or enjoyment of the property or as of the time of death of the decedent, whichever first occurs. If the recipient of the property fails to survive the decedent, the property is not taken into account in computing the intestate share to be received by the recipient's issue, unless the declaration or acknowledgment provides otherwise.

§ 2-111. [Debts to Decedent.]

A debt owed to the decedent is not charged against the intestate share of any person except the debtor. If the debtor fails to survive the decedent, the debt is not taken into account in computing the intestate share of the debtor's issue.

§ 2-112. [Alienage.]

No person is disqualified to take as an heir because he or a person through whom he claims is or has been an alien.

[§ 2-113. [Dower and Curtesy Abolished.]

The estates of dower and curtesy are abolished.]

§ 2-114. [Persons Related to Decedent Through Two Lines.]

A person who is related to the decedent through 2 lines of relationship is entitled to only a single share based on the relationship which would entitle him to the larger share.

Part 2
Elective Share of Surviving Spouse

§ 2-201. [Right to Elective Share.]

(a) If a married person domiciled in this state dies, the surviving spouse has a right of election to take an elective share of one-third of the augmented estate under the limitations and conditions hereinafter stated.

(b) If a married person not domiciled in this state dies, the right, if any, of the surviving spouse to take an elective share in property in this state is governed by the law of the decedent's domicile at death.

§ 2-202. [Augmented Estate.]

The augmented estate means the estate reduced by funeral and administration expenses, homestead allowance, family allowances and exemptions, and enforceable claims, to which is added the sum of the following amounts:

(1) The value of property transferred to anyone other than a bona fide purchaser by the decedent at any time during marriage, to or for the benefit of any

person other than the surviving spouse, to the extent that the decedent did not receive adequate and full consideration in money or money's worth for the transfer, if the transfer is of any of the following types:

(i) any transfer under which the decedent retained at the time of his death the possession or enjoyment of, or right to income from, the property;

(ii) any transfer to the extent that the decedent retained at the time of his death a power, either alone or in conjunction with any other person, to revoke or to consume, invade or dispose of the principal for his own benefit;

(iii) any transfer whereby property is held at the time of decedent's death by decedent and another with right of survivorship;

(iv) any transfer made to a donee within two years of death of the decedent to the extent that the aggregate transfers to any one donee in either of the years exceed $3,000.00.

Any transfer is excluded if made with the written consent or joinder of the surviving spouse. Property is valued as of the decedent's death except that property given irrevocably to a donee during lifetime of the decedent is valued as of the date the donee came into possession or enjoyment if that occurs first. Nothing herein shall cause to be included in the augmented estate any life insurance, accident insurance, joint annuity, or pension payable to a person other than the surviving spouse.

(2) The value of property owned by the surviving spouse at the decedent's death, plus the value of property transferred by the spouse at any time during marriage to any person other than the decedent which would have been includible in the spouse's augmented estate if the surviving spouse had predeceased the decedent to the extent the owned or transferred property is derived from the decedent by any means other than testate or intestate succession without a full consideration in money or money's worth. For purposes of this paragraph:

(i) Property derived from the decedent includes, but is not limited to, any beneficial interest of the surviving spouse in a trust created by the decedent during his lifetime, any property appointed to the spouse by the decedent's exercise of a general or special power of appointment also exercisable in favor of others than the spouse, any proceeds of insurance (including accidental death benefits) on the life of the decedent attributable to premiums paid by him, any lump sum immediately payable and the commuted value of the proceeds of annuity contracts under which the decedent was the primary annuitant attributable to premiums paid by him,

the commuted value of amounts payable after the decedent's death under any public or private pension, disability compensation, death benefit or retirement plan, exclusive of the Federal Social Security system, by reason of service performed or disabilities incurred by the decedent, any property held at the time of decedent's death by decedent and the surviving spouse with right of survivorship, any property held by decedent and transferred by contract to the surviving spouse by reason of the decedent's death and the value of the share of the surviving spouse resulting from rights in community property in this or any other state formerly owned with the decedent. Premiums paid by the decedent's employer, his partner, a partnership of which he was a member, or his creditors, are deemed to have been paid by the decedent.

(ii) Property owned by the spouse at the decedent's death is valued as of the date of death. Property transferred by the spouse is valued at the time the transfer became irrevocable, or at the decedent's death, whichever occurred first. Income earned by included property prior to the decedent's death is not treated as property derived from the decedent.

(iii) Property owned by the surviving spouse as of the decedent's death, or previously transferred by the surviving spouse, is presumed to have been derived from the decedent except to the extent that the surviving spouse establishes that it was derived from another source.

(3) For purposes of this section a bona fide purchaser is a purchaser for value in good faith and without notice of any adverse claim. Any recorded instrument on which a state documentary fee is noted pursuant to [insert appropriate reference] is prima facie evidence that the transfer described therein was made to a bona fide purchaser.

§ 2-203. [Right of Election Personal to Surviving Spouse.]

The right of election of the surviving spouse may be exercised only during his lifetime by him. In the case of a protected person, the right of election may be exercised only by order of the court in which protective proceedings as to his property are pending, after finding that exercise is necessary to provide adequate support for the protected person during his probable life expectancy.

§ 2-204. [Waiver of Right to Elect and of Other Rights.]

The right of election of a surviving spouse and the rights of the surviving spouse to homestead allowance, except property and family allowance, or any of them, may be waived, wholly or partially, before or after marriage, by a written contract, agreement or waiver signed by the party waiving after fair disclosure. Unless it provides to the contrary, a waiver of "all rights" (or equivalent language) in the property or estate of a present or prospective spouse or a complete property settlement entered into after or in anticipation of separation or divorce is a waiver of all rights to elective share, homestead allowance, exempt property and family allowance by each spouse in the property of the other and a renunciation by each of all benefits which would otherwise pass to him from the other by intestate succession or by virtue of the provisions of any will executed before the waiver or property settlement.

§ 2-205. [Proceeding for Elective Share; Time Limit.]

(a) The surviving spouse may elect to take his elective share in the augmented estate by filing in the Court and mailing or delivering to the personal representative, if any, a petition for the elective share within 9 months after the date of death, or within 6 months after the probate of the decedent's will, whichever limitation last expires. However, nonprobate transfers, described in Section 2-202(1), shall not be included within the augmented estate for the purpose of computing the elective share, if the petition is filed later than 9 months after death.

The Court may extend the time for election as it sees fit for cause shown by the surviving spouse before the time for election has expired.

(b) The surviving spouse shall give notice of the time and place set for hearing to persons interested in the estate and to the distributees and recipients of portions of the augmented net estate whose interests will be adversely affected by the taking of the elective share.

(c) the surviving spouse may withdraw his demand for an elective share at any time before entry of a final determination by the Court.

(d) After notice and hearing, the Court shall determine the amount of the elective share and shall order its payment from the assets of the augmented net estate or by contribution as appears appropriate under Section 2-207. If it appears that a fund or property included in the augmented net estate has not come into the possession of the personal representative, or has been distributed by the personal representative, the court nevertheless shall fix the liability of any person who has any interest in the fund or property or who has possession thereof, whether as trustee or otherwise. The proceeding may be maintained against fewer than all persons against whom relief could be sought, but no person is subject to contribution in any greater amount than he would have been if relief had been secured against all persons subject to contribution.

(e) The order or judgment of the court may be enforced as necessary in suit for contribution or payment in other courts of this state or other jurisdictions.

§ 2-206. [Effect of Election on Benefits by Will or Statute.]

A surviving spouse is entitled to homestead allowance, exempt property, and family allowance, whether or not he elects to take an elective share.

§ 2-207. [Charging Spouse With Gifts Received; Liability of Others For Balance of Elective Share.]

(a) In the proceeding for an elective share, values included in the augmented estate which pass or have passed to the surviving spouse, or which would have passed to the spouse but were renounced, are applied first to satisfy the elective share and to reduce any contributions due from other recipients of transfers included in the augmented estate. For purposes of this subsection, the electing spouse's beneficial interest in any life estate or in any trust shall be computed as if worth one half of the total value of the property subject to the life estate, or of the trust estate, unless higher or lower values for these interests are established by proof.

(b) Remaining property of the augmented estate is so applied that liability for the balance of the elective share of the surviving spouse is equitably apportioned among the recipients of the augmented estate in proportion to the value of their interests therein.

(c) Only original transferrees from, or appointees of, the decedent and their donees, to the extent the donees have the property or its proceeds, are subject to the contribution to make up the elective share of the surviving spouse. A person liable to contribution may choose to give up the property transferred to him or to pay its value as of the time it is considered in computing the augmented estate.

Part 3
Spouse and Children Unprovided For in Wills
§ 2-301. [Omitted Spouse.]

(a) If a testator fails to provide by will for his surviving spouse who married the testator after the execution of the will, the omitted spouse shall receive the same share of the estate he would have received if the decedent left no will unless it appears from the will that the omission was intentional or the testator provided for the spouse by transfer outside the will and the intent that the transfer be in lieu of a testamentary provision is shown by statements of the testator or from the amount of the transfer or other evidence.

(b) In satisfying a share provided by this section, the devises made by the will abate as provided in Section 3-902.

§ 2-302. [Pretermitted Children.]

(a) If a testator fails to provide in his will for any of his children born or adopted after the execution of his will, the omitted child receives a share in the estate equal in value to that which he would have received if the testator had died intestate unless:

(1) it appears from the will that the omission was intentional;

(2) when the will was executed the testator had one or more children and devised substantially all his estate to the other parent of the omitted child; or

(3) the testator provided for the child by transfer outside the will and the intent that the transfer be in lieu of a testamentary provision is shown by statements of the testator or from the amount of the transfer or other evidence.

(b) If at the time of execution of the will the testator fails to provide in his will for a living child solely because he believes the child to be dead, the child receives a share in the estate equal in value to that which he would have received if the testator had died intestate.

(c) In satisfying a share provided by this section, the devises made by the will abate as provided in Section 3-902.

Part 4
Exempt Property and Allowances
§ 2-401. [Homestead Allowance.]

A surviving spouse of a decedent who was domiciled in this state is entitled to a homestead allowance of [$5,000]. If there is no surviving spouse, each minor child and each dependent child of the decedent is entitled to a homestead allowance amounting to [$5,000] divided by the number of minor and dependent children of the decedent. The homestead allowance is exempt from and has priority over all claims against the estate. Homestead allowance is in addition to any share passing to the surviving spouse or minor or dependent child by the will of the decedent unless otherwise provided, by intestate succession or by way of elective share.

[§ 2-401A. [Constitutional Homestead.]

The value of any constitutional right of homestead in the family home received by a surviving spouse or child shall be charged against that spouse or child's homestead allowance to the extent that the family home is part of the decedent's estate or would have been but for the homestead provision of the constitution.]

§ 2-402. [Exempt Property.]

In addition to the homestead allowance, the surviving spouse of a decedent who was domiciled in this state is entitled from the estate to value not exceeding $3,500 in excess of any security interests therein in household furniture, automobiles, furnishings, appliances and personal effects. If there is no surviving spouse, children of the decedent are entitled jointly to the same value. If encumbered chattels are selected and if the value in excess of security interests, plus that of other exempt property, is less than $3,500, or if there is not $3,500 worth of exempt property in the estate, the spouse or children are entitled to other assets of the estate, if any, to the extent necessary to make up the $3,500 value. Rights to exempt property and assets needed to make up a deficiency of exempt property have priority over all claims against the estate, except that the right to any assets to make up a deficiency of exempt property shall abate as necessary to permit prior payment of homestead allowance and family allowance. These rights are in addition to any benefit or share passing to the surviving spouse or children by the will of the decedent unless otherwise provided, by intestate succession, or by way of elective share.

§ 2-403. [Family Allowance.]

In addition to the right to homestead allowance and exempt property, if the decedent was domiciled in this state, the surviving spouse and minor children whom the decedent was obligated to support and children who were in fact being supported by him are entitled to a reasonable allowance in money out of the estate for their maintenance during the period of administration, which allowance may not continue for longer than one year if the estate is inadequate to discharge allowed claims. The allowance may be paid as a lump sum or in periodic installments. It is payable to the surviving spouse, if living, for the use of the surviving spouse and minor and dependent children; otherwise to the children, or persons having their care and custody; but in case any minor child or dependent child is not living with the surviving spouse, the allowance may be made partially to the child or his guardian or other person having his care and custody, and partially to the spouse, as their needs may appear. The family allowance is exempt from and has priority over all claims but not over the homestead allowance.

The family allowance is not chargeable against any benefit or share passing to the surviving spouse or children by the will of the decedent unless otherwise provided, by intestate succession, or by way of elective share. The death of any person entitled to family allowance terminates his right to allowances not yet paid.

§ 2-404. [Source, Determination and Documentation.]

If the estate is otherwise sufficient, property specifically devised is not used to satisfy rights to homestead and exempt property. Subject to this restriction, the surviving spouse, the guardians of the minor children, or children who are adults may select property of the estate as homestead allowance and exempt property. The personal representative may make these selection if the surviving spouse, the children or the guardians of the minor children are unable or fail to do so within a reasonable time or if there are no guardians of the minor children. The personal representative may execute an instrument or deed of distribution to establish the ownership of property taken as homestead allowance or exempt property. He may determine the family allowance in a lump sum not exceeding $6,000 or periodic installments not exceeding $500 per month for one year, and may disburse funds of the estate in payment of the family allowance and any part of the homestead allowance payable in cash. The personal representative or any interested person aggrieved by any selection, determination, payment, proposed payment, or failure to act under this section may petition the Court for appropriate relief, which relief may provide a family allowance larger or smaller than that which the personal representative determined or could have determined.

Part 5
Wills

§ 2-501. [Who May Make a Will.]

Any person 18 or more years of age who is of sound mind may make a will.

§ 2-502. [Execution.]

Except as provided for holographic wills, writings within Section 2-513, and wills within Section 2-506, every will shall be in writing signed by the testator or in the testator's name by some other person in the testator's presence and by his direction, and shall be signed by at least 2 persons each of whom witnessed either the signing or the testator's acknowledgment of the signature or of the will.

§ 2-503. [Holographic Will.]

A will which does not comply with Section 2-502 is valid as a holographic will, whether or not witnessed, if the signature and the material provisions are in the handwriting of the testator.

§ 2-504. [Self-proved Will.]

(a) Any will may be simultaneously executed, attested, and made self-proved, by acknowledgment thereof by the testator and affidavits of the witnesses, each made before an officer authorized to administer oaths under the laws of the state where execution occurs and evidenced by the officer's certificate, under official seal, in substantially the following form:

I, _____, the testator, sign my name to this instrument this _____ day of _____, 19_____, and being first duly sworn, do hereby declare to the undersigned authority that I sign and execute this instrument as my last will and that I sign it willingly (or willingly direct another to sign for me), that I execute it as my free and voluntary act for the purposes therein expressed, and that I am eighteen years of age or older, of sound mind, and under no constraint or undue influence.

_____
Testator

We, _____, _____, the witnesses, sign our names to this instrument, being first duly sworn, and do hereby declare to the undersigned authority that the testator signs and executes this instrument as his last will and that he signs it willingly (or willingly directs another to sign for him), and that each of us, in the presence and hearing of the testator, hereby signs this will as witness to the testator's signing, and that to the best of our knowledge the testator is eighteen years of age or older, of sound mind, and under no constraint or undue influence.

_____
Witness

_____
Witness

The State of _____
County of _____

Subscribed, sworn to and acknowledged before me by _____, the testator and subscribed and sworn to before me by _____, and _____, witnesses, this _____ day of _____.

(Seal)

(Signed) _____
(Official capacity of officer)

(b) An attested will may at any time subsequent to its execution be made self-proved by the acknowledgment thereof by the testator and the affidavits of the witnesses, each made before an officer authorized to administer oaths under the laws of the state where the acknowledgment occurs and evidenced by the officer's certificate, under the official seal, attached or annexed to the will in substantially the following form:

The State of _____

County of _____

We,_____, _____, and _____, the testator and the witnesses, respectively, whose names are signed to the attached or foregoing instrument, being first duly sworn, do hereby declare to the undersigned authority that the testator signed and executed the instrument as his last will and that he had signed willingly (or willingly directed another to sign for him), and that he executed it as his free and voluntary act for the purposes therein expressed, and that each of the witnesses, in the presence and hearing of the testator, signed the will as witness and that to the best of his knowledge the testator was at that time eighteen years of age or older, of sound mind and under no constraint or undue influence.

_____
Testator

_____
Witness

_____
Witness

Subscribed, sworn to and acknowledged before me by _____, the testator, and subscribed and sworn to before me by _____, and _____, witnesses, this _____ day of _____.

(Seal)
(Seal)

(Signed) _____
(Official capacity of officer)

§ 2-505. [Who May Witness.]

(a) Any person generally competent to be a witness may act as a witness to a will.

(b) A will or any provision thereof is not invalid because the will is signed by an interested witness.

§ 2-506. [Choice of Law as to Execution.]

A written will is valid if executed in compliance with Section 2-502 or 2-503 or if its execution complies with the law at the time of execution of the place where the will is executed, or of the law of the place where at the time of execution or at the time of death the testator is domiciled, has a place of abode or is a national.

§ 2-507. [Revocation by Writing or by Act.]

A will or any part thereof is revoked
(1) by a subsequent will which revokes the prior will or part expressly or by inconsistency; or
(2) by being burned, torn, canceled, obliterated, or destroyed, with the intent and for the purpose of revoking it by the testator or by another person in his presence and by his direction.

§ 2-508. [Revocation by Divorce; No Revocation by Other Changes of Circumstances.]

If after executing a will the testator is divorced or his marriage annulled, the divorce or annulment revokes any disposition or appointment of property made by the will to the former spouse, any provision conferring a general or special power of appointment on the former spouse, and any nomination of the former spouse as executor, trustee, conservator, or guardian, unless the will expressly provides otherwise. Property prevented from passing to a former spouse because of revocation by divorce or annulment passes as if the former spouse failed to survive the decedent, and other provisions conferring some power or office on the former spouse are interpreted as if the spouse failed to survive the decedent. If provisions are revoked solely by this section, they are revived by testator's remarriage to the former spouse. For purposes of this section, divorce or annulment means any divorce or annulment which would exclude the spouse as a surviving spouse within the meaning of Section 2-802(b). A decree of separation which does not terminate the status of husband and wife is not a divorce for purposes of this section. No change of circumstances other than as described in this section revokes a will.

§ 2-509. [Revival of Revoked Will.]

(a) If a second will which, had it remained effective at death, would have revoked the first will in whole or in part, is thereafter revoked by acts under Section 2-507, the first will is revoked in whole or in part unless it is evident from the circumstances of the revocation of the second will or from testator's contemporary or subsequent declarations that he intended the first will to take effect as executed.

(b) If a second will which, had it remained effective at death, would have revoked the first will in whole or in part, is thereafter revoked by a third will, the first will is revoked in whole or in part, except to the extent it appears from the terms of the third will that the testator intended the first will to take effect.

§ 2-510. [Incorporation by Reference.]

Any writing in existence when a will is executed may be incorporated by reference if the language of the will manifests this intent and describes the writing sufficiently to permit its identification.

§ 2-511. [Testamentary Additions to Trusts.]

A devise or bequest, the validity of which is determinable by the law of this state, may be made by a will to the trustee of a trust established or to be established by the testator or by the testator and some other person or by some other person (including a funded or unfunded life insurance trust, although the trustor has reserved any or all rights of ownership of the insurance contracts) if the trust is identified in the testator's will and its terms are set forth in a written instrument (other than a will) executed before or concurrently with the execution of the testator's will or in the valid last will of a person who has predeceased the testator (regardless of the existence, size, or character of the corpus of the trust). The devise is not invalid because the trust is amendable or revocable, or because the trust was amended after the execution of the will or after the death of the testator. Unless the testator's will provides otherwise, the property so devised (1) is not deemed to be held under a testamentary trust of the testator but becomes a part of the trust to which it is given and (2) shall be administered and disposed of in accordance with the provisions of the instrument or will setting forth the terms of the trust, including any amendments thereto made before the death of the testator (regardless of whether made before or after the execution of the testator's will), and, if the testator's will so provides, including any amendments to the trust made after the death of the testator. A revocation or termination of the trust before the death of the testator causes the devise to lapse.

§ 2-512. [Events of Independent Significance.]

A will may dispose of property by reference to acts and events which have significance apart from their effect upon the dispositions made by the will, whether they occur before or after the execution of the will or before or after the testator's death. The execution or revocation of a will of another person is such an event.

§ 2-513. [Separate Writing Identifying Bequest of Tangible Property.]

Whether or not the provisions relating to holographic wills apply, a will may refer to a written statement or list to dispose of items of tangible personal property not otherwise specifically disposed of by the will, other than money, evidences of indebtedness, documents of title, and securities, and property used in trade or business. To be admissible under this section as evidence of the intended disposition, the writing must either be in the handwriting of the testator or be signed by him and must describe the items and the devisees with reasonable certainty. The writing may be referred to as one to be in existence at the time of the testator's death; it may be prepared before or after the execution of the will; it may be altered by the testator after its preparation; and it may be a writing which has no significance apart from its effect upon the dispositions made by the will.

Part 6
Rules of Construction

§ 2-601. [Requirement That Devisee Survive Testator by 120 Hours.]

A devisee who does not survive the testator by 120 hours is treated as if he predeceased the testator, unless the will of decedent contains some language dealing explicitly with simultaneous deaths or deaths in a common disaster, or requiring that the devisee survive the testator or survive the testator for a stated period in order to take under the will.

§ 2-602. [Choice of Law as to Meaning and Effect of Wills.]

The meaning and legal effect of a disposition in a will shall be determined by the local law of a particular state selected by the testator in his instrument unless the application of that law is contrary to the provisions relating to the elective share described in Part 2 of this Article, the provisions relating to exempt property and allowances described in Part 4 of this Article, or any other public policy of this State otherwise applicable to the disposition.

§ 2-603. [Rules of Construction and Intention.]

The intention of a testator as expressed in his will controls the legal effect of his dispositions. The rules of construction expressed in the succeeding sections of this Part apply unless a contrary intention is indicated by the will.

§ 2-604. [Construction That Will Passes All Property; After-Acquired Property.]

A will is construed to pass all property which the testator owns at his death including property acquired after the execution of the will.

§ 2-605. [Anti-lapse; Deceased Devisee; Class Gifts.]

If a devisee who is a grandparent or a lineal descendant of a grandparent of the testator is dead at the time of execution of the will, fails to survive the testator, or is treated as if he predeceased the testator, the issue of the deceased devisee who survive the testator by 120 hours take in place of the deceased devisee and if they are all of the same degree of kinship to the devisee they take equally, but if of unequal degree than those of more remote degree take by representation. One who would have been a devisee under a class gift if he had survived the testator is treated as a devisee for purposes of this section whether his death occurred before or after the execution of the will.

§ 2-606. [Failure of Testamentary Provision.]

(a) Except as provided in Section 2-605 if a devise other than a residuary devise fails for any reason, it becomes a part of the residue.

(b) Except as provided in Section 2-605 if residue is devised to two or more persons and the share of one of the residuary devisees fails for any reason, his share passes to the other residuary devisee, or to other residuary devisees in proportion to their interests in the residue.

§ 2-607. [Change in Securities; Accessions; Nonademption.]

(a) If the testator intended a specific devise of certain securities rather than the equivalent value thereof, the specific devisee is entitled only to:

(1) as much of the devised securities as is a part of the estate at time of the testator's death;

(2) any additional or other securities of the same entity owned by the testator by reason of action initiated by the entity excluding any acquired by exercise of purchase options;

(3) securities of another entity owned by the testator as a result of a merger, consolidation, reorganization or other similar action initiated by the entity; and

(4) any additional securities of the entity owned by the testator as a result of a plan of reinvestment.

(b) Distributions prior to death with respect to a specifically devised security not provided for in subsection (a) are not part of the specific devise.

As amended in 1987.

§ 2-608. [Nonademption of Specific Devises in Certain Cases; Unpaid Proceeds of Sale, Condemnation or Insurance; Sale by Conservator.]

(a) A specific devisee has the right to the remaining specifically devised property and:

(1) any balance of the purchase price (together with any security interest) owing from a purchaser to the testator at death by reason of sale of the property;

(2) any amount of a condemnation award for the taking of the property unpaid at death;

(3) any proceeds unpaid at death on fire or casualty insurance on the property; and

(4) property owned by testator at his death as a result of foreclosure, or obtained in lieu of foreclosure, of the security for a specifically devised obligation.

(b) If specifically devised property is sold by a conservator or an agent acting within the authority of a durable power of attorney for a principal who is under a disability, or if a condemnation award or insurance proceeds are paid to a conservator or an agent acting within the authority of a durable power of attorney for a principal who is under a disability as a result of condemnation, fire, or casualty, the specific devisee has the right to a general pecuniary devise equal to the net sale price, the condemnation award, or the insurance proceeds. This subsection does not apply if after the sale, condemnation or casualty, it is adjudicated that the disability of the testator has ceased and the testator survives the adjudication by one year. The right of the specific devisee under this subsection is reduced by any right he has under subsection (a).

As amended in 1987.

§ 2-609. [Non-Exoneration.]

A specific devise passes subject to any mortgage interest existing at the date of death, without right of exoneration, regardless of a general directive in the will to pay debts.

§ 2-610. [Exercise of Power of Appointment.]

A general residuary clause in a will, or a will making general disposition of all of the testator's property, does not exercise a power of appointment held by the testator unless specific reference is made to the power or there is some other indication of intention to include the property subject to the power.

§ 2-611. [Construction of Generic Terms to Accord with Relationships as Defined for Intestate Succession.]

Halfbloods, adopted persons, and persons born out of wedlock are included in class gift terminology and terms of relationship in accordance with rules for determining relationships for purposes of intestate succession. [However, a person born out of wedlock is not treated as the child of the father unless the person is openly and notoriously so treated by the father.]

§ 2-612. [Ademption by Satisfaction.]

Property which a testator gave in his lifetime to a person is treated as a satisfaction of a devise to that person in whole or in part, only if the will provides for deduction of the lifetime gift, or the testator declares in a contemporaneous writing that the gift is to be deducted from the devise or is in satisfaction of the devise, or the devisee acknowledges in writing that the gift is in satisfaction. For purpose of partial satisfaction, property given during lifetime is valued as of the time the devisee came into possession or enjoyment of the property or as of the time of death of the testator, whichever occurs first.

Part 7
Contractual Arrangements Relating to Death
(See also Article VI, Non-Probate Transfers)

§ 2-701. [Contracts Concerning Succession.]

A contract to make a will or devise, or not to revoke a will or devise, or to die intestate, if executed after the effective date of this Act, can be established only by (1) provisions of a will stating material provisions of the contract; (2) an express reference in a will to a contract and extrinsic evidence proving the terms of the contract; or (3) a writing signed by the decedent evidencing the contract. The execution of a joint will or mutual wills does not create a presumption of a contract not to revoke the will or wills.

Part 8
General Provisions

§ 2-801. [Renunciation of Succession.]

(a) A person or the representative of an incapacitated or protected person, who is an heir, devisee, person succeeding to a renounced interest, beneficiary under a testamentary instrument, or appointee under a power of appointment exercised by a testamentary instrument, may renounce in whole or in part the right of succession to any property or interest therein, including a future interest, by filing a written renunciation under this Section. The right to renounce does not survive the death of the person having it. The instrument shall (1) describe the property or interest renounced, (2) declare the renunciation and extent thereof, and (3) be signed by the person renouncing.

(b)(1) An instrument renouncing a present interest shall be filed not later than [9] months after the death of the decedent or the donee of the power.

(2) An instrument renouncing a future interest may be filed not later than [9] months after the event determining that the taker of the property or interest is finally ascertained and his interest is indefeasibly vested.

(3) The renunciation shall be filed in the [probate] court of the county in which proceedings have been commenced for the administration of the estate of the deceased owner or deceased donee of the power or, if they have not been commenced, in which they could be commenced. A copy of the renunciation shall be delivered in person or mailed by registered or certified mail to any personal representative, or other fiduciary of the decedent or donee of the power. If real property or an interest therein is renounced, a copy of the renunciation may be recorded in the office of the [Recorder of Deeds] of the county in which the real estate is situated.

(c) Unless the decedent or donee of the power has otherwise provided, the property or interest renounced devolves as though the person renouncing had predeceased the decedent or, if the person renouncing is designated to take under a power of appointment exercised by a testamentary instrument, as though the person renouncing had predeceased the donee of the power. A future interest that takes effect in possession or enjoyment after the termination of the estate or interest renounced takes effect as though the person renouncing had predeceased the decedent or the donee of the power. A renunciation relates back for all purposes to the date of the death of the decedent or the donee of the power.

(d)(1) The right to renounce property or an interest therein is barred by (i) an assignment, conveyance, encumbrance, pledge, or transfer of the property or interest, or a contract therefor, (ii) a written waiver of the right to renounce, (iii) an acceptance of the property or interest or benefit thereunder, or (iv) a sale of the property or interest under judicial sale made before the renunciation is effected.

(2) The right to renounce exists notwithstanding any limitation on the interest of the person renouncing in the nature of a spendthrift provision or similar restriction.

(3) A renunciation or a written waiver of the right to renounce is binding upon the person renouncing or person waiving and all persons claiming through or under him.

(e) This Section does not abridge the right of a person to waive, release, disclaim, or renounce property or an interest therein under any other statute.

(f) An interest in property existing on the effective date of this Section as to which the time for filing a renunciation under this Section would have begun to run were this Section in effect when the interest was created, may be renounced within [9] months after the effective date of this Section.

§ 2-802. [Effect of Divorce, Annulment, and Decree of Separation.]

(a) A person who is divorced from the decedent or whose marriage to the decedent has been annulled is not a surviving spouse unless, by virtue of a subsequent marriage, he is married to the decedent at the time of death. A decree of separation which does not terminate the status of husband and wife is not a divorce for purposes of this section.

(b) For purposes of Parts 1, 2, 3 & 4 of this Article, and of Section 3-203, a surviving spouse does not include:

(1) a person who obtains or consents to a final decree or judgment of divorce from the decedent or an annulment of their marriage, which decree or judgment is not recognized as valid in this state, unless they subsequently participate in a marriage ceremony purporting to marry each to the other, or subsequently live together as man and wife;

(2) a person who, following a decree or judgment of divorce or annulment obtained by the decedent, participates in a marriage ceremony with a third person; or

(3) a person who was a party to a valid proceeding concluded by an order purporting to terminate all marital property rights.

[§ 2-803. [Effect of Homicide on Intestate Succession, Wills, Joint Assets, Life Insurance and Beneficiary Designations.]

(a) A surviving spouse, heir or devisee who feloniously and intentionally kills the decedent is not entitled to any benefits under the will or under this Article, and the estate of decedent passes as if the killer had predeceased the decedent. Property appointed by the will of the decedent to or for the benefit of the killer passes as if the killer had predeceased the decedent.

(b) Any joint tenant who feloniously and intentionally kills another joint tenant thereby effects a severance of the interest of the decedent so that the share of the decedent passes as his

property and the killer has no rights by survivorship. This provision applies to joint tenancies [and tenancies by the entirety] in real and personal property, joint and multiple-party accounts in banks, savings and loan associations, credit unions and other institutions, and any other form of co-ownership with survivorship incidents.

(c) A named beneficiary of a bond, life insurance policy, or other contractual arrangement who feloniously and intentionally kills the principal obligee or the person upon whose life the policy is issued is not entitled to any benefit under the bond, policy or other contractual arrangement, and it becomes payable as though the killer had predeceased the decedent.

(d) Any other acquisition of property or interest by the killer shall be treated in accordance with the principles of this section.

(e) A final judgment of conviction of felonious and intentional killing is conclusive for purposes of this section. In the absence of a conviction of felonious and intentional killing the Court may determine by a preponderance of evidence whether the killing was felonious and intentional for purposes of this section.

(f) This section does not affect the rights of any person who, before rights under this section have been adjudicated, purchases from the killer for value and without notice property which the killer would have acquired except for this section, but the killer is liable for the amount of the proceeds or the value of the property. Any insurance company, bank, or other obligor making payment according to the terms of its policy or obligation is not liable by reason of this section unless prior to payment it has received at its home office or principal address written notice of a claim under this section.]

Part 9
Custody and Deposit of Wills

§ 2-901. [Deposit of Will With Court in Testator's Lifetime.]

A will may be deposited by the testator or his agent with any Court for safekeeping, under rules of the Court. The will shall be kept confidential. During the testator's lifetime a deposited will shall be delivered only to him or to a person authorized in writing signed by him to receive the will. A conservator may be allowed to examine a deposited will of a protected testator under procedures designed to maintain the confidential character of the document to the extent possible, and to assure that it will be resealed and left on deposit after the examination. Upon being informed of the testator's death, the Court shall notify any person designated to receive the will and deliver it to him on request; or the Court may deliver the will to the appropriate Court.

§ 2-902. [Duty of Custodian of Will; Liability.]

After the death of a testator and on request of an interested person, any person having custody of a will of the testator shall deliver it with reasonable promptness to a person able to secure its probate and if none is known, to an appropriate Court. Any person who wilfully fails to deliver a will is liable to any person aggrieved for the damages which may be sustained by the failure. Any person who wilfully refuses or fails to deliver a will after being ordered by the Court in a proceeding brought for the purpose of compelling delivery is subject to penalty for contempt of Court.

Part 10
Uniform International Wills Act
[International Will; Information Registration]

§ 1. [2-1001.] [Definitions.]

In this Act: [Part:]

(1) "International will" means a will executed in conformity with Sections 2 [2-1002] through 5 [2-1005].

(2) "Authorized person" and "person authorized to act in connection with international wills" mean a person who by Section 9 [2-1009], or by the laws of the United States including members of the diplomatic and consular service of the United States designated by Foreign Service Regulations, is empowered to supervise the execution of international wills.

§ 2. [2-1002.] [International Will; Validity.]

(a) A will is valid as regards form, irrespective particularly of the place where it is made, of the location of the assets and of the nationality, domicile, or residence of the testator, if it is made in the form of an international will complying with the requirements of this Act. [Part.]

(b) The invalidity of the will as an international will shall not affect its formal validity as a will of another kind.

(c) This Act [Part] shall not apply to the form of testamentary dispositions made by two or more persons in one instrument.

§ 3. [2-1003.] [International Will; Requirements.]

(a) The will must be made in writing. It need not be written by the testator himself. It may be written in any language, by hand or by any other means.

(b) The testator shall declare in the presence of two witnesses and of a person authorized to act in connection with international wills that the document is his will and that he knows the contents thereof. The testator need not inform the witnesses, or the authorized person, of the contents of the will.

(c) In the presence of the witnesses, and of the authorized person, the testator shall sign the will or, if he has previously signed it, shall acknowledge his signature.

(d) If the testator is unable to sign, the absence of his signature does not affect the validity of the international will if the testator indicates the reason for his inability to sign and the authorized person makes note thereof on the will. In that case, it is permissible for any other person present, including the authorized person or one of the witnesses, at the direction of the testator to sign the testator's name for him, if the authorized person makes note of this on the will, but it is not required that any person sign the testator's name for him.

(e) The witnesses and the authorized person shall there and then attest the will by signing in the presence of the testator.

§ 4. [2-1004.] [International Will; Other Points of Form.]

(a) The signatures must be placed at the end of the will. If the will consists of several sheets, each sheet must be signed by the testator or, if he is unable to sign, by the person signing on his behalf or, if there is no such person, by the authorized person. In addition, each sheet shall be numbered.

(b) The date of the will shall be the date of its signature by the authorized person. That date must be noted at the end of the will by the authorized person.

(c) The authorized person shall ask the testator whether he wishes to make a declaration concerning the safekeeping of his will. If so and at the express request of the testator, the place where he intends to have his will kept shall be mentioned in the certificate provided for in Section 5.

(d) A will executed in compliance with Section 3 shall not be invalid merely because it does not comply with this section.

§ 5. [2-1005.] [International Will; Certificate.]

The authorized person shall attach to the will a certificate to be signed by him establishing that the requirements of this Act [Part] for valid execution of an international will have been complied with. The authorized person shall keep a copy of the certificate and deliver another to the testator. The certificate must be substantially in the following form:

CERTIFICATE
(CONVENTION OF OCTOBER 26, 1973)

1. I, _____ (name, address and capacity), a person authorized to act in connection with international wills

2. Certify that on _____ (date) at _____ (place)

3. (testator) _____ (name, address, date and place of birth) in my presence and that of the witnesses

4. (a) _____ (name, address, date and place of birth)

(b) _____ (name, address, date and place of birth) has declared that the attached document is his will and that he knows the contents thereof.

5. I furthermore certify that:

6. (a) in my presence and in that of the witnesses

(1) the testator has signed the will or has acknowledged his signature previously affixed.

°(2) following a declaration of the testator stating that he was unable to sign his will for the following reason _____, I have mentioned this declaration on the will °and the signature has been affixed by _____ (name and address)

7. (b) the witnesses and I have signed the will;

8. °(c) each page of the will has been signed by _____ and numbered;

9. (d) I have satisfied myself as to the identity of the testator and of the witnesses as designated above;

10. (e) the witnesses met the conditions requisite to act as such according to the law under which I am acting;

11. °(f) the testator has requested me to include the following statement concerning the safekeeping of his will:

_____

12. PLACE OF EXECUTION

13. DATE

14. SIGNATURE and, if necessary, SEAL

°To be completed if appropriate

§ 6. [2-1006.] [International Will; Effect of Certificate.]

In the absence of evidence to the contrary, the certificate of the authorized person shall be conclusive of the formal validity of the instrument as a will under this Act. [Part. The absence or irregularity of a certificate does not affect the formal validity of a will under this Act. [Part.]

§ 7. [2-1007.] [International Will; Revocation.]

The international will shall be subject to the ordinary rules of revocation of wills.

§ 8. [2-1008.] [Source and Construction.]

Sections 1 [2-1001] through 7 [2-1007] derive from Annex to Convention of October 26, 1973, Providing a Uniform Law on the Form of an International Will. In interpreting and applying this Act [Part], regard shall be had to its international origin and to the need for uniformity in its interpretation.

§ 9. [2-1009.] [Persons Authorized to Act in Relation to International Will; Eligibility; Recognition by Authorizing Agency.]

Individuals who have been admitted to practice law before the courts of this state and who are in good standing as active law practitioners in this state, are hereby declared to be authorized persons in relation to international wills.

[§ 10. [2-1010.] [International Will Information Registration.]

The [Secretary of State] shall establish a registry system by which authorized persons may register in a central information center, information regarding the execution of international wills, keeping that information in strictest confidence until the death of the maker and then making it available to any person desiring information about any will who presents a death certificate or other satisfactory evidence of the testator's death to the center. Information that may be received, preserved in confidence until death, and reported as indicated is limited to the name, social security or any other individual-identifying number established by law, address, and date and place of birth of the testator, and the intended place of deposit or safekeeping of the instrument pending the death of the maker. The [Secretary of State], at the request of the authorized person, may cause the information it receives about execution of any international will to be transmitted to the registry system of another jurisdiction as identified by the testator, if that other system adheres to rules protecting the confidentiality of the information similar to those established in this State.]

Here ends Article II of the 1969 UPC.

ARTICLE III
PROBATE OF WILLS AND ADMINISTRATION

Part 1
General Provisions

§ 3-101. [Devolution of Estate at Death; Restrictions.]

The power of a person to leave property by will, and the rights of creditors, devisees, and heirs to his property are subject to the restrictions and limitations contained in this Code to facilitate the prompt settlement of estates. Upon the death of a person, his real and personal property devolves to the person to whom it is devised by his last will or to those indicated as substitutes for them in cases involving lapse, renunciation or other circumstances affecting the devolution of testate estate, or in the absence of testamentary disposition, to his heirs, or to those indicated as substitutes for them in cases involving renunciation or other circumstances affecting devolution of intestate estates, subject to homestead allowance, exempt property and family allowance, to rights of creditors elective share of the surviving spouse, and to administration.

ALTERNATIVE SECTION FOR COMMUNITY PROPERTY STATES

[§ 3-101A. [Devolution of Estate at Death; Restrictions.]

The power of a person to leave property by will, and the rights of creditors, devisees, and heirs to his property are subject to the restrictions and limitations contained in this Code to facilitate the prompt settlement of estates. Upon the death of a person, his separate property devolves to the persons to whom it is devised by his last will, or to those indicated as substitutes for them in cases involving lapse, renunciation or other circumstances affecting the devolution of estate estates, or in the absence of testamentary disposition to his heirs, or to those indicated as substitutes for them in cases involving renunciation or other circumstances affecting the devolution of intestate estates, and upon the death of a husband or wife, the decedent's share of their community property devolves to the persons to whom it is devised by his last will, or in the absence of testamentary disposition, to his heirs, but all of their community property which is under the management and control of the decedent is subject to his debts and administration, and that portion of their community property which is not under the management and control of the decedent but which is necessary to carry out the provisions of his will is subject to administration; but the devolution of all the above described property is subject to rights to homestead allowance, exempt property and family allowances, to renunciation, to rights of creditors, [elective share of the surviving spouse] and to administration.]

§ 3-102. [Necessity of Order of Probate For Will.]

Except as provided in Section 3-1201, to be effective to prove the transfer of any property or to nominate an executor, a will must be declared to be valid by an order of informal probate by the Registrar, or an adjudication of probate by the Court, except that a duly executed and unrevoked will which has not been probated may be admitted as evidence of a devise if (1) no Court proceeding concerning the succession of administration of the estate has occurred, and (2) either the devisee or his successors and assigns possessed the property devised in accordance with the provisions of the will, or the property devised was not possessed or claimed by anyone by virtue of the decedent's title during the time period for testacy proceedings.

§ 3-103. [Necessity of Appointment For Administration.]

Except as otherwise provided in Article IV, to acquire the powers and undertake the duties and liabilities of a personal representative of a decedent, a person must be appointed by order of the Court or Registrar, qualify and be issued letters. Administration of an estate is commenced by the issuance of letters.

§ 3-104. [Claims Against Decedent; Necessity of Administration.]

No proceeding to enforce a claim against the estate of a decedent or his successors may be revived or commenced before the appointment of a personal representative. After the appointment and until distribution, all proceedings and actions to enforce a claim against the estate are governed by the procedure prescribed by this Article. After distribution a creditor whose claim has not been barred may recover from the distributees as provided in Section 3-1004 or from a former personal representative individually liable as provided in Section 3-1005. This section has no application to a proceeding by a secured creditor of the decedent to enforce his right to his security except as to any deficiency judgment which might be sought therein.

§ 3-105. [Proceedings Affecting Devolution and Administration; Jurisdiction of Subject Matter.]

Persons interested in decedents' estates may apply to the Registrar for determination in the informal proceedings provided in this Article, and may petition the Court for orders in formal proceedings within the Court's jurisdiction including but not limited to those described in this Article. The Court has exclusive jurisdiction of formal proceedings to determine how decedents' estates subject to the laws of this state are to be administered, expended and distributed. The Court has concurrent jurisdiction of any other action or proceeding concerning a succession or to which an estate, through a personal representative, may be a party, including actions to determine title to property alleged to belong to the estate, and of any action or proceeding in which property distributed by a personal representative or its value is sought to be subjected to rights of creditors or successors of the decedent.

§ 3-106. [Proceedings Within the Exclusive Jurisdiction of Court; Service; Jurisdiction Over Persons.]

In proceedings within the exclusive jurisdiction of the Court where notice is required by this Code or by rule, and in proceedings to construe probated wills or determine heirs which concern estates that have not been and cannot now be open for administration, interested persons may be bound by the orders of the Court in respect to property in or subject to the laws of this state by notice in conformity with Section 1-401. An order is binding as to all who are given notice of the proceeding though less than all interested persons are notified.

§ 3-107. [Scope of Proceedings; Proceedings Independent; Exception.]

Unless supervised administration as described in Part 5 is involved, (1) each proceeding before the Court or Registrar is independent of any other proceeding involving the same estate; (2) petitions for formal orders of the Court may combine various requests for relief in a single proceeding if the orders sought may be finally granted without delay. Except as required for proceedings which are particularly described by other sections of this Article, no petition is defective because it fails to embrace all matters which might then be the subject of a final order; (3) proceedings for probate of wills or adjudications of no will may be combined with proceedings for appointment of personal representatives; and (4) a proceeding for appointment of a personal representative is concluded by an order making or declining the appointment.

§ 3-108. [Probate, Testacy and Appointment Proceedings; Ultimate Time Limit.]

No informal probate or appointment proceeding or formal testacy or appointment proceeding, other than a proceeding to probate a will previously probated at the testator's domicile and appointment proceedings relating to an estate in which there has been a prior appointment, may be commenced more than 3 years after the decedent's death, except (1) if a previous proceeding was dismissed because of doubt about the fact of the decedent's death, appropriate probate, appointment or testacy proceedings may be maintained at any time thereafter upon a finding that the decedent's death occurred prior to the initiation of the previous proceeding and the applicant or petitioner has not delayed unduly in initiating the subsequent proceeding; (2) appropriate probate, appointment or testacy proceedings may be maintained in relation to the estate of an absent, disappeared or missing person for whose estate a conservator has been appointed, at any time

within three years after the conservator becomes able to establish the death of the protected person; and (3) a proceeding to contest an informally probated will and to secure appointment of the person with legal priority for appointment in the event the contest is successful, may be commenced within the later of twelve months from the informal probate or three years from the decedent's death; and (4) if no proceeding concerning the succession or administration of the estate has occurred within 3 years after decedent's death, a formal testacy proceeding may be commenced at any time thereafter for the sole purpose of establishing a devise of property which the devisee or his successors and assigns possessed in accordance with the will or property which was not possessed or claimed by anyone by virtue of the decedent's title during the 3-year period, and the order of the Court shall be limited to that property. These limitations do not apply to proceedings to construe probated wills or determine heirs of an intestate. In cases under (1) or (2) above, the date on which a testacy or appointment proceeding is properly commenced shall be deemed to be the date of the decedent's death for purposes of other limitations provisions of this Code which relate to the date of death.

As amended in 1987.

§ 3-109. [Statutes of Limitation on Decedent's Cause of Action.]

No statute of limitation running on a cause of action belonging to a decedent which had not been barred as of the date of his death, shall apply to bar a cause of action surviving the decedent's death sooner than four months after death. A cause of action which, but for this section, would have been barred less than four months after death, is barred after four months unless tolled.

Part 2
Venue for Probate and Administration; Priority to Administer; Demand for Notice

§ 3-201. [Venue for First and Subsequent Estate Proceedings; Location of Property.]

(a) Venue for the first informal or formal testacy or appointment proceedings after a decedent's death is:

(1) in the [county] where the decedent had his domicile at the time of his death; or

(2) if the decedent was not domiciled in this state, in any [county] where property of the decedent was located at the time of his death.

(b) Venue for all subsequent proceedings within the exclusive jurisdiction of the Court is in the place where the initial proceeding occurred, unless the initial proceeding has been transferred as provided in Section 1-303 or (c) of this section.

(c) If the first proceeding was informal, on application of an interested person and after notice to the proponent in the first proceeding, the Court, upon finding that venue is elsewhere, may transfer the proceeding and the file to the other court.

(d) For the purpose of aiding determinations concerning location of assets which may be relevant in cases involving non-domiciliaries, a debt other than one evidenced by investment or commercial paper or other instrument in favor of a non-domiciliary is located where the debtor resides or, if the debtor is a person other than an individual, at the place where it has its principal office. Commercial paper, investment paper and other instruments are located where the instrument is. An interest in property held in trust is located where the trustee may be sued.

§ 3-202. [Appointment or Testacy Proceedings; Conflicting Claim of Domicile in Another State.]

If conflicting claims as to the domicile of a decedent are made in a formal testacy or appointment proceeding commenced in this state, and in a testacy or appointment proceeding after notice pending at the same time in another state, the Court of this state must stay, dismiss, or permit suitable amendment in, the proceeding here unless it is determined that the local proceeding was commenced before the proceeding elsewhere. The determination of domicile in the proceeding first commenced must be accepted as determinative in the proceeding in this state.

§ 3-203. [Priority Among Persons Seeking Appointment as Personal Representative.]

(a) Whether the proceedings are formal or informal, persons who are not disqualified have priority for appointment in the following order:

(1) the person with priority as determined by a probated will including a person nominated by a power conferred in a will;

(2) the surviving spouse of the decedent who is a devisee of the decedent;

(3) other devisees of the decedent;

(4) the surviving spouse of the decedent;

(5) other heirs of the decedent;

(6) 45 days after the death of the decedent, any creditor.

(b) An objection to an appointment can be made only in formal proceedings. In case of objection the priorities stated in (a) apply except that

(1) if the estate appears to be more than adequate to meet exemptions and costs of administration but inadequate to discharge anticipated unsecured claims, the Court, on petition of creditors, may appoint any qualified person;

(2) in case of objection to appointment of a person other than one whose priority is determined by will by an heir or devisee appearing to have a substantial interest in the estate, the Court may appoint a person who is acceptable to heirs and devisees whose interests in the estate appear to be worth in total more than half of the probable distributable value, or, in default of this accord any suitable person.

(c) A person entitled to letters under (2) through (5) of (a) above, and a person aged [18] and over who would be entitled to letters but for his age, may nominate a qualified person to act as personal representative. Any person aged [18] and over may renounce his right to nominate or to an appointment by appropriate writing filed with the Court. When two or more persons share a priority, those of them who do not renounce must concur in nominating another to act for them, or in applying for appointment.

(d) Conservators of the estates of protected persons, or if there is no conservator, any guardian except a guardian ad litem of a minor or incapacitated person, may exercise the same right to nominate, to object to another's appointment, or to participate in determining the preference of a majority in interest of the heirs and devisees that the protected person or ward would have if qualified for appointment.

(e) Appointment of one who does not have priority, including priority resulting from renunciation or nomination determined pursuant to this section, may be made only in formal proceedings. Before appointing one without priority, the Court must determine that those having priority, although given notice of the proceedings, have failed to request appointment or to nominate another for appointment, and that administration is necessary.

(f) No person is qualified to serve as a personal representative who is:

(1) under the age of [21];

(2) a person whom the Court finds unsuitable in formal proceedings

(g) A personal representative appointed by a court of the decedent's domicile has priority over all other persons except where the decedent's will nominates different persons to be personal representative in this state and in the state of domicile. The domiciliary personal representative may nominate another, who shall have the same priority as the domiciliary personal representative.

(h) This section governs priority for appointment of a successor personal representative but does not apply to the selection of a special administrator.

§ 3-204. [Demand for Notice of Order or Filing Concerning Decedent's Estate.]

Any person desiring notice of any order or filing pertaining to a decedent's estate in which he has a financial or property interest, may file a demand for notice with the Court at any time after the death of the decedent stating the name of the decedent, the nature of his interest in the estate, and the demandant's address or that of his attorney. The clerk shall mail a copy of the demand to the personal representative if one has been appointed. After filing of a demand, no order or filing to which the demand relates shall be made or accepted without notice as prescribed in Section 1-101 to the demandant or his attorney. The validity of an order which is issued or filing which is accepted without compliance with this requirement shall not be affected by the error, but the petitioner receiving the order or the person making the filing may be liable for any damage caused by the absence of notice. The requirement of notice arising from a demand under this provision may be waived in writing by the demandant and shall cease upon the termination of his interest in the estate.

Part 3
Informal Probate and Appointment Proceedings; Succession Without Administration

§ 3-301. [Informal Probate or Appointment Proceedings; Application; Contents.]

(a) Applications for informal probate or informal appointment shall be directed to the Registrar, and verified by the applicant to be accurate and complete to the best of his knowledge and belief as to the following information:

(1) Every application for informal probate of a will or for informal appointment of a personal representative, other than a special or successor representative, shall contain the following:

(i) a statement of the interest of the applicant;

(ii) the name, and date of death of the decedent, his age, and the county and state of his domicile at the time of death, and the names and addresses of the spouse, children, heirs and devisees and the ages of any who are minors so far as known or ascertainable with reasonable diligence by the applicant;

(iii) if the decedent was not domiciled in the state at the time of his death, a statement showing venue;

(iv) a statement identifying and indicating the address of any personal representative of the decedent appointed in this state or elsewhere whose appointment has not been terminated;

(v) a statement indicating whether the applicant has received a demand for notice, or is aware of any demand for notice of any probate or appointment proceeding concerning the decedent that may have been filed in this state or elsewhere; and

(vi) that the time limit for informal probate or appointment as provided in this Article has not expired either because 3 years or less have passed since the decedent's death, or, if more than 3 years from death have passed, circumstances as described by Section 3-108 authorizing tardy probate or appointment have occurred.

(2) An application for informal probate of a will shall state the following in addition to the statements required by (1):

(i) that the original of the decedent's last will is in the possession of the court, or accompanies the application, or that an authenticated copy of a will probated in another jurisdiction accompanies the application;

(ii) that the applicant, to the best of his knowledge, believes the will to have been validly executed;

(iii) that after the exercise of reasonable diligence, the applicant is unaware of any instrument revoking the will, and that the applicant believes that the instrument which is the subject of the application is the decedent's last will.

(3) An application for informal appointment of a personal representative to administer an estate under a will shall describe the will by date of execution and state the time and place of probate or the pending application or petition for probate. The application for appointment shall adopt the statements in the application or petition for probate and state the name, address and priority for appointment of the person whose appointment is sought.

(4) An application for informal appointment of an administrator in intestacy shall state in addition to the statements required by (1):

(i) that after the exercise of reasonable diligence, the applicant is unaware of any unrevoked testamentary instrument relating to property having a situs in this state under Section 1-301, or, a statement why any such instrument of which he may be aware is not being probated;

(ii) the priority of the person whose appointment is sought and the names of any other persons having a prior or equal right to the appointment under Section 3-203.

(5) An application for appointment of a personal representative to succeed a personal representative appointed under a different testacy status shall refer to the order in the most recent testacy proceeding, state the name and address of the person whose appointment is sought and of the person whose appointment will be terminated if the application is granted, and describe the priority of the applicant.

(6) An application for appointment of a personal representative to succeed a personal representative who has tendered a resignation as provided in Section 3-610(c), or whose appointment has been terminated by death or removal, shall adopt the statements in the application or petition which led to the appointment of the person being succeeded except as specifically changed or corrected, state the name and address of the person who seeks appointment as successor, and describe the priority of the applicant.

(b) By verifying an application for informal probate, or informal appointment, the applicant submits personally to the jurisdiction of the court in any proceeding for relief from fraud relating to the application, or for perjury, that may be instituted against him.

§ 3-302. [Informal Probate; Duty of Registrar; Effect of Informal Probate.]

Upon receipt of an application requesting informal probate of a will, the Registrar, upon making the findings required by Section 3-303 shall issue a written statement of informal probate if at least 120 hours have elapsed since the decedent's death. Informal probate is conclusive as to all persons until superseded by an order in a formal testacy proceeding. No defect in the application or procedure relating thereto which leads to informal probate of a will renders the probate void.

§ 3-303. [Informal Probate; Proof and Findings Required.]

(a) In an informal proceeding for original probate of a will, the Registrar shall determine whether:

(1) the application is complete;

(2) the applicant has made oath or affirmation that the statements contained in the application are true to the best of his knowledge and belief;

(3) the applicant appears from the application to be an interested person as defined in Section 1-201(20);

(4) on the basis of the statements in the application, venue is

(5) an original, duly executed and apparently unrevoked will is in the Registrar's possession;

(6) any notice required by Section 3-204 has been given and that the application is not within Section 3-304; and

(7) it appears from the application that the time limit for original probate has not expired.

(b) The application shall be denied if it indicates that a personal representative has been appointed in another [county] of this state or except as provided in subsection (d) below, if it appears that this or another will of the decedent has been the subject of a previous probate order.

(c) A will which appears to have the required signatures and which contains an attestation clause showing that requirements of execution under Section 2-502, 2-503 or 2-506 have been met shall be probated without further proof. In other cases, the Registrar may assume execution if the will appears to have been properly executed, or he may accept a sworn statement or affidavit of any person having knowledge of the circumstances of execution, whether or not the person was a witness to the will.

(d) Informal probate of a will which has been previously probated elsewhere may be granted at any time upon written application by any interested person, together with deposit of an authenticated copy of the will and of the statement probating it from the office or court where it was first probated.

(e) A will from a place which does not provide for probate of a will after death and which is not eligible for probate under subsection (a) above, may be probated in this state upon receipt by the Registrar of a duly authenticated copy of the will and a duly authenticated certificate of its legal custodian that the copy filed is a true copy and that the will has become operative under the law of the other place.

§ 3-304. [Informal Probate; Unavailable in Certain Cases.]

Applications for informal probate which relate to one or more of a known series of testamentary instruments (other than a will and one or more codicils thereto), the latest of which does not expressly revoke the earlier, shall be declined.

As amended in 1987.

§ 3-305. [Informal Probate; Registrar Not Satisfied.]

If the Registrar is not satisfied that a will is entitled to be probated in informal proceedings because of failure to meet the requirements of Sections 3-303 and 3-304 or any other reason, he may decline the application. A declination of informal probate is not an adjudication and does not preclude formal probate proceedings.

§ 3-306. [Informal Probate; Notice Requirements.]

(°) The moving party must give notice as described by Section 1-401 of his application for informal probate to any person demanding it pursuant to Section 3-204, and to any personal representative of the decedent whose appointment has not been terminated. No other notice of informal probate is required.

[(b) If an informal probate is granted, within 30 days thereafter the applicant shall give written information of the probate to the heirs and devisees. The information shall include the name and address of the applicant, the name and location of the court granting the informal probate, and the date of the probate. The information shall be delivered or sent by ordinary mail to each of the heirs and devisees whose address is reasonably available to the applicant. No duty to give information is incurred if a personal representative is appointed who is required to give the written information required by Section 3-705. An applicant's failure to give information as required by this section is a breach of his duty to the heirs and devisees but does not affect the validity of the probate.]

° This paragraph becomes (a) if optional subsection (b) accepted.

§ 3-307. [Informal Appointment Proceedings; Delay in Order; Duty of Registrar; Effect of Appointment.]

(a) Upon receipt of an application for informal appointment of a personal representative other than a special administrator as provided in Section 3-614, if at least 120 hours have elapsed since the decedent's death, the Registrar, after making the findings required by Section 3-308, shall appoint the applicant subject to qualification and acceptance; provided, that if the decedent was a non-resident, the Registrar shall delay the order of appointment until 30 days have elapsed since death unless the personal representative appointed at the decedent's domicile is the applicant, or unless the decedent's will directs that his estate be subject to the laws of this state.

(b) The status of personal representative and the powers and duties pertaining to the office are fully established by informal appointment. An appointment, and the office of personal representative created thereby, is subject to termination as provided in Sections 3-608 through 3-612, but is not subject to retroactive vacation.

§ 3-308. [Informal Appointment Proceedings; Proof and Findings Required.]

(a) In informal appointment proceedings, the Registrar must determine whether:

(1) the application for informal appointment of a personal representative is complete;

(2) the applicant has made oath or affirmation that the statements contained in the application are true to the best of his knowledge and belief;

(3) the applicant appears from the application to be an interested person as defined in Section 1-201(20);

(4) on the basis of the statements in the application, venue is proper;

(5) any will to which the requested appointment relates has been formally or informally probated; but this requirement does not apply to the appointment of a special administrator;

(6) any notice required by Section 3-204 has been given;

(7) from the statements in the application, the person whose appointment is sought has priority entitling him to the appointment.

(b) Unless Section 3-612 controls, the application must be denied if it indicates that a personal representative who has not filed a written statement of resignation as provided in Section 3-610(c) has been appointed in this or another [county] of this state, that (unless the applicant is the domiciliary personal representative or his nominee) the decedent was not domiciled in this state and that a personal representative whose appointment has not been terminated has been appointed by a Court in the state of domicile, or that other requirements of this section have not been met.

§ 3-309. [Informal Appointment Proceedings; Registrar Not Satisfied.]

If the Registrar is not satisfied that a requested informal appointment of a personal representative should be made because of failure to meet the requirements of Sections 3-307 and 3-308, or for any other reason, he may decline the application. A declination of informal appointment is not an adjudication and does not preclude appointment in formal proceedings.

§ 3-310. [Informal Appointment Proceedings; Notice Requirements.]

The moving party must give notice as described by Section 1-401 of his intention to seek an appointment informally: (1) to any person demanding it pursuant to Section 3-204; and (2) to any person having a prior or equal right to appointment not waived in writing and filed with the Court. No other notice of an informal appointment proceeding is required.

§ 3-311. [Informal Appointment Unavailable In Certain Cases.]

If an application for informal appointment indicates the existence of a possible unrevoked testamentary instrument which may relate to property subject to the laws of this state, and which is not filed for probate in this court, the Registrar shall decline the application.

§ 3-312. [Universal Succession; In General.]

The heirs of an intestate or the residuary devisees under a will, excluding minors and incapacitated, protected, or unascertained persons, may become universal successors to the decedent's estate by assuming personal liability for (1) taxes, (2) debts of the decedent, (3) claims against the decedent or the estate, and (4) distributions due other heirs, devisees, and persons entitled to property of the decedent as provided in Sections 3-313 through 3-322.

§ 3-313. [Universal Succession; Application; Contents.]

(a) An application to become universal successors by the heirs of an intestate or the residuary devisees under a will must be directed to the [Registrar], signed by each applicant, and verified to be accurate and complete to the best of the applicant's knowledge and belief as follows:

(1) An application by heirs of an intestate must contain the statements required by Section 3-301(a)(1) and (4)(i) and state that the applicants constitute all the heirs other than minors and incapacitated, protected, or unascertained persons.

(2) An application by residuary devisees under a will must be combined with a petition for informal probate if the will has not been admitted to probate in this State and must contain the statements required by Section 3-301(a)(1) and (2). If the will has been probated in this State, an application by residuary devisees must contain the statements required by Section 3-301(a)(2)(iii). An application by residuary devisees must state that the applicants constitute the residuary devisees of the decedent other than any minors and incapacitated, protected, or unascertained persons. If

the estate is partially intestate, all of the heirs other than minors and incapacitated, protected, or unascertained persons must join as applicants.

(b) The application must state whether letters of administration are outstanding, whether a petition for appointment of a personal representative of the decedent is pending in any court of this State, and that the applicants waive their right to seek appointment of a personal representative.

(c) The application may describe in general terms the assets of the estate and must state that the applicants accept responsibility for the estate and assume personal liability for (1) taxes, (2) debts of the decedent, (3) claims against the decedent or the estate, and (4) distributions due other heirs, devisees, and persons entitled to property of the decedent as provided in Sections 3-316 through 3-322.

§ 3-314. [Universal Succession; Proof and Findings Required.]

(a) The [Registrar] shall grant the application if:

(1) the application is complete in accordance with Section 3-313;

(2) all necessary persons have joined and have verified that the statements contained therein are true, to the best knowledge and belief of each;

(3) venue is proper;

(4) any notice required by Section 3-204 has been given or waived;

(5) the time limit for original probate or appointment proceedings has not expired and the applicants claim under a will;

(6) the application requests informal probate of a will, the application and findings conform with Sections 3-301(a)(2) and 3-303(a) (c)(d) and (e) so the will is admitted to probate; and

(7) none of the applicants is a minor or an incapacitated or protected person.

(b) The [Registrar] shall deny the application if letters of administration are outstanding.

(c) Except as provided in Section 3-322, the [Registrar] shall deny the application if any creditor, heir, or devisee who is qualified by Section 3-605 to demand bond files an objection.

§ 3-315. [Universal Succession; Duty of Registrar; Effect of Statement of Universal Succession.]

Upon receipt of an application under Section 3-313, if at least 120 hours have elapsed since the decedent's death, the [Registrar], upon granting the application, shall issue a written statement of universal succession describing the estate as set forth in the application and stating that the applicants (i) are the universal successors to the assets of the estate as provided in Section 3-312, (ii) have assumed liability for the obligations of the decedent, and (iii) have acquired the powers and liabilities of universal successors. The statement of universal succession is evidence of the universal successors' title to the assets of the estate. Upon its issuance, the powers and liabilities of universal successors provided in Sections 3-316 through 3-322 attach and are assumed by the applicants.

§ 3-316. [Universal Succession; Universal Successors' Powers.]

Upon the [Registrar's] issuance of a statement of universal succession:

(1) Universal successors have full power of ownership to deal with the assets of the estate subject to the limitations and liabilities in this [Act]. The universal successors shall proceed expeditiously to settle and distribute the estate without adjudication but if necessary may invoke the jurisdiction of the court to resolve questions concerning the estate.

(2) Universal successors have the same powers as distributees from a personal representative under Sections 3-908 and 3-909 and third persons with whom they deal are protected as provided in Section 3-910.

(3) For purposes of collecting assets in another state whose law does not provide for universal succession, universal successors have the same standing and power as personal representatives or distributees in this State.

§ 3-317. [Universal Succession; Universal Successors' Liability to Creditors, Other Heirs, Devisees and Persons Entitled to Decedent's Property; Liability of Other Persons Entitled to Property.]

(a) In the proportions and subject to limits expressed in Section 3-321, universal successors assume all liabilities of the decedent that were not discharged by reason of death and liability for all taxes, claims against the decedent or the estate, and charges properly incurred after death for the preservation of the estate, to the extent those items, if duly presented, would be valid claims against the decedent's estate.

(b) In the proportions and subject to the limits expressed in Section 3-321, universal successors are personally liable to other heirs, devisees, and persons entitled to property of the decedent for the assets or amounts that would be due those heirs, were the estate administered, but no allowance having priority over devisees may be claimed for attorney's fees or charges for preservation of the estate in excess of reasonable amounts properly incurred.

(c) Universal successors are entitled to their interests in the estate as heirs or devisees subject to priority and abatement pursuant to Section 3-902 and to agreement pursuant to Section 3-912.

(d) Other heirs, devisees, and persons to whom assets have been distributed have the same powers and liabilities as distributees under Sections 3-908, 3-909, and 3-910.

(e) Absent breach of fiduciary obligations or express undertaking, a fiduciary's liability is limited to the assets received by the fiduciary.

§ 3-318. [Universal Succession; Universal Successors' Submission to Jurisdiction; When Heirs or Devisees May Not Seek Administration.]

(a) Upon issuance of the statement of universal succession, the universal successors become subject to the personal jurisdiction of the courts of this state in any proceeding that may be instituted relating to the estate or to any liability assumed by them.

(b) Any heir or devisee who voluntarily joins in an application under Section 3-313 may not subsequently seek appointment of a personal representative.

§ 3-319. [Universal Succession; Duty of Universal Successors; Information to Heirs and Devisees.]

Not later than thirty days after issuance of the statement of universal succession, each universal successor shall inform the heirs and devisees who did not join in the application of the succession without administration. The information must be delivered or be sent by ordinary mail to each of the heirs and devisees whose address is reasonably available to the universal successors. The information must include the names and addresses of the universal successors, indicate that it is being sent to persons who have or may have some interest in the estate, and describe the court where the application and statement of universal succession has been filed. The failure of a universal successor to give this information is a breach of duty to the persons concerned but does not affect the validity of the approval of succession without administration or the powers or liabilities of the universal successors. A universal successor may inform other persons of the succession without administration by delivery or by ordinary first class mail.

§ 3-320. [Universal Succession; Universal Successors' Liability For Restitution to Estate.]

If a personal representative is subsequently appointed, universal successors are personally liable for restitution of any property of the estate to which they are not entitled as heirs or devisees of the decedent and their liability is the same as a distributee under Section 3-909, subject to the provisions of Sections 3-317 and 3-321 and the limitations of Section 3-1006.

§ 3-321. [Universal Succession; Liability of Universal Successors For Claims, Expenses, Intestate Shares and Devises.]

The liability of universal successors is subject to any defenses that would have been available to the decedent. Other than liability arising from fraud, conversion, or other wrongful conduct of a universal successor, the personal liability of each universal successor to any creditor, claimant, other heir, devisee, or person entitled to decedent's property may not exceed the proportion of the claim that the universal successor's share bears to the share of all heirs and residuary devisees.

§ 3-322. [Universal Succession; Remedies of Creditors, Other Heirs, Devisees or Persons Entitled to Decedent's Property.]

In addition to remedies otherwise provided by law, any creditor, heir, devisee, or person entitled to decedent's property qualified under Section 3-605, may demand bond of universal successors. If the demand for bond precedes the granting of an application for universal succession, it must be treated as an objection under Section 3-314(c) unless it is withdrawn, the claim satisfied, or the applicants post bond in an amount sufficient to protect the demandant. If the demand for bond follows the granting of an application for universal succession, the universal successors, within 10 days after notice of the demand, upon satisfying the claim or posting bond sufficient to protect the demandant, may disqualify the demandant from seeking administration of the estate.

Part 4
Formal Testacy and Appointment Proceedings

§ 3-401. [Formal Testacy Proceedings; Nature; When Commenced.]

A formal testacy proceeding is litigation to determine whether a decedent left a valid will. A formal testacy proceeding may be commenced by an interested person filing a petition as described in Section 3-402(a) in which he requests that the Court, after notice and hearing, enter an order probating a will, or a petition to set aside an informal probate of a will or to prevent informal probate of a will which is the subject of a pending application, or a petition in accordance with Section 3-402(b) for an order that the decedent died intestate.

A petition may seek formal probate of a will without regard to whether the same or a conflicting will has been informally probated. A formal testacy proceeding may, but need not, involve a request for appointment of a personal representative.

During the pendency of a formal testacy proceeding, the Registrar shall not act upon any application for informal probate of any will of the decedent or any application for informal appointment of a personal representative of the decedent.

Unless a petition in a formal testacy proceeding also requests confirmation of the previous informal appointment, a previously appointed personal representative, after receipt of notice of the commencement of a formal probate proceeding, must refrain from exercising his power to make any further distribution of the estate during the pendency of the formal proceeding. A petitioner who seeks the appointment of a different personal representative in a formal proceeding also may request an order restraining the acting personal representative from exercising any of the powers of his office and requesting the appointment of a special administrator. In the absence of a request, or if the request is denied, the commencement of a formal proceeding has no effect on the powers and duties of a previously appointed personal representative other than those relating to distribution.

§ 3-402. [Formal Testacy or Appointment Proceedings; Petition; Contents.]

(a) Petitions for formal probate of a will, or for adjudication of intestacy with or without request for appointment of a personal representative, must be directed to the Court, request a judicial order after notice and hearing and contain further statements as indicated in this section. A petition for formal probate of a will

(1) requests an order as to the testacy of the decedent in relation to a particular instrument which may or may not have been informally probated and determining the heirs,

(2) contains the statements required for informal applications as stated in the six subparagraphs under Section 3-301(a)(1), the statements required by subparagraphs (ii) and (iii) of Section 3-301(a)(2), and

(3) states whether the original of the last will of the decedent is in the possession of the Court or accompanies the petition.

If the original will is neither in the possession of the Court nor accompanies the petition and no authenticated copy of a will probated in another jurisdiction accompanies the petition, the petition also must state the contents of the will, and indicate that it is lost, destroyed, or otherwise unavailable.

(b) A petition for adjudication of intestacy and appointment of an administrator in intestacy must request a judicial finding and order that the decedent left no will and determining the heirs, contain the statements required by (1) and (4) of Section 3-301(a) and indicate whether supervised administration is sought. A petition may request an order determining intestacy and heirs without requesting the appointment of an administrator, in which case, the statements required by subparagraph (ii) of Section 3-301(a)(4) above may be omitted.

§ 3-403. [Formal Testacy Proceedings; Notice of Hearing on Petition.]

(a) Upon commencement of a formal testacy proceeding, the Court shall fix a time and place of hearing. Notice shall be given in the manner prescribed by Section 1-401 by the petitioner to the persons herein enumerated and to any additional person who has filed a demand for notice under Section 3-204 of this Code.

Notice shall be given to the following persons: the surviving spouse, children, and other heirs of the decedent, the devisees and executors named in any will that is being, or has been, probated, or offered for informal or formal probate in the [county,] or that is known by the petitioner to have been probated, or offered for informal or formal probate elsewhere, and any personal representative of the decedent whose appointment has not been terminated. Notice may be given to other persons. In addition, the petitioner shall give notice by publication to all unknown persons and to all known persons whose addresses are unknown who have any interest in the matters being litigated.

(b) If it appears by the petition or otherwise that the fact of the death of the alleged decedent may be in doubt, or on the written demand of any interested person, a copy of the notice of the hearing on said petition shall be sent by registered mail to the alleged decedent at his last known address. The Court shall direct the petitioner to report the results of, or make and report back concerning, a reasonably diligent search for the alleged decedent in any manner that may seem advisable, including any or all of the following methods:

(1) by inserting in one or more suitable periodicals a notice requesting information from any person having knowledge of the whereabouts of the alleged decedent;

(2) by notifying law enforcement officials and public welfare agencies in appropriate locations of the disappearance of the alleged decedent;

(3) by engaging the services of an investigator. The costs of any search so directed shall be paid by the petitioner if there is no administration or by the estate of the decedent in case there is administration.

§ 3-404. [Formal Testacy Proceedings; Written Objections to Probate.]

Any party to a formal proceeding who opposes the probate of a will for any reason shall state in his pleadings his objections to probate of the will.

§ 3-405. [Formal Testacy Proceedings; Uncontested Cases; Hearings and Proof.]

If a petition in a testacy proceeding is unopposed, the Court may order probate or intestacy on the strength of the pleadings if satisfied that the conditions of Section 3-309 have been met, or conduct a hearing in Open court and require proof of the matters necessary to support the order sought. If evidence concerning execution of the will is necessary, the affidavit or testimony of one of any attesting witnesses to the instrument is sufficient. If the affidavit or testimony of an attesting witness is not available, execution of the will may be proved by other evidence or affidavit.

§ 3-406. [Formal Testacy Proceedings; Contested Cases; Testimony of Attesting Witnesses.]

(a) If evidence concerning execution of an attested will which is not self-proved is necessary in contested cases, the testimony of at least one of the attesting witnesses, if within the state, competent and able to testify, is required. Due execution of an attested or unattested will may be proved by other evidence.

(b) If the will is self-proved, compliance with signature requirements for execution is conclusively presumed and other requirements of execution are presumed subject to rebuttal without the testimony of any witness upon filing the will and the acknowledgment and affidavits annexed or attached thereto, unless there is proof of fraud or forgery affecting the acknowledgment or affidavit.

§ 3-407. [Formal Testacy Proceedings; Burdens in Contested Cases.]

In contested cases, petitioners who seek to establish intestacy have the burden of establishing prima facie proof of death, venue, and heirship. Proponents of a will have the burden of establishing prima facie proof of due execution in all cases, and, if they are also petitioners, prima facie proof of death and venue. Contestants of a will have the burden of establishing lack of testamentary intent or capacity, undue influence, fraud, duress, mistake or revocation. Parties have the ultimate burden of persuasion as to matters with respect to which they have the initial burden of proof. If a will is opposed by the petition for probate of a later will revoking the former, it shall be determined first whether the later will is entitled to probate, and if a will is opposed by a petition for a declaration of intestacy, it shall be determined first whether the will is entitled to probate.

§ 3-408. [Formal Testacy Proceedings; Will Construction; Effect of Final Order in Another Jurisdiction.]

A final order of a court of another state determining testacy, the validity or construction of a will, made in a proceeding involving notice to and an opportunity for contest by all interested persons must be accepted as determinative by the courts of this state if it includes, or is based upon, a finding that the decedent was domiciled at his death in the state where the order was made.

§ 3-409. [Formal Testacy Proceedings; Order; Foreign Will.]

After the time required for any notice has expired, upon proof of notice, and after any hearing that may be necessary, if the Court finds that the testator is dead, venue is proper and that the proceeding was commenced within the limitation prescribed by Section 3-108, it shall determine the decedent's domicile at death, his heirs and his state of testacy. Any will found to be valid and unrevoked shall be formally probated. Termination of any previous informal appointment of a personal representative, which may be appropriate in view of the relief requested and findings, is governed by Section 3-612. The petition shall be dismissed or appropriate amendment allowed if the court is not satisfied that the alleged decedent is dead. A will from a place which does not provide for probate of a will after death, may be proved for probate in this state by a duly authenticated certificate of its legal custodian that the copy introduced is a true copy and that the will has become effective under the law of the other place.

§ 3-410. [Formal Testacy Proceedings; Probate of More Than One Instrument.]

If two or more instruments are offered for probate before a final order is entered in a formal testacy proceeding, more than one instrument may be probated if neither expressly revokes the other or contains provisions which work a total revocation by implication. If more than one instrument is probated, the order shall indicate what provisions control in respect to the nomination of an executor, if any. The order may, but need not, indicate how any provisions of a particular instrument are affected by the other instrument. After a final order in a testacy proceeding has been entered, no petition for probate of any other instrument of the decedent may be entertained, except incident to a petition to vacate or modify a previous probate order and subject to the time limits of Section 3-412.

§ 3-411. [Formal Testacy Proceedings; Partial Intestacy.]

If it becomes evident in the course of a formal testacy proceeding that, though one or more instruments are entitled to be probated, the decedent's estate is or may be partially intestate, the Court shall enter an order to that effect.

§ 3-412. [Formal Testacy Proceedings; Effect of Order; Vacation.]

Subject to appeal and subject to vacation as provided herein and in Section 3-413, a formal testacy order under Sections 3-409 to 3-411, including an order that the decedent left no valid will and determining heirs, is final as to all persons with respect to all issues concerning the decedent's estate that the court considered or might have considered incident to its rendition relevant to the question of whether the decedent left a valid will, and to the determination of heirs, except that:

(1) The court shall entertain a petition for modification or vacation of its order and probate of another will of the decedent if it is shown that the proponents of the later-offered will were unaware of its existence at the time of the earlier proceeding or were unaware of the earlier proceeding and were given no notice thereof, except by publication.

(2) If intestacy of all or part of the estate has been ordered, the determination of heirs of the decedent may be reconsidered if it is shown that one or more persons were omitted from the determination and it is also shown that the persons were unaware of their relationship to the decedent, were unaware of his death or were given no notice of any proceeding concerning his estate, except by publication.

(3) A petition for vacation under either (1) or (2) above must be filed prior to the earlier of the following time limits:

(i) If a personal representative has been appointed for the estate, the time of entry of any order approving final distribution of the estate, or, if the estate is closed by statement, 6 months after the filing of the closing statement.

(ii) Whether or not a personal representative has been appointed for the estate of the decedent, the time prescribed by Section 3-108 when it is no longer possible to initiate an original proceeding to probate a will of the decedent.

(iii) 12 months after the entry of the order sought to be vacated.

(4) The order originally rendered in the testacy proceeding may be modified or vacated, if appropriate under the circumstances, by the order of probate of the later-offered will or the order redetermining heirs.

(5) The finding of the fact of death is conclusive as to the alleged decedent only if notice of the hearing on the petition in the formal testacy proceeding was sent by registered or certified mail addressed to the alleged decedent at his last known address and the court finds that a search under Section 3-403(b) was made.

If the alleged decedent is not dead, even if notice was sent and search was made, he may recover estate assets in the hands of the personal representative. In addition to any remedies available to the alleged decedent by reason of any fraud or intentional wrongdoing, the alleged decedent may recover any estate or its proceeds from distributees that is in their hands, or the value of distributions received by them, to the extent that any recovery from distributees is equitable in view of all of the circumstances.

§ 3-413. [Formal Testacy Proceedings; Vacation of Order For Other Cause.]

For good cause shown, an order in a formal testacy proceeding may be modified or vacated within the time allowed for appeal.

§ 3-414. [Formal Proceedings Concerning Appointment of Personal Representative.]

(a) A formal proceeding for adjudication regarding the priority or qualification of one who is an applicant for appointment as personal representative, or of one who previously has been appointed personal representative in informal proceedings, if an issue concerning the testacy of the decedent is or may be involved, is governed by Section 3-302, as well as by this section. In other cases, the petition shall contain or adopt the statements required by Section 3-301(1) and describe the question relating to priority or qualification of the personal representative which is to be resolved. If the proceeding precedes any appointment of a personal representative, it shall stay any pending informal appointment proceedings as well as any commenced thereafter. If the proceeding is commenced after appointment, the previously appointed personal representative, after receipt of notice

thereof, shall refrain from exercising any power of administration except as necessary to preserve the estate or unless the Court orders otherwise.

(b) After notice to interested persons, including all persons interested in the administration of the estate as successors under the applicable assumption concerning testacy, any previously appointed personal representative and any person having or claiming priority for appointment as personal representative, the Court shall determine who is entitled to appointment under Section 3-203, make a proper appointment and, if appropriate, terminate any prior appointment found to have been improper as provided in cases of removal under Section 3-611.

Part 5
Supervised Administration

§ 3-501. [Supervised Administration; Nature of Proceeding.]

Supervised administration is a single in rem proceeding to secure complete administration and settlement of a decedent's estate under the continuing authority of the Court which extends until entry of an order approving distribution of the estate and discharging the personal representative or other order terminating the proceeding. A supervised personal representative is responsible to the Court, as well as to the interested parties, and is subject to directions concerning the estate made by the Court on its own motion or on the motion of any interested party. Except as otherwise provided in this Part, or as otherwise ordered by the Court, a supervised personal representative has the same duties and powers as a personal representative who is not supervised.

§ 3-502. [Supervised Administration; Petition; Order.]

A petition for supervised administration may be filed by any interested person or by a personal representative at any time or the prayer for supervised administration may be joined with a petition in a testacy or appointment proceeding. If the testacy of the decedent and the priority and qualification of any personal representative have not been adjudicated previously, the petition for supervised administration shall include the matters required of a petition in a formal testacy proceeding and the notice requirements and procedures applicable to a formal testacy proceeding apply. If not previously adjudicated, the Court shall adjudicate the testacy of the decedent and relating to the priority and qualifications of the personal representative in any case involving a request for supervised administration, even though the request for supervised administration may be denied. After notice to interested persons, the Court shall order supervised administration of a decedent's estate: (1) if the decedent's will directs supervised administration, it shall be ordered unless the Court finds that circumstances bearing on the need for supervised administration have changed since the execution of the will and that there is no necessity for supervised administration; (2) if the decedent's will directs unsupervised administration, supervised administration shall be ordered only upon a finding that it is necessary for protection of persons interested in the estate; or (3) in other cases if the Court finds that supervised administration is necessary under the circumstances.

§ 3-503. [Supervised Administration; Effect on Other Proceedings.]

(a) The pendency of a proceeding for supervised administration of a decedent's estate stays action on any informal application then pending or thereafter filed.

(b) If a will has been previously probated in informal proceedings, the effect of the filing of a petition for supervised administration is as provided for formal testacy proceedings by Section 3-401.

(c) After he has received notice of the filing of a petition for supervised administration, a personal representative who has been appointed previously shall not exercise his power to distribute any estate. The filing of the petition does not affect his other powers and duties unless the Court restricts the exercise of any of them pending full hearing on the petition.

§ 3-504. [Supervised Administration; Powers of Personal Representative.]

Unless restricted by the Court, a supervised personal representative has, without interim orders approving exercise of a power, all powers of personal representatives under this Code, but he shall not exercise his power to make any distribution of the estate without prior order of the Court. Any other restriction on the power of a personal representative which may be ordered by the Court must be endorsed on his letters of appointment and, unless so endorsed, is ineffective as to persons dealing in good faith with the personal representative.

§ 3-505. [Supervised Administration; Interim Orders; Distribution and Closing Orders.]

Unless otherwise ordered by the Court, supervised administration is terminated by order in accordance with time restrictions, notices and contents of orders prescribed for proceedings under Section 3-1001. Interim orders approving or directing partial distributions or granting other relief may be issued by the Court at any time during the pendency of a supervised administration on the application of the personal representative or any interested person.

Part 6
Personal Representative; Appointment, Control and Termination of Authority

§ 3-601. [Qualification.]

Prior to receiving letters, a personal representative shall qualify by filing with the appointing Court any required bond and a statement of acceptance of the duties of the office.

§ 3-602. [Acceptance of Appointment; Consent to Jurisdiction.]

By accepting appointment, a personal representative submits personally to the jurisdiction of the Court in any proceeding relating to the estate that may be instituted by any interested person. Notice of any proceeding shall be delivered to the personal representative, or mailed to him by ordinary first class mail at his address as listed in the application or petition for appointment or as thereafter reported to the Court and to his address as then known to the petitioner.

§ 3-603. [Bond Not Required Without Court Order, Exceptions.]

No bond is required of a personal representative appointed in informal proceedings, except (1) upon the appointment of a special administrator; (2) when an executor or other personal representative is appointed to administer an estate under a will containing an express requirement of bond or (3) when bond is required under Section 3-605. Bond may be required by court order at the time of appointment of a personal representative appointed in any formal proceeding except that bond is not required of a personal representative appointed in formal proceedings if the will relieves the personal representative of bond, unless bond has been requested by an interested party and the Court is satisfied that it is desirable. Bond required by any will may be dispensed with in formal proceedings upon determination by the Court that it is not necessary. No bond is required of any personal representative who, pursuant to statute, has deposited cash or collateral with an agency of this state to secure performance of his duties.

§ 3-604. [Bond Amount; Security; Procedure; Reduction.]

If bond is required and the provisions of the will or order do not specify the amount, unless stated in his application or petition, the person qualifying shall file a statement under oath with the Registrar indicating his best estimate of the value of the personal estate of the decedent and of the income expected from the personal and real estate during the next year, and he shall execute and file a bond with the Registrar, or give other suitable security, in an amount not less than the estimate. The Registrar shall determine that the bond is duly executed by a corporate surety, or one or more individual sureties whose performance is secured by pledge of personal property, mortgage on real property or other adequate security. The Registrar may permit the amount of the bond to be reduced by the value of assets of the estate deposited with a domestic financial institution (as defined in Section 6-101) in a manner that prevents their unauthorized disposition. On petition of the personal representative or another interested person the Court may excuse a requirement of bond, increase or reduce the amount of the bond, release sureties, or permit the substitution of another bond with the same or different sureties.

§ 3-605. [Demand For Bond by Interested Person.]

Any person apparently having an interest in the estate worth in excess of [$1,000], or any creditor having a claim in excess of [$1,000], may make a written demand that a personal representative give bond. The demand must be filed with the Registrar and a copy mailed to the personal representative, if appointment and qualification have occurred. Thereupon, bond is required, but the requirement ceases if the person demanding bond ceases to be interested in the estate, or if bond is excused as provided in Section 3-603 or 3-604. After he has received notice and until the filing of the bond or cessation of the requirement of bond, the personal representative shall refrain from exercising any powers of his office except as necessary to preserve the estate. Failure of the personal representative to meet a requirement of bond by giving suitable bond within 30 days after receipt of notice is cause for his removal and appointment of a successor personal representative.

§ 3-606. [Terms and Conditions of Bonds.]

(a) The following requirements and provisions apply to any bond required by this Part:

(1) Bonds shall name the [state] as obligee for the benefit of the persons interested in the estate and shall be conditioned upon the faithful discharge by the fiduciary of all duties according to law.

(2) Unless otherwise provided by the terms of the approved bond, sureties are jointly and severally liable with the personal representative and with each other. The address of sureties shall be stated in the bond.

(3) By executing an approved bond of a personal representative, the surety consents to the jurisdiction of the probate court which issued letters to the primary obligor in any proceedings pertaining to the fiduciary duties of the personal representative and naming the surety as a party. Notice of any proceeding shall be delivered to the surety or mailed to him by registered or certified mail at his address as listed with the court where the bond is filed and to his address as then known to the petitioner.

(4) On petition of a successor personal representative, any other personal representative of the same decedent, or any interested person, a proceeding in the Court may be initiated against a surety for breach of the obligation of the bond of the personal representative.

(5) The bond of the personal representative is not void after the first recovery but may be proceeded against from time to time until the whole penalty is exhausted.

(b) No action or proceeding may be commenced against the surety on any matter as to which an action or proceeding against the primary obligor is barred by adjudication or limitation.

§ 3-607. [Order Restraining Personal Representative.]

(a) On petition of any person who appears to have an interest in the estate, the Court by temporary order may restrain a personal representative from performing specified acts of administration, disbursement, or distribution, or exercise of any powers or discharge of any duties of his office, or make any other order to secure proper performance of his duty, if it appears to the Court that the personal representative otherwise may take some action which would jeopardize unreasonably the interest of the applicant or of some other interested person. Persons with whom the personal representative may transact business may be made parties.

(b) The matter shall be set for hearing within 10 days unless the parties otherwise agree. Notice as the Court directs shall be given to the personal representative and his attorney of record, if any, and to another parties named defendant in the petition.

§ 3-608. [Termination of Appointment; General.]

Termination of appointment of a personal representative occurs as indicated in Sections 3-609 to 3-612, inclusive. Termination ends the right and power pertaining to the office of personal representative as conferred by this Code or any will, except that a personal representative, at any time prior to distribution or until restrained or enjoined by court order, may perform acts necessary to protect the estate and may deliver the assets to a successor representative. Termination does not discharge a personal representative from liability for transactions or omissions occurring before termination, or relieve him of the duty to preserve assets subject to his control, to account therefor and to deliver the assets. Termination does not affect the jurisdiction of the Court over the personal representative, but terminates his authority to represent the estate in any pending or future proceeding.

§ 3-609. [Termination of Appointment; Death or Disability.]

The death of a personal representative or the appointment of a conservator for the estate of a personal representative, terminates his appointment. Until appointment and qualification of a successor or special representative to replace the deceased or protected representative, the representative of the estate of the deceased or protected personal representative, if any, has the duty to protect the estate possessed and being administered by his decedent or ward at the time his appointment terminates, has the power to perform acts necessary for protection and shall account for and deliver the estate assets to a successor or special personal representative upon his appointment and qualification.

§ 3-610. [Termination of Appointment; Voluntary.]

(a) An appointment of a personal representative terminates as provided in Section 3-1003, one year after the filing of a closing statement.

(b) An order closing an estate as provided in Section 3-1001 or 3-1002 terminates an appointment of a personal representative.

(c) A personal representative may resign his position by filing a written statement of resignation with the Registrar after he has given at least 15 days written notice to the persons known to be interested in the estate. If no one applies or petitions for appointment of a successor representative within the time indicated in the notice, the filed statement of resignation is ineffective as a termination of appointment and in any event is effective only upon the appointment and qualification of a successor representative and delivery of the assets to him.

§ 3-611. [Termination of Appointment by Removal; Cause; Procedure.]

(a) A person interested in the estate may petition for removal of a personal representative for cause at any time.

Upon filing of the petition, the Court shall fix a time and place for hearing. Notice shall be given by the petitioner to the personal representative, and to other persons as the Court may order. Except as otherwise ordered as provided in Section 3-607, after receipt of notice of removal proceedings, the personal representative shall not act except to account, to correct maladministration or preserve the estate. If removal is ordered, the Court also shall direct by order the disposition of the assets remaining in the name of, or under the control of, the personal representative being removed.

(b) Cause for removal exists when removal would be in the best interests of the estate, or if it is shown that a personal representative or the person seeking his appointment intentionally misrepresented material facts in the proceedings leading to his appointment, or that the personal representative has disregarded an order of the Court, has become incapable of discharging the duties of his office, or has mismanaged the estate or failed to perform any duty pertaining to the office. Unless the decedent's will directs otherwise, a personal representative appointed at the decedent's domicile, incident to securing appointment of himself or his nominee as ancillary personal representative, may obtain removal of another who was appointed personal representative in this state to administer local assets.

§ 3-612. [Termination of Appointment; Change of Testacy Status.]

Except as otherwise ordered in formal proceedings, the probate of a will subsequent to the appointment of a personal representative in intestacy or under a will which is superseded by formal probate of another will, or the vacation of an informal probate of a will subsequent to the appointment of the personal representative thereunder, does not terminate the appointment of the personal representative although his powers may be reduced as provided in Section 3-401. Termination occurs upon appointment in informal or formal appointment proceedings of a person entitled to appointment under the later assumption concerning testacy. If no request for new appointment is made within 30 days after expiration of time for appeal from the order in formal testacy proceedings, or from the informal probate, changing the assumption concerning testacy, the previously appointed personal representative upon request may be appointed personal representative under the subsequently probated will, or as in intestacy as the case may be.

§ 3-613. [Successor Personal Representative.]

Parts 3 and 4 of this Article govern proceedings for appointment of a personal representative to succeed one whose appointment has been terminated. After appointment and qualification, a successor personal representative may be substituted in all actions and proceedings to which the former personal representative was a party, and no notice, process or claim which was given or served upon the former personal representative need be given to or served upon the successor in order to preserve any position or right the person giving the notice or filing the claim may thereby have obtained or preserved with reference to the former personal representative. Except as otherwise ordered by the Court, the successor personal representative has the powers and duties in respect to the continued administration which the former personal representative would have had if his appointment had not been terminated.

§ 3-614. [Special Administrator; Appointment.]

A special administrator may be appointed:

(1) informally by the Registrar on the application of any interested person when necessary to protect the estate of a decedent prior to the appointment of a general personal representative or if a prior appointment has been terminated as provided in Section 3-609;

(2) in a formal proceeding by order of the Court on the petition of any interested person and finding, after notice and hearing, that appointment is necessary to preserve the estate or to secure its proper administration including its administration in circumstances where a general personal representative cannot or should not act. If it appears to the Court that an emergency exists, appointment may be ordered without notice.

§ 3-615. [Special Administrator; Who May Be Appointed.]

(a) If a special administrator is to be appointed pending the probate of a will which is the subject of a pending application or petition for probate, the person named executor in the will shall be appointed if available, and qualified.

(b) In other cases, any proper person may be appointed special administrator.

§ 3-616. [Special Administrator; Appointed Informally; Powers and Duties.]

A special administrator appointed by the Registrar in informal proceedings pursuant to Section 3-614(1) has the duty to collect and manage the assets of the estate, to preserve them, to account therefor and to deliver them to the general personal representative upon his qualification. The special administrator has the power of a personal representative under the Code necessary to perform his duties.

§ 3-617. [Special Administrator; Formal Proceedings; Power and Duties.]

A special administrator appointed by order of the Court in any formal proceeding has the power of a general personal representative except as limited in the appointment and duties as prescribed in the order. The appointment may be for a specified time, to perform particular acts or on other terms as the Court may direct.

§ 3-618. [Termination of Appointment; Special Administrator.]

The appointment of a special administrator terminates in accordance with the provisions of the order of appointment or on the appointment of a general personal representative. In other cases, the appointment of a special administrator is subject to termination as provided in Sections 3-608 through 3-611.

Part 7
Duties and Powers of Personal Representatives

§ 3-701. [Time of Accrual of Duties and Powers.]

The duties and powers of a personal representative commence upon his appointment. The powers of a personal representative relate back in time to give acts by the person appointed which are beneficial to the estate occurring prior to appointment the same effect as those occurring thereafter. Prior to appointment, a person named executor in a will may carry out written instructions of the decedent relating to his body, funeral and burial arrangements. A personal representative may ratify and accept acts on behalf of the estate done by others where the acts would have been proper for a personal representative.

§ 3-702. [Priority Among Different Letters.]

A person to whom general letters are issued first has exclusive authority under the letters until his appointment is terminated or modified. If, through error, general letters are afterwards issued to another, the first appointed representative may recover any property of the estate in the hands of the representative subsequently appointed, but the acts of the latter done in good faith before notice of the first letters are not void for want of validity of appointment.

§ 3-703. [General Duties; Relation and Liability to Persons Interested in Estate; Standing to Sue.]

(a) A personal representative is a fiduciary who shall observe the standards of care applicable to trustees as described by Section 7-302. A personal representative is under a duty to settle and distribute the estate of the decedent in accordance with the terms of any probated and effective will and this Code, and as expeditiously and efficiently as is consistent with the best interests of the estate. He shall use the authority conferred upon him by this Code, the terms of the will, if any, and any order in proceedings to which he is party for the best interests of successors to the estate.

(b) A personal representative shall not be surcharged for acts of administration or distribution if the conduct in question was authorized at the time. Subject to other obligations of administration, an informally probated will is authority to administer and distribute the estate according to its terms. An order of appointment of a personal representative, whether issued in informal or formal proceedings, is authority to distribute apparently intestate assets to the heirs of the decedent if, at the time of distribution, the personal representative is not aware of a pending testacy proceeding, a proceeding to vacate an order entered in an earlier testacy proceeding, a formal proceeding questioning his appointment or fitness to continue, or a supervised administration proceeding. Nothing in this section affects the duty of the personal representative to administer and distribute the estate in accordance with the rights of claimants, the surviving spouse, any minor and dependent children and any pretermitted child of the decedent as described elsewhere in this Code.

(c) Except as to proceedings which do not survive the death of the decedent, a personal representative of a decedent domiciled in this state at his death has the same standing to sue and be sued in the courts of this state and the courts of any other jurisdiction as his decedent had immediately prior to death.

§ 3-704. [Personal Representative to Proceed Without Court Order; Exception.]

A personal representative shall proceed expeditiously with the settlement and distribution of a decedent's estate and, except as otherwise specified or ordered in regard to a supervised personal representative, do so without adjudication, order, or direction of the Court, but he may invoke the jurisdiction of the Court, in proceedings authorized by this Code, to resolve questions concerning the estate or its administration.

§ 3-705. [Duty of Personal Representative; Information to Heirs and Devisees.]

Not later than 30 days after his appointment every personal representative, except any special administrator, shall give information of his appointment to the heirs and devisees, including, if there has been no formal testacy proceeding and if the personal representative was appointed on the assumption that the decedent died intestate, the devisees in any will mentioned in the application for appointment of a personal representative. The information shall be delivered or sent by ordinary mail to each of the heirs and devisees whose address is reasonably available to the personal representative. The duty does not extend to require information to persons who have been adjudicated in a prior formal testacy proceeding to have no interest in the estate. The information shall include the name and address of the personal representative, indicate that it is being sent to persons who have or may have some interest in the estate being administered, indicate whether bond has been filed, and describe the court where papers relating to the estate are on file. The information shall state that the estate is being administered by the personal representative under the [State] Probate Code without supervision by the Court but that recipients are entitled to information regarding the administration from the personal representative and can petition the Court in any matter relating to the estate, including distribution of assets and expenses of administration. The personal representative's failure to give this information is a breach of his duty to the persons concerned but does not affect the validity of his appointment, his powers or other duties. A personal representative may inform other persons of his appointment by delivery or ordinary first class mail.

As amended in 1987.

§ 3-706. [Duty of Personal Representative; Inventory and Appraisement.]

Within 3 months after his appointment, a personal representative, who is not a special administrator or a successor to another representative who has previously discharged this duty, shall prepare and file or mail an inventory of property owned by the decedent at the time of his death, listing it with reasonable detail, and indicating as to each listed item, its fair market value as of the date of the decedent's death, and the type and amount of any encumbrance that may exist with reference to any item.

The personal representative shall send a copy of the inventory to interested persons who request it. He may also file the original of the inventory with the court.

§ 3-707. [Employment of Appraisers.]

The personal representative may employ a qualified and disinterested appraiser to assist him in ascertaining the fair market value as of the date of the decedent's death of any asset the value of which may be subject to reasonable doubt.

Different persons may be employed to appraise different kinds of assets included in the estate. The names and addresses of any appraiser shall be indicated on the inventory with the item or items he appraised.

§ 3-708. [Duty of Personal Representative; Supplementary Inventory.]

If any property not included in the original inventory comes to the knowledge of a personal representative or if the personal representative learns that the value or description indicated in the original inventory for any item is erroneous or misleading, he shall make a supplementary inventory or appraisement showing the market value as of the date of the decedent's death of the new item or the revised market value or descriptions, and the appraisers or other data relied upon, if any, and file it with the Court if the original inventory was filed, or furnish copies thereof or information thereof to persons interested in the new information.

§ 3-709. [Duty of Personal Representative; Possession of Estate.]

Except as otherwise provided by a decedent's will, every personal representative has a right to, and shall take possession or control of, the decedent's property, except that any real property or tangible personal property may be left with or surrendered to the person presumptively entitled thereto unless or until, in the judgment of the personal representative, possession of the property by him will be necessary for purposes of administration. The request by a personal representative for delivery of any property possessed by an heir or devisee is conclusive evidence, in any action against the heir or devisee for possession thereof, that the possession of the property by the personal representative is necessary for purposes of administration. The personal representative shall pay taxes on, and take all steps reasonably necessary for the management, protection and preservation of, the estate in his possession. He may maintain an action to recover possession of property or to determine the title thereto.

§ 3-710. [Power to Avoid Transfers.]

The property liable for the payment of unsecured debts of a decedent includes all property transferred by him by any means which is in law void or voidable as against his creditors, and subject to prior liens, the right to recover this property, so far as necessary for the payment of unsecured debts of the decedent, is exclusively in the personal representative.

§ 3-711. [Powers of Personal Representatives; In General.]

Until termination of his appointment a personal representative has the same power over the title to property of the estate that an absolute owner would have, in trust however, for the benefit of the creditors and others interested in the estate. This power may be exercised without notice, hearing, or order of court.

§ 3-712. [Improper Exercise of Power; Breach of Fiduciary Duty.]

If the exercise of power concerning the estate is improper, the personal representative is liable to interested persons for damage or loss resulting from breach of his fiduciary duty to the same extent as a trustee of an express trust. The rights of purchasers and others dealing with a personal representative shall be determined as provided in Sections 3-713 and 3-714.

§ 3-713. [Sale, Encumbrance or Transaction Involving Conflict of Interest; Voidable; Exceptions.]

Any sale or encumbrance to the personal representative, his spouse, agent or attorney, or any corporation or trust in which he has a substantial beneficial interest, or any transaction which is affected by a substantial conflict of interest on the part of the personal representative, is voidable by any person interested in the estate except one who has consented after fair disclosure, unless (1) the will or a contract entered into by the decedent expressly authorized the transaction; or (2) the transaction is approved by the Court after notice to interested persons.

§ 3-714. [Persons Dealing with Personal Representative; Protection.]

A person who in good faith either assists a personal representative or deals with him for value is protected as if the personal representative properly exercised his power. The fact that a person knowingly deals with a personal representative does not alone require the person to inquire into the existence of a power or the propriety of its exercise. Except for restrictions on powers of supervised personal representatives which are endorsed on letters as provided in Section 3-504, no provision in any will or order of court purporting to limit the power of a personal representative is effective except as to persons with actual knowledge thereof. A person is not bound to see to the proper application of estate assets paid or delivered to a personal representative. The protection here expressed extends to instances in which some procedural irregularity or jurisdictional defect occurred in proceedings leading to the issuance of letters, including a case in which the alleged decedent is found to be alive. The protection here expressed is not by substitution for that provided by comparable provisions of the laws relating to commercial transactions and laws simplifying transfers of securities by fiduciaries.

§ 3-715. [Transactions Authorized for Personal Representatives; Exceptions.]

Except as restricted or otherwise provided by the will or by an order in a formal proceeding and subject to the priorities stated in Section 3-902, a personal representative, acting reasonably for the benefit of the interested persons, may properly:

(1) retain assets owned by the decedent pending distribution or liquidation including those in which the representative is personally interested or which are otherwise improper for trust investment;

(2) receive assets from fiduciaries, or other sources;

(3) perform, compromise or refuse performance of the decedent's contracts that continue as obligations of the estate, as he may determine under the circumstances. In performing enforceable contracts by the decedent to convey or lease land, the personal representative, among other possible courses of action, may:

(i) execute and deliver a deed of conveyance for cash payment of all sums remaining due or the purchaser's note for the sum remaining due secured by a mortgage or deed of trust on the land; or

(ii) deliver a deed in escrow with directions that the proceeds, when paid in accordance with the escrow agreement, be paid to the successors of the decedent, as designated in the escrow agreement;

(4) satisfy written charitable pledges of the decedent irrespective of whether the pledges constituted binding obligations of the decedent or were properly presented as claims, if in the judgment of the personal representative the decedent would have wanted the pledges completed under the circumstances;

(5) if funds are not needed to meet debts and expenses currently payable and are not immediately distributable, deposit or invest liquid assets of the estate, including moneys received from the sale of other assets, in federally insured interest-bearing accounts, readily marketable secured loan arrangements or other prudent investments which would be reasonable for use by trustees generally;

(6) acquire or dispose of an asset, including land in this or another state, for cash or on credit, at public or private sale; and manage, develop, improve, exchange, partition, change the character of, or abandon an estate asset;

(7) make ordinary or extraordinary repairs or alterations in buildings or other structures, demolish any improvements, raze existing or erect new party walls or buildings;

(8) subdivide, develop or dedicate land to public use; make or obtain the vacation of plats and adjust boundaries; or adjust differences in valuation on exchange or partition by giving or receiving considerations; or dedicate easements to public use without consideration;

(9) enter for any purpose into a lease as lessor or lessee, with or without option to purchase or renew, for a term within or extending beyond the period of administration;

(10) enter into a lease or arrangement for exploration and removal of minerals or other natural resources or enter into a pooling or unitization agreement;

(11) abandon property when, in the opinion of the personal representative, it is valueless, or is so encumbered, or is in condition that it is of no benefit to the state;

(12) vote stocks or other securities in person or by general or limited proxy;

(13) pay calls, assessments, and other sums chargeable or accruing against or on account of securities, unless barred by the provisions relating to claims;

(14) hold a security in the name of a nominee or in other form without disclosure of the interest of the estate but the personal representative is liable for any act of the nominee in connection with the security so held;

(15) insure the assets of the estate against damage, loss and liability and himself against liability as to third persons;

(16) borrow money with or without security to be repaid from the estate assets or otherwise; and advance money for the protection of the estate;

(17) effect a fair and reasonable compromise with any debtor or obligor, or extend, renew or in any manner modify the terms of any obligation owing to the estate. If the personal representative holds a mortgage, pledge or other lien upon property of another person, he may, in lieu of foreclosure, accept a conveyance or transfer of encumbered assets from the owner thereof in satisfaction of the indebtedness secured by lien;

(18) pay taxes, assessments, compensation of the personal representative, and other expenses incident to the administration of the estate;

(19) sell or exercise stock subscription or conversion rights; consent, directly or through a committee or other agent, to the reorganization, consolidation, merger, dissolution, or liquidation of a corporation or other business enterprise;

(20) allocate items of income or expense to either estate income or principal, as permitted or provided by law;

(21) employ persons, including attorneys, auditors, investment advisors, or agents, even if they are associated with the personal representative, to advise or assist the personal representative in the performance of his administrative duties; act without independent investigation upon their recommendations; and instead of acting personally, employ one or more agents to perform any act of administration, whether or not discretionary;

(22) prosecute or defend claims, or proceedings in any jurisdiction for the protection of the estate and of the personal representative in the performance of his duties;

(23) sell, mortgage, or lease any real or personal property of the estate or any interest therein for cash, credit, or for part cash and part credit, and with or without security for unpaid balances;

(24) continue any unincorporated business or venture in which the decedent was engaged at the time of his death (i) in the same business form for a period of not more than 4 months from the date of appointment of a general personal representative if continuation is a reasonable means of preserving the value of the business including good will, (ii) in the same business form for any additional period of time that may be approved by order of the Court in a formal proceeding to which the persons interested in the estate are parties; or (iii) throughout the period of administration if the business is incorporated by the personal representative and if none of the probable distributees of the business who are competent adults object to its incorporation and retention in the estate;

(25) incorporate any business or venture in which the decedent was engaged at the time of his death;

(26) provide for exoneration of the personal representative from personal liability in any contract entered into on behalf of the estate;

(27) satisfy and settle claims and distribute the estate as provided in this Code.

§ 3-716. [Powers and Duties of Successor Personal Representative]

A successor personal representative has the same power and duty as the original personal representative to complete the administration and distribution of the estate, as expeditiously as possible, but he shall not exercise any power expressly made personal to the executor named in the will.

§ 3-717. [Co-representatives; When Joint Action Required.]

If two or more persons are appointed co-representatives and unless the will provides otherwise, the concurrence of all is required on all acts connected with the administration and distribution of the estate. This restriction does not apply when any co-representative receives any receipts for property due the estate, when the concurrence of all cannot readily be obtained in the time reasonably available for emergency action necessary to preserve the estate, or when a co-representative has been delegated to act for the others. Persons dealing with a co-representative if actually unaware that another has been appointed to serve with him or if advised by the personal representative with whom they deal that he has authority to act alone for any of the reasons mentioned herein, are as fully protected as if the person with whom they dealt had been the sole personal representative.

§ 3-718. [Powers of Surviving Personal Representative.]

Unless the terms of the will otherwise provide, every power exercisable by personal co-representatives may be exercised by the one or more remaining after the appointment of one or more is terminated, and if one of 2 or more nominated as co-executors is not appointed, those appointed may exercise all the powers incident to the office.

§ 3-719. [Compensation of Personal Representative.]

A personal representative is entitled to reasonable compensation for his services. If a will provides for compensation of the personal representative and there is no contract with the decedent regarding compensation, he may renounce the provision before qualifying and be entitled to reasonable compensation. A personal representative also may renounce his right to all or any part of the compensation. A written renunciation of fee may be filed with the Court.

§ 3-720. [Expenses in Estate Litigation.]

If any personal representative or person nominated as personal representative defends or prosecutes any proceeding in good faith, whether successful or not he is entitled to receive from the estate his necessary expenses and disbursements including reasonable attorneys' fees incurred.

§ 3-721. [Proceedings for Review of Employment of Agents and Compensation of Personal Representatives and Employees of Estate.]

After notice to all interested persons or on petition of an interested person or on appropriate motion if administration is supervised, the propriety of employment of any person by a personal representative including any attorney, auditor, investment advisor or other specialized agent or assistant, the reasonableness of the compensation of any person so employed, or the reasonableness of the compensation determined by the personal representative for his own services, may be reviewed by the Court. Any person who has received excessive compensation from an estate for services rendered may be ordered to make appropriate refunds.

Part 8
Creditors' Claims

§ 3-801. [Notice to Creditors.]

(a) Unless notice has already been given under this section, a personal representative upon appointment [may] [shall] publish a notice to creditors once a week for three successive weeks in a newspaper of general circulation in the [county] announcing the appointment and the personal representative's address and notifying creditors of the estate to present their claims within four months after the date of the first publication of the notice or be forever barred.

(b) A personal representative may give written notice by mail or other delivery to a creditor, notifying the creditor to present his [or her] claim within four months after the published notice, if given as provided in subsection (a), or within 60 days after the mailing or other delivery of the notice, whichever is later, or be forever barred. Written notice must be the notice described in subsection (a) above or a similar notice.

(c) The personal representative is not liable to a creditor or to a successor of the decedent for giving or failing to give notice under this section.

As amended in 1989.

§ 3-802. [Statutes of Limitations.]

(a) Unless an estate is insolvent, the personal representative, with the consent of all successors whose interests would be affected, may waive any defense of limitations available to the estate. If the defense is not waived, no claim barred by a statute of limitations at the time of the decedent's death may be allowed or paid.

(b) The running of a statute of limitations measured from an event other than death or the giving of notice to creditors is suspended for four months after the decedent's death, but resumes thereafter as to claims not barred by other sections.

(c) For purposes of a statute of limitations, the presentation of a claim pursuant to Section 3-804 is equivalent to commencement of a proceeding on the claim.

As amended in 1989.

§ 3-803. [Limitations on Presentation of Claims.]

(a) All claims against a decedent's estate which arose before the death of the decedent, including claims of the state and any subdivision thereof whether due or to become due, absolute or contingent, liquidated or unliquidated, founded on contract, tort, or other legal basis, if not barred earlier by another statute of limitations or non-claim statute, are barred against the estate, the personal representative, and the heirs and devisees of the decedent, unless presented within the earlier of the following:

(1) one year after the decedent's death; or

(2) the time provided by Section 3-801(b) for creditors who are given actual notice, and within the time provided in 3-801(a) for all creditors barred by publication.

(b) A claim described in subsection (a) which is barred by the non-claim statute of the decedent's domicile before the giving of notice to creditors in this State is barred in this State.

(c) All claims against a decedent's estate which arise at or after the death of the decedent, including claims of the state and any subdivision thereof, whether due or to become due, absolute or contingent, liquidated or unliquidated, founded on contract, tort, or other legal basis, are barred against the estate, the personal representative, and the heirs and devisees of the decedent, unless presented as follows:

(1) a claim based on a contract with the personal representative, within four months after performance by the personal representative is due; or

(2) any other claim, within the later of four months after it arises, or the time specified in subsection (a)(1).

(d) Nothing in this section affects or prevents:

(1) any proceeding to enforce any mortgage, pledge, or other lien upon property of the estate;

(2) to the limits of the insurance protection only, any proceeding to establish liability of the decedent or the personal representative for which he is protected by liability insurance; or

(3) collection of compensation for services rendered and reimbursement for expenses advanced by the personal representative or by the attorney or accountant for the personal representative of the estate.

As amended in 1989.

§ 3-804. [Manner of Presentation of Claims.]

Claims against a decedent's estate may be presented as follows:

(1) The claimant may deliver or mail to the personal representative a written statement of the claim indicating its basis, the name and address of the claimant, and the amount claimed, or may file a written statement of the claim, in the form prescribed by rule, with the clerk of the Court. The claim is deemed presented on the first to occur of receipt of the written statement of claim by the personal representative, or the filing of the claim with the Court. If a claim is not yet due, the date when it will become due shall be stated. If the claim is contingent or unliquidated, the nature of the uncertainty shall be stated. If the claim is secured, the security shall be described. Failure to describe correctly the security, the nature of any uncertainty, and the due date of a claim not yet due does not invalidate the presentation made.

(2) The claimant may commence a proceeding against the personal representative in any Court where the personal representative may be subjected to jurisdiction, to obtain payment of his claim against the estate, but the commencement of the proceeding must occur within the time limited for presenting the claim. No presentation of claim is required in regard to matters claimed in proceedings against the decedent which were pending at the time of his death.

(3) If a claim is presented under subsection (1), no proceeding thereon may be commenced more than 60 days after the personal representative has mailed a notice of disallowance; but, in the case of a claim which is not presently due or which is contingent or unliquidated, the personal representative may consent to an extension of the 60-day period, or to avoid injustice the Court, on petition, may

order an extension of the 60-day period, but in no event shall the extension run beyond the applicable statute of limitations.

§ 3-805. [Classification of Claims.]

(a) If the applicable assets of the estate are insufficient to pay all claims in full, the personal representative shall make payment in the following order:

(1) costs and expenses of administration;

(2) reasonable funeral expenses;

(3) debts and taxes with preference under federal law;

(4) reasonable and necessary medical and hospital expenses of the last illness of the decedent, including compensation of persons attending him;

(5) debts and taxes with preference under other laws of this state;

(6) all other claims.

(b) No preference shall be given in the payment of any claim over any other claim of the same class, and a claim due and payable shall not be entitled to a preference over claims not due.

§ 3-806. [Allowance of Claims.]

(a) As to claims presented in the manner described in Section 3-804 within the time limit prescribed in 3-803, the personal representative may mail a notice to any claimant stating that the claim has been disallowed. If, after allowing or disallowing a claim, the personal representative changes his decision concerning the claim, he shall notify the claimant. The personal representative may not change a disallowance of a claim after the time for the claimant to file a petition for allowance or to commence a proceeding on the claim has run and the claim has been barred. Every claim which is disallowed in whole or in part by the personal representative is barred so far as not allowed unless the claimant files a petition for allowance in the Court or commences a proceeding against the personal representative not later than 60 days after the mailing of the notice of disallowance or partial allowance if the notice warns the claimant of the impending bar. Failure of the personal representative to mail notice to a claimant of action on his claim for 60 days after the time for original presentation of the claim has expired has the effect of a notice of allowance.

(b) After allowing or disallowing a claim the personal representative may change the allowance or disallowance as hereafter provided. The personal representative may prior to payment change the allowance to a disallowance in whole or in part, but not after allowance by a court order or judgment or an order directing payment of the claim. He shall notify the claimant of the change to disallowance, and the disallowed claim is then subject to bar as provided in subsection (a). The personal representative may change a disallowance to an allowance, in whole or in part, until it is barred under subsection (a); after it is barred, it may be allowed and paid only if the estate is solvent and all successors whose interests would be affected consent.

(c) Upon the petition of the personal representative or a claimant in a proceeding for the purpose, the Court may allow in whole or in part any claim or claims presented to the personal representative or filed with the clerk of the Court in due time and not barred by subsection (a) of this section. Notice in this proceeding shall be given to the claimant, the personal representative and those other persons interested in the estate as the Court may direct by order entered at the time the proceeding is commenced.

(d) A judgment in a proceeding in another court against a personal representative to enforce a claim against a decedent's estate is an allowance of the claim.

(e) Unless otherwise provided in any judgment in another court entered against the personal representative, allowed claims bear interest at the legal rate for the period commencing 60 days after the time for original presentation of the claim has expired unless based on a contract making a provision for interest, in which case they bear interest in accordance with that provision.

As amended in 1987.

§ 3-807. [Payment of Claims.]

(a) Upon the expiration of the earlier of the time limitations provided in Section 3-803 for the presentation of claims, the representative shall proceed to pay the claims allowed against the estate in the order of priority prescribed, after making provision for homestead, family and support allowances, for claims already presented that have not yet been allowed or whose allowance has been appealed, and for unbarred claims that may yet be presented, including costs and expenses of administration. By petition to the Court in a proceeding for the purpose, or by appropriate motion if the administration is supervised, a claimant whose claim has been allowed but not paid may secure an order directing the personal representative to pay the claim to the extent funds of the estate are available to pay it.

(b) The personal representative at any time may pay any just claim that has not been barred, with or without formal presentation, but is personally liable to any other claimant whose claim is allowed and who is injured by its payment if

(1) payment was made before the expiration of the time limit stated in subsection (a) and the personal representative failed to require the payee to give adequate security for the refund of any of the payment necessary to pay other claimants; or

(2) payment was made, due to negligence or willful fault of the personal representative, in such manner as to deprive the injured claimant of priority.

As amended in 1989.

§ 3-808. [Individual Liability of Personal Representative.]

(a) Unless otherwise provided in the contract, a personal representative is not individually liable on a contract properly entered into in his fiduciary capacity in the court of administration of the estate unless he fails to reveal his representative capacity and identify the estate in the contract.

(b) A personal representative is individually liable for obligations arising from ownership or control of the estate or for torts committed in the course of administration of the estate only if he is personally at fault.

(c) Claims based on contracts entered into by a personal representative in his fiduciary capacity, on obligations arising from ownership or control of the estate or on torts committed in the course of estate administration may be asserted against the estate by proceeding against the personal representative in his fiduciary capacity, whether or not the personal representative is individually liable therefor.

(d) Issues of liability as between the estate and the personal representative individually may be determined in a proceeding for accounting, surcharge or indemnification or other appropriate proceeding.

§ 3-809. [Secured Claims.]

Payment of a secured claim is upon the basis of the amount allowed if the creditor surrenders his security; otherwise payment is upon the basis of one of the following:

(1) if the creditor exhausts his security before receiving payment [unless precluded by other law] upon the amount of the claim allowed less the fair value of the security; or

(2) if the creditor does not have the right to exhaust his security or has not done so, upon the amount of the claim allowed less the value of the security determined by converting it into money according to the terms of the agreement pursuant to which the security was delivered to the creditor, or by the creditor and personal representative by agreement, arbitration, compromise or litigation.

§ 3-810. [Claims Not Due and Contingent or Unliquidated Claims.]

(a) If a claim which will become due at a future time or a contingent or unliquidated claim becomes due or certain before the distribution of the estate, and if the claim has been allowed or established by a proceeding, it is paid in the same manner as presently due and absolute claims of the same class.

(b) In other cases the personal representative or, on petition of the personal representative or the claimant in a special proceeding for the purpose, the Court may provide for payment as follows:

(1) if the claimant consents, he may be paid the present or agreed value of the claim, taking any uncertainty into account;

(2) arrangement for future payment, or possible payment, on the happening of the contingency or on liquidation may be made by creating a trust, giving a mortgage, obtaining a bond or security from a distributee, or otherwise.

§ 3-811. [Counterclaims.]

In allowing a claim the personal representative may deduct any counterclaim which the estate has against the claimant. In determining a claim against an estate a Court shall reduce the amount allowed by the amount of any counterclaims and, if the counterclaims exceed the claim, render a judgment against the claimant in the amount of the excess. A counterclaim, liquidated or unliquidated, may arise from a transaction other than that upon which the claim is based. A counterclaim may give rise to relief exceeding in amount or different in kind from that sought in the claim.

§ 3-812. [Execution and Levies Prohibited.]

No execution may issue upon nor may any levy be made against any property of the estate under any judgment against a decedent or a personal representative, but this section shall not be construed to prevent the enforcement of mortgages, pledges or liens upon real or personal property in an appropriate proceeding.

§ 3-813. [Compromise of Claims.]

When a claim against the estate has been presented in any manner, the personal representative may, if it appears for the best interest of the estate, compromise the claim, whether due or not due, absolute or contingent, liquidated or unliquidated.

§ 3-814. [Encumbered Assets.]

If any assets of the estate are encumbered by mortgage, pledge, lien, or other security interest, the personal representative may pay the encumbrance or any part thereof, renew or extend any obligation secured by the encumbrance or convey or transfer the assets to the creditor in satisfaction of his lien, in whole or in part, whether or not the holder of the encumbrance has presented a claim, if it appears to be for the best interest of the estate. Payment of an encumbrance does not increase the share of the distributee entitled to the encumbered assets unless the distributee is entitled to exoneration.

§ 3-815. [Administration in More Than One State; Duty of Personal Representative.]

(a) All assets of estates being administered in this state are subject to all claims, allowances and charges existing or established against the personal representative wherever appointed.

(b) If the estate either in this state or as a whole is insufficient to cover all family exemptions and allowances determined by the law of the decedent's domicile, prior charges and claims, after satisfaction of the exemptions, allowances and charges, each claimant whose claim has been allowed either in this state or elsewhere in administrations of which the personal representative is aware, is entitled to receive payment of an equal proportion of his claim. If a preference or security in regard to a claim is allowed in another jurisdiction but not in this state, the creditor so benefited is to receive dividends from local assets only upon the balance of his claim after deducting the amount of the benefit.

(c) In case the family exemptions and allowances, prior charges and claims of the entire estate exceed the total value of the portions of the estate being administered separately and this state is not the state of the decedent's last domicile, the claims allowed in this state shall be paid their proportion if local assets are adequate for the purpose, and the balance of local assets shall be transferred to the domiciliary personal representative. If local assets are not sufficient to pay all claims allowed in this state the amount to which they are entitled, local assets shall be marshalled so that each claim allowed in this state is paid its proportion as far as possible, after taking into account all dividends on claims allowed in this state from assets in other jurisdictions.

§ 3-816. [Final Distribution to Domiciliary Representative.]

The estate of a non-resident decedent being administered by a personal representative appointed in this state shall, if there is a personal representative of the decedent's domicile willing to receive it, be distributed to the domiciling personal representative for the benefit of the successors of the decedent unless (1) by virtue of the decedent's will, if any, and applicable choice of law rules, the successors are identified pursuant to the local law of this state without reference to the local law of the decedent's domicile; (2) the personal representative of this state, after reasonable inquiry, is unaware of the existence or identity of a domiciliary personal representative; or (3) the Court orders otherwise in a proceeding for a closing order under Section 3-1001 or incident to the closing of a supervised administration. In other cases, distribution of the estate of a decedent shall be made in accordance with the other Parts of this Article.

Part 9
Special Provisions Relating to Distribution

§ 3-901. [Successors' Rights if No Administration.]

In the absence of administration, (the heirs and devisees are entitled to the estate in accordance with the terms of a probated will or the laws of intestate succession. Devisees may establish title by the probated will to devised property. Persons entitled to property by homestead allowance, exemption or intestacy may establish title thereto by proof of the decedent's ownership, his death, and their relationship to the decedent. Successors take subject to all charges incident to administration, including the claims of creditors and allowances of surviving spouse and dependent children, and subject to the rights of others resulting from abatement, retainer, advancement, and adoption.

§ 3-902. [Distribution; Order in Which Assets Appropriated; Abatement.]

(a) except as provided in subsection (b) and except as provided in connection with the share of the surviving spouse who elects to take an elective share, shares of distributees abate, without any preference or priority as between real and personal property, in the following order: (1) property not disposed of by the will; (2) residuary devises; (3) general devises; (4) specific devises. For purposes of abatement, a general devise charged on any specific property or fund is a specific devise to the extent of the value of the property on which it is charged, and upon the failure or insufficiency of the property on which it is charged, a general devise to the extent of the failure or insufficiency. Abatement within each classification is in proportion to the amounts of property each of the beneficiaries would have received if full distribution of the property had been made in accordance with the terms of the will.

(b) If the will expresses an order of abatement, or if the testamentary plan or the express or implied purpose of the devise would be defeated by the order of abatement stated in subsection (a), the shares of the distributees abate as may be found necessary to give effect to the intention of the testator.

(c) If the subject of a preferred devise is sold or used incident to administration, abatement shall be achieved by appropriate adjustments in, or contribution from, other interests in the remaining assets.

[§ 3-902A. [Distribution; Order in Which Assets Appropriated; Abatement.]

(addendum for adoption in community property states)

[(a) and (b) as above.]

(c) If an estate of a decedent consists partly of separate property and partly of community property, the debts and expenses of administration shall be apportioned and charged against the different kinds of property in proportion to the relative value thereof.

[(d) same as (c) in common law state.]]

§ 3-903. [Right of Retainer.]

The amount of a non-contingent indebtedness of a successor to the estate if due, or its present value if not due, shall be offset against the successor's interest; but the successor has the benefit of any defense which would be available to him in a direct proceeding for recovery of the debt.

§ 3-904. [Interest on General Pecuniary Devise.]

General pecuniary devises bear interest at the legal rate beginning one year after the first appointment of a personal representative until payment, unless a contrary intent is indicated by the will.

§ 3-905. [Penalty Clause for Contest.]

A provision in a will purporting to penalize any interested person for contesting the will or instituting other proceedings relating to the estate is unenforceable if probable cause exists for instituting proceedings.

§ 3-906. [Distribution in Kind; Valuation; Method.]

(a) Unless a contrary intention is indicated by the will, the distributable assets of a decedent's estate shall be distributed in kind to the extent possible through application of the following provisions:

(1) A specific devisee is entitled to distribution of the thing devised to him, and a spouse or child who has selected particular assets of an estate as provided in Section 2-402 shall receive the items selected.

(2) Any homestead or family allowance or devise of a stated sum of money may be satisfied in kind provided (i) the person entitled to the payment has not demanded payment in cash; (ii) the property distributed in kind

is valued at fair market value as of the date of its distribution, and (iii) no residuary devisee has requested that the asset in question remain a part of the residue of the estate.

(3) For the purpose of valuation under paragraph (2) securities regularly traded on recognized exchanges, if distributed in kind, are valued at the price for the last sale of like securities traded on the business day prior to distribution, or if there was no sale on that day, at the median between amounts bid and offered at the close of that day. Assets consisting of sums owed the decedent or the estate by solvent debtors as to which there is no known dispute or defense are valued at the sum due with accrued interest or discounted to the date of distribution for assets which do not have readily ascertainable values, a valuation as of a date not more than 30 days prior to the date of distribution, if otherwise reasonable, controls. For purposes of facilitating distribution, the personal representative may ascertain the value of the assets as of the time of the proposed distribution in any reasonable way, including the employment of qualified appraisers, even if the assets may have been previously appraised.

(4) The residuary estate shall be distributed in any equitable manner.

(b) After the probable charges against the estate are known, the personal representative may mail or deliver a proposal for distribution to all persons who have a right to object to the proposed distribution. The right of any distributee to object to the proposed distribution on the basis of the kind or value of asset he is to receive, if not waived earlier in writing, terminates if he fails to object in writing received by the personal representative within 30 days after mailing or delivery of the proposal.

As amended in 1987.

§ 3-907. [Distribution in Kind; Evidence.]

If distribution in kind is made, the personal representative shall execute an instrument or deed of distribution assigning, transferring or releasing the assets to the distributee as evidence of the distributee's title to the property.

§ 3-908. [Distribution; Right or Title of Distributee.]

Proof that a distributee has received an instrument or deed of distribution of assets in kind, or payment in distribution, from a personal representative, is conclusive evidence that the distributee has succeeded to the interest of the estate in the distributed assets, as against all persons interested in the estate, except that the personal representative may recover the assets or their value if the distribution was improper.

§ 3-909. [Improper Distribution; Liability of Distributee.]

Unless the distribution or payment no longer can be questioned because of adjudication, estoppel, or limitation, a distributee of property improperly distributed or paid, or a claimant who was improperly paid, is liable to return the property improperly received and its income since distribution if he has the property. If he does not have the property, then he is liable to return the value as of the date of disposition of the property improperly received and its income and gain received by him.

§ 3-910. [Purchasers from Distributees Protected.]

If property distributed in kind or a security interest therein is acquired for value by a purchaser from or lender to a distributee who has received an instrument or deed of distribution from the personal representative, or is so acquired by a purchaser from or lender to a transferee from such distributee, the purchaser or lender takes title free of rights of any interested person in the estate and incurs no personal liability to the estate, or to any interested person, whether or not the distribution was proper or supported by court order or the authority of the personal representative was terminated before execution of the instrument or deed. This section protects a purchaser from or lender to a distributee who, as personal representative, has executed a deed of distribution to himself, as well as a purchaser from or lender to any other distributee or his transferee. To be protected under this provision, a purchaser or lender need not inquire whether a personal representative acted properly in making the distribution in kind, even if the personal representative and the distributee are the same person, or whether the authority of the personal representative had terminated before the distribution. Any recorded instrument described in this section on which a state documentary fee is noted pursuant to [insert appropriate reference] shall be prima facie evidence that such transfer was made for value.

§ 3-911. [Partition for Purpose of Distribution.]

When two or more heirs or devisees are entitled to distribution of undivided interests in any real or personal property of the estate, the personal representative or one or more of the heirs or devisees may petition the Court prior to the formal or informal closing of the estate, to make partition. After notice to the interested heirs or devisees, the Court shall partition the property in the same manner as provided by the law for civil actions of partition. The Court may direct the personal representative to sell any property which cannot be partitioned without prejudice to the owners and which cannot conveniently be allotted to any one party.

§ 3-912. [Private Agreements Among Successors to Decedent Binding on Personal Representative.]

Subject to the rights of creditors and taxing authorities, competent successors may agree among themselves to alter the interests, shares or amounts to which they are entitled under the will of the decedent or under the laws of intestacy, in any way that they provide in a written contract executed by all who are affected by its provisions. The personal representative shall abide by the terms of the agreement subject to his obligation to administer the estate for the benefit of creditors, to pay all taxes and costs of administration, and to carry out the responsibilities of his office for the benefit of any successors of the decedent who are not parties. Personal representatives of decedents' estates are not required to see to the performance of trusts if the trustee thereof is another person who is willing to accept the trust. Accordingly, trustees of a testamentary trust are successors for the purposes of this section. Nothing herein relieves trustees of any duties owed to beneficiaries of trusts.

§ 3-913. [Distributions to Trustee.]

(a) Before distributing to a trustee, the personal representative may require that the trust be registered if the state in which it is to be administered provides for registration and that the trustee inform the beneficiaries as provided in Section 7-303.

(b) If the trust instrument does not excuse the trustee from giving bond, the personal representative may petition the appropriate Court to require that the trustee post bond if he apprehends that distribution might jeopardize the interests of persons who are not able to protect themselves, and he may withhold distribution until the Court has acted.

(c) No inference of negligence on the part of the personal representative shall be drawn from his failure to exercise the authority conferred by subsections (a) and (b).

§ 3-914. [Disposition of Unclaimed Assets.]

(a) If an heir, devisee or claimant cannot be found, the personal representative shall distribute the share of the missing person to his conservator, if any, otherwise to the state treasurer to become a part of the state escheat fund.

(b) The money received by [state treasurer] shall be paid to the person entitled on proof of his right thereto or, if the [state treasurer] refuses or fails to pay, the person may petition the Court which appointed the personal representative, whereupon the Court upon notice to the [state treasurer] may determine the person entitled to the money and order the [treasurer] to pay it to him. No interest is allowed thereon and the heir, devisee or claimant shall pay all costs and expenses incident to the proceeding. If no petition is made to the [court] within 8 years after payment to the [state treasurer], the right of recovery is barred.]

§ 3-915. [Distribution to Person Under Disability.]

(a) A personal representative may discharge his obligation to distribute to any person under legal disability by distributing in a manner expressly provided in the will.

(b) Unless contrary to an express provision in the will, the personal representative may discharge his obligation to distribute to a minor or person under other disability as authorized by Section 5-501 or any other statute. If the personal representative knows that a conservator has been appointed or that a proceeding for appointment of a conservator is pending, the personal representative is authorized to distribute only to the conservator.

(c) If the heir or devisee is under disability other than minority, the personal representative is authorized to distribute to:

(1) an attorney in fact who has authority under a power of attorney to receive property for that person; or

(2) the spouse, parent or other close relative with whom the person under disability resides if the distribution is of amounts not exceeding [$10,000] a year, or property not exceeding [$10,000] in value, unless the court authorizes a larger amount or greater value.

Persons receiving money or property for the disabled person are obligated to apply the money or property to the support of that person, but may not pay themselves except by way of reimbursement for out of pocket expenses for goods and services necessary for the support of the disabled person. Excess sums must be preserved for future support of the disabled person. The personal representative is not responsible for the proper application of money or property distributed pursuant to this subsection.
As amended in 1987.

§ 3-916. [Apportionment of Estate Taxes.]

(a) For purposes of this section:

(1) "estate" means the gross estate of a decedent as determined for the purpose of federal estate tax and the estate tax payable to this state;

(2) "person" means any individual, partnership, association, joint stock company, corporation, government,

political subdivision, governmental agency, or local governmental agency;

(3) "person interested in the estate" means any person entitled to receive, or who has received, from a decedent or by reason of the death of a decedent any property or interest therein included in the decedent's estate. It includes a personal representative, conservator, and trustee;

(4) "state" means any state, territory, or possession of the United States, the District of Columbia, and the Commonwealth of Puerto Rico;

(5) "tax" means the federal estate tax and the additional inheritance tax imposed by and interest and penalties imposed in addition to the tax;

(6) "fiduciary" means personal representative or trustee.

(b) Except as provided in subsection (i) and, unless the will otherwise provides, the tax shall be apportioned among all persons interested in the estate. The apportionment is to be made in the proportion that the value of the interest of each person interested in the estate bears to the total value of the interests of all persons interested in the estate. The values used in determining the tax are to be used for that purpose. If the decedent's will directs a method of apportionment of tax different from the method described in this Code, the method described in the will controls.

(c)(1) The Court in which venue lies for the administration of the estate of a decedent, on petition for the purpose may determine the apportionment of the tax.

(2) If the Court finds that it is inequitable to apportion interest and penalties in the manner provided in subsection (b), because of special circumstances, it may direct apportionment thereof in the manner it finds equitable.

(3) If the Court finds that the assessment of penalties and interest assessed in relation to the tax is due to delay caused by the negligence of the fiduciary, the Court may charge him with the amount of the assessed penalties and interest.

(4) In any action to recover from any person interested in the estate the amount of the tax apportioned to the person in accordance with this Code the determination of the Court in respect thereto shall be prima facie correct.

(d)(1) The personal representative or other person in possession of the property of the decedent required to pay the tax may withhold from any property distributable to any person interested in the estate, upon its distribution to him, the amount of tax attributable to his interest. If the property in possession of the personal representative or other person required to pay the tax and distributable to any person interested in the estate is insufficient to satisfy the proportionate amount of the tax determined to be due from the person, the personal representative or other person required to pay the tax may recover the deficiency from the person interested in the estate. If the property is not in the possession of the personal representative or the other person required to pay the tax, the personal representative or the other person required to pay the tax may recover from any person interested in the estate the amount of the tax apportioned to the person in accordance with this Act.

(2) If property held by the personal representative is distributed prior to final apportionment of the tax, the distributee shall provide a bond or other security for the apportionment liability in the form and amount prescribed by the personal representative.

(e)(1) In making an apportionment, allowances shall be made for any exemptions granted, any classification made of persons interested in the estate and for any deductions and credits allowed by the law imposing the tax.

(2) Any exemption or deduction allowed by reason of the relationship of any person to the decedent or by reason of the purposes of the gift inures to the benefit of the person bearing such relationship or receiving the gift; but if an interest is subject to a prior present interest which is not allowable as a deduction, the tax apportionable against the present interest shall be paid from principal.

(3) Any deduction for property previously taxed and any credit for gift taxes or death taxes of a foreign country paid by the decedent or his estate inures to the proportionate benefit of all persons liable to apportionment.

(4) Any credit for inheritance, succession or estate taxes or taxes in the nature thereof applicable to property or interests includable in the estate, inures to the benefit of the persons or interests chargeable with the payment thereof to the extent proportionately that the credit reduces the tax.

(5) To the extent that property passing to or in trust for a surviving spouse or any charitable, public or similar purpose is not an allowable deduction for purposes of the tax solely by reason of an inheritance tax or other death tax imposed upon and deductible from the property, the property is not included in the computation provided for in subsection (b) hereof, and to that extent no apportionment is made against the property. The sentence immediately preceding does not apply to any case if the result would be to deprive the estate of a deduction otherwise allowable under Section 2053(d) of the Internal Revenue Code of 1954, as amended, of the United States, relating to deduction for state death taxes on transfers for public, charitable, or religious uses.

(f) No interest in income and no estate for years or for life or other temporary interest in any property or fund is subject to apportionment as between the temporary interest and the remainder. The tax on the temporary interest and the tax, if any, on the remainder is chargeable against the corpus of the property or funds subject to the temporary interest and remainder.

(g) Neither the personal representative nor other person required to pay the tax is under any duty to institute any action to recover from any person interested in the estate the amount of the tax apportioned to the person until the expiration of the 3 months next following final determination of the tax. A personal representative or other person required to pay the tax who institutes the action within a reasonable time after the 3 months' period is not subject to any liability or surcharge because any portion of the tax apportioned to any person interested in the estate was collectible at a time following the death of the decedent but thereafter became uncollectible. If the personal representative or other person required to pay the tax cannot collect from any person interested in the estate the amount of the tax apportioned to the person, the amount not recoverable shall be equitably apportioned among the other persons interested in the estate who are subject to apportionment.

(h) A personal representative acting in another state or a person required to pay the tax domiciled in another state may institute an action in the courts of this state and may recover a proportionate amount of the federal estate tax, of an estate tax payable to another state or of a death duty due by a decedent's estate to another state, from a person interested in the estate who is either domiciled in this state or who owns property in this state subject to attachment or execution. For the purposes of the action the determination of apportionment by the Court having jurisdiction of the administration of the decedent's estate in the other state is prima facie correct.

(i) If the liabilities of persons interested in the estate as prescribed by this act differ from those which result under the federal estate tax law, the liabilities imposed by the federal law will control and the balance of this Section shall apply as if the resulting liabilities had been prescribed herein.

Part 10
Closing Estates

§ 3-1001. [Formal Proceedings Terminating Administration; Testate or Intestate; Order of General Protection.]

(a) A personal representative or any interested person may petition for an order of complete settlement of the estate. The personal representative may petition at any time, and any other interested person may petition after one year from the appointment of the original personal representative except that no petition under this section may be entertained until the time for presenting claims which arose prior to the death of the decedent has expired. The petition may request the Court to determine testacy, if not previously determined, to consider the final account or compel or approve an accounting and distribution, to construe any will or determine heirs and adjudicate the final settlement and distribution of the estate. After notice to all interested persons and hearing the Court may enter an order or orders, on appropriate conditions, determining the persons entitled to distribution of the estate, and, as circumstances require, approving settlement and directing or approving distribution of the estate and discharging the personal representative from further claim or demand of any interested person.

(b) If one or more heirs or devisees were omitted as parties in, or were not given notice of, a previous formal testacy proceeding, the Court, on proper petition for an order of complete settlement of the estate under this section, and after notice to the omitted or unnotified persons and other interested parties determined to be interested on the assumption that the previous order concerning testacy is conclusive as to those given notice of the earlier proceeding, may determine testacy as it affects the omitted persons and confirm or alter the previous order of testacy as it affects all interested persons as appropriate in the light of the new proofs. In the absence of objection by an omitted or unnotified person, evidence received in the original testacy proceeding shall constitute prima facie proof of due execution of any will previously admitted to probate, or of the fact that the decedent left no valid will if the prior proceedings determined this fact.

§ 3-1002. [Formal Proceedings Terminating Testate Administration; Order Construing Will Without Adjudicating Testacy.]

A personal representative administering an estate under an informally probated will or any devisee under an informally probated will may petition for an order of settlement of the estate which will not adjudicate the testacy status of the decedent. The personal representative may petition at any time, and a devisee may petition after one year, from the appointment of the original personal representative, except that no petition under this section may be entertained until the time for presenting claims which arose prior to the death of the decedent has expired. The petition may request the Court to consider the final account or compel or approve an accounting and distribution, to construe the will and adjudicate final settlement and distribution of the estate. After notice to all devisees and the personal representative and hearing, the Court may enter an order or orders, on appropriate conditions, determining the persons entitled to distribution of the estate under the will, and, as circumstances require, approving settlement and directing or approving distribution of the estate and discharging the personal representative from further claim or demand of any devisee who is a party to the proceeding and those he represents. If it appears that a part of the estate is intestate, the proceedings shall be dismissed or amendments made to meet the provisions of Section 3-1001.

§ 3-1003. [Closing Estates; By Sworn Statement of Personal Representative.]

(a) Unless prohibited by order of the Court and except for estates being administered in supervised administration proceedings, a personal representative may close an estate by filing with the court no earlier than six months after the date of original appointment of a general personal representative for the estate, a verified statement stating that the personal representatives or a previous personal representative, has:

(1) determined that the time limited for presentation of creditors' claims has expired.

(2) fully administered the estate of the decedent by making payment, settlement or other disposition of all claims which were presented, expenses of administration and estate, inheritance and other death taxes, except as specified in the statement, and that the assets of the estate have been distributed to the persons entitled. If any claims remain undischarged, the statement must state whether the personal representative has distributed the estate subject to possible liability with the agreement of the distributees or state in detail other arrangements that have been made to accommodate outstanding liabilities; and

(3) sent a copy of the statement to all distributees of the estate and to all creditors or other claimants of whom the personal representative is aware whose claims are neither paid nor barred and has furnished a full account in writing of the personal representative's administration to the distributees whose interests are affected thereby.

(b) If no proceedings involving the personal representative are pending in the Court one year after the closing statement is filed, the appointment of the personal representative terminates.

As amended in 1989.

§ 3-1004. [Liability of Distributees to Claimants.]

After assets of an estate have been distributed and subject to Section 3-1006, an undischarged claim not barred may be prosecuted in a proceeding against one or more distributees. No distributee shall be liable to claimants for amounts received as exempt property, homestead or family allowances, or for amounts in excess of the value of his distribution as of the time of distribution. As between distributees, each shall bear the cost of satisfaction of unbarred claims as if the claim had been satisfied in the course of administration. Any distributee who shall have failed to notify other distributees of the demand made upon him by the claimant in sufficient time to permit them to join in any proceeding in which the claim was asserted against him loses his right of contribution against other distributees.

§ 3-1005. [Limitations on Proceedings Against Personal Representative.]

Unless previously barred by adjudication and except as provided in the closing statement, the rights of successors and of creditors whose claims have not otherwise been barred against the personal representatives for breach of fiduciary duty are barred unless a proceeding to assert the same is commenced within 6 months after the filing of the closing statement. The rights thus barred do not include rights to recover from a personal representative for fraud, misrepresentation, or inadequate disclosure related to the settlement of the decedent's estate.

§ 3-1006. [Limitations on Actions and Proceedings Against Distributees.]

Unless previously adjudicated in a formal testacy proceeding or in a proceeding settling the accounts of a personal representative or otherwise barred, the claim of a claimant to recover from a distributee who is liable to pay the claim, and the right of an heir or devisee, or of a successor personal representative acting in their behalf, to recover property improperly distributed or its value from any distributee is forever barred at the later of three years after the decedent's death or one year after the time of its distribution thereof, but all claims of creditors of the decedent, are barred one year after the decedent's death. This section does not bar an action to recover property or value received as the result of fraud.

Amended in 1989.

§ 3-1007. [Certificate Discharging Liens Securing Fiduciary Performance.]

After his appointment has terminated, the personal representative, his sureties, or any successor of either, upon the filing of a verified application showing, so far as is known by the applicant, that no action concerning the estate is pending in any court, is entitled to receive a certificate from the Registrar that the personal representative appears to have fully administered the estate in question. The certificate evidences discharge of any lien on any property given to secure the obligation of the personal representative in lieu of bond or any surety, but does not preclude action against the personal representative or the surety.

§ 3-1008. [Subsequent Administration.]

If other property of the estate is discovered after an estate has been settled and the personal representative discharged or after one year after a closing statement has been filed, the Court upon petition of any interested person and upon notice as it directs may appoint the same or a successor personal representative to administer the subsequently discovered estate. If a new appointment is made, unless the Court orders otherwise, the provisions of this Code apply as appropriate; but no claim previously barred may be asserted in the subsequent administration.

Part 11
Compromise of Controversies

§ 3-1101. [Effect of Approval of Agreements Involving Trusts, Inalienable Interests, or Interests of Third Persons.]

A compromise of any controversy as to admission to probate of any instrument offered for formal probate as the will of a decedent, the construction, validity, or effect of any probated will, the rights or interests in the estate of the decedent, of any successor, or the administration of the estate, if approved in a formal proceeding in the Court for that purpose, is binding on all the parties thereto including those unborn, unascertained or who could not be located. An approved compromise is binding even though it may affect a trust or an inalienable interest. A compromise does not impair the rights of creditors or of taxing authorities who are not parties to it.

§ 3-1102. [Procedure for Securing Court Approval of Compromise.]

The procedure for securing court approval of a compromise is as follows:

(1) The terms of the compromise shall be set forth in an agreement in writing which shall be executed by all competent persons and parents acting for any minor child having beneficial interests or having claims which will or may be affected by the compromise. Execution is not required by any person whose identity cannot be ascertained or whose whereabouts is unknown and cannot reasonably be ascertained.

(2) Any interested person, including the personal representative or a trustee, then may submit the agreement to the Court for its approval and for execution by the personal representative, the trustee of every affected testamentary trust, and other fiduciaries and representatives.

(3) After notice to all interested persons or their representatives, including the personal representative of the estate and all affected trustees of trusts, the Court, if it finds that the contest or controversy is in good faith and that the effect of the agreement upon the interests of persons represented by fiduciaries or other representatives is just and reasonable, shall make an order approving the agreement and directing all fiduciaries subject to Its jurisdiction to execute the agreement. Minor children represented only by their parents may be bound only if their parents join with other competent persons in execution of the compromise. Upon the making of the order and the execution of the agreement, all further disposition of the estate is in accordance with the terms of the agreement.

Part 12
Collection of Personal Property by Affidavit and Summary Administration Procedure for Small Estates

§ 3-1201. [Collection of Personal Property by Affidavit.]

(a) Thirty days after the death of a decedent, any person indebted to the decedent or having possession of tangible personal property or an instrument evidencing a debt, obligation, stock or chose in action belonging to the decedent shall make payment of the indebtedness or deliver the tangible personal property or an instrument evidencing a debt, obligation, stock or chose in action to a person claiming to be the successor of the decedent upon being presented an affidavit made by or on behalf of the successor stating that:

(1) the value of the entire estate, wherever located, less liens and encumbrances, does not exceed $5,000;

(2) 30 days have elapsed since the death of the decedent;

(3) no application or petition for the appointment of a personal representative is pending or has been granted in any jurisdiction; and

(4) the claiming successor is entitled to payment or delivery of the property.

(b) A transfer agent of any security shall change the registered ownership on the books of a corporation from the decedent to the successor or successors upon the presentation of an affidavit as provided in subsection (a).

§ 3-1202. [Effect of Affidavit.]

The person paying, delivering, transferring, or issuing personal property or the evidence thereof pursuant to affidavit is discharged and released to the same extent as if he dealt with a personal representative of the decedent. He is not required to see to the application of the personal property or evidence thereof or to inquire into the truth of any statement in the affidavit. If any person to whom an affidavit is delivered refuses to pay, deliver, transfer, or issue any personal property or evidence thereof, it may be recovered or its payment, delivery, transfer, or issuance compelled upon proof of their right in a proceeding brought for the purpose by or on behalf of the persons entitled thereto. Any person to whom payment, delivery, transfer or issuance is made is answerable and accountable therefor to any personal representative of the estate or to any other person having a superior right.

§ 3-1203. [Small Estates; Summary Administrative Procedure.]

If it appears from the inventory and appraisal that the value of the entire estate, less liens and encumbrances, does not exceed homestead allowance, exempt property, family allowance, costs and expenses of administration, reasonable funeral expenses, and reasonable and necessary medical and hospital expenses of the last illness of the decedent, the personal representative, without giving notice to creditors, may immediately disburse and distribute the estate to the persons entitled thereto and file a closing statement as provided in Section 3-1204.

§ 3-1204. [Small Estates; Closing by Sworn Statement of Personal Representative.]

(a) Unless prohibited by order of the Court and except for estates being administered by supervised personal representatives, a personal representative may close an estate administered under the summary procedures of Section 3-1203 by filing with the Court, at any time after disbursement and distribution of the estate, a verified statement stating that:

(1) to the best knowledge of the personal representative, the value of the entire estate, less liens and encumbrances, did not exceed homestead allowance, exempt property, family allowance, costs and expenses of administration, reasonable funeral expenses, and reasonable, necessary medical and hospital expenses of the last illness of the decedent;

(2) the personal representative has fully administered the estate by disbursing and distributing it to the persons entitled thereto; and

(3) the personal representative has sent a copy of the closing statement to all distributees of the estate and to all creditors or other claimants of whom he is aware whose claims are neither paid nor barred and has furnished a full account in writing of his administration to the distributees whose interests are affected.

(b) If no actions or proceedings involving the personal representative are pending in the Court one year after the closing statement is filed, the appointment of the personal representative terminates.

(c) A closing statement filed under this section has the same effect as one filed under Section 3-1003.

ARTICLE IV
FOREIGN PERSONAL REPRESENTATIVES; ANCILLARY ADMINISTRATION

Part 1
Definitions

§ 4-101. [Definitions.]

In this Article

(1) "local administration" means administration by a personal representative appointed in this state pursuant to appointment proceedings described in Article III.

(2) "local personal representative" includes any personal representative appointed in this state pursuant to appointment proceedings described in Article III and excludes foreign personal representatives who acquire the power of a local personal representative pursuant to Section 4-205.

(3) "resident creditor" means a person domiciled in, or doing business in this state, who is, or could be, a claimant against an estate of a nonresident decedent.

Part 2
Powers of Foreign Personal Representatives

§ 4-201. [Payment of Debt and Delivery of Property to Domiciliary Foreign Personal Representative Without Local Administration.]

At any time after the expiration of sixty days from the death of a nonresident decedent, any person indebted to the estate of the nonresident decedent or having possession or control of personal property, or of an instrument evidencing a debt, obligation, stock or chose in action belonging to the estate of the nonresident decedent may pay the debt, deliver the personal property, or the instrument evidencing the debt, obligation, stock or chose in action, to the domiciliary foreign personal representative of the nonresident decedent upon being presented with proof of his appointment and an affidavit made by or on behalf of the representative stating:

    (1) the date of the death of the nonresident decedent,

    (2) that no local administration, or application or petition therefor, is pending in this state,

    (3) that the domiciliary foreign personal representative is entitled to payment or delivery.

§ 4-202. [Payment or Delivery Discharges.]

Payment or delivery made in good faith on the basis of the proof of authority and affidavit releases the debtor or person having possession of the personal property to the same extent as if payment or delivery had been made to a local personal representative.

§ 4-203. [Resident Creditor Notice.]

Payment or delivery under Section 4-201 may not be made if a resident creditor of the nonresident decedent has notified the debtor of the nonresident decedent or the person having possession of the personal property belonging to the nonresident decedent that the debt should not be paid nor the property delivered to the domiciliary foreign personal representative.

§ 4-204. [Proof of Authority-Bond.]

If no local administration or application or petition therefor is pending in this state, a domiciliary foreign personal representative may file with a Court in this State in a [county] in which property belonging to the decedent is located, authenticated copies of his appointment and of any official bond he has given.

§ 4-205. [Powers.]

A domiciliary foreign personal representative who has complied with Section 4-204 may exercise as to assets in this state all powers of a local personal representative and may maintain actions and proceedings in this state subject to any conditions imposed upon nonresident parties generally.

§ 4-206. [Power of Representatives in Transition.]

The power of a domiciliary foreign personal representative under Section 4-201 or 4-205 shall be exercised only if there is no administration or application therefor pending in this state. An application or petition for local administration of the estate terminates the power of the foreign personal representative to act under Section 4-205, but the local Court may allow the foreign personal representative to exercise limited powers only to preserve the estate. No person who, before receiving actual notice of a pending local administration, has changed his position in reliance upon the powers of a foreign personal representative shall be prejudiced by reason of the application or petition for, or grant of, local administration. The local personal representative is subject to all duties and obligations which have accrued by virtue of the exercise of the powers by the foreign personal representative and may be substituted for him in any action or proceedings in this state.

§ 4-207. [Ancillary and Other Local Administrations; Provisions Governing.]

In respect to a non-resident decedent, the provisions of Article III of this Code govern (1) proceedings, if any, in a Court of this state for probate of the will, appointment, removal, supervision, and discharge of the local personal representative, and any other order concerning the estate; and (2) the status, powers, duties and liabilities of any local personal representative and the rights of claimants, purchasers, distributees and others in regard to a local administration.

Part 3
Jurisdiction Over Foreign Representatives

§ 4-301. [Jurisdiction by Act of Foreign Personal Representative.]

A foreign personal representative submits personally to the jurisdiction of the Courts of this state in any proceeding relating to the estate by (1) filing authenticated copies of his appointment as provided in Section 4-204, (2) receiving payment of money or taking delivery of personal property under Section 4-201, or (3) doing any act as a personal representative in this state which would have given the state jurisdiction over him as an individual. Jurisdiction under (2) is limited to the money or value of personal property collected.

§ 4-302. [Jurisdiction by Act of Decedent.]

In addition to jurisdiction conferred by Section 4-301, a foreign personal representative is subject to the jurisdiction of the courts of this state to the same extent that his decedent was subject to jurisdiction immediately prior to death.

§ 4-303. [Service on Foreign Personal Representative.]

(a) Service of process may be made upon the foreign personal representative by registered or certified mail, addressed lo his last reasonably ascertainable address, requesting a return receipt signed by addressee only. Notice by ordinary first class mail is sufficient if registered or certified mail service to the addressee is unavailable. Service may be made upon a foreign personal representative in the manner in which service could have been made under other laws of this state on either the foreign personal representative or his decedent immediately prior to death.

(b) If service is made upon a foreign personal representative as provided in subsection (a), he shall be allowed at least [30] days within which to appear or respond.

Part 4
Judgments and Personal Representative
§ 4-401. [Effect of Adjudication For or Against Personal Representative.]

An adjudication rendered in any jurisdiction in favor of or against any personal representative of the estate is as binding on the local personal representative as if he were a party to the adjudication.

ARTICLE V
PROTECTION OF PERSONS UNDER DISABILITY AND THEIR PROPERTY

Part 1
General Provisions and Definitions
§ 5-101. [Facility of Payment or Delivery.]

(a) Any person under a duty to pay or deliver money or personal property to a minor may perform the duty, in amounts not exceeding $5,000 a year, by paying or delivering the money or property to:

(1) the minor if 18 or more years of age or married;

(2) any person having the care and custody of the minor with whom the minor resides;

(3) a guardian of the minor; or

(4) a financial institution incident to a deposit in a state or federally insured savings account or certificate in the sole name of the minor with notice of the deposit to the minor.

(b) This section does not apply if the person making payment or delivery knows that a conservator has been appointed or proceedings for appointment of a conservator of the estate of the minor are pending.

(c) Persons, other than the minor or any financial institution, receiving money or property for a minor, are obligated to apply the money to the support and education of the minor, but may not pay themselves except by way of reimbursement for out-of-pocket expenses for goods and services necessary for the minor's support. Any excess sums must be preserved for future support and education of the minor and any balance not so used and any property received for the minor must be turned over to the minor when majority is attained. A person who pays or delivers money or property in accordance with provisions of this section is not responsible for the proper application thereof.

§ 5-102. [Delegation of Powers by Parent or Guardian.]

A parent or guardian of a minor or incapacitated person, by a properly executed power of attorney, may delegate to another person, for a period not exceeding 6 months, any power regarding care, custody or property of the minor child or ward, except the power to consent to marriage or adoption of a minor ward.

§ 5-103. [General Definitions.]

As used in Parts 1, 2, 3 and 4 of this Article:

(1) "Claims," in respect to a protected person, includes liabilities of the protected person, whether arising in contract, tort, or otherwise, and liabilities of the estate which arise at or after the appointment of a conservator, including expenses of administration.

(2) "Court" means the [_____] court.

(3) "Conservator" means a person who is appointed by a Court to manage the estate of a protected person and includes a limited conservator described in Section 5-419(a).

(4) "Disability" means cause for a protective order as described in Section 5-401.

(5) "Estate" includes the property of the person whose affairs are subject to this Article.

(6) "Guardian" means a person who has qualified as a guardian of a minor or incapacitated person pursuant to parental or spousal nomination or court appointment and includes a limited guardian as described in Sections 5-209(e) and 5-306(c), but excludes one who is merely a guardian ad litem.

(7) "Incapacitated person" means any person who is impaired by reason of mental illness, mental deficiency, physical illness or disability, advanced age, chronic use of drugs, chronic intoxication, or other cause (except minority) to the extent of lacking sufficient understanding or capacity to make or communicate responsible decisions.

(8) "Lease" includes an oil, gas, or other mineral lease.

(9) "Letters" includes letters of guardianship and letters of conservatorship.

(10) "Minor" means a person who is under [21] years of age.

(11) "Mortgage" means any conveyance, agreement, or arrangement in which property is used as collateral.

(12) "Organization" includes a corporation, business trust, estate, trust, partnership, association, 2 or more persons having a joint or common interest, government, governmental subdivision or agency, or any other legal entity.

(13) "Parent" includes any person entitled to take, or who would be entitled to take if the child died without a will, as a parent by intestate succession from the child whose relationship is in question and excludes any person who is only a stepparent, foster parent, or grandparent.

(14) "Person" means an individual or an organization.

(15) "Petition" means a written request to the Court for an order after notice.

(16) "Proceeding" includes action at law and suit in equity.

(17) "Property" includes both real and personal property or any interest therein and means anything that may be the subject of ownership.

(18) "Protected person" means a minor or other person for whom a conservator has been appointed or other protective order has been made as provided in Sections 5-407 and 5-408.

(19) "Protective proceeding" means a proceeding under the provisions of Part 4 of this Article.

(20) "Security" includes any note, stock, treasury stock, bond, debenture, evidence of indebtedness, certificate of interest or participation in an oil, gas, or mining title or lease or in payments out of production under such a title or lease, collateral trust certificate, transferable share, pivoting trust certificate or, in general, any interest or instrument commonly known as a security, or any certificate of interest or participation, any temporary or interim certificate, receipt or certificate of deposit for, or any warrant or right to subscribe to or purchase any of the foregoing.

(21) "Visitor" means a person appointed in a guardianship or protective proceeding who is trained in law, nursing, or social work, is an officer, employee, or special appointee of the Court, and has no personal interest in the proceeding.

(22) "Ward" means a person for whom a guardian has been appointed. A "minor ward" is a minor for whom a guardian has been appointed.

§ 5-104. [Request for Notice; Interested Person.]

Upon payment of any required fee, an interested person who desires to be notified before any order is made in a guardianship proceeding, including any proceeding subsequent to the appointment of a guardian under Section 5-312, or in a protective proceeding under Section 5-401, may file a request for notice with the clerk of the court in which the proceeding is pending. The clerk shall mail a copy of the request to the guardian and to the conservator if one has been appointed. A request is not effective unless it contains a statement showing the interest of the person making it and the address of that person or an attorney to whom notice is to be given. The request is effective only as to proceedings occurring after the filing. Any governmental agency paying or planning to pay benefits to the person to be protected is an interested person in protective proceedings.

Part 2
Guardians of Minors

§ 5-201. [Appointment and Status of Guardian of Minor.]

A person may become a guardian of a minor by parental appointment or upon appointment by the Court. The guardianship status continues until terminated, without regard to the location from time to time of the guardian or minor ward.

§ 5-202. [Parental Appointment of Guardian for Minor.]

(a) The parent of an unmarried minor may appoint a guardian for the minor by will, or other writing signed by the parent and attested by at least 2 witnesses.

(b) Subject to the right of the minor under Section 5-203, if both parents are dead or incapacitated or the surviving parent has no parental rights or has been adjudged to be incapacitated, a parental appointment becomes effective when the guardian's acceptance is filed in the Court in which a nominating instrument is probated, or, in the case of a nontestamentary nominating instrument, in the Court at the place where the minor resides or is present. If both parents are dead, an effective appointment by the parent who died later has priority.

(c) A parental appointment effected by filing the guardian's acceptance under a will probated in the state of the testator's domicile is effective in this State.

(d) Upon acceptance of appointment, the guardian shall give written notice of acceptance to the minor and to the person having the minor's care or the minor's nearest adult relative.

§ 5-203. [Objection by Minor of Fourteen or Older to Parental Appointment.]

A minor 14 or more years of age who is the subject of a parental appointment may prevent the appointment or cause it to terminate by filing in the Court in which the nominating instrument is filed a written objection to the appointment before it is accepted or within 30 days after receiving notice of its acceptance. An objection may be withdrawn. An objection does not preclude appointment by the Court in a proper proceeding of the parental nominee or any other suitable person.

§ 5-204. [Court Appointment of Guardian of Minor; Conditions for Appointment.]

(a) The Court may appoint a guardian for an unmarried minor if all parental rights have been terminated or suspended by circumstances or prior Court order. A guardian appointed pursuant to Section 5-202 whose appointment has not been prevented or nullified under Section 5-203 has priority over any guardian who may be appointed by the Court, but the Court may proceed with another appointment upon a finding that the parental nominee has failed to accept the appointment within 30 days after notice of the guardianship proceeding.

(b) If necessary, and on appropriate petition or application, the Court may appoint a temporary guardian who shall have the full authority of a general guardian of a minor, but the authority of a temporary guardian may not last longer than 6 months. The appointment of a temporary guardian for a minor may occur even though the conditions described in subsection (a) have not been established.

§ 5-205. [Venue.]

The venue for guardianship proceedings for a minor is in the court at the place where the minor resides or is present at the time the proceedings are commenced.

§ 5-206. [Procedure for Court-appointment of Guardian of Minor.]

(a) A minor or any person interested in the welfare of the minor may petition for appointment of a guardian.

(b) After the filing of a petition, the Court shall set a date for hearing, and the petitioner shall give notice of the time and place of hearing the petition in the manner prescribed by Section 1-401 to:

(1) the minor, if 14 or more years of age and not the petitioner;

(2) any person alleged to have had the principal care and custody of the minor during the 60 days preceding the filing of the petition; and

(3) any living parent of the minor.

(c) Upon hearing, if the Court finds that a qualified person seeks appointment, venue is proper, the required notices have been given, the conditions of Section 5-204 (a) have been met, and the welfare and best interest of the minor will be served by the requested appointment, it shall make the appointment and issue letters. In other cases, the Court may dismiss the proceedings or make any other disposition of the matter that will serve the best interest of the minor.

(d) If the Court determines at any time in the proceeding that the interests of the minor are or may be inadequately represented, it may appoint an attorney to represent the minor, giving consideration to the preference of the minor if the minor is 14 or more years of age.

§ 5-207. [Court Appointment of Guardian of Minor; Qualifications; Priority of Minor's Nominee.]

The Court may appoint as guardian any person whose appointment would be in the best interest of the minor. The Court shall appoint a person nominated by the minor, if the minor is 14 or more years of age, unless the Court finds the appointment contrary to the best interest of the minor.

§ 5-208. [Consent to Service by Acceptance of Appointment; Notice.]

By accepting a parental or court appointment as guardian, a guardian submits personally to the jurisdiction of the Court in any proceeding relating to the guardianship that may be instituted by any interested person. The petitioner shall cause notice of any proceeding to be delivered or mailed to the guardian at the guardian's address listed in the Court records and to the address then known to the petitioner. Letters of guardianship must indicate whether the guardian was appointed by court order or parental nomination.

§ 5-209. [Powers and Duties of Guardian of Minor.]

(a) A guardian of a minor ward has the powers and responsibilities of a parent regarding the ward's support, care, and education, but a guardian is not personally liable for the ward's expenses and is not liable to third persons by reason of the relationship for acts of the ward.

(b) In particular and without qualifying the foregoing, a guardian shall:

(1) become or remain personally acquainted with the ward and maintain sufficient contact with the ward to know of the ward's capacities, limtations, needs, opportunities, and physical and mental health;

(2) take reasonable care of the ward's personal effects and commence protective proceedings if necessary to protect other property of the ward;

(3) apply any available money of the ward to the ward's current needs for support, care, and education;

(4) conserve any excess money of the ward for the ward's future needs, but if a conservator has been appointed for the estate of the ward, the guardian, at least quarterly, shall pay to the conservator money of the ward to be conserved for the ward's future needs; and

(5) report the condition of the ward and of the ward's estate that has been subject to the guardian's possession or control, as ordered by the Court on petition of any person interested in the ward's welfare or as required by Court rule.

(c) A guardian may:

(1) receive money payable for the support of the ward to the ward's parent. Guardian, or custodian under the terms of any statutory benefit or insurance system or any private contract, devise, trust, conservatorship, or custodianship, and money or property of the ward paid or delivered pursuant to Section 5-101;

(2) if consistent with the terms of any order by a court of competent jurisdiction relating to detention or commitment of the ward, take custody of the person of the ward and establish the ward's place of abode within or without this State;

(3) if no conservator for the estate of the ward has been appointed, institute proceedings, including administrative proceedings, or take other appropriate action to compel the performance by any person of a duty to support the ward or to pay sums for the welfare of the ward;

(4) consent to medical or other professional care, treatment, or advice for the ward without liability by reason of the consent for injury to the ward resulting from the negligence or acts of third persons unless a parent would have been liable in the circumstances;

(5) consent to the marriage or adoption of the ward; and

(6) if reasonable under all of the circumstances, delegate to the ward certain responsibilities for decisions affecting the ward's well-being.

(d) A guardian is entitled to reasonable compensation for services as guardian and to reimbursement for room, board, and clothing personally provided to the ward, but only as approved by order of the Court. If a conservator, other than the guardian or one who is affiliated with the guardian has been appointed for the estate of the ward, reasonable compensation and reimbursement to the guardian

may be approved and paid by the conservator without order of the Court controlling the guardian.

(e) In the interest of developing self-reliance on the part of a ward or for other good cause, the Court, at the time of appointment or later, on its own motion or on appropriate petition or motion of the minor or other interested person, may limit the powers of a guardian otherwise conferred by this section and thereby create a limited guardianship. Any limitation on the statutory power of a guardian of a minor must be endorsed on the guardian's letters or, in the case of a guardian by parental appointment, must be reflected in letters that are issued at the time any limitation is imposed. Following the same procedure, a limitation may be removed and appropriate letters issued.

§ 5-210. [Termination of Appointment of Guardian; General.]

A guardian's authority and responsibility terminates upon the death, resignation or removal of the guardian or upon the minor's death, adoption, marriage or attainment of majority, but termination does not affect the guardian's liability for prior acts or the obligation to account for funds and assets of the ward. Resignation of a guardian does not terminate the guardianship until it has been approved by the Court. A parental appointment under an informally probated will terminates if the will is later denied probate in a formal proceeding.

§ 5-211. [Proceedings Subsequent to Appointment; Venue.]

(a) The Court at the place where the ward resides has concurrent jurisdiction with the Court that appointed the guardian or in which acceptance of a parental appointment was filed over resignation, removal, accounting and other proceedings relating to the guardianship.

(b) If the Court at the place where the ward resides is neither the appointing court nor the court in which acceptance of appointment is filed, the court in which proceedings subsequent to appointment are commenced in all appropriate cases shall notify the other court, in this or another state, and after consultation with that court determine whether to retain jurisdiction or transfer the proceedings to the other court, whichever is in the best interest of the ward. A copy of any order accepting a resignation or removing a guardian must be sent to the appointing court or the court in which acceptance of appointment is filed.

§ 5-212. [Resignation, Removal, and Other Post-appointment Proceedings.]

(a) Any person interested in the welfare of a ward or the ward, if 14 or more years of age, may petition for removal of a guardian on the ground that removal would be in the best interest of the ward or for any other order that is in the best interest of the ward. A guardian may petition for permission to resign. A petition for removal or for permission to resign may, but need not, include a request for appointment of a successor guardian.

(b) Notice of hearing on a petition for an order subsequent to appointment of a guardian must be given to the ward, the guardian, and any other person as ordered by the court.

(c) After notice and hearing on a petition for removal or for permission to resign, the Court may terminate the guardianship and make any further order that may be appropriate.

(d) If the Court determines at any time in the proceeding that the interest of the ward is or may be inadequately represented, it may appoint an attorney to represent the minor, giving consideration to the preference of the minor if the minor is 14 or more years of age.

Part 3
Guardians of Incapacitated Persons

§ 5-301. [Appointment of Guardian for Incapacitated Person by Will or Other Writing.]

(a) The parent of an unmarried incapacitated person may appoint by will, or other writing signed by the parent and attested by at least 2 witnesses, a guardian of the incapacitated person. If both parents are dead or the surviving parent is adjudged incapacitated, a parental appointment becomes effective when, after having given 7 days prior written notice of intention to do so to the incapacitated person and to the person having the care of the person or to the nearest adult relative, the guardian files acceptance of appointment in the court in which the will is [informally or formally] probated, or in the case of a non-testamentary nominating instrument, in the Court at the place where the incapacitated person resides or is present. The notice shall state that the appointment may be terminated by filing a written objection in the Court, as provided by subsection (d). If both parents are dead, an effective appointment by the parent who died later has priority.

(b) The spouse of a married incapacitated person may appoint by will, or other writing signed by the spouse and attested by at least 2 witnesses, a guardian of the incapacitated person. The appointment becomes effective when, after having given 7 days prior written notice of intention to do so to the incapacitated person and to the person having care of the incapacitated person or to the nearest adult relative, the guardian files acceptance of appointment in the Court in which the will is informally or formally probated or, in the case of non-testamentary nominating instrument, in the Court at

the place where the incapacitated person resides or is present. The notice shall state that the appointment may be terminated by filing a written objection in the Court, as provided by subsection (d). An effective appointment by a spouse has priority over an appointment by a parent.

(c) An appointment effected by filing the guardian's acceptance under a will probated in the state of the decedent's domicile is effective in this State.

(d) Upon the filing in the Court in which the will was probated or, in the case of a non-testamentary nominating instrument, in the Court at the place where the incapacitated person resides or is present, of written objection to the appointment by the incapacitated person for whom a parental or spousal appointment of guardian has been made, the appointment is terminated. An objection does not prevent appointment by the Court in a proper proceeding of the parental or spousal nominee or any other suitable person upon an adjudication of incapacity in proceedings under the succeeding sections of this Part.

As amended in 1987.

§ 5-302. [Venue.]

The venue for guardianship proceedings for an incapacitated person is in the place where the incapacitated person resides or is present at the time the proceedings are commenced. If the incapacitated person is admitted to an institution pursuant to order of a court of competent jurisdiction, venue is also in the [county] in which that Court is located.

§ 5-303. [Procedure for Court Appointment of a Guardian of an Incapacitated Person.]

(a) The incapacitated person or any person interested in the welfare of the incapacitated person may petition for appointment of a guardian, limited or general.

(b) After the filing of a petition, the Court shall set a date for hearing on the issue of incapacity so that notices may be given as required by Section 5-304, and, unless the allegedly incapacitated person is represented by counsel, appoint an attorney to represent the person in the proceeding. The person so appointed may be granted the powers and duties of a guardian ad litem. The person alleged to be incapacitated must be examined by a physician or other qualified person appointed by the Court who shall submit a report in writing to the Court. The person alleged to be incapacitated also must be interviewed by a visitor sent by the Court. The visitor also shall interview the person who appears to have caused the petition to be filed and any person who is nominated to serve as guardian and visit the present place of abode of the person alleged to be incapacitated and the place it is proposed that the person will be detained or reside if the appointment is made and submit a report in writing to the Court. The Court may utilize the service of any public or charitable agency as an additional visitor to evaluate the condition of the allegedly incapacitated person and to make appropriate recommendations to the Court.

(c) A person alleged to be incapacitated is entitled to be present at the hearing in person. The person is entitled to be represented by counsel, to present evidence, to cross examine witnesses, including the Court-appointed physician or other qualified person and any visitor [, and to trial by jury]. The issue may be determined at a closed hearing [or without a jury] if the person alleged to be incapacitated or counsel for the person so requests.

(d) Any person may apply for permission to participate in the proceeding, and the Court may grant the request, with or without hearing, upon determining that the best interest of the alleged incapacitated person will be served thereby. The Court may attach appropriate conditions to the permission.

§ 5-304. [Notice in Guardianship Proceeding.]

(a) In a proceeding for the appointment of a guardian of an incapacitated person, and, if notice is required in a proceeding for appointment of a temporary guardian, notice of hearing must be given to each of the following:

(1) the person alleged to be incapacitated and spouse, or, if none, adult children, or if none, parents;

(2) any person who is serving as guardian, conservator, or who has the care and custody of the person alleged to be incapacitated;

(3) in case no other person is notified under paragraph (1), at least one of the nearest adult relatives, if any can be found; and

(4) any other person as directed by the Court.

(b) Notice of hearing on a petition for an order subsequent to appointment of a guardian must be given to the ward, the guardian and any other person as ordered by the Court.

(c) Notice must be served personally on the alleged incapacitated person. Notices to other persons as required by subsection (a)(1) must be served personally if the person to be notified can be found within the state. In all other cases, required notices must be given as provided in Section 1-401.

(d) The person alleged to be incapacitated may not waive notice.

§ 5-305. [Who May Be Guardian; Priorities.]

(a) Any qualified person may be appointed guardian of an incapacitated person.

(b) Unless lack of qualification or other good cause dictates the contrary, the Court shall appoint a guardian in accordance with the incapacitated person's most recent nomination in a durable power of attorney.

(c) Except as provided in subsection (b), the following are entitled to consideration for appointment in the order listed:

(1) the spouse of the incapacitated person or a person nominated by will of a deceased spouse or by other writing signed by the spouse and attested by at least 2 witnesses;

(2) an adult child of the incapacitated person;

(3) a parent of the incapacitated person, or a person nominated by will of a deceased parent or by other writing signed by a parent and attested by at least two witnesses;

(4) any relative of the incapacitated person with whom the person has resided for more than 6 months prior to the filing of the petition; and

(5) a person nominated by the person who is caring for or paying for the care of the incapacitated person.

(d) With respect to persons having equal priority, the Court shall select the one it deems best qualified to serve. The Court, acting in the best interest of the incapacitated person, may pass over a person having priority and appoint a person having a lower priority or no priority.

§ 5-306. [Findings; Order of Appointment.]

(a) The Court shall exercise the authority conferred in this Part so as to encourage the development of maximum self-reliance and independence of the incapacitated person and make appointive and other orders only to the extent necessitated by the incapacitated person's mental and adaptive limitations or other conditions warranting the procedure.

(b) The Court may appoint a guardian as requested if it is satisfied that the person for whom a guardian is sought is incapacitated and that the appointment is necessary or desirable as a means of providing continuing care and supervision of the person of the incapacitated person. The Court, on appropriate findings, may (i) treat the petition as one for a protective order under Section 5-401 and proceed accordingly, (ii) enter any other appropriate order, or (iii) dismiss the proceedings.

(c) The Court, at the time of appointment or later, on its own motion or on appropriate petition or motion of the incapacitated person or other interested person, may limit the powers of a guardian otherwise conferred by Parts 1, 2, 3 and 4 of this Article and thereby create a limited guardianship. Any limitation on the statutory power of a guardian of an incapacitated person must be endorsed on the guardian's letters or, in the case of a guardian by parental or spousal appointment, must be reflected in letters issued at the time any limitation is imposed. Following the same procedure, a limitation may be removed or modified and appropriate letters issued.

§ 5-307. [Acceptance of Appointment; Consent to Jurisdiction.]

By accepting appointment, a guardian submits personally to the jurisdiction of the Court in any proceeding relating to the guardianship that may be instituted by any interested person. Notice of any proceeding must be delivered or mailed to the guardian at the address listed in the Court records and at the address as then known to the petitioner.

§ 5-308. [Emergency Orders; Temporary Guardians.]

(a) If an incapacitated person has no guardian, an emergency exists, and no other person appears to have authority to act in the circumstances, on appropriate petition the Court may appoint a temporary guardian whose authority may not extend beyond [15 days] [the period of effectiveness of ex parte restraining orders], and who may exercise those powers granted in the order.

(b) If an appointed guardian is not effectively performing duties and the Court further finds that the welfare of the incapacitated person requires immediate action, it may appoint, with or without notice, a temporary guardian for the incapacitated person having the powers of a general guardian for a specified period not to exceed 6 months. The authority of any permanent guardian previously appointed by the Court is suspended as long as a temporary guardian has authority.

(c) The Court may remove a temporary guardian at any time. A temporary guardian shall make any report the Court requires. In other respects the provisions of Parts 1, 2, 3 and 4 of this Article concerning guardians apply to temporary guardians.

§ 5-309. [General Powers and Duties of Guardian.]

Except as limited pursuant to Section 5-306(c), a guardian of an incapacitated person is responsible for care, custody, and control of the ward, but is not liable to third persons by reason of that responsibility for acts of the ward. In particular and without qualifying the foregoing, a guardian has the same duties, powers and responsibilities as a guardian for a minor as described in Section 5-209(b), (c) and (d).

§ 5-310. [Termination of Guardianship for Incapacitated Person.]

The authority and responsibility of a guardian of an incapacitated person terminates upon the death of the guardian or ward, the determination of incapacity of the guardian, or upon removal or resignation as provided in Section 5-311. Testamentary appointment under an informally probated will terminates if the will is later denied probate in a formal proceeding. Termination does not affect a guardian's liability for prior acts or the obligation to account for funds and assets of the ward.

§ 5-311. [Removal or Resignation of Guardian; Termination of Incapacity.]

(a) On petition of the ward or any person interested in the ward's welfare, the Court, after hearing, may remove a guardian if in the best interest of the ward. On petition of the guardian, the Court, after hearing, may accept a resignation.

(b) An order adjudicating incapacity may specify a minimum period, not exceeding six months, during which a petition for an adjudication that the ward is no longer incapacitated may not be filed without special leave. Subject to that restriction, the ward or any person interested in the welfare of the ward may petition for an order that the ward is no longer incapacitated and for termination of the guardianship. A request for an order may also be made informally to the Court and any person who knowingly interferes with transmission of the request may be adjudged guilty of contempt of court.

(c) Upon removal, resignation, or death of the guardian, or if the guardian is determined to be incapacitated, the Court may appoint a successor guardian and make any other appropriate order. Before appointing a successor guardian, or ordering that a ward's incapacity has terminated, the Court shall follow the same procedures to safeguard the rights of the ward that apply to a petition for appointment of a guardian. As amended in 1987.

§ 5-312. [Proceedings Subsequent to Appointment; Venue.]

(a) The Court at the place where the ward resides has concurrent jurisdiction with the Court that appointed the guardian or in which acceptance of a parental or spousal appointment was filed over resignation, removal, accounting, and other proceedings relating to the guardianship, including proceedings to limit the authority previously conferred on a guardian or to remove limitations previously imposed.

(b) If the Court at the place where the ward resides is not the Court in which acceptance of appointment is filed, the Court in which proceedings subsequent to appointment are commenced, in all appropriate cases, shall notify the other Court, in this or another state, and after consultation with that Court determine whether to retain jurisdiction or transfer the proceedings to the other Court, whichever may be in the best interest of the ward. A copy of any order accepting a resignation, removing a guardian, or altering authority must be sent to the Court in which acceptance of appointment is filed.

Part 4
Protection of Property of Persons
Under Disability and Minors

§ 5-401. [Protective Proceedings.]

(a) Upon petition and after notice and hearing in accordance with the provisions of this Part, the Court may appoint a conservator or make any other protective order for cause as provided in this section.

(b) Appointment of a conservator or other protective order may be made in relation to the estate and affairs of a minor if the Court determines that a minor owns money or property requiring management or protection that cannot otherwise be provided or has or may have business affairs that may be jeopardized or prevented by minority, or that funds are needed for support and education and that protection is necessary or desirable to obtain or provide funds.

(c) Appointment of a conservator or other protective order may be made in relation to the estate and affairs of a person if the Court determines that (i) the person is unable to manage property and business affairs effectively for such reasons as mental illness, mental deficiency, physical illness or disability, chronic use of drugs, chronic intoxication, confinement, detention by a foreign power, or disappearance; and (ii) the person has property that will be wasted or dissipated unless property management is provided or money is needed for the support, care, and welfare of the person or those entitled to the person's support and that protection is necessary or desirable to obtain or provide money.

As amended in 1988.

§ 5-402. [Protective Proceedings; Jurisdiction of Business Affairs of Protected Persons.]

After the service of notice in a proceeding seeking the appointment of a conservator or other protective order and until termination of the proceeding, the Court in which the petition is filed has:

(1) exclusive jurisdiction to determine the need for a conservator or other protective order until the proceedings are terminated;

(2) exclusive jurisdiction to determine how the estate of the protected person which is subject to the laws of this State must be managed, expended, or distributed to or for the use of the protected person, the protected person's dependents, or other claimants; and

(3) concurrent jurisdiction to determine the validity of claims against the person or estate of the protected person and questions of title concerning any estate asset.

§ 5-403. [Venue.]

Venue for proceedings under this Part is:

(1) in the court at the place in this State where the person to be protected resides whether or not a guardian has been appointed in another place; or

(2) if the person to be protected does not reside in this State, in the Court at any place where property of the person is located.

§ 5-404. [Original Petition for Appointment or Protective Order.]

(a) The person to be protected or any person who is interested in the estate, affairs, or welfare of the person, including a parent, guardian, custodian, or any person who would be adversely affected by lack of effective management of the person's property and business affairs may petition for the appointment of a conservator or for other appropriate protective order.

(b) The petition must set forth to the extent known the interest of the petitioner; the name, age, residence, and address of the person to be protected; the name and address of the guardian, if any; the name and address of the nearest relative known to the petitioner; a general statement of the person's property with an estimate of the value thereof, including any compensation, insurance, pension, or allowance to which the person is entitled; and the reason why appointment of a conservator or other protective order is necessary. If the appointment of a conservator is requested, the petition must also set forth the name and address of the person whose appointment is sought and the basis of the claim to priority for appointment.

§ 5-405. [Notice.]

(a) On a petition for appointment of a conservator or other protective order, the requirements for notice described in Section 5-304 apply, but

(i) if the person to be protected has disappeared or is otherwise situated so as to make personal service of notice impracticable, notice to the person must be given by publication as provided in Section 1-401, and

(ii) if the person to be protected is a minor, the provisions of Section 5-206 also apply.

(b) Notice of hearing on a petition for an order subsequent to appointment of a conservator or other protective order must be given to the protected person, any conservator of the protected person's estate, and any other person as ordered by the Court.

§ 5-406. [Procedure Concerning Hearing and Order on Original Petition.]

(a) Upon receipt of a petition for appointment of a conservator or other protective order because of minority, the Court shall set a date for hearing. If the Court determines at any time in the proceeding that the interests of the minor are or may be inadequately represented, it may appoint an attorney to represent the minor, giving consideration to the choice of the minor if 14 or more years of age. An attorney appointed by the Court to represent a minor may be granted the powers and duties of a guardian ad litem.

(b) Upon receipt of a petition for appointment of a conservator or he other protective order for reasons other than minority, the Court shall set a date for hearing. Unless the person to be protected has chosen counsel, the Court shall appoint an attorney to represent the person who may be granted the powers and duties of a guardian ad litem. If the alleged disability is mental illness, mental deficiency, physical illness or disability, chronic use of drugs, or chronic intoxication, the Court may direct that the person to be protected be examined by a physician designated by the Court, preferably a physician who is not connected with any institution in which the person is a patient or is detained. The Court may send a visitor to interview the person to be protected. The visitor may be a guardian ad litem or an officer or employee of the Court.

(c) The Court may utilize, as an additional visitor, the service of any public or charitable agency to evaluate the condition of the person to be protected and make appropriate recommendations to the Court.

(d) The person to be protected is entitled to be present at the hearing in person. The person is entitled to be represented by counsel, to present evidence, to cross-examine witnesses, including any Court-appointed physician or other qualified person and any visitor [, and to trial by jury]. The issue may be determined at a closed hearing [or without a jury] if the person to be protected or counsel for the person so requests.

(e) Any person may apply for permission to participate in the proceeding and the Court may grant the request, with or without hearing, upon determining that the best interest of the person to be protected will be served thereby. The Court may attach appropriate conditions to the permission.

(f) After hearing, upon finding that a basis for the appointment of a conservator or other protective order has been established, the Court shall make an appointment or other appropriate protective order.

§ 5-407. [Permissible Court Orders.]

(a) The Court shall exercise the authority conferred in this Part to encourage the development of maximum self-reliance and independence of a protected person and make protective orders only to the extent necessitated by the protected person's mental and adaptive limitations and other conditions warranting the procedure.

(b) The Court has the following powers that may be exercised or through a conservator in respect to the estate and business affairs of a protected person:

(1) While a petition for appointment of a conservator or other protective order is pending and after preliminary hearing and without notice to others, the Court may preserve and apply the property of the person to be protected as may be required for the support of the person or dependents of the person.

(2) After hearing and upon determining that a basis for an appointment or other protective order exists with respect to a minor without other disability, the Court has all those powers over the estate and business affairs of the minor which are or may be necessary for the best interest of the minor and members of the minor's immediate family.

(3) After hearing and upon determining that a basis for an appointment or other protective order exists with respect to a person for reasons other than minority, the Court, for the benefit of the person and members of the person's immediate family, has all the powers over the estate and business affairs which the person could exercise if present and not under disability, except the power to make a will. Those powers include, but are not limited to, power to make gifts; to convey or release contingent and expectant interests in property, including marital property rights and any right of survivorship incident to

joint tenancy or tenancy by the entirety; to exercise or release powers held by the protected person as trustee, personal representative, custodian for minors, conservator, or donee of a power of appointment; to enter into contracts; to create revocable or irrevocable trusts of property of the estate which may extend beyond the disability or life of the protected person; to exercise options of the protected person to purchase securities or other property; to exercise rights to elect options and change beneficiaries under insurance and annuity policies and to surrender the policies for their cash value; to exercise any right to an elective share in the estate of the person's deceased spouse and to renounce or disclaim any interest by testate or intestate succession or by transfer.

(c) The Court may exercise or direct the exercise of the following powers only if satisfied, after notice and hearing, that it is in the best interest of the protected person, and that the person either is incapable of consenting or has consented to the proposed exercise of power:

(1) to exercise or release powers of appointment of which the protected person is donee;

(2) to renounce or disclaim interests;

(3) to make gifts in trust or otherwise exceeding 20 percent of any year's income of the estate; and

(4) to change beneficiaries under insurance and annuity policies.

(d) A determination that a basis for appointment of a conservator or other protective order exists has no effect on the capacity of the protected person.

§ 5-408. [Protective Arrangements and Single Transactions Authorized.]

(a) If it is established in a proper proceeding that a basis exists as described in Section 5-401 for affecting the property and business affairs of a person, the Court, without appointing a conservator, may authorize, direct or ratify any transaction necessary or desirable to achieve any security, service, or care arrangement meeting the foreseeable needs of the protected person. Protective arrangements include payment, delivery, deposit, or retention of funds or property; sale, mortgage, lease, or other transfer of property; entry into an annuity contract, a contract for life care, a deposit contract or a contract for training and education; or addition to or establishment of a suitable trust.

(b) If it is established in a proper proceeding that a basis exists as described in Section 5-401 for affecting the property and business affairs of a person, the Court, without appointing a conservator, may authorize, direct, or ratify any contract, trust, or other transaction relating to the protected person's property and business affairs if the Court determines that the transaction is in the best interest of the protected person.

(c) Before approving a protective arrangement or other transaction under this section, the Court shall consider the interests of creditors and dependents of the protected person and, in view of the disability, whether the protected person needs the continuing protection of a conservator. The Court may appoint a special conservator to assist in the accomplishment of any protective arrangement or other transaction authorized under this section who shall have the authority conferred by the order and serve until discharged by order after report to the Court of all matters done pursuant to the order of appointment.

§ 5-409. [Who May Be Appointed Conservator; Priorities.]

(a) The Court may appoint an individual or a corporation with general power to serve as trustee or conservator of the estate of a protected person. The following are entitled to consideration for appointment in the order listed:

(1) a conservator, guardian of property, or like other fiduciary appointed or recognized by an appropriate court of any other jurisdiction in which the protected person resides;

(2) an individual or corporation nominated by the protected person 14 or more years of age and of sufficient mental capacity to make an intelligent choice;

(3) the spouse of the protected person;

(4) an adult child of the protected person;

(5) a parent of the protected person, or a person nominated by the will of a deceased parent;

(6) any relative of the protected person who has resided with the protected person for more than 6 months before the filing of the petition; and

(7) a person nominated by one who is caring for or paying benefits to the protected person.

(b) A person in priorities (1), (3), (4), (5), or (6) may designate in writing a substitute to serve instead and thereby transfer the priority to the substitute. With respect to persons having equal priority, the Court shall select the one it deems best qualified to serve. The Court, acting in the best interest of the protected person, may pass over a person having priority and appoint a person having a lower priority or no priority.

§ 5-410. [Bond.]

The Court may require a conservator to furnish a bond conditioned upon faithful discharge of all duties of the trust according to law, with sureties it shall specify. Unless otherwise directed, the bond must be in the amount of the aggregate capital value of the property of the estate in the conservator's control, plus one year's estimated income, and minus the value of securities deposited under arrangements requiring an order of Court for their removal and the value of any land which the fiduciary, by express limitation of power, lacks power to sell or convey without Court authorization. The Court, in lieu of sureties on a bond, may accept other collateral for the performance of the bond, including a pledge of securities or a mortgage of land.

§ 5-411. [Terms and Requirements of Bonds.]

(a) The following requirements and provisions apply to any bond required under Section 5-410.

(1) Unless otherwise provided by the terms of the approved bond, sureties are jointly and severally liable with the conservator and with each other.

(2) By executing an approved bond of a conservator, the surety consents to the jurisdiction of the Court that issued letters to the primary obligor in any proceeding pertaining to the fiduciary duties of the conservator and naming the surety as a party respondent. Notice of any proceeding must be delivered to the surety or mailed by registered or certified mail to the address listed with the Court at the place where the bond is filed and to the address as then known to the petitioner.

(3) On petition of a successor conservator or any interested person, a proceeding may be initiated against a surety for breach of the obligation of the bond of the conservator.

(4) The bond of the conservator is not void after the first recovery but may be proceeded against from time to time until the whole penalty is exhausted.

(b) No proceeding may be commenced against the surety on any matter as to which an action or proceeding against the primary obligor is barred by adjudication or limitation.

§ 5-412. [Effect of Acceptance of Appointment.]

By accepting appointment, a conservator submits personally to the jurisdiction of the Court in any proceeding relating to the estate which may be instituted by any interested person. Notice of any proceeding must be delivered to the conservator or mailed by registered or certified mail to the address as listed in the petition for appointment or as thereafter reported to the Court and to the address as then known to the petitioner.

§ 5-413. [Compensation and Expenses.]

If not otherwise compensated for services rendered, any visitor, attorney, physician, conservator, or special conservator appointed in a protective proceeding and any attorney whose services resulted in a protective order or in an order that was beneficial to a protected person's estate is entitled to reasonable compensation from the estate.

§ 5-414. [Death, Resignation, or Removal of Conservator.]

The Court may remove a conservator for good cause, upon notice and hearing, or accept the resignation of a conservator. Upon the conservator's death, resignation, or removal, the Court may appoint another conservator. A conservator so appointed succeeds to the title and powers of the predecessor.

§ § 5-415. [Petitions for Orders Subsequent to Appointment.]

(a) Any person interested in the welfare of a person for whom a conservator has been appointed may file a petition in the appointing court for an order:

(1) requiring bond or collateral or additional bond or collateral, or reducing bond;

(2) requiring an accounting for the administration of the trust;

(3) directing distribution;

(4) removing the conservator and appointing a temporary or successor conservator; or

(5) granting other appropriate relief:

(b) A conservator may petition the appointing court for instructions concerning fiduciary responsibility.

(c) Upon notice and hearing, the Court may give appropriate instructions or make any appropriate order.

§ 5-416. [General Duty of Conservator.]

A conservator, in relation to powers conferred by this Part, or implicit in the title acquired by virtue of the proceeding, shall act as a fiduciary and observe the standards of care applicable to trustees.

§ 5-417. [Inventory and Records.]

(a) Within 90 days after appointment, each conservator shall prepare and file with the appointing Court a complete inventory of the estate subject to the conservatorship together with an oath or affirmation that the inventory is believed to be complete and accurate as far as information permits. The conservator shall provide a copy thereof to the protected person if practicable and the person has attained the age of 14 years and has sufficient mental capacity to understand the arrangement. A copy also shall be provided to any guardian or parent with whom the protected person resides.

(b) The conservator shall keep suitable records of the administration and exhibit the same on request of any interested person.

§ 5-418. [Accounts.]

Each conservator shall account to the Court for administration of the trust not less than annually unless the Court directs otherwise, upon resignation or removal and at other times as the Court may direct. On termination of the protected person's minority or disability, a conservator shall account to the Court or to the formerly protected person or the successors of that person. Subject to appeal or vacation within the time permitted, an order after notice and hearing allowing an intermediate account of a conservator adjudicates as to liabilities concerning the matters considered in connection therewith; and an order, following notice and hearing, allowing a final account adjudicates as to all previously unsettled liabilities of the conservator to the protected person or the protected person's successors relating to the conservatorship. In connection with any account, the Court may require a conservator to submit to a physical check of the estate, to be made in any manner the Court specifies.

As amended in 1987.

§ 5-419. [Conservators; Title by Appointment.]

(a) The appointment of a conservator vests in the conservator title as trustee to all property, or to the part thereof specified in the order, of the protected person, presently held or thereafter acquired, including title to any property theretofore held for the protected person by custodians or attorneys-in-fact. An order specifying that only a part of the property of the protected person vests in the conservator creates a limited conservatorship.

(b) Except as otherwise provided herein, the interest of the protected person in property vested in a conservator by this section is not transferable or assignable by the protected person. An attempted transfer or assignment by the protected person, though ineffective to affect property rights, may generate a claim for restitution or damages which, subject to presentation and allowance, may be satisfied as provided in Section 5-427.

(c) Neither property vested in a conservator by this section nor the interest of the protected person in that property is subject to levy, garnishment, or similar process other than an order issued in the protective proceeding made as provided in Section 5-427.

§ 5-420. [Recording of Conservator's Letters.]

(a) Letters of conservatorship are evidence of transfer of all assets, or the part thereof specified in the letters, of a protected person to the conservator. An order terminating a conservatorship is evidence of transfer of all assets subjected to the conservatorship from the conservator to the protected person, or to successors of the person.

(b) Subject to the requirements of general statutes governing the filing or recordation of documents of title to land or other property, letters of conservatorship and orders terminating conservatorships, may be filed or recorded to give record notice of title as between the conservator and the protected person.

§ 5-421. [Sale, Encumbrance, or Transaction Involving Conflict of Interest; Voidable; Exceptions.]

Any sale or encumbrance to a conservator, the spouse, agent, attorney of a conservator, or any corporation, trust, or other organization in which the conservator has a substantial beneficial interest, or any other transaction involving the estate being administered by the conservator which is affected by a substantial conflict between fiduciary and personal interests is voidable unless the transaction is approved by the Court after notice as directed by the Court.

§ 5-422. [Persons Dealing with Conservators; Protection.]

(a) A person who in good faith either assists or deals with a conservator for value in any transaction other than those requiring a Court order as provided in Section 5-407 is protected as if the conservator properly exercised the power. The fact that a person knowingly deals with a conservator does not alone require the person to inquire into the existence of a power or the propriety of its exercise, but restrictions on powers of conservators which are endorsed on letters as provided in Section 5-425 are effective as to third persons. A person is not bound to see the proper application of estate assets paid or delivered to a conservator.

(b) The protection expressed in this section extends to any procedural irregularity or jurisdictional defect occurred in proceedings leading to the issuance of letters and is not a substitution for protection provided by comparable provisions of the law relating to commercial transactions or to simplifying transfers of securities by fiduciaries.

§ 5-423. [Powers of Conservator in Administration.]

(a) Subject to limitation provided in Section 5-425, a conservator has all of the powers conferred in this section and any additional powers conferred by law on trustees in this State. In addition, a conservator of the estate of an unmarried minor [under the age of 18 years], as to whom no one has parental rights, has the duties and powers of a guardian of a minor described in Section 5-209 until the minor attains [the age of 18 years] or marries, but the parental rights so conferred on a conservator do not preclude appointment of a guardian as provided in Part 2.

(b) A conservator without Court authorization or confirmation, may invest and reinvest funds of the estate as would a trustee.

(c) A conservator, acting reasonably in efforts to accomplish the purpose of the appointment, may act without Court authorization or confirmation, to

(1) collect, hold, and retain assets of the estate including land in another state, until judging that disposition of the assets should be made, and the assets may be retained even though they include an asset in which the conservator is personally interested;

(2) receive additions to the estate;

(3) continue or participate in the operation of any business or other enterprise;

(4) acquire an undivided interest in an estate asset in which the conservator, in any fiduciary capacity, holds an undivided interest;

(5) invest and reinvest estate assets in accordance with subsection (b);

(6) deposit estate funds in a state or federally insured financial institution, including one operated by the conservator;

(7) acquire or dispose of an estate asset, including land in another state, for cash or on credit, at public or private sale, and manage, develop, improve, exchange, partition, change the character of, or abandon an estate asset;

(8) make ordinary or extraordinary repairs or alterations in buildings or other structures; demolish any improvements; and raze existing or erect new party walls or buildings;

(9) subdivide, develop, or dedicate land to public use; make or obtain the vacation of plats and adjust boundaries; adjust differences in valuation or exchange or partition by giving or receiving considerations; and dedicate easements to public use without consideration;

(10) enter for any purpose into a lease as lessor or lessee with or without option to purchase or renew for a term within or extending beyond the term of the conservatorship;

(11) enter into a lease or arrangement for exploration and removal of minerals or other natural resources or enter into a pooling or unitization agreement;

(12) grant an option involving disposition of an estate asset and take an option for the acquisition of any asset;

(13) vote a security, in person or by general or limited proxy;

(14) pay calls, assessments, and any other sums chargeable or accruing against or on account of securities;

(15) sell or exercise stock-subscription or conversion rights;

(16) consent, directly or through a committee or other agent, to the reorganization, consolidation, merger, dissolution, or liquidation of a corporation or other business enterprise;

(17) hold a security in the name of a nominee or in other form without disclosure of the conservatorship so that title to the security may pass by delivery, but the conservator is liable for any act of the nominee in connection with the stock so held;

(18) insure the assets of the estate against damage or loss and the conservator against liability with respect to third persons;

(19) borrow money to be repaid from estate assets or otherwise; advance money for the protection of the estate or the protected person and for all expenses, losses, and liability sustained in the administration of the estate or because of the holding or ownership of any estate assets, for which the conservator has a lien on the estate as against the protected person for advances so made;

(20) pay or contest any claim; settle a claim by or against the estate or the protected person by compromise, arbitration, or otherwise; and release, in whole or in part, any claim belonging to the estate to the extent the claim is uncollectible;

(21) pay taxes, assessments, compensation of the conservator, and other expenses incurred in the collection, care, administration, and protection of the estate;

(22) allocate items of income or expense to either state income or principal, as provided by law, including creation of reserves out of income for depreciation, obsolescence, or amortization, or for depletion in mineral or timber properties;

(23) pay any sum distributable to a protected person or dependent of the protected person by paying the sum to the distributee or by paying the sum for the use of the distributee to the guardian of the distributee, or, if none, to a relative or other person having custody of the distributee;

(24) employ persons, including attorneys, auditors, investment advisors, or agents, even though they are associated with the conservator, to advise or assist in the performance of administrative duties; act upon their recommendation without independent investigation; and instead of acting personally, employ one or more agents to perform any act of administration, whether or not discretionary;

(25) prosecute or defend actions, claims, or proceedings in any jurisdiction for the protection of estate assets and of the conservator in the performance of fiduciary duties; and

(26) execute and deliver all instruments that will accomplish or facilitate the exercise of the powers vested in the conservator.

§ 5-424. [Distributive Duties and Powers of Conservator.]

(a) A conservator may expend or distribute income or principal of the estate without Court authorization or confirmation for the support, education, care, or benefit of the protected person and dependents in accordance with the following principles:

(1) The conservator shall consider recommendations relating to the appropriate standard of support, education, and benefit for the protected person or dependent made by a parent or guardian, if any. The conservator may not be surcharged for sums paid to persons or organizations furnishing support, education, or care to the protected person or a dependent pursuant to the recommendations of a parent or guardian of the protected person unless the conservator knows that the parent or guardian derives personal financial benefit therefrom, including relief from any personal duty of support or the recommendations are clearly not in the best interest of the protected person.

(2) The conservator shall expend or distribute sums reasonably necessary for the support, education, care, or benefit of the protected person and dependents with due regard to (i) the size of the estate, the probable duration of the conservatorship), and the likelihood that the protected person, at some future time, may be fully able to be wholly self-sufficient and able to manage business affairs and the estate; (ii) the accustomed standard of living of the protected person and dependents; and (iii) other funds or sources used for the support of the protected person.

(3) The conservator may expend funds of the estate for the support of persons legally dependent on the protected person and others who are members of the protected person's household who are unable to support themselves, and who are in need of support.

(4) Funds expended under this subsection may be paid by the conservator to any person, including the protected person, to reimburse for expenditures that the conservator might have made, or in advance for services to be rendered to the protected person if it is reasonable to expect the services will be performed and advance payments are customary or reasonably necessary under the circumstances.

(5) A conservator, in discharging the responsibilities conferred by Court order and this Part, shall implement the principles described in Section 5-407(a), to the extent possible.

(b) If the estate is ample to provide for the purposes implicit in the distributions authorized by the preceding subsections, a conservator for a protected person other than a minor has power to make gifts to charity and other objects as the protected person might have been expected to make, in amounts that do not exceed in total for any year 20 percent of the income from the estate.

(c) When a minor who has not been adjudged disabled under Section 5-401(c) attains majority, the conservator, after meeting all claims and expenses of administration, shall pay over and distribute all funds and properties to the formerly protected person as soon as possible.

(d) If satisfied that a protected person's disability, other than minority, has ceased, the conservator, after meeting all claims and expenses of administration, shall pay over and distribute all funds and properties to the formerly protected person as soon as possible.

(e) If a protected person dies, the conservator shall deliver to the Court for safekeeping any will of the deceased protected person which may have come into the conservator's possession, inform the executor or beneficiary named therein of the delivery, and retain the estate for delivery to a duly appointed personal representative of the decedent or other persons entitled thereto. If, 40 days after the death of the protected person, no other person has been appointed personal representative and no application or petition for appointment is before the Court, the conservator may apply to exercise the powers and duties of a personal representative in order to be able to proceed to administer and distribute the decedent's estate. Upon application for an order granting the powers of a personal representative to a conservator, after notice to any person nominated personal representative by any will of which the applicant is aware, the Court may grant the application upon determining that there is no objection and endorse the letters of the conservator to note that the formerly protected person is deceased and that the conservator has acquired all of the powers and duties of a personal representative. The making and entry of an order under this section has the effect of an order of appointment of a personal representative [as provided in Section 3-308 and Parts 6 through 10 of Article III], but the estate in the name of the conservator, after administration, may be distributed to the decedent's successors without prior re-transfer to the conservator as personal representative.

§ 5-425. [Enlargement or Limitation of Powers of Conservator.]

Subject the restrictions in Section 5-407(c), the Court may confer on a conservator at the time of appointment or later, in addition to the powers conferred by Sections 5-423 and 5-424, any power that the Court itself could exercise under Sections 5-407(b)(2) and 5-407(b)(3). The Court, at the time of appointment or later, may limit the powers of a conservator otherwise conferred by Sections 5-423 and 5-424 or previously conferred by the Court and may at any time remove or modify any limitation. If the Court limits any power conferred on the conservator by Section 5-423 or Section 5-424, or specifies, as provided in Section 5-419(a), that title to some but not all assets of the protected person vest in the conservator, the limitation or specification of assets subject to the conservatorship must be endorsed upon the letters of appointment.

§ 5-426. [Preservation of Estate Plan; Right to Examine.]

In (i) investing the estate, (ii) selecting assets of the estate for distribution under subsections (a) and (b) of Section 5-424, and (iii) utilizing powers of revocation or withdrawal available for the support of the protected person and exercisable by the conservator or the Court, the conservator and the Court shall take into account any estate plan of the protected person known to them, including a will, any revocable trust of which the person is settlor, and any contract, transfer, or joint ownership arrangement originated by the protected person with provisions for payment or transfer of benefits or interests at the person's death to another or others. The conservator may examine the will of the protected person.

§ 5-427. [Claims Against Protected Person; Enforcement.]

(a) A conservator may pay or secure from the estate claims against the estate or against the protected person arising before or after the conservatorship upon their presentation and allowance in accordance with the priorities stated in subsection (c). A claim may be presented by either of the following methods:

(1) The claimant may deliver or mail to the conservator a written statement of the claim indicating its basis, the name and mailing address of the claimant, and the amount claimed; or

(2) The claimant may file a written statement of the claim, in the form prescribed by rule, with the clerk of Court and deliver or mail a copy of the statement to the conservator.

(b) A claim is deemed presented on the first to occur of receipt of the written statement of claim by the conservator or the filing of the claim with the Court. A presented claim is allowed if it is not disallowed by written statement mailed by the conservator to the claimant within 60 days after its presentation. The presentation of a claim tolls any statute of limitation relating to the claim until 30 days after its disallowance.

(c) A claimant whose claim has not been paid may petition the [appropriate] Court for determination of the claim at any time before it is barred by the applicable statute of limitation and, upon due proof, procure an order for its allowance, payment, or security from the estate. If a proceeding is pending against a protected person at the time of appointment of a conservator or is initiated against the protected person thereafter, the moving party shall give notice of the proceeding to the conservator if the proceeding could result in creating a claim against the estate.

(d) If it appears that the estate in conservatorship is likely to be exhausted before all existing claims are paid, the conservator shall distribute the estate in money or in kind in payment of claims in the following order:

(1) costs and expenses of administration;

(2) claims of the federal or state government having priority under other laws;

(3) claims incurred by the conservator for care, maintenance, and education, previously provided to the protected person or the protected person's dependents;

(4) claims arising prior to the conservatorship;

(5) all other claims.

(e) No preference may be given in the payment of any claim over any other claim of the same class, and a claim due and payable is not entitled to a preference over claims not due; but if it appears that the assets of the conservatorship are adequate to meet all existing claims, the Court, acting in the best interest of the protected person, may order the conservator to give a mortgage or other security on the conservatorship estate to secure payment at some future date of any or all claims in class 5.

§ 5-428. [Personal Liability of Conservator.]

(a) Unless otherwise provided in the contract, a conservator is not personally liable on a contract properly entered into in fiduciary capacity in the course of administration of the estate unless the conservator fails to reveal the representative capacity and identify the estate in the contract.

(b) The conservator is personally liable for obligations arising from ownership or control of property of the estate or for torts committed in the course of administration of the estate only if personally at fault.

(c) Claims based on (i) contracts entered into by a conservator in fiduciary capacity, (ii) obligations arising from ownership or control of the estate, or (iii) torts committed in the course of administration of the estate, may be asserted against the estate by proceeding against the conservator in fiduciary capacity, whether or not the conservator is personally liable therefor.

(d) Any question of liability between the estate and the conservator personally may be determined in a proceeding for accounting, surcharge, or indemnification, or other appropriate proceeding or action.

§ 5-429. [Termination of Proceedings.]

The protected person, conservator, or any other interested person, may petition the Court to terminate the conservatorship. A protected person seeking termination is entitled to the same rights and procedures as in an original proceeding for a protective order. The Court, upon determining after notice and hearing that the minority or disability of the protected person has ceased, shall terminate the conservatorship. Upon termination, title to assets of the estate passes to the formerly protected person or to successors. The order of termination must provide for expenses of administration and direct the conservator to execute appropriate instruments to evidence the transfer.

§ 5-430. [Payment of Debt and Delivery of Property to Foreign Conservator without Local Proceedings.]

(a) Any person indebted to a protected person or having possession of property or of an instrument evidencing a debt, stock, or chose in action belonging to a protected person may pay or deliver it to a conservator, guardian of the estate, or other like fiduciary appointed by a court of the state of residence of the protected person upon being presented with proof of appointment and an affidavit made by or on behalf of the fiduciary stating:

(1) that no protective proceeding relating to the protected person is pending in this State; and

(2) that the foreign fiduciary is entitled to payment or to receive delivery.

(b) If the person to whom the affidavit is presented is not aware of any protective proceeding pending in this State, payment or delivery in response to the demand and affidavit discharges the debtor or possessor.

§ 5-431. [Foreign Conservator; Proof of Authority; Bond; Powers.]

If a conservator has not been appointed in this State and no petition in a protective proceeding is pending in this State, a conservator appointed in the state in which the protected person resides may file in a Court of this State in a [county] in which property belonging to the protected person is located, authenticated copies of letters of appointment and of any bond. Thereafter, the domiciliary foreign conservator may exercise as to assets in this State all powers of a conservator appointed in this State and may maintain actions and proceedings in this State subject to any conditions imposed upon non-resident parties generally.

Part 5
Durable Power of Attorney

§ 5-501. [Definition.]

A durable power of attorney is a power of attorney by which a principal designates another his attorney in fact in writing and the writing contains the words "This power of attorney shall not be affected by subsequent disability or incapacity of the principal, or lapse of time," or "This power of attorney shall become effective upon the disability or incapacity of the principal," or similar words showing the intent of the principal that the authority conferred shall be exercisable notwithstanding the principal's subsequent disability or incapacity, and, unless it states a time of termination, not withstanding the lapse of time since the execution of the instrument.

As amended in 1984.

§ 5-502. [Durable Power of Attorney Not Affected by Lapse of Time, Disability or Incapacity.]

All acts done by an attorney in fact pursuant to a durable power of attorney during any period of disability or incapacity of the principal have the same effect and inure to the benefit of and bind the principal and his successors in interest as if the principal were competent and not disabled. Unless the instrument states a time of termination, the power is exercisable notwithstanding the lapse of time since the execution of the instrument.

As amended in 1987.

§ 5-503. [Relation of Attorney in Fact to Court-appointed Fiduciary.]

(a) If, following execution of a durable power of attorney, a court of the principal's domicile appoints a conservator, guardian of the estate, or other fiduciary charged with the management of all of the principal's property or all of his property except specified exclusions, the attorney in fact is accountable to the fiduciary as well as to the principal. The fiduciary has the same power to revoke or amend the power of attorney that the principal would have had if he were not disabled or incapacitated.

(b) A principal may nominate, by a durable power of attorney, the conservator, guardian of his estate, or guardian of his person for consideration by the court if protective proceedings for the principal's person or estate are thereafter commenced. The court shall make its appointment in accordance with the principal's most recent nomination in a durable power of attorney except for good cause or disqualification.

§ 5-504. [Power of Attorney Not Revoked Until Notice.]

(a) The death of a principal who has executed a written power of attorney, durable or otherwise, does not revoke or terminate the agency as to the attorney in fact or other person, who, without actual knowledge of the death of the principal, acts in good faith under the power. Any action so taken, unless otherwise invalid or unenforceable, binds successors in interest of the principal.

(b) The disability or incapacity of a principal who has previously executed a written power of attorney that is not a durable power does not revoke or terminate the agency as to the attorney in fact or other person, who, without actual knowledge of the disability or incapacity of the principal, acts in good faith under the power. Any action so taken, unless otherwise invalid or unenforceable, binds the principal and his successors in interest.

§ 5-505. [Proof of Continuance of Durable and Other Powers of Attorney by Affidavit.]

As to acts undertaken in good faith reliance thereon, an affidavit executed by the attorney in fact under a power of attorney, durable or otherwise, stating that he did not have at the time of exercise of the power actual knowledge of the termination of the power by revocation or of the principal's death, disability, or incapacity is conclusive proof of the non-revocation or nontermination of the power at that time. If the exercise of the power of attorney requires execution and delivery of any instrument that is recordable, the affidavit when authenticated for record is likewise recordable. This section does not affect any provision in a power of attorney for its termination by expiration of time or occurrence of an event other than express revocation or a change in the principal's capacity.

ARTICLE VI
NONPROBATE TRANSFERS ON DEATH

(The original Article reproduced here was revised in 1989. The revised version has been adopted by Arizona, Colorado, Florida, Montana, Nebraska, New Mexico, and North Dakota.)

Part 1
Provisions Relating to Effect of Death

§ 6-101. [Nonprobate Transfers on Death.]

(a) A provision for a nonprobate transfer on death in an insurance policy, contract of employment, bond, mortgage, promissory note, certificated or uncertificated security, account agreement, custodial agreement, deposit agreement, compensation plan, pension plan, individual retirement plan, employee benefit plan, trust, conveyance, deed of gift, marital property agreement, or other written instrument of a similar nature is nontestamentary. This subsection includes a written provision that:

(1) money or other benefits due to, controlled by, or owned by a decedent before death must be paid after the decedent's death to a person whom the decedent designates either in the instrument or in a separate writing, including a will, executed either before or at the same time as the instrument, or later;

(2) money due or to become due under the instrument ceases to be payable in the event of death of the promisee or the promisor before payment or demand; or

(3) any property controlled by or owned by the decedent before death which is the subject of the instrument passes to a person the decedent designates either in the instrument or in a separate writing, including a will, executed either before or at the same time as the instrument, or later.

(b) This section does not limit rights of creditors under other laws of this State.

Part 2
Multiple-Person Accounts

SUBPART 1
DEFINITIONS AND
GENERAL PROVISIONS

§ 6-201. [Definitions.]

In this part:

(1) "Account" means a contract of deposit between a depositor and a financial institution, and includes a checking account, savings account, certificate of deposit, and share account.

(2) "Agent" means a person authorized to make account transactions for a party.

(3) "Beneficiary" means a person named as one to whom sums on deposit in an account are payable on request after death of all parties or for whom a party is named as trustee.

(4) "Financial institution" means an organization authorized to do business under state or federal laws relating to financial institutions, and includes a bank, trust company, savings bank, building and loan association, savings and loan company or association, and credit union.

(5) "Multiple-party account" means an account payable on request to one or more of two or more parties, whether or not a right of survivorship is mentioned.

(6) "Party" means a person who, by the terms of an account, has a present right, subject to request, to payment from the account rather than as a beneficiary or agent.

(7) "Payment" of sums on deposit includes withdrawal, payment to a party or third person pursuant to check or other request, and a pledge of sums on deposit by a party, or a set-off, reduction, or other disposition of all or part of all account pursuant to a pledge.

(8) "POD designation" means the designation of (i) a beneficiary in an account payable on request to one party during the party's lifetime and on the party's death to one or more beneficiaries, or to one or more parties during their lifetimes and on death of all of them to one or more beneficiaries, or (ii) a beneficiary in an account in the name of one or more parties as trustee for one or more beneficiaries if the relationship is established by the terms of the account and there is no subject of the trust other than the sums on deposit in the account, whether or not payment to the beneficiary is mentioned.

(9) "Receive," as it relates to notice to a financial institution, means receipt in the office or branch office of the financial institution in which the account is established, but if the terms of the account require notice at a particular place, in the place required.

(10) "Request" means a request for payment complying with all terms of the account, including special requirements concerning necessary signatures and regulations of the financial institution; but, for purposes of this part, if terms of the account condition payment on advance notice, a request for payment is treated as immediately effective and a notice of intent to withdraw is treated as a request for payment.

(11) "Sums on deposit" means the balance payable on on account, including interest and dividends earned, whether or not included in the current balance, and any deposit life insurance proceeds added to the account by reason of death of a party.

(12) "Terms of the account" includes the deposit agreement and other terms and conditions, including the form, of the contract of deposit.

§ 6-202. [Limitation on Scope of Part.]

This part does not apply to (i) an account established for a partnership, joint venture, or other organization for a business purpose, (ii) an account controlled by one or more persons as an agent or trustee for a corporation, unincorporated association, or charitable or civic organization, or (iii) a fiduciary or trust account in which the relationship is established other than by the terms of the account.

§ 6-203. [Types of Account; Existing Accounts.]

(a) An account may be for a single party or multiple parties. A multiple-party account may be with or without a right of survivorship between the parties. Subject to Section 6-212(c), either a single-party account or a multiple-party account may have a POD designation, an agency designation, or both.

(b) An account established before, on, or after the effective date of this part, whether in the form prescribed in Section 6-204 or in any other form, is either a single-party account or a multiple-party account, with or without right of survivorship, and with or without a POD designation or an agency designation, within the meaning of this part, and is governed by this part.

§ 6-204. [Forms.]

(a) A contract of deposit that contains provisions in substantially the following form establishes the type of account provided, and the account is governed by the provisions of this part applicable to an account of that type:

UNIFORM SINGLE- OR MULTIPLE-PARTY ACCOUNT FORM

PARTIES [Name One or More Parties]:

—————————————   —————————————

OWNERSHIP [Select One and Initial]:

————   SINGLE-PARTY ACCOUNT

————   MULTIPLE-PARTY ACCOUNT

Parties own account in proportion to net contributions unless there is clear and convincing evidence of a different intent.

RIGHTS AT DEATH [Select One and Initial]:

————   SINGLE-PARTY ACCOUNT

At death of party, ownership passes as part of party's estate.

————   SINGLE-PARTY ACCOUNT WITH POD (PAY ON DEATH) DESIGNATION

[Name one Or More Beneficiaries]:

—————————————   —————————————

At death of party, ownership passes to POD beneficiaries and is not part of party's estate.

————   MULTIPLE-PARTY ACCOUNT WITH RIGHT OF SURVIVORSHIP

At death of party, ownership passes to surviving parties.

————   MULTIPLE-PARTY ACCOUNT WITH RIGHT OF SURVIVORSHIP AND POD (PAY ON DEATH) DESIGNATION

[Name One or More Beneficiaries]:

—————————————   —————————————

At death of last surviving party, owner-ship passes to POD beneficiaries and is not part of last surviving party's estate.

————   MULTIPLE-PARTY ACCOUNT WITHOUT RIGHT OF SURVIVORSHIP

At death of party, deceased party's ownership passes as part of deceased party's estate.

AGENCY (POWER OF ATTORNEY) DESIGNATION [Optional]

Agents may make account transactions for parties but have no ownership or rights at death unless named as POD beneficiaries.

[To Add Agency Designation To Account, Name One or More Agents]:

—————————————   —————————————

[Select One And Initial]:

————   AGENCY DESIGNATION SURVIVES DISABILITY OR INCAPACITY OF PARTIES

————   AGENCY DESIGNATION TERMINATES ON DISABILITY OR INCAPACITY OF PARTIES

(b) A contract of deposit that does not contain provisions in substantially the form provided in subsection (a) is governed by the provisions of this part applicable to the type of account that most nearly conforms to the depositor's intent.

§ 6-205. [Designation of Agent.]

(a) By a writing signed by all parties, the parties may designate as agent of all parties on an account a person other than a party.

(b) Unless the terms of an agency designation provide that the authority of the agent terminates on disability or incapacity of a party, the agent's authority survives disability and incapacity. The agent may act for a disabled or incapacitated party until the authority of the agent is terminated.

(c) Death of the sole party or last surviving party terminates the authority of an agent.

§ 6-206. [Applicability of Part.]

The provisions of Subpart 2 concerning beneficial ownership as between parties or as between parties and beneficiaries apply only to controversies between those persons and their creditors and other successors, and do not apply to the right of those persons to payment as determined by the terms of the account. Subpart 3 governs the liability and set-off rights of financial institutions that make payments pursuant to it.

SUBPART 2
OWNERSHIP AS BETWEEN PARTIES AND OTHERS

§ 6-211. [Ownership During Lifetime.]

(a) In this section, "net contribution" of a party means the sum of all deposits to an account made by or for the party, less all payments from the account made to or for the party which have not been paid to or applied to the use of another party and a proportionate share of any charges deducted from the account, plus a proportionate share of any interest or dividends earned, whether or not included in the current balance. The term includes deposit life insurance proceeds added to the account by reason of death of the party whose net contribution is in question.

(b) During the lifetime of all parties, an account belongs to the parties in proportion to the net contribution of each to the sums on deposit, unless there is clear and convincing evidence of a different intent. As between parties married to each other, in the absence of proof otherwise, the net contribution of each is presumed to be an equal amount.

(c) A beneficiary in an account having a POD designation has no right to sums on deposit during the lifetime of any party.

(d) An agent in an account with an agency designation has no beneficial right to sums on deposit.

§ 6-212. [Rights at Death.]

(a) Except as otherwise provided in this section, on death of a party sums on deposit in a multiple-party account belong to the surviving party or parties. If two or more parties survive and one is the surviving spouse of the decedent, the amount to which the decedent, immediately before death, was beneficially entitled under Section 6-211 belongs to the surviving spouse. If two or more parties survive and none is the surviving spouse of the decedent, the amount to which the decedent, immediately before death, was beneficially entitled under Section 6-211 belongs to the surviving parties in equal shares, and augments the proportion to which each survivor, immediately before the decedent's death, was beneficially entitled under Section 6-211, and the right of survivorship continues between the surviving parties.

(b) In an account with a POD designation:

(1) On death of one of two or more parties, the rights in sums on deposit are governed by ubsection (a).

(2) On death of the sole party or the last survivor of two or more parties, sums on deposit belong to the surviving beneficiary or beneficiaries. If two or more beneficiaries survive, sums on deposit belong to them in equal and undivided shares, and there is no right of survivorship in the event of death of a beneficiary thereafter. If no beneficiary survives, sums on deposit belong to the estate of the last surviving party.

(c) Sums on deposit in a single-party account without a POD designation, or in a multiple-party account that, by the terms of the account, is without right of survivorship, are not affected by death of a party, but the amount to which the decedent, immediately before death, was beneficially entitled under Section 6-211 is transferred as part of the decedent's estate. A POD designation in a multiple-party account without right of survivorship is ineffective. For purposes of this section, designation of an account as a tenancy in common establishes that the account is without right of survivorship.

(d) The ownership right of a surviving party or beneficiary, or of the decedent's estate, in sums on deposit is subject to requests for payment made by a party before the party's death, whether paid by the financial institution before or after death, or unpaid. The surviving party or beneficiary, or the decedent's estate, is liable to the payee of an unpaid request for payment. The liability is limited to a proportionate share of the amount transferred under this section, to the extent necessary to discharge the request for payment.

§ 6-213. [Alteration of Rights.]

(a) Rights at death under Section 6-212 are determined by the type of account at the death of a party. The type of account may be altered by written notice given by a party to the financial institution to change the type of account or to stop or vary payment under the terms of the account. The notice must be signed by a party and received by the financial institution during the party's lifetime.

(b) A right of survivorship arising from the express terms of the account, Section 6-212, or a POD designation, may not be altered by will.

§ 6-214. [Accounts and Transfers Nontestamentary.]

Except as provided in Part 2 of Article II (elective share of surviving spouse) or as a consequence of, and to the extent directed by, Section 6-215, a transfer resulting from the application of Section 6-212 is effective by reason of the terms of the account involved and this part and is not testamentary or subject to Articles I through IV (estate administration).

§ 6-215. [Rights of Creditors and Others.]

(a) If other assets of the estate are insufficient, a transfer resulting from a right of survivorship or POD designation under this part is not effective against the estate of a deceased party to the extent needed to pay claims against the estate and statutory allowances to the surviving spouse and children.

(b) A surviving party or beneficiary who receives payment from an account after death of a party is liable to account to the personal representative of the decedent for a proportionate share of the amount received to the extent necessary to discharge the claims and allowances described in subsection (a) remaining unpaid after application of the decedent's estate. A proceeding to assert the liability may not be commenced unless the personal representative has received a written demand by the surviving spouse, a creditor, a child, or a person acting for a child of the decedent. The proceeding must be commenced within one year after death of the decedent.

(c) A surviving party or beneficiary against whom a proceeding to account is brought may join as a party to the proceeding a surviving party or beneficiary of any other account of the decedent.

(d) Sums recovered by the personal representative must be administered as part of the decedent's estate. This section does not affect the protection from claims of the personal representative or estate of a deceased party provided in Section 6-226 for a financial institution that makes payment in accordance with the terms of the account.

§ 6-216. [Community Property and Tenancy by the Entireties.]

(a) A deposit of community property in an account does not alter the community character of the property or community rights in the property, but a right of survivorship between parties married to each other arising from the express terms of the account or Section 6-212 may not be altered by will.

(b) This part does not affect the law governing tenancy by the entireties.

SUBPART 3
PROTECTION OF FINANCIAL INSTITUTIONS

§ 6-221. [Authority of Financial Institution.]

A financial institution may enter into a contract of deposit for a multiple-party account to the same extent it may enter into a contract of deposit for a single-party account, and may provide for a POD designation and an agency designation in either a single-party account or a multiple-party account. A financial institution need not inquire as to the source of a deposit to an account or as to the proposed application of a payment from an account.

§ 6-222. [Payment on Multiple-Party Account.]

A financial institution, on request, may pay sums on deposit in a multiple-party account to:

(1) one or more of the parties, whether or not another party is disabled, incapacitated, or deceased when payment is requested and whether or not the party making the request survives another party; or

(2) the personal representative, if any, or, if there is none, the heirs or devisees of a deceased party if proof of death is presented to the financial institution showing that the deceased party was the survivor of all other persons named on the account either as a party or beneficiary, unless the account is without right of survivorship under Section 6-212.

§ 6-223. [Payment on POD Designation.]

A financial institution, on request, may pay sums on deposit in an account with a POD designation to:

(1) one or more of the parties, whether or not another party is disabled, incapacitated, or deceased when the payment is requested and whether or not a party survives another party;

(2) the beneficiary or beneficiaries, if proof of death is presented to the financial institution showing that the beneficiary or beneficiaries survived all persons named as parties; or

(3) the personal representative, if any, or, if there is none, the heirs or devisees of a deceased party, if proof of death is presented to the financial institution showing that the deceased party was the survivor of all other persons named on the account either as a party or beneficiary.

§ 6-224. [Payment to Designated Agent.]

A financial institution, on request of an agent under an agency designation for an account, may pay to the agent sums on deposit in the account, whether or not a party is disabled, incapacitated, or deceased when the request is made or received, and whether or not the authority of the agent terminates on the disability or incapacity of a party.

§ 6-225. [Payment to Minor.]

If a financial institution is required or permitted to make payment pursuant to this part to a minor designated as a beneficiary, payment may be made pursuant to the Uniform Transfers to Minors Act.

§ 6-226. [Discharge.]

(a) Payment made pursuant to this part in accordance with the type of account discharges the financial institution from all claims for amounts so paid, whether or not the payment is consistent with the beneficial ownership of the account as between parties, beneficiaries, or their successors. Payment may be made whether or not a party, beneficiary, or agent is disabled, incapacitated, or deceased when payment is requested, received, or made.

(b) Protection under this section does not extend to payments made after a financial institution has received written notice from a party, or from the personal representative, surviving spouse, or heir or devisee of a deceased party, to the effect that payments in accordance with the terms of the account, including one having an agency designation, should not be permitted, and the financial institution has had a reasonable opportunity to act on it when the payment is made. Unless the notice is withdrawn by the person giving it, the successor of any deceased party must concur in a request for payment if the financial institution is to be protected under this section. Unless a financial institution has been served with process in an action or proceeding, no other notice or other information shown to have been available to the financial institution affects its right to protection under this section.

(c) A financial institution that receives written notice pursuant to this section or otherwise has reason to believe that a dispute exists as to the rights of the parties may refuse, without liability, to make payments in accordance with the terms of the account.

(d) Protection of a financial institution under this section does not affect the rights of parties in disputes between themselves or their successors concerning the beneficial ownership of sums on deposit in accounts or payments made from accounts.

§ 6-227. [Set-off.]

Without qualifying any other statutory right to set-off or lien and subject to any contractual provision, if a party is indebted to a financial institution, the financial institution has a right to set-off against the account. The amount of the account subject to set-off is the proportion to which the party is, or immediately before death was, beneficially entitled under Section 6-211 or, in the absence of proof of that proportion, an equal share with all parties request is made or received, and whether or not the authority of the agent terminates on the disability or incapacity of a party.

Part 3
Uniform TOD Security Registration Act
§ 6-301. [Definitions.]

In this part:

(1) "Beneficiary form" means a registration of a security which indicates the present owner of the security and the intention of the owner regarding the person who will become the owner of the security upon the death of the owner

(2) "Register," including its derivatives, means to issue a certificate showing the ownership of a certificated security or, in the case of an uncertificated security, to initiate or transfer an account showing ownership of securities.

(3) "Registering entity" means a person who originates or transfers a security title by registration, and includes a broker maintaining security accounts for customers and a transfer agent or other person acting for or as an issuer of securities.

(4) "Security" means a share, participation, or other interest in property, in a business, or in an obligation of an enterprise or other issuer, and includes a certificated security, an uncertificated security, and a security account.

(5) "Security account" means (i) a reinvestment account associated with a security, a securities account with a broker, a cash balance in a brokerage account, cash, interest, earnings, or dividends earned or declared on a security in an account, a reinvestment account, or a brokerage account, whether or not credited to the account before the owner's death, or (ii) a cash balance or other property held for or due to the owner of a security as a replacement for or product of an account security, whether or not credited to the account before the owner's death.

§ 6-302. [Registration in Beneficiary Form; Sole or Joint Tenancy Ownership.]

Only individuals whose registration of a security shows sole ownership by one individual or multiple ownership by two or more with right of survivorship, rather than as tenants in common, may obtain registration in beneficiary form.

Multiple owners of a security registered in beneficiary form hold as joint tenants with right of survivorship, as tenants by the entireties, or as owners of community property held in survivorship form, and not as tenants in common.

§ 6-303. [Registration in Beneficiary Form; Applicable Law.]

A security may be registered in beneficiary form if the form is authorized by this or a similar statute of the state of organization of the issuer or registering entity, the location of the registering entity's principal office, the office of its transfer agent or its office making the registration, or by this or a similar statute of the law of the state listed as the owner's address at the time of registration. A registration governed by the law of a jurisdiction in which this or similar legislation is not in force or was not in force when a registration in beneficiary form was made is nevertheless presumed to be valid and authorized as a matter of contract law.

§ 6-304. [Origination of Registration in Beneficiary Form.]

A security, whether evidenced by certificate or account, is registered in beneficiary form when the registration includes a designation of a beneficiary to take the ownership at the death of the owner or the deaths of all multiple owners.

§ 6-305. [Form of Registration in Beneficiary Form.]

Registration in beneficiary form may be shown by the words "transfer on death" or the abbreviation "TOD," or by the words "pay on death" or the abbreviation "POD," after the name of the registered owner and before the name of a beneficiary.

§ 6-306. [Effect of Registration in Beneficiary Form.]

The designation of a TOD beneficiary on a registration in beneficiary form has no effect on ownership until the owner's death. A registration of a security in beneficiary form may be canceled or changed at any time by the sole owner or all then surviving owners without the consent of the beneficiary.

§ 6-307. [Ownership on Death of Owner.]

On death of a sole owner or the last to die of all multiple owners, ownership of securities registered in beneficiary form passes to the beneficiary or beneficiaries who survive all owners. On proof of death of all owners and compliance with any applicable requirements of the registering entity, a security registered in beneficiary form may be registered in the name of the beneficiary or beneficiaries who survive the death of all owners. Until division of the security after the death of all owners, multiple beneficiaries surviving the death of all owners hold their interests as tenants in common. If no beneficiary survives the death of all owners, the security belongs to the estate of the deceased sole owner or the estate of the last to die of all multiple owners.

§ 6-308. [Protection of Registering Entity.]

(a) A registering entity is not required to offer or to accept a request for security registration in beneficiary form. If a registration in beneficiary form is offered by a registering entity, the owner requesting registration in beneficiary form assents to the protections given to the registering entity by this part.

(b) By accepting a request for registration of a security in beneficiary form, the registering entity agrees that the registration will be implemented on death of the deceased owner as provided in this part.

(c) A registering entity is discharged from all claims to a security by the estate, creditors, heirs, or devisees of a deceased owner if it registers a transfer of the security in accordance with Section 6-307 and does so in good faith reliance (i) on the registration, (ii) on this part, and (iii) on information provided to it by affidavit of the personal representative of the deceased owner, or by the surviving beneficiary or by the surviving beneficiary's representatives, or other information available to the registering entity. The protections of this part do not extend to a reregistration or payment made after a registering entity has received written notice from any claimant to any interest in the security objecting to implementation of a registration in beneficiary form. No other notice or other information available to the registering entity affects its right to protection under this part.

(d) The protection provided by this part to the registering entity of a security does not affect the rights of beneficiaries in disputes between themselves and other claimants to ownership of the security transferred or its value or proceeds.

§ 6-309. [Nontestamentary Transfer on Death.]

(a) A transfer on death resulting from a registration in beneficiary form is effective by reason of the contract regarding the registration between the owner and the registering entity and this part and is not testamentary.

(b) This part does not limit the rights of creditors of security owners against beneficiaries and other transferees under other laws of this State.

§ 6-310. [Terms, Conditions, and Forms for Registration.]

(a) A registering entity offering to accept registrations in beneficiary form may establish the terms and conditions under which it will receive requests (i) for registrations in beneficiary form, and (ii) for implementation of registrations in beneficiary form, including requests for cancellation of previously registered POD beneficiary designations and requests for reregistration to effect a change of beneficiary. The terms and conditions so established may provide for proving death, avoiding or resolving any problems concerning fractional shares, designating primary and contingent beneficiaries, and substituting a named beneficiary's descendants to take in the place of the named beneficiary in the event of the beneficiary's death. Substitution may be indicated by appending to the name of the primary beneficiary the letters LDPS, standing for "lineal descendants per stirpes." This designation substitutes a deceased beneficiary's descendants who survive the owner for a beneficiary who fails to so survive, the descendants to be identified and to share in accordance with the law of the beneficiary's domicile at the owner's death governing inheritance by descendants of an intestate. Other forms of identifying beneficiaries who are to take on one or more contingencies, and rules for providing proofs and assurances needed to satisfy reasonable concerns by registering entities regarding conditions and identities relevant to accurate implementation of registrations in beneficiary form, may be contained in a registering entity's terms and conditions.

(b) The following are illustrations of registrations in beneficiary form which a registering entity may authorize:

(1) Sole owner-sole beneficiary: John S. Brown TOD (or POD) John S. Brown Jr.

(2) Multiple owners-sole beneficiary: John S. Brown Mary B. Brown JT TEN TOD John S. Brown Jr.

(3) Multiple owners-primary and secondary (substituted) beneficiaries: John S. Brown Mary B. Brown JT TEN TOD John S. Brown Jr SUB BENE Peter Q. Brown or John S. Brown Mary B. Brown JT TEN TOD John S. Brown Jr LDPS.

§ 6-311. [Application of Part.]

This part applies to registrations of securities in beneficiary form made before or after [effective date], by decedents dying on or after [effective date].

Glossary

401(k) plan A company-sponsored retirement plan in which an employee agrees either to take a salary reduction or to forgo a bonus to provide money for retirement.

A

abates 1. Destroy or completely end. 2. Greatly lessen or reduce.

adeemed Take away.

ademption 1. Disposing of something left in a will before death, with the effect that the person it was left to does not get it. 2. The gift, before death, of something left in a will to a person who was left it.

administrator A person appointed by the court to supervise the estate (property) of a dead person. If the supervising person is named in the dead person's will, the proper name is executor.

administering an estate Settling and distributing the estate of a deceased person.

administrator *ad litem* Person appointed by a court to furnish a necessary party to a lawsuit in which a deceased has an interest.

administrator of goods not administered (Latin) "Of the goods not (already taken care of)." An administrator appointed to hand out the property

of a dead person whose executor (person chosen to hand it out) has died. Also called *administrator de bonis non* or *administrator d.b.n.*

administrator *pendente lite* Temporary administrator appointed before the adjudication of testacy or intestacy to preserve the assets of an estate.

administrator with the will annexed (Latin) "With the will attached." An administrator who is appointed by a court to supervise handing out the property of a dead person whose will does not name executors (persons to hand out property) or whose named executors cannot or will not serve. Also known as *administrator w.w.a., administrator cum testamento annexo,* and *administrator c.t.a.*

administratrix Female appointed to administer the estate of an intestate decedent.

advance directives A document such as a durable power of attorney, health-care proxy, or living will that specifies your health-care decisions and who will make decisions for you if you cannot make your own. Advance directives often specify a DNR (do-not-resuscitate) order.

affinity Relationship by marriage. For example, a wife is related by affinity to her husband's brother.

agent A person authorized (requested or permitted) by another person to act for him or her; a person entrusted with another's business.

alternate valuation method Under federal tax rules, the administrator of a dead person's property may set a value for the property based on the date of death or on the "alternate valuation date," the day the property is sold or given out. If six months go by before the property is disposed of, the choice is between the value as of the day of death and six months after, so long as the later value is less than the earlier.

ambulatory Movable; capable of being changed or revoked; able to walk.

anatomical gift A donation of all or part of a human body.

ancillary administration A proceeding in a state where a dead person had property, but which is different from the state where that person lived and has her main estate administered.

annuity 1. A fixed sum of money, usually paid to a person at fixed times for a fixed time period or for life. 2. A retirement annuity is a right to receive payments starting at some future date, usually retirement, but sometimes a fixed date. 3. An account with an investment or insurance company that is tax free until retirement.

antilapse statutes State laws that prevent lapsed legacies and lapsed devises.

appearance 1. The coming into court as a party (plaintiff or defendant) to a lawsuit. A person who does this "appears." 2. The formal coming into court as a lawyer in a specific lawsuit; often also called "entering" the case.

appointee The person who is to receive the benefit under a power of appointment.

appointive property Property that is an estate asset that will be given out by power of appointment.

appointment The act of putting into effect a power of appointment.

attest Swear to; act as a witness to; certify formally, usually in writing.

attestation The act of witnessing the signing of a document and signing that you have witnessed it.

attestation clause A clause, usually at the end of a document, that witnesses the signing of the document with a signature of attestation.

attorney-in-fact Any person who acts formally for another person.

B

bastard A child born out of lawful wedlock.

beneficiaries 1. A person (or organization, etc.) for whose benefit a trust is created. 2. A person to whom an insurance policy is payable. 3. A person who inherits under a will. 4. Anyone who benefits from something or who is treated as the real owner of something for tax or other purposes.

beneficiary (cestui que trust) (French) "He or she who." For example, a cestui que trust is a person who has a right to the property, money, and proceeds being managed by another. The modern phrase is "beneficiary of a trust."

bequeath To give property, usually not real estate, by a will.

bequest A gift by will, usually of personal property.

bond A document that promises to pay money if a particular future event happens, or a sum of money that is put up and will be lost if that event happens.

C

caveat (Latin) "Beware;" warning.

charitable remainder annuity trust (CRAT) Trust in which a fixed amount of income is given to a beneficiary at least annually, and the entire remainder is given to charity.

charitable remainder trust Trust in which the settlor or a beneficiary retains the income from the trust for a period of time (usually for life), after which the trust principal is given to a charity.

charitable remainder unitrust (CRUT) Trust in which a percentage—not less than five percent—of the value of the trust property is determined annually and given to a beneficiary, with the entire remainder going to charity.

charitable trust A trust set up for a public purpose such as to support a school, church, or charity. Also called a *public trust.*

chose in action A right to recover a debt or to get damages that can be enforced in court. These words also apply to the thing itself that is being sued on; for example, an accident, a contract, stocks, etc.

citation A notice to appear in court.

codicil A supplement or addition to a will that adds to it or changes it.

collateral consanguinity On the side. Kinship that includes uncles, aunts, and all persons similarly related, but not direct ancestors such as grandparents.

community property Property owned in common (both persons owning it all) by a husband and wife. "Community property states" are those states that call most property acquired during the marriage the property of both partners no matter whose name it is in.

consanguinity Having a blood relationship; kinship.

conservator A guardian or preserver of another person's property appointed by a court because the other person cannot legally manage it.

constructive trust A situation in which a person holds legal title to property, but the property should, in fairness, actually belong to another person (because the title was gained by fraud, by a clerical error, etc.). In this case, the property may be treated by a court as if the legal owner holds it in trust for the "real" owner.

conveyance in trust Trust created by a settlor's transfer of legal title to trust property to a trustee for the benefit of either the settlor or someone else.

credit-shelter trust Trust under which a deceased spouse's estate passes to a trust rather than to the surviving spouse, thereby reducing the possibility of the surviving spouse's estate being taxable. Also called an *A-B trust,* a *bypass trust,* or an *exemption equivalent trust.*

crummey powers Powers that give trust beneficiaries the right to withdraw each year the money that is contributed to the trust.

curtesy A husband's right to part of his dead wife's property. This right is regulated by statute and varies from state to state.

CUSIP number Nine-digit number assigned to all stocks and bonds traded on major exchanges and many unlisted securities.

cy pres (French) "As near as possible." When a dead person's will can no longer legally or practically be carried out, a court may (but is not obligated to) order that the dead person's estate be used in a way that most nearly does what the person would have wanted. The doctrine of *cy pres* is now usually applied only to charitable trusts.

D

decedent A dead person.

declaration of trust A written statement by a person owning property that said property is held for another person. This is one way of setting up a trust.

degree of kindred The relationship between a deceased person and her relatives to determine who are most nearly related by blood.

demonstrative legacy A gift of a specific sum of money in a will that is to be paid out of a particular fund where, if the fund has no money, the gift becomes a general legacy on an equal footing with other general legacies.

descendants People who are of the bloodline of an ancestor.

descent 1. Inheritance from parents or other ancestors. 2. Getting property by inheritance of any type, rather than by purchase or gift.

devise 1. The gift of land by will. 2. Any gift by will.

devisee A person to whom land is given by will.

devisor A person who makes a gift of land in a will.

directive to physicians Another name for a living will.

disclaimer The refusal, rejection, or renunciation of a claim, a power, or property.

disinterred Unearthed.

dispositive provisions Provisions that clearly settle the disposition of the testator's property.

distribution Division by shares; for example, giving out what is left of a dead person's estate after taxes and debts are paid.

divestiture 1. Derive, take away, or withdraw. 2. Sell or otherwise dispose of legal title. For example, you can divest yourself of a car by selling it.

domicile A person's permanent home, legal home, or main residence. The words *abode, citizenship, habitancy,* and *residence* sometimes mean the same as domicile and sometimes not.

donee A person to whom a gift is made or to whom a power is given.

donor A person making a gift to another or giving another person power to do something.

dower A wife's right to part of her dead husband's property. This right is now regulated by statute and varies from state to state.

durable power of attorney A power of attorney that lasts as long as a person remains incapable of making decisions, usually about health care. It is a form of advance directive.

E

education IRAs Accounts that can be established for children under the age of 18 for a child's elementary through postsecondary education.

employer identification number (EIN) Number assigned by the IRS to identify an estate; used in place of a Social Security number.

endowment insurance An insurance policy that pays a set amount at a set time or, if the person insured dies, pays the money to a beneficiary.

equitable title Ownership of a beneficial interest, with legal title belonging to another. Also known as *beneficial title.*

escheats When the state gets property because no owner can be found. For example, if a person dies and no person can be found who can legally inherit that person's property, the government gets it by escheat.

estate planning Carrying out a person's wishes for property to be passed on at her death and gaining maximum legal benefit from that property by using the laws of wills, trusts, insurance, property, and taxes.

executor A person selected by a person making a will to administer the will and to hand out the property after the person making the will dies.

executor de son tort (French) "Of his own wrong." A person who takes on a duty, such as being executor of a will, without any right to take on the duty, will be held responsible for all actions he takes as executor.

executrix A female executor.

exempt property Certain property of a decedent that passes to the surviving spouse or children without being subject to the claims of general creditors.

exordium clause The introductory clause of a will, stating that it is a valid will, etc. Also known as a *publication clause.*

express trusts A trust with terms stated in oral or written words.

extinction Put to an end.

F

fair market value The price to which a willing seller and a willing buyer would agree for an item in the ordinary course of trade.

family allowance A state-set percentage of an estate that is given to the immediate family (or the spouse) even if the will gives them less. Also known as a *widow's allowance.*

family limited partnership A partnership of family members in which one or more family members are general partners and one or more family members are limited partners.

fiduciary A person who manages money or property for another person and in whom that other person has a right to place great trust.

fiduciary capacity The position of a person who manages money or property for another person. This position implies trust, power, confidence, responsibility, and good faith on the part of both parties.

fiduciary relationship Any relationship between persons in which one person acts for another in a position of trust; for example, lawyer and client or parent and child.

filius nullius A child of nobody.

forced heir A person who cannot be deprived of a share of an estate unless the testator (person making a will) has a recognized legal cause for disinheriting the person.

forced share The share a surviving spouse may choose to take in the estate of a deceased spouse. Also known as an *elective share*.

formal proceedings Proceedings conducted before a judge with notice to interested persons (UPC § 1–201(15)).

G

general legacy A gift of money from the general assets of an estate.

general partners Members of a partnership who run the business and have liability for all partnership debts.

generation-skipping transfer tax A tax imposed when property exceeding an amount set by Congress is transferred to a person who is two or more generations below the donor or decedent.

gross estate The total value of a dead person's property from which deductions are subtracted (and to which certain gifts made during life are added) to determine the amount on which federal estate and gift taxes will be paid.

gross estate tax Tentative estate tax computed by applying the unified rate schedule to the sum of the taxable estate and all taxable gifts.

guardian A person who has the legal right and duty to take care of another person or that person's property because that other person (for example, a child) cannot. The arrangement is called *guardianship*.

guardians of a child's person One who has the care and custody of a child or person who is mentally or physically incapacitated.

guardians of a child's property One who has the responsibility of caring for a child's or incapacitated person's property.

H

half blood A relationship between people who have one parent in common but not both parents in common.

head of household A special category of federal taxpayer. To be taxed at head of household rates, you must meet several requirements; for example, unmarried or legally separated, pay over half the support of your dependents, etc. Also known as *householder*.

health care proxy Written statement authorizing an agent or surrogate to make medical treatment decisions for a principal in the event of the principal's incapacity.

health-care declaration Another name for a living will.

heirs Persons who inherit property; persons who have a right to inherit property; or those who have a right to inherit property only if another person dies without leaving a valid, complete will.

heirs at law Those persons who would have inherited had the decedent died intestate.

holographic will A will that is entirely in the handwriting of the signer. Some states require a holographic will to be signed, witnessed, and in compliance with other formalities before it is valid. Other states require less.

homestead exemption State laws allowing a head of a family to keep a home and some property safe from creditors other than mortgage holders, or to allow certain persons (such as those over a certain age) to avoid paying real estate or inheritance taxes on their homes.

I

illegitimate child Describes a child born to an unmarried mother.

implied trusts A trust that exists by analyzing surrounding circumstances or the action of person(s) involved; a trust known indirectly by the words of another person. Also known as *involuntary trusts*.

Incidents of ownership Indications of ownership of life insurance, such as the power to change the beneficiary, surrender or cancel the policy, assign the policy, revoke an assignment, pledge the policy for a loan, or obtain a loan against the policy's cash surrender value.

income in respect of the decedent All gross income that a decedent would have received, had he not died, that was not properly includable on the decedent's final income tax return.

incorporation by reference Making a document a part of something else by mere mention. For example, if document A says that "document B is incorporated by reference," then document B becomes a part of document A even though the words in document B are not rewritten into document A.

independent probate Informal probate proceedings. Referred to in some states as *probate in common form*.

informal proceedings Proceedings conducted without notice to interested persons by an officer of the court acting as a registrar for probate of a will or appointment of a personal representative (UPC § 1–201(19)).

in personam jurisdiction Jurisdiction over the person.

in rem proceedings Action directed against a property to enforce rights in a thing as opposed to one brought to enforce rights against another person.

insolvent 1. The condition of being unable to pay debts as they come due. 2. Having liabilities far greater than assets.

intangible property Property that is really a right, rather than a physical object; for example, bank accounts, stocks, copyrights, "goodwill" of a business, etc.

inter vivos gift An ordinary gift, as opposed to a gift made shortly before dying.

intestacy The status of the estate or property of a person who dies without having a valid will.

intestate 1. Without a will. Dying intestate is dying without having a valid will or one that covers all of the dead person's property. 2. One who dies without a valid will.

intestate succession The distribution of inheritances to heirs according to a state's laws about who should collect. This is done when there is no valid will or when the will does not cover some of a dead person's property.

inventory A detailed list of articles of property.

irrevocable Incapable of being called back, stopped, or changed.

irrevocable living trust Living trust that cannot be revoked or amended by the settlor once it has been established.

issue Descendants (children, grandchildren, etc.).

J

Joint tenants Persons who each hold a share of land that remains the property of the surviving joint owners when a joint owner dies. The joint owners have equal shares that they received at the same time by way of the same conveyance. This form of ownership is called a joint tenancy or a joint tenancy with the right of survivorship.

joint will A single instrument that serves as the will of two or more people.

Jurisdiction 1. The geographical area within which a court (or a public official) has the right and power to operate. 2. The persons about whom and the subject matters about which a court has the right and power to make decisions that are legally binding.

K

Keogh plan A tax-free retirement account for persons with self-employment income.

kiddie tax Slang for a federal tax on certain unearned income (over a certain amount) of children under 14. The income is taxed at the parent's highest rate to discourage income shifting.

L

lapsed devises A gift of real property in a will that fails because the devisee predeceased the testator.

lapsed legacies A gift in a will that fails because the legatee predeceased the testator.

legacy A gift by will, usually of money.

legal title Full and absolute ownership without an equitable or beneficial interest.

legatee A person who inherits personal property in a will.

legator A person who makes a gift of personal property in a will.

letter of instruction A letter written by a testator to accompany a will, giving detailed information that is not contained in the will.

letters of administration A formal document appointing the administrator of the estate of a person who has died intestate.

letters testamentary A formal document appointing the executor of the estate of a person who has died testate.

life estate An ownership interest in property (an estate) that lasts until a named person or persons die.

limited partners Members of a partnership who partly or fully finance a business, take no part in running it, and have no liability for partnership debts beyond the money they put in or promise to put in.

limited-payment life insurance Insurance for which premiums are paid only for the limited period required by the policy, such as 10, 20, or 30 years. After that period, the policy is paid up.

Lineal consanguinity In a line. Blood relationships such as father and son, grandson and grandmother, etc.

living trust An ordinary (regular or usual) trust as opposed to one created under a will upon death. Inter vivos (Latin) for "between the living." Also known as an *inter vivos trust.*

living will An advance directive by which you authorize your possible future removal from an artificial life support system.

long-term care insurance An insurance policy designed to provide money to pay for nursing home and custodial care when an insured becomes chronically ill.

M

marital deduction The amount of money a wife or husband can inherit from the other without paying estate or gift taxes.

marital deduction trust Trust designed to make optimal use of the federal tax marital deduction.

marshaling of assets Collecting assets and claims and arranging the debts into the proper order of priority and then dividing up the assets to pay them off. This is done by an executor or administrator of a dead person's estate.

medical directive *See* advance directive.

mutual wills Wills that are done together and bilateral (two-sided, two-way, or done one for the other).

N

net estate tax Amount of estate tax that must be paid to the government; determined by deducting certain allowable credits, including a unified credit of $192,000, from the gross estate tax.

next of kin 1. Persons most closely related to a dead person. 2. All persons entitled to inherit from a person who has not left a will.

no-contest (Latin) "In threat"; "in terror;" "by threat." An *in terrorem* clause in a will "threatens" a beneficiary with revocation of that person's bequest if he or she contests the will. Also known as an *in terrorem* clause.

nonmarital child A child born out of lawful wedlock.

nuncupative wills An oral will. It is valid in a few states.

O

organ-tissue donor's card Document, signed by a donor in the presence of two witnesses, donating all or part of the donor's body; the donation takes effect upon or after death.

P

parol Oral; not in writing. For example, parol evidence is oral evidence (the evidence a witness gives). It usually refers to evidence about an agreement's meaning that is not clear from the written contract.

pay-on-death (POD) account A trust created by putting money into a bank account in your name as trustee for another person. You can take it out when you want, but if you do not take it out before you die, it becomes the property of that other person.

pecuniary legacy (bequest) A monetary legacy; a bequest of money.

per capita (Latin) "By heads." By the number of individual persons, each equally.

per stirpes (Latin) "By roots;" by right of representation. Describes a method of dividing a dead person's estate by giving out shares equally "by representation" or by family groups. For example, if John leaves $3,000 to Mary and Sue, and Mary dies, leaving two children (Steve and Jeff), a *per stirpes* division would give $1,500 to Sue and $750 each to Steve and Jeff.

personal property Having to do with movable property, as opposed to land and buildings.

personal representative A general term for the executor or administrator of a dead person's property.

petition for administration Written application by one or more heirs, next of kin, or creditors asking the court to appoint the petitioner as administrator (-trix) of the estate.

petition for administration with the will annexed Written application by someone other than the person nominated as personal representative in a will, asking the court to prove and allow the will and to appoint the petitioner as administrator(-trix).

petition for probate Formal, written application asking the court to prove and allow the will and to appoint the petitioner, who is nominated in the will, as executor (-trix) thereof.

posthumous issue A child born after the death of the father.

postmortem planning Estate planning done after a person dies.

pour-over trust Provision in a will in which the testator(-trix) leaves a gift to the trustee of an existing living trust.

power of appointment The power to decide who gets certain money or property or how it will be used. This power is usually given to a specific person in a deed or will.

power of attorney A document authorizing a person to act as attorney *in fact* for the person signing the document.

precatory trust A trust expressing a wish; it is advisory only and not legally binding in most situations.

preliminary letters testamentary Certificate, used in some states, giving a preliminary executor the same powers that are given to an ordinary executor, with some limitations, when a delay in probate is anticipated.

prenuptial agreement An antenuptial (before marriage) agreement. A contract between persons about to marry, usually stating the way property will be handled during the marriage, the way it will divide in case of divorce, and the limits on spousal support obligations.

pretermitted child A child (or sometimes any descendant) either unintentionally left out of a will or born after the will is made. Some states have pretermission statutes that allow a child left out by mistake to take a share of the parent's property.

principal A person or anyone else who has another person (an agent) do things for him or her.

probate court A court that handles matters of wills and estates of a dead person. It sometimes handles the problems of minors and others who are not legally competent to manage their affairs. Some states designate this same court as the *court of chancery*, the *surrogate court*, or the *orphan's court*.

probate estate Real and personal property that was owned by the decedent either solely or with others as a tenant in common.

probate in solemn form Formal probate proceedings.

probate jurisdiction The authority of the court to process the handling of the will and the estate of a dead person. A probate court handles these matters and sometimes handles the problems of minors and others who are not legally competent to manage their affairs.

probate property Property that was owned by the decedent either severally or as a tenant in common with another.

probated The process of handling the will and the estate of a dead person.

probating a will Process of proving or establishing before the probate court that the document being offered for official recognition as the will of the decedent is in fact genuine.

profit à prendre Describes the right to take the growing crops of another person's land.

proponent The person who offers something, puts something forward, or proposes something.

public administrator An official appointed to administer an estate when no one appears who is entitled to act as administrator.

purchase money mortgages A buyer's financing of part of a purchase by giving a mortgage on the property to the seller as security for the loan.

Q

qualified disclaimer Under federal tax law, an irrevocable and unqualified refusal by a person to accept an interest in property. It is effective only if it is in writing, received within a specified time, received prior to the acceptance of any benefits, and legally effective to pass the disclaimed interest to another person without direction from the person making the disclaimer.

qualified terminable interest property (QTIP) Trust that gives all trust income to the surviving spouse for life, payable at least annually, and which meets the requirements of I.R.C. § 2056(b)(7).

R

real property Land, buildings, and things permanently attached to land and buildings. Also called realty.

reciprocal wills Wills that are mutual (done together) and bilateral (two-sided, two-way, or done one for the other). For example, reciprocal wills are wills made by two persons, and enforceable against each other because each person put something in his will that the other asked for.

registry of Deeds An office where deeds, mortgages, and other instruments affecting title to real property are kept.

registry of Probate An office where the records of all probate activities are kept.

republishing Reestablishing the validity of a will that has been revoked.

residuary clause Clause in a will that disposes of all items not specifically given away (the "leftovers").

resulting trust A trust created by law (rather than by agreement) for reasons of fairness when one person holds property for another.

revocable living trust Living trust in which the settlor retains the right to alter, amend, or revoke the trust during the settlor's lifetime.

revoking Wiping out the legal effect of something by taking it back, canceling, rescinding, etc.

Roth IRAs Retirement accounts that are similar to traditional IRAs except that distributions are not required and are tax free when taken after age 59½ if the account has been in existence for five years or longer.

rule against perpetuities A law preventing any attempt to control the disposition of your property by will that is meant to last longer than the life of a person alive when you die (or at least conceived by then) plus 21 years. Enacted in most states.

S

satisfaction Property given by a parent to an heir that the parent intends to deduct from the child's eventual share of the parent's estate. Also known as *advancement.*

self-proof clause A clause in a will containing affidavits of the testator and witnesses that allow a will to be proved without testimony.

settlor A person who sets up a trust by providing money or property for it.

severally Separate, individual, independent.

signature clause The clause in a will that falls immediately before the testator's signature.

simplified employee pension plan (SEP) An employer's contribution to an employee's IRA that meets certain federal requirements. Self-employed persons often use a SEP.

skip person Person receiving the property in a generation-skipping transfer.

slayer statutes State laws provide that one who is convicted of murdering another cannot inherit from the victim's estate.

sound mind Whole, healthy mental condition of a person. Sane; mentally competent.

special administrator An administrator who is appointed when necessary to preserve the estate or to secure its proper administration (UPC § 3-614).

specific devise A gift of a particular, exact piece(s) of real estate (land).

specific legacy Exact. A gift in a will of a precisely identifiable object such as "the family Bible."

spendthrift A person who spends money wildly and whose property the state may allow a trustee to look after.

spendthrift trust A trust set up for the protection of a person's property against himself, or creditor. These trusts are also set up privately through wills and trusts to enable one person to give money or property to another without fear that it will be squandered.

split-gift provision Provision in the Internal Revenue Code under which spouses may consent to treat gifts of one spouse as if made one-half by each spouse, thereby doubling the amount that may be given away tax free each year.

sprinkling trust A trust that gives income to many persons at different times. Also known as a *spray trust* or *discretionary trust.*

subscribe Sign a document (as the person who wrote it, as a witness, etc.).

successor personal representative Personal representative, other than a special administrator, who is appointed to succeed a previously appointed personal representative (UPC § 1–201(41)).

supervised administration Process in which an estate is settled under the continuing surveillance of the court from beginning to end.

surety A person or company that insures or guarantees that another person's debt will be paid by becoming liable (responsible) for the debt when it is made.

surety bond A bond that contains an agreement by a third party (*surety*) to pay an obligation if the principal defaults.

surrogate A person who stands in for, takes the place of, or represents another.

surrogate decision-making laws Laws, passed by most states, that permit a close relative or friend to make health-care decisions for patients who have no advance directives.

T

tangible personal property Personal property that is physically real, capable of being touched.

tangible property Property, real or personal, that is capable of being physically touched.

taxable estate The property of a dead person (or a gift) that will be taxed after subtracting for allowable expenses, deductions, and exclusions.

tenancy in partnership Form of co-ownership of property belonging to members of a partnership.

tenants by the entirety Like joint tenants except that they must also be husband and wife and that neither has a share of the land, but both hold the entire land as one individual owner.

tenants in common Persons who each hold a share of land that can be passed on to heirs or otherwise disposed of. This form of ownership is called a tenancy in common.

term life insurance Life insurance that ends at the end of a certain time period.

testament A will.

testamentary capacity The mental ability needed to make a valid will.

testamentary dispositions A bequest or devise. Giving any form of property by will.

testamentary trust A trust created in a will, which takes effect when the testator dies.

testator A person who makes a will.

testatrix A female who makes a will.

testimonium clause The part of a deed or other document that contains who signed and when and where it was signed.

The Uniform Simultaneous Death Act Uniform law, adopted by most states, that sets forth rules to be followed when the passage of property depends upon the time of one's death, and there is no sufficient evidence that the people died other than at the same time.

Totten trust A savings account in the name of the depositor as trustee for another person called a beneficiary.

traditional IRAs Bank or investment accounts into which some persons may set aside a certain amount of their earnings each year and have the interest taxed only later when withdrawn.

trust An arrangement by which one person holds legal title to money or property for the benefit of another.

trust res Money or property set aside in a trust or set aside for special purposes. Also known as *trust corpus*, *trust principal*, *trust property*, or *trust fund*.

trustee A person who holds money or property for the benefit of another person (*see* trust).

U

Uniform Anatomical Gifts Act (UAGA) Uniform law that provides a simplified manner of making a testamentary donation of vital organs for medical research or transplant.

uniform laws Laws in various subject areas, proposed by the Commission on Uniform State Laws and the American Law Institute, adopted in whole or in part by many states. Sometimes called *model acts*.

Uniform Probate Code (UPC) Uniform law designed to modernize and standardize the laws relating to the affairs of decedents, minors, and certain other persons who need protection.

Uniform Transfers to Minors Act (UTMA) Formerly called Uniform Gifts to Minors Act (UGMA). A uniform law that provides an inexpensive, easy mechanism for transferring property to minors.

universal (adjustable-premium whole) life insurance Type of whole life insurance that allows the policyholder flexibility in choosing and changing terms of the policy.

unsupervised administration Method of administering an estate, under the UPC, without court action unless such action is requested by an interested person.

V

vests 1. Give an immediate, fixed, and full right. 2. Take immediate effect.

voluntary administrator Person who undertakes the informal administration of a small intestate estate.

voluntary executor Person who undertakes the informal administration of a small testate estate.

voluntary trusts With complete free will; intentional. In this sense, a voluntary trust is one set up intentionally, rather than imposed by law.

W

ward A person for whom a guardian has been appointed.

whole life insurance Life insurance with continuing premium payments (which stop if the policy becomes fully paid), a sum paid at death, and, usually, a cash surrender value.

will A document in which a person disposes his or her property after death.

Index

IMPORTANT! READ CAREFULLY: This End User License Agreement ("Agreement") sets forth the conditions by which Cengage Learning will make electronic access to the Cengage Learning-owned licensed content and associated media, software, documentation, printed materials, and electronic documentation contained in this package and/or made available to you via this product (the "Licensed Content"), available to you (the "End User"). BY CLICKING THE "I ACCEPT" BUTTON AND/OR OPENING THIS PACKAGE, YOU ACKNOWLEDGE THAT YOU HAVE READ ALL OF THE TERMS AND CONDITIONS, AND THAT YOU AGREE TO BE BOUND BY ITS TERMS, CONDITIONS, AND ALL APPLICABLE LAWS AND REGULATIONS GOVERNING THE USE OF THE LICENSED CONTENT.

1.0   SCOPE OF LICENSE

1.1   Licensed Content. The Licensed Content may contain portions of modifiable content ("Modifiable Content") and content which may not be modified or otherwise altered by the End User ("Non-Modifiable Content"). For purposes of this Agreement, Modifiable Content and Non-Modifiable Content may be collectively referred to herein as the "Licensed Content." All Licensed Content shall be considered Non-Modifiable Content, unless such Licensed Content is presented to the End User in a modifiable format and it is clearly indicated that modification of the Licensed Content is permitted.

1.2   Subject to the End User's compliance with the terms and conditions of this Agreement, Cengage Learning hereby grants the End User, a nontransferable, nonexclusive, limited right to access and view a single copy of the Licensed Content on a single personal computer system for noncommercial, internal, personal use only. The End User shall not (i) reproduce, copy, modify (except in the case of Modifiable Content), distribute, display, transfer, sublicense, prepare derivative work(s) based on, sell, exchange, barter or transfer, rent, lease, loan, resell, or in any other manner exploit the Licensed Content; (ii) remove, obscure, or alter any notice of Cengage Learning's intellectual property rights present on or in the Licensed Content, including, but not limited to, copyright, trademark, and/or patent notices; or (iii) disassemble, decompile, translate, reverse engineer, or otherwise reduce the Licensed Content.

2.0   TERMINATION

2.1   Cengage Learning may at any time (without prejudice to its other rights or remedies) immediately terminate this Agreement and/or suspend access to some or all of the Licensed Content, in the event that the End User does not comply with any of the terms and conditions of this Agreement. In the event of such termination by Cengage Learning, the End User shall immediately return any and all copies of the Licensed Content to Cengage Learning.

3.0   PROPRIETARY RIGHTS

3.1   The End User acknowledges that Cengage Learning owns all rights, title and interest, including, but not limited to all copyright rights therein, in and to the Licensed Content, and that the End User shall not take any action inconsistent with such ownership. The Licensed Content is protected by U.S., Canadian and other applicable copyright laws and by international treaties, including the Berne Convention and the Universal Copyright Convention. Nothing contained in this Agreement shall be construed as granting the End User any ownership rights in or to the Licensed Content.

3.2   Cengage Learning reserves the right at any time to withdraw from the Licensed Content any item or part of an item for which it no longer retains the right to publish, or which it has reasonable grounds to believe infringes copyright or is defamatory, unlawful, or otherwise objectionable.

4.0   PROTECTION AND SECURITY

4.1   The End User shall use its best efforts and take all reasonable steps to safeguard its copy of the Licensed Content to ensure that no unauthorized reproduction, publication, disclosure, modification, or distribution of the Licensed Content, in whole or in part, is made. To the extent that the End User becomes aware of any such unauthorized use of the Licensed Content, the End User shall immediately notify Cengage Learning. Notification of such violations may be made by sending an e-mail to infringement@cengage.com.

5.0   MISUSE OF THE LICENSED PRODUCT

5.1   In the event that the End User uses the Licensed Content in violation of this Agreement, Cengage Learning shall have the option of electing liquidated damages, which shall include all profits generated by the End User's use of the Licensed Content plus interest computed at the maximum rate permitted by law and all legal fees and other expenses incurred by Cengage Learning in enforcing its rights, plus penalties.

6.0   FEDERAL GOVERNMENT CLIENTS

6.1   Except as expressly authorized by Cengage Learning, Federal Government clients obtain only the rights specified in this Agreement and no other rights. The Government acknowledges that (i) all software and related documentation incorporated in the Licensed Content is existing commercial computer software within the meaning of FAR 27.405(b)(2); and (2) all other data delivered in whatever form, is limited rights data within the meaning of FAR 27.401. The restrictions in this section are acceptable as consistent with the Government's need for software and other data under this Agreement.

7.0   DISCLAIMER OF WARRANTIES AND LIABILITIES

7.1   Although Cengage Learning believes the Licensed Content to be reliable, Cengage Learning does not guarantee or warrant (i) any information or materials contained in or produced by the Licensed Content, (ii) the accuracy, completeness or reliability of the Licensed Content, or (iii) that the Licensed Content is free from errors or other material defects. THE LICENSED PRODUCT IS PROVIDED "AS IS," WITHOUT ANY WARRANTY OF ANY KIND AND CENGAGE LEARNING DISCLAIMS ANY AND ALL WARRANTIES, EXPRESSED OR IMPLIED, INCLUDING, WITHOUT LIMITATION, WARRANTIES OF MERCHANTABILITY OR FITNESS FOR A PARTICULAR PURPOSE. IN NO EVENT SHALL CENGAGE LEARNING BE LIABLE FOR: INDIRECT, SPECIAL, PUNITIVE OR CONSEQUENTIAL DAMAGES INCLUDING FOR LOST PROFITS, LOST DATA, OR OTHERWISE. IN NO EVENT SHALL CENGAGE LEARNING'S AGGREGATE LIABILITY HEREUNDER, WHETHER ARISING IN CONTRACT, TORT, STRICT LIABILITY OR OTHERWISE, EXCEED THE AMOUNT OF FEES PAID BY THE END USER HEREUNDER FOR THE LICENSE OF THE LICENSED CONTENT.

8.0   GENERAL

8.1   Entire Agreement. This Agreement shall constitute the entire Agreement between the Parties and supercedes all prior Agreements and understandings oral or written relating to the subject matter hereof.

8.2   Enhancements/Modifications of Licensed Content. From time to time, and in Cengage Learning's sole discretion, Cengage Learning may advise the End User of updates, upgrades, enhancements and/or improvements to the Licensed Content, and may permit the End User to access and use, subject to the terms and conditions of this Agreement, such modifications, upon payment of prices as may be established by Cengage Learning.

8.3   No Export. The End User shall use the Licensed Content solely in the United States and shall not transfer or export, directly or indirectly, the Licensed Content outside the United States.

8.4   Severability. If any provision of this Agreement is invalid, illegal, or unenforceable under any applicable statute or rule of law, the provision shall be deemed omitted to the extent that it is invalid, illegal, or unenforceable. In such a case, the remainder of the Agreement shall be construed in a manner as to give greatest effect to the original intention of the parties hereto.

8.5   Waiver. The waiver of any right or failure of either party to exercise in any respect any right provided in this Agreement in any instance shall not be deemed to be a waiver of such right in the future or a waiver of any other right under this Agreement.

8.6   Choice of Law/Venue. This Agreement shall be interpreted, construed, and governed by and in accordance with the laws of the State of New York, applicable to contracts executed and to be wholly preformed therein, without regard to its principles governing conflicts of law. Each party agrees that any proceeding arising out of or relating to this Agreement or the breach or threatened breach of this Agreement may be commenced and prosecuted in a court in the State and County of New York. Each party consents and submits to the nonexclusive personal jurisdiction of any court in the State and County of New York in respect of any such proceeding.

8.7   Acknowledgment. By opening this package and/or by accessing the Licensed Content on this Web site, THE END USER ACKNOWLEDGES THAT IT HAS READ THIS AGREEMENT, UNDERSTANDS IT, AND AGREES TO BE BOUND BY ITS TERMS AND CONDITIONS. IF YOU DO NOT ACCEPT THESE TERMS AND CONDITIONS, YOU MUST NOT ACCESS THE LICENSED CONTENT AND RETURN THE LICENSED PRODUCT TO CENGAGE LEARNING (WITHIN 30 CALENDAR DAYS OF THE END USER'S PURCHASE) WITH PROOF OF PAYMENT ACCEPTABLE TO CENGAGE LEARNING, FOR A CREDIT OR A REFUND. Should the End User have any questions/comments regarding this Agreement, please contact Cengage Learning at Delmar.help@cengage.com.

CD-ROM & DVD-ROM Setup Instructions

1. Insert disc into CD-ROM or DVD-ROM drive. The program should start automatically. If it does not, go to step 2.
2. From My Computer, double-click the icon for the CD or DVD drive.
3. Double-click the start.exe file to start the program.